2.00

5,000 NEW ANSWERS
TO QUESTIONS

5,000 NEW ANSWERS TO QUESTIONS

BY

Frederic J. Haskin

Author of ANSWERS TO QUESTIONS, THE AMERICAN
GOVERNMENT, THE IMMIGRANT, THE PANAMA
CANAL, UNCLE SAM AT WORK (*Motion Picture*)

GROSSET & DUNLAP
PUBLISHERS : : NEW YORK

Printed in the United States of America

CONTENTS

INTRODUCTION

Here is a book by the public for the public.

Pupils of little red school houses in the mountains of remote regions and professors at universities, miners who toil beneath the earth's surface and heads of great industrial enterprises, newsboys and bankers, keepers of cross-road stores and great merchants, dentists and statesmen—a multitude of individuals in every walk and condition of life—constitute the authors of one half the volume.

This half reflects every shade of desire for information, from the wish to settle a wager or satisfy curiosity to the most profound hunger after knowledge. Such impulses are responsible for all the body of learning which is the heritage of generations of mankind.

Hundreds of authorities, including officials of the Government of the United States, representatives of other governments, heads of organizations, searchers after scientific and philosophic truth, producers of the world's literature, makers of music, all skilled in their fields, constitute the authors of the second half of this book. They have supplied the answers to more than five thousand questions.

The asker and the answerer may have dwelt thousands of miles apart, in spheres of life as separate as the planets. In many cases, neither ever heard of the other before, never knew such a collaborator existed. These strangers have become fellow-contributors to this volume which expresses both.

The task of matching answerer against questioner, of seeking to the ends of the earth if need be for the information which will supply the knowledge sought, has been organized at one of the world's greatest fountain heads of learning—Washington, the National Capital. Under the directorship of Frederic J. Haskin, an information bureau has for years been conducted for the purpose of providing a clearing house of facts for the readers of newspapers.

Inasmuch as American newspapers constitute in themselves a university of the people, open to all without matriculation fee, examination, or tuition, their readers form the greatest student body in the world. Each day presents to them new topics and each new topic suggests questions. To provide a means whereby those searching for fuller knowledge may receive guidance, the Haskin Information Service was established and, since its organization, has answered hundreds of thousands of questions on every conceivable subject.

The questions and answers of a single day's operation would make a book. Not all would have a general appeal. Those included in this volume are but a few which it is believed are representative, on the one hand, of what people want to know and, on the other, of what they may rely upon. Each day brings a fresh grist and each day the Haskin Information Service reaches out to bring in the requisite information. Each day brings many questions never asked before. The entire process is a moving pageant.

Thus, this is a book by the public for the public.

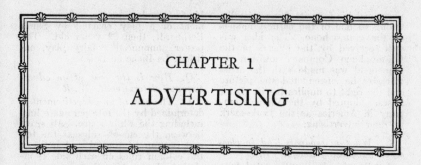

CHAPTER 1

ADVERTISING

Q. *What newspapers carry the largest volume of advertising? G. B.*

A. For the six months ended July 31, 1932, the leaders were: The Washington Star with 10,769,133 agate lines; Baltimore Sun, 9,245,078 agate lines; New York Times, 8,900,913 agate lines; Detroit News, 8,640,576 agate lines, and the Chicago Tribune, 7,957,080 agate lines.

Q. *How much money is spent for advertising in this country? G. E. W.*

A. It has been estimated by the Committee on Recent Economic Changes that annual expenses for all kinds of advertising in the United States total over $1,500,000,000.

Q. *Are many daily newspapers equipped to do color printing? G. R.*

A. The Editor and Publisher of December 10, 1932, says that 363 daily newspapers in the United States are now equipped to run color as an additional service to advertisers.

Q. *Which industries invest the most money in newspaper advertising? P. A.*

A. The tobacco industry leads. It is followed by the automobile industry, food industry, and toilet goods in the order named.

Q. *How did the word kodak originate? A. D.*

A. The name was coined by the inventor, George Eastman, for a trade-mark. K was a favorite letter with him and he tried out different combinations of letters beginning and

ending with k until he finally selected the word kodak.

Q. *Is the use of the comic strip in advertising a new idea? W. F.*

A. Not particularly. "Printers' Ink" says it has been done for at least twenty years.

Q. *Who wrote the Spotless Town verses that were used in advertising several years ago? D. S. A.*

A. J. K. Fraser, who is now president of the Blackman Company.

Q. *Name the government bureaus interested in stopping fraudulent advertising. A. T. A.*

A. The Post Office Department, the Department of Justice, and the Federal Trade Commission are all endeavoring to curb fradulent advertising.

Q. *Does billboard advertising conflict with newspaper and magazine advertising? C. O. A.*

A. In most instances, the billboard medium is employed in a reminder capacity, supplementary to newspaper or magazine advertising, which is usually employed in a primary way.

Q. *Can you give the origin of the picture of a dog listening to the talking machine? C. C. V.*

A. The idea was originally conceived by an English artist named Francis Beauraud, who appeared at the offices of the Gramophone Company, Ltd., of London, with a finely executed oil painting. This painting

1

portrayed his favorite fox terrier listening to one of the earliest models of the gramophone. The idea was well received by the officers of the Gramophone Company and an arrangement was made with the artist whereby he surrendered the picture and the right to duplicating it. Later it was adopted by the Victor Company in America as the trade-mark in their advertising.

Q. What newspapers lead in classified advertising linage? B. L.

A. For the six months ended June 30, 1932, the Los Angeles Times headed the list with 1,800,247 agate lines. It was followed by the Brooklyn Eagle with 1,527,282 agate lines; Los Angeles Examiner, 1,462,155 agate lines; San Francisco Examiner, 1,383,-943 agate lines; Washington Star, 1,296,645 agate lines; New York World-Telegram 1,173,694.

Q. What is meant by an agate line? F. N.

A. An agate line is a line of agate type, and the basis on which advertising matter is figured as to size, cost, and volume. There are fourteen agate lines to an inch of space, one column wide.

Q. What are the colored glowing advertising signs now seen so frequently? S. L.

A. The use of neon tubes in sign writing is a recent development. The signs are made in the form of long tubes twisted into the shapes of letters and figures. They may be given various colors by the admixture of other gases.

Q. Please give the history of posters. P. C.

A. Actually, the poster or placard can trace its ancestry back almost to the dawn of civilization. Egyptian wall-paintings, mural decorations, and inscriptions, produced over 3000 years B.C., have been discovered by archaeologists. The modern poster began with Jules Cheret, a Frenchman, born in Paris in 1836, self taught as a draughtsman. In 1867 the world saw his first modern poster, an announcement of a play enacted by Sarah Bernhardt, then 22 years old. The poster announced a fairy play, entitled: La Biche au Bois.

Q. How is the cost of an advertisement determined? W. R.

A. The cost of an advertisement is determined by the rate per agate line, including the white space. All space between the cut-off rules at the top and bottom of the ad and between the column rules on each side is included. In marking the space an advertisement is to occupy the depth in agate lines and width in columns is indicated, i.e. 100 x 2 being 100 lines deep and two columns wide.

Q. How many advertising agencies are there in the United States? R. M. B.

A. There are about 1200 advertising agencies in the United States, of which approximately 800 are recognized by the American Newspaper Publishers' Association.

Q. Are most advertisements set by hand? D. W.

A. In modern newspaper plants most advertising, including the heads and much of the display type, is now set on machines.

Q. What is the newspaper's chief source of revenue? C. R. T.

A. Newspapers derive their chief source of revenue from the sale of their advertising space.

Q. Does a newspaper accept all and any advertising offered it? B. N. R.

A. Newspapers reserve the right to accept or reject any advertising offered them, and to edit the copy as to text, display type, and illustration, to conform to their rules and regulations. Many advertisements are refused.

Q. What is the Better Business Bureau? D. W. K.

A. The Better Business Bureau is an agency semi-public in character that aims to protect the public against merchants who make false or misleading statements in their advertising, and against the promoters and sellers of fake stocks and other alleged securities. This organization which is a unit only in the common purpose and methods of operations, is composed of the National Better Business Bureau and local bureaus in some 40-odd cities. Each local bureau is a distinct entity supported by, and owing allegiance to only its own community, and it is not a member of, or subsidiary to, the National Better Business Bureau. The bureaus are financed by merchants, manufacturers, and other financial interests. Their activities are furthered immeasurably by the cooperation of newspapers and other publications. The slogan of the monthly magazine of the National organization is "To increase public confidence in business by promoting fair play in advertising and selling."

Q. What is a blind advertisement? I. D.

A. In most cases this variety of advertisement discloses neither the name of the firm advertising nor much of the nature of its business.

Q. When a box appears on the front page of a newspaper to the left of the name of the paper, what is it called? D. B.

A. It is called the left ear. It is rarely sold to advertisers.

Q. Is the name, Bull Durham, trade-marked? W. H.

A. The American Tobacco Company says that the trade name consists of the words Bull Durham used singly or collectively, with, or without, the picture of the bull, which trade-mark is the property of the company.

Q. Who sponsored the first authorized voice advertisement by radio? When was this done? M. E. W.

A. The National Broadcasting Company says that to the best of its knowledge a talk on real estate, spon-sored by the Queensboro Realty Corporation of Jackson Heights, L. I., was the first sponsored voice advertisement on the air. This was done in the latter part of 1922 over WEAF, which it believes was the first station in the United States to accept a talk for broadcast advertising. At that time, WEAF was owned and operated as an experimental station by the American Telephone & Telegraph Co.

Q. Does Europe use outdoor advertising to the extent that it is used in America? E. E. P.

A. Observers say that Europe outstrips America in many forms of advertising. Poster boards abound, and many clever and ingenious ways of attracting the eye are used which are new to Americans.

Q. What column in an American newspaper corresponds to the English Agony Column? D. C.

A. The Personal Column of an American newspaper carries somewhat similar items to those of the Agony Column of the London Times, but there is no exact equivalent.

Q. Are there laws regulating the use of advertising signs along highways in the United States? M. A. D.

A. Almost all states have statutory provisions for the regulation of advertising signs along public highways.

Q. How did the trade-mark, 4711, originate? V. N.

A. The firm of Muhlens and Kroff began using 4711 as a trade-mark in 1792 to designate cologne water made from a family recipe. Its address at the time was 4711 Glockenstrasse, Cologne, Germany.

Q. Why is a clock used for advertising purposes always set at twenty minutes after eight? C. B.

A. This position of the hands of a clock is selected for the reason that it furnishes the greatest facility to meet the requirements for painting the longer name above the hands and the shorter word below. The minute hand has been varied in position from 17 to 25 minutes after eight.

Q. *Who was the model for the Campbell's soup kids?* M. A. G.

A. Grace Drayton, the artist, says that she used herself as a model. She had, from childhood, drawn comical presentments of herself and these finally brought her fame.

Q. *Whose trade-mark is Rexall?* F. G. B.

A. Some 20 years ago a number of druggists formed a cooperative company, the purpose of which was to manufacture products of which they all approved. The company was called the United Drug Company, and a trade-mark was coined from the Latin word Rex—meaning king, by adding "all" meaning "King of All." There are now more than 7,000 druggists in the organization.

Q. *How long have there been advertising agencies?* B. C. E.

A. In New York City, as early as 1850, there were agencies which arranged rates with newspapers, gathered information as to the extent and character of newspaper circulation, etc., for the guidance of clients. It was after the Civil War, however, with the development of the patent medicine industry, that the business took on a wider and more complicated form.

Q. *When did newspapers begin to carry advertisements?* N. E. D.

A. In the 17th century small advertisements appeared in newspapers for books, tea, coffee, or medicine. A heavy stamp tax hampered the growth of newspapers and advertising in England until 1855. In America, advertisements appeared in the early colonial papers. Brief notices told of new goods just imported from England, coffee, slave sales, runaway slaves and servants, or lost cattle. Newspaper advertising on a large scale dates from the establishment of the New York Sun in 1833, followed shortly by the New York Herald, the Philadelphia Public Ledger, and the New York Tribune.

Q. *Why is purple so rarely used in advertising?* A. M. E.

A. An authority says that while this color is distinctive, its suggestion of mourning makes it inappropriate for most advertising.

Q. *When was commercial art first employed?* M. G.

A. It has been stated that the origin of advertising can be traced to the walls of public buildings in Egypt in the days of Egyptian supremacy.

Q. *How did the Arm and Hammer trade-mark originate?* M. W. W.

A. This trade-mark was adopted about seventy-five years ago by the Vulcan Mills. It was an appropriate emblem to choose, as Vulcan was the god of smithy.

Q. *How long have advertising mediums been used?* M. T.

A. Advertising is of great antiquity. Egyptian advertising over 4000 years old has been discovered. Picture advertisements were used for the most part up to the time of and through the Middle Ages The earliest newspaper advertisement is said to have been in Germany, 1591.

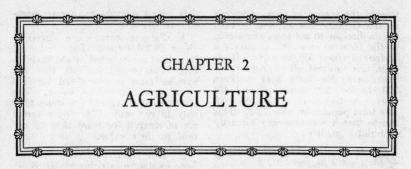

CHAPTER 2
AGRICULTURE

Q. Have many new crops been brought into this country since colonial days? P. N.

A. The Department of Agriculture has sent plant explorers to all sections of the earth, and many new species are being adapted to this country. Until it became active in the matter only two plants, sorghum and alfalfa, had been added to the list since colonial days.

Q. What state has the greatest percentage of land that can be cultivated? F. S.

A. Iowa claims the largest proportion of actually arable land.

Q. Where is the best wheat grown? F. B. A.

A. A Canadian, Herman Trelle, of Wembley, Alberta, has won the world's wheat prize at the International Grain and Hay Show at Chicago. Canada has taken this prize 17 times in 21 years.

Q. Which causes more crop damage in the United States, hail storms or tornadoes? W. B.

A. The average annual damage done by hail is three or four times that done by tornadoes. The hail losses on ten leading agricultural crops amount to $47,500,000 in an average year.

Q. Does hay shrink more in a stack in a field or in a barn? B. G.

A. In Colorado, hay which was stored in barns for eight months shrank 12.2 per cent, while hay in a

stack for eight months shrank 17 per cent. This principle applies generally to all hay.

Q. Is wild rice really a form of rice? D. N.

A. It is not a true rice. The grains are longer and less rounded than those of true rice and the husk is somewhat darker in color. Wild rice is usually served as a vegetable, especially with game.

Q. Will grains of wheat which are found in old Egyptian tombs sprout if planted? J. D.

A. Seeds of most types of grain remain viable generally for at least 20 years, in some cases perhaps longer, but it is utterly impossible for wheat placed in the tombs of Egyptian kings to be planted several thousand years later and germinate. No case has ever been recorded of the germination of seeds more than 25 years old.

Q. Why is Liverpool a leading wheat market? S. L. F.

A. The reason for the importance of Liverpool as a leading wheat market is that Great Britain is one of the principal industrial nations of the world and consequently needs a great supply of wheat to feed her population, her own crop being insufficient.

Q. Is it true that some of the Russian farms are of enormous size? I. B. C.

A. Louis Fischer in an article on Russia tells of the collectivized farms.

5

One of the largest of these is known as the Gigant. An airplane is used by its director to get from one sector of the farm to another. It covers a surface of about 550,000 acres. However, this was not all cultivated this year. On this farm 3541 workers, 220 tractors, 230 combines, and 450 tractor seeding drills were employed. The total population was 17,000. This means that it was necessary virtually to build a small city.

Q. *Is farming the basic industry of the United States?* M. T.

A. Throughout most of the history of the United States, farming was regarded as the basic industry. With the rise of manufacturing, however, particularly since 1900, the value of manufactured products has exceeded the value of farm products. Today, only a fraction of the working people are employed on farms whereas, earlier in our history, nearly all were so employed. While farming remains practically indispensable, it is no longer the basic industry. If a single industry were to be selected among the manufacturing industries, it would be steel, as that includes iron and coal. The United States now is classed as an industrial rather than an agricultural nation. Many states, taken individually, would still show farming as the basic industry. For the world, agriculture must still be regarded as basic, since from agriculture comes food without which there could be no other industry.

Q. *How does the value of American farms now compare with that ten years ago?* A. C. M.

A. The 1930 farm census shows the average value of American farms has dropped from $10,284 a farm in 1920 to $7,614, and from $69.39 an acre in 1920 to $48.52 an acre. The value of land and buildings dropped $18,400,-000,000 in the decade.

Q. *What are the working hours of women on farms?* H. M. R.

A. The average for the summer is 13.1 hours daily, and for the winter, 11.5 hours.

Q. *How heavily are farms mortgaged?* E. S.

A. Farm mortgages are placed at about $9,360,000,000. Total value of farm land is estimated at $34,000,000,-000. This would indicate that the average farm is mortgaged for less than one-third of its value. The Department of Agriculture states that only 12 per cent of American farms are mortgaged for *more than 75 per cent* of their value.

Q. *Has farm relief long been an issue in American politics?* D. B.

A. It has been an issue from the early days, when both major parties looked upon demands for farm relief with suspicion, as representing a threat of communism. Later, the Republicans espoused the cause. The first homestead act was vetoed by President Buchanan, a Democrat, on the ground that the measure "had the savor of the subversive doctrines fermenting in Europe." Not until after Mr. Lincoln became President did a homestead act become law.

Q. *How many farms in this country use electric power?* J. G. F.

A. It is estimated that between 600,000 and 700,000 farms in the United States use electric power.

Q. *How large is the Fishman wheat farm in Kansas?* T. A. T.

A. Simon Fishman is known as the wheat king of Greeley County and operates wheat farms totalling 30,000 acres. He says that he went West on the advice of Horace Greeley.

Q. *How large is the farm in Montana operated by Thomas Campbell?* H. D.

A. It is 95,000 acres in extent.

Q. *By whom are most of the mortgages on farms in the United States held?* A. S.

A. Life insurance companies hold 22.9 per cent; mortgage annuities, 10.4; commercial banks, 10.8; federal land banks, 12.1; stock land banks, 7.0; active farmers, 3.6; retired farmers, 10.6; other individuals, 15.4; other agencies, 7.2.

Q. What is the farmers' holiday which has been discussed in the newspapers? W. N.

A. It is a voluntary agreement of large groups of farmers to stop raising produce for the market. Its purpose is to create a shortage which will raise prices which farmers declare have been below the cost of production.

Q. What is the most valuable farm product? E. L. R.

A. Milk. The value for a recent year is given officially as $2,045,000,-000, compared with $1,546,000,000 for hogs, the second most valuable farm product, and $1,375,700,000 for cotton, the third in rank.

Q. What is the new cover crop which is being used in Florida? P. H. M.

A. Crotalaria is the crop which is gaining wide popularity as a cover crop in citrus groves and young tung-oil groves. The plant is native to Africa, India, South America, and Mexico.

Q. What is a Kulak? T. S. C.

A. In Soviet Russia a Kulak family is one whose means of production is valued at $700 or more. In 1928, any farmer who raised $250 worth of foodstuffs or more, after deducting $10 a head for family consumption, was considered a Kulak. Such farmers are to be taxed until their wealth is reduced to the common level.

Q. What is the gross income from farms? T. H.

A. The Bureau of Agricultural Economics says that in 1931 the gross income was $6,955,000,000. The gross income for 1932 is estimated at $5,240,000,000.

Q. When were potatoes and sugar bringing the highest prices? H. L. O.

A. The Bureau of Home Economics says that the highest market price ever paid for potatoes was in June

1920 in Chicago when they sold for approximately $9.14 per hundred pounds. The highest price ever paid for sugar was at the same time and the price was 26.7 cents per pound.

Q. Can the Chinese Litchi nut be grown in the United States? M. E.

A. The litchi or Lichi grows successfully only in southern China, Cochin-China, and the Philippines. It has been grown experimentally in southern Florida, and southern California, but will not thrive except in a tropical climate.

Q. How much flour does a bushel of wheat make? R. H. W.

A. A bushel of wheat usually weighs 60 pounds and can be made into 42 pounds of flour, 8⅗ pounds of bran, and 9⅗ pounds of shorts.

Q. How high does the bush grow from which tea leaves are taken? F. T. K.

A. As cultivated in China, it is an evergreen shrub growing to a height of from 3 to 5 feet.

Q. Who sponsors the national corn-husking contests? H. W.

A. They are held under the jurisdiction of the American Association of Middle-Western Farm Newspapers.

Q. Can Irish potatoes be grown from seed? B. G. R.

A. Irish potatoes produce blossoms which in turn produce seeds. However, as in the case of so many other cultivated plants, potato plants will not bear true from seed and a very inferior type of potato would result from planting and growing the seed. Only by planting and growing the tuber as is customarily done can the potato plant be made to reproduce accurately.

Q. Is there any record of the age attained by grape vines? F. W.

A. One of the royal grape vines at Hampton Court, near London, was planted in 1768, during the reign of George III, and is still yielding a fine crop each year. The girth of this ancient vine at ground level is 81 inches, the largest of any vine ever known. Its main branch is 114 feet long. This sturdy old vine is located near the Thames River and its roots are believed to have descended into the bed of that stream. The celebrated vine at the San Gabriel Mission in California is but three years younger and has a circumference of 72 inches.

Q. *What is the oldest cultivated fiber plant?* R. T. L.

A. Hemp is said to be. It was grown in China as early as 2800 B.C.

Q. *What kinds of plant patents have been issued?* J. T.

A. The first was issued August 18, 1931, and was for a variety of rose. Many of the patents are in the horticultural field.

Q. *How much of a supply of raw cotton do the cotton mills and manufacturers of cotton goods keep on hand?* I. E. K.

A. The Bureau of Agricultural Economics says that cotton mills and manufacturers of cotton textiles customarily have only three months supply of cotton on hand at a time.

Q. *What was the level of farm wages during the 1932 depression?* R. C. L.

A. In 1932 farm wages were the lowest in thirty years. Wages per day without board varied from a minimum in South Carolina of 55 cents to a maximum in Massachusetts and Rhode Island of $2.60. Wages per month with board ranged from $12.30 in South Atlantic States to $29.40 in Far Western States.

Q. *How many acres of average farm land does it require to produce a year's food for a farm horse?* R. L. M.

A. The Bureau of Animal Industry says that under good corn belt conditions it requires approximately two and one-half acres to produce a year's food for a farm horse of 1350 pounds. The amount of food eaten by a horse in a year and the number of acres required to produce it vary, of course, depending upon the amount of work a horse does and the productivity of the land. The figures cited are, however, a good average figure for fertile land. Expressed differently, the year's requirements in food for a farm horse are 3000 pounds of grain, 5000 pounds of roughage, and six months of pasture.

Q. *In what month is the largest amount of cotton shipped out of New Orleans?* C. L.

A. For a three-year period, the month of heaviest shipments was December.

Q. *What country and what city consume the most vegetables, especially asparagus and cucumbers?* J. E. T.

A. The United States consumes more vegetables than any other country in the world. The largest market for asparagus and cucumbers is New York City.

Q. *What is Alaska's best crop?* E. O. R.

A. Perhaps no crop is more generally cultivated than the potato.

Q. *What is the difference between the yam and the sweet potato?* B. F.

A. They are two distinct types of edible plants. The sweet potato is the root of a vine of the morning-glory family, while the yam is the root of a plant of a distinct family, Dioscoreaceae. The only species in this country is Dioscorea villosa, which occurs wild in the southern states. The yam and sweet potato are similar except that the latter has a more delicate taste and is preferred by many for food, having been cultivated for generations.

Q. *What percentage of the world's cotton consumption is in the United States?* N. D.

A. The United States consumes almost 30 per cent, Continental Europe about 27 per cent, Asia 27 per cent, and the United Kingdom about 11 per cent, leaving about four or five per cent for other parts of the world.

Q. When was cotton first cultivated in the South? D. H.

A. Cotton cultivation began about 1621.

Q. Does the peanut grow upon a shrub or tree? A. S.

A. It grows upon a vine. As the blossoms appear they are covered with earth and the nuts develop in the ground, somewhat like potatoes. Unlike the potato, however, the nut is attached to the branch and not to the root of the vine.

Q. How is copra made? J. T.

A. Copra is the dried meat of the coconut, which is detached from the shell and dried. One thousand nuts yield from 440 to 550 pounds of copra, containing approximately ten per cent of water. The copra is dried either by exposure to the air and sun, or by some artificial drying process, such as kiln drying, or subjection to a current of hot air in a heated tunnel.

Q. How many potatoes does it take to feed the average person in New York City? C. W.

A. The approximate average per capita consumption of potatoes in the New York area is .18 bushel per month, which amounts to about 10.8 pounds.

Q. What is the acid in tomatoes? C. F.

A. While there are other acids present in small amounts, the principal one is citric acid.

Q. What are the standard grades for asparagus sizes approved by the Federal Food and Drug Administration? S. F.

A. They run from Giant which is one inch at the base of the stalk to Tiny which indicates a stalk three eighths of an inch. Intermediate grades are Colossal, Mammoth, Large, and Medium.

Q. Is rhubarb a fruit or a vegetable? R. N.

A. It is a vegetable, since the edible part is prepared from the leaf stalks of the plant. Botanically, a fruit is the seed of a plant, or the seeds and the case which contains or holds them.

Q. Can turnips be kept for winter use by pickling, as cabbage is made into sauerkraut? D. H.

A. A similar process is satisfactory. Firm, sweet, juicy turnips should be used. They should be ground or shredded and mixed with salt at the rate of four ounces of salt to ten pounds of turnips. Pack in stone jars, weigh down, and store at a low temperature.

Q. What is the pomato? T. M. L.

A. It is a plant produced by the late Luther Burbank, obtained by cleft grafting tomato scions onto potato roots. These two vegetables are closely related, being two different species of the same genus (Solanum), and Mr. Burbank succeeded in producing both tomatoes and potatoes on the same plant. The pomato has never had any commercial importance, but is interesting as an example of plant breeding. Both the fruit and the tubers are edible, but such a plant could hardly be made to produce both tomatoes and potatoes of good flavor, or in commercial quantity.

Q. Please explain how mushrooms are dried. C. M.

A. Mushrooms may be preserved entire by drying them in the sun or in an oven. All moisture must be removed before the material is packed in a perfectly tight container. Mushrooms so preserved, after a preliminary soaking in tepid water or milk may be cooked as if fresh.

Q. What causes hollow spots in large potatoes? B. M.

A. If hollow spots appear in large potatoes this may be due to too rich soil and too much rain, which together give a rapid growth and form hollow spots. Some varieties of potatoes are more subject to this defect than others.

Q. *What makes peppers so hot?* M. W.

A. It is a glucoside contained in the peppers close to the spot where the seed is attached. The pungent principle derived from this glucoside is an essential oil.

Q. *What is the name for the eye of the bean?* A. A.

A. The Latin word for the eye or the scar at the point of attachment of a seed to its base, is hilum: plural, hila. Literally it means a little thing or trifle.

Q. *Is endive a cross between two other plants or is it a vegetable in a class of its own?* G. D.

A. It is a distinct species of vegetable, not obtained by crossing with any other plant. It is an herb of the chicory family and is known botanically as Cichorium endivia.

Q. *How many farms are served with automotive equipment?* G. O'B.

A. Fifty-eight per cent of all farms in the United States have automobiles; 13.4 per cent have motor trucks, and 13.3 per cent have tractors.

Q. *To whom did George Washington bequeath the River Farm?* T. D. S.

A. It was bequeathed to his grand nephews, Fayette Washington and Charles Augustine Washington. This farm is now known as Collingwood, and is owned by Mrs. Mark Ried Yates.

Q. *Where is the Berkshire Industrial Farm?* C. T.

A. It is near Canaan, New York. The Berkshire Farm gives to destitute, neglected, and imperiled boys the environment and training which will make them useful and self-supporting men. This work was founded nearly half a century ago by those who felt it was better to prevent juvenile delinquency than to permit it to ripen into criminality. Thousands of happy and successful graduates of the Farm are a tribute to its training. The Berkshire Farm, which is national and non-sectarian, is supported by voluntary contributions.

Q. *Has Henry Ford taken up farming?* F. M.

A. Mr. Ford is doing intensive farming on a 3000-acre tract of land in Lenawee County, Michigan. A group of farms has been purchased by him and will be operated as an experiment designed to solve some of the problems of agriculture.

Q. *What is the Hohenheim System?* N. R.

A. It is an intensive system of pasture fertilization and management in dairy farming extensively used in Europe. Under this system, the pasture is divided into small fields which are fertilized and grazed in rotation. It has been proved highly successful. The idea was introduced in Germany some 30 years ago, but gets its name from Hohenheim, Germany, where it was thoroughly investigated by Professor Warmbold in 1916.

Q. *How big a harrow can be used with a tractor?* F. R.

A. Harrows to be drawn by tractors have been built that are 65 feet wide and have 16 sections.

Q. *How large an acreage does it take to constitute a farm?* H. L.

A. In taking the census, anything from three acres up is considered a farm. No tract smaller than this is recorded as a farm unless it produced at least $250 in crops in a year.

Q. *What kind of rice is paddy?* T. M.

A. Paddy is unhusked rice, whether growing or gathered.

Q. *When was the sickle first used to reap grain?* W. A. A.

A. The grain sickle appears in some of the earliest hieroglyphics or picture writing and is known to have been included in a rude form in the earliest implements used by man.

Q. What is Yogo? D. P.

A. It is a new winter wheat which is being given a limited trial in Montana.

Q. Who made the first steel plows in this country? C. M. B.

A. About 1797 John Newbold demonstrated a cast-iron plow. It was similar to cast-iron plows which had been demonstrated shortly before in England. Records indicate that farmers feared detrimental effects from so much iron in contact with the soil, and evidently this first American cast-iron plow was never repaired after its moldboard became broken. The obstinate quality of the soil in the Mississippi Valley led to the use of steel instead of iron strips on the moldboards of plows. John Deere, 1837, and William Parlin, 1842, were pioneers in the steel plow business of the middle west. Much credit is due also to James Oliver who, beginning his experiments in 1853, greatly advanced the process for chilling cast-iron plow points.

Q. How much popped corn will one pint of popcorn make? T. H.

A. It should, if in good condition, make 15 to 20 pints. Popcorn should not be stored in a warm or heated room, as it will become too dry. This can be somewhat overcome by sprinkling with water before popping. If it has become very dry the corn may be placed out of doors in a shaded place where it can absorb moisture from the air.

Q. What percentage of the originally planted agricultural crop is a complete failure due to adverse conditions, such as extreme wet, extreme dry, or hail storms? W. W.

A. Formal estimates of abandonment are made by the Department of Agriculture for only two crops—winter wheat, for which the ten-year average abandonment has been 12.1 per cent, equivalent to 5,245,000 acres per year; cotton, for which the ten-year average estimated abandonment has been 3.4 per cent, equivalent to 1,430,000 acres per year. Average abandonment for remaining crops probably does not exceed an average of 1.5 per cent a year, which would be equivalent to approximately 4,300,000 acres.

Q. What is Kaffir corn? W. C. S.

A. It is a variety of Indian millet, Andropogon sorghum, cultivated in South Africa.

Q. Why are silos usually round? J. K.

A. The rectangular type is less popular because the silage may spoil in the corners.

Q. Would the same amount of pop corn weigh the same whether raw or popped? B. D.

A. Corn pops because of the expansion of steam within the kernel, and a certain amount of moisture is lost from the popped kernel. A volatile oil is also given off, as indicated by the characteristic odor of popping corn. A pound of pop corn will therefore weigh slightly less after it is popped, although this may not be enough to detect on an ordinary pound scale.

Q. Is grohoma a kind of wheat? M. R.

A. The Division of Cereal Investigation says that the grain called grohoma is not a wheat but a grain sorghum which originated in Oklahoma and which is now grown in surrounding states such as Kansas and Texas.

Q. In what years were there wheat corners on the Chicago Board of Trade? R. E. D.

A. They include the Hutchinson Corner, 1888; the Leiter Corner, 1898; and the Patten Corner, 1909.

Q. Why isn't flax grown in this country for the manufacture of linen? L. E.

A. It is grown to some extent, but the climate is not very suitable. Flax is a fibre which requires more moisture than any other for its successful manipulation.

Q. *Please give a recipe for salting peanuts in the shell.* J. O. C.

A. Peanuts may be salted in the shell by soaking in a ten per cent salt solution before roasting.

Q. *What is abaca?* C. R.

A. Abaca is a native name for Manila hemp.

Q. *What is copra used for?* F. S.

A. Copra is the kernel of the coconut dried for exporting. It is used in the manufacture of soap, candles, and cocoa butter, to a limited extent for addition to other food products, and as a fodder.

Q. *How did the Indians parch corn?* N. S.

A. The preparation of maize as food, by the Indians, involved almost numberless processes, varying with the tribes. In general, when maize reached the edible stage the ears were roasted in pit ovens, and after the feasting the surplus of roasted ears was dried for future use. The mature grain was milled raw or parched, the meal entering into various mushes, cakes, pones, wafers, and other bread. The grain was soaked in lye obtained from wood ashes to remove the horny envelope and was then boiled, forming hominy; this in turn was often dried, parched, and ground, reparched and reground, making a concentrated food of great nourishing power in small bulk, which was consumed dry, or in water as gruel.

Q. *Is sea-island cotton being grown?* S. L. F.

A. Sea-island cotton was formerly grown on the islands along the eastern coasts of South Carolina and Georgia. It had to be abandoned there because of the ravages of the boll weevil and is now confined to the drier islands of the West Indies where it was reintroduced from the United States. A little cotton of this type is grown experimentally at Yuma, Arizona.

Q. *How much hay in the United States is lost from spontaneous combustion?* A. A.

A. Fully one-tenth of the harvested hay crop of the United States is lost from the time it is cut until it is used as a result of spontaneous heating.

Q. *In the trading in cotton futures, is more than the actual production dealt in?* W. F. K.

A. The actual amount of cotton future trading is generally estimated as eight to ten times greater than the actual annual production.

Q. *How many acres of land are under cultivation in India?* R. D.

A. Two hundred and fifty-seven million acres are under cultivation. About one-third of this is in rice.

Q. *What is meant by the term liming as generally used in reference to the improvement of soil?* M. L.

A. The term liming as generally used means the application to the soil of the element known to chemists as calcium in one or two forms—either calcium carbonate, more commonly known as carbonate of lime, or calcium oxide, the ordinary burned lime of commerce. Carbonate or magnesium mixed with carbonate of lime, as in dolomitic or magnesian limestone, and the mixed oxides resulting from burning such limestones are included also under the term lime.

Q. *What is the cheapest first grade cotton sold in the United States?* J. S.

A. The Bureau of Agricultural Economics says that the lowest price for which middling or first grade cotton ever sold in this country was in 1842 when it brought four and one-half cents a pound on the New Orleans Cotton Exchange. The records of the Bureau extend back through the year 1831, and this is the lowest price recorded in all the years since that year. The second lowest price occurred twice—in the years 1847 and 1898. This was four and three-fourths cents a pound.

Q. What percentage of the asparagus raised is canned? V. H. C.

A. About 50 per cent of the asparagus raised in the United States is consumed in the canning industry.

Q. How long ago did people discover that the tomato is edible? H. L.

A. About 1850, people began to eat tomatoes. Before that time it was the general belief that tomatoes were poisonous.

Q. How is cotton applied to roads? R. S.

A. In surfacing roads with cotton fabric, the road is first scarified and given the desired grade. When the surface becomes firm, it is swept clean of loose particles, and a prime coat of light tar applied. While the tar is still sticky, the cotton fabric is spread in longitudinally overlapping strips, and covered with hot asphaltic oil applied by means of a pressure distributor. This is covered with coarse sand, gravel or finely crushed stone, which is then carefully rolled and evened.

Q. Is the vitamin content of spinach or other greens reduced by the addition of vinegar? L. A. H.

A. Vinegar used on greens will not destroy the vitamins. Generally, the more acid the product, the less danger there is of vitamin destruction.

Q. Where was the eggplant first grown? T. R. S.

A. The eggplant is said to be a native of southern Asia where it has been cultivated since remote antiquity.

Q. What vegetables will grow in Alaska? G. F.

A. The growing of hardier vegetables has been demonstrated throughout most of Alaska south of the Arctic Circle. Radishes, mustard, turnips, kale, and lettuce can be grown anywhere. Carrots, parsnips, parsley, peas, cress, cabbage, cauliflower, Brussels sprouts, onions, spinach, beets, potatoes, rhubarb, and such herbs as caraway, mint, catnip, sage, and thyme, may be grown along the coast region and in the interior of Alaska if garden sites are selected with reference to shelter and exposure to the sun.

Q. Why is shoe-peg corn given this name? J. E.

A. It is used to indicate a type of grain in the corn similar in appearance to a shoe peg.

Q. What is long sauce? F. D. S.

A. Long sauce denotes beets, carrots, parsnips, etc., as distinguished from short sauce, the shorter vegetables.

Q. Is red cotton grown in this country? W. C. J.

A. This type of cotton is grown in Alabama and Mississippi. It was introduced into this country because of a supposed immunity to attacks from the boll weevil, but is not immune. The theory arose from the fact that red cotton is a late flowering cotton and boll weevils seem to prefer early flowering varieties.

Q. Should green beans be called string beans or snap beans? B. D.

A. Since the new varieties of beans are stringless, a better name for them is snap beans.

Q. How many pounds are there in a bale of cotton? R. T.

A. It has an average gross weight of 500 pounds and a net weight of 478 pounds.

Q. Are beet leaves edible? C. E.

A. Beet leaves are more valuable food than beet roots. Care should be taken in selecting only leaves which have no diseased or dead-looking spots.

Q. What percentage of opium does lettuce contain? H. E. Q.

A. Contrary to popular belief, lettuce contains no opium.

Q. *What are the raw vegetables which should be fed to young children?* H. A.

A. The Bureau of Home Economics suggests finely chopped cabbage, finely chopped celery, grated carrots, chopped lettuce, chopped watercress, and peeled tomatoes.

Q. *What does it cost to raise potatoes?* W. R. F.

A. It costs about $120 to grow an acre of potatoes under modern conditions.

Q. *Was cotton grown in the United States to any extent at the time of the Revolutionary War?* S. T.

A. According to McMaster, cotton in 1784 was never seen growing except in gardens among rose bushes and vines. A little had been sent to Liverpool five years before the beginning of the war. In 1784 eight bags were sent to Liverpool, but the customs officers seized them claiming that it was well known that so much cotton could never have come from America.

Q. *Is a toadstool poisonous and a mushroom non-poisonous?* H. A.

A. The terms toadstool and mushroom in popular usage refer indiscriminately to any type of fungus correctly known as mushroom. Toadstool is really a nickname, and although it is used by some people to refer to poisonous varieties, it actually has no such distinction.

Q. *Were potatoes brought to America from Europe or taken to Europe from America?* L. M. N.

A. Potatoes were introduced into Europe from America.

Q. *How large a part of California is under cultivation?* O. M.

A. One-third of the land in California is under cultivation, and probably almost one-third more could be cultivated with irrigation. California leads all states in irrigation, having spent millions of dollars on projects and having over four million acres under irrigation.

Q. *How long has the human race cultivated crops?* D. M.

A. Agriculture is believed to be the earliest occupation of man. It can be traced back to prehistoric times when primitive man began to select particular plants as preferable to others for his use as food. Records on ancient monuments have enabled us to trace the history of agriculture in Egypt back to at least 3000 B.C.

Q. *Is the practice of liming soils of comparatively recent origin?* I. L. S.

A. The practice of applying lime to soils to increase crop yields has been more or less common in many parts of this country since its first settlement. It has been followed in many parts of Europe for centuries, and dates back more than 3000 years.

Q. *Is cotton or burlap more durable for cotton-picking sacks and sheets?* W. D.

A. A cotton-picking sack made of cotton lasts 3.6 times as long as a sack made of burlap, and a picking sheet made of cotton is 1.8 times as durable as one made of burlap, according to estimates by the Bureau of Agricultural Economics, U. S. Department of Agriculture.

Q. *What is mulching?* K. L. R.

A. For many years Hawaiian sugar planters made a practice of leaving the crop refuse, such as leaves and tops, between the rows of growing cane. This served the double purpose of conserving the moisture in the soil and keeping down the weed growth. Later the experiment was made of covering the ground between the rows with a cheap grade of asphalt paper and still later the entire field was so covered when it was found that the stiff shoots of the cane would penetrate the paper, while weeds would not. These differing processes are known as mulching. The same thing is now done with the pineapple crop, holes being made in the paper so that the pineapples can grow through. Experiments made in the United States in mulching various vegetables are said to have resulted in production increases of from 30 to 500 or 600 per cent. It is said that twelve days after a rain soil protected with paper mulch will contain as much as 20 per cent more moisture than unmulched soil in the same vicinity.

Q. Is a cane-brake an indication of poor soil or of good soil? N. M.

A. A cane-brake is an indication of rich land.

Q. How many acres of the soil of the United States have been surveyed and classified? P. S.

A. The Department of Agriculture says that nearly a billion acres have been surveyed and that the work is progressing at the rate of 15,000,000 acres a year.

Q. How much fertility is wasted by erosion of soil in comparison with what it takes to make an average crop? C. W. C.

A. The Department of Agriculture says that approximately twenty-one times as much plant food is washed away by erosion yearly as is taken out of the soil by plants. Furthermore this plant food can not be put back since it has been washed completely off the soil.

Q. How long have artichokes been generally used in the United States? A. K.

A. John Randolph, Jr., writing what has been called the "earliest American book on kitchen gardening," in Virginia about 1765, discussed the cultivation of artichokes as if they were as common as cabbages. It is noted that Thomas Jefferson mentioned them among the vegetables common in the Washington city markets when he was President.

Q. Has cauliflower much food value? B. S.

A. Cauliflower, while low in fuel value, is rich in vitamins A, B, and C. It contains, also, considerable calcium and phosphorus, which are needed for healthy bones and teeth. Its water content is 92 per cent.

Q. Are parsnips poison when they come up the second year? F. C. H.

A. Parsnips are not poisonous. Occasionally cattle, or even humans, mistake water hemlock for parsnips, and when the water hemlock is eaten it frequently causes serious stomach disorders.

Q. What color are sugar beets? A. E.

A. Sugar beets are white.

Q. In what parts of the country can two crops of potatoes be grown in a season? D. B.

A. In the southern states, from southern New Jersey to Texas, and as far north as the Ohio and Missouri Rivers, and in California the growing season is long enough to produce two crops of potatoes a year by the practical application of the dormancy-breaking treatments.

Q. What is the bean that is used in chop suey? M. T.

A. It is the mung bean. This is an oriental bean grown primarily in China and Japan. The bean sprouts grow to be from one to one and one-half inches long. It is only the bean sprout that is used, as practically all of the bean goes to sprout. For sprouting, the beans should be soaked 24 hours in water and then placed in a well-drained container and kept at a medium temperature for about ten days. The bean should be moistened daily.

Q. Please give some information about truffles. B. J. H.

A. Truffles range from the size of a filbert to that of a potato. Although white truffles are somewhat in demand, it is the black or queen truffles of England and France which are in most demand, those of the French province of Perigord being considered the finest. Truffles are practically never cultivated, in spite of various attempts, but are occasionally cared for in situ.

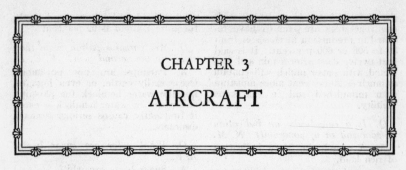

CHAPTER 3

AIRCRAFT

Q. *Do landing or starting planes have the right of way at an airport?* J. H.

A. Descending planes always have the right of way, on the theory that those on the ground can never know how important it is for a plane to effect a speedy landing.

Q. *Who was the first woman to fly an airplane in the United States?* D. T.

A. Dr. Jessica Raiche of Santa Ana, California, was the first. She flew an airplane at Mineola Field, Long Island, in 1910.

Q. *How are altitude records of aviators verified?* R. H. T.

A. When an aviator attempts to break an official record he carries a barograph which has been sealed. When he lands the barograph unopened is sent to the Bureau of Standards or some similar organization where it is opened and tested.

Q. *At what height can a man in a balloon hear sounds made on the earth?* G. H. N.

A. The Weather Bureau says since no definite experiments are known to have been made to determine the height in question, no positive answer may be given. Experience of army balloonists shows that shouting voices may be heard in a balloon at a height of 5000 feet where the wind is not unusually strong. Birds singing in the trees have been heard at 10,000 feet, and the whistles of railroad trains have been heard between 15,000 and 20,000 feet. High pitched sounds are heard best. On cloudy, calm days when the balloon is in the clouds or just above them, the sounds, at least in some cases, seem to be heard to somewhat greater altitudes.

Q. *Is the German Do-X an amphibian plane?* A. N. B.

A. It is not. An amphibian plane is one which can alight on either land or water due to its collapsible wheels. The Do-X can land only on water.

Q. *How many Americans made emergency parachute jumps from balloons during the World War?* R. N.

A. One hundred and seventeen such jumps were made in the zone of operations. Of this number 59 were made from balloons which had been attacked and set on fire by enemy aircraft, and 58 from balloons which had been attacked but did not catch fire.

Q. *Is there such a thing as an air ambulance?* F. S. K.

A. The United States Army Air Service has ambulance airplanes. They are painted white with a red cross on the side. Twelve patients, a doctor, and attendant, can be carried in the cabins.

Q. *Are the quarters for the crew of the Akron inside or outside the dirigible?* A. L. M.

A. The crew's quarters, the radio cabin, the galley, mess rooms, etc., are inside the hull of the Akron. The control car is forward, projecting below the stream line of the lower half, and is built as an integral part of the structure. Here the commander and his staff are stationed to direct operations. The car has been made only large enough comfortably to take care of these operations, thereby reducing the air resistance to a minimum.

Q. Why is it harder to fly from Europe to America than it is to fly the other way? C. M. J.

A. The nature of the winds created by the motion of the earth and the heat of the sun will always be an obstacle in flying from east to west. The earth in turning on its axis from west to east drags along its envelope of atmosphere in the same direction as the atmosphere rotates from the United States toward Europe. The prevailing winds in summer and winter also move in the same direction. European aviators even in perfect flying weather have no tail winds to increase their speed in taking off from Europe, but find themselves constantly flying westward into the winds which cause a loss of speed and an extra expenditure of gasoline.

Q. When an airship is fastened to a mooring mast, why doesn't the gas cause the unanchored end to rise? C. G.

A. Airships are kept on an even keel when they are not in motion because the lift is even throughout.

Q. Who was the first man to fly over the Alps? B. C. B.

A. George Chavez made the first successful flight in 1910. He followed the Simplon Pass, and made a flight which remains a high light in aviation, but lost his life through a mishap in landing his plane.

Q. What did American aviators accomplish in the World War? T. D.

A. American aviators engaged in over 2100 combats. There were 12,830 pursuit flights, 6672 observation flights, and 1174 bombing flights. Enemy positions and strategic points were photographed 17,845 times. From these plates 585,000 prints were made.

Q. Please name the leading French ace, German ace, and American ace. A. W. M.

A. The leading French ace of the World War was Lieut. Rene Fonck, who was credited with 75 air victories. The leading German ace was Capt. Manfred Von Richthofen, who was credited with 80 air victories. This is the largest number credited to any ace during the World War. Capt. Edward B. Rickenbacker was the leading American ace. He was credited with 25 air victories.

Q. How much does it cost to swing open the doors of the airship dock of the U. S. S. Akron? B. R.

A. The cost of the electricity used in swinging the doors at either end of the dock is about one dollar.

Q. What kind of ground is chosen for a gliderport? C. R. E.

A. A gliderport is distinguished from an airport in that an airport is a level piece of land which has the least possible number of approach obstructions, while the gliderport should be entirely surrounded by high hills so that these motorless flying machines may be taken off from the top of the hills in any wind direction and flown to the level ground in the center.

Q. Where was the first aviation repair shop established? P. H.

A. This is not on record. The first one officially recognized by the United States Department of Commerce was the Boeing Station at Cheyenne, Wyoming. It was recognized March 26, 1930.

Q. Where is the Daniel Guggenheim Airship Institute? B. S. S.

A. It was dedicated recently in Akron, Ohio. The institute was created with a fund of $250,000 furnished by the Daniel Guggenheim Foundation for the Promotion of

Aeronautics, established in 1926 by the late Daniel Guggenheim, together with $100,000 advanced by the city of Akron. The institute has the world's largest vertical wind tunnel for testing airship models.

Q. *Why are balloon races held?* B. T.

A. Balloon racing is important because it is an important contribution to the training of dirigible airship pilots and, like automobile racing in the automobile industry, is a test for new improvements on airships.

Q. *Who named the dirigible Akron?* G. A.

A. The U. S. S. Akron was named by Secretary of the Navy Adams in 1930. It was named after the City of Akron, Ohio, where it was built.

Q. *Has the Graf Zeppelin made a trip across the Southern States?* L. S.

A. The Graf Zeppelin has only made one trip over the United States. On this trip she passed over Los Angeles, California, El Paso, Texas, Chicago, Illinois, and New York City, N. Y. She did not cross the Southern States.

Q. *When was Richard E. Byrd made a Rear Admiral?* C. B. K.

A. His status on the expedition to the South Pole was Commander, and in December, 1929, he was promoted by Congress to the rank of Rear Admiral.

Q. *What was the total number of flyers belonging to the Lafayette Escadrille during the World War and how many were killed?* G. A.

A. The total number was 210. Of these 65 died and 19 were wounded.

Q. *Are De Haviland airplanes still used by the Army Air Corps?*

A. More than a thousand were in use for a few years after the World War. The number has diminished until the last few which were occasionally used for training purposes are no longer in use.

Q. *What keeps a glider in the air?* E. H. S.

A. The modern glider is a soaring plane. It is for all practical purposes an extremely light airplane without an engine, while the construction is greatly simplified, all parts being made as light as consistent with strength, and the lifting surface so designed and set as to give high lift at low speeds. The fact remains that the craft is sustained in the air by means of the lift on its surface caused by its motion relative to the airship.

Q. *Where do the Marines learn to fly airplanes?* E. S.

A. They learn to fly at Pensacola Field, Florida.

Q. *Why is a tandem airplane so called?* H. V.

A. In a tandem airplane the rear motors push and the front motors pull. Since they are arranged one behind the other, the name tandem is used because it denotes that line-up.

Q. *Who invented the autogiro?* E. T. S.

A. It was invented by the Spanish inventor Juan de la Cierva.

Q. *How far did Jackson and O'Brine travel in making their airplane endurance record?* H. G.

A. In August, 1930, they established the record flight of 647 hours and 28 minutes and covered a distance of 42,008 miles.

Q. *How does an airship collect water to compensate for the weight of the fuel burned?* R. M. D.

A. The water recovery apparatus used on airships consists of a condenser which collects the water of combustion formed by the combination of the hydrogen in the gasoline with the oxygen of the air. When ordinary aviation gasoline is used, about 140 pounds of water is formed in burning 100 pounds of fuel. The condensing method simply cools the engine exhaust gas to within a few degrees of air temperature and separates entrained moisture from the gases as they leave the apparatus.

Q. When was the Army aviation field in Texas completed? F. R.

A. Randolph Field was finished in 1931. It is popularly denominated "The West Point of the Air." As Randolph Field is developed, all student training will be concentrated there.

Q. What word describes the shape of the new Goodyear hangar at Akron, Ohio? A. L.

A. It is approximately semi-paraboloid. Its shape has been well-described as "a half-egg." The length is 1175 feet between center lines of door tracks; its width, 325 feet, center to center of arch pins; and its height, 197½ feet from center of lower to center of top pins. The height from the floor to the platform at the top is 211 feet. The floor area is 364,000 square feet, the largest single uninterrupted floor area yet built. The volume is approximately 55,000,000 cubic feet.

Q. How big is the ordinary parachute? F. I. H.

A. The standard airplane parachute when opened has an umbrella spread of 24 feet.

Q. What is the insignia that denotes a United States military airplane? W. V. W.

A. The insignia is round with a five-pointed star and a red circle inside the star. The specifications state that the inner circle shall be red and that portion of the star not covered by the inner circle shall be white, and that the portion of the circumscribed circle not covered by either the star or the inner circle shall be blue.

Q. How many persons had crossed the Atlantic by air before Charles Lindbergh made his solo flight? J. A. C.

A. Sixty-four persons had crossed previously. Several airplanes and the English dirigible, R 34, had made trips across.

Q. How does the Sperry Pilot work? W. W.

A. The Sperry Pilot or Robot Pilot is composed of gyroscopes sensitive to the slightest change of position, electrical switches upon which the gyroscopes react, electric motors which are the Robot's muscles, and rods and pulleys which serve him for arms and legs in operating the controls. The Mechanical Pilot can fly a plane with unerring precision in any of the three dimensions of flight. The instrument not only maintains the plane in level flight, but also keeps it on the desired course. Human hands are required only on the take-off and landing.

Q. How many people can the Do-X carry comfortably? F. C. B.

A. This giant plane carried 169 persons in a test flight over Lake Constance, Switzerland. The plane has three decks, and can provide comfortable accommodations for 100 persons.

Q. What airplane was the first to make a non-stop flight from Europe to North America? D. J. B.

A. The Bremen is the first airplane to make a non-stop flight from Europe to North America. It took off from the airport at Dublin, Ireland, and flew across the Atlantic to Newfoundland and came to a forced landing at Greenly Island, off the coast of Labrador, in the Strait of Belle Isle, after a continuous flight of 36 hours and 35 minutes.

Q. Did the United States purchase the Los Angeles from Germany? A. N.

According to Armistice terms the United States was entitled to two rigid airships. These were destroyed by the Germans before being taken over by this government. As the United States wanted a sample of their best work, a request was made to the Council of Ambassadors through Myron T. Herrick, United

States Ambassador to France, that these two rigid airships be replaced. We first asked for one with 100,000 cu.m. capacity, but the Powers objected, so a compromise was made on one of 70,000 cu.m., which is larger than either of the two destroyed. The ZR-3 was constructed solely for the United States, and did not cost our nation anything except accessories which amounted to approximately $50,000.

Q. Is it true that it rains inside the Goodyear Zeppelin Dock at Akron when it is clear outside? P. E.

A. The dock is so large (55,000,000 cubic feet) that sudden changes of temperature cause clouds to form inside the hangar and rain falls.

Q. If an airplane could stand still in the air, would the earth pass in view beneath it? W. J.

A. An airplane rising above the earth's surface remains within the earth's atmosphere and moves with the earth. Therefore, even were it possible for a plane to remain stationary for twenty-four hours, it would be carried with the earth as the latter turns on its axis and moves around the sun.

Q. What is the speed of propellers used on passenger airplanes? A. L. P.

A. The average speed of propellers in commercial use today lies between 1600 and 1850 revolutions per minute.

Q. What was Lindbergh's time in crossing the ocean? G. H.

A. The flying time for Lindbergh's transatlantic flight was 33 hours and 29 minutes.

Q. How far has an aviator fallen before opening his parachute in a safe descent? J. W. G.

A. The record for delayed parachute jumps is held by E. S. "Spud" Manning, who has since been killed. After an official calibration of the barograph he carried on a leap March 1, 1931, it was proved that he fell 15,265 feet before opening his parachute. The previous record of 9600 feet was held by Rex Hardin.

Q. How did the round-the-world flight by airplane compare in time with Magellan's trip? N. M. S.

A. Wiley Post and Harold Gatty circled the globe in 8 days, 15 hours, and 51 minutes; a record breaking 15,128-mile flight. The flight was made from June 23 to July 1, 1931. Magellan's round-the-world voyage was made in 1519 to 1522. The trip took 1083 days.

Q. Who was the first victim of the airplane? R. G.

A. As far as we have been able to ascertain, the first death caused by an airplane in the history of American aviation was that of Lieut. Selfridge. Quoting from "American Air Service: "Then on September 17, 1908, came the first fatal accident; the propeller blade broke when the machine was at a height of about 75 feet, the plane careened, glided 35 feet, and then pitched forward to the ground, killing Lieutenant Selfridge and injuring Orville Wright."

Q. What is it about an airplane which makes the roaring noise? E. R.

A. The primary source of noise in an airplane is the propeller, and the secondary source is the engine.

Q. Who was the first woman to own and operate a flying school in the United States? H. P.

A. Miss Catherine Stinson. She opened a flying school in San Antonio, Texas, soon after the World War started in 1914.

Q. Please tell something of the outfitting of the Byrd Expedition. C. L. S.

A. The Byrd Expedition to the South Pole sailed in a fleet of four ships—the City of New York, the Eleanor Bolling, the Sir James Clark Ross, and the C. A. Larsen. It was the most elaborately equipped expedition that has ever undertaken polar research. More than a million dollars was spent in outfitting. Besides the ships' crews, there were 82 scientists, engineers, aviators, and radio experts. The larders contained 1200 different items, including 30 tons of poultry and beef, 5 tons of ham and bacon, and 60 tons of groceries. There were 4 planes, including a Ford trimotored plane and 3 smaller planes for scout work, as well as snow motors and caterpillar tractors. Seventy-nine dogs were taken along.

Q. Does Colonel Lindbergh hold his title through state or federal appointment? L. C.

A. Colonel Lindbergh was promoted to the rank of Colonel in the United States Army Air Corps Reserve in June, 1927, when the President of the United States approved the recommendation of the Secretary of War for Lindbergh's appointment as Colonel. The commission was presented by the Secretary of War at ceremonies held later in St. Louis.

Q. What causes the highest per cent of accidents to airplanes carrying passengers? B. G.

A. Weather conditions. Fog is one of the greatest menaces to fliers.

Q. What equipment has the Akron for carrying airplanes? C. L. J.

A. The storage hangar of the Akron is 75 by 60 feet in size and is located about one-third of the ship's length from the nose. It will carry five planes. These may be released through a T-shaped opening in the ship's bottom by a trapeze arrangement while the ship is in flight. They may be picked up again on the trapeze and hauled into the compartment by a winch.

Q. When was an airplane first used to drop bombs? A. P. D.

A. The Air Corps News says that from all accounts this occurred in 1911 during the Italian campaign in Tripoli. The next use of the aerial bomb was by the Spanish forces in the Moroccan Campaign. A German airplane used the first bombs in the World War in a raid on Paris, August 30, 1914.

Q. To whom was issued the first aviator's license? E. J. C.

A. Glenn H. Curtiss. The first license as an air pilot in America was issued to him, June 8, 1911.

Q. How many guns could the airship Akron carry? M. J. W.

A. Seven gun emplacements have been located on this airship so as to cover all angles of approach and some of these emplacements will carry more than one gun. The final choice of guns, their arrangement, and means for ammunition stowage and supply are matters that will require to be worked out on the basis of actual experience.

Q. How is soaring accomplished in a glider? W. W.

A. Soaring consists of taking advantage of rising air currents along a hill or ridge under certain clouds or along the shores of large bodies of water and riding these air currents for altitude and distance.

Q. What causes a tail spin? D. D.

A. A tail spin is the result of a stall. After stalling, an airplane falls off on one wing, the nose drops, and the airplane revolves in the opposite direction to which the rudder is applied. The tail revolves, making the nose the approximate center of the turn. If the rudder is applied to the left wing, it becomes a left spin, and if to the right wing, it becomes a right spin. A tail spin is used as a stunt and also as a means of losing altitude. It becomes dangerous only when the pilot loses control of the plane.

Q. Why didn't Lindbergh fly to Paris by way of the Azores? J. S.

A. The route he chose is about 473 miles shorter than by the Azores. The reason for this, technically stated, is that in the higher latitudes the shortest distance between two points, because of the earth's curvature, is not on the east and west parallel, but on the arc of a circle which would divide the earth in two equal parts and pass through the points in question.

Q. When was the first seaplane made? D. D.

A. The first seaplane, The Loon, was constructed by Glenn Curtiss, and tried out by him in 1908. It was not until 1911, however, that the pontoon attachment was perfected.

Q. What is the highest rating that an airport is given by the Department of Commerce? O. L. H.

A. The "A-1-A" of the Department of Commerce is the highest rating. The Rickenbacker Airport, Sioux City, Iowa, was the first commercial airport to attain this standing. It is not necessary for every landing field used regularly by planes to have this rating.

Q. Is an airplane a dirigible? E. B.

A. An airplane is a dirigible craft just as an automobile or a bicycle. Dirigible means capable of being directed. Therefore anything the speed and direction of which can be controlled is properly a dirigible.

Q. In making a landing is the airplane headed into the wind? W. T.

A. Landings are made with the airplane headed into the wind, as when taking off. The force of the wind slows up the plane and helps in making landings.

Q. What is meant by blind flying? T. L. N.

A. An aviator is flying "blind" when he cannot see, either because of the construction of his plane, or because of weather conditions, such as fog, rain, etc. When flying "blind" an aviator guides his plane by means of instruments. The most important of these instruments is the earth indicator compass. Other essential instruments are a turn indicator, a bank indicator, and a drift meter. While the precision of these instruments is great, they are by no means perfectly accurate. Skill is required to read the scales.

Q. How are airplanes catapulted off ships? S. S.

A. There are two methods of catapulting airplanes off ships, the gun-powder catapult and the compressed air catapult. These devices work in much the same way as does a sling shot. The plane is placed on a car which is on a track on the deck of a ship. The releasing of compressed air or of gunpowder at the back of the plane assists it to pick up the necessary flying speed.

Q. How are airplanes assisted in landing on the deck of a ship? J. M. D.

A. Airplanes are enabled to land on the deck of aircraft carriers by means of cables stretched crosswise and lengthwise across the deck. The plane as it descends, lets fall a large hook which catches in the wires, thus retarding the speed of the plane.

Q. What are the specifications of the Navy Airships U.S.S. Akron, and U.S.S. Macon? A. L.

A. Except for minor changes in the Macon the ships are identical. The specifications are: length 785 feet; maximum diameter 132.9 feet; number of gas cells 12; number of engines 8; maximum speed 72.8 m.p.h. (at 3000 feet altitude).

Q. What is dope used for on an airplane? M. Z.

A. Dope is a somewhat viscous solution of cellulose nitrate. The name dope is given to that substance used as an application on the fabric covering of the wings of an airplane, for the purpose of shrinking and protection. A dope must shrink so that the tautness of the dope-covered fabric is satisfactory for flying. The tautness should also remain fairly constant under various weather conditions. The dope film must act as a protective covering for the fabric to prevent rapid deterioration.

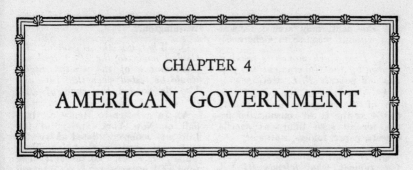

CHAPTER 4

AMERICAN GOVERNMENT

Q. What is the oldest republic in the world? T. M. G.

A. The United States of America is the world's oldest existing republic that began with a President as its chief executive.

Q. How many members of Congress named Smith have there been? D. J.

A. There have been 99 members of Congress named Smith, of whom 17 have been Senators. There have been three members named Smyth.

Q. How many Jews are there in Congress? S. M. B.

A. The Senate has no Jewish members. The House of Representatives had seven Jews in the second session of the 72nd Congress, and ten were elected to the 73rd Congress.

Q. What is the Bill of Rights? H. G. F.

A. The first ten amendments to the Constitution of the United States.

Q. What was the Government paying in rentals in Washington, D. C., before the new building program got under way? L. U.

A. In 1929, the year prior to the occupancy of the first of the new buildings, the rental bill was $1,-381,388.

Q. Which Presidents, besides Washington, made short inaugural addresses? J. M. G.

A. Washington's second inaugural address was the shortest on record—

134 words. Lincoln's second address contained 588 words; Johnson's, 362; Arthur's, 431.

Q. How does the per capita cost of running our Government now compare with its cost in the early days? S. M.

A. Randolph Leigh in an article on The American Constitution says that for the first year the Government was organized—1789—the per capita cost was approximately 20 cents, while at present it is about $38 per inhabitant.

Q. Has there ever been a House of Commons in this country? N. W.

A. The National Government never has had a body so named, but in the early history of North Carolina the lower branch of its legislature was called the House of Commons.

Q. Who has made the longest speech in the Senate? L. S. K.

A. The longest continuous speech in the Senate was on the Ship Purchase Bill in 1915 when Senator Smoot talked for 11 hours and 25 minutes.

Q. Can the Secretary of State take action with respect to recognizing a government without the consent of Congress? E. A. A.

A. The State Department says that recognition of a foreign government, being expressly a part of the executive function conferred upon the President by the Constitution,

23

the Secretary of State, on behalf of the President, may accord recognition without recourse to Congress.

Q. *How much money is spent in a year by the Government for pencils and paper?* F. L. McG.

A. The General Supply Committee of the Treasury gives $1,362,-880.04 as the latest consolidated figure for all such things as pencils, erasers, paper, folders, stationery, etc.

Q. *If a suit is brought against the Government who defends it?* A. C. R.

A. The Department of Justice defends the Government in all suits brought against it.

Q. *What is the actual cost of Congress to the country?* W. S.

A. The actual expenditures for the Senate and the House of Representatives in 1931 were $3,419,720.28 and $8,268,583.88 respectively.

Q. *How fast does a reading clerk read in the House of Representatives?* H.

A. A reading clerk in the House says that the speed of the average reading clerk is governed by the reading matter under consideration. A fair average speed might be estimated as 100 words a minute.

Q. *Has any Chief Justice of the United States other than Chief Justice White been a Catholic?* T. R.

A. Roger Brooke Taney was a Roman Catholic. Each of these two men had an unusually long term, their combined years of service amounting to 39 years.

Q. *How many foreign consulates are there in New York City?* R. E. M.

A. There are 57.

Q. *Who was the first foreign diplomat to be recalled at the request of this Government?* L. T.

A. Citizen Genet, French minister to the Congress of the United States, who was recalled by the French Government at the request of President Washington.

Q. *What was the statement McCauley made to the effect that the Government of the United States would be tested when the Huns and Vandals flooded the country?* W. S. T.

A. In a letter to Henry S. Randall of New York, author of the Life of Jefferson, dated May 23, 1857, published in the New York Times, March 24, 1860, he said: "The time will come when New England will be as thickly peopled as Old England; hundreds of thousands of artisans will assuredly be sometimes out of work. Then the institutions of America will fairly be brought to the test. The rich will be robbed to feed the poor. Either some Caesar or Napoleon will seize the reigns of government with a strong hand; or your republic will be as fearfully plundered and laid waste by barbarians in the twentieth century as the Roman Empire was in the fifth, with this difference that the Huns and Vandals who ravaged the Roman Empire came from without and that your Huns and Vandals will have been engendered within your own country and by your own institutions."

Q. *What is meant by the word veto, with respect to the President's power?* T. E. B.

A. The word is from the Latin and means "I forbid." The first veto was by Washington, who vetoed "An act for the apportionment of the Representatives among the several States."

Q. *Is the same prayer offered each day at the opening of the sessions of Congress?* B. O. E.

A. The prayers are extemporaneous and differ from day to day.

Q. *How long has there been a reclamation service of the United States?* D. W.

A. The Reclamation Bureau celebrated its thirtieth birthday on the

17th of June, 1932. On that date in 1902, the reclamation act under which the bureau functions was approved by President Roosevelt.

Q. *What does the mileage of Members of Congress cost the Government yearly?* C. T. N.

A. Transportation allowances to Members of Congress are said to exceed $175,000 annually.

Q. *Who held the greatest number of Federal offices before becoming President?* B. M. H.

A. This appears to be Thomas Jefferson who served as a member of the Provisional Congress, Delegate to the Continental Convention, United States Senator, Minister to a foreign nation, Cabinet Member, Vice-President, and President. If both federal and state offices were considered, the record would be held by Martin Van Buren.

Q. *Why is the statement of the proposed receipts and expenditures of the United States called a budget?* A. C.

A. The word budget means a bag or pouch and was applied to the black leather bag in which the English Chancellor of the Exchequer carried his statements of accounts to the House of Parliament. The term later was applied to the contents of the bag itself. To open the budget was a parliamentary term as early as the 17th century.

Q. *Does each Member of Congress have a page?* J. S.

A. He does not. At the present time there are 21 pages in the House of Representatives, and 20 in the Senate.

Q. *Do Senators and Representatives in Congress occupy the same seats?* C. S. T.

A. Senators are assigned desks when sworn in and they may retain these throughout their terms. Senior Senators occupy the more desirable seats. In the House there are no individual seats or desks. Each Rep-

resentative formerly had a seat assigned to him but, as the membership increased, this became impracticable and the House of Commons system was adopted. In both Houses Republicans and Democrats sit right and left of the middle aisle.

Q. *Have Britishers a greater representation in their House of Commons than Americans have in the House of Representatives?* T. W.

A. In Great Britain there is a member for approximately each 70,000 of population, while in the United States there is a member for each 280,674.

Q. *What office or position was Emmett Scott appointed to by Secretary of War Baker during the World War and for how long?* R. C. N.

A. Emmett Scott was appointed by the Secretary of War to occupy the position of special assistant to the Secretary of War. It was Mr. Scott's duty to advise in matters pertaining to negro soldiers. He held this position as assistant to Secretary of War Baker from 1917 to 1919.

Q. *Is there a clause in the Constitution prohibiting members of certain religions from becoming President of the United States?* A. G.

A. There is not. Article VI of the Constitution states that "no religious test shall ever be required as a qualification to any office or public trust under the United States.

Q. *How long did the longest filibuster last in the Senate of the United States?* L. S. K.

A. The longest on record was the one conducted by Senator La Follette and others in 1917, March 3 and 4, lasting approximately 27 hours on the question of arming merchant ships.

Q. *What State has the smallest legislature? The largest?* F. S.

A. The size of State senates varies from 17 in Delaware to 67 in Minnesota, and the number of members in the lower houses ranges from 35 in Delaware to 421 in New Hampshire.

Q. *What are some of the other professions of members represented in Congress besides that of law?* G. J.

A. In the Senate, in 1932, there were six farmers, three livestock men, and eight bankers. There were 36 farmer members of the House, 26 bankers, 16 editors and publishers, six contractors and builders, 11 insurance and real estate, three coal operators, and 21 members of business firms.

Q. *What is the longest term of office of any government official?* F. G.

A. The Comptroller General of the United States and the Assistant Comptroller General have the longest tenure. They hold their offices for 15 years.

Q. *Please describe the mace in the House of Representatives.* R. S.

A. The mace is about three feet long and consists of 13 ebony rods representing the 13 original colonies. It is bound together with transverse bands of silver in imitation of the thongs that bound the fasces of ancient Rome. The shaft is surmounted by a globe of solid silver about five inches in diameter upon which rests a massive silver eagle.

Q. *What is the Curtis-Reed Bill?* M. C.

A. The Curtis-Reed Bill which is offered in place of the Reed-Sterling Bill of the 68th Congress would create a Secretary of Education with a place in the Cabinet of the President, and would make a total initial appropriation of $1,500,000 to maintain the new department.

Q. *How is it determined who is the Dean of the Diplomatic Corps?* M. W.

A. The Diplomatic Corps is formed and the Ambassador who has been in the country in his official capacity for the longest time is the Dean. The ranking of diplomats changes often, as there are many changes in the Corps. This is an international practice.

Q. *Please explain the American budget system.* E. V. R.

A. A budget system was adopted in the United States in 1921 and the Bureau of Budget was created. The bill authorizing the establishment of the budget makes the President the head of the budget system, creates the Bureau of Budget, requires that the President submit the budget to Congress at the beginning of the regular session each year, and requires that Congress be told at that time exactly what the revenues and expenditures for the year are to be, and what is the state of the public debt.

Q. *Who administers the oath of office to the Speaker of the House of Representatives in Congress?* F. M.

A. It is usually administered by the oldest member in point of service, called the Father of the House.

Q. *Where is the original copy of the Constitution?* A. S. S.

A. On the second floor of the Library of Congress the original Constitution of the United States and of the Declaration of Independence are on permanent exhibition.

Q. *What inscriptions are being placed on the new building for the Supreme Court of the United States?* W. S.

A. The Office of the Architect of the Capitol says that the inscriptions for the West and East Porticoes, respectively, are as follows: "Equal Justice Under Law" "Justice The Guardian of Liberty." Decision has not been reached as to inscriptions to be placed in other parts of the building.

Q. *Does the Constitution of the United States give citizens the right to vote?* K. T.

A. It does not. This right is reserved to the States. The Federal

Constitution says that, in granting such right, the States shall not discriminate on account of race, religion, or sex. This safeguard was inserted in the Constitution because, in the colonies, local governments forbade Jews, Catholics, Quakers and Baptists the franchise.

Q. *At what age are the Justices of the United States Supreme Court eligible for retirement?* J. C. R.

A. They are eligible for retirement at the age of 70 years on full pay.

Q. *Was the League of Nations projected by Woodrow Wilson before he attended the Versailles Conference?* H. B.

A. The project of the League of Nations had long been an ideal of the War President. It is item fourteen in the famous Fourteen Points.

Q. *Why is a member of Congress referred to on the floor as the gentleman from New York, for example, instead of by name?* E. W.

A. It is the custom in the British Parliament, as well as the United States Congress, and in fact, in all large deliberative bodies, to avoid the use of the personal name in debate or procedure. The original purpose of this was to avoid any possible breach to personalities and to prevent an action for libel from being brought by an individual, who might hold that his name had been slandered.

Q. *What was the origin of the practice of paying mileage to defray the expenses of Senators and Representatives in Congress while traveling to and from Washington to attend sessions?* D. H.

A. The principle of mileage was established in the days of the earliest British Parliaments. Englishmen who received the King's writ, summoning them to Parliament, were privileged to kill two deer in the Crown forests en route to and from sessions to provide them with venison.

Q. *What salary does the Chaplain of the Senate receive? The Chaplain of the House of Representatives?* M. H.

A. Each receives $1680 per annum.

Q. *How many times have Presidents appointed judges to the United States Supreme Court and had them rejected by the Senate?* M. H. D.

A. Since the creating of the Court in 1789, nine appointees have been rejected by the Senate.

Q. *What are the different forms of civilized government?* M. K.

A. The principal forms of government in the world today are—limited monarchies, as Great Britain; absolute monarchies, as Abyssinia; republics, as the United States; dictatorships, such as Italy and Russia; protectorates such as Morocco. In addition there are several independent principalities, and the Soviet Socialistic governments.

Q. *What course does a bill have to take to become a Federal law?* C. H. B.

A. The routing chart of normal course of a bill introduced in the House of Representatives follows: draughting room; introduced; referred to committee; hearing of witnesses, debated in committee; debated on floor of House; passed House, published as House bill; introduced in Senate; printed as Act of House; referred to committee; debated in committee; debated on floor of Senate; passed Senate; signed by President; printed as slip law; printed in session laws; printed in statutes-at-large.

Q. *Must revenue bills and appropriation bills originate in the House of Representatives of our Congress?* S. M. K.

A. The Constitution provides that all revenue bills shall originate in the House of Representatives. It is customary for appropriation bills to originate there also. This, however, is not necessary.

Q. *Has the mileage for Members of Congress been changed often?* C. E. B.

A. The following rates were established: 1791, 30 cents per mile; 1795, 35 cents per mile; 1818, 40 cents per mile; 1866, 20 cents per mile; 1932, 15 cents per mile (economy cut).

Q. *Please give the total cost of each government department.* G. R. B.

A. In 1931 they were as follows: Department of Agriculture, $296,865,-944.69; Department of Commerce, $61,477,117.63; Department of the Interior, $71,500,359.20; Department of Justice, $44,835,003.16; Department of Labor, $12,181,885.62; Navy Department, $354,071,004.10; Post Office Department, $145,725,910.71; Department of State, $16,024,646.48; Treasury Department, $1,346,850,037.49; War Department, $489,241,835.68.

Q. *How does the Government's appropriation for public works this year compare with three or four years ago?* J. W. F.

A. Expenditures of the Federal Government on public works in 1928 amounted to $260,000,000. This includes public buildings, harbor, flood control, highway, waterway, aviation, merchant and naval ship construction. The amount spent in 1932 was approximately $780,000,000.

Q. *Was William Randolph Hearst ever elected to Congress?* J. A. C.

A. He served in the 58th and 59th Congresses from 1903 to 1907. He was elected from the 11th New York District.

Q. *Can you give me the main features of President Wilson's famous fourteen points?* A. M. N.

A. Briefly they are: 1, non secret treaties; 2, freedom of the seas; 3, no economic barriers; 4, reduction of armaments; 5, impartial adjustment of colonial claims with consideration of the rights of the populations of the colonies, as well as the countries involved; 6, evacuation of Russian territory; 7, evacuation and restoration of Belgium; 8, evacuation and restoration of invaded portions of France and return of Alsace-Lorraine; 9, readjustment of Italian frontiers along lines of nationality; 10, autonomy for the subject peoples of Austria-Hungary; 11, evacuation of Rumania, Serbia, and Montenegro; 12, autonomy of the subject races of Turkey; 13, establishment of an independent Poland; 14, general association of nations.

Q. *When did the first Congress of the United States meet and actually start functioning?* P. A. D.

A. On Wednesday, March 4, 1789, some of the members of each House appeared and took their seats. A quorum was not present in either House, so both adjourned. They met and adjourned from day to day until April 1, upon which day a quorum was present in the House of Representatives, whereupon it was organized. Upon April 6, a quorum was present in the Senate, and its official business was begun.

Q. *Is there a school in the Capitol for the Senate and House pages?* M. T. H.

A. A classroom has been installed on the terrace of the House wing of the Capitol, and here the boys, whose work prevents them from attending public school, are tutored.

Q. *Is it possible to impeach a Justice of the Supreme Court?* L. E. J.

A. It is possible to impeach or accuse a Justice of the United States Supreme Court or any other national official. The Constitution makes provision as to the bringing of the impeachment by a member of the House and the trial of the accused by the Senate sitting as a court.

Q. *Who composed the electoral commission to decide whether Hayes or Tilden should be President, in 1876?* D. M. C.

A. The commission was composed of five members of the Senate, five members of the House of Representatives, and five Justices of the United States Supreme Court.

Q. By what authority can the President of the United States call an extra session of Congress? T. C.

A. The Constitution provides for this. Article II, Section 3, says: ". . . he may, on extraordinary occasions, convene both Houses, or either of them. . . ."

Q. What are the largest bureaus in the government service? G. E. B.

A. Among the largest are: Veterans' Bureau; Bureau of Internal Revenue; Bureau of Standards; Patent Office; Bureau of the Census; Bureau of Plant Industry; and Bureau of Animal Industry.

Q. What are the salaries, hours, and duties of the Senate pages? P. E. H.

A. The page boys in the Senate are paid $3.30 per day while the Senate is in session. Their hours are concurrent with those of the Senate, but it is necessary for them to report somewhat earlier than the hour at which the Senate convenes. Their duties are those of messengers, generally. Under the laws of the District of Columbia, they are required to attend school for 15 hours each week. Some attend night school and others attend classes conducted by an instructor at the Capitol in the mornings.

Q. How are Members of Congress chosen for committee assignments? M. P.

A. Members of Congress are permitted to express a preference for committee assignments, but the Committee on Committees has the final decision as to the membership of these committees.

Q. Are letters sent to a Senator in Washington opened by him or by his secretary? T. H.

A. It is customary for a Senator's secretary to open his mail whether the letters are received at his home or at his office. Ordinarily the best way to approach a Senator is through his secretary and, generally speaking, any confidential matter may be taken up with the secretary. Most Senators prefer to take up as many things as possible in writing since there are so many demands upon their time for interviews.

Q. Were the men who wrote the Constitution men of marked ability at that time? E. W.

A. Elson says: "An abler body of statesmen has not assembled in modern times than that which made our Constitution in 1787, nor has any assembly met with truer motives, or produced a grander result. The whole number of delegates was 55, and there was scarcely a man among them who had not been distinguished in the state or in the field, who had not been a governor, a member of Congress, or a commander in the army."

Q. How much has the cost of government in the United States increased in recent years? A. L. F.

A. The late President Calvin Coolidge in the Saturday Evening Post, March 26, 1932, said: "The total cost of national, state and local government was $13,048,000,000 in 1929, a raise from $2,919,000,000 in 1923. This was a difference in per capita cost from $30.24 to $107.37." Of the 1932–33 national budget, 72 per cent of estimated expenditures was for war debts, war pensions, or defense.

Q. Do Congressmen have passes on the railroads? W. W.

A. United States Senators and Representatives are not granted passes on railroads. The Government allows them mileage for each session of Congress.

Q. What was the Kansas-Nebraska Bill? D. V.

A. The Kansas-Nebraska Bill was an act passed by Congress in 1854, which provided for the organization of the Territories of Kansas and Nebraska. It introduced the principle of squatter sovereignty, or local option on the slavery question, for the people of the Territories, thus abrogating the Missouri Compromise of 1820. It disrupted finally the Whig Party, led to the rise of the Republican Party, and was an important link in the chain of events leading to the Civil War.

Q. How many proposed amendments have been introduced in Congress since the adoption of the Constitution? F. W. A.

A. It is impossible to say how many amendments to the United States Constitution have been introduced to Congress since 1789. A great many amendments are reported each session and referred to committees where they die a natural death. William Tyler Page says that 24 amendments to the Constitution have been submitted to the States for ratification since 1776. Of these, twenty have been duly ratified and are now part of the Constitution.

Q. What was the object of the Clayton-Bulwer Treaty? Y. T.

A. The object of this treaty was to facilitate and project the construction of a canal at Nicaragua, between the Atlantic and Pacific Oceans. It was later abrogated by the Hay-Pauncefote Treaty of 1902.

Q. What is the term of office of the Treasurer of the United States? K. E. L.

A. The Treasurer is appointed by the President of the United States, and no length of term of office is specified.

Q. Did Secretary of State Stimson serve in the World War? F. D. M.

A. Henry Lewis Stimson has the title of Colonel which he received during the World War. He saw active service in France.

Q. Please give the origin of the Australian ballot. E. G.

A. It was first proposed to the legislature of South Australia by a member, Francis S. Dutton. The plan was elaborated and became a law under the name of the Elections Act of that legislature in 1857.

Q. Who was Anson Burlingame? P. E. J.

A. He was a member of the Free-soil and Know-nothing parties, and was one of the founders of the present Republican Party. He served as a member of Congress from Massachusetts and was sent as Minister to China in 1861. Later he was in the employ of the Chinese government. It was at this time that a treaty of commerce and amity was signed between the United States and China, 1868.

Q. Why are Members of Congress spoken of as solons? W. E. S.

A. The name, Solon, was borne by an Athenian who was noted for his learning and wisdom in counsel. He was also known as the law-giver of Athens, and to him was entrusted the task of revising the Athenian constitution. This accounts for the name being applied to the Members of the United States Congress.

Q. Could members of the President's Cabinet be permitted to sit in Congress without amending the Constitution? S. W.

A. Our Government, by Garner and Capen, says that members of the Cabinet cannot at the same time be members of either House of Congress. They could, however, be allowed to occupy seats for the purpose of advocating or opposing the enactment of laws affecting their departments and for giving explanations to Congress and defending their policies against attack. This privilege could be allowed without amending the Constitution.

Q. When were the various government departments established? M. P.

A. Four of the departments are older than the Government under the Constitution. These are Department of Foreign Affairs, Treasury, War and Post Office. They were re-established by the First Congress under the Constitution, changing the Department of Foreign Affairs to Department of State. The Office of Attorney General was also established in 1789, and in 1870 the name was changed to Department of Justice. The Department of the Navy was established in 1798; Department of the Interior, 1849; Department of Agriculture, 1889; Department of Commerce (and Labor), 1903; Department of Labor, 1913.

Q. Are the men who become officers of the Government usually college graduates? M. C. C.

A. It has been estimated the percentage of college graduates among Government officials of the United States has been as follows: 55 per cent of our Presidents; 36 per cent of Members of Congress; 47 per cent of Speakers of the House; 54 per cent of Vice Presidents, 62 per cent of Secretaries of State; 50 per cent of our Secretaries of the Treasury; 65 per cent of Attorneys General; and 69 per cent of Supreme Court Justices.

Q. How many amendments were made to the Constitution during Woodrow Wilson's term? G. E. H.

A. Three amendments became effective during President Wilson's term—the 17th, 18th, and 19th. The 17th, providing for the direct election of Senators, had been submitted to the States for ratification during President Taft's administration but went into effect in May, 1913. The 18th, or Prohibition Amendment, and the 19th, giving nation-wide suffrage to women, were proposed, ratified, and became effective in 1920.

Q. Which states gain and which lose in the House of Representatives under the apportionment of the Fifteenth Census? M. R. H.

A. The following gain: California, 9, New Jersey, 2, Oklahoma, 1, Michigan, 4, Ohio, 2, North Carolina, 1, Texas, 3, Connecticut, 1, Washington, 1, New York, 2, Florida, 1, (total 27). The following states will lose Representatives: Missouri, 3, Alabama, 1, Minnesota, 1, South Carolina, 1, Georgia, 2, Indiana, 1, Mississippi, 1, South Dakota, 1, Wisconsin, 1, Iowa, 2, Kansas, 1, Nebraska, 1, Tennessee, 1, Kentucky, 2, Maine, 1, North Dakota, 1, Vermont, 1, Pennsylvania, 2, Massachusetts, 1, Rhode Island, 1, Virginia, 1, (total 27).

Q. Why is it necessary to have a Constitutional Amendment in order to eliminate the "Lame Duck Session" of Congress? D. B.

A. It cannot be eliminated without Constitutional Amendment because of the fact that the length of the Congressional term is provided for in the Constitution. The date of beginning that term cannot be changed without either lengthening or shortening the Congressional and Presidential terms of office. A Constitutional Amendment is therefore necessary.

Q. When John Marshall was appointed Chief Justice of the United States, who took his place as Secretary of State? P. E.

A. Marshall's nomination was confirmed by the Senate, January 27, 1801. This left but a few weeks of President Adams' term. The President asked Marshall to continue to attend to the duties of Secretary of State, which he did until Adams went out of office. He drew but one salary for this period of double duty, taking the pay of the Chief Justice of the Supreme Court.

Q. When a city is granted a charter must it adopt the kind of charter specified by the state legislature or can it frame its own charter? F. D. C.

A. In some states a number of different charters have been framed by the legislatures and cities are permitted a choice of these. In other States, each city of a certain class is permitted to frame its own charter which, when it is approved by the voters, goes into effect, provided it does not conflict with the state laws or constitution. In a few States the legislatures specify the charter forms for cities of various classes.

Q. What are the credentials that an ambassador presents to a ruler? S. F.

A. An ambassador is sent by the head of a sovereign state as his personal representative to negotiate with a foreign government and to care for the interests of his own country. The credentials consist of a sealed letter addressed from his sovereign or ruler to the one to whom he is accredited and embody a general assurance that his ruler will confirm whatever is done by the ambassador in his name.

Q. Has an amendment to the Constitution ever been repealed? H. G. N.

A. Up to the present time no amendment to the Constitution has been repealed.

Q. What is an item veto? L. L.

A. Some States and municipalities give to their governors or mayors, the power to strike out items in appropriation bills without vetoing the whole bill or ordinance. There is no such leeway given to the President with respect to acts of Congress.

Q. What is meant by the franking privilege? C. D. G.

A. Congress gives to its membership, to certain other government officials, and also on occasions to those whom it especially desires to honor, the privilege of sending through the mails unstamped literature and correspondence. To Congressional Members and public officials this applies, however, only to their public correspondence.

Q. What right has a Territorial Delegate in each House of Congress? H. B. B.

A. A Territorial Delegate sits in the House of Representatives. Each organized Territory has the right to one Delegate. Delegates may be appointed to committees and have the

right to speak on any subject, but not to vote.

Q. What is meant when it is said that Senators are paired? M. M.

A. Sometimes a Senator belonging to one party agrees with a Senator belonging to the other party that neither will vote if the other is absent, the theory being that they would always vote on opposite sides of the question. This is called a pair. Sometimes pairs are secured on a particular vote only. For instance, if a Senator in favor of a certain piece of legislature is ill or unavoidably detained, his friends arrange for someone on the opposite side of the question not to vote. This insures for each a record as to whether or not he favors a particular piece of legislation. While many are opposed to general pairs, as the first is called, all are glad to arrange a pair for a specific measure if a Senator is unavoidably prevented from being present to vote.

Q. On what kind of cloth is the Constitution of the United States written? J. G.

A. It is not written on cloth. It is engrossed on parchment.

Q. What are the duties of a floor leader? H. I. J.

A. A floor leader is a member designated by his party caucus to have charge of the party strategy in the House of Congress of which he is a member. He follows the proceedings carefully and accurately, in order to speak effectively when necessary. He has the duty of arranging the order in which other members of his party may speak on a given measure.

Q. Who proposed the creation of the first executive departments and the first amendments to the Constitution? D. B.

A. Madison proposed the resolutions for the creation of the first three executive departments, and a series of twelve amendments to the Constitution out of which the first ten were finally adopted.

CHAPTER 5

ANIMALS

Q. What animal runs the fastest?
I. D.

A. The cheetah or hunting leopard of India is credited with being the swiftest four-footed animal. This applies especially to short distant runs, since the cheetah has not a great deal of endurance for continued speed. For short distances, however, it can run down any antelope or deer after which it starts.

Q. How many zoological gardens are there in the United States? A. E.

A. While various cities have collections of animals, there are only nineteen which would be included in a list of principal zoos.

Q. What is the smallest ruminant known? W. D.

A. The royal antelope, also called dik-dik, is the smallest, standing only 12 inches high at the shoulder. It is a native of West Africa.

Q. What animals besides the giraffe can make no sound? V. B.

A. The giraffe is unique among mammals in this respect. All other mammals, practically all birds, some reptiles and amphibians, and some fish, have the power of making some sound with the vocal cords.

Q. What is a panda? E. L. C.

A. This Asiatic animal is one of the rarest of mammals, with the face of a raccoon, feet like a cat, and body similar to that of the bear. There are two specimens at the Field Museum in Chicago. These were captured by Theodore and Kermit Roosevelt near the border of Tibet.

Q. What animals change their fur or plumage to white in the winter time? G. G.

A. The ermine, the ptarmigan, the Arctic fox, and the polar hare.

Q. Can moles see? J. McC.

A. Neither external eyes nor ears are ordinarily in evidence in the American mole. If not totally blind the common mole of the eastern United States can at best merely distinguish between light and darkness, as the remains of its organs of sight lie wholly beneath the skin.

Q. How far down will a gopher dig a hole? Z. S.

A. About three feet straight down.

Q. Do earthworms make any sound? W. F.

A. Angleworms do make a slight sound. It can be closely imitated by moistening the lips and then opening and closing them without moving the jaw. Whether or not they hear has not been decided, but they do not see in the true sense of the word as they have no eyes.

Q. What is the easiest way to tell a goat from a sheep? F. D. C.

A. It is usually easy to distinguish them, but certain hair breeds of sheep are to the layman only distinguishable from goats by the direction of the tail, which is upward in goats and downward in sheep.

33

Q. *What is the correct way to pick up a rabbit.* C. T. L.

A. It should be picked up by the scruff of its neck. It is incorrect to pick up a rabbit, especially a full grown one, by its ears, since this is a strain on the ears.

Q. *Which of the large animals get up with their forefeet first.* E. T. C.

A. All of the ruminants or cud-chewers, namely cattle, sheep, goats, deer, antelope, and camels, invariably get up with their hind legs first, while other large quadrupeds use the opposite procedure with forelegs first.

Q. *Does the alligator make any other noise besides hissing?* D. B.

A. The alligator is noted for the pronounced roaring or bellowing noise which it makes when angered or disturbed. This is remarkable since it is the only saurian or reptile of the alligator group which is known to make a distinctive noise.

Q. *Have the smooth-looking seals on the rocks off the coast of Maine any hair?* F. H. W.

A. All seals have hair. The coat of the hair seal is quite different from that of the fur seal in that the hairs are of the same length and lie down very closely and smoothly to the skin. Being of a uniform color, the hair seal's coat therefore looks very much like skin when wet.

Q. *Do all mammals have four limbs?* P. C.

A. Normally they are four in number, but the hind pair are suppressed in whales and sea-cows. The limbs assume the form of legs for terrestrial progression, wings for flight, and paddles for swimming. There are about 600 genera and 5000 species of mammals extant.

Q. *Do people ever eat rattle-snakes?* E. C. S.

A. This is quite a common performance among the Indians of Mexico and many travelers have tasted the unusual dish and pronounced the flesh of rattlesnakes to be not unlike that of the white meat of the chicken. The poison of the rattlesnake is contained in certain glands and does not affect the flesh of the reptile.

Q. *What is the word for fear of cats?* H. M.

A. The term for this feeling is aelurophobia.

Q. *How does an ape differ from a monkey?* A. O. S.

A. The terms in popular language are more or less interchangeable. Correctly speaking, however, ape refers to any of the large anthropoid primates which are entirely tailless, and monkey to any of the smaller members of this order with either short or long tails.

Q. *What color is a coyote?* A. M.

A. The standard color of the coyote is brown or tan. Its larger cousin, the timber-wolf, is a grey color.

Q. *What animals are considered beasts of burden?* E. M.

A. A beast of burden is any animal domesticated for use in transportation, draft, or agriculture. The outstanding species which have been used for this purpose are: The ox and the horse, in practically all parts of the world; the camel, in the desert countries of North Africa and southwestern Asia; the dog, in countries where larger draft-animals do not exist; the reindeer, in the Arctic regions; and the alpaca and llama in the mountainous countries in western South America.

Q. *How long do crabs, leeches, and spiders live?* W. E. D.

A. The span of life of a crab is 20 years; of a leech, 20 years; of a spider, 10 to 15 years.

Q. *Do all mammals have hair?* L. M.

A. Hair is the characteristic covering of mammals. Hairs are not wanting on any mammals, but vary greatly in abundance, some being densely clothed while others possess it only on limited parts of the body.

Q. Can the native home of a tiger be determined by its fur when made into a rug? H. E.

A. There is considerable difference in the skins of tigers. The Bengal tiger has a short coat of dark orange-brown color with black stripes. Tigers from other parts of India are of the same color, but have longer hair. Those further north, such as in China and Mongolia, are not only larger in size but have very long soft hair of orange-brown with white flanks and are generally marked with black stripes.

Q. If earthworms are not rained down how do they get into rain barrels? W. R. W.

A. While tornadoes might occasionally account for earthworms and other creatures coming down with rain, it is more logical to reach a different conclusion. Any of the 40 to 50 kinds of birds which feed on earthworms might carry them to the roof or eaves of buildings where they are washed or fall into the gutters and then find their way into the rain barrels.

Q. How long has the new rat powder recommended by the Department of Agriculture been on the market? L. T.

A. Red-squill powder was placed on the American market in 1926. It has been found efficacious and has the added recommendation of being relatively harmless to human beings and domestic animals.

Q. Are all camels properly called dromedaries? J. G. G.

A. There are two types of camels—the one-humped or Arabian, and the two-humped or Bactrian. The former is sometimes also called the dromedary. As correctly used, the word dromedary applies only to the one-humped variety. The number of humps is the outstanding difference between these two types, but in addition, the Bactrian camel is more

heavily set, shorter, and has much longer hair of a darker color than the Arabian variety.

Q. What is a gibbon? M. B.

A. A gibbon is any of several apes constituting the genus Hylobates. They are the lowest of the anthropoid apes, and the smallest and most perfectly arboreal in habits of that group. Their arms are very long, and they have distinct ischial callosities, but no tail or cheek pouches. They are found in southeastern Asia and the East Indies. A number of species or varieties are known, as the siamang, wou-wou, and hoolock.

Q. What are the habits of jackals in lion country? J. B.

A. Jackals are wild dogs of several species, particularly Canis aureus of southeastern Europe, southern Asia, and northern Africa. They are smaller, usually more yellowish, and much more cowardly than wolves, and hunt in packs at night. Jackals feed on carrion and on small animals including poultry. They frequently devour the carcass of large animals killed by lions and are often seen in large numbers in lion country. Jackals can be tamed and by some are believed to be the progenitors of domestic dogs.

Q. What is the largest bison head on record? T. M.

A. The head of Old Tex, famous bison bull of the Yellowstone herd, is the biggest. It measures 35½ inches on its outside spread. The right horn is 21½ inches long; the left horn is 23 inches long. The circumference of the right horn at the base is 16 inches, while the left is 15¼ inches, and the inside spread is 30½ inches. Old Tex was killed in 1926 because of old age and his head is on display in the new museum at Fishing Bridge, on the shores of Yellowstone Lake.

Q. What do gorillas eat when in the wild state? A. M. C.

A. Gorillas inhabit dense forests in their native west African haunts, and they are almost entirely vegetarian. They feed mostly on fruits and tender shoots, and occasionally raid plantations.

Q. Do many people drink goats' milk? R. M. D.

A. The use of goats' milk is common in Switzerland, Germany, Cuba, Mexico, and other countries. It is used in our own country in certain sections and the larger cities. The goat takes up little room and produces quite a quantity of good milk. Goats' milk has been used extensively in infant hospitals and other places as a substitute for cows' milk.

Q. What are cabinet skins? T. G.

A. The term, cabinet skin, refers to any skin or part of a skin that is kept in a cabinet or drawer for scientific purposes and is not mounted.

Q. What is a wash-bear? R. L.

A. It is a raccoon.

Q. Were buffaloes ever found in South America? H. G. S.

A. The American bison was never native south of Mexico. In fact, the South American continent is very poor in any members of the ox family except a few small deer. The Indian water buffalo, a relative of the American bison, has been introduced with success into some parts of tropical America, but this is an Old World animal.

Q. When were reindeer imported into Alaska? H. A.

A. Through the efforts of Dr. Sheldon Jackson, a missionary, 16 Siberian reindeer were brought into the Bering Sea region in 1891 and 171 reindeer in 1892. By 1902, 1280 had been imported, when the Russian Government forbade further exportations. The number increased to over 400,000, of which about 100,000 have been used for food and clothing.

Q. How are the Pacific Ocean seals protected? D. D.

A. The fur seals of the North Pacific Ocean are protected by the North Pacific Seal Convention of July 7, 1911, among the United States, Great Britain, Japan, and Russia.

Q. How large do gila monsters grow? A. R. H.

A. Some of them attain a length of two feet.

Q. How many vertebrae are there in the neck of a giraffe? W. V.

A. There are seven vertebrae in the neck of a giraffe? This number is not greater than in other quadrupeds, and the neck has no extraordinary flexibility, although its form and movements are very graceful. The length, therefore, is due to the elongation of each cervical vertebra.

Q. What should be fed to a young alligator? M. G.

A. Alligators are first given a diet of earthworms and minnows. Upon this they are kept for two months, when dead mice are occasionally given them. As soon as they show an increase in size, the quantity of food is correspondingly increased. Earthworms are then excluded from the menu, while small rodents are given frequently, in alternation with frogs, fish, and scraps of beef. Young rats and sparrows are soon added to the list. They are usually fed twice a week, and at most three times a week.

Q. How many poisonous species of lizards are there in the United States? E. P.

A. The gila monster, a large lizard of the Arizona and New Mexico deserts, is the only poisonous lizard in this country.

Q. Is it true that a monkey cannot swim? H. C.

A. Monkeys can swim, but water is distasteful to them.

Q. Please give some information about the kinkajou, commonly called the honey bear. E. B. R.

A. The kinkajou is a member of the raccoon family. It is a native of the forests of the warmer parts of South and Central America. It is about three feet long and has a slender body, a long tail, large eyes, and soft yellowish-brown fur, and is nocturnal and arboreal in habits. It feeds on fruit, honey, eggs, and small birds and mammals. It is often tamed as a pet.

Q. *What animals were there in North America when it was discovered?* B. G.

A. There were bears, wolves, lynx, bison, reindeer, moose, bighorn, white goat, beaver, and the majority of the rodents. There were also the puma, skunk, and muskox.

Q. *Are animals other than horses spoken of as thoroughbred?* T. D. L.

A. Other animals which are recorded or eligible to be recorded are spoken of as pure bred.

Q. *Are there tigers in Africa?* P. B.

A. There are no tigers in Africa except in captivity. Tigers are native only to eastern and southern Asia and the adjacent islands.

Q. *Can water buffalo survive entirely on land?* B. B.

A. Although it is true that the water buffalo is very fond of water and remains near it as much as possible, it can live quite easily without being in water. It must have water to drink like all other animals, but lying in water is a matter of comfort and not of sustaining life.

Q. *Is there such an animal as a flying fox?* C. J. B.

A. A flying fox is any of various, very large fruit-eating bats, so called from the foxlike face.

Q. *What kind of an animal is it which is heard in the spring and is called a peeper?* G. W. S.

A. It is a tree-frog. It is a small climbing frog about two inches in length, of a color which matches tree bark so closely that it is seldom recognized. It has an opposable thumb,

and a sucking disc on the end of each toe, which enables it to climb trees, although it seldom ascends more than 20 feet.

Q. *Does a pocket gopher carry dirt in its pouch?* P. A.

A. The pocket gopher has large cheek pouches which do not communicate with the mouth, and are lined on the inside with fur. The gopher uses these pouches not for carrying dirt but for the conveyance of food supplies.

Q. *What is the name given to a calf whose mother is not known?* E. R.

A. Maverick is the word used in referring to an unbranded animal, especially a motherless calf, formerly customarily claimed by the first person branding it. The name is said to be derived from Samuel Maverick, a cattle owner in Texas who did not brand his cattle, his ranch being on an island.

Q. *Does the female reindeer have horns?* R. D.

A. Reindeer and caribou are the only members of the deer family in which both sexes have horns.

Q. *What is the weight of a newly born black bear?* T. F.

A. At birth a black bear cub weighs from 9 to 12 ounces which is about $\frac{1}{200}$ to $\frac{1}{250}$ of its mother's weight. It is about 8 inches long, blind, and covered with a dark hair so thin that it is practically naked.

Q. *How long should it take to milk a cow?* E. R. F.

A. The time required to milk a cow is between 2½ and 15 minutes, the average being approximately six minutes. The difference in the time is caused by the temper of the cow in letting down her milk and is not dependent on the ability of the milker.

Q. *Is bear meat palatable?* S. J.

A. It is considered quite savory and palatable. It has always been a favorite article of diet among American Indians in regions inhabited by bears, and is relished by sportsmen and hunters in bear country.

Q. *What is the name of the whiskers of a cat?* W. K.

A. They are setae.

Q. *Where and when was the eradication of bovine T. B. started?* A. L.

A. The Bureau of Animal Industry says that eradication of tuberculosis in cattle was started in Pennsylvania in 1892 and 1893. The general campaign was not started until 1917, in which campaign fifteen or twenty states participated.

Q. *Do bears have tails?* J. P.

A. They have rudimentary tails.

Q. *When are deer born in the Adirondacks?* J. S.

A. Usually in May—sometimes in the latter part of April or the early part of June. The young fawns are spotted when born and the spots remain until about the age of four months. Young fawns, like many other hoofed animals, have ridiculously long legs and very large ears. They are usually under the care of their mother until the spots disappear.

Q. *If a pure bred dog mates with a mongrel, will her puppies always be part mongrel?* J. E. L.

A. The Bureau of Animal Industry says that it is contrary to generic belief that the previous mating of a pure bred dog has any effect upon the off-spring when the female is mated with a pure bred.

Q. *Has a cow teeth?* S. D.

A. It has a full set of lower teeth and upper teeth except front teeth.

Q. *What sort of dog is the borzoi?* F. D.

A. The borzoi or Russian wolfhound is a lithe, active dog, 28 to 31 inches high at the shoulders and weighing from 75 to 105 pounds. The hair is silky and loose, and in color,

borzois are combinations of black, white, and tan. They are substantially the same as the ancient long-haired greyhounds of the Arabs and Persians, but the coat has lengthened in adaptation to a cold climate.

Q. *Why does a dog stick its tongue out when it pants?* S. T.

A. This is an unconscious effort to increase the evaporating surface of the body. Heat required to evaporate perspiration caused by exertion cools the body.

Q. *Are elk browsing or grazing animals?* E. B.

A. They are both. They feed not only on pasturage, but on the leaves and tender young shoots of trees and shrubs.

Q. *Has "blind as a bat" any foundation in fact?* E. F.

A. This is a mistaken simile. All have efficient eyes, those of the Oriental fruit-eating sorts being of a size natural to their fox-like countenances. In our more familiar insect-eating species they are likely to be small, bead-like, and nearly hidden in the very soft fur with which these animals are clothed; the old English and German names "flitting mice" were not bad ones.

Q. *What is the normal temperature of a dog?* M. E.

A. The normal temperature of dogs is higher than that of people. It is usually about 101 degrees. Young dogs and small ones have slightly higher temperatures than old and large animals.

Q. *Why are horses tails docked? Is part of the bone removed?* R. J. S.

A. It was primarily intended for style and never had any utilitarian aspect. It is now generally discredited by horse breeders, although hackney and coach horses are still subjected to this treatment. Docking—for a full grown horse especially —is a serious operation, necessitating amputation of the tail bone. There are approximately 15 vertebrae in a horse's tail and in docking the last five or six are customarily removed.

Q. *How many teeth does a dog have?* C. T.

A. It has forty-two permanent teeth.

Q. *At what depth do sponges grow? Are they found in beds?* J. S.

A. They are found at all depths, the deeper water yielding sponges of better texture and longer wear. They are not found in beds. Divers walk along the bottom of the sea, tearing the sponges from the rocks or coral to which they cling. Sponges are one of the lowest forms of animal life.

Q. *How is a hunting dog broken to gunfire?* H. C.

A. Breaking a dog to gunfire is usually accomplished when it is quite young and is done by gradually accustoming the dog to the noise of the fire. A small arm is used at first and is fired at some distance from the dog, gradually working up to closer distances and larger arms.

Q. *Was Jumbo the largest elephant ever measured?* R. S.

A. Jumbo, the famous elephant of the Barnum and Bailey Circus, was 10 feet 10 inches tall and weighed approximately six tons. Jumbo was one of the largest elephants ever in captivity, but there are records of larger elephants which were not taken alive, but killed. One elephant shot in East Africa measured 11 feet 8½ inches at the shoulder, had a total length from trunk to end of tail of 15 feet 5 inches, and a girth of forefoot of 5 feet 5¼ inches.

Q. *What gaits should a saddle horse have?* M. M.

A. The Bureau of Animal Industry says there are two kinds of gaited saddle horses. The three-gaited horse is the most common. The gaits are the walk, trot, and canter. A five-gaited horse must walk, trot, canter, rack, or single-foot, and in addition must be trained in one of the following three slow gaits: the running walk, the slow pace, or fox-trot. Occasionally a horse can walk, trot, rack, canter, and is trained in all of the three slow gaits. Such a horse may be called a seven-gaited horse.

Q. *What is galyak fur?* A. H.

A. It is the pelt of aborted lambs of either of the two breeds of Asiatic-Russian sheep known as Bokhara and Karakul. It is an inferior fur since the hair has just begun to show above the skin. A moire effect is sometimes, although not usually, present.

Q. *How long is an elephant considered young?* T. F.

A. The Burmese who are much accustomed to breeding elephants say that the term of life is approximately 150 years for normal elephants. The period from birth to 25 years is considered infancy and extreme youth; from 25 to 35 years immature period; 35 to 45 years full grown period; 45 to 50 middle aged period; and 50 to 60 years and over period of old age and decline.

Q. *Is there a species of sheep with a broad tail that has to be supported?* J. J. M.

A. The broad-tailed, or fat-tailed sheep found in many parts of Asia, are chiefly characterized by the enormous accumulation of fat on each side of the tail bone. The tail is esteemed a great delicacy, and to protect it from being injured by dragging on the ground, it is sometimes supported by a board or small pair of wheels. The fat of the tail is often used in place of butter.

Q. *In what countries are there lions?* P. D.

A. In prehistoric times the lion was distributed over the greater part of Europe, and within the historic period it has inhabited all of Africa, southern Asia, and possibly Greece. At the present time, it is found in most parts of Africa, in Mesopotamia, and in Gujarat in northwest India.

Q. *Why are lions called man-eaters?* J. M. B.

A. Some lions form the habit of coming into native villages and carrying off people. This gives them the name of man-eating lions. However, this is true of few lions.

Q. *What is the stick called with which an elephant is prodded by the man driving it?* H. A. B.

A. An elephant driver is called a mahout and the stick is an ankus. This goad is a stick about two feet long, capped with a sharp spike and hook. It resembles a short-handled boat hook.

Q. *What kind of dog is a Dobermann Pinscher?* E. L.

A. It is a cross between the German shepherd dog and fox terrier (G. Pinscher), named from the first breeder, Dobermann.

Q. *How much does a lion weigh?* E. T. L.

A. The average male lion weighs about 500 pounds.

Q. *Are there white elephants?* L. M.

A. White elephants are merely light-skinned Asiatic elephants, and may occur as the offspring of normally colored parents. This type of elephant is very valuable in Siam, where it is much revered and kept in the royal stables of the monarch and his family.

Q. *Compared with a cow, how much does a sheep eat?* V. F.

A. The Bureau of Animal Industry says that the usual ratio of food eaten by sheep to food eaten by cattle is seven sheep to one cow.

Q. *How old a breed is the King Charles Spaniel?* C. T. D.

A. This is a fairly popular toy breed, which is at least 300 years old, since specimens of it occur in French paintings of the 17th Century. Princess Henriette of Orleans, the sister of King Charles II of England, is reputed to have introduced this breed into England, hence its name.

Q. *Is a bat a bird?* J. T.

A. The bat is not a bird but a mammal; that is, it is warm blooded, covered with hair, gives birth to its young alive, and suckles them, but at the same time has the digits of its four limbs enormously elongated into wing-like structures over which a thin membrane of skin is stretched. Bats are therefore the only true flying mammals.

Q. *Is the Yale bulldog a mythical dog?* E. A. K.

A. The Yale University Athletic Association says that the Eli mascot is no myth. Handsome Dan was his name and he was owned by Andrew B. Graves of the class of '92. Handsome Dan was the official Yale football mascot for over ten years. He was a big, white, brindle bulldog and when he died his skin was stuffed and it now adorns an important position in the Yale trophy room.

Q. *What is the most humane way to kill a horse?* J. L. W.

A. The Bureau of Animal Industry says that the most humane way is to shoot him in the forehead.

Q. *Why are guinea pigs used for experiments in medical laboratories?* J. K.

A. Guinea pigs are used in laboratories because they are susceptible to many of the diseases of man. They are also small animals and can be easily handled and are not vicious.

Q. *How heavy do hogs grow?* S. S.

A. There are authenticated records of hogs of 1250 pounds or more, and reports which have not been investigated by the Bureau of Animal Industry of a few which have approached 1500 pounds.

Q. *What kind of a dog is a Saluki?* P. A. R.

A. The Bureau of Animal Industry says that the Saluki or gazelle hound is a very old breed of Asiatic origin. The word Saluki means hound or running dog. This breed of dog has been used in the near and middle east for centuries in hunting and killing gazelles, hence its other name of gazelle hound.

Q. *Why are bats of value?* B. K.

A. They are great destroyers of insects and furnish guano which is a valuable fertilizer.

Q. *Are lion's skins used much as furs?* J. I. S.

A. The principal use of a lion's skin is for rugs with the heads mounted. In some parts of Africa, however, they are still the insignia of royalty, and their use as cloaks or garments is restricted to the reigning monarch.

Q. *Why are whippets always run in short races?* L. L. F.

A. A whippet can run 200 yards in 12 seconds. It is never permitted to run long races, since with its speed it would soon tire.

Q. *Were horses native to North America?* J. J.

A. The horse was not native to the western hemisphere in historic times, although a pre-equine mammal did occur here several million years ago. The wild horses on the western plains of this continent today are descended from domesticated horses brought to America by Cortez and other Spanish conquistadores.

Q. *Where do bats go in the daytime?* H. K.

A. Bats spend the hours of daylight in eaves, ruins, hollow trees, garrets, and similar hiding places. They sometimes resort to caverns in vast numbers. At dusk they fly forth alone or in pairs searching for food.

Q. *How many bones are there in a horse?* A. D.

A. The number of bones in the body of a horse is somewhat variable according to whether the teeth or certain parts of the skull and other portions of the body are included as separate bones. There are approximately 216 bones in a horse's skeleton, or if the teeth are included, there are 256 separate pieces.

Q. *Is it true that the sable and ermine are the fur of the same animal, one taken in the summer, the other in the winter?* E. W.

A. It is not true. The animals which yield these furs are cousins—both species are of the weasel family. Ermine is from the genus Mustele and sable from the genus Putorius.

Q. *How many elephants are there in the United States?* M. A. C.

A. The National Zoological Park says that the number of elephants in this country is approximately 150, most of them in circuses.

Q. *Are live toads really found imbedded in rock?* J. C.

A. Dr. Leonhard Stejneger of the Smithsonian Institution says that the facts are: Toads for the purposes of hibernation dig holes in the ground or crawl into fissures of rocks. Occasionally such specimens are found after blasting operations and the conclusion hastily drawn that the toad had been living inside the solid rock.

Q. *Should a dog be taught to bring game to his master?* F. H.

A. A dog should not be taught to bring in the game. The reason for this is that when the dog points where the hunter gets the game, it is extremely annoying to have the dog dashing back and forth looking for the game and bringing it to the master. In the case of birds if the dog goes after the first bird killed he will usually frighten the rest of the flock, giving the hunter a poor chance of bringing down a great number.

Q. *What is the difference between a tortoise and a turtle?* E. B.

A. In popular usage the terms are more or less interchangeable. Strictly speaking tortoise refers to members of the order which live on land, and turtle to the aquatic species.

Q. *Where is the largest snake in captivity?* R. A. L.

A. Dr. Raymond L. Ditmars of the New York Zoological Park says that the largest snake he knows of in captivity is a 21-foot reticulated python which is now in the New York Zoological Park. It weighs about 175 pounds.

Q. *What is the word for a group of rabbits to correspond with a flock of birds?* W. S. S.

A. The term is colony.

Q. *What is the name of the German army officer who popularized the so-called police dog in the United States?* D. L.

A. This has been accredited to Capt. Max von Stephanitz, the world authority on shepherds. Thirty-one years ago he formed his famous Society for German Shepherds which grew from a small local club to an organization with headquarters in Munich and branches all over the world.

Q. *What kind of a snake is a bush master?* R. D. S.

A. The bush master is one of the largest members of the rattlesnake family, reaching a length of from 8 to 12 feet. It inhabits the Amazon River of northern South America, being specially common in the Guianas. It is extremely venomous, with very large fangs, and has a tail terminating in a spine which makes a rustling sound as the snake moves.

Q. *Where did the Texas longhorn cattle originate?* C. F. P.

A. The Bureau of Animal Industry says that these cattle were descendants of the Andalusian cattle brought to this country by the Spanish explorers and conquerors. A number of them escaped and ran wild and multiplied until there were so many of them in the Southwest that they actually competed with the bison for the pasture land. Like all other large wild animals of the West, the Texas longhorn cattle have largely disappeared with the advance of civilization until now there are very few left. One group of them is preserved in the Wichita National Forest in Oklahoma.

Q. *Can snakes bite and breathe under water?* E. Z.

A. Snakes do not breathe under water, but the Biological Survey says that it is possible for a swimming snake to strike a swimming man. It is said that the cottonmouth snake strikes in the water. There are species of sea snakes that strike only when in the water.

Q. *How do the tusks of Indian elephants compare with those of African elephants?* D. M.

A. The tusks of African elephants are somewhat larger. An Indian elephant's tusks may be 9 feet long and 100 pounds in weight, while those of a full grown African elephant are rarely less than 10 feet in length and weigh as much as 220 pounds. These are average figures and individuals may greatly surpass them.

Q. *What snake is the most poisonous?* H. A. B.

A. The most poisonous snake in the world is generally conceded to be the King Cobra of India. This snake has its evil reputation not only on account of the extreme virulence of its poison, but also because of its vicious and aggressive disposition which makes it doubly dangerous.

Q. *Are zebras black with white stripes or white with black stripes?* B. D.

A. The basic color of a zebra is white, and his stripes are black. This is proved by the fact that when a zebra is crossed with a donkey the offspring are almost invariably of a light tan color with heavy black stripes on the legs and faint black stripes on the neck and body. The stripes in various species are of varying width.

CHAPTER 6

ART

Q. *How much did the French Government pay for Whistler's portrait of his mother?* N. G.

A. Six hundred and twenty-five dollars.

Q. *Why was Gilbert Stuart's Athenaeum portrait of Washington unfinished?* M. McL.

A. The tradition is that the picture was left in this condition in order that the painter might retain it in his studio as a nest egg from which to make copies. After his death it was sold by his family for $1500 and given to the Boston Athenaeum.

Q. *Was "Liberty Enlightening the World," the statue in New York harbor, brought to this country as a finished statue?* D. L.

A. After being exhibited in Paris, the statue was taken down, and the pieces were packed in 210 cases and shipped to New York on the vessel, Isere.

Q. *Who was the first outstanding marine painter in this country?* F. H. K.

A. Winslow Homer was the first to be generally acclaimed, and many critics regard him as the best of the American marine painters.

Q. *What is the origin of the female figure known as Britannia?* R. E. C.

A. The first known representation of Britannia as a female figure sitting on a globe is on a Roman coin of Antoninus Pius, died 161 A.D. It reappeared on the copper coins of Charles II in 1665. The model at this time was Miss Stewart, afterwards created Duchess of Richmond. The engraver was Philip Roehrer.

Q. *Did Michelangelo sign his sculpture?* C. G.

A. The only piece signed by the sculptor is his Pieta.

Q. *What was Velasquez's device in art?* P. K.

A. "Verdad no pintura—truth not painting."

Q. *How far from Los Angeles is the art gallery which contains The Blue Boy?* F. R. G.

A. The Huntington estate, where the art collection of the late Henry Huntington is located, is in the city of San Marino about 15 miles from the heart of Los Angeles.

Q. *Who painted the picture of the Revolution that has three figures, one playing a fife, one a drum, and one carrying a flag?* J. C.

A. This picture, entitled The Spirit of '76, was painted by A. M. Willard.

Q. *How long did it take Leonardo da Vinci to paint the Last Supper?* B. H. L.

A. About two years. It was painted between 1496 and 1498 on the end wall of the Refectory of the Dominican Convent of Saint Maria delle Grazie at Milan. It was originally executed on a badly prepared stucco ground and began to deteriorate a few years after its completion. It has been restored at least four times, and it is now believed that it will suffer no further injury.

Q. *Please explain about the Bronze Horses of Venice.* M. C.

A. They are supposed to belong to some Graeco-Roman triumphal quadriga. These were brought to Venice by Doge Enrico Dandolo in 1204. They have had numerous adventures. During the World War they were taken down from the place before St. Mark's Cathedral and safely hidden.

Q. *What painter refused to sign a canvas saying, "My work is all over it"? What does this mean?* E. T.

A. Gilbert Stuart seldom signed a canvas because, as he said, "My work is all over it." It is said that there is as much individualism expressed in brush strokes as in handwriting.

Q. *How much did Raphael receive for The Transfiguration?* F. B. L.

A. Raphael's remuneration was $1650. This was considered a large sum.

Q. *Whose statue stands in Uniontown, Pennsylvania? It is a short man holding a beaver hat.* H. W. J.

A. The statue is of the Marquis de Lafayette for whom that county was named. He made several visits to that county during and after the War of the Revolution. The statue was made by a wood-carver and placed on a dome of a Court House erected about 1840. When the present Court House was built, the statue was resurrected from the basement of the old Court House and placed on a pedestal on the present Court House lawn.

Q. *In the color scheme used by the early Egyptians what colors were prisoners painted?* N. A.

A. Prisoners were painted yellow. Birds were blue and green; water was blue; men and women were painted red, the men being redder than the women.

Q. *What was Rembrandt's first painting?* D. D.

A. In the Stuttgart Gallery there is a signed and dated picture of St. Paul in Prison which is Rembrandt's earliest piece with an ascertained date—1627.

Q. *What remuneration did Munkacsy receive for his first painting?* T. C.

A. The entire family of a tailor was the subject of his first painting. For it, he received a winter coat.

Q. *Who did the mural decorations in the Boston Public Library?* C. S. E.

A. The Boston Public Library has many unusually beautiful mural decorations. John Sargent, Edwin Abbey, and John Elliott were among the American painters of distinction who were invited to decorate this building. The celebrated French artist Puvis de Chevannes is also represented. Sargent contributed, among many notable works, "The Frieze of the Prophets." The widow of John Elliott in her recently published biography of her husband tells in detail of his work which is on permanent exhibition in the building. Edwin Abbey chose for his theme the Quest of the Holy Grail. His murals are in the delivery room of the Library.

Q. *Who made the statuary group in front of Gallaudet College in Washington?* R. A. S.

A. This group, composed of Thomas Hopkins Gallaudet and his first pupil, Alice Cogswell, is the work of Daniel Chester French. Both teacher and pupil are represented making the letter "A" in the sign language of the deaf.

Q. *What is the oldest known fresco?* W. A.

A. Ruth de Rochement says in "Evolution in Art": The oldest known fresco that deserves to be called a painting belongs to Roman times and represents a Roman marriage ceremony—the Aldobrandini Marriage, now in the Vatican.

Q. How much did Millet realize for his great picture, The Angelus? T. V.

A. He sold it for 1800 francs—about $360. Later it brought 800,000 francs, or about $160,000, at auction.

Q. Please name the Apostles who appear in Leonardo da Vinci's "Last Supper." B. B.

A. Reading from left to right they are: Saints Bartholomew, James the Less, Andrew, Judas, Peter, and John; The Christ; Saints Thomas, James the Greater, Philip, Matthew, Thaddeus, and Simon.

Q. Where did Velasquez study to be a painter? S. W. K.

A. Albert Hechman says that Velasquez—"one of the greatest painters of all times—was virtually self-taught, save for a little instruction he received from some local painters in his birthplace."

Q. How many portraits did Sully paint? L. L. B.

A. Thomas Sully was one of the best known of the early portrait painters in this country. He was extremely prolific. There are over 2000 listed Sully portraits, and 500 subject paintings.

Q. Was the Sistine Madonna painted for the Sistine Chapel? F. E. S.

A. The Sistine Madonna has no connection with the Sistine Chapel in the Vatican. The painting was executed by Raphael for the order known as the "Black Monks of San Sisto," who lived in a little town in Italy called Piacenza.

Q. How is an etching made? A. H.

A. An etching is made by scratching the lines of a picture on a metal plate by means of acid and wax, filling the scratches with ink and printing the impressions upon paper by pressure against the plate. A number of prints can be made from one etching.

Q. What does the title, Mona Lisa, mean? S. V.

A. The title Mona is an abbreviation of the longer word Madonna which means My Lady. Lisa is a proper name. Mona Lisa is the name of a famous portrait by Leonardo da Vinci.

Q. What is meant by "values" in speaking of a picture? F. R. L.

A. The term refers to degrees of light and shade or of color intensity.

Q. What is the significance of Watts' painting called Hope? J. B.

A. In The Outline of Art, by the late Sir William Orpen, this painting is spoken of as follows: "Blindfolded with lyre in hand and sitting on the globe in the dim twilight of the world, Hope strives to get all the music possible out of the last remaining string."

Q. Why is the model of an elephant so popular? B. N.

A. The elephant has figured in Oriental mythology from a very early period. It is a symbol of temperance, eternity, and sovereignty.

Q. Who coined the term Renaissance as applied to a period of art history? Do the Italians use it? M. S.

A. Vasari coined the term. The Italians use instead, Quattrocento and Cinquecento.

Q. About how much do the paintings and sculpture of living American artists bring in a year? C. H. R.

A. In 1930 American artists realized $20,000,000 for their works of art.

Q. How large is the panoramic painting of the World War? A. D. H.

A. It is 402 feet long and 45 feet high. It was painted by twenty-eight French artists with the assistance of more than one hundred other artists under the direction of Pierre Carrier-Belleuse and Auguste-Francois Gorguet. It contains six thousand life-size portraits of World War heroes and leaders.

Q. *What was the first nude bronze of the Renaissance?* T. A.

A. Donatello's David.

Q. *Where is there a reproduction in this country of a room in Pompeii?* T. B.

A. The Metropolitan Museum of Art in New York City has a room from a house in Pompeii which was actually brought from the ruins of Pompeii and reconstructed in the Gallery.

Q. *Is there a new picture gallery in Vatican City?* C. S. T.

A. A new building designed to house scientifically many fine works of art has recently been constructed. It was formally opened by the Pope.

Q. *Were halos used before the pictures of Christian Saints and Christ were made?* R. B.

A. There is evidence that aureoles or halos were in use in earliest times as an attribute to the deities. Aureoles have been found with the pictures of the gods on some of the coins of the Indian kings Kanishka, Huvishka, and Vasudeva, 58 B.C. to A.D. 41. They are also found in the depiction of Egyptian deities from which their use spread to the Greeks and Romans.

Q. *How much does it cost to get into the Metropolitan Museum of Art in New York?* S. K.

A. There is no fee except on Mondays and Fridays when the admission charge is twenty-five cents.

Q. *What are the most famous paintings of the Madonna?* B. V. R.

A. Among the most famous Madonnas are: Raphael's Sistine Madonna, Madonna of the Goldfinch, and Madonna of the Chair; Holbein's Madonna of Burgomeister Meyer; Murillo's Madonna; Andrea del Sar-to's Madonna of the Sack; and Leonardo da Vinci's Virgin of the Rocks.

Q. *Who sat for The Spanish Beggar by Sargent?* D. B.

A. Carmela Bertogna, a Spanish girl, whom Sargent saw in the south of France.

Q. *In Raphael's day in Rome who had the greater following, he or Michelangelo?* E. M. D.

A. Raphael had by far the larger following.

Q. *Who made the first bronze equestrian statue?* S. D.

A. Donatello's statue of Gattemelata was the first attempted since the days of antiquity.

Q. *What is meant by genre in art?* H. R.

A. It is a style of painting or sculpture representing everyday life and manners in a realistic way.

Q. *Why did Munkacsy devote so much time to painting pictures of Christ?* A. L. R.

A. When the Hungarian painter was a lad, he was dissatisfied with representations of the Christ which he saw. They seemed "effeminate personifications of too much humility." He wished to paint "such a man as could be severe to the wrongdoer, even while he was forgiving and tender to the repentant." To counteract the effect of the paintings of which Munkacsy disapproved, he himself painted pictures which have Christ's life for themes.

Q. *How long was Tintoretto a pupil of Titian?* T. G. N.

A. The youthful art student remained but ten days in Titian's studio.

Q. *Who was Countess Potocka and who painted the famous portrait of her?* M. K. K.

A. Sophie de Witt, Countess Potocka, was a famous beauty, known chiefly from Anton Graff's pastel portrait of her made in Berlin where she lived for some time and where she died. She was the daughter of a Greek shoemaker of Constantinople. She married a Russian general and, after her divorce from him, married Count Stanislas Felix Potocka.

Q. When the Pennell collection of Whistleriana was first exhibited at the Library of Congress was it as well received as was the London exhibition? S. D.

A. Joseph and Elizabeth Pennell who gave the collection to the Library have written: "When the Whistler Memorial Exhibition was held in London, it was visited by thousands daily. The King and Queen asked to come. It was opened by Ambassadors and supported by the press. Here (in Washington) in the first weeks, not a thousand people visited the exhibition. But one Ambassador has come near it—naturally, M. Jusserand, the French Ambassador; but one Minister, M. Peter, the Swiss Minister. . . ."

Q. How many people visit the Corcoran Art Gallery in Washington, D. C., each year? G. C.

A. It has about 160,000 visitors annually.

Q. Was Leonardo da Vinci buried in Italy? E. B. N.

A. The artist was buried in the royal chapel of St. Florentin at Amboise.

Q. What is the meaning of the famous painting, The Huguenot? E. G. C.

A. Briefly, the explanation of the painting called The Huguenot is as follows: By order of the Duc de Guise, issued before St. Bartholomew's Day, "all good Catholics" were enjoined to wear a white scarf as a distinguishing badge. The young woman pleads with her lover as she strives to fasten the symbolic white scarf. The lover will die in the morning. As one writer suggests, the picture is reminiscent of the famous line, "I could not love thee, dear, so much, loved I not honour more."

Q. Who originated the style of painting called "Sante Conversazione"? C. C. W.

A. Palma Vecchio is generally credited with originating the style.

Q. What is meant by an aquatint? A. W. B.

A. It is a process of etching on copper or steel plates by means of nitric acid, producing an effect resembling a fine drawing in water colors, sepia, or India ink.

Q. What is the significance of the figure in the Chopin Memorial Monument, unveiled in Warsaw last fall? Hovering over the figure is a great bird, or it may be the drooping branches of a tree. P. H.

A. The Legation of Poland says that this monument is a statue of Chopin sitting beneath a willow tree, his whole attitude showing enraptured listening to the music of the wind sighing through the rustling willow branches.

Q. Who posed for the canvas known as "Pinkie"? N. A.

A. The model was Mary Moulton Barrett, the aunt of Elizabeth Barrett Browning. The artist was the famous Sir Thomas Lawrence.

Q. Who suggested the painting of Botticelli's "Allegory of Spring"? F. F.

A. This popular picture was suggested by a passage from Lucretius. It was painted for Cosimo de Medici's villa at Castello.

Q. Who was the founder of historic painting among the Greeks? M. E. D.

A. De Pauw says: "As Homer was the founder of epic poetry, so was Polygnotus the founder of historic painting."

Q. Is the Colossus of Rhodes meant to represent anyone? J. D.

A. It represented Helios, the Sun God. The statue was the work of Chares of Lindus. It was erected by the Rhodians at a cost of 300 talents, apparently as a thank offering after the successful defense of the city against Demetrius Poliorceles. It was set up about 280 B.C., but 56 years later was overthrown by an earthquake and lay in ruins until 653 A.D., when the Arabs captured the city and sold the metal to a Jewish merchant.

Q. *Who was the sculptor of the Lion of Lucerne?* E. M. B.

A. The Lion of Lucerne was copied from a model by Bertel Thorwaldsen, the famous Danish sculptor. The Swiss artist was named Ahorn. The statue was dedicated in 1821. The lion was chiseled out of solid rock as a memorial to the Swiss guards who died in heroic defense of the Tuileries.

Q. *What are pictographs and petroglyphs?* H. S.

A. Pictographs are representations or figures painted upon some surface, while petroglyphs are symbols carved in or on some surface.

Q. *Who, among the Greek artists, invented foreshortening?* J. W.

A. Credit for this is given to Cimon of Cleonae.

Q. *What artists decorated the Basilica of St. Francis at Assisi?* M. W.

A. This "cradle of Italian art" was decorated by Guinta, an artist from Pisa; Cavallina, Roman mosaicist; Cimabue and Giotto from Florence; Simone di Marinto and the Lorenzetti.

Q. *Who is Clotilde Zanetta?* L. E. M.

A. Clotilde Zanetta is a young Chilean sculptor who has gained favor by the unusual beauty of her statues which are usually of holy subjects. She studied in Cincinnati under the direction of Mr. Clement H. Barnhorn who has permitted the placing of two of her figures, The Virgin and St. Joseph, by his own masterpiece, The Crucifixion group, in the new church of Santa Monica.

Miss Zanetta has also designed figures for the altar of the Gothic chapel of the Fenwick Club in Cincinnati. The charm of her work lies in the extreme height and slenderness of her figures as well as the pure beauty of expression found in their faces.

Q. *Where is the statue to Balto in New York City?* M. E. McC.

A. On December 15, 1925, a statue to Balto was unveiled in Central Park, New York City.

Q. *What are the six rules of painting as laid down by Hsieh Ho in the 5th century?* M. G.

A. The celebrated "Six Canons of Painting" which has been the basis of art criticism in the Far East throughout subsequent centuries are, translated freely, (1) life motion engendered by spiritual harmony; (2) use of the brush in rendering bone-structure; (3) delineation of forms in conformity with the objects; (4) application of colors appropriate to the kinds; (5) spacing based on proper planning; (6) copying of classic pictures, thereby preserving tradition.

Q. *Who posed for the young Christ in Hunt's "Finding of Christ in the Temple"?* M. J. E.

A. Hunt visited all the Jewish schools in London. He finally found a lad in the school at Red Lion Square whom he used as the model.

Q. *How is a smooth, glossy finish obtained in a painting?* C. M. M.

A. The preparation used to give a smooth, glossy texture or finish to paintings is poppy oil mixed with turpentine.

Q. *What is the interpretation of the etching, Melancholia, by Alfred Durer?* A. R. L.

A. Endless speculation has been aroused by this most famous of Durer's engravings, but, in spite of many theories advanced as to its meaning, it remains to this day an unsolved enigma.

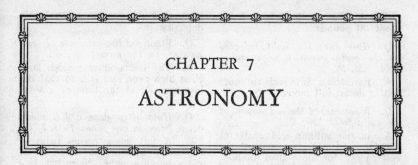

CHAPTER 7

ASTRONOMY

Q. How bright is moonlight? D. T.

A. The total brightness of the moon is reckoned as equal to a 100 candle-power lamp at a distance of 22 yards.

Q. When a meteorite falls to the earth, to whom does it belong? J. S.

A. Courts have decided that meteorites belong to the owners of the land on which they are found.

Q. How close will a modern telescope bring the moon for observation? B. L.

A. The enormous instrument at Mt. Wilson, with an enlargement of 2500 diameters, brings the moon within approximately 31 miles of the earth.

Q. Are there living creatures on Mars? R. B.

A. The late Prof. Lowell was a proponent of the theory that Mars may be inhabited, but there are yet few astronomers who regard it as proved. Life as we know it on earth depends on a number of special conditions, among which are a favorable temperature and a supply of water and of oxygen. Oxygen and water appear to be very scarce on Mars and the temperature unsatisfactory.

Q. How large was the meteoric stone that fell in Arkansas? J. C.

A. The Paragould meteorite that fell on February 17, 1930, on a farm at Paragould, Arkansas, weighs 820 pounds. It has been purchased and presented to the Field Museum of Natural History in Chicago by Stanley Field, the president of that institution.

Q. How long does it take each planet to go around the sun? E. C.

A. Mercury, 88 days; Venus, 225 days; Earth, 365 days; Mars, 687 days; Jupiter 11⅞ years; Saturn, 29½ years; Uranus, 84 years; Neptune, 165 years.

Q. Who first calculated the distance around the earth? B. M.

A. Eratosthenes (C. 275–195 B.C.) of Cyrene, was the first astronomer to attempt to measure the distance around the earth. His calculations of the circumference came surprisingly near the truth, the degree of error being only a little more than 23 minutes.

Q. As our sun is a star among millions of other stars, which are divided in groups or constellations, in what group or constellation does our sun belong? J. H.

A. The sun, the center of our solar system, is not in any constellation. The stars in the heavens are merely divided into constellations for convenience in studying them.

Q. How many pieces were found of the meteorite that fell in Arizona in 1912? J. C. W.

A. A meteorite fell in Arizona on the 19th of July, 1912. The largest fragment weighed 14 pounds. Upwards of 14,000 separate stones were gathered, the total weight being about 481 pounds.

Q. *How does the light reflected by the earth compare with moonlight?* M. P.

A. Earthshine is equal to more than a dozen full moons.

Q. *What caused the red sunsets of the early 80's?* W. R.

A. In the autumn and winter of 1883, a vivid red glow suffused the western sky for more than an hour after the sun set. Volcanic dust and gaseous matter from an eruption of Krakatoa in Sunda Strait were the probable cause.

Q. *Are the fixed stars in motion?* F. C.

A. All stars are in motion. Fixed stars are so called because they appear to change their positions so slowly in comparison with the planets.

Q. *Why can the sun be seen before it is actually above the horizon?* R. G.

A. Refraction always increases the apparent altitude of a celestial body and it is for this reason that the sun can be seen above the horizon when it is really below.

Q. *Why is the tail of a comet always on the side away from the sun?* J. V.

A. It is believed that the tail consists of extremely rarefied matter which is thrown off by the comet and then powerfully repelled by the sun. It is called the tail on account of its appearance.

Q. *What power is being exerted to keep the earth rotating upon its axis?* J. M. J.

A. No energy at all is being exerted to keep the earth rotating on its axis. All that is necessary for continued motion is that no force be acting to stop it; and that is the case, except that the tides have a retarding effect, which is so minute that it is only within the last hundred years that astronomers succeeded in detecting it.

Q. *What are the extremes of temperature on the moon?* N. W.

A. The temperature reaches 265° F. at high noon and falls to 196° below zero F., at the time of a total eclipse.

Q. *How often does a full moon occur twice in one month?* J. J. W.

A. A full moon occurs twice in the same month ten times in 28 years, on an average. Since 1900 this has happened in July, 1901, March, 1904, November, 1906, August, 1909, May, 1912, January, 1915, March, 1915, September, 1917, July, 1920, April, 1923, October, 1925. In this list, the Greenwich civil day has been used.

Q. *Is it true that thousands of tons of iron shot out of the sky in Siberia some years ago?* J. L.

A. This is a fact. It was caused by a falling meteorite crashing to earth in Yenesei province in Central Siberia. It exploded as it neared the earth and illuminated the country for nearly 500 miles. The heat from this body could be felt for a distance of 300 miles. It was the largest falling star in history. If it had struck New York City every building and subway would have been destroyed and every bit of life wiped out.

Q. *When was Greenwich Observatory founded?* T. N. A.

A. It was established by King Charles II in 1675. The direction of the observatory is under the charge of the Astronomer-Royal, who is assisted by eight astronomers and a staff of computers.

Q. *How far from the earth is the new planet, 1932 H. A?* E. C.

A. 1932 H. A. is not a planet but a planetoid. Dr. Frost of Yerkes Observatory estimated its distance from the earth at about 7,000,000 miles, but its discoverer, Dr. Karl Reinmuth of the University of Heidelburg, believes it to be only 4,000,-

000 miles distant. It is the closest known heavenly body to the earth, with the exception of the moon. Its diameter is estimated to be no more than 10 miles.

Q. What is meant by saros in speaking of eclipses? T. H.

A. It is a time interval of 18 years 10 days, being 223 times the time elapsing between two successive new moons and 242 times the period of the moon in its orbit around the earth. Therefore, it is the principal period between eclipses—any eclipse which occurs is repeated after 18 years 10 days.

Q. How many asteroids are there? S. G.

A. More than 1000 have been discovered. These tiny planets range in diameter from 480 miles to three miles or less. Most of them have been named and catalogued.

Q. What is a parsec? M. T.

A. It is a unit of length used in expressing the distance of stars. One parsec is almost exactly 206,265 times the mean distance of the earth from the sun. A star is at a distance of one parsec from the earth if its annual parallax amounts to one second of arc.

Q. How much does the earth weigh? R. S.

A. Dr. Paul R. Heyl, of the Bureau of Standards, worked for several years on a new figure for the gravitational constant from which the weight of the earth is calculated. Dr. Heyl announced that the estimated weight of the earth is 5,997,000,000,-000,000,000,000 tons.

Q. How are sites for observatories chosen? B. R.

A. Several factors are taken into consideration. A site is chosen where there is a large number of clear nights in the year, where the air is free from dust and haze, where the altitude is high enough for the site to be above part of the air, where a dry climate assures cloudless skies, and where the smoke and artificial lights of cities are absent. To this must be added the factor of "good seeing" as opposed to "poor seeing."

Q. What is a planetoid? N. L.

A. It is one of the group of small planets whose orbits lie between those of Mars and Jupiter. These are also called asteroids.

Q. How does the light of the moon compare with sunlight? D. McC.

A. The earth gets about 1/600,000 as much light from the full moon as from the sun.

Q. Which is the darkest hour of the night? S. F.

A. The Naval Observatory says that no light is received from the sun when it is 18 degrees or more below the horizon, and during those hours there is none that is regularly the darkest.

Q. Why do scientists entertain the idea of a rocket flight to the moon, instead of an airplane? A. H.

A. An airplane would be useless without air in which to travel. In space the only kind of propulsion considered practical is the kick of an explosion, for the push then is against the gases formed by the explosion instead of the push against the air which is employed in airplanes.

Q. What is meant by the Universe? G. P. G.

A. The term universe is generally used in reference to the entire world of stars and nebulae, not only visible to the naked eye but hundreds of thousands besides so distant that their existence is revealed only by the greatest telescopes and the most sensitive photographic plates. The term actually includes also our own solar system.

Q. What is meant by an astronomical unit? M. A.

A. The astronomical unit is 92,-900,000 miles or the mean distance from the earth to the sun. It is used in astronomy as a measurement of distance.

Q. *What is meant by a reflector type of telescope?* I. L. R.

A. There are two classes of telescopes, refracting and reflecting. Refracting telescopes transmit the rays through a combination of lenses called the object glass, while the reflectors bring them to a focus by reflection from a concave mirror. In the axis of the telescope is a small mirror having its focus coincident with that of the large reflector and transmitting the light received from the latter back through a hole in the center of the large mirror to the eye piece beyond.

Q. *What causes the brilliant colors at sunset?* F. K.

A. Sunset colors are caused by the excess of rays of long wave length, red and orange chiefly, which pass more readily over the long path through the dense lower strata of the atmosphere, which must be traversed at sunset, than the short wave length rays, blue and violet, which are obstructed not only by the atmosphere, but also by dust particles and impurities suspended in it. The finest sunset colors are produced when there is the greatest amount of dust and impurities in the air through which the sunlight passes. No sunset is perfectly colorless.

Q. *Please tell me something of the new 200-inch telescope?* M. G.

A. It is being erected by the California Institute of Technology in co-operation with the Carnegie Institution of Washington. Much of the work is being done in a specially constructed building in Pasadena. To complete the telescope 13 mirrors from 2 to 16 feet in diameter will be required.

Q. *What is the zodiacal light?* L. J. P.

A. The zodiacal light is a soft, hazy wedge of light reaching from the horizon along the ecliptic just as

twilight is ending or as dawn is beginning. Its base is 20° or 30° wide and it generally can be followed 90° from the sun. Sometimes it is seen as a narrow, very faint, band entirely around the sky. The spring months are most favorable for observing the zodiacal light in the evening, and the autumn months for observing it in the morning.

Q. *How many times in a year is the moon eclipsed?* S. B.

A. Never more than three eclipses of the moon occur in a year, and in some years none at all. The moon is eclipsed only when it is near one of the nodes of its orbit at the time of full moon, the nodes being the two points at which the moon's orbit passes through the plane of the earth's orbit.

Q. *What is false dawn?* A. B. M.

A. False dawn is the zodiacal light, supposed to be due to the reflection of sunlight from fine particles of matter entirely outside the earth's atmosphere. It is best seen in low latitudes, especially in the pure air of tropical and subtropical deserts.

Q. *What comet has the smallest orbit?* M. L. H.

A. Encke's comet has the smallest known, since it returns about every 3.3 years.

Q. *Is there a meteor shower which occurs every hundred years?* D. P.

A. There is none whose period of return is once in a hundred years. The Leonids are especially brilliant about every thirty-three years. The earth meets the thicker part of the swarm three times in about one hundred years.

Q. *Why is it believed that the moon has no atmosphere?* T. M.

A. Its absence is proved by the fact that, at the time of an eclipse of the sun, the moon's limb is perfectly dark and sharp, with no apparent distortion of the sun due to refraction. Similarly, when a star is occulted by the moon, it disappears suddenly and not somewhat gradually as it would if its light were being more and more extinguished by an atmosphere. There are other indications which lead to the same conclusions.

Q. Are comets often visible in the daytime to the naked eye? J. McG.

A. In the last hundred years, only two comets have been sufficiently brilliant to be seen by day with the unaided eye. One of these was in February, 1843, the other in September, 1882.

Q. Where is the hole made by the fall of an enormous meteor in one of the western states? A. S. S.

A. Probably you refer to Coon Butte, which is a large depression near Canon Diabolo, Arizona. The crater is 4000 feet across, and 550 feet deep. Since several tons of meteoric iron have been found nearby, it is believed that the crater was formed by the fall of an enormous meteorite, although this has not been definitely established. Borings have so far failed to locate any large mass within it.

Q. How can one judge the power of a telescope? G. E.

A. To determine the power of a telescope, focus it on a brick wall. With a little practice one can keep both eyes open in which case one sees the wall directly with one eye, and sees the wall through the instrument with the other. If the magnified brick is as large as ten unmagnified, the power of the telescope is ten. The telescope should be at least 100 feet from the wall.

Q. Why was the new planet given the name, Pluto? R. L. W.

A. Roger Lowell Putnam, trustee of Lowell Observatory, says that the name Pluto for the new planet was selected after a large number of suggested names had been narrowed down to three—Minerva, Pluto, and Cronus. Mr. Putnam said the various scientists interested felt that the line of Roman gods for whom other planets are named should not be broken. The name Pluto is symbolic of the dark and distant regions through which the planet travels in its orbit about the sun.

Q. What star is called the morning star? B. F.

A. This popular and poetic name is given to the planets Jupiter, Mars, Saturn, and Venus, when one of them rises shortly before the sun and is a conspicuous object in the sky before dawn.

Q. Why do stars seem to be pointed? M. E. H.

A. The apparent points of stars when seen by the naked eye are merely due to scintillation which arises from inequalities of the earth's atmosphere.

Q. Are there any planetariums in the United States? K. J. M.

A. Chicago and Philadelphia have the distinction of being the first American cities to have these mechanical marvels. Max Adler, a former Sears-Roebuck official, gave Chicago $500,000 to purchase a Zeiss planetarium for that city. It is on an island near the Field Museum. Samuel S. Fels, philanthropist, has provided a planetarium for Philadelphia as a part of the new Science Museum of the Franklin Institute. Los Angeles is also to have a Planetarium.

Q. What part of the sun's heat does the earth receive? M. P.

A. Less than one two-billionth of the sun's energy is intercepted by the earth, since its energy radiates in all directions.

Q. Please define the stratosphere. W. R. C.

A. It is the upper portion of the atmosphere above 11 kilometers, more or less, depending on latitude, season, and weather, in which temperature changes but little with altitude and clouds of water never form, and in which there is practically no convection or distribution of the atmospheric equilibrium causing winds. It is often called the isothermal region; that is, region of equal temperature.

Q. How and how soon does a sunspot affect the earth? E. D. A.

A. The fact has been established that some connection exists between sunspots and magnetic storms on the earth, such storms generally, though not always, occurring when there is a large spot near the central meridian of the sun. These storms frequently recur at intervals of 27.3 days, which is the period of the sun's synodic revolution. The average time of the commencement of a magnetic storm is about 30 hours after the passage of the spot over the central meridian of the sun.

Q. Does the moon have any effect upon the temperature of the earth? E. K.

A. The Naval Observatory says that the direct effect of the moon on the temperature of the earth is entirely inappreciable.

Q. How long a time is a sun spot visible? E. H. H.

A. After appearing on the sun's eastern limb spots remain visible for about two weeks. By solar rotation they are carried behind the western limb. If still existing they reappear again about a fortnight later. Spots are at times seen to form on the sun's visible hemisphere.

Q. When a tide reaches its highest point does it remain so for a length of time or does it turn immediately? J. B.

A. The Coast and Geodetic Survey says that the tide begins to fall immediately after reaching its highest point, but the vertical motion is so slow at the times of both high and low waters that the change of elevation is not usually perceptible until some minutes later. The apparent stand of the water at these times depends largely upon the range of tide and is independent of the distance from the equator. The smaller the range of tide, the longer is the apparent stand at the times of high and low waters.

Q. Of what did Galileo make his first telescope? V. N.

A. A spectacle lens was placed at each end of a piece of organ pipe. The telescope magnified only three times.

Q. It is claimed that the sun is the source of all energy. How can the energy of a waterfall be traced to the sun? D. L.

A. The Naval Observatory says that the energy of a waterfall comes from water which has fallen from the clouds in the form of rain or snow; and these clouds are caused by evaporation which is the result of the sun's energy acting in the form of heat on the surface of oceans, lakes, etc.

Q. How can one tell a star from a planet? O. P.

A. A planet may be distinguished from a star in three ways—first, the stars twinkle and the planets usually do not. However, this rule is far from infallible. Second, when magnified by a telescope, the planets show disks of perceptible area, while the stars appear as glittering points. This distinction holds for all the principal planets, but fails for most of the many minor planets, or asteroids. Third, the stars maintain practically the same relative positions for years while a planet changes its position among them perceptibly from night to night or, seen in a telescope, in the course of a few hours or even minutes.

Q. How many stars are there in the Southern Cross? I. T.

A. The Southern Cross is a constellation situated near the Antarctic Circle. It consists of four bright stars. The two brilliant stars which mark the summit and foot have nearly the same right ascension. The constellation, therefore, is almost vertical when passing the meridian, and these two stars act as pointers to the Antarctic Circle. The constellation becomes visible at about north latitude 30°, but haze and fog near the sea horizon will usually obscure it until a latitude six or seven degrees farther south has been reached.

Q. Isn't the sun really the distance that it travels in the time it takes its light to reach us, ahead of where we see it? J. K.

A. It is true that any heavenly body appears to be in the place it occupied when the light by which it is seen left the body, not in the place it occupies when this light reaches the earth; but the difference in direction between its apparent place and its true place is so small as to be imperceptible to the naked eye.

Q. Please give a few of the known facts about the newly discovered planet, Pluto. A. H.

A. Present distance from the earth—41 astronomical units, or 3,813,000,000 miles. Mass—Known to be smaller than at first believed, but not computed; tentatively believed about the same as the earth. Orbit—Elliptical, its plane inclined to that of the other major planets at about 31 degrees 21 minutes. Size of orbit—Long diameter, roughly 433 astronomical units, or 433 times 93,000,000 miles. Time required for complete circuit of orbit—3200 years. Length of time to remain in view of earth—probably a century more. Time it will then remain hidden—roughly, 3000 years.

Q. What difference in ultra-violet rays is there in winter and summer sunshine? P. F. S.

A. It depends upon the latitude. George H. Maughan of Cornell University says that in central New York, from October to March, the sun shines during only one-third of the daylight hours, and along with the decrease in sunshine goes a greater decrease in the effect of ultra-violet rays. Winter sun contains less than one-tenth of effective ultra-violet as does June sunshine.

Q. How does gravity on the sun compare with gravity on the earth? H. F. O.

A. The force of gravity at the sun's surface is twenty-seven and two-thirds as great as gravity at the surface of the earth.

Q. How much is the earth slowing down in rotating on its axis? D. M. R.

A. The rate of rotation is not constant, but is gradually decreasing with a consequent lengthening of the sidereal day, amounting to about 1/1000 of a second per century.

Q. What was the power of the telescope through which Galileo found four satellites of Jupiter? A. R.

A. This telescope, constructed by Galileo, magnified 33 diameters.

Q. How far away is the horizon? G. C.

A. The actual distance of the horizon depends upon the height above sea level of the eyes of the observer. The horizon is always as far away as one can see. The higher one goes up from a given point, the greater the distance of the horizon. The observer looking out over the land or sea from a high place can see more of the earth's round surface before the curve of the surface takes things beyond the range of vision. If one stands on a cliff 100 feet high at the seashore and looks toward a point where a ship is coming toward the shore, the ship can be seen much sooner than if one stands at sea level. In exact words, one sees actually more of the earth's surface the higher one is, because with the increase of elevation, one's position in relation to the curvature of the earth's surface changes.

Q. Is there any explanation for the counter-glow or Gegenschein? L. J. R.

A. The spectrum of the Gegenschein as observed by Fath of Lick

Observatory in 1908 seems identical with that of sunlight and there is little doubt, according to some astronomers, that the illumination is caused by the reflection of sunlight by a belt of small bodies revolving in orbits which lie mostly within that of Venus, but some of which may extend beyond the earth.

Q. Does the sun rotate upon its axis? A. R. H.

A. The sun rotates upon its axis from west to east. It is inclined at an angle of 7° to the plane of the ecliptic.

Q. What heavenly bodies are included in the solar system? V. B.

A. The solar system is the sun, with the group of celestial bodies, which, held by its attraction, revolve around it. This group comprises so far as is known, 9 major planets attended by 26 satellites, about 700 minor planets or asteroids, also comets and meteors.

Q. How long would it take to travel to the sun by train? B. R. K.

A. Dr. Paul W. Merrill, astronomer at the Mt. Wilson Laboratory, Pasadena, computed that an express train would take 200 years to reach the sun from our earth.

Q. Is the taking of astronomical observations and the making of calculations hard on the eyes? J. N. H.

A. On the whole, astronomical work is apt to over-strain the eyes; (a) from excessive light of the sun, when it is an object of study; (b) from the extreme faintness of some stellar objects; and (c) from the danger of too much use of the microscope in measuring astronomical photographs.

Q. What is the difference between a total eclipse of the sun and an annular eclipse? A. S. B.

A. Annular eclipse—when the moon is more distant than usual, so that around its disk is a thin ring of true sunlight unobscured. Total eclipse—when the moon is at the critical distance where its conical shadow, passing over the earth, falls short of certain regions (annular eclipse visible) but touches others in between (totality visible).

Q. Why does the eclipse of the sun, when seen through steam, look red? L. L.

A. When light passes through a medium containing numerous small particles, a certain proportion of the light is scattered sideways by these particles, and the shorter the wave length, the greater will be the scattering. The blue light is therefore scattered to a much greater extent than the red light. The light as it travels onward is thus gradually robbed of its blue portion and will appear red. This effect is readily seen by looking at a street lamp from a short distance in a fog.

Q. Do many people visit the Planetarium in Chicago? R. P.

A. In the first year of its existence, the Adler Planetarium was visited by three-quarters of a million people.

Q. How is the word digit used in astronomy? J. H.

A. The Naval Observatory says the word digit (Latin digitus), means astronomically the twelfth part of the diameter of the sun or moon and was formerly used to express the magnitude of an eclipse. The word is now obsolete in this connection.

Q. Why isn't the earth's orbit perfectly round? M. C. F.

A. The Naval Observatory says that it has been proved, first by Sir Isaac Newton, that a spherical body attracted gravitationally only by another spherical body will move in a circle, ellipse, parabola, or hyperbola, but this proof is a matter of higher mathematics. The orbits of the planets are not perfect ellipses, because the elliptical motion of each of them that would result from the attraction of the sun alone is disturbed by the attraction of the other planets.

Q. Is the space between the earth and sun dark or light? F. A. A.

A. Space is perpetual night. If space happened to be in the orbit of a heavenly body, when it occupied that particular spot, there would be light, since the atmosphere surrounding planets and planetoids causes them to reflect the light of the sun.

Q. In the Arctic regions is the moon above the horizon when it is full? J. K. C.

A. The Naval Observatory says at either pole the moon is above the horizon continuously for about two weeks, and then below the horizon continuously for about two weeks. At the Arctic and Antarctic Circles there are some years when for a few days in each month the moon does not set, and a few days when it does not rise; otherwise at these circles it rises and sets daily. In the polar regions, during the winter months, the moon is generally above the horizon when it is full and below the horizon when it is new; and the reverse is the case during the summer months.

Q. Are there active volcanoes on the moon? Z. McL.

A. It is not known that there are active volcanoes on the moon. The surface of the moon shows a great number of so-called craters. No universal agreement has as yet been reached to explain the existence of these craters. If they are of volcanic origin, the activity which occurred on the moon must have enormously surpassed anything known on the earth. In view of the fact that there are no lava flows, and that in most cases the material around a crater would not fill it, the volcanic theory of their origin has not been universally accepted.

Q. When was the orbit of comets first computed according to the law of gravitation? E. T. C.

A. The comet of 1680 was the first one whose orbit was computed on the basis of the law of gravitation. Newton made the calculations and found that its period of revolution was about 600 years. At its perihelion it passed through the sun's corona at a distance of only 140,000 miles from its surface. It flew along this part of its orbit at the rate of 370 miles per second and its tail, 100,000,000 miles long, changed its direction to correspond with the motion of the comet in its orbit.

Q. Of what is the moon made? S. C. C.

A. The measured cooling rate of the moon suggests that its surface is largely pumice, or a material with similar radiational properties.

Q. Are there any so-called interplanetary ships in process of construction? W. J. B.

A. Experiments in interplanetary communication are being conducted in several localities in the United States and in Europe. Prof. Robert H. Goddard is building a rocket plane in New Mexico. He has stated that it was impossible to say when it would be ready. Cleve Shaffer has been studying rocket propulsion in San Francisco and Harvey V. Bull at the University of Syracuse, New York. A rocket is also being built by the American Interplanetary Society in the vicinity of New York City, under the direction of Edward Bendray, David Lesser, H. F. Pierce, and Dr. H. H. Sheldon, of New York University. A rocket flying field known as the Raketen Flugplatz has been established near Berlin, Germany, where experiments are being conducted and rocket ships are being built.

Q. Can a sundial constructed for one latitude be used in another?

A. The Naval Observatory says if the sundial was constructed for the location at which it is to be set up, the face of the dial should be truly horizontal and the style set north and south. If, however, the dial was constructed for some other latitude, the dial, set up as above, and keeping its east and west line truly horizontal should be tilted from the horizontal position through an angle equal to the difference between the latitude of the place at which the dial is being set up and the latitude for which the dial was constructed, the north point being depressed if the latitude of construction is larger than the local latitude, the north end being elevated if the latitude of construction is less than the local latitude. The latitude for which the dial was constructed, if not marked on it, should be ascertained from the manufacturer or by measuring the angle between the style and the face of the dial.

Q. How is the temperature of the moon determined? J. T. B.

A. Modern observatories are equipped with instruments whereby the temperature of the moon can be measured. The temperature of the moon depends upon the amount of heat it receives, the amount it reflects, and its rate of radiation. It is easy to measure with some approximation the amount of heat the earth receives from the moon, but it is not easy to determine what part is reflected and what part radiated. When the moon passes into the earth's shadow so that the direct rays of the sun are cut off, then all the heat received from the moon is that radiated and this can be measured, and from the amount received, and the rate at which it decreases as the eclipse continues, it is possible to determine approximately the rate at which the moon loses heat by radiation, and from this the temperature to which it has been raised. Observations show that the amount of heat received from the moon diminishes very rapidly after it passes into the earth's shadow. This indicates that its radiation is very rapid.

Q. What is an astrolabe? E. G.

A. Astrolabe was the name formerly given to any circular instrument for observing the stars. Astrolabes were of two kinds—spherical and planispheric. They were used mainly during the 15th, 16th, and 17th centuries.

Q. What determines the size of halos around the sun and moon? L. K. W.

A. There are two kinds of rings about the sun and moon. Those that are close in—only one to four or five diameters of the moon, say, away—which we call coronas, are caused by water droplets. The smaller the droplets, the larger the ring. The other rings, the true halos, occurring much farther away, are caused by ice crystals. There are several such rings, but each one always has the same angular size. This size depends on the shape of the crystal (usually, but not always, a short six-sided column with flat ends perpendicular to the sides), the course of the light through the crystal, and the amount of bending this light undergoes as it enters a face of the crystal at a given slope.

Q. Please name the eleven motions of the earth. M. H.

A. Popular Astronomy, by Flammarion and Gore, gives the following as the eleven principal motions of the earth (other authorities might regard their numbers as greater or less than eleven): rotation on its axis; revolution about the sun; precession of the equinoxes; motion around the center of gravity of earth and moon; nutation; variation in the obliquity of the ecliptic; variation in the eccentricity; motion of the perihelion; planetary perturbations; motion of the sun around the center of gravity of the solar system; and the sun's motion through space.

Q. Can the hour be told in advance when the earth will go through the densest part of the Leonids? C. P.

A. The exact hour at which the earth meets the densest positions of the swarm of meteors known as the Leonids cannot be predicted in advance. The earth comes nearest to the orbit of the Leonids November 14–15 each year, but as the meteors are more or less bunched in their orbit and are continually changing their positions due to the attraction of the planets, the time when they will be encountered in largest numbers is uncertain. The intensity of the display also varies considerably from year to year as the earth meets different portions of the swarm each year.

Q. *If the star of Bethlehem was not of supernatural origin, what star could it have been?* M. C.

A. According to Kepler the star in question was probably a conjunction of Jupiter and Saturn in the constellation Pisces, the two planets being so close as to seem like a single star. This conjunction is recorded as having occurred about 7 B.C. and might possibly coincide with the birth of Christ. Another theory is that the star of Bethlehem was a recurrent star the last appearance of which was in 1572 when it appeared in Cassiopeia. This star is reported to appear about every 350 years. A third theory is that the star was Venus which varies in brightness but is the brightest of all known stars.

Q. *What causes the earth's magnetism?* R. K.

A. It is not known whether the earth's magnetism arises chiefly from substances in the magnetized condition exhibited by the natural magnet, the lodestone, and by the artificial magnet, or as a result of electric currents circulating approximately in the direction from east to west within the earth. All we know is that the earth acts like a magnet and is therefore surrounded by a magnetic field, whose lines of force extend far out into space.

Q. *Does the moon ride higher in the heavens some years than it does in others?* O. A. L.

A. The moon reaches a maximum distance north of the equator at intervals of about twenty-seven and one-third days. For about 9.3 years nearly every maximum distance north is greater than the preceding maximum distance north, and then for the next 9.3 years nearly every one is less than the preceding, the great-est maximum, so to speak, being about 28° 35′, and the least maximum 18° 20′. About thirteen and two-thirds days after each maximum distance north the moon reaches a maximum distance south, of about the same amount. Maximum north or south may be at any phase of the moon.

Q. *How can I locate the North Star?* C. A. P.

A. The North Star may be found by observing the direction of the Pointers or two end stars of the Big Dipper; also, by remembering that the North Star is the last star in the handle of the Little Dipper.

Q. *What is the zodiac?* N. T. O.

A. It is an imaginary belt encircling the heavens and extending about 8° on each side of the ecliptic, within which are the larger planets. It is divided into twelve parts, called signs of the zodiac, which formerly corresponded to twelve constellations bearing the same names.

Q. *How can we know that stars are still in existence when it takes so many years for their light to reach us?* L. C. V.

A. We do not know positively that any star which we see is now actually in existence; but the continued existence of the stars generally may be assumed since no cause is known why they should cease to exist.

Q. *Are most of the known stars north of the celestial equator?*

A. The Naval Observatory says that recent investigations appear to indicate that there are more visible stars south of the equator than north, but this cannot be stated positively.

Q. *Please give the different characters outlined by the stars.* L. M.

A. Some of the better known constellations are: Andromeda—The chained lady; Cassiopeia—Lady seated in chair holding up arms in supplication; Aquila—Eagle; Auriga—Waggoner; Cygnus—Swan; Lyra—

Lyre; Pegasus—Winged horse; Sagitta—Arrow; Ursa major—Great bear; Aquarius—Water bearer; Canis major—Great dog; Crux—Cross; Orion—Great hunter; Pisces—The fishes.

Q. Since the Yerkes 40-inch refractor is spoken of as the largest in the world, what became of the two 49-inch objectives built in France for the World's Fair in Paris? E. T. B.

A. The Director of Yerkes Observatory says that the Yerkes 40-inch refractor is the largest of its type in actual use. The objectives, built in France were worthless for actual observations and were never installed in an observatory. If he is not mistaken, these lenses were offered for sale and it was expected that they could be reduced in size and refigured to give more satisfactory images.

Q. Why is it that some places have two tides a day while others have only one? L. A. W.

A. Each body of water has a natural period of oscillation which depends upon its length and depth and it will respond best to that disturbing force which has a period approximating its natural period of oscillation. Hence some waterways respond better to semi-daily tide producing forces, while others respond better to the daily tide producing forces. Over the greater part of the Gulf of Mexico there is generally but one high and one low water in a day. Among other places at which there is usually but one tide a day may be mentioned St. Michael, Alaska; Do-Son, French Indo-China; Batavia, Java; and Manila, P. I.

Q. Does light have weight? C. P. G.

A. Astronomical observations appear to show that a beam of light, from a distant star, is deflected when passing near a second celestial body (planet), as if the beam were of the nature of a stream of matter. These observations corroborate theoretical predictions that a light ray shows weight in a gravitational field. That light produces a definitely measurable pressure on a mirror reflecting it, shows that it has beyond doubt the property of inertia.

Q. Please name stars that are blue, red, white, and yellow. R. W. I.

A. The Pole Star and Procyon appear white in color; Betelgeux and Antares red; Capella and Alpha Ceti yellowish; Vega and Sirius blue.

Q. What is the solar system? L. R.

A. The solar system is the sun, with the group of celestial bodies, which, held by its attraction, revolve around it. This group comprises, so far as is known, 9 major planets attended by 26 satellites, about 700 minor planets or asteroids, also comets and meteors.

Q. What is meant by the "green flash" at sunset? H. A. B.

A. The index of refraction of air is greater for green light than for red. Thus, when the horizon is sharp and clear just as the sun disappears, the color changes from reddish yellow to green and we view what is known as the "green flash."

Q. What would happen if two heavenly bodies should collide? E. R. R.

A. A collision between any two heavenly bodies would produce a vast amount of heat, some of which would of course reach the earth, if the collision took place within the solar system.

Q. Who was the first astronomer in the United States? M. O.

A. David Rittenhouse born at Germantown, Pennsylvania, on April 8, 1732. As an astronomer he is noteworthy for having introduced the use of spider lines in the focus of a transit instrument. He died in 1796.

CHAPTER 8

AUTHORS

Q. How much did Harriet Beecher Stowe profit by the dramatization of her novel, Uncle Tom's Cabin? E. D. N.

A. Mrs. Stowe, in her total disregard of the theatre, had failed to reserve to herself the dramatic rights of the book. Consequently, it was at the call of any producer who wished to have it. Throughout the play's immensely profitable life she never received a dollar in theatrical royalties.

Q. Has Pearl Buck, who wrote The Good Earth, spent much of her life in China? N. C.

A. She was born in China, the daughter of American missionaries, and has spent the greater part of her life there. When she was seventeen she was sent to America to complete her education. She returned to China and married John Lossing Buck, an American missionary and teacher. They live in Nanking.

Q. Is Gertrude Atherton a descendant of Benjamin Franklin? B. C. M.

A. It is often stated that she is. Mrs. Atherton says, however, that her mother was descended from a brother of Benjamin Franklin.

Q. Please relate the story of Irvin Cobb's letters to editors written when he needed work. A. A. R.

A. Cobb grew tired "studying the wall-paper designs in the anterooms" of New York newspaper editors. He therefore sent a duplicate letter to thirteen editors, asking for work. Five editors responded offering him a job. Cobb chose one on the Evening Sun.

Q. Are the three children in the family of Kathleen Norris her own? K. H.

A. They are the two daughters and son of the poet, William Rose Benet, whose first wife was the sister of Kathleen Norris.

Q. Did Conan Doyle know, when he began a Sherlock Holmes story, how it would end? R. L.

A. The author answered this question: "Of course I do. One could not possibly steer a course if one did not know his destination."

Q. For whom were the first of Thornton Burgess' popular Bedtime Stories written? G. F. L.

A. For the small son of the author.

Q. Where was Dr. Henry Van Dyke at the time that he wrote his poem, America For Me? L. S. R.

A. Dr. Van Dyke says that he wrote it in Paris in 1909 at the end of a year's service as American professor at the Sorbonne.

Q. Where can one hear a pure Colonial dialect spoken in the United States? I wish to reproduce it in a novel. J. Y. M.

A. In the back districts of North Carolina an almost pure dialect of our Colonial period is spoken.

Q. When did Kipling live in the United States? A. V.

A. He visited the United States and married in 1892, the daughter of H. W. Balestier of New York. He lived for several years in Vermont.

Q. Who won the 1932 Nobel Prize for literature?

A. John Galsworthy.

Q. What did the Negro poet, Countee Cullen, say about his wish to be regarded? C. B.

A. The young poet thus answers your query: "A number of times I have said I wanted to be a poet and known as such and not as a Negro poet. Somehow or other, however, I find my poetry of itself treating of the Negro, of his joys and his sorrows—mostly the latter—and of the heights and depths of the emotion which I feel as a Negro."

Q. What is a ghost writer? M. Z.

A. He is a person who is employed to write an article, a story, or a book, but whose name does not appear as the author. The ostensible author is a person who has won some distinction either in the field of literature or in some other line of endeavor.

Q. Where did Thornton Wilder write the Bridge of San Luis Rey? C. D.

A. This novel was written while Thornton Wilder was at the MacDowell Colony at Peterborough, New Hampshire.

Q. Was Sir Walter Scott dependent upon his writings for his living? N. D.

A. For 25 years Scott was subsheriff, a sort of justice of Selkirkshire, and was also a clerk of the court in Edinburgh. The two positions paid him about $8000 a year, and took little of his time.

Q. Does Harold Bell Wright believe in immortality? F. E. N.

A. The novelist says: "I believe in immortality because I know that nothing—not even the things which we call material—dies in the sense that it ceases to exist."

Q. What was Sir Walter Scott paid for Ivanhoe? P. G.

A. He is said to have received $1500. The novel contained nearly 150,000 words.

Q. Please name some writers who have been in prison. V. R.

A. Among them are St. Paul, Henry David Thoreau, John Bunyan, Oscar Wilde, Sir Walter Raleigh, O. Henry, and, of moderns, John Galsworthy.

Q. Did John Galsworthy write of his own experience in Justice? D. J.

A. The Golden Book says that one day he put on old clothes, wrapped a brick in brown paper, stopped in front of a tempting-looking plate-glass window and let fly. Under an assumed name he spent the next six months in prison, and the play Justice was the result.

Q. Who are the immortal eight referred to in English literature? M. V.

A. They are: Milton, Shakespeare, Coleridge, Shelley, Keats, Byron, Browning, and Tennyson.

Q. What prompted Rudyard Kipling to write The Houses? J. A. H.

A. The inner meaning of the poem is an appeal to the dominions and colonies to stand together and stand by the mother country. It was written in 1898 at the first signs of growing independence of political action on the part of the dominions. The idea is expressed in the couplet —"If my house be taken, thine tumbleth down; If thy house be forfeit, mine followeth soon."

Q. Was Walter Winchell, the columnist, ever on the stage? B. E. L.

A. With George Jessel, Eddie Cantor, and a third East Side boy, Walter Winchell sang tenor in a quartet in one of the earliest nickelodeon movie houses. Subsequently they were signed up by Gus Edwards, the vaudeville impresario, and performed as part of a Newsboys' Sextet.

Q. *Is the author of The Birds' Christmas Carol still living?* N. I. U.

A. Kate Douglas Wiggin died August 24, 1923.

Q. *What legal step must a person take in order to write under an assumed name?* L. C. T.

A. A writer who wishes to use a pseudonym goes through no process of law.

Q. *Please name some London-born writers.* W. L. T.

A. The following, among others, were born in London: Bacon, Blake, Browne, Browning, Byron, Chaucer, Crashaw, Defoe, De Morgan, Donne, Gaskell, Gibbon, Gray, Herrick, Hunt, Huxley, Jonson, Keats, Lamb, Milton, More, Morris, Newman, Pater, Pinero, Pope, Mrs. Radcliffe, Rossetti, Ruskin, Shirley, Spenser, Swinburne, Walpole, and Zangwill.

Q. *Was Joseph Conrad's father an educated man?* F. C.

A. His father, a country squire, was a distinguished poet and literary critic. His mother was a gentlewoman.

Q. *Did some story suggest to Stevenson the plot of Dr. Jekyll and Mr. Hyde?* T. A. B.

A. Dr. W. J. Long says that Stevenson was in this instance indebted to E. A. Poe's story "William Wilson."

Q. *Was Lord Byron's childhood unhappy?* R. G.

A. His father was a reckless, dissipated spendthrift, who deserted his wife and child. His mother convulsively clasped her son to her one moment and threw the scissors and tongs at him the next, calling him "the lame brat," in reference to his club foot.

Q. *What is Meredith's epitaph?* I. B.

A. A line of his novel "Vittoria" is carved on his tombstone: "Life is but a little holding, lent to do a mighty labor."

Q. *When did E. P. Roe live?* A. K.

A. This American clergyman and novelist was born in 1838 and died in 1888. His novels possessed but moderate literary merit, but were wholesome and usually of absorbing interest.

Q. *How long was the identity of the author of the Waverly Novels kept a secret?* E. C. D.

A. Thirteen years.

Q. *In Shakespeare's day, what were the school hours?* P. R. C.

A. In summer, from six in the morning until six at night; in winter, from daybreak until dusk.

Q. *How long did it take Lewis Carroll to relate Alice in Wonderland?* M. E.

A. Almost the entire narrative was told at one sitting on the afternoon of June 2, 1862. The poems were later added to the story.

Q. *Which writer has the larger reading public, Victor Hugo or Balzac?* J. H. S.

A. It is said that outside of France Victor Hugo has been more widely read, while in France Balzac has had the larger following.

Q. *Who is the author of the lines: "That no life lives forever, That dead men rise up never; That even the weariest river winds somewhere safe to sea"?* E. L.

A. Algernon Charles Swinburne.

Q. *Please name two famous men of letters who did not excel as students in their school days.* C. D. L.

A. David Thoreau answers the requirements; so also, James Barrie. Of the latter it is said that "he was an indifferent pupil seldom opening his books except to draw pictures in them."

Q. *Did Rudyard Kipling revise The Light That Failed, giving it a happy ending? B. H.*

A. It is a fact that under pressure of his reading public, Rudyard Kipling wrote a happy ending for The Light That Failed. When Sir Johnston Forbes-Robertson produced the play in this country, he used the happy ending.

Q. *Has Jean Capart (author of a book on Tut-ankh-amen) first-hand knowledge of the tomb excavated by Lord Carnarvon? T. C.*

A. Professor Jean Capart is a distinguished Egyptologist. Lord Carnarvon invited Professor Capart to accompany Queen Elizabeth of Belgium when Her Majesty went to Egypt to be present when the tomb of the King was opened.

Q. *What was Voltaire's object in writing Candide? V. K.*

A. Candide is a satire which Voltaire wrote to attack the current theory that "all is for the best in this best of all possible worlds."

Q. *Who wrote "Drink to me only with thine eyes"? C. A. A.*

A. It is from the Greek of Philostratus, translated by Ben Jonson.

Q. *Where is Poictesme, of which country James Branch Cabell writes so engagingly? W. W.*

A. It has no geographical location, being a fictitious place within a short distance of France.

Q. *Is Henry Handel Richardson an Englishman? T. H.*

A. The author of Ultima Thule is an Australian woman, born in Melbourne.

Q. *Who were Jack London's parents? M. L. G.*

A. Jack London was the son of a trapper, John London, and his second wife, Flora Wellman London. The father lived in Springfield County, Pennsylvania, and the mother in Massillon, Ohio. The elder London was of English extraction and his wife English and Welsh.

Q. *Where is Gene Stratton Porter's Limberlost Cabin? F. M.*

A. Limberlost Cabin was built on Sylvan Lake near Rome City in the northeastern part of Indiana.

Q. *What is Sax Rohmer's real name? M. McL.*

A. Sax Rohmer is the pseudonym of Arthur S. Ward.

Q. *How many children has Rudyard Kipling? M. W.*

A. The son of Rudyard Kipling was posted as missing in action during the World War. His fate is not known. The remaining child is a daughter, who was married about 1927 to the British Military Attache to the Court of Spain.

Q. *What is the nationality of Michael Arlen? Of Sabatini? L. O. L.*

A. Michael Arlen is a pseudonym. His name is Dikran Konyoumdjean. He is an Armenian. Rafael Sabatini is an Italian.

Q. *Is Winston Churchill who wrote "The Crisis" and "Richard Carvel" the same person as the English statesman by that name? L. B.*

A. No. These are two individuals. The novelist is an American.

Q. *When did the author of 'Twas the Night before Christmas live? L. V.*

A. C. C. Moore was born in New York City, July 15, 1779. He died at Newport, Rhode Island, July 10, 1863.

Q. *Please give a biography of Erich Maria Remarque. H. S.*

A. Remarque was born in Onasbruck, Westphalia, the son of a family of French emigres who settled in the Rhineland during the French Revolution. He is a Roman Catholic. Left school at eighteen, and went into the army, straight to the Western Front. The book All Quiet on the Western Front, was written to get rid of the depression of his own thoughts. It has been translated into twenty languages and more than two million copies sold.

Q. How old was John Burroughs when he wrote "Waiting," Keats when he wrote "On Death"? At what age did Lowell write "Thenodia"? M. V.

A. John Burroughs was 25; Keats was 18; Lowell was 20.

Q. How old was the author of In Flanders' Fields at the time of his death? C. C.

A. He was forty-five. John David McCrae was a Canadian physician, son of an army officer. He volunteered in 1914 and crossed with the Canadian Field Artillery. He served in the field and later in a hospital as second in command. He died of pneumonia.

Q. How long did it take Milton to write Paradise Lost?

A. It was composed between the years 1658 and 1665 and published in 1667. It was conceived, however, as early as 1640.

Q. Why is George W. Russell called A. E.? F. H.

A. The letters A. E. have been used as a pen name by Mr. Russell, Irish essayist, philanthropist, and speaker, for a great many years. His earliest literary effort was signed AEon. The printer could not decipher his handwriting, so set up only the first two letters. Russell adopted this and used it for subsequent work.

Q. Who is Abbe Ernest Dimnet? M. V. M.

A. He is a French divine and author. One of his best known works is The Art of Thinking.

Q. Please give a short sketch of James Joyce. W. L. K.

A. James Joyce was born in Dublin in 1882 and educated at Dublin University. His first book was a collection of lyrics, Chamber Music, in 1907. Dubliners, his only volume of short stories, appeared in 1914. In 1916, A Portrait of the Artist as a Young Man was published, and in 1921, Ulysses.

Q. When did Sir Walter Scott publish his first book? W. D.

A. In 1799, when he was 28 years old.

Q. When did Omar Khayyam write the Rubaiyat? H. P.

A. Omar Khayyam was born in the latter half of the 11th century and died within the first quarter of the 12th century A.D. Exactly when the Rubaiyat was written is not known.

Q. What name did Richard Harding Davis give himself when a correspondent in the Russo-Japanese War? C. Y.

A. As John Fox, Jr., once wrote: "Nine months passed, and we never heard the whistle of a bullet or shell. Dick called himself a 'cherry-blossom correspondent' and when our ship left those shores each knew that the other went to his stateroom and in bitter chagrin and disappointment, wept quite childishly."

Q. How did De Quincey classify literature? S. R. W.

A. The English writer classified all literature as the literature of knowledge and the literature of power.

Q. Did Olive Schreiner ever write under a pseudonym? C. E. T.

A. The Story of an African Farm was published in 1883 by Chapman and Hall under the pseudonym of Ralph Iron.

Q. Where was Oscar Wilde buried? N. W.

A. At first he was buried by his friend, Robert Ross, in a grave which was leased for a few years in Bagneux Cemetery, Paris. Later a permanent resting-place was secured in the Pere Lachaise Cemetery.

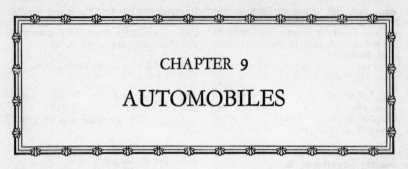

CHAPTER 9

AUTOMOBILES

Q. *Are there more bathtubs or automobiles in proportion to the American population?* G. N.

A. The United States has one bathtub for every 6.3 persons and one automobile for every 4.5 persons.

Q. *How many men have piloted automobiles at a speed greater than 200 miles per hour?* B. H. T.

A. Until 1933, only five men have qualified for this record. They were Major H. O. D. Segrave, Daytona, Florida, 203.97 miles an hour; Roy Keech, Daytona, Florida, 207.55 miles per hour; Frank Lockhart, Daytona, Florida, officially exceeded 200 miles per hour in trials but was killed when trying to beat the Keech record; Lee Bible, Daytona, Florida, 204 miles per hour; Captain Malcolm Campbell, 245.73 miles per hour.

Q. *What is the average life of an automobile?* R. W.

A. The average life of an automobile is seven years.

Q. *How many cars are used by Federal, State, and local governments in the United States?* C. K. L.

A. In 1932 all departments of the Federal Government together used approximately 29,000 vehicles. The total number of vehicles operated by State and local governments was approximately 143,000.

Q. *Why are automobiles prohibited in Bermuda?* J. M.

A. Automobiles are prohibited in Bermuda because the people do not desire to have the noise and confusion which arise from automotive traffic.

Q. *What is the earliest age at which a person can get an automobile driver's license?* P. A.

A. In several states a license may be obtained at the early age of 14.

Q. *What is the average license tax received from motor vehicles?* N. B.

A. The National Industrial Conference Board says that 25,800,000 motor vehicles were registered in 1931, and that the average license tax receipts amounted to $13.34.

Q. *How many automobile manufacturers are there now?* C. F. K.

A. In 1932 there were 144 companies reporting their production to the National Automobile Chamber of Commerce. Of this number 42 manufactured passenger cars, and 113 commercial vehicles. Eleven of these companies manufactured both.

Q. *How nearly is the world motorized from the automobile point of view?* H. S.

A. In 1931 there was one automobile for every 56 persons in the world. In the United States the ratio is one car to every 4.5 persons.

Q. *What is floating power in an automobile?* C. C.

A. Floating power is a method of mounting an engine in the car frame. The motor is suspended in perfect balance on two mountings of rubber and steel. By allowing the motor to oscillate on its natural axis within prescribed limits, torque reaction or vibration is insulated from the frame and body.

Q. Does it cost more to drive an automobile at sixty miles an hour than at forty? J. L. F.

A. The Chicago Motor Club has come to the conclusion, after an exhaustive investigation, that it may safely be said that a mile-a-minute in an automobile is from three to four times more expensive than when the speedometer says forty to forty-five. The conclusion was arrived at after checks made at various speeds. These results were cited: Oil consumption at fifty-five miles per hour is seven times greater than it is at thirty; tire wear at fifty is twice as much as at forty; gasoline consumption at fifty-five is one-fourth more than at thirty. In addition there is the wear and tear on the car at the higher speeds.

Q. Will the impact be greater when two automobiles meet going at the same rate of speed or when one is going slowly and the other faster? P. M. D.

A. If two automobiles collide head on, when traveling at the same rate of speed, greater impact results than if one automobile collides with a slower vehicle.

Q. How can an automobile radiator be entirely cleared of alcohol? L. R. R.

A. Drain the alcohol from it and then fill the radiator with a solution of sal soda. Run the solution in the radiator about half an hour, drain, and flush with clear water.

Q. At what age do drivers of automobiles have the most accidents? T. H. C.

A. Operators under 20 years old have the most accidents in proportion to their number. The next group is between 20 and 30. Although drivers who are 30 or over comprise 63.6 per cent of the 4,000,000

licensed drivers in the United States they are responsible for only 51.4 per cent of the accidents which result in personal injury.

Q. Can a trip be made to South America by automobile? R. L. P.

A. It is not feasible. Such a trip has been made but only under great hardships. As yet, in 1933, the Pan-American Highway has only been surveyed.

Q. At what speed does an automobile use the least gas? A. J. W.

A. The faster an automobile runs the more gasoline it uses. The most economical speed for an automobile of any make is 25 miles an hour.

Q. What harm does it do to automobile tires to carry too much or too little air? E. T.

A. Too little pressure breaks down the side walls of the casing while too much pressure reduces the tire area placed in contact with the pavement and bumpy riding and greater tire wear result.

Q. How can a windshield be given a good polish? M. C.

A. Use equal parts of denatured alcohol and ether. Apply this mixture to the glass with a clean woolen cloth. Rub briskly, then sprinkle a little jeweler's rouge upon a piece of chamois skin and polish.

Q. When was the first automobile race? V. G.

A. What might be so termed was the endurance run in Chicago in 1895, sponsored by a Chicago newspaper. Six cars started over a course of 54 miles, and two finished. Four of the cars were gasoline driven and two were propelled by electricity. Charles Z. Duryea, the winner of the $500 prize, finished in 10 hours and 23 minutes.

Q. How many tourist camps are there in the United States? J. T.

A. There are many which are not counted, but the Motor Tourist Camp Manual lists 15,000 in the

United States and Canada. It also includes dude ranches, camps for boys, girls, and adults, and fishing and hunting camps. Some 2000 airports and plane landings are listed.

Q. How are automobiles timed for speed at Daytona Beach? C. M.

A. Automobiles are timed at Daytona Beach by a trap laid at the start of the mile, and a wire at the end of the mile. These are connected with an instrument in the judge's stand which clicks the time when the car passes over the trap and the wire. The average is then made between the north and south trips.

Q. When was the pneumatic tire invented? H. K.

A. In 1888 the pneumatic tire was invented by Dunlop, and at once came into universal use on the bicycle. In England and on the continent, an automobile casing, containing an inner inflated tube, was attached to the wheel rim; while in America a single tube cemented to the rim was more generally used, and to this day holds its place on the bicycle. With the advent of the automobile, a new field was opened for the pneumatic rubber tire.

Q. What is the average weight of the rubber worn off an automobile tire in driving one mile over a paved street? R. R.

A. The Bureau of Standards says that it depends on the size of tire, load, speed, temperature, and condition of pavement. For a 4.40 inch tire as used on an ordinary light car, the amount of rubber worn off is in round numbers about 0.0003 pound per mile or about 2 grains.

Q. How many automobile races on dirt tracks are there in this country during the year? R. B.

A. The Contest Board of the American Automobile Association sanctions over 100 dirt track races a year. Its jurisdiction covers the whole of the United States and these races are held during the year in different parts of the country. All motors under 400 cubic inch displacement are eligible to enter in these events unless the promoter limits his field to a certain specification.

Q. When were balloon tires first used? O. O. E.

A. They were first developed and perfected by the Firestone Tire and Rubber Company in 1923.

Q. What is the length of the automobile race track in Indianapolis, and what kind of a surface does it have? H. M. T.

A. It is 2½ miles around the track, and the surface is brick.

Q. Does it take more gas to run an automobile carrying five passengers than it does when there is only one person in the car? Z. F. R.

A. The heavier the load placed in an automobile, the more the motor is taxed and more fuel is required to pull the load.

Q. When was the first electric-driven automobile produced? L. K.

A. The first electric automobile made its appearance in 1892. William Morrison of Des Moines, Iowa, was the maker.

Q. How much do automobile accidents cost the people of the United States in a year? J. B.

A. The annual cost of the consequences of America's automobile accidents totaled $2,500,000,000 in 1931. This figure includes the deaths, the injuries which disabled for life, the injuries from which the victims will recover, and the damage to property. The per capita cost is $20.

Q. What is the approximate temperature of an automobile engine piston and rings at full speed? At idling speed? W. W.

A. The Bureau of Standards says that at full load and speed the temperature at the center of the crown of an automobile engine piston may exceed 250° C. for aluminum pistons and 400° C. for cast iron pistons.

Skirt temperatures at the same time may be about 100° with temperatures in the neighborhood of the rings at about 150° to 200° or more. Under idling conditions, temperatures are more nearly uniform and probably do not exceed about 150° at any point.

Q. Can a person drive a car in Europe with an American driver's license? J. H.

A. American driving licenses are not accepted in all countries of Europe as authority to operate a motor vehicle, therefore an International Traveling Pass, which is a general license for the car and driver, must be obtained. This document is available in most European countries for twelve months from the date of issue, and eliminates the necessity of re-registering the vehicle and obtaining a driving license in each country, thus saving its holder a great deal of time, trouble, and expense.

Q. How long must an automobile manufacturer make parts for a discontinued car? G. V.

A. For five years.

Q. How old was Henry Ford when his car was put on this market? F. H. W.

A. Henry Ford began his experiments as a mere boy. He was 40 years of age before he offered the Ford car to the world. His first car was completed in 1892; his second car in 1896. Until 1903 he worked quietly and experimented. He then introduced the famous "999."

Q. What per cent of the automobile drivers are women? R. S. B.

A. It is estimated that between 24 and 25 per cent of the drivers in the United States are women.

Q. What is the average cost of operating an automobile? W. L.

A. The American Road Builders' Association, from detailed cost records, reported on about 800 automobiles operated in various parts of the United States over all types of sur-

facing, finds the cost in cents per mile to be: light fours, 6.02; medium fours, 6.42; heavy fours, 7.20; light sixes, 7.38; medium sixes, 8.40; heavy sixes, 9.45.

Q. Are hand signals considered important in safe driving of automobiles? F. C.

A. They are an indispensable part of vehicle operation. Drivers should give hand signals as automatically as they feed gas to the engine. A hand signal should be given before each stop, turning movement, starting a parked car into lane of traffic, and before any unexpected or unusual move.

Q. Do racing cars have brakes? H. A. T.

A. The rules of the Contest Board of the American Automobile Association provide that racing cars shall be equipped with a motor-driven reverse mechanism and two independently operated sets of brakes.

Q. What was the Ford Motor Company called before it bore this name? C. E.

A. The Detroit Automobile Company was organized by Henry Ford, and was the predecessor of the present company.

Q. What is the liquid which drops from the exhaust pipe on an automobile? A. W.

A. When gas is carbureted there is one part of gas to 15 parts of air sucked in through the carburetor. This air contains oxygen. In combination with the hydrogen atoms in the gas the oxygen atoms form water. This water comes out of the exhaust as a vapor, which is sometimes condensed again into drops of water.

Q. How long does it take to assemble a Ford Model A motor and a passenger car? S. S.

A. The Ford Motor Company says that under normal production schedule it requires approximately one hour and fifty-five minutes to assemble the Model A motor. Under similar conditions a passenger car spends from thirty-five to forty minutes on the final assembly line.

Q. How many new automobile drivers are there in a year? S. C. H.

A. The Silvertown Safety League estimates that about 2,000,000 drivers are added each year.

Q. What causes back-firing in an automobile engine? E. E. S.

A. Generally speaking, back-firing is caused by a weak mixture which burns so slowly that the flame continues until the opening of the admission valve again, when it ignites the incoming charge in the intake pipe and shoots back to the carburetor.

Q. Who was the inventor of the automobile electric starter? A. K. C.

A. The credit for the first practical self-starter for automobiles is largely due to Mr. Charles F. Kettering. This starter was adopted by Cadillac during the year 1911 and proved to be the first successful electric self-starter on the market.

Q. What State was first to license automobiles? L. G.

A. New York State was the first State to license motor vehicles, beginning in 1901 and collecting $954 that year.

Q. Who is called the Henry Ford of England? P. D. B.

A. Sir William Morris, Bart., is known as the Henry Ford of England. His plants are located at Cowley, England. His plants now turn out about 60,000 cars a year, which is about ⅜ of the total output. He specializes in light, low-powered cars, and it is said that his employees are paid above the average wage.

Q. If larger wheels are put on an automobile and nothing else is changed, will it increase the speed? H. L. L.

A. The Bureau of Standards says that putting larger wheels on an automobile would probably have very little effect. The car speed would be increased at a given engine speed and this might make the car a little faster on level road, but speed really depends on power, not on wheel diameter.

Q. Were automobiles ever barred from Central Park in New York City? B. F. R.

A. In 1899 an ordinance of the City of New York barred Central Park to horseless vehicles.

Q. Of the early automobile companies, how many are still in existence? T. B. S.

A. There are about a dozen still in existence using the same names that were known in the early days. Some have been absorbed and the names changed, and over a thousand companies have come into existence, only to find the going too hard, and have failed.

Q. Can an automobile be fixed so that it can be driven by a man who has only one leg? J. R. L.

A. A gear shift can be adjusted so that a man with one leg may drive it. This may be done by putting the clutch pedal and brake pedal together.

Q. Does an automobile have much more power with the cut out open? F. N.

A. The power is slightly increased by opening the cut out of an automobile, but at ordinary speeds there is very little gain.

Q. Why was the Chevrolet car so named? R. E. R.

A. It was named after Louis Chevrolet, who built the first Chevrolet in a small work shop on Grand River Avenue in Detroit, Michigan, in 1911.

Q. What is meant by a stock car in automobile parlance? W. L. L.

A. The American Automobile Association says that a stock car is a manufacturer's model of car that is in regular production, is regularly catalogued in the current catalogues of the manufacturer, is advertised in the regular schedule of advertising, and is identical in technical details and in other respects with the required production of said model as specified in certain rules.

Q. What disposition was made of the famous "999" racing Ford, driven in Detroit races in 1902 by Barney Oldfield? H. A. D.

A. The Ford racing car No. 999 is in the possession of Mr. Henry Ford and forms a part of his collection in the Dearborn Museum.

Q. Why is the back seat in some automobiles called the rumble seat? M. L. E.

A. The term rumble seat was first applied to the seat in a carriage behind the body of the carriage, which was provided for servants. Doubtless it was called this because of the continuous low heavy noise which was made by a carriage or wagon as it rolled over the road.

Q. When did the number of automobiles in the United States reach a million? C. C.

A. It was not until 1912 that the million mark was reached, and not until 1916 that the production of a million cars in one year was accomplished.

Q. What is meant by free wheeling? G. R. M.

A. It means the disconnection of the engine and rear wheels so that the car runs as though the engine had been thrown out of gear.

Q. What is meant by bootleg gasoline? O. L.

A. There are two kinds. One is gasoline smuggled into a State and sold tax-free to a dealer. The second is gasoline unlawfully substituted in dispensing devices bearing the trademark and brand name of established

companies, and often adulterated with kerosene or other low grade fuels to increase the volume.

Q. What were some of the names suggested for the vehicle that is called the automobile? C. C. E.

A. Originally it was known as the horseless carriage. Up to 1899 many names were proposed and rejected for the new invention. Some of them were: carleck, electromobile. gasmobile, auto carriage, autovic, locomotive, cabine, victorine, ipsomotor, sineque, autogo, kineter, and autokinet.

Q. When were the Packard, Peerless, Pierce-Arrow, Cadillac, Buick, and Stutz automobiles first made? S. G.

A. Packard, 1900; Peerless, 1900; Pierce-Arrow, 1901; Cadillac, 1902; Buick, 1904; Stutz, 1911.

Q. Why is it not practicable to run automobiles with natural gas? G. F.

A. The Bureau of Standards says that automobiles could be run successfully on natural gas but the gas would have to be compressed into steel cylinders which would add considerable weight. The amount of natural gas equivalent to five gallons of gasoline would require enormous containers if it were not compressed.

Q. How many dealers in automobiles are there in the United States? H. N.

A. There are about 48,000 according to latest statistics.

Q. What is the average reduction in prices on last year's automobiles? T. R. E.

A. Manufacturers estimate that the 1932 automobiles, taking everything into consideration, were about 30 per cent cheaper than automobiles had ever been before.

CHAPTER 10

BEVERAGES

Q. What was the most expensive drink ever known? A. B.

A. Aesop, son of Clodius Aesopus, dissolved in vinegar a pearl valued at $40,000 in order to have the satisfaction of consuming the most expensive drink ever known.

Q. Having no food, would a person keep alive longer on wine or water? C. T.

A. The Public Health Service says that a person can live longer on water than on wine, because wine unless diluted with water would not satisfy his thirst.

Q. What is used to color soft drinks? W. K.

A. Most soft drinks are artificially colored with so-called certified dyes, harmless, and suitable for use in beverages and other foods.

Q. How far does water have to run over gravel in order to purify itself? G. T.

A. A Columbia University report says that there is no rule which would prove over how many feet of sand, stone, or pebbles water would have to run before it became pure. Such statements as that water purifies itself every two hundred feet, or even every ten miles, are wholly without foundation and should be emphatically contradicted.

Q. What was the first intoxicating drink known? C. B. N.

A. Dr. Harvey W. Wiley said that wine is the oldest and most impor-

tant of fermented beverages. He said: "It could not escape early discovery, because fruits of all kinds, when crushed and left to natural causes, undergo the alcoholic fermentation. Primitive man must, therefore, have been acquainted with the properties of the fermented juice of fruits, especially of grapes. Wine was known in the remotest historical times, as evidenced by references to it in the earliest preserved literature."

Q. Is milk as heavy as water? H. H. P.

A. Milk is slightly heavier than water, its specific gravity ranging from 1.029 to 1.034 at 60° F.

Q. Why does a person get thirsty? A. E. P.

A. The pneumo-gastric, or tenth cranial nerve, supplies the stomach with the desire. When the body becomes dehydrated, or the amount of water runs below normal, this nerve conveys to the brain the sensation of thirst.

Q. In the old days was whiskey ever used as ballast? A. M. H.

A. In the pre-Volstead days it was not uncommon for a distillery to ship barrels of whiskey as ballast on an ocean voyage in order to age it. The Kentucky distillers used to have their whiskey placed on board the Ohio River steamers, also as ballast. The rocking of the boat caused a chemical reaction that expedited the aging process.

Q. *How many persons in the United States consume intoxicating beverages?* M. M.

A. Lewis E. Lawes says that it has been estimated that in 1932 forty million people in the United States were persistent violators of the 18th Amendment.

Q. *Who first made ginger ale?* J. E. G.

A. Cantrell & Cochrane first manufactured it. It was originated by chemists to use as a substitute for ginger beer for the British troops in India.

Q. *What is the name of the device used in testing the alcoholic content of beer?* O. T. P.

A. It is the ebulliometer.

Q. *Can a person tell that water is poisonous merely by looking at it?* M. G. G.

A. It is not possible. Water may appear perfectly clear and yet be polluted. A sample should be analyzed by a commercial chemist or by the local Public Health Service.

Q. *What was the alcoholic content of beer before prohibition?* J. W. P.

A. The Bureau of Prohibition has said that the approximate alcoholic content of beer prior to prohibition was from 4 to 9 per cent.

Q. *Are two glasses of water daily considered enough for a person to drink?* E. W.

A. The Public Health Service says from six to eight glasses a day is considered the required amount.

Q. *Who made the first beer?* J. M.

A. The scanty records of ancient Babylon going back to 5000 or 6000 B.C. show that beer made from barley, and from barley and spelt, was extensively drunk there, even by laborers and by women in the harem. It was used in medicine in Babylon and Egypt, and had spices and bittering substances added to it. In Abyssinia and Nubia, Herodotus and Strabo both wrote that the people lived on millet and barley "whereof they also made a beverage." Tacitus said that beer was the usual drink of the Germans, and Pliny mentions the use of it in Gaul and Spain; he also writes, "They employ the foam which thickens upon the surface as a leaven"—probably the first reference to beer yeast for baking purposes.

Q. *Is water a food?* D. A.

A. The National Institute of Health says that it is necessary to define the word food before attempting to say whether water is a food. If by food is meant an element which nourishes the body, water would not be considered a food. If defined as an element necessary to maintain life in the body, water is a food.

Q. *What per cent of water is there in cow's milk?* R. M.

A. Cow's milk is 13 per cent solids and 87 per cent water.

Q. *Why does milk boil quicker than water?* B. F. C.

A. Because of a difference in specific gravity.

Q. *How long has chocolate been in use?* W. B. P.

A. Chocolate for eating is comparatively a modern development. As a beverage it has been used since the discovery of America. The Aztecs made a cold frothy drink from cacao beans. It is only since 1700, however, that milk has been used in preparing the drink.

Q. *Why is gin sometimes called synthetic?* J. K.

A. Because it is made by mixing its component parts and is not distilled.

Q. *When did the present method of preserving grape juice without fermentation start?* E. C.

A. While the Romans and the Greeks preserved grape juice, the present commercial industry was founded in Vineland, N. J., about

1870. The industry has grown considerably in the United States since the passing of the Volstead Act.

Q. Who invented whiskey? J. W. M.

A. It is not known who invented whiskey. It has been prepared for many centuries both in Ireland and in Scotland. The name is probably from the Celtic uisgebeatha, which was contracted to usquebaugh, a liquor which was extensively used during the 17th and 18th centuries. It was not quite the same as modern whiskey.

Q. What is the basis for believing that the restoration of legal traffic in liquor would produce a government income of half a billion dollars? W. L.

A. The taxes collected on distilled spirits and fermented liquors in 1919, the year before prohibition went into effect, totaled about $490,000,000.

Q. How many calories are contained in an average bottle of carbonated beverage? W. B. W.

A. A half-pint bottle of the average carbonated beverage contains enough sugar to yield about 150 calories, or about ⅟₂₀th of our required daily energy-yielding foods.

Q. How much money do all the bootleggers make in a year? D. R. K.

A. Edward Dean Sullivan estimates that in 1929 bootleggers netted over $2,000,000,000 from the sale of intoxicating beverages.

Q. How many bottles of soft drinks does the average person drink in a year? G. P.

A. More than 90. This average would include infants, as the total consumption in the United States is more than 11,000,000,000 bottles of non-alcoholic beverages annually.

Q. What is the difference between lager beer and other types? H. M.

A. The term lager indicates a special brewing process. Lager beer is produced from bottom fermentation while other types are produced by top fermentation. The fermentation also takes place at a lower temperature. Lager beer is aged longer than other types and takes it name from the fact. Lager is an early Germanic word for storehouse, and therefore lager beer is storehouse beer.

Q. How much revenue does Great Britain collect from the liquor tax? M. T.

A. The official figures for 1931 give the amount as $650,000,000.

Q. Is as much money spent for liquor in Russia as in the days of the Empire? E. M. O.

A. The Soviet Union Information Bureau says: "In 1913 the Czarist government collected 511,300,000 rubles in excise duties on vodka, beer, and other alcoholic drinks, or 62.9 per cent of the total revenue from excise duties. In 1927–28 the Soviet government collected 697,600,000 chervonetz rubles from the same source (that is, about 350,000,000 rubles, in terms of the pre-war ruble), which amounted to 50.3 per cent of the total revenue from excise duties. As regards the production of vodka, 4,636,000 hectoliters were produced in 1913, as against 1,804,000 hectoliters in 1926–27. The consumption per person in 1927–28 was 40 per cent of what it was in Czarist days."

Q. What is the difference in alcoholic content of beer by weight and by volume? J. R. S.

A. The Bureau of Prohibition says that the difference is as follows: Alcoholic content by weight is less than by volume. For instance, 50 per cent alcohol by volume would average 45 per cent alcohol by weight. Therefore, 2¾ per cent beer by volume would equal 2.47 per cent alcoholic content by weight and 4 per cent beer by volume would equal 3.6 per cent beer by weight.

Q. Is vermouth distilled or fermented? P. S.

A. It is neither. Like tea, it is steeped.

Q. Why is a liquid fit to drink called potable? C. B.

A. It is from the Latin potare, meaning to drink.

Q. What is vodka made of? E. O. W.

A. Vodka is a Russian distilled alcoholic liquor, commonly made from rye, sometimes from potatoes, and rarely from barley. Sometimes, in Russia, the term is applied to any kind of whiskey or brandy.

Q. What is done with the alcohol taken out of near beer? H. O. P.

A. Most near beer is made as follows: Regular beer is made and then dealcoholized by heating. The alcohol is usually conserved, but can be allowed to escape into the atmosphere. The alcohol conserved is then sold for industrial alcohol.

Q. What is meant by fortified wine? R. T.

A. It is wine to which grape brandy or ethyl alcohol has been added.

Q. When camping we boil water and find that it has a flat taste. Is there any remedy for this? E. N.

A. This may be remedied by pouring the water from one vessel into another a number of times, which procedure permits the water to aerate itself. However, even if the water has a slightly flat taste, you will be assured that it is safe to drink.

Q. What is the Bratt System of liquor control? C. E. W.

A. Legislation controlling liquor in Sweden is known as the Bratt System. Under the 1917 law private trade lost the right to retail wines or spirits, and since 1919 the home retail trade has become the monopoly of the system companies. It then became necessary to monopolize the wholesale trade also and to eliminate all private pecuniary interest from both branches of the liquor trade through limited dividend companies. There were in 1928, 120 local companies whose policy was controlled by the local authorities, thus giving a measure of local option. The boards of the system companies are composed of two members appointed by the parent society, two appointed by the municipal authorities, and a fifth member, the chairman, appointed by the state board of control. These boards supervise all the companies and have general responsibility for the enforcement of the law.

Q. Who invented Coca Cola and who named it? R. D. S.

A. Dr. J. S. Pemberton of Atlanta, Georgia, was the originator of Coca Cola. In 1886 he perfected the beverage and put it on the market. An associate, F. M. Robinson, suggested the name Coca Cola.

Q. How much grain was used in this country in the manufacture of liquor before prohibition? E. McV.

A. In 1917 the following amount was used: 2533 bushels of wheat; 4,239,677 bushels of malt; 2,375,439 bushels of rye; 33,973,268 bushels of corn; 6730 bushels of oats.

Q. Who invented ice cream soda? L. T. D.

A. It is not definitely recorded just who first suggested ice cream soda in its present form. Snow-cooled beverages were known to the Jews, ancient Greeks, and Romans. It is recorded that in Rome a certain Quintus Maximus Gurges, nicknamed the glutton, wrote a recipe for a similar preparation in one of his books.

Q. How long have Russian samovars been in use? S. A. N.

A. The samovar is a large urn with a tin of burning charcoal in the center to boil the water. The Russians use this in making tea. They have used samovars nearly a hundred years.

Q. Please explain how an olla works. O. W. W.

A. The desert cooler, or olla, of the Southwest is a porous earthenware jar which holds from five to ten gallons of water. It is hung in the sun and the rapid evaporation, which is the result of the porous material of the jar, keeps the water cold.

Q. *Was wine made in the same way in ancient times that it is in modern?* S. F. P.

A. The actual making of wine in ancient times does not appear to have differed very much in principle from the methods obtaining at the present day. Plastering appears to have been known at an early date and when the juice of the grapes was too thin for the production of a good wine, it was occasionally boiled down with a view to concentration. The first wine receptacles were made of skins or hides, treated with oil or resin to make them impervious. Later, earthenware vessels were employed, but the wooden cask, not to mention the glass bottle, was not generally known until a much later date.

Q. *Will wine or whiskey age in sealed glass bottles?* B. T.

A. Wine improves in sealed bottles when kept under proper conditions, but whiskey does not change or improve when sealed in glass containers.

Q. *Is it true that water itself is intoxicating?* F. I. H.

A. Water in excess is an intoxicant, according to Science Service. With the aid of an extract from one of the ductless glands, and also without such assistance in controlling thirst, Dr. Leonard G. Rowntree, of the Mayo Clinic, has proved that excessive water drinking by either humans or animals may result in intoxication. "Water intoxication," he says, "is hard to produce, as nature has provided against the accumulation of water in the body in poisonous amounts. Through thirst the intake of water is regulated to the body's needs. Unless the intake is greatly in excess the output through the kidneys and the skin takes care of the surplus. The convulsions of water poisoning are cerebral in origin and of extreme violence at times, usually lasting from 1 to 10 or 15 minutes."

Q. *What does plastering mean as used in wine making?* J. S.

A. Wine is treated with plaster of Paris to improve the color and keeping qualities.

Q. *How was the liquor called Bacardi named?* W. W. G.

A. Bacardi is a Cuban liquor invented by a well known Cuban by that name, a native of Santiago de Cuba, Province of Oriente. The liquor is called Ron Bacardi in Cuba, while the drink made from it is called Daiquiri cocktail.

Q. *Are any wines made without sugar?* M. F.

A. The Bureau of Industrial Alcohol says that many famous brands of wine are made without the addition of sugar, the natural grape sugar being sufficient to produce the desired alcoholic content in what are called dry wines.

Q. *Are the people of Russia permitted to manufacture alcoholic drinks?* L. E. M.

A. The Soviet Union Information Bureau says: "The people are not allowed to make alcoholic drinks. The making of vodka and other alcoholic beverages is a government monopoly, a step which was taken mainly to combat the production and consumption of bootleg liquor. Alcoholic beverages are sold under severe restrictions regarding the quantity to one person, and so on. The sale to minors or intoxicated persons is prohibited. It is planned to cut down the production of spirits each year, so that in fifteen years it will be done away with entirely."

Q. *Where were carbonated beverages first sold?* H. A. B.

A. The first carbonated beverage was produced by an American, Townsend Speakman, a Philadelphia druggist, who supplied most of the medicines for General Washington's armies. Mr. Speakman, at the request of a then prominent Philadelphia physician, Dr. Philip Cyng Physick, undertook to invent apparatus to produce carbonated water. Dr. Physick had become interested in the medicinal possibilities of carbonated water because of experiments commenced by Joseph Priestley, the famous English scientist, in 1772, and desired to prescribe it for one of his patients. Mr. Speakman succeeded in producing carbonated water and Dr. Physick prescribed its liberal use by his patients.

Q. What is applejack? T. M.

A. Dr. Harvey Wiley, in his book on beverages, says that when the juice of apples is fermented the product is known as hard cider. When this is subjected to distillation, apple brandy is produced, commonly known by the term, applejack.

Q. What States prohibit the prescribing of alcoholic beverages by physicians?

A. In December, 1931, the following States prohibited the prescription of alcoholic beverages by physicians: Maine, Delaware, West Virginia, North Carolina, South Carolina, Georgia, Florida, Alabama, Mississippi, Indiana, North Dakota, Nebraska, Kansas, Oklahoma, Arkansas, Utah, Arizona, New Mexico, Washington, Oregon, Idaho, and the Territory of Alaska.

Q. Do Germans or Englishmen drink more beer, more spirits? D. H.

A. Englishmen are heavier beer drinkers and Germans heavier drinkers of hard liquors. The per capita beer consumption of the United Kingdom is 77.4 liters compared with 67.6 for Germany, while the English consumption of spirits is 1.6 liters compared with 2.1 for Germany. Germans also drink more wine. England ranks first as a beer consumer, Austria second, and Germany third.

Q. What happens to tea if it is allowed to stand too long? C. D.

A. Tea should never stand longer than three minutes after freshly boiled water has been poured over the leaves. In three minutes the leaves give up all of their flavor and aroma, and all their caffeine. Caffeine is the substance that gives the tea its pleasant strengthening effect. If the tea steeps over three minutes, too much tannin is obtained. With an over-supply of tannin in the tea, it often appears cloudy.

Q. What do authorities claim to be the most popular beverage in the world? N. A. S.

A. Tea.

Q. How many oranges does it take to make one quart of orange juice? J. D. D.

A. A dealer in orange beverages says that oranges are graded from numbers 96 through 344. This particular orange juice company uses oranges size 176 and finds that from this size each orange gives two ounces of juice, 16 oranges are needed to make one quart. This may vary, due to the widely varying juice content of different oranges.

Q. Will the gas in carbonated water escape if left in open tanks? V. B.

A. Most of it will. A small proportion will stay, however. The amount which remains depends upon the temperature of the air, a cool temperature being preferable.

CHAPTER 11

BIRDS

Q. *How many varieties of birds are there in the world?* A. L.

A. There are about 20,000 species of birds in the world, about 800 of them being in the United States.

Q. *Are English sparrows good to eat?* H. B.

A. Their flesh is palatable, and although their bodies are small, their numbers make up for their size. In the Old World they have been served for centuries.

Q. *Is the turkey the national bird?* M. L. F.

A. The turkey is not the national bird. This distinction belongs to the American bald eagle, which is represented in the Great Seal of the United States and also on United States currency.

Q. *What birds have become extinct in the United States within the last two hundred years?* C. B.

A. The passenger pigeon in the 1880's, Labrador duck in the 1840's, and the great auk in the 1840's.

Q. *How much fish does a pelican eat in a day?* M. A. T.

A. In Fort Myers, Florida, there is a tame pelican which takes its meals at a local fish market. The proprietor says that it consumes about ten pounds of fish daily.

Q. *Do birds ever fly across the Atlantic Ocean?* W. A.

A. There are definite records of birds which have flown across the At-

lantic. The longest flight known for a banded bird was an Atlantic tern which flew from Labrador to Natal, South Africa. It was banded on July 23, 1928, and found dead on the beach in Natal, November 14, 1928.

Q. *How long have the starlings been in this country?* B. M.

A. The starlings now found in almost every part of the United States are believed to be the descendants of fifty pairs of starlings that were released in Central Park, New York City, in 1890 and 1891.

Q. *How many feathers has a 25-pound turkey?* E. G.

A. A turkey has 3860 feathers.

Q. *Are the American egret and snowy heron increasing in numbers or are they dying out?* T. I. P.

A. It is the opinion of the Department of Agriculture that the American egret and the snowy heron are on the increase. Both are on the protected list throughout the year and are found in a number of refuges and protected rookeries. They are now seen further north than usual. Some have been seen as far north as Massachusetts.

Q. *Where can I get some information about the strange birds called hoatzins?* M. L.

A. An amazing account of his visit to one of the haunts of these strange creatures is given by William Beebe in his book, "Jungle Peace." Mr. Beebe says the hoatzin is prob-

78

ably the most remarkable and interesting bird living in the world today. It has successfully defied time and space. There has been less change in it than in any other form of organic life. Mr. Beebe says that these queer birds renew for our inspection the youth of bird life upon the earth. His book contains an enthusiastic foreword by Theodore Roosevelt, and the chapters on the hoatzin are masterful accounts of a phase of outdoor life which no other writer has ever been able to equal.

Q. Should a person try to return a banded pigeon to its owner? R. P.

A. Pigeons are generally banded by fanciers who raise them for sale and racing purposes. These owners show little interest in the fate of a bird that fails to return to its proper loft, as they consider such failures indicative of lack of strength or homing instinct.

Q. What is the name of the bird which often alights on the back of the rhinoceros? S. M.

A. It is called a rhinoceros bird or beef-eater. It feeds on the ticks and insects found on animals.

Q. Where did chimney swifts nest before human habitations were built? F. E. L.

A. The chimney swift is a bird which has acquired a new method of nesting with the advance of civilization. Before chimneys were common the chimney swift used to nest in dead trees. It has the unusual power of flying straight up and down, which makes it possible for it to get in and out of vertical apertures.

Q. What bird won the greatest fame during the World War? B. B.

A. Unquestionably the most famous bird of the World War was Cher Ami, credited with saving Major Whittlesey's Lost Battalion. Released with a message on October 21, 1918, at 2:35 P.M., during intense artillery action, Cher Ami delivered a message 40 kilometers distant in 25 minutes and was the only pigeon

to get through the enemy's fire. Although wounded in the breast, and the leg which carried the precious message was shot away, the tiny tube, still intact, hung to the exposed ligaments. Later he crossed the seas with the doughboys on the Ohioan transport and died in June, 1919, from the effects of the wounds.

Q. How many kinds of humming-birds are there? J. A. E.

A. What humming-birds lack in size, they try to make up in number. There are nearly five hundred species, and they are found only in the New World. They are tropical, but in warm weather, and the season of flowers, they migrate as far north as Alaska, and as far south as Patagonia. Our country makes an acceptable summer home for about sixteen species.

Q. Swallows have a nest on a window cap of our veranda and are hatching eggs. Will there be time for the fledglings to learn to fly? I calculate it will have to be done within seven weeks. F. E. P

A. The Biological Survey says that the birds described are probably cliff swallows, and that the period of seven weeks is not too short for the young to be ready for their flight. Incubation ordinarily requires two weeks, the young birds remain in the nest two weeks, and have then three weeks left to develop their strength, which is sufficient time. It is likely that this is the second brood of the summer.

Q. What do birds eat when snow covers the ground? E. D. K.

A. Birds find insects in the bark of trees. They also feed on soft parts of seeds.

Q. Are some birds when hatched able to care for themselves? H. F.

A. Terms are applied to birds with regard to the condition of their young when hatched. Altricial means having young born naked, helpless, and requiring their parents' care, while precocial applies to those birds whose young are covered with down, and can hunt for their own food. Game and water birds are precocial, while perching birds are altricial.

Q. What American bird lines its nest with snake skin? F. L. S.

A. The Biological Survey says that there are several American birds which use snake skin in their nests. This is not exactly used for the purpose of lining them, and in fact, the exact purpose cannot be accurately guessed, though it may be with an idea of adornment. The Great Crested Flycatcher always uses snake skin and the Tufted Titmouse often does.

Q. Where is the albatross found? P. M. H.

A. The albatross, which is the largest sea bird, attaining a length of four feet, a weight of 25 pounds, and the unique wing-spread of 17 feet is most common in the Southern Hemisphere. Two species, however, the black-footed albatross and the short-tailed albatross, occur in the north Pacific from California to Alaska.

Q. How fast do racing pigeons travel? How long does it take them to return to the home loft? J. F. K.

A. The Biological Survey says that the average speed of racing pigeons is 40 miles an hour although speeds of 60 and 70 miles an hour are known. The usual distance for pigeon races is around 500 miles and in these races a good many birds return to the loft in one or two days. The record distance from which a homing pigeon has returned to its loft is over 2000 miles.

Q. Why is the meat of some birds such as the dove all dark in color, while that of others is part light and part dark? B. D. R.

A. The Biological Survey says very little data have been compiled regarding the reason that some birds have all dark flesh and others part light and part dark. It has been ob-served, however, that birds in which the power of flight is well developed have more dark meat than others.

Q. What kinds of birds has Central Australia? C. L. S.

A. Central Australia is arid and barren and not well suited to bird life. The only bird which can be said to be characteristic of this region is the Emu, a large bird related to the ostrich of Africa which is flightless and capable of considerable running speed. The Emu has long silky feathers which fall over the rear portion of its body with a characteristic skirt-like appearance. Next to the ostrich it is the largest living bird.

Q. Why was the bird sanctuary in Florida established by Edward Bok? J. G. M.

A. The purpose for which this sanctuary was established and the tower built was to create symbols of pure beauty and to express the appreciation and gratitude of Edward Bok to the American people for their kindness and generosity. The motto chosen for it was "I come here to find myself; it is so easy to get lost in the world," by John Burroughs.

Q. How long have people provided shelters for birds? W. H. G.

A. Early records of Asia Minor testify to the use of doves and pigeons for carrying messages, and it is reasonable to believe that shelters were provided for the birds. The shelves for swallows in Japanese temples and feeding towers with nesting places maintained by the Brahmans of India were early indications that birds were taken care of. The American Indians were known to hang gourds on trees for purple martins and other insectivorous birds.

Q. What are phoebes? P. H.

A. The phoebes are a species of birds among the first to arrive in the North as a herald of Spring. They live almost entirely upon insects—click beetles, May beetles, and weevils.

Q. *When was the fact of bird migration first recognized?* A. L.

A. In an article called "New Light on Bird Migration" Witmer Stone of the Academy of Natural Sciences says: "The semi-annual migration of birds has attracted the attention of mankind from the earliest days. In the Old Testament we read the words of the prophet, Jeremiah: 'the stork in the heaven knoweth her appointed times, and the turtle (i.e. turtle dove), and the crane, and the swallow observe the time of their coming.' Both Homer and Aristotle refer tc the subject, the latter discussing it at length and advancing the theory of hibernation to account for the sudden appearance and disappearance of certain birds."

Q. *Why do birds throw back their heads when drinking?* J. G.

A. The pigeon is the only bird that drinks by suction. All other birds take the water into their mouths and throw their heads back in order to swallow.

Q. *Why aren't English skylarks imported into this country?* E. M. G.

A. Permits are not issued by this country allowing the importation of the English skylark, since it is considered an undesirable bird. The habits of the skylark are similar to those of the starling.

Q. *Are birds increasing or decreasing in this country?* C. H.

A. The Biological Survey says that the number of small birds in the United States is increasing while the number of large birds is decreasing. Large birds have been hunted more than small ones and they suffer more when woods and forests are cleared.

Q. *What fish-eating birds are seen in the Florida Everglades?* H. F.

A. The Biological Survey says that the following are among those seen: snakebirds, curlews, ibises, cranes, king-fishers, herons, wild ducks, and geese.

Q. *Are owls blind in the daytime?* V. M.

A. Owls can see in the daytime, but not so well as at night. They are nocturnal birds and their eyes are adapted for seeing in the dark. Therefore the bright light of day partially blinds them.

Q. *Does gravity affect birds while they are flying?* T. B.

A. Certainly. Birds would fall to earth unless they exerted themselves against the pull of gravity by flying or taking advantage of upward currents of air.

Q. *How much does a grown ostrich weigh?* L. F.

A. An average full grown ostrich weighs about 300 pounds.

Q. *Which has the sharpest eyes, a vulture, an eagle, or a hawk?* M. B.

A. The Biological Survey says that eagles, hawks, and vultures are so closely related that it is a very fine point to tell which has the keenest eyesight. The eyesight of the vulture is not quite as powerful as that of the eagle or hawk. The eagle will possibly ascend to a higher altitude than the hawk, and this is perhaps the reason for believing that its eyesight is the sharper of the two. These two birds have more powerful eyesight than any other animal.

Q. *How many feathers are in a peacock's tail?* W. H.

A. The tail consists of 18 feathers.

Q. *What are totipalmate birds?* S. D.

A. Those having toes completely webbed, such as the pelican.

Q. *Where is the largest bird house and collection of live birds?* L. E. W.

A. The largest individual bird house shown in available records is the one in the National Zoölogical Park, Washington, D. C., which has 15 indoor cages and 22 outdoor cages, and was erected at a total cost of $132,000. The National Zoölogical

Park, however, does not have the largest collection of birds, as the following figures will show: Washington, D. C., 350 species; Philadelphia, 500 to 600; New York, N. Y., 700; London, 1000; Berlin, 1000.

Q. Are the night-hawk and whippoorwill the same bird? B. E. T.

A. In spite of their similarity in appearance and habits, the nighthawk and the whippoorwill are two distinct species of birds. The nighthawk has no call and appears chiefly at sunset, while the whippoorwill, whose peculiar call is so well known, likes to fly after dusk.

Q. About what per cent of an egg is the shell? D. D.

A. Approximately 11.2 per cent of every egg is shell.

Q. How can one distinguish between harmful and beneficial species of hawks? T. L.

A. Hawks with long tails and rounded wings are destroyers of game birds and poultry; while the hawks with broad fan-shaped tails and square wings kill only insects and rodents.

Q. Have birds ever had teeth? H. A.

A. The first birds, which developed from the flying reptiles, all possessed teeth. As they progressed into the later stages of bird evolution, however, the teeth were lost, and there are now no living birds with teeth.

Q. How much Canadian territory is set aside as bird sanctuaries? F. T.

A. About 560,000 square miles. In these sanctuaries no shooting, trapping, or killing of birds is permitted.

Q. What are some of the fabulous birds of prey? S. V.

A. Probably the best known of the fabulous birds of prey were the roc, which was a bird so enormous that it obscured the sun where it flew, and carried away men in its talons; the phoenix, which was a bird with a beautiful voice and a long tail like a peacock's, and was supposed to rise from the ashes of fire; and the harpy, which was a terrible bird, with a woman's face and breast and great claws like an eagle's and pursued men who had sinned.

Q. When an egg as large as a pea is found in a hen which has been killed, how long would it have been before the egg was laid? G. L.

A. It takes from 18 to 20 hours for an egg to mature and be laid.

Q. How much does a dozen eggs weigh? M. K. O.

A. Eggs generally weigh from 23 to 25 ounces to the dozen, but may vary from 18 to 32 ounces.

Q. How did the fowl get the name of turkey? M. M.

A. It is one of the common mistakes in popular nomenclature which creep into a language due to a misconception about the animal in question. This bird was originally called a Turk because it was thought that it originated in that country just as Columbus called the natives of the West Indies Indians because he thought he had reached India. The name is misleading but it stuck, and became popular.

Q. How many geese are necessary to furnish one pound of goose feathers for pillows? E. B. T.

A. The best goose feathers are procured from the live bird in the spring, about six birds of average size furnishing one pound of feathers.

Q. What is the legend of the swallow? T. N. A.

A. According to Scandinavian tradition, this bird hovered over the Cross, of our Lord, crying "Svala! svale!" (Console! console!) whence it was called svalow, the bird of consolation. Aelian says the swallow was sacred to the Penates, or household gods. It is still considered good luck if a swallow builds under the eaves of one's house.

CHAPTER 12

BOOKS

Q. When was "Tom Sawyer" written? J. N.

A. "Tom Sawyer" was begun as a book in 1874 and by July 5, 1875, the story was finished. It appeared late in December, 1876.

Q. What is the meaning of the title of John Masefield's book, "Odtaa"? A. M. B.

A. The title is composed of the initial letters of the well known phrase "One damn thing after another."

Q. What is the first book known to have had illustrations? M. S. R.

A. The earliest known is the wonderful set of Egyptian papyrus rolls called the "Book of the Dead," written fifteen centuries before Christ.

Q. Had Browning's "How They Brought the Good News from Ghent" any foundation in fact? H. T.

A. It was purely an imaginary incident.

Q. What is vellum? A. G.

A. Vellum is a fine parchment, usually calfskin, which is used for expensive bindings for books and also for written manuscripts. It is clear white in color.

Q. How many books on magic did Houdini bequeath to the Library of Congress? D. A.

A. The collection as received comprises 1620 volumes and pamphlets and 107 volumes of periodicals on magic and 3286 books and pamphlets and 134 volumes of periodicals on the psychic.

Q. Were the characters and places real in Owen Wister's book, "The Virginian"? J. S.

A. Owen Wister said: "No character in the book is derived from any definite character in life. No geography in the book that has an imaginary name definitely refers to any real geography. The whole book may be styled the result of impressions of people and things covering from eight to nine years."

Q. How much is spent for books and pamphlets in the United States in a year? W. H. F.

A. Approximately $180,000,000.

Q. What was the first American biography of importance? I. S. F.

A. Chief Justice Marshall's "Life of Washington" was the first biography of any scope and dignity.

Q. How long a time was occupied in writing "From Man to Man"? M. T. S.

A. Olive Schreiner, the author, worked on her novel through a period covering fifty years.

Q. Is "Alice in Wonderland" the most popular book for children? J. R. K.

A. Opinions differ on this subject, but when over 50 famous authors were asked by a New York newspaper to name which book they had read as children and still liked, "Alice in Wonderland" was the overwhelming favorite. Grimms' Fairy Tales ranked second in popularity, followed by Swiss Family Robinson, Little Women, David Copperfield, and Andersen's Fairy Tales.

Q. *How many illuminated manuscripts of the so-called classical period exist?* A. E. R.

A. There are only three classical manuscripts in existence—the two Vergil Manuscripts now in The Vatican, and the "Ambrosian Iliad" now in Milan.

Q. *Where is the original of Samuel Pepys' diary?* T. A. J.

A. Six of the original volumes are the property of Magdalene College, Cambridge. They are displayed to a limited number of visitors upon request.

Q. *What is the earliest volume of United States laws?* F. F.

A. The Colonies complied and printed their own law books and King's rulings, but probably the first book pertaining to the United States at large is the "Reports of the Attorney General of United States—1795."

Q. *What is the inside margin of the pages of a book called, where they are bound?* G. I. C.

A. It is called the gutter.

Q. *What is meant by a diamond edition?* J. B.

A. It is said of an edition in a small volume or volumes printed in small type.

Q. *Where is the "House of Seven Gables"?* E. M.

A. It is in Salem, Mass.

Q. *Was the printer of the "Wicked Bible" punished in any way?* W. C.

A. According to Dr. Rosenbach, only four copies of the "Wicked Bible," printed in 1631, escaped the public executioner. The printer was fined 300 pounds by Archbishop Laud.

Q. *What occasioned the choice of "The Rosary" as the song sung in the novel by this name?* A. T.

A. Mrs. Barclay paused while writing her novel to ask her daughter what song Jane Champion should sing. The daughter casually selected Nevin's composition.

Q. *In this country, is there a collection of first editions of Shakespeare that is unusually valuable?* U. L.

A. G. H. Hale, writing of the Huntington Library and Art Gallery, says that the collection of first and intermediate editions of Shakespeare on deposit in this library "equals that of the British Museum."

Q. *Where do the Yahoos come from?* M. N.

A. The Yahoos are fictitious characters in Swift's "Gulliver's Travels." They are slaves of the Houyhnhnms or horsefolk, and possess the form of both man and horse. They are a satire on the human race.

Q. *What is the real setting of "The Gold Bug"?* T. L. D.

A. Authorities generally agree that the action of the story occurs on Sullivan's Island. Here Poe remained an entire year.

Q. *What books should boys and girls read before they reach the age of sixteen?* A. M. F.

A. It is not possible to furnish a complete list, but the following are selected from a reading course for boys and girls compiled by the Bureau of Education: Little Women, Louisa M. Alcott; Robinson Crusoe, Daniel Defoe; Tanglewood Tales, Hawthorne; Alice in Wonderland, Lewis Carroll; Just So Stories, Kipling; Heidi, Johanna Spyri; The Arabian Nights; The Adventures of Odysseus and the Tale of Troy, Padriac Colum; The Oregon Trail, Francis Parkman; The Adventures of Tom Sawyer, Mark Twain; The

Story of Dr. Doolittle, Hugh Lofting; and Ivanhoe, Sir Walter Scott.

Q. *What book did Abraham Lincoln regard as the best text book for an American boy?* A. M. D.

A. Dr. W. E. Barton said that Lincoln so regarded Murray's "English Reader."

Q. *Were any books carried in the "Friendship"?* A. K.

A. A copy of "Skyward," Commander Byrd's autobiography, was taken by Miss Earhart in the "Friendship" as a gift to Mrs. Frederick Guest who was to have made the flight.

Q. *What is the longest serial ever printed?* C. A. L.

A. Probably the world's record for printing the longest serial story is accorded to the New Era of Parker, South Dakota. It took this weekly paper twenty-two years and eight months to print the Holy Bible in its entirety.

Q. *Was a particular incident the inspiration of Goethe's Werther?* J. L. M.

A. It is said that this character was suggested by the suicide of the son of Johann Friedrich Wilhelm Jerusalem, a German Protestant divine.

Q. *In "Tales from Shakespeare" by Charles and Mary Lamb, is it known which person wrote each tale?* N. F. S.

A. Charles Lamb wrote the tragedies and his sister, Mary, wrote the comedies. The book was published in 1807, and has become an English classic of a minor order.

Q. *How long have bookplates been used?* P. T.

A. They are ancient. Some of the small tablets found in Assyrian libraries must have been bookplates. Japan had them in the 10th century. Modern bookplates are nearly contemporaneous with printing. The earliest actually known is a hand-colored heraldic wood-cut of about 1480.

Q. *Wasn't "Monsieur Beaucaire," Booth Tarkington's first successful novel?* S. W. T.

A. Tarkington first won recognition with "The Gentleman from Indiana."

Q. *When was Wallace's "Ben Hur" published?* L. I. R.

A. In 1880.

Q. *Do many books contain grammatical and typographical mistakes?* M. T.

A. It is said that publishers have never been able to bring out a book entirely free from errors. The book nearest perfection is the Bible which, due to its many reprintings, has offered many opportunities to correct mistakes.

Q. *Where was "The Garden of Allah" written?* N. V. G.

A. Much of the novel was written in a peasant's house above Taormina.

Q. *Was "Camille" originally a play or a novel?* D. C.

A. It first appeared as a novel in 1848 and was dramatized the following year.

Q. *When did Florence Barclay write "The Rosary"?* S. S.

A. In 1905, during a severe illness which confined Mrs. Barclay to her room for nine months, she wrote this novel. It was not published for some years.

Q. *Many people attribute the authorship of "Rules of Civility and Decent Behavior in Company and Conversation" to George Washington. Is this correct?* N. D.

A. It is not. Helen Nicolay, the distinguished biographer of Washington, says: "The book really comes down from the days of Erasmus, having been translated back and forth between Latin and French, and finally into English."

Q. *What is a picaresque novel?*
R. L.

A. The picaresque novel (Spanish, picaro, a rogue) is a story of adventure in which rascally tricks play a prominent part. This type of fiction came from Spain.

Q. *Why is a book called a volume?* *E. L.*

A. Egypt developed papyrus, a book was written on one long strip of papyrus, which was then rolled and tied. This accounts for the word, volume, which comes from the Latin word meaning to roll.

Q. *What is forage painting used in bookbinding?* *W. L.*

A. This is a corruption of the word fore edge used to describe the delicate painting or decoration applied to the extreme front edges of the book. When the book was closed only blotches or masses of colors showed but when the leaves of the book were partially spread delicate tracery, artistic designs, and sometimes elaborate pictures were revealed. Samuel Mearne, bookbinder to King Charles II of England, is credited with originating this form of decoration.

Q. *What is the favorite character in "Alice in Wonderland" of the original Alice?* *A. H.*

A. Mrs. Hargreaves stated on her visit to this country that she always had a special fondness for the Cheshire Cat. On sailing, the Cunard Company had a special flag made for her with the smiling cat on a background of white.

Q. *Please tell something of the earliest encyclopedias.* *G. E.*

A. Pliny's Natural History was notable of the encyclopedias of antiquity. It retained its popularity through the Middle Ages and was the source of much information in medieval compilations, one of which was the "Etymologies" of St. Isadore" (Ca. 560–636). Two centuries later Rabanus Maurus published his "Concerning the Universe," which was largely a condensation of Isadore. The greatest of medieval encyclopedias was the "Speculum Majus" by Vincent of Bauvais, chaplain and librarian of Louis IX of France.

Q. *Did the real "Alice" of "Alice in Wonderland" marry?* *A. S. D.*

A. She married and became the mother of three sons. Two were lost in the World War.

Q. *How can the soiled leaves of a book be cleaned?* *P. E. T.*

A. They may be cleaned by using a mixture of benzol (not benzene or gasoline) and calcined magnesia. Pour the benzol on the magnesia until it becomes a crumbling mass. Then apply to the soiled spots, rubbing it lightly with the tip of the finger. When the benzol has evaporated, brush off the remaining powder. Finger marks can often be removed by using a soft rubber.

Q. *What is meant by a signed edition of books?* *R. K. G.*

A. A signed edition of a book means merely that the author has placed his autograph in each copy of the edition. This is thought to enhance the value of each book.

Q. *Which of his novels did Sir Walter Scott regard as the best?* *G. C. A.*

A. Scott said that his most rapid work was his best. "Guy Mannering," that admirable picture of Scottish life and manners, was written in only six weeks.

Q. *In how many volumes is "The Domesday Book" contained?* *R. N.*

A. In two—"The Great Domesday Book" and "The Little Domesday Book."

Q. *When were bookplates first made by American engravers?* *C. L.*

A. For many years after the settling of this country, bookplates used by Americans for their libraries were imported from England. The earliest dated and signed bookplate by a native engraver is that of Thomas Dering, engraved in 1740 by Nathaniel Hurd of Boston.

Q. *When was the first story written containing the character, Sherlock Holmes?* F. B.

A. Sherlock Holmes made his first appearance in "A Study in Scarlet," published in 1887.

Q. *When originally published, was "Robinson Crusoe" divided into chapters?* N. W.

A. In its original form, there was no chapter division.

Q. *Outside of the Shakespeare Libraries, where is the largest collection of Shakespeareana in this country?* A. F. R.

A. Marsden J. Perry, of Providence, R. I., has the largest private collection in the United States.

Q. *Where is the manuscript of Franklin's autobiography?* B. W.

A. The Huntington Library and Art Gallery, San Marino, California, includes this manuscript in its collection.

Q. *When was the Uncle Remus character introduced by Joel Chandler Harris?* R. N.

A. He first appeared in "Uncle Remus: His Songs and Sayings" in 1880.

Q. *For what purpose was "Lamentations" written?* S. N.

A. It was a book composed for professional mourners to use in leading the wailing of the faithful over the fall of Jerusalem.

Q. *Was "The Good Earth" written first in Chinese?* N. W.

A. Mrs. Buck is bilingual. She says that the story came to her in Chinese and she translated it into English as she wrote.

Q. *How many words are there in "War and Peace"?* B. H.

A. Tolstoi's novel runs to a half million words.

Q. *When was the first book on first aid published?* D. C.

A. In 1633 by Stephen Bradwell.

Q. *Please give some of the big prices paid for novels which have appeared in the movies.* R. E.

A. The Authors' League Bulletin says that Rupert Hughes was paid $75,000 for "Ladies Man"; $25,000 was paid for "All Quiet on the Western Front"; "The Front Page" cost $125,000; "Street Scene," $150,000; and "Cimarron," $125,000.

Q. *When was Parson Weems' biography of Washington published?* M. A. B.

A. It first appeared in 1800.

Q. *How does Walt Whitman's "Leaves of Grass" rank in American literature?* M. L.

A. Carl Sandburg says: "In certain particulars it stands by itself and is the most peculiar and noteworthy monument amid the work of American literature. . . . Walt Whitman is the only established epic poet of America. He is the single American figure that both American and European artists and critics most often put in a class or throw into a category with Shakespeare, Dante, and Homer." As opposed to this view, it should be stated that this same volume still has its critics who claim that it is the most deeply damned book that ever came from an American printing press.

Q. *What is the name of the book which Mrs. Herbert Hoover, together with her husband, translated?* A. W.

A. It was "de Re Metallica" from the Latin of Georg Agricola, 1556.

Q. *When was the book, "Moby Dick," written?* A. B. C.

A. This book by Herman Melville was published in 1851.

Q. *Why are the chapters in Dickens' "Christmas Carol" called staves?* C. F.

A. Stave is another word for stanza or verse of a poem or song.

Since a carol is literally a song celebrating the nativity of Christ, it is
quite appropriate that the subdivisions be termed staves.

Q. *How many lines are there in
the translation of the "Odyssey"? In
"Beowulf"? K. S. C.*

A. In the translation of the
"Odyssey" by Alexander Pope, there
are 631 lines. "Beowulf" has over
3000 lines. According to the former
method of printing this poem, it has
about 6365 lines. It was written in
half lines.

Q. *What kind of liquid can be
spread over printed pages to preserve
them? E. J.*

A. The Bureau of Standards says
that in large libraries, it is customary
to paste a very thin silk fabric over
the pages, using good mucilage as
the adhesive. The fabric is like
chiffon. The Bureau does not know
of any liquid that is entirely satisfactory. Varnish would be good if
it did not penetrate the paper more
in some places than in others, and
thus cause a blotchy appearance.

Q. *Into how many languages has
"The Rosary" been translated? M. T.*

A. Into eight.

Q. *What is the "Flateyjarbok"?
A. E.*

A. It is a collection of sagas, once
preserved in the island of Flatey,
Iceland, but now in the Royal Library in Copenhagen. It was written
in 1380–95 by two priests of Iceland
and is one of the main sources for
the belief that the Norsemen discovered America.

Q. *When did the first New York
City Directory appear? M. T.*

A. In 1786. It had 846 names,
not going above Roosevelt and
Cherry Streets on the East Side or
Dey Street on the West.

Q. *Which of Hawthorne's books is
considered his best? G. S.*

A. Opinions differ, but some authorities say that in "The Scarlet
Letter" Hawthorne reached the full-
ness of his power.

Q. *Please give in inches the following book sizes: 32 mo.; 12 mo.;
8 vo.; elephant folio. E. C. C.*

A. Books are defined respectively
as—folio, quarto, octavo, duodecimo,
sextodecimo, octodecimo, vigesimo-
quarto, trigesimo-secundo, etc. These
terms are founded upon the number
of times a sheet is folded. For example, a folio sheet forms 2 leaves,
a quarto 4 leaves, etc. The dimensions are as follows: 32 mo.—3⅛ x
4¾; 12 mo.—5 x 7½; 8 vo.—the
sizes of octavo books differ according
to the paper; for example, cap octavo
is 4¼ x 7 inches; demy, 5¼ x 8, etc.;
royal 8 vo.—6½ x 10; 4 to.—9½ x
12; elephant folio—23 x 28.

Q. *Is the "Comedie Humaine" a
book? If so, who is the author?
C. S.*

A. The "Comedie Humaine" is a
series of novels by Balzac, so designated by their author, and intended
to form a picture of the manners and
morals of the period. The first volume appeared in 1829, but it was
not until 1842 that Balzac adopted
the general title. The author intended to present a panorama of his
time in France. He wrote nearly
100 novels without completing his
herculean task.

Q. *What is meant by "the great
American novel"? B. E. O.*

A. It is a phrase applied to a
novel not yet written, but dreamed
of by all who are interested in
American literature.

Q. *What are illuminated manuscripts? V. B.*

A. They are those whose texts
are brightened and heightened by
vignettes and otherwise decorated in
colors or in gold and silver. Fifteen
centuries before Christ the papyrus
rolls of the Book of the Dead were
illuminated with brilliantly colored
scenes. Later, as writing became
alphabetic, the important letters
were illuminated.

Q. Who was Trilby and why the expression "Trilby foot"? E. G.

A. Trilby, a model, was the heroine of a novel by du Maurier, and a Trilby foot means a small perfectly formed foot.

Q. On what is the Alexandrian codex written? S. L. L.

A. Books Before Typography says: "The famous Alexandrian codex, one of the earliest known copies of the Bible, is written on antelope skin."

Q. Was the character of Uncle Tom in "Uncle Tom's Cabin" drawn from life? S. T.

A. Mrs. Stowe said that her first conception of the character came from writing letters for her colored cook in Ohio to the husband, a slave in Kentucky. Afterward she used some incidents from the autobiography of Josiah Henson. The character of Uncle Tom, therefore, was a fictional one, imbued with traits with which Mrs. Stowe was familiar. The death of Uncle Tom was her own invention.

Q. When was the first arithmetic text book published? S. M. G.

A. "Cocker's Arithmetic," the first complete manual for "numerists" was published on the third of September, 1677, by Sir Roger L'Estrange. The author, who died before it was published, became proverbial in England as a master of mathematical subjects. His book was a "best seller" for nearly a century.

Q. How many printed books are there in existence that were made before 1500? L. L.

A. It is thought that there are but 101. Nearly one-third of these rare books are owned by the Library of Congress.

Q. What parts of "Little Women" are true? M. F.

A. Miss Alcott said that her family really lived most of it. "Facts in the stories that are true, though often changed as to time and place:

Little Women—The early plays and experiences; Beth's death; Jo's literary and Amy's artistic experiences; Meg's happy home; John Brooke and his death; Dennis' character. Mr. March did not go to war, but Jo did. Mrs. March is all true, only not half good enough. Laurie is not an American boy, though every lad I ever knew claimed the character. He was a Polish boy met abroad in 1865. Mr. Lawrence is my grandfather, Col. Joseph May. Aunt March is no one."

Q. What was the first book printed by Benjamin Franklin? R. B.

A. It was "The Rise, Increase and Progress of the Christian People Called Quakers" by William Sewel.

Q. When was the first book catalog issued? E. M.

A. In 1498 Aldus of Venice printed on a folio sheet the description, titles, and prices of his publications.

Q. How expensive were the first books printed? B. S.

A. There is record of two printers in 1478 agreeing to publish 930 copies of the Bible. Just how long these Bibles were in preparation is debatable, but the first record of sales in that locality, Venice, year 1492, and by the same printers gives the selling price at 6 to 12 ducats, or $30 to $60.

Q. In what year was "Webster's New International Dictionary" revised and the obsolete and rare words placed in a separate section of the page? D. M.

A. The G. & C. Merriam Co. says that the divided page was adopted in the edition that was published in 1909.

Q. Was "The Hoosier Schoolmaster" ever published serially? T. C.

A. In a copy of the first edition of this book given to Hamlin Garland, the author inscribed these lines: This story was published in

Hearth and Home in October, November, and December of 1871, and in book form, December 15. It sold about ten thousand copies the first six months, and about ten thousand in each of the two following half-years. It was pirated and sold in England in an edition of 10,000 copies, and has since been reprinted there with no profit to the author. Madame Blanc rendered it into French for the Revue des Deux Mondes. It was published in book covers in French, German, and Danish, and perhaps other tongues. This copy has all the original crudities, exuberances, and violations of artistic canons that have helped to give the book a sale of more than a hundred thousand in the United States. These facts are set down here for my good friend, Mr. Hamlin Garland, with the sincere regards of Edward Eggleston.

Q. What suggested the title of Thackeray's "Vanity Fair"? M. N.

A. It was the appropriate name for the book and was chosen from Pilgrim's Progress: "And the name of that town is Vanity; and at that town there is a fair kept, called Vanity Fair."

Q. Into how many languages has "The Message to Garcia" been translated? V. S.

A. At the time that Hubbard wrote a foreword for an edition, he said that forty million copies had been distributed and that it had been translated into Russian, German, Spanish, Turkish, Chinese, Japanese, and Hindu.

Q. Who first condensed the classics? R. C. D.

A. Dr. Rossiter Johnson, author, editor, and President of the People's University Extension Society of New York, is said to be the first person to experiment with abbreviating famous novels. It is stated that as early as 1876 he startled critics and book-lovers by making abbreviated editions of standard novels, omitting passages not necessary to the action of the story.

Q. What is a bookplate? L. T.

A. It is a printed or engraved label, bearing the owner's name and a decorative design, which is pasted inside the front cover of a book. The most popular size for a bookplate is 2 by 2¾ inches.

Q. What was the first encyclopedia? C. G.

A. The first encyclopedia written in English and with the articles alphabetically arranged was a "Universal English Dictionary of Arts and Sciences," by John Harris, a London clergyman, published in 1704.

Q. Is the expression "dime novel" used in England? L. T.

A. England has its own equivalent "penny dreadful."

Q. About what period of English history is "Lorna Doone" written? B. L.

A. It is a romance of Exmoor in the Stuart times from about 1673 to 1687.

Q. Please give me the name of an authoritative book on the American Indian. K. D. V.

A. "The Story of the Red Man," by Flora Warren Seymour, a member of the Board of Indian Commissioners, is said to be an excellent account of the various Indian tribes. Her book is also valuable as a record of the Government's relations with the Indians.

Q. In Barrie's "Peter and Wendy" is the name Wendy Scotch? C. A. M.

A. J. A. Hammerton in his book, "Barrie: The Story of a Genius," states that the name of Wendy came into use because the little daughter of W. E. Henley was trying to describe Sir James Barrie, who used to visit her home, as "friendly." The best effort she could make to pronounce it was Wendy.

CHAPTER 13

BRIDGES

Q. *How many bridges are there across the Mississippi River?* R. B.

A. There are 130.

Q. *How long did it take to build Brooklyn Bridge?* M. P.

A. The construction on Brooklyn Bridge commenced June 3, 1870. The bridge was formally opened on May 24, 1883.

Q. *How high above the railroad tracks is the Royal Gorge Suspension Bridge?* L. N. S.

A. This Colorado bridge is 1,053 feet above the railroad tracks, and when built was the highest in the world.

Q. *What part of the cost of the Philadelphia-Camden bridge was paid by Philadelphia?* G. N. R.

A. Philadelphia paid one-half of Pennsylvania's share in the cost.

Q. *Who conceived the idea of a bridge of granite across the Potomac at Washington, D. C., which would symbolize the union of the North and South?* W. A. B.

A. This was a cherished hope and plan of President Jackson's. The construction of the Arlington Memorial Bridge made this dream a reality.

Q. *How many bridges has the city of Pittsburgh?* S. E. McL.

A. Pittsburgh might be called the City of Bridges. Within the city proper and owned by the city, there are about 125 bridges. In the metro-politan district, Alleghany County owns 331. There are also a number which are the property of railroads and street railway companies. Considering these, the metropolitan district has over 500 bridges and viaducts.

Q. *Are there bridges over the Jordan?* D. A.

A. There are two. One below Lake Merom is the one over which the road passes from Damascus to Galilee. The other bridge is below the Lake of Tiberias.

Q. *How much longer is the George Washington-Hudson River Bridge in the summer than in the winter?* H. R.

A. The 3500 foot main span steel-work has been fabricated to a definite length at the normal temperature of 68° F. For the assumed maximum summer temperature of 105° F., this steelwork will lengthen a total of ten inches; for the assumed minimum winter temperature of –5° F., it will shorten a total of twenty inches. In other words, for a range in temperature of 110° F., there is a range in linear motion of thirty inches.

Q. *Does the Brooklyn Bridge sway at all?* J. S. S.

A. The action of the suspension bridge is that of a rope spanning between supports; for any load it finds the appropriate curve of equilibrium and is stable in that position. But as the adjustment to varying

position of load results from change
of curve, the roadway hung from the
cable distorts, that is, the bridge is
very flexible. It therefore may
swing.

*Q. How long is the pontoon bridge
at Dardanelle, Ark.? G. D. B.*

A. This bridge across the Arkansas River is approximately one-half
mile long and eight feet wide. It
was built about 1895.

*Q. Is the New George Washing-
ton Bridge across the Hudson the
largest suspension bridge in the world
now? S. L.*

A. After a survey of similar
structures throughout the world, the
National Geographic Society has
stated that this bridge has that distinction. With the longest span of
3500 feet between supports, it has
no rival among suspension bridges.
The Ambassador Bridge, connecting
Detroit and Sandwich, Ontario, is
second with a central span of 1850
feet. It is longer over all than the
Hudson bridge, however, as from entrance to exit it stretches 9000 feet,
compared to the George Washington's 8700 feet. The Philadelphia-
Camden Bridge has a central span of
1750 feet with longer approaches,
giving it an over all of 9500 feet.

*Q. How many natural bridges are
there in the United States? W. F.*

A. There are more than fifty
natural bridges of considerable size
and interest.

Q. Where is the Rialto? L. D.

A. It is the largest and finest
bridge in Venice, connecting the
island of Rialto with the isle of St.
Mark across the Grand Canal. It
dates from 1588.

*Q. Will a body of soldiers cross-
ing a suspension bridge cause it to
break? M. J. S.*

A. Engineering Societies Library
says that soldiers marching in step
across a bridge might cause failure
of the bridge due to too great a load
or due to vibration. If the type is

known, together with certain other
details of its construction, it is possible for a bridge engineer to calculate whether or not the bridge will
break. It is sometimes possible to
produce oscillations in a bridge by
men marching in step and these oscillations may be sufficient cause to
break down the bridge. In 1850 a
suspension bridge at Angers, France,
gave way when 487 soldiers were
marching over it, and 226 were
killed.

*Q. How was the first line put
across the Niagara Gorge to start
the first suspension bridge? W. S. T.*

A. Theodore G. Hulett, who
supervised the construction of the
first suspension bridge across Niagara,
relates that a premium of $10 was
offered to the first boy who should
successfully fly over the gorge his
kite string and fasten its end to a
tree on either side. A boy named
Homan Walsh, a resident of Lincoln,
Nebraska, was successful. The following day a stronger line was drawn
over by the kite string and then a
rope of sufficient strength to haul
over the iron cable. By means of
this rope the iron cable was carried
across and its ends secured to the
solid rock. It crossed the gorge five
miles above Lewiston.

*Q. What is a bascule bridge?
E. D.*

A. A bascule bridge is the type of
drawbridge in which two sections divide and the driveways of them are
lifted into the air.

*Q. When was the Million Dollar
Bridge in Washington, D. C., named
the William Howard Taft Bridge?
T. C.*

A. This was the Connecticut Avenue Bridge and the name was officially changed to William Howard
Taft Bridge, April 7, 1931.

*Q. When was the Fabrician Bridge
built? K. C.*

A. The Fabrician Bridge in Rome
is a stone bridge joining Aesculapius
Island with the left bank of the

Tiber, built in 62 B.C. by Lucius Fabricius. It is the only bridge built in Rome during the Roman period which has lasted to our day. It is known to modern Romans as the Ponte dei Quattro Capi.

Q. *Under how much pressure can men work within a caisson?* A. S.

A. It cannot be stated exactly. Pressure within a caisson, used for subaqueous workers must be increased by one atmosphere to fifteen pounds per square inch for every 33½ feet that the caisson is submerged below the surface. Hence at a depth of 100 feet, a worker in a caisson must be subjected to a pressure of 60 pounds per square inch. At the St. Louis Bridge, where a pressure was employed equal to 4½ atmospheres, out of 600 workmen, 119 were affected with caisson disease, and 14 died.

Q. *Who built the Benson Foot Bridge on the Columbia River Highway and what did it cost?* G. W. C.

A. It was constructed in 1914 by Mr. S. Benson, a prominent citizen of Portland, Oregon, at his own expense, and presented to Multnomah County. For this reason there are no figures available on the cost.

Q. *Where is Hell Gate Bridge?* C. E. H.

A. It extends across the East River at Hell Gate, New York, connecting Long Island with the mainland. Its total length is 18,000 feet. It is 135 feet above the water. The bridge was opened March 1, 1917. The cost of construction was $12,-000,000.

Q. *Has London Bridge ever fallen down?* P. T.

A. London Bridge has never actually fallen down. Old London Bridge, begun about 1170, was completed in 1209. It carried a row of timber houses, which were frequently burned down, but the main structure existed until the beginning of the 19th Century. The old bridge was the center for booksellers and other

tradesmen. On it stood the Chapel of St. Thomas of Canterbury, and a tower on which the heads of traitors were exposed to view. The present London Bridge was begun in 1824, and completed in 1831. It is borne on 5 granite arches; is 928 feet long; 65 feet wide; and 56 feet above the river.

Q. *What are the dimensions of the new bridge over the Potomac River at Washington?* E. E. H.

A. The dimensions of the new Arlington Memorial Bridge are as follows: length, 2138 feet; total breadth, 90 feet; breadth of roadway, 60 feet; breadth of sidewalks, 15 feet on each side; height above water in center, 45 feet; length of center span (the one which contains the draw) 184 feet.

Q. *Will Bear Mountain Bridge revert to the State or will it always be a privately owned bridge?* P. J. M.

A. It will revert to the State of New York thirty years from the date of its completion.

Q. *How great a load will the pontoon bridge of the Army carry?* D. G.

A. Model 1926 will carry a 7½ ton tank or truck. Reinforced by an extra boat in the middle of each span, the bridge will carry a gross load of 12 tons. One bridge company has 3 platoons. The equipment of one platoon will construct a bridge 220 feet long.

Q. *What bridge was it that had to be rebuilt recently because of defective wire in the cables?* S. R. C.

A. There were two instances recently of bridges which had to be torn down and rebuilt before they were completed, owing to defective wire in the cables. They were the Detroit-Windsor International Bridge and the Mount Hope Bridge connecting the island, on which stands Newport, Rhode Island, with the mainland. In the construction a new processed heat-treated steel wire was used and found defective. In both cases it had to be removed and replaced by the cold drawn wire. The defects were not discovered until the cables were completed and considerable progress had been made in the erection of the steel work, but in time to save a collapse.

Q. *Please give the length of the James River Bridge, the Lake Ponchartrain Bridge and the Gandy Bridge. G. A. H.*

A. The James River Bridge project includes three bridges, totalling 5⅔ miles in length. The largest of the bridges is 4½ miles in length. The Lake Ponchartrain Bridge is 5 miles in length. The Gandy Bridge at Tampa, Florida, is also a concrete highway, 10,000 feet shorter than the Lake Ponchartrain Bridge.

Q. *How was the hanging bridge near Canyon City, Colorado, built? W. G. S.*

A. The hanging bridge of the Denver and Rio Grande Railroad was designed and built by C. Shaler Smith in 1879. By placing the bridge close to one wall it was possible to support the floor system on that side on a bench wall and one girder span. But on the other side three girder spans were used, supported by eyebar hangers suspended from two A frames supported from the two sides of the gorge. This bridge is situated in Royal Gorge, near Canyon City, Colorado.

Q. *If a train is approaching a drawbridge on the Passaic River, and a boat wants to go through the draw, which one has the right of way? D. J. L.*

A. The opening of drawbridges over the Passaic is governed by regulations of the War Department. This regulation reads as follows: "The draw of any bridge used solely for United States mail, passenger, and express trains need not be opened for a vessel reaching said draw less than five minutes before the scheduled arrival of any such train until such train passes, unless

the bridge tender has notice that the train is delayed more than five minutes."

Q. *Where is the Rainbow Bridge? V. R.*

A. This bridge is located within the Navajo Indian Reservation, in San Juan County, Utah. The bridge is 309 feet above the water and its span is 279 feet. The bridge is unique among the natural bridges of the world in that it is not only a symmetrical arch below, but presents a curved surface above, thus having the appearance of a rainbow.

Q. *Why was a pontoon bridge built between Coblenz and Ehrenbreitstein? L. F.*

A. The Schiffsbrucke which connects Coblenz with Ehrenbreitstein was so constructed because a movable bridge was considered advantageous for so important a position in case of invasion. Boats are used in place of stationary piers to support the ends of the beams carrying the roadway platform. The bridge is 485 yards long.

Q. *Why are bridges over small streams often built like a letter S. A. B. C.*

A. The Bureau of Public Roads says that often small highway bridges are built in the shape of the letter S because the road approaches the stream at an angle (not a right angle), and it is desirable to cross the stream at a right angle with the channel.

Q. *How many bridges beside London Bridge are there across the river Thames at London, England? A. W.*

A. Fourteen road-bridges cross the Thames within the county of London. London Bridge of the present was completed in 1831, the Tower Bridge in 1894. Other great bridges are Southwark, Blackfriars, Hungerford, Westminster, Waterloo, Lambeth, Vauxhall, Victoria, Albert, Battersea, Wandsworth, Putney, and Hammersmith.

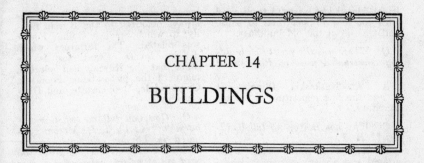

CHAPTER 14

BUILDINGS

Q. *After what is the Washington Memorial near Alexandria, Virginia, modeled?* A. S.

A. It is modeled after the ancient towers which were used as beacons to guide mariners into harbor, as exemplified in those of Rhodes. The building consists of four colonnaded stories of diminishing perimeters tapering from the base through successive stages to the observation tower provided at the top.

Q. *Where is Sweetheart Abbey?* A. D.

A. It is on the way from London to Glasgow to the west of the Nith Estuary. The abbey, now in ruins, was founded by Devorguila in 1275 and derives its name from the fact that she had the heart of her husband, John Baliol, who died in 1269 buried here in her own tomb.

Q. *What is the land worth on which the new Department of Commerce is built in Washington?* L. E. R.

A. The ground was purchased in 1910 at a cost of $2,459,831. The Assessor's Office of the District gives $5,365,065 as the land value for the site.

Q. *Exactly what is a penthouse?* H. W.

A. It is a shed-like structure, usually clinging to the side of a building, having a sloping roof and corbelled floor. It sometimes is used immediately over a doorway. Also a small shed built as a temporary shelter in an open field is classed as a penthouse. The term is now applied to living quarters built on the roof of a tall building.

Q. *How many houses were there in Rome when it was considered the first city in Europe?* D. M.

A. At the beginning of the Christian Era the actual number of domiciles in Rome was 1,950,000.

Q. *What is the significance of the Latin numerals which precede the names of the States on the frieze on the Lincoln Memorial Building in Washington, D. C.?* H. R.

A. They indicate the date on which the States either accepted the Constitution or were admitted to the Union.

Q. *Are there any round churches?* D. E. D.

A. There are five remaining in England, the largest being the Temple Church in London.

Q. *How much space does the average office tenant occupy?* B. M.

A. The National Association of Real Estate Boards says that less than 1000 square feet of office space is used for the usual tenant.

Q. *Why are buildings in Russia blown up instead of being torn down?* M. R. B.

A. They are dynamited because the importance of the new project is so great, and the value of the old material is relatively so small, that it is considered less wasteful to proceed with the new project than to pause and tear down the old buildings.

Q. *Where was the first brick building constructed west of Pittsburgh?* W. H.

A. At Kaskaskia, Illinois. It housed the first legislature of Illinois Territory.

Q. *Why has Boston no tall buildings?* R. T.

A. Boston is built upon filled ground and a city ordinance forbids the erection of skyscrapers. The Customs House, however, might be termed a skyscraper, but it was built by the Federal Government upon Federal property.

Q. *Are there any windowless buildings?* G. M.

A. Buildings of this kind artificially lighted and ventilated are being planned and a few are in existence. A film studio erected by UFA, near Berlin, is without windows and the plans for the large Travel and Transport Building at the Chicago World's Fair in 1933 called for steel walls without windows.

Q. *What business building contains the most floor space?* D. T.

A. The Chicago Merchandise Mart is the largest business building of its type ever constructed. It has a million more feet of floor space than any other such building.

Q. *How high must one go in an office building to get away from street noises?* R. T. L.

A. Under average city conditions, street noises are not disturbing from the tenth or twelfth floor up.

Q. *Is the house where "My Old Kentucky Home" was written, still standing?* D. S.

A. Federal Hill, the old Rowan homestead at Bardstown, Kentucky, where Foster wrote this masterpiece, is standing and in an excellent state of preservation. The State of Kentucky has made it a shrine. The house was completed in 1795, and has always belonged to the Rowan family, to which Stephen Collins Foster was related. The furniture, which delights lovers of antiques, is the same that the Rowans had selected, many of the pieces being Sheraton, Chippendale, Heppelwhite, and Duncan Phyfe.

Q. *Can you tell me whether the house offered by J. P. Morgan, situated in London, England, to the United States Government to be used by it as an embassy was ever accepted?* O. A. K.

A. The building in London offered by J. P. Morgan as an embassy for the United States was accepted and is now being used.

Q. *I wish some information about the Shewe Dagon Pagoda in Rangoon, Burma.* I. P.

A. It is one of the most magnificent Buddhist pagodas on earth. It is the mecca of the followers of the Great Enlightened One in that part of Asia. It is literally covered with gold leaf. The long flight of stairs which leads to the shrine is covered by a series of wonderfully carved teak roofs supported by pillars of wood and masonry. The pagoda has no interior, being a solid mass of brick raised over a relic chamber. Carpenter describes the structure as "a gilded mountain ending in a spire nearly four hundred feet high." A great shining umbrella from which hang more than 1500 bells of gold and others of silver is a feature of this pagoda.

Q. *When was Morro Castle built?* S. J. H.

A. The Morro Castle in Havana is a picturesque fortress, built about 1633 on a jutting promontory, 200 feet above the water opposite the narrow harbor entrance to Havana. It was built by the Spanish and although the Dutch captured the city of San Juan in 1635 they did not capture Morro. It remained in Spanish possession until the Spanish-American War.

Q. *How far can you ride in one elevator in the Empire State Building?* M. R.

A. It is possible to ride for 80 floors in one elevator in the Empire State Building, which is 102 stories and 1248 feet high above the street. The express elevator travels from the first to the eightieth floor in less than one minute. There are smaller tower elevators from the 80th to the 86th floor where the observatory roof is located and a mast elevator from the 86th to the 102nd floor.

Q. *How large is the new British Embassy in Washington?* C. E. B.

A. Located on a four-acre tract, it is a gigantic rambling structure with Queen Anne as its motif. The conception of Sir Edmund Lutyens, it has been carried out in fisher brick —a dull particolored brick—and limestone. Variety and beauty of design characterize the building. There are 97 rooms, 28 with baths, as well as several showers and a swimming pool in the back garden near the tennis courts. There are two nurseries, rooms for maids, footmen, and chauffeurs. And there are libraries, sitting rooms, a drawing room, a long dining room and the ball room.

Q. *At the time the Declaration of Independence was adopted, what was the building known as Independence Hall used for?* E. G.

A. It was the State House or Capitol of Pennsylvania.

Q. *Please give some information concerning the English castle which has been built in Richmond, Virginia.* P. A. D.

A. The Virginia Historical Society says that several years ago Mr. and Mrs. Alexander W. Weddell purchased the remnants of Warwick Priory situated in the town of Warwick, England, the Priory at this time being in great disrepair and the materials of which it was built being offered for sale. This material Mr. and Mrs. Weddell had sent carefully to this country and from it have had assembled a most beautiful Elizabethan manor house, but it is in no sense a castle. One end of the building is a replica of Sulgrave Manor. It is known as Virginia House.

Q. *How large is the Washington Cathedral to be? What is the inscription on the foundation stone?* F. C.

A. Measuring from the exterior of the Apse to the western entrance, the Cathedral will be 534 feet long. It will have a total area of 71,000 square feet. Its central tower will be 262 feet high and the western towers will be 195 feet high. The foundation stone, laid in 1907, was brought from Bethlehem and is engraved with this inscription: "The Word was Made Flesh and Dwelt Among Us."

Q. *Who was the architect for the Folger Shakespeare Memorial Library?* T. W. C.

A. It was Mr. Paul P. Cret in consultation with Mr. Alexander B. Trowbridge. The building is classic in spirit though not an archaeological imitation of any particular period of classic architecture, and in certain details is suggestive of a restrained modernism.

Q. *Please describe the Nebraska State Capitol at Lincoln.* N. G.

A. This structure is a notable innovation in American state edifices. It is a broad, low main building, 400 feet square, constructed around four courts. In the center rises an impressive square tower, 400 feet high. The façade, with it setback, suggests that of the Pitti Palace at Florence (1430); while the tower indicates modern German influence, recalling, at the same time, the turreted structure over the crossing in the older cathedral at Salamanca, Spain. Bertram Grosvenor Goodhue was the architect.

Q. *Is Uncle Tom's cabin still in existence?* M. T. P.

A. The remains of the original log cabin stand near the old General Kennedy home, nine miles from Lancaster, Kentucky. A room on the upper floor of the Kennedy mansion is said to have been occupied by Harriet Beecher Stowe during the time she was in Kentucky gathering material for the story. The old slave block from which Uncle Tom and many other slaves were sold, is to be seen at Washington, Kentucky.

Q. *Please give some information about Dick's Castle across from West Point, New York. W. O. H.*

A. Dick's Castle near Nelsonville, New York, was intended for a residence. The building is a massive concrete structure of Spanish architecture containing many spacious rooms. It was about two-thirds completed, but from neglect and exposure the concrete has begun to deteriorate and break down. If completed, this building would have been one of the largest and most beautiful residences in America, or at least along the Hudson.

Q. *How many people travel in the elevators in the Chicago Merchandise Mart every day? T. B. D.*

A. Approximately 40,000 persons are served daily by the elevators in this building.

Q. *Who built Blarney Castle? J. A. W.*

A. Blarney Castle was built about 1446 by Cormac McCarthy. It has walls which in places are as thick as 18 feet. The fame of the castle is bound up in the civil history of the country and the War of the Great Rebellion. The famous Blarney Stone is near the top of the wall. Promises and flattering speeches delayed the surrender of the castle in medieval times and from this fact it is supposed that the tradition concerning the Blarney Stone arose.

Q. *What building is considered the first skyscraper? T. H.*

A. The Home Insurance Building in Chicago. It was a twelve-story building which has been razed. It was erected in 1885. In order to decide what building should be so designated, a committee of architects defined a skyscraper as a building embodying the principles of skeleton construction in which a metal frame or cage, composed of girders, beams, and columns, supports all internal and external loads and carries all stresses directly to the foundations.

Q. *What is the building in Harrisburg, Pa., that has on its walls a history of the world? J. R. K.*

A. The New Educational Building Forum has on its semicircular wall a tabloid history of the world in 30,000 words written by Eric Gugler, a New York artist. Chronological tables, alternating with mural maps, depict the ancient occidental civilizations and so on through the progress of the ages up to August, 1914. The Forum, which seats 2000 people, is built along classic Greek lines. It was destroyed by fire when nearing completion and its total cost, including work done twice because of this, is estimated at over $4,000,-000.

Q. *When was the old Waldorf-Astoria built? What style was its architecture? H. P.*

A. The old Waldorf-Astoria Hotel was a red brick and sandstone structure in the German Renaissance style. The Waldorf section on 33rd Street was erected in 1893 by the Hon. William Waldorf Astor, occupying the site of the town house of his father, John Jacob Astor. The 34th Street section, known as the Astoria, was built in 1897 by Col. John Jacob Astor and occupied the site of the house of his father, William B. Astor. The Empire State Building now stands on this site.

Q. *Was the Crystal Palace in New York copied from the one near London? T. A. G.*

A. It has often been stated that the prototype of the Crystal Palace in New York was the famous Crystal Palace, Sydenham, near London. The Sydenham Palace was opened in 1854 whereas the Crystal Palace in New York had been opened on July 14th of the preceding year.

The New York Crystal Palace was destroyed by fire in 1858.

Q. *Does England own Newstead Abbey, the ancestral home of Lord Byron?* B. T.

A. Sir Julian Cahn owns Newstead Abbey. He purchased it from C. I. Fraser who has owned it since 1912. In the purchase were included a circular table at which part of Childe Harold was written, a copy of Byron's earliest poems, and a number of other treasures. Sir Julian Cahn is to present Newstead Abbey to the British nation as a memorial to Lord Byron who inherited it when he was only ten years old.

Q. *Who is restoring Robert E. Lee's early home?* M. J. B.

A. The Daughters of the Confederacy are restoring Stratford-on-the-Potomac, the birthplace of Robert E. Lee. It is said to be the largest mansion in the State of Virginia, and is the only example of this particular old English type of home in America. It was built in 1729 and 1730.

Q. *Is the Hickok home now a state memorial in Illinois?* P. R.

A. The State of Illinois purchased the Hickok Homestead in the village of Troy, LaSalle County, Ill., and established it on August 29, 1930, as a memorial institution in honor of James Butler Hickok, a pioneer law-enforcement officer, known in history as "Wild Bill" Hickok. The 55th General Assembly voted an appropriation of $10,000 for the purchase of the homestead and the erection of a monument thereon.

Q. *Who operated the hotel, What Cheer House, built on a hull of an old ship in San Francisco Bay?* E. J.

A. The San Francisco Chamber of Commerce says that this famous old hotel provided rough comfort for miners and ranchers. It was operated by Robert B. Woodward, who also later conducted the well known pleasure park, Woodward's Gardens.

The What Cheer House was located at Sacramento and Leidesdorff Streets in San Francisco. It is reported that this hotel was the first in San Francisco to be run on the European plan. At one time it contained the only library in town, which was frequented by Mark Twain and Bret Harte.

Q. *Who built the famous Jumel Mansion in New York City?* C. E. H.

A. It was built by Roger Morris in 1758 for his bride, Mary Philipse of Yonkers.

Q. *How long will adobe houses last?* W. L. S.

A. Adobe houses have stood for hundreds of years. The secret of longevity is a dry stone foundation.

Q. *Are there any buildings as tall as twelve stories in Mexico?* E. H.

A. Mexico is a land of low buildings, but a large life insurance company is erecting an office building in Mexico City that will be 12 stories.

Q. *What is a recessional building?* G. K.

A. The recessional building is a term applied to the new style of architecture, seen for example, in many of the New York structures. As the building increases in height, the width of the floors is reduced, so that seemingly the building tapers.

Q. *Is the Taj Mahal an Indian style of architecture? By whom was it planned?* F. H. J.

A. The Taj Mahal was planned by Ustad Isa, a Persian, and is Persian architecture rather than Indian. It is of white marble outside and jeweled mosaic inside.

Q. *What is the estimated life of the modern skyscrapers?* G. L.

A. The Architectural Record says that the average skyscraper is estimated to continue in existence from 25 to 30 years. This brief period of existence is due to the rapid growth and changes in our cities and does not indicate failure due to construction. The modern skyscraper, with proper care to protect the steel frame-work and footings, should exist a century or longer. Precautions are taken against destructive agencies by painting the steelwork and encasing steel in terra cotta or concrete. Electrolysis has been found to be injurious to the life of steel and this may be a destructive factor (about which little is known) which, under certain conditions, may shorten the life of the skyscraper to half a century or so.

Q. *Please give some information concerning the Hoover War Memorial Library. N. H.*

A. This library is at Leland Stanford University. A building on the campus houses the library which is the most complete of this kind in the United States and perhaps in the world. The building was opened soon after the war. Additions to the collection of books are constantly being made.

Q. *In what historic building in Kentucky is there a self-supporting circular stone stairway? T. S. H.*

A. In the Old State Capitol at Frankfort, built in 1829.

Q. *After what building was the Scottish Rite Temple in Washington, D. C., modeled? A. M. T.*

A. It is said to be reminiscent of the Mausoleum of Halicarnassus, which was one of the seven wonders of the ancient world. It was designed by John Russell Pope.

Q. *What part of a building is the belvedere? U. H. B.*

A. Belvedere is a term designating the whole or a part of the upper story of an Italian building, open on one or more sides so as to command a view. The word means beautiful view.

Q. *Has the Library of Louvain which was destroyed during the World War been restored? A. D.*

A. The Library of Louvain was reopened on July 18, 1929. Various nations gave books which were already in place at the time of the opening. Germany replaced 300,000 volumes. The British donation amounted to 55,000 books. France gave 33,000; Japan collected 20,000 pounds for the reconstruction of the Library. The building of the Louvain Library began in the summer of 1928.

Q. *Please give examples of Gothic, Norman-Gothic, Renaissance, Romanesque, and Byzantine architecture in Washington, D. C. H. E. K.*

A. Gothic: (English) The Washington Cathedral, Mount St. Alban's. Norman-Gothic: Smithsonian Institution. Renaissance: Library of Congress. Romanesque: Sacred Heart Church. Byzantine: The Catholic Shrine (Cathedral), Catholic University.

Q. *How much money did Henry Clay Folger leave for the Folger Shakespeare Memorial? P. W.*

A. He left a trust fund of $10,000,-000. The library building cost more than $1,000,000 and is considered one of the most beautiful in the world.

Q. *Has America a distinctive architecture of its own? C. E. A.*

A. Philip Newell Youtz says that it has. Even in its colonial phase, old world designs were subtly changed to suit the new country. Today American architecture is an epitome of American life. The skyscraper, the modern factory, power house, grain elevator, railway terminal, school building, hospital, and theatre are all examples of original American thought and design.

Q. *What building is considered the most perfect specimen of pure Gothic architecture? R. N. T.*

A. The Sainte Chapelle in Paris. It was built by Louis IX in 1245.

Q. *In what country was the Porcelain Tower located? C. E. S.*

A. The Porcelain Tower was an octagonal structure in Nanking, China, erected in the early part of the fifteenth century. It had nine stories, faced with variegated porcelain, from which bells and lamps were hung. The tower was destroyed by the Taipings in 1853.

Q. What is the diameter of the dome of St. Peter's in Rome and of St. Paul's in London? L. A. V.

A. St. Peter's is between 136 and 138 feet in internal diameter. The inner shell of St. Paul's is 102 feet in diameter.

Q. Why doesn't the Leaning Tower of Pisa fall? S. F.

A. The fact that the Leaning Tower of Pisa stands depends on the law of statics which ensures the stability of the leaning buildings whose parts are firmly bound together and whose center of gravity does not project beyond the limits of the supporting foundation. The leaning tower has a spiral stairway within, which is built with increased height on the sides of the lean and decreased height on the sides opposite the lean, thus throwing a greater weight of masonry on the side opposed to the lean.

Q. Does Clarence Saunders still own the "pink palace" he built at Memphis? M. H. N.

A. The palatial residence built by Mr. Saunders at the height of his prosperity as the originator of a chain grocery system, was sold at auction. It now belongs to the city which is making it over into a museum.

Q. How many rooms are there in the Palace of Versailles? C. S.

A. The exact number isn't a matter of record. There are between 1800 and 2000 rooms in the palace.

Q. Where is Sandringham House and how long has it been a possession of the King and Queen of England? G. M.

A. Sandringham House is at Sandringham, a village in Norfolk, England. The estate, of some 7000 acres, was acquired in 1861 by the late King Edward, when Prince of Wales, for about $1,250,000. It was rapidly made into a model and modern place. Sandringham House is a picturesque building of brick and stone in Elizabethan style, standing in a park of 200 acres. On a tablet is inscribed: "That house was built by Albert Edward and Alexandra, his wife, in the year of our Lord 1870."

Q. How should houses be built in order to receive the most sunlight, directly north, south, etc., or on a diagonal? J. G. N.

A. Their orientation should be north and south, east and west.

Q. Is the Parthenon still standing? M. T.

A. The Parthenon continues to stand on the Acropolis in Athens. It was seriously damaged by an explosion many years ago. In 1932 the Parthenon was illuminated for the first time in history. This was in honor of a special celebration which occurred in Athens.

Q. Who described architecture as frozen music? I. G.

A. Goethe.

Q. What is the real name of the Flatiron Building in New York City? P. V. C.

A. The name carved in stone on the building is the Fuller Building.

Q. What are the names of the male and female figures used in architecture on pillars? A. B.

A. The female figures used as supports in architecture are known as caryatids. The male figures are known as atlantes.

Q. How long has it been since Independence Hall was opened to the public as a museum? What sort of collection does it have? H. I.

A. Independence Hall was formally thrown open as a public historical museum July 4, 1876. The collection consists of furniture, manuscripts, musical instruments, water colors, missiles, maps, coins, currency, weapons, metals, prints, wearing apparel, utensils, and books.

Q. How many feet of telephone and telegraph wire are there in the Empire State Building? E. O.

A. There are more than 17,000,-000 feet of telephone and telegraph wire and cable in the Empire State Building.

Q. Who designed the bronze doors at the east entrance to the Capitol in Washington? B. L.

A. They were designed and modeled by the American artist, Randolph Rogers in Rome in 1858, and were cast by Von Muller in Munich.

Q. Why is an acorn so often seen in carving on Colonial houses and gates? A. H. D.

A. It was considered a symbol of hospitality.

Q. Why is it possible to hear a whisper or low voice across the dome of St. Paul's Cathedral, London? J. W.

A. Whispering galleries are generally the result of accident. There are two general types—the focussing and the conducting. The dome of St. Paul's Cathedral in London is of the second type. A whisper close to and along the smooth concave wall is continually deflected inward upon itself by the wall, is prevented from spreading and is thus conducted with only slightly diminished intensity to the other side of the dome. The sound traveling by great circles, concentrates again at the opposite end of the diameter of which the sound is produced.

Q. Who built the Alamo? W. J. L.

A. The Alamo is a Franciscan mission house built about 1722. After 1793 it was used on occasions as a fort and was renamed Fort Alamo. It consisted of an oblong plaza some 2½ acres in area enclosed by a wall 8 feet high and 33 inches thick, a church, a hospital building, a convent and a walled convent yard about 100 feet square.

Q. Was the Reims Cathedral completely destroyed during the World War? L. C.

A. It was not completely destroyed, but severely damaged. It took years to restore it. Many Americans contributed to the cost of restoration.

Q. Where is the Pohick Church? W. W.

A. Pohick Church, parish church of Mount Vernon, is six miles from the Mansion, on the highway between Washington and Richmond. It was built from plans drawn by George Washington (1768–70), a vestryman there for 20 years. Among the rectors of the church was Parson Weems, who recorded stories of Washington's boyhood, such as that of the cherry tree. The church was used as a stable during the Civil War, but is now well restored. It contains the original baptismal font which was lost for many years but finally reclaimed from a farmyard. The pew of Washington is reserved.

Q. Please give me some information about the Bok Tower. E. C.

A. The Mountain Lake Sanctuary in Florida is the work of Frederick Law Olmsted, the New England landscape architect. The Singing Tower with its carillon of 71 bells is of pink marble and coquina stone. It is the work of Milton B. Medary, the Philadelphia architect. The construction of the tower which is 205 feet high was begun in January, 1927, and was practically completed in February, 1929. It took fifteen months to make the 71 perfectly tuned bells. These were manufactured in England and weigh from 17 pounds to 12 tons. Mr. Anton Brees is bell master. The purpose for which this Sanctuary was established and the Tower built is to create symbols of pure beauty and to express appreciation and gratitude of Edward Bok to the American people for their kindness and generosity.

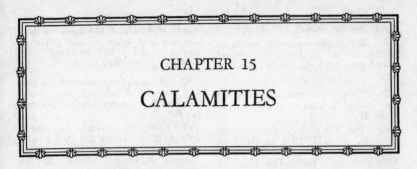

CHAPTER 15

CALAMITIES

Q. What was the Krakatoa disaster? M. O. U.

A. In 1883 the volcano of Krakatoa in the Sunda Strait erupted with what authorities believed to be the most violent volcanic explosion of which there is record. Dust from this eruption was gradually distributed over nearly the entire world, and the sound of the volcanic explosions was heard 3000 miles away.

Q. What percentage of the accidents in this country could be prevented? F. G. T.

A. Experts say that about 60 per cent of the accidents per year could be prevented.

Q. How many people were killed in 4th of July accidents in 1932? L. R. G.

A. The deaths of 245 persons were reported. Those injured who may have died later are not included in this number. Only 10 of these were fireworks fatalities. There were 119 motor vehicle deaths, 90 drownings, and 26 deaths from other accidents.

Q. In what way would it be helpful if earthquakes could be predicted? R. M.

A. The Coast and Geodetic Survey says that the possibility of predicting earthquakes accurately is extremely remote. However, when any natural peril is understood, protection becomes largely an engineering problem, and such problems can be solved. Natural phenomena may not be subject to human control, but their disastrous effects can be minimized by taking protective measures based on careful scientific research.

Q. In an automobile accident, would a person who was awake or asleep at the time fare better? J. M. P.

A. The Public Health Service says that in such an accident the person who is awake and could brace himself would probably suffer greater injuries than the person who was asleep and relaxed.

Q. How many people were killed and injured in the earthquake at Managua, Nicaragua, in 1931? W. E. A.

A. More than 750 bodies were recovered and buried, and more than 6000 were treated for injuries.

Q. Was Captain Smith saved when the Titanic sank? R. H. W.

A. Captain Smith perished with his ship. It is reported that he swam to help a drowning child and after carrying it safely to a life-boat, returned to his ship and sank with it.

Q. Where were the wireless messages that told of the Titanic disaster received? P. J. H.

A. The Wanamaker Station in New York City received the first message of the Titanic disaster from the Olympic. President Taft ordered all radio stations in the vicinity of Wanamaker's to close down so that there might be no interference with official news.

Q. How far back can traditions of the Flood be traced? T. T. S.

A. The Sumerian story seems to be the oldest. In India the earliest record goes back to the 6th century B.C.

Q. Were more passengers lost on the General Slocum or the Eastland? T. R. W.

A. The General Slocum disaster occurred, June 15, 1904, in the East River, New York City, and over 1000 lives were lost. The Eastland disaster, occurring in the Chicago River at Chicago, July 24, 1915, cost 812 lives.

Q. I have heard that the children of Poland contributed generously to the relief of Mississippi Flood Sufferers. Will you please give me some of the details? P. G.

A. For the relief of juvenile flood sufferers in the Mississippi Valley the children of the various schools throughout Poland contributed $1,178.45. The fund was sent through the Polish-American Society at Warsaw to Secretary Herbert Hoover. A second contribution was received for the same purpose and from the same source amounting to $735.81—a total contribution of $1914.26.

Q. In what year was the earthquake which destroyed Messina, Sicily? J. N.

A. It occurred on December 28, 1908.

Q. Were any of the crew saved when the ship with Lord Kitchener on board was lost at sea? C. A. M.

A. The Cruiser Hampshire, on which Lord Kitchener lost his life, was sunk by a German mine off the West Orkney Islands, June 5, 1916. Only 12 sailors survived. These were able to reach the shore on a raft.

Q. How far from the edge of the polar ice cap was the Italia wrecked? C. J.

A. As far as we have been able to ascertain, the position of the Italia at the time it was wrecked was directly between Kings Bay and the North Pole, about 300 miles north of the southern edge of the polar ice cap and about five hundred miles north of Kings Bay.

Q. When did the floor of the Boston dance hall collapse that caused the death of many of the dancers? G. B.

A. It was in the early morning of July 4, 1925. About 200 people were precipitated into the wreck of the burning building. Almost 50 lost their lives.

Q. What was the last message cabled from St. Pierre just before Mount Pelée erupted? G. E. M.

A. The operator at St. Pierre cabled "Red-hot stones are falling here, don't know how long I can hold out." The message was sent the morning of May 6, 1902. May 8, the city was in ruins.

Q. What was the Pemberton Mill disaster? D. M.

A. On January 10, 1860, the Pemberton Mill at Lawrence, Massachusetts, collapsed and fire ensued. About 100 lives were lost and several times that number of persons were injured.

Q. How many men are injured in coal mines each year? R. C.

A. The Bureau of Mines estimates that more than 100,000 men are injured by accidents in coal mines each year. About 2000 of these injuries result fatally.

Q. What year and month was the great explosion at the Naval Ammunition Depot, Dover, New Jersey? W. K. R.

A. July 10, 1926.

Q. How is it possible to tell what kind of disaster caused a city to be buried? M. O.

A. The soil that covers a buried city sometimes indicates the manner in which it was buried—for instance, if the city is buried in sand, it is reasonable to believe that some terrific sand storm enveloped it. On the other hand, if the overlaying earth is volcanic in character, it is indicated that some eruption caused the loss of the city. For many cases historical records are available telling of the nature of the catastrophe.

Q. How many people were lost when the Lady Elgin sank on Lake Michigan? E. E. M.

A. The Steamer Lady Elgin was sunk on Lake Michigan, September 8, 1860, after a collision with the Schooner Augusta. Of the 385 persons abroad, 287 were lost—among them Mr. Herbert Ingram, Member of the British Parliament and founder of the London Illustrated News, and his son.

Q. How many people become permanently disabled through accident and disease each year? E. D.

A. The Federal Board for Vocational Education says that in the United States 335,000 become physically handicapped each year.

Q. When was the Napier earthquake? M. S. F.

A. The town of Napier, a resort of New Zealand, was destroyed by severe earthquake lasting almost three minutes, on February 3, 1931. A cliff some 300 feet high slid into the sea, carrying with it private dwellings, burying the general hospital and raising the harbor bottom.

Q. What caused the Galveston flood? I. A. S.

A. A West Indian hurricane blowing steadily for 18 hours and reaching a velocity of 135 miles per hour piled up enormous waves which swept over the city.

Q. Did the ferry boat which blew up in East River ever carry tourists on trips around the Island? J. N. F.

A. The ferry, Observation, which exploded in East River, September 9, 1932, was formerly in the sightseeing service, carrying tourists around Manhattan Island. At the time of its destruction, however, it was employed as a ferry to carry iron workers from the Bronx to their work at the new Riker's Island Penitentiary in East River.

Q. How does the accidental fatality rate per thousand in the United States compare with other countries? D. H.

A. It is highest in this country. Canada comes next, then Australia and Switzerland, then New Zealand, Scotland, England and Wales, Germany, Italy, Sweden, Norway, and France.

Q. Does England ever have earthquakes? C. D.

A. It has them occasionally. On August 15, 1926, a series of shocks was felt throughout the midland counties of England.

Q. Please give a short account of the Vermont flood. H. C.

A. The New England floods commenced on November 2, 1927, after three days of heavy rain in northern Vermont. The Lamoilee and Winooski Rivers became flooded causing nine deaths in the former and 86 in the latter valley. Waterbury, Bolton, Richmond, Montpelier, Barrie, Ducksbury, and Johnson were the principal towns suffering. The estimated property damage was $30,-000,000. Springfield, Westfield, Brockton, Worcester, Becket, and Millbury were the principal towns in Massachusetts suffering.

Q. Has Floyd Collins' body been removed from the cave in which he lost his life? W. R. H.

A. The body of Floyd Collins was lifted from the cave, in which he had been entombed on April 23, 1925, and buried near Crystal Cave, Kentucky.

Q. How many lives were lost when the Sultana sank? E. F. W.

A. The steamer Sultana was lost as a result of an explosion on April 27, 1865. The majority of the passengers, numbering 2300 and including 1965 Union soldiers and officers from Confederate prisons, lost their lives. A few were saved by clinging to floating wreckage and a few more were picked up by men who rowed out in skiffs.

Q. Who was blamed for the collision between the S–51 and the City of Rome? J. L. R.

A. The Board of Investigation held the City of Rome entirely to blame for the accident.

Q. In how many cases are automobile accidents due to mechanical failure in the automobile? H. G.

A. In 1,281,400 accidents studied, in only 56,330 cases were the accidents due to mechanical difficulties. This is only one time in twenty-three.

Q. What kind of buildings withstand earthquake shocks the best? L. M.

A. The subject of earthquake-proof construction has been studied much of late. Houses so called have roofs that are exceedingly light, chimneys that are short and thick. Arches are avoided, and rafters run from the ridge pole to the floor-sills. The essential point, as was shown in the Japanese earthquake of 1923, is that the building should be so framed and braced that it will move bodily as one block with its foundation. The modern steel-brick buildings offer good resistance to both earthquake and fire, and nearly half of those in Tokyo escaped unharmed.

Q. Was a man ever blown through the top of the tube and the bed of the river and came out alive during the building of one of the tunnels under the New York rivers? M. L.

A. Tunnel engineers say that such an occurrence took place twice under the East River; the first time in 1905 while boring the tunnel from the Battery to Joralemon Street, Brooklyn, and another time in 1916 while boring the tunnel from Whitehall Street at the Battery to Monta-

gue Street, across the river in Brooklyn. In the 1905 incident the tunnel worker was recovered. In the 1916 mishap three sand-hogs were blown through the heading where a soft spot in the river bed opened up and permitted the air pressure to escape; one came out alive, the second man was found dead in the river, and the body of the third man was never recovered.

Q. Which of the Mississippi floods came the nearest to the flood height established in 1927? T. B. W.

A. That of 1882 came close to it. On a twin tree on the Mississippi a home-made flood gage shows the mark set in 1927 as the highest. Below it are 1882, 1884, 1897, 1922, and 1912 in the order named.

Q. Were more lives lost in the Iroquois disaster than in any other theater fire? R. F. C.

A. There have been several greater disasters than the Iroquois, which cost 575 lives. In 1836 a theater in Petrograd burned with a loss of 700 lives; in 1845 a Canton, China, theater fire cost 1670 lives; in 1872 a similar disaster in Trenton, N. J., cost 600 lives; and in 1881, one in Vienna, Austria, 640 lives.

Q. Does the sound of an explosion or the force of the concussion travel faster? P. E. H.

A. The Bureau of Standards says that the noise and the shock occur simultaneously. There is an interesting record of an observer in England who was looking down and across a stretch of open country from a hill during a bright sunshiny day, and suddenly noticed a long narrow shadow rushing toward him silently across the valley. As it passed him he heard the sudden report of a heavy explosion and felt the jar of it. A powder magazine several miles away had exploded, as he learned later. The "shadow" was the result of the increased density of the air in the compression waves.

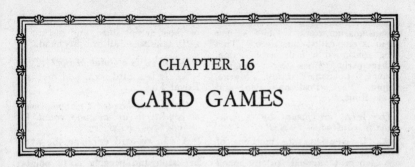

CHAPTER 16

CARD GAMES

Q. *How many people in the United States now play Bridge?* **P. C. C.**

A. There are no actual statistics on the subject, but it is the belief of card experts that Bridge—Auction and Contract—now has more players than all other card games combined.

Q. *When a hostess plays in a card game and has the high score should she keep the prize?* **A. C.**

A. If she is giving a card party her score card is not totaled. She does not compete for the prize. If the hostess is merely entertaining a card club in her turn, she does compete for the prize, and keeps it if she wins.

Q. *Why was the contract match between the Culbertsons and Lenz and Jacoby fixed at 150 rubbers?* **T. H. N.**

A. Because it was assumed that in 150 rubbers the element of luck in the distribution of the cards would be approximately even as between the teams and the result therefore would be a test of the systems and skill of the players.

Q. *What is meant by the still pack in cards?* **G. M.**

A. The still pack is the one not in play when two packs of cards are used in a game.

Q. *What is a kibitzer in a bridge game?* **A. R.**

A. Kibitzer is a Yiddish slang term for one who meddles with others' affairs. In bridge playing, it is specifically a person who, although not a player, makes suggestions and gives unasked advice to the players.

Q. *What is meant by a psychic bid in Contract Bridge?* **P. B.**

A. It is a bid without the values to justify it, made for the purpose of confusing adversaries.

Q. *What kind of a card game is Patience?* **F. B. R.**

A. Patience is a synonym for Solitaire. There are many games that are forms of Solitaire or Patience.

Q. *Does a redouble close the bidding in Auction or Contract? Can a player bid who has passed several times?* **E. B. M.**

A. In Auction and Contract Bridge, a redouble has the same standing as a bid or a double. It opens the bidding for the other three players. Any player may bid in his turn no matter how many times he has passed.

Q. *What was the first card game played?* **R. R.**

A. Cards for playing games of chance are of the most remote antiquity and have almost universal usage. There is evidence that they were in use in Egypt at the time of Joseph; that their use extended as far east as Hindustan and China at a period long before their introduction into Europe is well attested. The design and number of cards in a pack varied. Even the names of most of the old games are found only in antiquarian works. Chief among them is one called "primiero." This long continued a fashionable game. Other early games were: Mauve, Piquet, Loadan, Noddy, Macke, Oupre, Gleek, Post and Pan, and Bank Rout.

Q. What are meant by conventions in card games? S. S.

A. Conventions are methods of bidding, leading, or playing which are generally agreed to by good players, and which have special significance.

Q. When was Hoyle first published? W. O. H.

A. Edmond Hoyle lived from 1672 to 1769. Little is known of his early life. It is thought that he was educated for the law. He lived in London for many years, where he taught games. In 1742 he published "A Short Treatise on the Game of Whist" which went through many editions and became the world's authority. Other games have been added, until "Hoyle" has grown to mean "a set of rules" and includes many games that have been invented since Edmond Hoyle's death.

Q. What is the basis for the idea some people have that if a Bridge player gets a hand that has neither an Ace nor a face card in it he may demand a new deal? C. L.

A. It was probably handed down as one of the traditions of the game of Whist, and it is possible that in some places some people did play Whist on that basis. However, there was never such a rule in the laws of Whist, Bridge, Auction Bridge or Contract Bridge.

Q. In playing draw poker, if you hold three cards and ask for three cards instead of two, is your hand dead? J. J. W.

A. The hand is not dead. If a player asks for too many cards and receives them, the error may be corrected if discovered before he has looked at them and before the next player receives his cards. Otherwise he must accept them, and discard so as to take them all into his hand.

Q. What is a Quint Major? T. T.

A. It is a card term and means a Royal Flush.

Q. In two-handed Cribbage, what is considered an average count for a hand? C. F. B.

A. In six-card cribbage the average expectation of the non-dealer for his hand and pegging is 12 points; for the dealer, in hand, crib, and play, 17 points. Each player having had a deal their scores should be about 29. If a player is 29 or more he is said to be "at home," and if he is 7 or more points ahead of his opponent on even deals he is said to be "safe at home."

Q. How long has Contract Bridge been played? N. K.

A. About 17 years. Americans who went abroad found that players were experimenting with a form of Contract Bridge. About 1915 the Whist Club of New York considered codifying the game but decided that the time had not arrived to do so. Little more was heard of Contract until the summer of 1926 when it became very popular in Newport and Southampton. In the fall its popularity spread to New York City. It is now played in all parts of the country.

Q. How many packs of playing cards are made in a year? N. D. J.

A. About 50,000,000.

Q. A bets that there are more hands that will beat four tens than there are that will beat four aces. Does he win? L. N.

A. A loses. There are thirty-two hands that will beat four aces and only twenty-four that will beat four tens. Only straight flushes will beat four aces and there are thirty-two in which aces do not figure (the aces being held against the possible combinations). There are only twenty straight flushes that can be made without the use of the tens. Add to this number the four sets of fours that will beat the four tens and the result is that you have only twenty-four hands that will beat four tens.

Q. In speaking of a person who is an unusually good card player, should one say that he is a shark or a sharp? F. K.

A. A shark is a slang term for one who excels in something. A sharp is a term for an expert, but seems to have the idea of cheating.

Q. Is it fair to exact a penalty for infraction of a rule at Contract, when the same misplay has been made previously without penalty? C. S.

A. It is fair. Players are not obliged to exact penalties. But the fact that some players are too easy-going or negligent to do so should not influence a player who chooses to demand a penalty. All players should be prepared to pay penalties cheerfully when guilty of infractions of the rules.

Q. What is Tarok? I think it is some kind of a game. J. P. R.

A. Tarok is a game of cards that is very popular in Austria and Germany. It is also played in some parts of France. Tarok requires a special deck of cards and the rules are very complicated.

Q. In Auction and Contract Bridge should the Dummy place his trumps on the table before the first lead has been made? E. C.

A. No cards should be exposed until the first lead has been made.

Q. When was the game of cribbage first played? B. C.

A. Little is known concerning the history of cribbage. It appears to be of English origin and was formerly known as Noddy. It was mentioned under that name in an epilogue by Sir John Harrington in 1616. The earliest description of the game is found in the "Compleat Gamster," 1674. The place and time of the first game of cribbage is not recorded,

nor the reason for the use of 31 as a limit. Originally, 61 was used as a stopping point.

Q. In Five Hundred, if the bidder has a lower score than the opponents, and both make enough points to win the game, which side wins? T. C.

A. The score is not counted until the hand is completed. Then the bidder scores first and wins the game if he makes his bid and it is sufficient to bring his score to 500.

Q. Is Russian Bank played with one deck of cards or with two? H. G.

A. It is usually played with two packs. There is a variation of the game which is played with one pack.

Q. What is the official name for the game called Contract? C. D.

A. Contract Bridge is the official name.

Q. Should Dummy leave his seat to watch his partner play the hand? A. S.

A. He should not. Dummy has the same status in the playing of the hand as the other players, with a few exceptions, and should keep his seat and follow the play.

Q. What is the "Mississippi Heart Hand"? J. H. T.

A. Milton C. Work says that it is a hand supposed to have been used by gamblers on the Mississippi steamers and is apparently a very strong hand, but in reality is badly beaten by the adversaries. It is the type of hand that people who take chances on playing cards with steamer or train pick-ups may expect to have run in on them.

Q. Does a rubber of Contract take longer to play than a rubber of Auction? M. W.

A. Some rubbers in either game are very short, others may last a comparatively long time. The length of the average rubber of Auction is twenty minutes, and Contract about twenty-four minutes.

Q. *In 500 Rum, is the Ace played in sequence with the King and Queen or with the deuce and trey?* G. K.

A. It may be used either way. When played with the King and Queen an Ace counts fifteen, but when played with deuce and trey it counts only one point.

Q. *How is the past tense of the Poker term, ante, spelled?* V. O.

A. Anteed.

Q. *Are the laws for Contract Bridge the same as those for Auction Bridge?* A. M.

A. They are essentially the same except for scoring. Tricks, honors, games, rubbers, slams, doubles, premiums, and penalties are different, and there is a basic difference that only the number of tricks contracted for can be scored toward game.

Q. *What is a good rule to follow in stud poker as to whether to stay in the pot and draw cards?* J. H.

A. Conservative players say that one should not draw unless his buried card is at least as high as any exposed card of the other players, or unless he has a pair. Like most rules for playing winning poker, however, this rule is more honored in the breach than in the observance.

Q. *What are the proper hours for a bridge tea?* M. M. B.

A. A bridge tea is usually from two until five-thirty o'clock. At the conclusion of the game sandwiches, tea, salad, with possibly mints and candy, are served. Usually, guests who could not come to play bridge, are asked to come in for tea.

Q. *Who invented the informatory double in Auction Bridge?* T. S.

A. Wilbur C. Whitehead invented the informatory double rules and all their ramifications.

Q. *What is meant by milking the cards?* N. B. C.

A. Instead of shuffling playing cards, taking the top and bottom cards from the pack at the same time, with forefinger and thumb, and showering them on the table is called milking the cards.

Q. *In pinochle, what is the past tense of the word, meld?* O. R.

A. The past tense is formed in the usual way. It is melded.

Q. *In Contract Bridge, if a player bids six tricks, or seven tricks, but does not say he is bidding a small slam, or a grand slam, and makes his contract, will his slam be counted as a slam?* D. E. S.

A. Certainly. A bid of six is a small slam bid, or a bid of seven is a grand slam bid, whether or not the player so announces.

Q. *In five-card cribbage, two-handed, doesn't the player who loses the cut for the deal get something to offset the advantage of the deal?* F. S.

A. The non-dealer on the first hand of each game is allowed to peg three holes as a compensation for the advantage his adversary derives from having the first deal.

Q. *In Auction and Contract Bridge, is it permissible for the Declarer to pass his hand across for Dummy to see before the play begins?* W. C.

A. There is no rule against it, but it is an offensive practice. It disqualifies Dummy from participating in the play of the hand.

Q. *Who suggested the suit values which are used in Contract Bridge?* C. B.

A. They constitute what is called the Vanderbilt count, after its originator, Harold S. Vanderbilt.

Q. *What is High-Low Poker?* N. B.

A. It is a form of Draw Poker. The pot is equally divided between the high and low hands, the high hand getting the odd chip if there is one. The players do not declare whether they are competing for high or low until the betting is over.

Hands are not shown until all have declared.

Q. *After the still pack of cards is shuffled when playing Bridge, at which side of the next dealer should the cards be placed?* J. H. B.

A. They are put at the left of the next dealer. When it is time for him to deal, he lifts the cards and places them between himself and the player at his right to be cut.

Q. *What is the name given to taking a score overlooked by an opponent at Cribbage?* E. K. E.

A. The term is muggins.

Q. *What is meant by one side getting the squeeze in a bridge score?* C. L.

A. When fractions of 100 points are counted as 100 or zero, the side which gains thereby is said to get the squeeze.

Q. *In stud poker, should the first bet be made on the buried cards or on the first exposed cards?* L. M.

A. Stud poker may be played either way. The more usual way, however, is to make the first bet on the first round of exposed cards.

Q. *In playing Poker with Deuces wild, which hand win—A. has three aces and B. has an Ace and two Deuces?* G. L. H.

A. In a tie the hand containing fewer wild cards wins. Three natural Aces beat one Ace and two Deuces.

Q. *What is meant by wide cards in Cribbage?* B. C.

A. The term is applied to cards too far apart to be likely to form sequences.

Q. *In Contract Bridge, is there a penalty if a player hesitates noticeably before playing to a trick when he has only one card of the suit in his hand?* L. E.

A. This is an offense against the ethics of the game. No player should hesitate unnecessarily in order to create a wrong impression concerning his hand. There is no penalty. Such a player should be avoided.

Q. *What is the name of the game something like Bridge, in which one bids to lose tricks?* H. G.

A. Nada is such a game. Bids are to lose 7, 8, 9, or 10 tricks. If a player thinks he can lose 11, he bids nil; if he can lose 12 he bids grand nil; and to lose all 13, he bids nada.

Q. *In 500 Rum, who wins the game, the player who declares Rum or the one having the most points, when both are over 500?* G. K.

A. If in the final hand, two or more players score 500 or more, player having the most points wins.

Q. *When the Joker is used in Auction Pitch, what is the order in which the points are scored?* D. W.

A. High, Low, Jack, Joker, Game.

Q. *In Contract Bridge, when a bidder who has been doubled fails to make his contract, the bonus differs according to vulnerability. Does the status of the doubler affect the score?* C. J. R.

A. It is the bidder who is penalized according to whether his side is not vulnerable or vulnerable. The status of the opponents is not considered.

Q. *In Cassino, playing a four-handed partnership game, can a partner assist in a build which has already been started, even though he has not the card in his hand to take the trick?* T. T.

A. The rules provide that this may be done.

Q. *Can the penalty tricks for a revoke in Contract Bridge be counted by the declarer if his bid was not sufficient to go game?* K. J. G.

A. The rule provides that the penalty tricks for a revoke shall count exactly as if won in play and assist the declarer to make his contract or to go game, but they cannot be counted to assist the declarer to go game when his bid is not sufficient to go game because they could not be counted that way if they were won in play. If they give him a total number of tricks in excess of his contract, such excess is counted above the line.

Q. In playing Poker, when a premium is decided upon for "fours," must the hand be called in order to collect the premium? L. D.

A. It need not. The holder collects whether the hand is called or not.

Q. Are grand slams often bid and made in Contract Bridge? C. T. N.

A. Even experts rarely bid for a grand slam and the less expert player should never do so. No system of card accounting provides a method where lower but frequently essential cards may be located in advance.

Q. In Poker if two flushes are held of identical cards, which suit is higher? A. H.

A. In Poker, all suits are of the same value. Should two or more hands of identical value be held, the pot is divided.

Q. In playing Poker with the Joker, what is the best hand? J. R. M.

A. The highest hand is composed of four aces and the Joker. All "fives" are better than any straight flush. In cases of ties, a hand made with natural cards is better than a hand made with the Joker.

Q. Must the goulash be played in Contract Bridge? E. H.

A. It is optional. Some players like this innovation while others dislike it. Goulashes should not be played unless the majority of the players desire it.

Q. In Cribbage, if the last card makes thirty-one, does it count two for the thirty-one and one for last card? W. A. W.

A. There is no count for last card if it makes thirty-one.

Q. Will there be any more changes in the rules for Contract Bridge? W. A.

A. Contract is a new game. It is being studied for soundness by many experts. It is quite probable that further changes will be made.

Q. In Contract Bridge, does the bonus for the rubber go to the side that wins the two games, or the side that wins the rubber on account of having higher score through penalties? M. C.

A. The bonus for the rubber is put in the honor column of the side that wins two games. The scores are then added, and the side that has the net score (the difference between their total points) is considered the winner of the rubber.

Q. Should the person who cuts the cards in Contract Bridge complete the cut? J. C. C.

A. The rules for Auction and Contract Bridge provide that "The dealer presents the pack to the player on his right, who lifts off a portion from the top and places it toward the dealer beside the bottom portion. The dealer then completes the cut by placing the bottom portion on the top portion."

Q. When was a pack of cards first called a deck of cards? B. W.

A. The origin of the term is obscure. The word is from the Anglo-Saxon "theccan" meaning a cover, and the earliest recorded use in application to playing cards is in 1593, Shakespeare's Henry VI.

Q. What is a jump-shift in Contract Bridge? N. L.

A. It is a raise or shift made by a bid higher than needed merely to overcall the last preceding bid.

Q. In cutting for deal in Cribbage, can one player turn the next card to another player's cut? O. F.

A. According to the laws of Cribbage, a cut must consist of at least four cards. In cutting for deal, the player cutting first must not cut more than half the pack.

CHAPTER 17

CHEMISTRY

Q. Can matter be destroyed? C. E. M.

A. It is an accepted fact by the majority of scientists today that matter can neither be destroyed nor created. It may be changed, rearranged, adapted, in innumerable ways, but this does not involve actual creation or destruction.

Q. How many basic odors are there? C. E.

A. It has been stated that there are but four fundamental odors. The chemists advancing this idea call them fragrant, burnt, acid, and caprylic. The last is the odor of certain evil-smelling chemicals.

Q. What is the greatest solvent? V. N.

A. Water is the greatest of all solvents. It dissolves to a greater or lesser extent almost all substances with which it comes in contact.

Q. What were the last elements discovered? F. M. S.

A. The last two elements discovered were 87 in 1930 and 85 in 1931. The 92 elements are now all known.

Q. What is the lowest temperature to which ice can be brought? N. J. B.

A. Ice can exist at any temperature below freezing point.

Q. What is fire? L. S.

A. Fire may be described as the visible light and heat that are evolved by the action of high tem-

perature on certain bodies. Burning or combustion results from the chemical reaction between the elements composing the fuel and the oxygen in the air.

Q. What is ambergris used for? N. E. L.

A. Ambergris is a fatty substance essential in the manufacture of high-grade perfumes and is very valuable. It has been used as a food also. English literature speaks of a favorite old dish as being eggs and ambergris.

Q. Why is it that water won't burn when it contains a combustible gas (hydrogen)? W. O.

A. Because it has already burned. Water is hydrogen dioxide resulting from the combustion of hydrogen and oxygen.

Q. Who invented cellophane? J. J.

A. Its inventor is Dr. J. E. Brandenberger, a Swiss chemist, born in 1872, and Doctor of the University of Berne, Switzerland.

Q. What is the hardest element or ore next to the diamond? G. A. M.

A. Corundum ranks next to the diamond in hardness, the relative degree of hardness being as nine to ten.

Q. What is dry ice? F. R. C.

A. Dry ice is solid compressed carbon dioxide snow whose temperature is -114° F. It is considered a superior, though more expensive, refrigerant than water ice since it melts to a gas directly.

Q. *How long had phosphorus been known before matches were invented?* G. W. R.

A. The discovery of phosphorus preceded by eight hundred years any effort to obtain light by friction of phosphorus and sulphur.

Q. *What is the heaviest element?* L. D.

A. Osmium is the heaviest element known.

Q. *Can liquid air be frozen like water?* J. S. F.

A. The Bureau of Standards says that liquid air may be frozen.

Q. *How can an atom be split? Can the process be observed?* A. T.

A. Atoms are split by using other atoms as projectiles. The actual process cannot be observed, only the results of the splitting process are observable. The usual method of splitting atoms is to direct a stream of alpha particles (high speed helium nuclei) at the substance, the atoms of which are to be disrupted.

Q. *How can I repair my celluloid spectacle frames which have been broken?* C. C.

A. The Bureau of Standards says that the simplest and most effective way to repair celluloid spectacle frames is to apply a drop of glacial acetic acid to the broken ends, then in a few minutes press them firmly together and allow them to dry.

Q. *Please explain how the neon signs are made.* E. E. I.

A. Neon is a colorless, inactive gas, which occurs in the atmosphere. Neon has the property of glowing with a peculiarly brilliant fiery-red tint, when an electric current is passed through it in a near vacuum. For advertising purposes the gas is put into hollow tubes which are twisted by a combined heat and blowing process into the required shapes to make script letters. The air is removed by a vacuum pump. If a few drops of mercury are inserted in the tube of neon, the light becomes a brilliant blue; in a yellow-tinted tube it appears green.

Q. *At what temperature does glass melt?* G. McQ.

A. Glass is melted from raw materials at temperatures from 1350° to 1400° C. Plate glass softens at about 570° C.

Q. *I would like to have a formula for a paste or cement to put on the tips of the fingers of canvas gloves to make them last.* S. T.

A. Impregnation of the finger tips of the gloves in a cellulose nitrate cement may make them last. A number of such cements are on the market. If these are found to make the finger tips too stiff, the addition of castor oil to the cement before applying will make them softer.

Q. *What can be added to a rinse water to render clothes fireproof?* D. B.

A. Fabrics may be steeped in almost any saline solution, such as borax, alum, sal ammoniac, etc. The addition of about one ounce of alum or sal ammoniac to the last water used to rinse textile materials or the addition of a lesser quantity to the starch used to stiffen them, renders them so little combustible that they will not readily take fire or burst into flame if kindled.

Q. *What causes merchandise to fade when exposed to the sun?* M. G.

A. Colored merchandise is faded by the action of sunlight and skylight. The ultra-violet, violet, and blue radiation produce most of the fading, though some materials fade from exposure to yellow, orange, or red radiation. The more intense the radiation, the greater the fading. The fading of textiles is usually considerably greater when they are exposed to light in a moist condition.

For that reason, it is customary to dry colored goods that have been laundered either indoors or in the shade and as rapidly as possible.

Q. Is it true that a new paint has been invented which will indicate automatically when machinery becomes overheated? A. M. P.

A. P. B. Cochrane, Westinghouse research engineer, has invented a new red paint that suddenly turns black at 150 degrees. It remains black until the machinery on which it is used becomes cool again, when it resumes its brilliant red color.

Q. Why does plain glass seem to become iridescent with age? C. W. T.

A. The Bureau of Standards says that glass frequently changes color on exposure to sunlight and the surface may weather or decompose slightly on exposure to certain types of atmospheric conditions. The color change is generally from the initial color of the glass to a purplish tint. This is thought to be the result of the action of sunlight on the manganese which was used to decolorize the glass. The weathering produces a scum on the surface of the glass and renders it less transparent but does not in general change its color.

Q. What is the electronic theory? F. T.

A. The electronic theory is the theory that the chemical atom is not the smallest possible part of an element, but is composed of electrons describing orbital and vibratory motions.

Q. Why isn't liquid air on the market? E. J. S.

A. Liquid air is not an article of commerce as it cannot be stored for any length of time. It is prepared in research laboratories and the laboratories of large universities.

Q. How are sponge rubber novelties made? E. D.

A. The Bureau of Standards says that in the manufacture of sponge rubber, a substance such as ammonium carbonate is mixed in the rubber compound. The gas which is liberated during vulcanization produces the porous condition in the finished product.

Q. When was nitrogen discovered? G. B.

A. Nitrogen was first recognized as a distinct substance by Daniel Rutherford of the University of Edinburgh in 1772. His demonstration consisted in showing what when a small animal breathes the air in an enclosed space for a while, and the carbon dioxide produced is removed by absorption, there still remains a gas that is incapable of supporting respiration.

Q. In how many forms is carbon found? S. W.

A. The element, carbon, is found in three distinct forms: in a soft, amorphous condition resulting from the burning of wood, coal, or other vegetable substance as in charcoal or lampblack; in the form of graphite or black lead; and in a crystallized form as the diamond, which is the hardest substance known.

Q. When salt is placed on ice, why does a thin coating of water form immediately? L. S.

A. The presence of a solute tends to prevent the freezing of a solution, for freezing means the separation of a part of the pure solvent in the form of ice. Therefore solutions can be frozen only at temperatures below those of the pure solvents. A saturated salt solution freezes only at -21°, to give a mixture of pure ice and pure salt, both in solid form. Hence, ice and salt cannot permanently exist together above that temperature.

Q. What is the best solvent for ordinary writing ink which has dried as on steel pens? T. H. B.

A. The deposit left by the drying of ordinary writing ink on steel pens consists of iron sulphate, gallic and tannic acids, dye, phenol, and perhaps some gummy matter. There may also be substances formed by the oxidation and polymerization of the gallic and tannic acids. No one liquid will remove all of these substances. Hydrochloric or sulphuric acid will loosen the deposit, but will corrode the pens and be bad for the skin and clothing.

Q. *What is the Brownian movement?* R. K.

A. The name is given to the irregular agitation seen when minute solid particles, suspended in a liquid are viewed under a high magnifying power. It is named for Robert Brown, who observed it in 1827. Many particles which are put into a fluid, instead of sinking steadily are endowed with a vigorous motion which is haphazard and irregular. The particles move to and fro, rotate, rise, and sink, but show no tendency to rest, maintaining indefinitely the same average state of agitation.

Q. *Kindly advise us the nature of the chemical used in the making of a certain type of envelopes so as to render a portion of the envelope transparent.* W. W. U.

A. One-piece window envelopes are made by treating the portion of the paper to be used as a window with a material to make that portion transparent. Ordinary paper may be made transparent by treating with oils or clear varnish. Clear linseed oil varnish is suitable for this purpose. Treating the paper with oil or paraffin or molten paraffin wax is often satisfactory for such purposes.

Q. *How many electrons are there in an atom?* C. H.

A. Physicists of today state that there is evidence that all atoms known have in them a certain definite number of negative electrons and exactly the same number of positive electrons. For instance, the lead atom consists of a positive nucleus charge of 82 units about which 82 electrons revolve; zinc, a nucleus charge of 30 units with 30 revolving electrons; helium, a nucleus charge of 2 units with 2 revolving electrons; sulphur, a nucleus charge of 16 units with 16 revolving electrons; platinum, 78; gold, 79; radium, 88, and so forth.

Q. *Where does the element, Hafnium, get its name?* B. M.

A. Hafnium, which is element No. 72, takes its name from Hafniae, the Latin name for Copenhagen, where the research work of Coster and Hevesy, discoverers of the element, was performed.

Q. *How are maps or other printed matter made washable?* L. B. B.

A. There is a large number of methods in use for rendering paper moisture-resistant. Among the methods applicable to printed papers are coating with clear varnish or lacquer, immersing in a bath of paraffin or oil, surface-sizing with glue and hardening with formaldehyde, or parchmentizing by passing through a bath of zinc chloride or sulphuric acid and subsequently washing and drying.

Q. *Who devised the periodic law of chemistry?* J. C. M.

A. It was devised by Mendeleev. It states that the properties of the elements, as well as the forms and properties of their compounds, are in periodic dependence on or form a periodic function of the atomic weights of the elements. This law enabled Mendeleev to foretell the existence and even the properties of several unknown elements since discovered.

Q. *What is the substance so often used as a substitute for ice for skating exhibitions?* J. R. L.

A. Ordinary photographer's hypo has lately been used to make artificial ice for skating purposes. The chemical is spread on the ground, groomed with a hot iron, cooled and is then ready for skating. Hypo is a compound of sodium thiosulfate with a considerable quantity of water. At normal temperatures it is a dry and glassy, but somewhat soft solid of much the same texture as ice.

Q. *How large a sheet of cellophane weighs an ounce? A. E. M.*

A. It depends upon the thickness of the cellophane. A sheet of No. 300 plain transparent cellophane 40 inches by 33 inches will weigh one ounce.

Q. *Why does ice become white when scraped? V. J.*

A. Ice becomes white when scraped because the scraping leaves a multitude of small irregular surfaces which reflect the light in all directions, giving the white appearance.

Q. *What is the quantum theory? T. J. H.*

A. It is the theory that radiation from a body is emitted only in discrete units, called quanta, and, according to some forms of the theory, that absorption occurs in the same discontinuous manner. This theory is now widely accepted by scientists. It has, however, been criticized by Frank Wigglesworth Clark.

Q. *Is there an ingredient which, when added to a mixture of liquids, renders them unanalyzable? M. G.*

A. There are liquids which of themselves without the addition of another ingredient, are practically unanalyzable. For instance, nobody has completely unraveled coal tar or blood serum. By this is meant that although it is possible to determine the percentages of carbon, hydrogen and other elements in these materials, no chemist would claim that he has separated all of the individual compounds they contain and has determined their amounts.

Q. *Please give information on coloring or tinting kerosene or gasoline red, green, and golden. M. A.*

A. Oil-soluble dyes are used for coloring kerosene and gasoline. Several red, orange, and yellow oil-soluble dyes are available. The use of the only green dye which is suitable for this purpose is covered by U. S. Patent 1654259. Several American dye manufacturers make these dyes.

Q. *Are all atoms the same size? E. G.*

A. Different kinds of atoms may vary in size but atoms of the same kind are uniform.

Q. *What causes paint to crack in small lines in all directions? T. B. F.*

A. Paint that is cracked in small hair lines sometimes running parallel, and often running crosswise on the grain, usually indicates improper drying between coats or an improper composition in the paint. Quite often this is due to applying a quick-drying top coat over a slow drying or improperly dried undercoat. The top coat cannot contract and expand uniformly with the undercoat. Sometimes a paint containing a large proportion of zinc oxide in the top coat may be the cause.

Q. *What substance (chemical or drug) when placed in gasoline renders it non-explosive? F. G.*

A. Two volumes of carbon tetrachloride added to one volume of ordinary motor gasoline will give a non-inflammable mixture. High test gasoline will require a larger amount of carbon tetrachloride.

Q. *Please name three substances which become liquid quickly when exposed to moist air. W. B.*

A. Calcium chloride, magnesium chloride, and caustic potash are examples of deliquescent substances.

Q. *Are rubber articles made by pouring melted rubber into molds? F. J.*

A. Contrary to what seems to be the quite common impression, rubber goods are not cast by pouring the melted material into molds. Instead the crude rubber is worked between steam-heated rolls and at the same time the sulphur and other ingredients are mixed in. The warm plastic mixture is then molded and heated to vulcanize the rubber, that is, to cause the sulphur to combine with it.

Q. What is it that the scientists call atomic energy? A. McC.

A. The atomic theory shows that an atom contains in suspense a vast amount of energy. The particles which make up the atom—itself too small to be visible—revolve in a world of their own. It is believed that if their orbit could be interrupted, they would throw off a tremendous force. The experiments attempting to split the atom which are noted in newspapers from time to time are directed toward investigation of this energy.

Q. What causes shellac to foam when brushing? W. L. D.

A. The foam is caused by air bubbles entrapped in the brush or in the shellac. They should be worked out.

Q. Do gasoline and kerosene have a chemical formula or symbol? E. A.

A. There can be no disputing the statement that neither gasoline nor kerosene is a chemical individual. Therefore neither has a chemical formula.

Q. What is meant by a 5 per cent solution? C. E. W.

A. The Bureau of Standards says that the term per cent solution is used loosely in two or three ways. For instance a 5 per cent solution of calcium chloride means, to some chemists, a solution made up by dissolving 5 grams of the salt in 100 cubic centimeters of water. It may also mean a solution made by dissolving 5 grams of the salt in enough water to make 100 cc. In the strict sense, a 5 per cent solution is one of such strength that 100 parts by weight contain 5 parts by weight of the salt.

Q. Who devised the system of abbreviations of chemicals in formulas? G. T. D.

A. Chemical equation writing was devised by Jons Jakob Berzelius, a Swedish chemist, who lived from 1779–1848. He began the system of using initial letters of the Latin and occasionally Greek names of elements as symbols for them and adding a small numeral subscript to show the number of atoms of each present in a compound.

Q. Who invented the so-called floating brick supposed to be only one-fifth as heavy as those used in building now? L. U.

A. The light weight clay brick referred to above was developed by Dr. Charles T. Burgess, Founder and Director of the Burgess Laboratories, Madison, Wisconsin. For information concerning this product it is suggested that an inquiry be sent to the Burgess Laboratories.

Q. What are the names of the two recently discovered elements? R. R. S.

A. Element 85 has been named Alabamine and element 87 Virginium.

Q. Why will baking powder put out a fire? A. K.

A. Baking powder is thrown on a small fire because the heat will decompose it, producing carbon dioxide, while the acid salts themselves will fuse and coat the burning materials and extinguish the fire.

Q. What is an empirical formula? P. F.

A. It is a chemical formula expressing merely the results of a quantitative analysis.

CHAPTER 18

CHILDREN

Q. Have any President's children been born in the White House? G. W.

A. Esther Cleveland who was President Cleveland's second child was born in the White House, September 9, 1893.

Q. How many triplets are born in this country each year? O. L.

A. In 1928, in the Birth Registration Area, there were 2,208,784 births. Of these there were 25,619 cases of twin births, 285 of triple births, and 1 quadruple birth.

Q. What was the baptismal name of Virginia Dare, the first white child born in this country? B. L.

A. The baptismal name of Virginia Dare was Manteo for a friendly Indian chief who was baptised the Sunday before her baptism which took place on Sunday, August 20, 1587.

Q. What are the names of the children of Franklin D. Roosevelt? R. O.

A. James, Anna Eleanor (Mrs. Curtis Dall), Elliot, Franklin D., and John A.

Q. What was the name of the boy who was the hero of the bus tragedy in Colorado in 1931? L. R.

A. On March 27, 1931, near Towner, 5 school children and their bus driver froze to death in a blizzard. Bryan Untiedt saved 15 of the children by keeping them walking and active. He was later invited to the White House by President Hoover.

Q. Did Vice-President Curtis spend his boyhood among the Indians? D. H.

A. Charles Curtis, left a motherless child by the death of his mother when he was but three years old, went to live among the Kaws with his grandmother, the Princess Julie.

Q. Who was called "the sunshine of the White House"? J. K.

A. Mary Donelson, the grandchild of Andrew Jackson. It was a lock of Mary's hair that Jackson sent when he was asked for something precious to be placed in the cornerstone of the Treasury Building.

Q. Were Indian parents devoted to their children? B. D.

A. Both the father and mother of Indian children were entirely devoted to them, and bestowed upon them every mark of affection and solicitude. Children crippled by accident were treated by parents and companions with great tenderness.

Q. Name some famous infant prodigies. C. H.

A. Infant prodigies seem to be more numerous among musicians. Some of the better known ones are Mozart who composed minuets before he was four; Beethoven, who played in public at eight and composed works which were published at ten; Hummel, who gave concerts at nine; Schubert, who composed at 11;

Chopin, who played a concerto in public before he was nine; Mendelssohn, who began to compose systematically at 12. One of the most remarkable boy prodigies was William Henry West Betty who appeared on the stage at 11 years of age in the heaviest Shakespearean parts. It is said that the House of Commons actually adjourned to witness his Hamlet.

Q. How is the birth of twins regarded by the Indians? I. P.

A. Twins are usually regarded as uncanny and are rather feared as possessing occult power. Formerly the birth of twins was regarded as abnormal by some tribes and one or both were killed.

Q. Who were the "Children of the Mist"? A. M.

A. A wild race of Scotch Highlanders in Scott's Legend of Montrose. Landseer has painted a picture with the same title.

Q. When is National Child Health Day? D. L.

A. The first of May or May Day is known as National Child Health Day.

Q. Is deafness common among children?

A. According to surveys made in 1927 by the American Federation of Organizations for the Hard of Hearing, there are in the United States not less than 3,000,000 children with impaired hearing. Of these 3,000,000 children, between 300,000 and 400,000 have hearing difficulties sufficiently advanced to need special classes in lip reading, in order to be able readily to understand the spoken word. Sometimes a child who seems unresponsive when spoken to, and slow in school, is not stupid. He is only suffering because of difficulty in hearing.

Q. How fast does the average child learn to talk? B. R.

A. Elizabeth Cleveland says that the child begins to use single words at from 10 months to a year old. At 23 months he should be using simple phrases. By the time he is three he has a large vocabulary, 500 to 1500 words, and can converse well enough for his own practical purposes.

Q. When a baby is learning to walk, should he be taught to "toe out"? N. D.

A. He should not. The feet should be straight forward. The child who toes out throws his weight on the inside of the foot instead of on the ball and will almost surely develop flatfoot.

Q. Should a child be dressed more warmly indoors in the winter time than in the summer time? H. H.

A. The Children's Bureau says that if the house is well heated—68° to 70° F.—he should wear practically what he wears on cool days in summer. If the house is poorly heated or floors are drafty, he will need warmer clothes. However, many children are dressed too warmly indoors. Warm outer garments should be provided for outdoor wear according to temperature.

Q. Should a child be wakened from a nap, if he seems to be sleeping too long? O. D. C.

A. After a child is three years of age, too long a daytime nap usually interferes with night sleeping. One and one-half hours is considered adequate. The child should then be gently wakened.

Q. Are there many children born after the death of the father? T. F.

A. Life insurance figures show that one child out of every 280 children born in the United States is born after its father's death.

Q. How much does a baby actually sleep? H. G. F.

A. A new born infant may sleep as much as 22 hours out of the 24; at the age of one year this sleep period has dropped to 13¾ hours.

Q. Is a child of five too young to be permitted to spend money? E. D.

A. The Children's Bureau says that at that age a child should discriminate between a penny and a dime and be permitted to make occasional purchases in order to learn the handling of money.

Q. Do children ever die of rickets? T. P.

A. The Public Health Service says that they rarely do, but this disease seems to render children more susceptible to infectious diseases. The lack of lime and phosphorus causes rickets. While a proper amount of these elements may be present in the diet, it is apparently vitamin D that is the factor which makes them assimilable.

Q. Please list the given names of Robert E. Lee's children. M. N. B.

A. They were George Washington Custis, Mary, William Henry Fitzhugh, Anne Carter, Eleanor Agnes, Robert Edward, and Mildred Childe.

Q. Are there as many children under one year of age now as there were ten years ago? B. C.

A. The Bureau of the Census says that the number has decreased. In 1920, there were 2,257,255 infants under a year old, while in 1930 there were 2,190,791.

Q. What is the purpose of the Girl Scouts? A. L.

A. The Girl Scouts, a national association, is non-sectarian and nonpartisan. The object of the organization is to give girls, through natural, wholesome pleasures, those habits of mind and body, which will make them useful, responsible women, ready and willing to take a definite part in the home, civic, and national affairs of their country.

Q. Is the birthrate in the large cities of the world increasing or declining? L. B.

A. The Metropolitan Life Insurance Company has made a survey in 42 of the world's large cities and reports that in only two, Glasgow and Rio de Janeiro, had there been any increase in 1931 compared with 1930. In 24 of these cities the birthrate declined at least 5 per cent. In Boston the decline was 22 per cent and in Detroit, 17 per cent.

Q. Who was the first white boy born in Kentucky? N. F. W.

A. The first white male child born in Kentucky was Daniel Boone's son.

Q. What time of year do children grow the most rapidly? O. V. S.

A. A Swedish physiologist, Dr. Gustav Nylin, says that children grow most rapidly in height in the spring and put on weight fastest in the late fall and winter.

Q. When were incubators first used for babies? B. N. C.

A. The first incubator designed for rearing children too weak to survive under normal conditions, or those prematurely born, was that of Dr. Tarnier, constructed in 1880, and first used at the Paris Maternity Hospital.

Q. Is there any truth in the statement that children form 75 per cent of our motion picture audiences? C. H.

A. As a matter of fact, only eight per cent are children. Impartial surveys made by disinterested organizations show that in the Manhattan theater district of New York City, for instance, the proportion of the children in the audience, by actual count, is as low as three to four per cent and in the residential urban districts it is eight per cent.

Q. How many children has Mr. Garner? W. W.

A. Speaker Garner has one son, Tully, who manages the Garner properties in Uvalde, Texas.

Q. What do the four H's stand for in 4-H Clubs? W. S.

A. The 4-H Clubs were organized by the Department of Agriculture in

1909. They were made up of groups of farm children who, prior to 1909, were under the supervision of agriculture agents. The Government fosters their activities. The four H's stand for the following: The First H: Is to train the head to think, to reason. The Second H: To train the heart to sympathize and feel. The Third H: To train the hand to execute the thoughts of the head. The Fourth H: Health to resist disease.

Q. How many children has Sir Oliver Lodge? A. L. M.

A. He had 11 children. His son, Raymond, was killed in the World War.

Q. Do the youths of today select their own clothes and other supplies without parental supervision? S. G.

A. A survey of the buyers of boy's merchandise between the ages of 14 and 21 brought out the facts that more than half of the youths chose their clothing, shoes, sporting goods, radios, and musical instruments without parental aid.

Q. How tall are Don Jaime and Don Juan, sons of former King Alphonso?

A. Princess Pilar in her new book says that Don Jaime is well over six feet and his younger brother is even taller.

Q. Are there more than two kinds of twins? J. B. B.

A. There are three: identical, unlike, and Siamese.

Q. How many children has the former Crown Prince of Germany? T. N. W.

A. Six—William, Louis-Ferdinand, Hubert, Frederick, Alexandrine, and Cecilie.

Q. What has been the decrease in child labor in the past ten years? E. R.

A. In 1920 the number of employed children up to the age of 18 was as follows: 10–13 years, 378,063;

14–15 years, 682,795; 16–17 years, 1,712,648. This is 17 per cent of the total child population of the country. In 1930 the figures were: 10–13 years, 235,328; 14–15 years, 431,790; 16–17 years, 1,478,855. This is 11.3 per cent of the total child population.

Q. Please name a person who was a child prodigy and became a great thinker or writer. H. T.

A. John Stuart Mill may be taken as an example. His father began to teach him Greek at the age of three, Latin at seven, and algebra, geometry, and calculus at twelve. He began the study of logic at twelve and political economy at thirteen. He became a leading English social and political reformer, philosopher, and economist.

Q. Should the collecting instinct in children be fostered? W. M. J.

A. Angelo Patri discusses this at length, and says in part: "This instinct to collect is the germ of his responsibility towards his family. He must get and keep so that others, later on, may have what they will need. If he does not follow this instinct, and do his hoarding and sorting and valuing, he will lose that valuable phase of his growth. To be sure, he has no appreciation of this. It is fun for him. But his heart is in his treasure."

Q. Should babies' teeth be cared for?

A. It is important that the first teeth be cared for, because they not only furnish food for the second teeth but form the arch responsible for their regularity.

Q. Please tell about the Children's Crusade. J. H.

A. This expedition was undertaken in 1212 by a great army of about 50,000 children, boys and girls, most of whom were less than twelve years of age. A French shepherd lad, Stephen by name, declared that God had called him to the rescue of the Holy Land. He it was who led the children. Upon reaching Marseilles, they were bitterly disappointed because they had expected the sea to divide and give them safe passage to the Holy Land. Many of the children made their way home. Merchants, however, lured several thousand on board seven vessels. The children were promised free passage to Palestine. Off Sardinia two of the vessels were wrecked. The other five carried the children to Alexandria where they were sold into slavery.

Q. How long have births been registered in England? A. J. S.

A. It is believed to have been inaugurated by Thomas Cromwell in 1522, but the statutes concerning registration are of a comparatively modern date. The first Registrar-General was appointed in 1836.

Q. When did the Siamese twins live? J. A.

A. Eng and Chang, the original Siamese twins, were born in 1811 and lived until 1874.

Q. How many of Count Tolstoi's children survived him? M. D.

A. At the time of the distribution of his property, nine children were living. They were: Screzha, Grinenka, Tanya, Masha, Ilya, Lyova, Andryusha, Sasha, and Vanichka.

Q. How old is Paulina Longworth? G. L.

A. Paulina Longworth was born February 14, 1925.

Q. How many children had Senator and Mrs. Dwight Morrow? M. E. H.

A. There are four Morrow children—Elizabeth R., Anne S. (now Mrs. Charles A. Lindbergh); Dwight W., Jr., and Constance C.

Q. How is intelligence distributed according to Galton's law of filial regression? T. S. G.

A. The Galton law of filial regression states that the tendency of the children of unusual parents is to approximate more nearly to the common type of the family or stock. Hereditary characteristics are derived as follows: one-half from the parents; one-quarter from the grandparents; one-eighth from the great grandparents, etc.

Q. What are some of the best known children's books? L. A.

A. Heidi, Alice in Wonderland, Little Women, Child's Garden of Verses, and Little Lord Fauntleroy are among the children's books which might be classified as among children's classics.

Q. Please name the children of Premier Mussolini of Italy. E. K.

A. They are: Edda—now the Princess Ciano (her husband is a young nobleman in the Italian diplomatic service)—Vittorio, Bruno, Romano, and Anna Maria.

Q. How should each food dollar be divided so that the children in a family will have the food they need? O. P.

A. Milk, one-fourth, 25¢. Vegetables, one-fifth, 20¢. These should include canned tomatoes at least twice a week, cabbage at least twice a week, and potatoes, greens, and other vegetables as often as possible. Cereals, bread and beans, one-fifth, 20¢. Fats and sugars, one-fifth, 20¢. Fats include lard, salt pork, margarine, vegetable oil. Small quantities of eggs, meat, fish, cheese, and accessories such as salt, baking powder, tea, coffee and cocoa, 15¢. Each child under two years must have at least two teaspoonsful of cod liver oil each day. He should have three or four. This must be purchased extra.

Q. Have any states rejected the Child Labor Amendment? V. A.

A. The Child Labor Amendment has been rejected by both Houses in Connecticut, Delaware, Florida, Georgia, Indiana, Kansas, Kentucky, Maine, Maryland, Massachusetts, Minnesota, Missouri, New Hampshire, North Carolina, Pennsylvania, South Carolina, South Dakota, Tennessee, Texas, Utah, Vermont, Virginia, Washington, West Virginia.

Q. Do scientists find that the young boys of today are shorter than their grandparents were when they were boys? B. K.

A. Dr. Horace Gray of the Institute for Juvenile Research in Chicago says, "The American boys of today are at least two inches taller than their grandpas were when they were boys." Measurements of the heights of over 1000 boys of American-born parents were compared with the heights of boys measured over 50 years ago by another scientist. The increase in height may be attributed to the increasing knowledge of health and disease control, thinks Dr. Gray.

Q. Are more children born in hospitals or at home? R. R.

A. Many more are born at home. In the United States, out of 2,200,000 births in a year, about 1,500,000 are born at home.

Q. What causes children to tell lies? M. T.

A. Children tell lies for different reasons. One class of lies is due to a misunderstanding or misapprehension by the child of what has happened to him or what has been said to him. Tense may be the cause of other lies. The child may not know the difference between "I did" and "I will" and "I mean to." Another class of lies is due to confusion of the fancied with the real. A child may believe that his dreams were actual events. A fourth type of children's lies is deception where a conscious substitution of the untrue for the true is made. One reason for deception is fear. Another is to gain his own way without friction. A

third reason is to attract attention, while a fourth is the desire to preserve one's self-respect or the respect of one's associates. A child often lies to avoid ridicule.

Q. What were the ten don'ts for parents published in a Department of Labor bulletin? B. P.

A. These don'ts for parents were given by Dr. D. A. Thon of the Boston Habit Clinics for children. They were: don't be over-solicitous; don't baby your children too much; don't give your children everything they demand; don't bribe; don't cheat; don't make meaningless threats; don't talk about or laugh at the children in their presence; don't be cold and repelling; don't be discourteous; don't disagree over discipline problems before the child.

Q. What effect has a depression on child labor? N. T.

A. Certain indices of the trend of child labor in New York State, namely, employment certificate, school attendance, and inspections records show a decrease in child labor during the depression years. Similar statistics for the next few years will be of especial interest in showing whether this represents a permanent decline in child labor or merely a temporary fluctuation due to scarcity of jobs.

Q. How often should a baby be weighed? B. B.

A. He should be weighed every week until he is three months old, and after that age, at least once a month. A healthy normal baby gains from five to eight ounces a week for the first three months, and from four to six ounces for the next three months. At six months, a baby has usually doubled his weight.

CHAPTER 19

CLOTHING

Q. What size hat do most men wear? M. R. L.

A. It is estimated that 25 per cent of the hats sold to men are size 6⅞.

Q. What is meant by a custom-made garment? A. E. S.

A. This designation is given to a garment made to order to individual measure.

Q. Are suspenders worn with evening clothes? W. F. J.

A. It is customary since the trousers hang better than they would if a belt were worn.

Q. Why is not spider's silk used commercially? L. McC.

A. Spider's silk is not manufactured because of the spider's cannibalistic tendencies. It would require a separate box for each one, therefore the process would be too costly.

Q. What was the color of Martha Washington's wedding dress? H. T. H.

A. It was a yellow silk brocade with bunches of red and blue flowers and a shaded vine. One piece of this is owned by Mrs. James Henderson Peter of Bethesda, Maryland, whose husband is a descendant of Mrs. Washington.

Q. Why is a certain style of undergarment for women called a teddy-bear? S. N. O.

A. Several explanations are offered. The most credible is that a manufacturer of ladies' underthings in New York, by the name of Theodore Baer, invented this style of lingerie.

Q. What is the highest price paid for one pair of women's hosiery? A. H. R.

A. The highest on record is $2000. This pair of stockings consisted of clocks made up of real diamonds.

Q. What size shoe is worn by the average American woman? M. C.

A. The average size of women's shoes is now placed at six and one-half.

Q. How much cloth will a pound of cotton make? P. R.

A. Differences of weaving govern, but it has been figured that a pound of cotton should make three and a half yards of sheeting, three and three-fourths yards of muslin, nine and a half yards of lawn, seven and a half yards of calico, five and a half yards of gingham, or fifty-seven spools of thread.

Q. When were overalls first made, especially the blue ones? J. E. J.

A. Jean cloth has been in use for workman's clothing—call them overalls or by other names—since the 16th century. The name is derived from the City of Jaen, one of the Moorish capitals of Spain, which was the seat of a large textile industry in the 16th century. The first blue overalls in this country were made about 1880.

Q. *What clothes should a woman wear, who is going to travel by airplane?* **E. A. M.**

A. A woman wears exactly the same clothes she would wear for a train trip. The cabin planes are heated in cold weather, so it is merely a question of preference. A tailored suit, sport clothes, or dress of suitable color and weight will be satisfactory.

Q. *Did Mrs. Bloomer invent the garment that bears her name?* **D. R.**

A. Mrs. Bloomer in her writings gave credit to Mrs. Elizabeth Miller Smith for designing the costume, which she copied. Mrs. Elizabeth Cady Stanton and Mrs. Lucy Stone also adopted it for a time.

Q. *How are the sizes of women's stockings determined?* **A. M.**

A. Size eight is eight inches from top of the toe to end of the heel. Each larger size is a half inch longer. Men's hose are measured in the same way.

Q. *Why is a certain kind of riding breeches called jodhpurs?* **D. McP.**

A. The name is derived from the Indian town of Jodhpur where they first became popular.

Q. *Of what kind of paper were the paper suits made that Germans wore during the War?* **E. E. M.**

A. Cloth made of cellulose yarn was used to make the so-called paper suits worn in Germany during the War. The cellulose is transformed into paper and cut into strips and these strips are spun. The waste from other fibrous materials such as cotton and flax are introduced to make a thread in the manufacture of the yarn.

Q. *Are pigskin gloves really made from the skin of pigs?* **U. S. E.**

A. They are made from the skins of wild pigs such as the peccary, of the southwestern United States and Mexico. The bramble scratches on these gloves are supposed to be an indication that the skins are actually from wild animals.

Q. *What styles in men's attire are directly attributable to Beau Brummel?* **M. B.**

A. He is credited with making universal and permanent the conventions of short unpowdered hair, long trousers, a tailed coat, and the use of dark colors for coat and vest.

Q. *When were neckties first generally worn?* **M. R.**

A. Neckties, formerly known as cravats, were first extensively worn in Europe during the French Revolution. The custom was borrowed from the Croats or Crabats, as they were called, in the 17th century.

Q. *How much silk thread does it take to make a pair of all silk women's hosiery?* **R. W.**

A. It requires 19,700 feet of silk thread for a pair of 4-thread woman's hose; 9900 feet of 8-thread; and 6500 feet of 10-thread. Hosiery made with cotton welts, heel, sole, and toe would naturally contain less silk.

Q. *What are Persian shawls?* **M. G.**

A. Strictly speaking a Persian shawl is one which is woven of the native wools of Persia, dyed with the native vegetable colorings and woven on the native hand looms. Paisley shawls are reproductions of these native shawls and given their title from the fact that many of the finest and best were made in Paisley, Scotland, which for a great many years conducted an enormous business in this commodity. This shawl was popular from about 1820 until 1870.

Q. *Where did our early settlers get their shoes?* **G. H. J.**

A. Shoes were brought to America by the first settlers. The Indians wore moccasins and the white men adopted them until Thomas Beard, a London shoemaker, came to Massachusetts in 1629, bringing a supply of leather, as well as a kit of tools, and became the first shoemaker on record in the colony. Many early settlers made their own shoes. Some raised the cattle and tanned the leather of which their shoes were made.

Q. *How are full fashioned stockings made?* B. M.

A. This hosiery is knitted flat. The leg is made on one machine and then transferred to a footer, after which the entire stocking is seamed.

Q. *How do riding boots, hunting boots, and polo boots differ from each other?* A. P.

A. A riding boot is stiff one-half way down the leg but there is a soft place between the stiffness and the foot that shows creases after being worn a few times. A hunting boot is laced all the way. A polo boot looks like a riding boot but is stiff all the way. It is not so comfortable for general riding as a regular riding boot, as the soft place above the foot gives flexibility.

Q. *Exactly what causes wool garments to shrink?* E. Y. V.

A. Shrinkage of woolens may be caused by having the soap washing bath, or the rinses, too warm. It may also be caused by too free use of soap in washing or rather by failure to remove the soap in rinsing. Garments shrunken from this cause may often be remedied by passing through a fairly strong and warm alkali bath made by adding two ounces of powdered borax to five gallons of water, followed by rinsing to remove the soap and the "felting" effect on the fabric caused by it. A very common cause of shrinkage is in drying the wet cleaned work at too high a temperature.

Q. *Which furs are for dress wear and which for sports wear?* L. D.

A. The style of the garment determines this to some extent. Generally speaking, furs for dress wear are: American broadtail (processed lamb), broadtail, caracul, astrakhan, weasel, ermine, squirrel, chinchilla, and mole. Furs for sports wear: muskrat, raccoon, civet cat, skunk, opossum, the leopard and his kindred, Russian pony and korova, suslik, antelope and gazelle, goat and kid, chipmunk and burunduk. Dependable coat furs for most occasions are: Alaska seal, Hudson seal (dyed muskrat), sealine and near seal (dyed coney), mink, kolinsky, beaver, nutria, krimmer, and Persian lamb.

Q. *Why are silk trains run on a faster schedule than other trains?* E. D.

A. Silk is costly, the price in New York fluctuates, and the insurance rate is high. It is therefore important that no time be lost in transit.

Q. *How long since shoddy was first used?* W. W.

A. The shoddy trade was begun at Batley, Yorkshire, England, in 1813 by Benjamin Law. It also was among the earliest products of American woolen mills.

Q. *Can a new style of wearing apparel be patented?* D. R.

A. The Patent Office says that wearing apparel is patentable subject matter.

Q. *Why are some shoes called brogues?* H. T.

A. Brogues were originally heavy coarse shoes, and took their name from the Gaelic word brog which meant a shoe.

Q. *Are Panama hats made in Panama?* J. W. H.

A. They are made to some extent in Panama, but by far the largest proportion of them is made in Ecuador.

Q. *How long has waterproof clothing been in use?* N. A. L.

A. The art of painting over textile fabrics with oily preparations to make them waterproof is probably nearly as old as textile manufacture itself. There are several processes, many based on that contained in Dr. Stenhouse's patent of 1864. Waterproofing by the application of a thin layer of rubber was first suggested by

Besson, in France in 1793. His method was improved upon by Mackintosh and Hancock in Glasgow and by Goodyear in the United States.

Q. *What part of the clothing is meant when speaking of widow's weeds?* K. J.

A. Mourning garb is an equivalent expression. It refers to the entire costume.

Q. *For whom was the Prince Albert coat named?* R. N. W.

A. The long double-breasted frock coat for men is named after Prince Albert, the Prince Consort of Queen Victoria.

Q. *In what country are the most fur coats worn?* M. D.

A. Despite the fact that the climate of the United States could not be termed rigorous, the demand for fur coats is so great that this country consumes more fur than any other in the world.

Q. *How did a certain style of hat happen to be called a derby?* T. R. C.

A. This stiff felt hat, with a dome-shaped crown and stiff rim, was first worn at the Earl of Derby's race track.

Q. *What are the lengths used by manufacturers of baby dresses?* A. G.

A. The following measures are used by one large manufacturer of baby dresses: infants' first dress, 20 inches; one year, 16 inches; two years, 17 inches; three years, 18 inches.

Q. *Why do women's coats button from right to left, while men's coats fasten from left to right?* E. S.

A. The Haberdasher says: "The story connected with the placing of buttons on men's and women's coats is an interesting one. Tradition hands us the following, and it is reasonable enough to be believed: In former times when men wore swords on all occasions, it was frequently necessary to be quick on the draw. The weapon, of course, was invariably fastened at the left and in order to draw it from its scabbard with quick dispatch, such emergencies made it necessary to place the coat buttons at the right. Obviously, fumbling would have been fatal. As the left hand reached to the right in order to unbutton the coat, the right hand went to the left and drew the sword. Now for the ladies who also enter into this pleasant legend in a most agreeable way: As has been the custom since time immemorial, it is the practice of women to hold a baby in the hollow of her left arm which engages both the arm and the hand. It becomes clear that if the woman's jacket is to be unbuttoned easily it must be done with the right hand without disturbing the position of the child; hence the necessity of buttoning the jacket toward the left which permits usage of the free right arm in either buttoning or unbuttoning her garments."

Q. *How does the weight of a man's clothing compare with that of a woman's?* F. N.

A. In a recent experiment it was found that the average weight of women's clothing was 2½ pounds, and of men's 8½ pounds. A man's shoes often weigh more than the total weight of a woman's apparel.

Q. *What is put in silk materials to make them seem heavier?* E. R.

A. Silks are weighted by the addition of solutions of tin or iron salts. They make the silk seem heavier, with more body. However, they decrease the wearing quality of the silk.

Q. *How long does it take to make a hula skirt?* B. K.

A. To make a real hula costume it requires from 40 to 80 ti plant leaves, depending on the size of the dancer. It takes approximately three hours to weave a skirt, the life of which is three days.

CHAPTER 20

COMMERCE

Q. *Where did the founder of the ten cent stores get his idea?* **D. R.**

A. Frank Winfield Woolworth while still a young man worked in a dry goods store and waited on a counter where five and ten cent articles were sold. This gave him the idea and in February, 1879, he opened a store in Utica, New York, where he dealt only in articles which cost five and ten cents.

Q. *When was the first Chamber of Commerce organized?* **P. L. D.**

A. Chambers of Commerce originated on the Continent of Europe with the disintegration of the old guild system. The first Chamber of Commerce on record is that of Marseilles, France, which grew out of a committee of merchants established in 1599. The movement spread to the United States where the first Chamber of Commerce, that of New York City, was organized in 1768.

Q. *What was the first manufactured product exported from this country?* **C. P.**

A. Captain John Smith sent from Jamestown wood made into panels for wainscoting. This is the earliest manufactured product exported.

Q. *What were the differences on the tariff question between Alexander Hamilton and Thomas Jefferson?* **S. E.**

A. Alexander Hamilton looked toward the development of an industrial nation and believed in the protection of infant industries by a tar- iff levy. Thomas Jefferson believed in the philosophy of individualism and hoped that the country would remain a simple agricultural state. In 1793, however, he advocated high tariffs against England.

Q. *Can returning travelers bring in two hundred dollars worth of purchases free of duty?* **J. A. B.**

A. The Customs Service states that no change has been made in the one hundred dollars worth of importations which may be brought in by each American tourist coming into the United States. It has been proposed to raise this amount to two hundred dollars, but the change has not been made.

Q. *How long has it been the practice to give mortgages as security for debts?* **A. W. D.**

A. The American Architect says: "The oldest existing mortgage record is said to be one found in 1893 by an archeological expedition of the University of Pennsylvania. It is a clay tablet stating that in 430 B.C. an inhabitant of Nippur, Babylon, borrowed thirty bushels of dates from a fellow townsman and pledged his ancestral lands as security for their return. It has been definitely established, however, that similar agreements were in common use as long ago as 2200 B.C."

Q. *What is a favorable balance of trade?* **G. T.**

A. When exports of merchandise exceed imports a balance is due, and there is a favorable balance of trade in favor of the country which has sold more than it has bought.

Q. What is the origin of the word tariff? S. M.

A. According to popular etymological ideas, the name tariff is derived from Tarifa, Spain, a port near Gibraltar where duties were levied on all merchandise on ships passing through the Strait of Gibraltar. Another theory is that the word tariff comes from the Arabic tarif meaning knowledge, information, and inventory; hence, a schedule of duties.

Q. How much money is spent for candy in the United States? O. D.

A. Each year between $750,000,000 and $1,000,000,000 worth of candy is purchased.

Q. What is Tata Sons, Limited? E. B.

A. This is an Indian house founded by the late Jamsetji N. Tata, a Parsi merchant and industrial pioneer. The headquarters are in Bombay, and the combined capital of their undertakings is estimated at $250,000,000, providing employment for nearly 250,000 people.

Q. Is there any line of retail buying in which men make more purchases than women? W. L. L.

A. A survey of 12 classes of retail establishments — department stores, drug stores, grocery stores, silks, pianos, leather goods, automobiles, hardware, electrical supplies, men's socks, jewelry, men's neckwear —showed that in only two lines, automobiles and hardware, do men make more purchases. Men purchased 59 per cent of the automobiles and 51 per cent of the hardware.

Q. Do our exports exceed our imports? R. N.

A. The only month during 1930 and 1931 when our exports did not exceed our imports was August. The exports for the year ending December, 1931, were $333,957,000 in excess of our imports. The exports have exceeded the imports every year since 1893.

Q. Is the jewelry trade heavier at any particular time of year? P. C.

A. About 31.2 per cent of the jewelry sales are made in December. The two months having the next largest sale are June 7.9 per cent and November with 7.4 per cent.

Q. Please give the dates of the opening of some of the large chain store systems. L. M.

A. The first of the existing chain store systems appears to have been the Great Atlantic and Pacific Tea Company which was founded in 1858. The Jones Brothers Tea Company was established in 1872; Woolworth's Five and Ten Cent Stores in 1879; James Butler Company's Grocery Chain in 1882; McCrory Grocery Chain in 1882; Kresge Company in 1885; United Cigar Stores in 1901; J. C. Penney Stores in 1902; and the United Drug Company in 1902.

Q. What is the largest privately owned business in the world? R. T. F.

A. The House of Mitsui, in Japan, is said to be the greatest business enterprise in the world. Takatoshi Mitsui, the great, began with a dry-goods store where he established the first fixed price, spot cash, no credit system. He sold cloth in any length desired, instead of only kimono lengths. The house is ruled by the senior Baron Hachiroyemon, 14th Baron Mitsui, but the prime minister of the Mitsui empire is Baron Takuma Dan, frequently referred to as the Morgan of Japan. Baron Dan was graduated from the Massachusetts Institute of Technology. The aggregate wealth of the House of Mitsui has been estimated at 2,000,000,000 yen, or $1,000,000,000.

Q. Please tell something of the origin of the wholesale grocery business. F. T. C.

A. The early history of the wholesale grocery business is confined principally to England. The immediate forerunner of the grocery was the pepperer or spicer, whose trade was well established in London by 1180. The earliest use of the word, grocer, occurs in 1310 in the city record report of London. During the Middle Ages all trades were formed into guilds, and the Grocers' Company of London was founded in 1345. From this time, the growth of the trade was rapid.

Q. From what countries is the value of our imports greatest? T. W.

A. Imports from Canada, Brazil, Germany, United Kingdom, and Japan were valued at more than $100,000,000 each for the calendar year 1931.

Q. Who had the first department store? H. L. A.

A. The modern department store is an evolution of the village general store. Rowland H. Macy is credited with having conceived the department store idea in America and was probably the first in the world. He opened an establishment at 204 Sixth Avenue, New York City, in 1858. At first it was devoted exclusively to fancy goods and gradually hats, dress goods, jewelry, toilet ware, and other departments were added. For many years this was the only store in New York to carry soaps and perfumes. Wanamaker's in Philadelphia was opened in 1861 as Oak Hall. Marshall Field & Company was organized in Chicago in 1881.

Q. Do more cities call their organization a Chamber of Commerce or a Board of Trade? C. T.

A. The modern tendency is toward the term, Chamber of Commerce. Other names used are Board of Trade, Business Men's Association, Commercial Club, Association of Commerce, Board of Commerce, and Merchants' Association.

Q. To what countries do we send most of our exports? I. F.

A. The countries to which we sent goods valued at more than $100,000,-000 for the year ending December 31, 1931, are Canada, France, Germany, United Kingdom, Soviet Russia, and Japan.

Q. When was the trade acceptance first used in America? J. L. C.

A. The acceptance in America dates back to the time when England sent goods to Virginia and the boats took back tobacco.

Q. From what countries do we import coffee? D. E. M.

A. Coffee is imported into the United States from Brazil, Colombia, Venezuela, Central America, Mexico, Netherland East Indies, Aden, West Indies and Bermudas.

Q. Are there any commodities leaving the United States upon which export duties are placed? F. T. D.

A. The United States has no export tariffs.

Q. Is the capacity of the Panama Canal sufficient to handle the commerce at present? R. S.

A. The present capacity of the Panama Canal is ample for the handling of any traffic likely to develop for many years to come, according to the annual report of the Governor of the Panama Canal for the fiscal year ended June, 1932.

Q. Does the expression free trade as commonly used mean absolutely free exchange? H. M. I.

A. As commonly used, free trade refers to exchange restricted only by moderate revenue duties.

Q. How was the Sears-Roebuck firm started? W. J. H.

A. Mr. Roebuck was originally employed by Richard W. Sears as a watch repair man. At that time Mr. Sears was doing business in the name of the R. W. Sears Watch Company, which business he sold out, agreeing not to go into the mail order watch business again, in his own name for three years. In the meantime he used the name of A. C. Roebuck and had advertised under that name considerably until the three years expired. He then changed the name to Sears, Roebuck and Company at Minneapolis. Mr. Roebuck was really never financially interested in the business to any extent, but was in its employ.

Q. *Is the commerce between the United States and Hawaii of more value than that between the United States and either Alaska or Porto Rico? C. W. N.*

A. The value of exports to Hawaii is greater than to either Alaska or Porto Rico. In 1929 and 1931 the value of imports from Hawaii was greater, but in 1930 those from Porto Rico slightly exceeded those from Hawaii.

Q. *How many camels or mules travel in a caravan? S. A. I.*

A. The number of camels or mules in a single caravan varies from 40 or so up to 600 and more. Sometimes as on the reopening of a long closed route it reaches 1000.

Q. *What is a cartel? E. H.*

A. A cartel is a form of combination among manufacturers by which the independent firms and establishments in a particular trade or process contract to regulate their output and in certain cases their prices.

Q. *When was the Department of Commerce separated from the Department of Labor? D. L.*

A. The Department of Commerce succeeded the earlier Department of Commerce and Labor by the Act of Congress approved on March 4, 1913.

Q. *Is the Secretary of Commerce a member of the President's Cabinet? H. D.*

A. The Secretary of Commerce is a member of the President's Cabinet, but he is not in line of succession to the Presidency.

Q. *What is the Amtorg Trading Corporation? T. F.*

A. The Amtorg Trading Corporation is composed of representatives in the United States of the principal trusts, syndicates, trading agencies, and other economic organizations of the Union of Soviet Socialist Republics, with the exception of the All-Russian Textile Syndicate and cooperative organizations.

Q. *What are the two most important industries of Alaska and what is their value? B. D.*

A. During the fiscal year of 1932 there were 49,524 skins of fur seals taken in Alaska. These brought a total of $546,219.20. Gold valued at $9,507,000 was mined in Alaska during the last fiscal year. This was an increase of about $1,000,000 over the previous fiscal year.

Q. *How many soda fountains are there in the United States? K. N.*

A. It is estimated that there are approximately 100,000 soda fountains in the United States.

Q. *How much money is spent for flowers each year? C. N.*

A. The total approximate sales of the 9,391 florists listed in the 1930 Census of Distribution were $177,488,-758 in 1929.

Q. *What proportion of our exports and imports are shipped in foreign vessels? D. C.*

A. For the year ending December, 1931, 64.1% of our exports and 66.1% of our imports were carried in foreign vessels. This, of course, refers to the water-borne commerce.

Q. *What is the purpose of the Chamber of Commerce of the United States? W. N. S.*

A. The purpose of the Chamber of Commerce of the United States is to encourage trade and commercial intercourse between the States and the insular possessions of the United States and also with foreign nations. It is also interested in the cooperation between Chambers of Commerce, Boards of Trade, and other commercial and manufacturing organizations. It is interested in promoting uniformity and equity in business usage laws and the proper consideration and concentration of opinion on questions affecting finance and commerce.

Q. *What was the immediate cause of the financial crisis of 1837?* M. L. B.

A. President Jackson, after he had vetoed the Act of Congress renewing the charter of the United States Bank, directed the Secretary of the Treasury to deposit no more federal revenues in the Bank and to withdraw the government's cash from its vaults in payment of bills. The national funds were distributed among certain state banks.

Q. *When was the first depression in the United States?* M. E.

A. The first so-called depression in the United States was the one of 1785 to 1789.

Q. *What is included in good will when a business is sold?* B. E. F.

A. Crowell's Dictionary of Business and Finance defines it as the evaluation placed upon the reputation, patronage, drawing power, and other intangible advantages possessed by a business concern in operation, including name and good disposition of its customers. The purchase value of good will is based on the average annual net profits for a period of years.

Q. *Are our importations from the Hawaiian Islands important?* M. C. L.

A. More than 1,900,000,000 pounds of sugar and 484,276,079 pounds of canned pineapple were imported from the Hawaiian Islands in 1931.

Q. *Do customers having charge accounts pay bills as promptly during a depression?* H. J.

A. Nearly as promptly. Figures for several months in 1932 indicate an average of 78 days of credit being used in 7 lines of trade compared with 75 days before the depression deepened, a delay of only 3 additional days. While this is small for each average customer it means that millions of dollars of cash due to merchants are tied up at interest 3 days longer.

Q. *Do customs duties form an important source of our federal revenue?* I. S.

A. Until 1913 there was no other more important sources of revenue to the Federal Government than customs duties. Since that time, however, the income tax has become a more important source of revenue.

Q. *How did Webster stand on the question of tariff?* M. T.

A. In early debates in Congress Daniel Webster opposed protection. Later he came to favor protection and made every effort to secure advantageous rates for his constituents.

Q. *Please give the popular names of some of the best known tariff acts.* T. G.

A. The high protective tariff of 1828 known as the tariff of abominations, the compromise tariff of 1833, the Walker tariff of 1836, the McKinley Act of 1890, the Wilson-Gorman Act of 1894, the Dingley Act of 1897, the Payne-Aldrich tariff of 1909, the Underwood tariff of 1913, the Smoot-Hawley tariff of 1930.

Q. *What is a commercial treaty?* H. T. W.

A. A commercial treaty is a contract between countries relative to trade. Definite arrangements are made by each contracting party toward the other.

Q. *How serious did the depression of 1873 seem to the people living through it?* E. R.

A. Rhodes thus described the situation in the five years from 1873 to 1878: "A long dismal tale of declining markets, exhaustion of capital, a lowering in value of all kinds of property, including real estate, constant bankruptcies, close economy in business, and grinding frugality in living, idle mills, furnaces and factories, former profit-earning iron mills reduced to the value of a scrap heap, laborers out of employment, reductions of wages, strikes and lockouts, the great railroad riots of 1877, suffering of the unemployed, depression and despair." Recovery was fairly rapid.

Q. What is a corporation? S. O. R.

A. In English law a corporation is an association of persons which is treated in many respects as if it were itself a person. A corporation may own land, but the individual members of the corporation have no rights therein. A corporation may owe money, but the incorporators as individuals are under no obligation to pay the debt.

Q. What is an index number? C. D. H.

A. A number, generally a percentage, designed to indicate the general level of prices at any given date. It is formed from ratios of the prices of various staples at the date in question, as compared with some previous date which has been adopted as a standard, and for which the index has been fixed at 100.

Q. Please list the principal Soviet imports and exports to and from the United States. D. L.

A. Imports into the United States: Agricultural products such as flax, raw silk, lentils, dried mushrooms, bristles and horsehair; furs, fish products, hides and leather, lumber and pulpwood; mined products such as manganese, iron, and chrome ores, barytes, asbestos, anthracite coal, platinum, potash, granite, kaolin; rugs and handicraft products, linen textiles, confectionery and biscuits, certain chemicals. Exports to Soviet Russia: Machinery and equipment for practically all kinds of factories; transport equipment; raw materials such as non-ferrous metals, alloy steels, diamonds for drilling, paints and dyes, chemicals.

Q. What caused the triumph of the high protective tariff in 1816? A. E.

A. The agricultural States of what was at that time the west, namely Ohio and Kentucky, were won to the side of the high tariff by the home market argument, the essence of which was that protection through promoting manufactures would increase the farmer's home market so that he need not depend on a foreign market to dispose of his surplus.

Q. May a tariff measure originate in the Senate? P. M.

A. Since the tariff is classed as a revenue measure, it must under the provisions of the Constitution originate in the House of Representatives.

Q. Does a drop in foreign trade follow decreased industrial production? W. B.

A. The shrinkage in volume of foreign trade since 1929 has closely followed the drop in industrial production. Comparative figures show that industrial production has declined about 45 per cent since 1929 and the physical volume of exports has declined about the same amount.

Q. Must goods manufactured in a foreign country be marked to show foreign manufacture? A. S. L.

A. The Tariff Act provides that every article imported into the United States, and its immediate container, and the package in which such article is imported, shall be marked, stamped, branded, or labeled, in legible English words, in a conspicuous place in such manner as to indicate the country of origin of such article.

CHAPTER 21

CRIMINOLOGY

Q. Is it possible to tell a crook by his looks? P. C.

A. After many surveys, scientists are approaching the conclusion that there is no such thing as a criminal type.

Q. How many people go to prison every year? M. G.

A. It is estimated that four hundred thousand enter and leave our penal institutions each year.

Q. Whose signature is most often forged? R. L.

A. Madeline Laurier says that probably the signature which has been forged more often than any other in history is that of Antonius Stradivarius, maker of famous Stradivarius violins.

Q. How many speak-easies are there in New York? T. A. V.

A. Major Maurice Campbell, former Prohibition Administrator in New York, declared that in 1931 there were 36,000 speak-easies in New York City, 52,000 in New York State, and 222,000 in the United States. This estimate he declared to be conservative.

Q. What are some of the steps that can be taken to prevent crime? F. W.

A. H. E. Barnes says: "First step in preventing crime is to see that the human individual is well born; second, adequate education; third, sufficient manual or vocational education to provide means of making a living; fourth, efficient methods of aiding backward children who might become victims of criminal suggestions."

Q. In what age group are most of the criminals in the United States? B. P.

A. Persons between the ages of fifteen and thirty constitute 50 per cent of the population, yet they constitute 73 per cent of our criminals.

Q. Has the increase in crime in this country been more rapid than the increase in population? E. D.

A. While the population gain of the United States in the last 20 years has been 45 per cent, law-breaking, according to the courts, has increased 700 per cent in this same period.

Q. When gangsters kill an enemy of their kind, why do they place a nickel or a dime in his hand? D. M.

A. The small coin placed in this way is the gangsters' symbol of how cheaply they estimate their victim.

Q. Which States provide for the sterilization of criminals? N. M.

A. In 1932 the United States Public Health Service said: "With reference to the sexual sterilization of mental defectives, the information available to this office indicates that the following States have sterilization laws: Alabama, Arizona, California, Connecticut, Delaware, Idaho, Indiana, Iowa, Kansas, Maine, Michigan, Minnesota, Mississippi, Montana, Nebraska, New Hampshire, North Carolina, North Dakota, Oregon, South Dakota, Utah, Virginia, Washington, West Virginia, and Wisconsin."

Q. Is kidnaping a federal offense? F. M.

A. Under the provisions of an act of Congress approved by the President on June 22, 1932, any person involved in transporting a person illegally seized in interstate or foreign commerce and holding such person for ransom or reward, is guilty of violating a federal law. Cases of this nature are investigated by the Bureau of Investigation of the Department of Justice.

Q. Are many crimes committed in Alaska? N. A. B.

A. It is said that Alaska has been free from murders and other serious crimes to an extent unsurpassed by any other part of the United States.

Q. How long has capital punishment been used? D. E. W.

A. Capital punishment as a lawful procedure has existed since the history of mankind. It is laid down in the Mosaic Law in the books of Leviticus and Deuteronomy.

Q. What countries do not have capital punishment?

A. There are now 16 countries where there is no death sentence. The death sentence has been abolished in Holland, Norway, Sweden, Portugal, Rumania, Austria, Latvia, Lithuania, Argentina, Brazil, Colombia, Honduras, and Uruguay. It has been abrogated by disuse in Denmark, Belgium, and Finland.

Q. What punishments were given to criminals in Rome? F. P. R.

A. The following punishments were meted out to the offender in ancient Rome: the mulcta or fine; vincula, imprisonment or fetters; verbera, or stripes; talio or infliction of punishment similar to injury, i.e., limb for a limb; infamia, public disgrace, by which the delinquent, besides being scandalized, was rendered incapable of holding public office and deprived of other privileges of Roman citizenship; exilium, banishment; death, either civil or natural. Natural death was brought about by beheading, scourging, strangling, or throwing the criminal headlong from the Tarpeian rock, or from a place in a prison, from the Robur.

Q. What State uses lethal gas in dispatching criminals? J. R.

A. It is form of capital punishment used in Nevada.

Q. Are more crimes punishable by death in England or in America? M. P. O.

A. The only crimes for which capital punishment may now be inflicted, according to the law of England, are high treason and murder. By United States statutes nine crimes may be so punished, including treason, murder, arson, rape, piracy, and robbery of the mail.

Q. What is the derivation of yegg, meaning a robber? J. G. W.

A. The term seems to have referred first to a tramp who made a business of robbery and was taken from gypsy argot. When a particularly clever thief was found among a gypsy tribe he was selected as the yegg or chief thief, the name having come from one John Yegg.

Q. What form of execution is used in Cuba? W. E. L.

A. The Cuban Embassy says that the execution in Cuba, when the death penalty is carried out, depends upon the status of the man sentenced. If the condemned man is a member of the army, he is shot by a squad of soldiers. In case of a civilian being condemned to death, the execution is carried out by garrote. Garrote is a chair similar to the electric chair, which has a collar of iron and hide which is fitted to the neck of the victim. This collar is attached to a large screw, which, on moving, compresses and suffocates, causing death by strangulation or broken neck. Generally the victim is declared dead within ten or twelve minutes after the execution. It is a very old system of penalty, used in Spain since 1832.

Q. *What is the difference between probation and parole?* C. J. S.

A. Quoting Judge Kavanagh: "Probation lets one who has been adjudged guilty of crime go from the court room without any punishment at all. Parole means forgiving the rest of the punishment after a guilty person has suffered a part."

Q. *Why is a person sometimes called a stool pigeon?* M. McC.

A. A stool pigeon is a pigeon used as a decoy to draw other pigeons into a net. Hence, the term is applied to a person used as a decoy for others, especially to one who acts as a spy for the police.

Q. *Where is the largest collection of finger prints of criminals?* W. G.

A. The National Division of Identification and Information of the United States Department of Justice has what is believed to be the largest and most complete collection of criminal finger print records of current value existing in the world. This collection consists of over one and one-half million finger print records and of more than two and one-half million card-index records.

Q. *For what offense are most criminals sent to prison for the first time?* A. T.

A. A survey of the inmates of many penitentiaries made by an official of the Juvenile Court showed that petty larceny was the outstanding first offense of the prisoners examined.

Q. *Among what type of people are crimes of violence usually committed?* H. V. Z.

A. A survey of prisons revealed the fact that the illiterate classes constituted the main body of those being punished for crimes of violence, while the educated classes were more fully represented by those serving time for crimes against property.

Q. *What is a person called who is an habitual criminal?* P. T.

A. A confirmed criminal is called a recidivist. In the United States, the term is also applied to a person serving a second term in prison.

Q. *Who was the "Duke of Exeter's daughter"?* A. W.

A. When the rack as an instrument of torture was introduced into England in 1447 by John Holland, Duke of Exeter, who was at that time constable of the Tower of London, it speedily became known as "the Duke of Exeter's daughter."

Q. *How many people are necessary to constitute a riot?* H. T. T.

A. In law, a riot is the tumultuous disturbance of the peace by an unlawful assembly of three or more persons in the execution of some private object.

Q. *How many murders were committed in Canada in 1930?* P. L.

A. Two hundred and fifty-seven were killed through malice or carelessness of others. Of these, 184 were dealt with by the criminal court and 73 did not reach the courts.

Q. *How many cases of kidnaping have there been in the United States recently?* B. G.

A. Joseph A. Gerk, Chief of Police of St. Louis, in February, 1932, told Congress that there were 282 cases of kidnaping reported officially in twenty-eight of the forty-eight States in 1931 and at least 3000 cases not reported. Gerk's survey revealed that although some 2000 were actively and gainfully employed in kidnaping in 1931, only sixty-five were convicted.

Q. *Why are criminals usually executed at night or in the early morning?* H. G.

A. The reason that electrocutions take place in the late afternoon or evening is that during the day the convicts are working and are not in their cells. A pending execution in a penitentiary exerts a depressing influence over the convicts and to avoid any outbreak or manifestation on their part, the hour is deferred until the prisoners are in their individual cells.

Q. *Are there as many suicides as murders in the United States?* R. A.

A. Public Safety says that in a recent year there were 10,354 homicides and 16,991 suicides.

Q. *What is meant by the torture called "the question"?* L. D. T.

A. "The question" was one of the most dreaded forms of torture. A hard leather funnel was forced down the victim's throat by a callous assistant and bucket after bucket of water was poured into it. The "simple question," usually given to women, was limited to six quarts of water.

Q. *Are homicide and murder one and the same?* S. L.

A. Homicide is a broader term. It signifies the killing of one person by another. Murder is intentional and unlawful homicide.

Q. *What is the difference between a thief and a robber?* S. A. L.

A. A thief is one who deprives another of property secretly or without open force, as opposed to a robber who uses open force or violence. A burglar is a thief who forces an entrance into a building.

Q. *In what country is a criminal tried for a crime committed on the high seas?* W. A. McL.

A. He is tried under the jurisdiction of the nation whose flag the ship flies.

Q. *Is alternating or continuous current used in electrocutions?* L. C. D.

A. Both alternating and continuous current are used in electrocutions. Experiments at Sing Sing have resulted in the conclusion that no human body can withstand an alternating current of 1500 volts and that a current of 300 has produced death, while for the continuous current it may be necessary that as much as 3000 volts be used.

Q. *How many murders are committed in the United States?* R. K.

A. According to a report by J. Edgar Hoover, Director of the Bureau of Investigation of the Department of Justice, in 1930, the average number of murders has risen from three a day at the beginning of the year to nearly five a day in September. This report is based on returns from 58 cities with a population of 100,000 or more.

Q. *Please tell something about Dick Turpin.* J. W. P.

A. He was born in Hempstead, Essex County, England, 1706. His father was an innkeeper and apprenticed Richard to a butcher. He stole his master's cattle and on being discovered fled and joined a gang of highwaymen. He was associated with Tom King whom he fatally shot while trying to protect him from arrest. He escaped for some time, but was finally captured and executed.

Q. *What are the seven grave offenses reported most frequently to the United States police?* B. S. H.

A. Felonious homicide, including (a) murder, nonnegligent manslaughter, and (b) manslaughter by negligence; rape; robbery; aggravated assault; burglary—breaking or entering; larceny—theft, including (a) thefts of $50 and over and (b) thefts of under $50; and auto theft.

Q. *Are there any States in the United States in which there have never been lynchings?* T. L.

A. The Federal Council Bulletin says that five States have never had a recorded lynching. They are Connecticut, Massachusetts, New Hampshire, Rhode Island, and Vermont.

Q. *Does Germany have as many murders as Great Britain?* E. B.

A. It has more. In 1928, Great Britain had 138 and Germany had 1264.

Q. For what kind of crimes are the greatest number of federal prisoners serving time? E. R. A.

A. Among the long-term prisoners, the liquor-law violators form the largest group. They form almost half of the total. Drug-law violators and those convicted of violating the Motor Vehicle Theft Act, added to the prohibition violators, account for almost 80 per cent of the number of prisoners received.

Q. How many men were in the Jesse James gang? How old was Jesse James when he was killed? A. R. L.

A. The members of his gang consisted generally of eight or nine persons and included Jesse and Frank James, Cole Younger, James Younger, Clell Miller, James White, James Koughman, and later Robert Younger. He was killed in 1882 at the age of thirty-five.

Q. What form of execution is used in France? M. C.

A. The guillotine is still in use.

Q. Who was the man who forged Shakespearian manuscripts to the point of deceiving his own father? L. D.

A. William Henry Ireland, 1777–1835, was the son of Samuel Ireland, who was an author, engraver, and dealer in rare books and curios. Young Ireland first forged manuscripts to tease his father. Upon finding how credulous he was these forgeries were foisted upon the public. Many scholars were deceived for a time, but exposure followed. The disgrace was said to have hastened his father's death.

Q. What is an Oregon boot? E. R. L.

A. The Oregon boot was invented by William H. Leininger of Oregon and patented in 1876. It was a shackle for securing prisoners with more safety and less discomfort. When attached it was of compact cylindrical shape without projecting parts and supported by a frame of steel fitted around the top of the shoe.

Q. What was the tribute of Lieut. Becker to his wife before his electrocution for the Rosenthal murder? D. S.

A. Before his electrocution on July 30, 1915, he said: "I am proud to have been the husband of the purest, the noblest woman that ever lived—Helen Becker. This acknowledgment is the only legacy I can leave her." Mrs. Becker's statement was: "In all the ten years of our married life, I never had occasion to regret that I was his wife."

Q. Who was Jack the Ripper? F. A. W.

A. He was believed to be the author of a number of murders which took place in London in the latter part of the 19th century. Notwithstanding special work by Scotland Yard and private detectives, the murderer was never captured.

Q. At what age are most women prisoners committed? G. A. S.

A. From 21 to 24 years of age.

Q. Can a foreigner be deported for committing a crime after he has been naturalized in this country? W. B.

A. After an alien becomes a naturalized citizen he is not subject to deportation.

Q. Was Fra Diavolo a real person? T. N.

A. He was a monk, but was expelled from his order. He then became the leader of a troop of Neapolitan highwaymen.

Q. What are bilboes? C. H.

A. This name was given to a bar of iron with sliding shackles once used to fetter prisoners.

Q. What happens when jewels taken from smugglers are not redeemed? F. F. H.

A. If not redeemed, they are forfeited and sold at public auction at the port where they were seized.

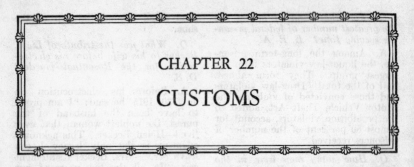

CHAPTER 22

CUSTOMS

Q. What was the origin of the bride's shower? L. H.

A. It is said to have had its origin in Holland. A Dutch father refused to give his daughter a dowry if she married a poor miller whom she loved. The friends of the young couple, poor themselves, decided to make them gifts with which they could go to housekeeping. In this way the young people were provided for, and the custom of having showers was inaugurated.

Q. Why is President von Hindenburg the godfather of so many children? E. R. W.

A. He follows an old custom of the Prussian kings and stands as godfather for each seventh child in a German family. He is said to be godfather to more than 14,000 children.

Q. When was a seal first used for impressing documents? R. L. L.

A. The custom of using seals on documents has prevailed for centuries in the East. The earliest examples of seals are found among the antiquities of Egypt, Babylonia, and Assyria. The use of the signet was required by Roman law for legal purposes. The custom died out by the 7th century A.D., but was revived in the Middle Ages.

Q. While traveling in India I observed that the Hindus carry small brass bowls. Why is this? G. K.

A. Every Hindu, even a child, carries his individual drinking bowl.

The bowl is generally filled with water. The custom arises from the fact that no Hindu may drink water which has been drawn by a person of the wrong caste, nor may he drink water upon which a low-caste person has looked.

Q. Were napkins used in the days of the ancient Greeks? G. R. B.

A. In place of napkins, small pieces of bread were used. They were then thrown on the floor for dogs to eat.

Q. What is the origin of notches in coat lapels? T. B. A.

A. The notch is said to have originated through the rivalry of General Moreau with Napoleon, Moreau's followers having devised it as a secret badge of their partisanship.

Q. What is the origin of the custom of presenting the keys of a city? W. W. W.

A. The custom of presenting the keys of a city goes back to medieval times when every fortified town in Europe was surrounded by walls and people could only enter or leave by the gates. The keys were kept by the mayor or the military commander and the surrendering of the keys indicated the giving over of the city. It thus became the custom figuratively to surrender the city to distinguished visitors by handing them a key. Hall's Chronicle, Henry VI, page 162, says, "All the townes in Acquitayne delivered their keys and became vassals."

Q. Is there any civilized country where the men of today wear earrings? J. A. B.

A. Earrings are still worn by some fishermen on the Belgian coast. They are very rarely worn by men elsewhere, but are sometimes seen in the ears of gypsies, and a few Italians and Spaniards.

Q. Where were masks first worn at fancy dress balls? H. W.

A. The use of masks at costume balls originated in Italy, where the domino or half mask, worn by ladies, became very popular.

Q. Is the image of Guy Fawkes still burned in England? B. W.

A. It is still the custom in England to burn the effigy of Guy Fawkes on the 5th of November, Guy Fawkes Day.

Q. How is the fire walking ceremony of Tahiti explained? R. C. T.

A. The late S. P. Langley of the Smithsonian Institution who witnessed the fire walking ceremony in Tahiti said that the stones used in the ceremony were tested and found to be of vesicular basalt, whose most distinctive features are its porosity and non-conductibility. He found that these stones could be heated red-hot at one end while the remaining part was comparatively cool. He was of the opinion that while the lower stones of the pit were glowing, the upper layer was fairly cool.

Q. What is the origin of the round robin? A. D. B.

A. Boswell traced it to a sailors' custom followed when they entered into a conspiracy so as not to let it be known who put his name first or last to the paper.

Q. In George Washington's day, was it customary for all men to dress as he did? E. M. E.

A. In Washington's day the citizens of the upper class dressed much as he did. Between 1790 and 1800 there occurred a change in the style of garb worn by men. A round hat, short coat, light waistcoat, and pantaloons reaching to the ankles and fastened by buttons, comprised the attire of a gentleman. The hair was short and unpowdered.

Q. Who introduced the custom of wearing black as mourning? C. J.

A. It was originated by Anne, the Queen of Charles VIII of France. On the death of her husband in 1498, she surrounded her coat-of-arms with black in token of widowhood and clothed herself in black, contrary to the prevailing habit which was for widows to wear white.

Q. Is the tonsure an ancient custom? A. C. C.

A. Among the priests of Isis and Serapis the tonsure was the custom. It entered Christianity through monasticism.

Q. What pewter articles were used in this country in colonial days? C. E. D.

A. During the 18th century the following pewter articles were used: Porringers, plates, salts, platters, sugar bowls, dram cups, tea pots, pepper casters, butter plates, and quart and pint pots. Spoons appeared in the latter part of the century. In the early 1800's old and new silver teaspoons are listed. Tankards and flagons were on the earliest list, but pitchers appeared early in the 1800's.

Q. Why did the custom of placing flowers on graves originate? W. H.

A. The ancients believed that the dead enjoyed the fragrance of the flowers.

Q. Why did the Puritans and Pilgrims wear such plain clothes? D. E. T.

A. The simplicity of dress of the Pilgrims and Puritans of New England was largely the result of the superseding of Puritanism as an ideal in England early in the 17th century. Clothing was stripped of all ornamentation or frivolity and so remained during Cromwell's life. The hardships endured by the early New England colonists also made it necessary for them to adopt simple and practical clothing.

Q. What is the origin of the salutation, "How do you do"? J. W. G.

A. It is not known definitely. Murray's Dictionary indicates that an older form of this expression was "How do you"? This authority traces the inquiry back to 1563.

Q. Why is red associated with the Christmas season? M. E.

A. Red is regarded as the most cheerful of all colors. It is said to react the most quickly on the optic nerve. Decorations available at the winter solstice include holly, the berries of which are red. It grew to be the custom to use holly and berries of a similar nature in preparing for the festival of Christmas. By virtue of the association of ideas, red came to be connected with the Christmas season.

Q. Why do waiters wear white cotton gloves? C. T. M.

A. This custom harks back to the day of Louis XIV. In the palace of Versailles the kitchens were so far from the royal suite that food was brought on heated heavy silver platters with dome-shaped covers. The footmen wore thick white gloves in carrying these dishes. As the court did, so also did its imitators.

Q. What was meant by a drunkard's cloak? L. N.

A. This was an old English punishment for drunkenness. A spirits barrel was hung on the drunkard with holes in the sides through which his hands were thrust. He could neither sit nor lie down.

Q. Why is a bottle of champagne or water used to christen a vessel? N. C. W.

A. The custom of breaking a bottle of champagne on the prow of a ship when it is launched is a relic of the ancient libation which was practiced when ships were launched.

The ancients consecrated the ship to the god whose image she bore. The action of blessing ships is alluded to by the Monks of St. Denys. In July, 1418, the Bishop of Bangor was sent to Southampton to bless the King's ship to insure successful voyages. In this country, water or some other liquid has usually taken the place of wine since Prohibition went into effect.

Q. Do many people still send valentines? W. S.

A. A survey made in Park Row, New York City, the nation's wholesale valentine center, showed that sales for 1932 amounted to from five to seven million dollars.

Q. Why did people wear patches on their faces? D. T.

A. These bits of silk or courtplaster were worn to set off the complexion by contrast. Both the beaux and belles of the 17th and early 18th century wore them as adornments.

Q. What does the English expression, maundy money, mean? H. G.

A. It is the alms given on Maundy Thursday, the Thursday before Good Friday, in connection with the annual system of washing the feet of the poor on this day by the sovereign of Great Britain. This was the custom for some centuries. The foot washing is obsolete, but alms are still distributed. Formerly special silver coins of the value of one, two, three, or four pence were struck annually for the maundy alms.

Q. How long has mourning been worn? What colors other than black have been used? M. E.

A. The custom of wearing mourning is of the greatest antiquity. Allusion is made to it in the first chapter of Genesis and throughout the Bible the shaving of the head, the wearing of sackcloth, the sprinkling of the body with ashes, the rending of the garments are mentioned. In China the mourning color is white. In early Egypt it was yellow; Ethiopia, brown; Turkey, violet.

Q. Why do the natives cast berries into the crater of Kilauea? S. G.

A. The custom of casting chelo berries into the crater of the volcano is a very ancient one in Hawaii. The object is to propitiate the Goddess Pele. The Goddess Pele appears in various guises. Formerly it was believed that she would never allow the volcano to harm any individuals, but the recent flows of lava have shown this to be untrue. Red flags are often placed to mark the boundaries of the village and a live pig is tied in front as a sacrifice to the goddess. Kilauea is merely a crater on the eastern slope of Mauna Loa, which is the largest volcano in the world, though not the loftiest.

Q. How long have wigs been worn in English courts of justice? C. M. S.

A. English barristers and judges adopted wigs as part of their ceremonial costume during the 17th century. The custom is an ancient one. Wigs were worn by the Egyptians as a royal and official headdress.

Q. Why do European housebuilders put a tree on top of a house when the ridge pole is placed? S. O.

A. The origin of the custom of placing a flag or tree when the highest part of any structure is completed, the Editor of Contractors' and Engineers' Monthly believes, originated in Germany. It is simply a good luck omen and was designed to protect the building from evil spirits. In other countries, it is still the custom for the owner to treat the workmen to drinks as soon as the tree is placed on the ridge pole.

Q. How ancient is the custom of saying grace before meals? M. H.

A. There is evidence of this ancient custom's being observed as early as the 3rd century.

Q. What is the origin of the use of a cross instead of a signature? E. N. K.

A. The cross with or without the signature has been used on documents since early medieval times. It was regarded as equivalent to an oath and therefore attested to the truth of the statements made therein.

Q. Can you tell me anything of the superstition that it is bad luck to walk under a ladder? E. S.

A. Nothing definite is known concerning the origin of the superstition in regard to walking under a ladder. According to some authorities, the idea is traceable to the fact that Christ was taken down from the Cross by means of a ladder. There is a general belief in England that if a woman walks under a ladder she will not be married within the year. It is more probable, however, that the idea is associated with the possible danger of falling objects, since persons employing a ladder for work generally carry tools which might fall on a passerby.

Q. How did hand clapping originate? M. C.

A. It comes from the Romans who had a set ritual of applause for public performance, expressing degrees of approval—snapping the finger and thumb, clapping with the flat or hollow palm, waving the flap of the toga or a handkerchief. At the close of a play, the chief actor called out—"Valete et plaudite," and the audience chanted their applause.

Q. What is the origin of the judicial oath? J. E. D.

A. The custom of an official's taking an oath of office faithfully to administer the laws did not originate with the Christian religion. From the earliest record of the Jews such oaths were required.

Q. Which is the proper way to hang a horseshoe over the door and why? B. P.

A. The usual method of nailing up a horseshoe to bring good luck is having the two ends pointing downwards. This is because some persons think its protective powers to be due to its resemblance to the nimbus or halo frequently seen in pictures of angels or saints. The superstition regarding the horseshoe as an emblem of luck is believed to be connected with the custom of the ancient Romans. They used to drive nails into the walls of their houses as an antidote against the plague. In the Middle Ages, horseshoes were used over the doorways of houses in order to keep out witches.

Q. How long has it been the custom of the Romans to make a pilgrimage to Tasso's tomb? W. C.

A. This custom has been observed since 1595. Tasso died on the day before that on which he was to ascend the Campidoglio to receive the poet's crown. A votive lamp has recently been placed on a slender marble pedestal before Tasso's tomb.

Q. Why is an opal considered ill luck? B. M.

A. The opal has not always been regarded as an unlucky stone. The superstition regarding its bad luck began in the 14th century at the time of the Black Death, particularly in Venice. At that time the opal was a favorite of the Italian jewelers, but it was said that opals worn by those stricken with the disease became suddenly brilliant and that their luster departed upon the death of the owner. Thus the opal became associated with death and was an object of dread.

Q. Why do people knock on wood? S. B.

A. Knocking on wood seems to have originated in the custom of touching wood upon every occasion of happiness or good fortune, in gratitude to Christ who died on a wooden cross. Through some association of ideas, the custom of touching or knocking on wood came to be looked upon as a means of protection.

Q. What is the origin of the hand salute of the soldier? M. V. A.

A. This salute is believed to have originated in feudal days when a queen of love and beauty was chosen at the close of tournaments and jousts. The knights, passing in review before the throne of beauty, raised their mailed fists to shade their eyes, intimating that they were dazzled by the beauty of the queen.

Q. Why is it considered bad luck to break a mirror? M. C.

A. Lillian Eicher says in her book "Customs of Mankind": "Since very early times the mirror has been used in divination, in attempts to read future or past. An early belief was that one saw the will of the gods in a mirror. To break one accidentally, therefore, was interpreted as an effort of the gods to prevent a person from seeing into the future. This was construed as a warning that the future held unpleasant things. Among highly superstitious people the breaking of a mirror came to be looked upon as a death omen. Somehow this superstitious belief has prevailed and still exists even among educated people."

Q. When was the wooden figure first used in front of cigar stores? W. C. T.

A. John L. Morrison, editor, and a collector of wooden Indians, says: "Wooden Indians are not indigenous to American soil. As early as the reign of James I the wooden Indian was a familiar sight in England. Of the early wooden Indians in America, an odd, cupid-like Pocahontas that once stood guard on Hancock Street, Boston, dates from 1730. The pioneer authenticated appearance of a cigar-store show figure was in 1770, when Christopher Demuth opened a tobacco-shop in Lancaster, Pa. This figure was not an Indian, but a delicate, minuet-type gentleman, extending a snuff-box invitingly."

Q. Why is 13 considered an unlucky number? F. O.

A. From early times and in many nations it has been customary to avoid this number. Some authorities trace this superstition to the Last Supper of the Lord and His Disciples at which thirteen were present. In Norse mythology Loki once intruded at a banquet in Valhalla making the number of guests thirteen. Balder, one of those at the feast, was subsequently slain.

Q. How long have Christmas cards been in use? C. C.

A. Thomas L. Masson says that they have been in use about eighty-two years, the first one of which he knows having been designed in 1846 by J. C. Horsely, R. A. It was not however until after 1860 that they came into general use, John Leighton, in 1862, having made designs for Messrs. Goodall of London.

Q. When did people begin paying rent? P. D. K.

A. We find no exact records of the first rent paid. It is said that when the Germans conquered parts of Gaul, the land was parceled out to chiefs, lieutenants, and private soldiers. In return the holders of the lands promised military service when needed. Some of the land was given to favorites who were allowed to pay in money instead of service, and the system was established. Rent was certainly known in the days when Rome flourished, there being Latin names for rent under long leasehold tenure; rent of a farm; ground rent; rent of state lands; and the annual rent payable for the right to the perpetual enjoyment of anything built on the surface of the land.

Q. Why is a broom used to symbolize victory? E. A.

A. The custom of hanging up a broom to indicate a victory is probably connected with the old naval custom of hanging a broom at the masthead of ships about to be sold, that is, swept away. It is said that Adm. Van Der Tromp hoisted a broom to signify his intention of sweeping the British fleet off the seas.

Q. What is the origin of the legend about St. Swithin's Day? A. K.

A. Saint Swithin was an English bishop of Winchester. At his request, he was buried after his death outside his church at Winchester. When a century later he was canonized, his body was exhumed and buried within the church. There is a legend that this was to have been done on July 15th, but delayed on account of violent rains which continued for 40 days. This has given rise to the popular superstition that if it rains on Saint Swithin's Day, it continues to rain for 40 days.

Q. Is it true that bodies were sometimes buried upright? E. B. S.

A. The custom of burying in an upright position does not belong to any particular age or people, but was carried out at the request of some individuals. From the remains found at Stonehenge and Cannae, it is evident that bodies were buried in a sitting posture at a very early period. Charlemagne also decreed that he be buried in this position. Georges Clemenceau's father was buried in an upright position.

Q. How did the custom of casting a shoe after a bride originate? R. E.

A. This custom had its origin in Israel where the delivery of a shoe was used as a testimony in transferring a possession. The throwing of the shoe on property was a symbol of new ownership. From these ancient practises came the old customs in England and Scotland of throwing an old shoe after a bride on her departure for a new home, symbolizing that the parents gave up all right of dominion over their daughter.

Q. How did the custom of having surnames begin? J. U.

A. Surnames originated in various ways. Originally individuals were only known by their Christian names, then certain distinguishing names began to be added. Some surnames are descriptive of the place of residence of some ancestor; others refer to some peculiarity either in character or dress. It is believed by authorities on the subject that surnames came to be adopted in England about the year 1000 A.D., coming mainly from Normandy. After Henry II in 1160 had enfranchised the land, hereditary names became common and were used more generally. Surnames were used prior to this time to a limited extent in Rome and Greece. In this case, family or clan names were hereditary, whereas surnames remained individual. Surnames were legally recognized in England by the Statute of Additions, passed during the reign of Henry V.

Q. *What is the origin of the ceremony on board ship when the equator is crossed?* A. R.

A. The ceremony that takes place on board ship on crossing the equator is known as crossing the line, and is performed for those who have never crossed the equator before. It is a very ancient practice and was probably begun as a worship of some deity. The Greeks sacrificed on nearly every prominent cape. During the Middle Ages the ceremony of receiving a visit from Neptune had come into prominence. It was not performed at the equator, but on arriving in the tropics, crossing the Arctic Circle, etc. It is not mentioned in connection with any of the voyages of Columbus but in 1529 the French created a sort of order of knighthood known as Chevaliers de la Mer.

Q. *Why was the custom of driving on the right side of the road established in America?* J. F. E.

A. Gould in his "Right and Left-Handedness" is of the opinion that it is due to the fact that the earliest colonists were not preponderatingly English. Among the first Puritan settlers there were many Dutch and to them France added her complement. They were from the continent where the custom of passing to the right had long been prevalent. During the early period of colonization, the people were accustomed to traveling afoot and even in England it was customary for pedestrians to go to the right while vehicles went to the left. This custom of going to the right probably became fairly well established in America before vehicles were used to any great extent. When large wagons or schooners came into use, the driver being right-handed sat upon the near wheel-horse. He therefore sat on the right to operate the brake with his right hand or foot. This was important in traveling over hilly country or ungraded roads. It can thus readily be seen that under these various influences the custom of going right at all times became firmly established.

Q. *Why are after-dinner-toasts and toastmasters so called?* C. F.

A. The custom of drinking to health and success to undertakings at banquets dates back to the invasion of the Romans. The word toast appears to have originated from the practice of putting bits of toast in the wine, the guests partaking of such a sippet with the draught of wine as soon as the felicitation had passed the lips.

Q. *Why is rice showered on newly married couples?* J. P.

A. The custom comes from India, rice being with the Hindus an emblem of fecundity.

Q. *When was the wedding ring first used?* M. J. N.

A. The origin of the wedding ring is unknown. The Egyptians were probably the first to use rings and in their hieroglyphics a circle represents eternity. The Romans used a plain iron ring which was placed upon the finger of the bride by the bridegroom. Among the Anglo-Saxons the groom gave a pledge or wed to the bride at the betrothal and this pledge was a ring placed on the right hand. It was worn on the right hand until the wedding when it was changed to the other. It is recorded that the wedding ring was used by Christians as early as 860 A.D.

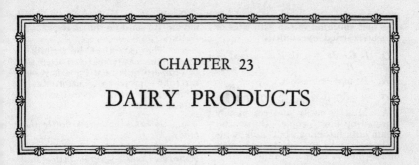

CHAPTER 23

DAIRY PRODUCTS

Q. How many children of today get enough milk? P. N.

A. At the White House Conference on Child Health it was reported that only 57 per cent of the American children have enough milk each day, 3½ per cent have none at all, and the other 39½ per cent have far too little.

Q. Is more cream used on Sundays than on week days? B. P.

A. It depends somewhat on the location of the consumer. The average American family uses three times as much cream on Sunday, but less milk. At Christmas and Thanksgiving three or four times as much cream is used.

Q. Will cows give more milk if milked three times a day instead of twice? H. S. D.

A. Such a milking schedule produces more milk. In observed cases the increase has been from 10 to 25 per cent.

Q. Was there ever a cow with a window in its stomach? D. C. N.

A. The cow with the so-called window in her stomach is dead. She belonged to Pennsylvania State College whose veterinarian cut an opening into the rumen or largest stomach. When healed a rubber stopper was inserted to close the opening. Through this window samples of food could be taken out at any time for chemical analysis and the processes of digestion studied. The cow's death was said to be natural and not caused by this experimental work upon her.

Q. What causes the holes in Swiss cheese? F. W. S.

A. After the salting process, the Swiss cheeses are placed in a room at about 70° F., in which the typical fermentation produces gas holes or eyes due to the development of certain anaerobic bacteria, during a period of about two weeks. The finished product appears on the market with the cut surface showing eyes one-half inch or more in diameter.

Q. When were glass milk bottles first used in the United States? G. C. G.

A. The Bureau of Dairy Industry says that milk was first sold in glass containers in the year 1878 in Brooklyn, N. Y. A product known as the common sense bottle appeared in 1889. It was very similar to that used today.

Q. What is ghee? N. D.

A. This is a kind of clarified butter used in India and other Eastern countries. It is prepared from milk of buffaloes or cows, and after a certain process, put into closed pots, where it is said to keep for years.

Q. How old is the trade of buttermaking? T. I.

A. Butter-making was known for at least two thousand years prior to the beginning of the Christian Era. It was used as a medicine and as an ointment for bathing. Sometimes it was burned in lamps in place of oil. The first churning was in skin bags or pouches carried by animals.

Q. *Is Grade A milk Pasteurized or raw?* J. H.

A. It may be either.

Q. *Is milk fattening?* C. T.

A. Milk is easily and completely digested by most people. Butter and cream are fattening, but milk adds little weight to the adult, if the rest of the diet is correctly adjusted.

Q. *How is Pennsylvania Pot Cheese made?* F. A.

A. It is made from fresh curd prepared by breaking up and heating the curd of sour, clabbered milk. When cooled sufficiently the curd is placed in a receptacle and allowed to stand for three or four days until it has become colored throughout. It is then put into a kettle over a fire; salt, milk, and usually caraway seed are added, and the whole is stirred vigorously until it becomes of the consistency of thick molasses, or until it strings when a spoon is withdrawn from it. The mass can then be put into molds to remain until it becomes cool, or placed in a vessel for keeping. It gets hard with cooling and will retain the shape of the mold.

Q. *At what age does a cow produce the maximum amount of milk?* M. K.

A. A cow matures in milk production in six years and produces the maximum amount of milk in from six to ten years. A cow in good health may live fifteen or twenty years, or even longer, but her usefulness usually begins to wane when she passes the age of twelve or thirteen.

Q. *How cold should a refrigerator be in order that milk will keep well?* D. A.

A. The Bureau of Home Economics says that a temperature of 45° F. or below is desirable. If the milk is to be used within 24 hours, a temperature of 50° F. is satisfactory.

Q. *What is in buttermilk which makes it suitable for babies?* M. E. B.

A. The casein of buttermilk is often more easily digested than that of ordinary milk, and for this reason, carefully prepared buttermilk is sometimes a food of special value for babies and invalids.

Q. *Do other countries bottle their milk?* F. H. S.

A. Mexico and South American countries bottle very little milk. England and Canada use many bottles similar to ours. Germany bottles little milk, but some European countries use bottles.

Q. *What minerals are present in milk?* T. T.

A. Mineral constituents of milk that are especially important to the body are phosphorus, iron, and lime.

Q. *What is the fuel value of whole milk and buttermilk?* A. G. G.

A. Whole milk contains 315 calories per pound, and buttermilk contains 160.

Q. *Are there more germs in cream than in milk?* P. S.

A. Germs (bacteria) in milk rise with the cream, and when cream is separated from milk, 60 per cent of all the germs will be found in the cream. Therefore, it is wise to buy pasteurized cream, or scald raw cream.

Q. *Give the origin of the Ice Cream Sundae.* D. S. C.

A. In the soda parlor of E. C. Berners at Two Rivers, Wis., over 50 years ago the clerk sold a dish of vanilla ice cream and set it before a boy named George Hallaner. The boy had a great idea. He saw a bottle of chocolate syrup which was used for chocolate sodas. "Put some of that chocolate syrup over the ice cream," the boy suggested. This astonished the owner of the soda parlor, but he did what the boy asked. Not only the boy, but other customers liked it, and the dessert became popular. The only difficulty was the expense of giving both the chocolate syrup and the ice cream. Other dealers protested. So it was decided to sell this dessert for a nickel only on Sunday. Some days later a little girl came into the store. She wanted ice cream "with stuff on it," she said. The proprietor explained that he served it only on Sunday. "Then it must be Sunday because I want that kind," insisted the child. And because of the child's demand, soon all the ice cream parlors in that vicinity were calling the new dish a "Sundae."

Q. Is it true that cows give more milk than formerly? A. F. H.

A. A hundred years ago the best cows did not give to exceed 2000 pounds of milk a year, whereas the best dairies today average 5000 pounds per cow.

Q. How should butter be stored for winter use? W. S.

A. The Department of Agriculture says that Pasteurized sweet cream should be used, churned at a low temperature, and the butter washed so that it will be firm and waxy. Rolls or prints of butter should be wrapped in parchment butter paper, placed in a stone crock, and covered with strong brine. Butter should be stored in as cool a place as is available and in place free from odors likely to be absorbed by the butter.

Q. What is meant by loose milk? D. K.

A. The term is applied to milk which is not sold in sealed bottles—milk which is sold from large containers.

Q. How long should the milk fed to a baby be kept hot in a thermos bottle? E. M. G.

A. The Division of Dairy Industry says that milk fed to babies should never be heated and kept in a thermos bottle. It is suggested, however, that two thermos bottles,

one filled with very hot water and the other with the proper baby formula, be used. At feeding time the water in the thermos bottle should be poured off into a saucepan and the milk poured into the hot thermos. The bottle can then be placed into the saucepan of hot water. This is the only satisfactory way to heat a baby formula.

Q. Is there a test which shows whether milk has been watered? W. L. F.

A. The regular Babcock test for determining the amount of fat in milk checked by the test of specific gravity will successfully indicate whether milk has been watered or not. Watered milk will obviously have a considerably lesser content of fat and its specific gravity will likewise be altered.

Q. How far can milk be shipped by railroad and received in good condition? J. C.

A. The distance milk can be shipped by railroad and received in good condition, depends upon the quality of milk shipped and the temperature maintained during shipment. It is possible to ship from San Francisco, Calif., to New York City. The same answer applies to the refrigerator car. High-grade milk maintained at a temperature of 40° F. will keep a week in the modern refrigerator car with little change in quality.

Q. Is there more than one name for hand cheese? M. O. S.

A. Hand cheese is so named because originally it was molded by hand into its final shape. It is a sour-milk cheese, very popular among German races, and manufactured in many countries. There are many local names for hand cheeses, among which are the following: Thuringia Caraway cheese; Ihlefeld, made in Mecklenburg; Livlander, made in Russia; Olmutzer Bierkase; Dresdener Bierkase; Satz, made in Saxony; Tyrol sour cheese; Berliner Kuhkase; and Alt Kuhkase.

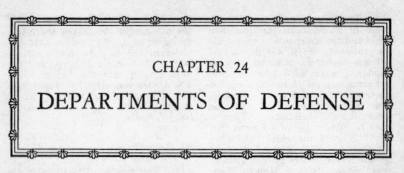

CHAPTER 24

DEPARTMENTS OF DEFENSE

Q. *What does it cost the Government to maintain an individual soldier for a year?* M. G.

A. During the fiscal year 1930, the average cost to the United States Government to maintain each of its soldiers was $724.14. This estimate is based on pay, subsistence, clothing, and medical care.

Q. *How fast does the Army travel under its own locomotion?* D. A.

A. The average number of miles per hour which a regiment of infantry, cavalry, or field artillery fully equipped travels is as follows: Infantry, 2½ miles; cavalry, 4 miles at walk, 8 miles at trot, or 6 miles per hour average; field artillery, 4 miles per hour.

Q. *What does the United States pay for battleships, cruisers, destroyers, and submarines?* L. K.

A. Battleships cost about $27,000,-000; cruisers, $12,500,000; destroyers, $1,750,000; and submarines, $5,600,-000.

Q. *What is the largest ship in the United States Navy?* R. J. D.

A. The U.S.S. Saratoga, airplane carrier, is the flag ship of the Carrier Division, and is the largest ship of the United States Navy.

Q. *When was the first order issued that the hair of the soldiers of the American Army should be cut short?* R. K.

A. In 1801 Brigadier General James Wilkinson ordered that the hair be cut short and also that the whiskers should not be lower than the bottom of the ear. The order regarding whiskers was rescinded in 1853 and the cadets at West Point alone compelled to be clean shaven.

Q. *What was the first organized army in the history of the world?* V. M. S.

A. Historians say that Egypt was the first country to have a military organization. Sesostris or Rameses III was the first military organizer of Egypt (1620 B.C.). Palamedes in 1193 B.C. was the first to form an army in a regular line of battle. The first guards and regular troops of a standing army were formed by Saul in 1093 B.C.

Q. *Is there any person living who collects a pension from the War of 1812?* K. K.

A. On December 11, 1932, there were seven women receiving pensions as the result of service of husbands or fathers in the War of 1812.

Q. *Why are the Marines so called?* A. C.

A. The word is derived from the old French word marin, meaning sea soldier. The United States Marine Corps is an independent branch of the military service, and though under the direction of the Navy Department, may be detailed by order of the President for service with the Army. The duties assigned to the Marine Corps are to garrison the Navy Yards and Naval Stations and

150

the defenses erected for their protection. To furnish all battleships and cruisers and other vessels, when necessary, a detachment for guard duty and also to assist in the handling of the ships' guns. A mobile force is always held in readiness at the Marine Barracks as the first line for foreign service when the occasion may arise.

Q. What does it cost the United States to fire one of its 16-inch guns, its 14-inch, 12-inch, and 6-inch? W. C. B.

A. The cost per round for the 16-inch gun is $2030.10; 14-inch gun, $1345.68; 12-inch gun, $962.25; 6-inch gun, $104.64.

Q. Is the use of gases in warfare a recent development? F. P. I.

A. Many efforts have been made in the past to use various gases—chiefly sulphur dioxide—in warfare. As early as 431 B.C. the Spartans, in besieging the cities of Belium and Platea, burned pitch and sulphur under the walls of these cities in order to break down their defense by suffocation of the troops of the cities.

Q. When branding was practised as a form of punishment in the Army what part of the body was branded? V. P.

A. For many years when branding was used in the Army as a punishment for desertion, the letter D was marked on the left side of a deserter two inches below the armpit. It was not, properly speaking, branded on his side, but marked with ink, gunpowder, or some other substance which would leave a stain that could not be obliterated without destroying the skin at the part. This practice has been abolished.

Q. When was a powder horn a part of the equipment of our Army? E. R.

A. A powder horn was part of the equipment which a colonial militiaman was required to have at hand for service at a moment's warning. Requirement was continued by Act of

Congress May 8, 1792. The requirement was not repealed until 1820, and the use of the powder horn was continued until during the Mexican War in 1847.

Q. When was the first practical machine gun made? L. A.

A. The first modern practical machine gun was invented by Dr. Gatling of Chicago in 1862, and it was put into general use about 1870.

Q. What color is a dishonorable discharge from the National Guard? W. B. S.

A. The various discharges from the National Guard are the same color as the Regular Service: Honorable discharge, white; discharge without honor, blue; dishonorable discharge, yellow.

Q. What is the largest number of Marines that the United States has had in Nicaragua at one time? How many have been killed? E. B.

A. During the American occupation in Nicaragua, there were at the peak, July 11, 1928, 5365 Marines and 456 Naval Officers and men. Twenty-seven Marines were killed, 15 died of wounds, and 59 were wounded, but not fatally.

Q. Who calls out the National Guard? Who orders it to appear in processions? F. B. M.

A. The Governor of a State is the only one who has the authority to call out the National Guard. National Guard units often voluntarily offer to walk in parades and such public administrations, but they cannot be commanded to do so except by the Governor.

Q. How many colored regiments are there in the United States Army? N. S.

A. There are four.

Q. What is the life of a big gun? W. H. P.

A. The Department of War says that the life of a big gun is 200 to 500 rounds. This does not mean, however, that the gun is absolutely worthless after 500 rounds, only that it has to be relined. A big gun would be considered a 14- or 16-inch gun.

Q. *Is it true that thousands of soldiers deserted from the American Army while in France?* J. H. S.

A. Among more than 2,000,000 men who went overseas there were but approximately 1200 deserters.

Q. *How long ago did our Army stop shooting men who were sentenced to death by court martial?* R. J. M.

A. The practice was discontinued about the time of the Civil War.

Q. *Are guns fired at sunrise and sunset at our army posts?* I. W. P.

A. A gun is fired at sunset at all United States military forts when the flag is lowered at retreat. No gun is fired at sunrise.

Q. *Can an enlisted man purchase his discharge from the Army? If so, what does it cost?* K. S.

A. In time of peace, in certain situations and conditions, discharges are thus allowed. Length of service and place stationed enter into the price which ranges from $15 for a Philippine Scout after 11 years' service to $170 after one year's service in the Philippines or China. Sometimes part of the payment is waived, when the authorities find it justifiable.

Q. *What percentage of our recruits for service in the World War was illiterate?* J. D. O.

A. Of the whole army about 25 per cent was illiterate.

Q. *Where are United States Army proving grounds located?* L. M.

A. The Army proving grounds are at Aberdeen, Md.; Port Clinton, Ohio; and Savanna, Ill.

Q. *When was the Naval Academy established?* C. E.

A. The United States Naval Academy at Annapolis, Maryland, was established in 1845, by a special act of Congress. The origin of this technical educational institution was due primarily to the efforts of George Bancroft, Secretary of the Navy.

Q. *After what length of service can an Army officer retire?* N. W. G.

A. An officer cannot retire at his own request with less than thirty years' service. It is compulsory that he retire at the age of 64.

Q. *What is the name of the school in France which corresponds to West Point?* J. M.

A. Saint Cyr is the French Military Academy. France also maintains other supplementary military schools.

Q. *Why are Army recruits called rookies?* G. M. C.

A. They are so named from the term "rookery" which in English military slang refers to the quarters in the barracks occupied by subalterns.

Q. *Please give an estimate of the cost of World War Veterans Rehabilitation, including bonus.* D. R. C.

A. The United States Veteran Bureau has expended a total of $5,589,-358,342 for the relief of veterans, their dependents and beneficiaries. Of this amount $925,599,616 has been disbursed from allotments deducted from service men's pay and from insurance premiums. In addition to these disbursements, to May 9, 1931, the Bureau has made loans direct to veterans on their adjusted service certificates, amounting to approximately $977,000,000.

Q. *How many torpedoes are necessary to sink a modern battleship?* A. T.

A. Usually four or five are required.

Q. *What is the origin of the name for the Sam Browne Belts?* G. C.

A. General Samuel Joseph Browne was an English officer prominent in the early Indian Campaigns and the Indian Mutiny. He served in India throughout the Great Indian Mutiny and Sepoy Wars, during which he was twice wounded and lost an arm at the Battle of Seeporah, which nearly cost him his life. It was the loss of his arm which caused him to devise a new sort of saber belt, which was later generally adopted by the British Army, and also by other military forces. This is the belt, which with some modification, is to-day known as the "Sam Browne" in the United States Army. The proper designation of the word, according to the War Department, is "Belt, Officers Model, 1921."

Q. How many doctors were there in the Medical Corps of the United States Army during the World War? O. H.

A. At one time there were 30,-591 commissioned doctors in the Medical Corps.

Q. When were headstones first furnished by the Government for soldier's graves? J. A. J.

A. Under Act of Congress, March 3, 1873, the Secretary of War was authorized to furnish suitable headstones for soldiers, sailors and marines, buried in national cemeteries. By an Act of Congress passed in 1879, the order was extended to those who were buried in private, village, and city cemeteries.

Q. Why are an officer's boots hung over the saddle of his horse, heels forward, in the funeral procession? J. F. N.

A. It indicates that it is the officer's last march and that the end of his earthly journey has been reached.

Q. Can compensation and insurance claims of World War veterans be litigated? F. S. A.

A. The Veterans Administration says that compensation claims may not be litigated. The judgment of the Administrator is final. Insurance claims can be litigated under Section 19 of the World War Veteran's Act. However, if a veteran is dissatisfied with the Regional Rating Board's decision, he may appeal the case to the Board of Review at the Administrative Board of Appeals in Washington, D. C. The time limit for appealing the case is one year from the date of filing claim.

Q. How many veterans are treated without cost in government hospitals for disabilities not connected with their service? C. M. L.

A. In the fiscal year ending June 30, 1931, there were 99,123 veterans treated for non-service connected disabilities at an expense to the Government of $22,756,459.81.

Q. Why do sailors wear flaring trousers? G. E.

A. Sailors wear bell-bottom trousers in order that they may be easily rolled up when scrubbing the decks or when wading in the water.

Q. Why were the American soldiers called Sammy? G. A. F.

A. Various stories are told as to the origin of this nickname. One of the most plausible is that when the United States troops disembarked in France the French children called, "Ce sont les amis! Ce sont les amis!" To the unaccustomed ears of the marching Americans it sounded as though the children were calling out "Sammy! Sammy!" and they took it to mean themselves.

Q. How does the amount of money spent by the United States Government for veterans' relief compare with a like expenditure in other countries? B. M.

A. The appropriations of our Government exceed those of all other countries combined. The men mobilized in this country totaled 4,-355,000, while the armies of Germany, France, Great Britain, Italy and Canada totaled 34,244,636.

Q. How many sailors are there on a battleship? F. C. W.

A. There are approximately 1400 sailors on a battleship.

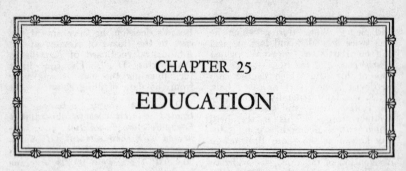

CHAPTER 25

EDUCATION

Q. *What was the first educational endowment in America?* **D. T.**

A. The bequeathing of 250 acres of land, an adjacent salt marsh, and eight milk cows comprised the first educational endowment in America. It was left by Benjamin Symmes to found a free school in Elizabeth County, Virginia. Mr. Symmes died in 1634.

Q. *Please give a brief and comprehensive definition of education.* **T. H. R.**

A. One of the prize winning definitions of education published in the Forum is as follows: Education is the knowledge, acquired through the systematic and harmonious cultivation of one's natural powers, which gives one the ability to adjust himself satisfactorily to his physical and intellectual environment.

Q. *What per cent of the people of the United States have a college education?* **H. R. A.**

A. The Office of Education says that one person in 72 of the total population for 1930 has been graduated from a college. One person in 16 of the total population has been graduated from high school and not from college.

Q. *What is the oldest scholarship in the United States?* **E. A.**

A. Harvard University offers the oldest scholarship in the United States, according to data gathered by Miss Ella B. Ratcliffe of the Office of Education. This scholarship, given

by Lady Mowlson of London, England, was established in 1643.

Q. *How long does it take an illiterate adult to learn to write?* **R. D.**

A. In the Moonlight Schools, there were few mountain women who could not write a simple letter after three weeks' instruction. Many learned in less time.

Q. *How rapidly can one take stenographic dictation?* **J. R. M.**

A. A record was made by Charles L. Swem, who wrote at the rate of 282 words a minute with 99.29% accuracy.

Q. *Is there a college in Alaska?* **R. J. A.**

A. The Alaska Agricultural College and School of Mines is at Fairbanks, Alaska. It is probably the farthest northern college of the world.

Q. *How is the school problem met in the sparsely settled districts of Canada?* **M. McD.**

A. A Canadian Pacific railway passenger car has been converted into a complete schoolroom and teacher's home and serves a limited district. It brings education to the children of railway section men and others not in organized school districts. The car is stationed at a place for two or three days, where it receives pupils from several miles around, before leaving for the next point, and the teacher gives the children lessons to work out at home before his return. The car contains schoolroom, teacher's bedroom, dining room and kitchen, bookcases, blackboards and maps.

Q. *Do boys study home economics? F. H. C.*

A. It is estimated by the Bureau of Education that over 7000 high school boys are taking courses in home economics.

Q. *What university is the southern-most in the world? L. S.*

A. Otago University, Dunedin, New Zealand, has this distinction.

Q. *What is the largest foundation in the United States? A. F.*

A. The Carnegie Corporation of New York is the largest, with a capital of $159,860,783. The Rockefeller Foundation is second with a capital of $147,373,921.

Q. *Who was the first college president in the United States? M. M. R.*

A. In 1638, the regular course of academic studies at Harvard began, degrees being conferred four years after. Nathaniel Eaton, with the title of master or professor, was the first in charge. He was appointed in 1637, but two years later was dismissed from the institution and was followed by Rev. Henry Dunster, the first college executive in the United States to bear the title of president.

Q. *Has the school which Henry Ford attended as a boy been opened? N. K. L.*

A. The Old Scotch Settlement School at which Mr. Ford was a pupil in his childhood has been reopened as a part of the Ford Historical Museum. It is reported that the first thing Ford did after the opening exercises was to carve his name on the desk where he sat years ago.

Q. *What is the Rockefeller Foundation? J. L. E.*

A. It is a philanthropic trust, incorporated by Act of New York Legislature of May 14, 1913. The purpose is "To promote the well-being of mankind throughout the world," through charitable, religious, missionary, and educational activities, as well as through research and publications. The Foundation offers fellowships in graduate medicine and public health. In granting the Rockefeller fellowships individual cases are dealt with as there is no established system of granting them and no public announcement is made.

Q. *What is probably the oldest free school in continuous operation in the United States? A. B.*

A. A school built by George Washington in 1785 and still in use by the public school system of Alexandria, Va. Robert E. Lee was a pupil in the school from 1818 to 1824.

Q. *Where is the oldest university in the western hemisphere? D. M. G.*

A. Lima, Peru, claims the oldest university in the western hemisphere, the University of San Marcos, which was founded in 1551.

Q. *What scholarship was awarded the boy who discovered Pluto? J. M.*

A. Clyde Tombaugh, discoverer of the new planet, was given the Edwin Emory Slosson $500 scholarship in science. Almost entirely self-educated, Tombaugh has been honored by the Royal Astronomical Society of Great Britain for his discovery and is now on the staff of Mount Wilson Observatory at Pasadena, Calif.

Q. *Please give some information about the school built by the President near his summer camping place. K. H.*

A. The President Herbert Hoover Community School was built upon privately owned land, which was donated for the purpose of erecting the school. It was equipped by Mr. and Mrs. Hoover with the money donated by them and their friends. It is located at Criglersville, Virginia.

Q. *When was the first school for delinquent girls established?* R. I. K.

A. The first school in the United States for girls only was established at Lancaster, Mass., in 1854.

Q. *Do all colleges give the same examinations to pre-medical students?* J. R.

A. The examinations are not always the same, as each school can make its own individual requirements. George Washington University uses the College Entrance Board examination and says that a number of schools do use this same examination.

Q. *What are the aims of the Daniel Guggenheim Fund for the Promotion of Aeronautics?* C. M.

A. Its general purposes may be broadly defined as follows: To promote aeronautical education both in higher institutions of learning and among the general public; to assist in the extension of fundamental aeronautical science; to assist in the development of commercial aircraft and aircraft equipment; to further the application of aircraft in business, industry, and other economic and social activities of the Nation.

Q. *How is a person's intelligence quotient figured?* A. J.

A. The intelligence quotient or I. Q. of a person is determined by multiplying the mental age by 100 and dividing by the actual age. Thus the intelligence quotient of a normal person is 100. A person with an I. Q. below 80 is rated as subnormal, while one with an I. Q. above 120 is rated as gifted.

Q. *What is the purpose of the Juilliard Musical Foundation? Where is it located?* M. R. B.

A. Its object is to promote the interests of music by aiding exceptional students through the granting of scholarships and fellowships as well as assisting selected musical en-

terprises of national significance by means of money grants. The address is 49 East 52nd St., New York, N. Y.

Q. *What per cent of the national income is expended for education?* S. S.

A. The cost of public elementary and secondary education is 2.4 per cent of the total national income.

Q. *How is the Office of Education divided into departments?* V. W.

A. The following is a partial list: Administration; Research and Investigation (a) Colleges, (b) American School Systems, (c) Foreign School Systems, (d) Special Problems, (e) Statistical; Editorial; Library; Service; General Surveys.

Q. *How long has dentistry been taught in special schools?* H. N. S.

A. Among the ancients the desire to preserve teeth, to retain loose teeth, and to disguise dental disfigurement gave birth to the art of dentistry. Until well into the 19th century apprenticeship afforded the only means of acquiring a knowledge of dentistry, but in November, 1840, the Baltimore College of Dentistry was established. This was the first college in the world for the systematic education of dentists. The charter of the Baltimore College of Dental Surgery specified that there should be at least one annual term of instruction, of not less than four months in length. The first academic year opened on November 3, 1840, with five students; instruction was continued until the latter part of February, and the first class of two students graduated on March 9, 1841.

Q. *What is the Cranbrook Foundation?* C. K.

A. The Cranbrook Foundation is an educational center for boys established in 1927 by George G. Booth, newspaper publisher of Detroit, and his wife. It comprises five schools and a church on his country estate, 12 miles north of Detroit. The estate contains 225 acres, of which all but that portion devoted to the home of Mr. and Mrs. Booth was conveyed to the foundation. The total outlay involves approximately $10,000,000.

Q. What college received a collection of original Browning autograph letters? T. T. M.

A. Wellesley College has such a collection which contains 284 letters from Robert Browning and 287 from Elizabeth Barrett Browning.

Q. Is there a school in Florida where the students have some classes under water? A. T. C.

A. At the University of Miami students of marine biology have laboratory work under water. Specially constructed boats with glass bottoms are used to make trips to the marine gardens where the students can see how the creatures that live in the ocean exist. On these expeditions the attire consists of bathing suits and shoes and a diving helmet. The necessary supply of oxygen is supplied by means of pumps on the boat.

Q. In what language are the schools in Russia conducted? L. B. F.

A. In the teaching in various schools throughout the country a total of seventy national tongues is used. Out of every 1000 pupils 624 are taught in the Russian language, 175 in Ukranian, 36 in White Russian, 27 in Tartar, 19 in Georgian, 14 in Armenian, 10 in Azerbaijan-Turkish, 9 in Uzbek; the rest scattered.

Q. What is the name and scope of the institution in Germany which took Lenin's brain for scientific study? G. L.

A. It is the Kaiser Wilhelm Institute for Brain Research in Buch. The Institute is administered by the Kaiser Wilhelm Association for the Advancement of Science, founded in 1911 to foster scientific research dissociated from the encumbrance of university teaching. This organization sponsors some thirty research institutes in addition to the Institute for Theoretical Physics, headed by Einstein.

Q. Where in the East is there a college giving a course in personality? R. E.

A. The School of Commerce, Accounts and Finance of New York University, New York City, offers such a course. It is designed primarily for business men and women.

Q. Why was the Carlisle Indian School discontinued? M. B.

A. The Indian Office says that the Carlisle Indian School was originally an old army post which the War Department turned over for a school in the East for Indians about 1880. The agreement was that when needed the Indian Office would give back the post to the War Department. This was done in the latter part of the war and the school was used for rehabilitation work. The date was December 21, 1918.

Q. Is there a place where a boy can borrow money to help him get a college education? J. E. B.

A. Student Loan Funds have been established by privately endowed societies, by associations, by States, and by large denominations, so that a deserving student will have no trouble in obtaining a loan to pay or help pay his college expenses. The Office of Education has published a bulletin on self help for college students which contains a complete list of sources of loans, and information in general on this subject.

Q. Please describe the school system at the Lawrenceville School. D. W.

A. It is an American college preparatory school at Lawrenceville, New Jersey. It was originally founded in 1810, but refounded in 1882, when the house system was adopted. In scope it corresponds to such English schools as Harrow and

Rugby and has about 400 pupils and about 36 masters. There are 13 masters' houses, with an Upper House and the Hamill House for the boys of the upper form, managed by boards of directors appointed by the boys themselves.

Q. *Which university has a fund for research on venereal disease?* W. L.

A. The University of Chicago has the A. B. Kuppenheimer Fund of one million dollars for that purpose.

Q. *When did William and Mary College become coeducational?* F. F.

A. Young women were admitted upon equal terms with young men at William and Mary College for the first time in September, 1918.

Q. *After whom was McGill University, Canada's leading institution of learning, named?* B. S.

A. James McGill was born in Scotland in 1744. He came to Canada in 1770 and entered the fur trade. He accumulated a fortune as a merchant, became a member of Parliament, and was a brigadier general in the War of 1812 against the United States. He died in 1813 leaving a will providing for the establishment of The Royal Institution for the Advancement of Learning. This official name has given place to the name of McGill University.

Q. *What is the heuristic method?* J. A.

A. Heuristic is derived from the Greek heuretikos meaning ingenious. Heuristic method is one which incites the pupil to find out things for himself and use his own initiative.

Q. *Does it interfere with a boy's scholarship for him to work his way through college?* T. H. M.

A. A survey by Datus C. Smith, Jr., director of student employment at Princeton, shows that undergraduates working their way through that university win more than their proportionate share of Phi Beta Kappa memberships. While one-fifth of the members of the junior and senior classes in one year were actively engaged in remunerative work, one-fourth of those elected that year to Phi Beta Kappa were registered with the student employment section. Twenty-two per cent of the honors awarded for excellent scholarship went to students who were making all or a great part of their college expenses.

Q. *What should a person study in college who is interested in journalism?* M. B. S.

A. A curriculum in journalism usually consists of two groups of courses. Subjects for background are English, history, economics, government, science, language, philosophy, psychology, and technical subjects such as reporting, copy reading, editorial writing, newspaper management, feature writing, law of the press, and history of American journalism.

Q. *What constitutes an educated man?* D. L. H.

A. Wm. H. Danforth selected the following from "The Marks of an Educated Man": "An educated man cultivates the open mind; never laughs at new ideas; knows the secret of getting along with other people; cultivates the habit of success; knows as a man thinketh, so is he; knows popular notions are always wrong; always listens to the man who knows; links himself with a great cause; builds an ambition picture to fit his abilities; keeps busy at his highest natural level; knows it is never too late to learn; never loses faith in the man he might have been; achieves the masteries that make him a world citizen; and lives a great religious life."

Q. *How does one secure a teaching position in the Detached Territories?* D. B. B.

A. Application for teaching positions in the Detached Territories should be made to the following offices: Alaska, Department of Interior, Washington, D. C.; Hawaii, Superintendent of Public Instruction, Honolulu, Hawaii; Panama Canal Zone, Panama Canal, Washington, D. C.; Philippine Service, Civil Service Commission, F at 7th St., N. W., Washington, D. C.; Porto Rico, Chief of the Bureau of Insular Affairs, Washington, D. C.; Virgin Islands, Governor of the Virgin Islands, St. Thomas, Virgin Islands.

Q. What is meant by "education on the instalment plan"? K. S.

A. It is a plan by which the school and college expenses are collected monthly from the parents by a funding corporation, which turns the sums over to the colleges. In this way the payments are distributed throughout the school year.

Q. What is the purpose of the Leopold Schepp Foundation? F. B.

A. It is to encourage the best impulses in a boy's life; to help in a substantial way those who wish to make the most of their opportunities. The foundation invites boys of 13, 14, and 15 years of age to sign the required pledge to abstain from gambling and drinking, provided it is their honest intention to keep the pledge faithfully for three years, when they will be entitled to receive the sum of $200 each. The foundation awards five annual scholarships to boys and the income of $1,000,000 for scholarships for girls.

Q. When and by whom was Wellesley College founded? W. M.

A. Wellesley was founded by Henry Fowle Durant, a Boston lawyer, with the announced purpose "of giving to young women opportunities for education equivalent to those usually provided in colleges for young men." The first charter was granted by the Commonwealth of Massachusetts on March 17, 1870, under the name of Wellesley Female Seminary. This name was changed to Wellesley College by act of legislature, March 7, 1873.

Q. What kind of a school is the Massachusetts Nautical School? W. E. G.

A. The Massachusetts Nautical School is a state training school for American Merchant Marine officers. It was established in 1892.

Q. What became of the money which George Washington willed to endow a university in the District of Columbia? L. E. G.

A. In his will he left fifty shares of stock in the Potomac (Canal) Company for the endowment of a university to be established in the District of Columbia "to which the youth of fortune and talents from all parts thereof might be sent for the completion of their Education in all the branches of polite literature;— in arts and Sciences,—in acquiring knowledge in the principles of Politics & good Government." In furtherance of that hope and project of the first President of the United States, Columbian College, now named George Washington University, was established. The stock which General Washington willed toward such an institution became valueless owing to the failure of the canal properties, and it was necessary for "the College," established in the District of Columbia, to obtain funds from other sources.

Q. Are Indian students admitted free to Dartmouth College? E. G.

A. Boys of predominantly Indian blood who have succeeded in meeting the entrance requirements and have been selected for admission to Dartmouth College are given free tuition.

Q. What is the name of the school in Alabama which has neither grades nor promotions? R. L. M.

A. The School of Organic Education at Fairhope, Alabama, is organized along such lines. It was begun twenty-five years ago as an experiment by Mrs. Marietta Johnson, who developed it according to her belief that education is life, and a school program should be life-giving to the body as well as mind. No standards are set up to measure a child's achievements in this curriculum, consequently there are no grades, marks, or promotions.

Q. *What is a book machine?* L. G.

A. It is a typewriter so arranged that typing may be done in a book.

Q. *When were kindergartens started?* E. S.

A. The kindergarten was suggested and organized by Frederich Froebel, a German educationalist, around the middle of the 19th century. The first kindergarten was opened by Froebel in the year 1840 in the village of Blakenburg in the Thuringian Forest. The pioneer movement for the establishment of kindergartens in the United States was led by Miss Elizabeth Peabody of Boston, who on becoming interested in Froebel's writings, went to Germany in 1867 to study his system. The first public kindergarten was opened in Boston in 1870, but shortly abandoned. The first permanent successful attempt to make the kindergarten a part of the public school system was begun in St. Louis in 1873 under the leadership of Miss Susan Blow and Dr. W. T. Harris.

Q. *What is the name of the school in New York City in which Mrs. Franklin Roosevelt is interested, and what subjects did she teach?* H. L. D.

A. Mrs. Roosevelt taught history, drama, and English two days each week at the Todhunter School, in New York City.

Q. *Is there a college in which both students and teachers support themselves by other than educational pursuits?* P. C.

A. The Nashville Agricultural Normal Institute at Madison, Tenn., was established nearly twenty-eight years ago with the definite purpose of making it possible for worthy young men and women who have no money to obtain the benefits of a thorough education. The institution has no money endowment and never has had any. Neither has it ever solicited any money either for the purpose of paying teachers' salaries or supporting any student in school. On the contrary it operates a farm of about nine hundred acres and something like 25 or 26 other productive industries, from which faculty and students alike must earn their support. There are over three hundred students in attendance, all of whom have the opportunity of working their way through school and at the same time doing regular college work.

Q. *How is Howard University financed?* G. G.

A. The Federal Government makes annual appropriations toward its upkeep. In addition, there is also income from tuition and other fees, and the university has several endowment funds.

Q. *How much money did William and Mary give for the founding of William and Mary College?* P. M. G.

A. William and Mary College was founded in 1693. An old history of this college says that William gave 2000 pounds toward the building. To the endowment of the college William and Mary also gave 1985 pounds. This money was raised out of quit-rents of the colonies. The quit-rent was the rent paid to the superior by the under person in exchange for his service.

Q. *Why was Dartmouth College given this name?* N. B.

A. Dartmouth College at Hanover, New Hampshire, was the outgrowth of Joshua Moor's Indian Charity School opened by Rev. Eleaser Wheelock at Lebanon, Connecticut, in 1754. A sum of 10,000 pounds was collected in Great Britain and placed in trust. With the endowment Dr. Wheelock decided to extend the sphere of his work and to admit English students. The institution was moved to Hanover in 1785. In the charter the name of Dartmouth College was adopted as a compliment to Lord Dartmouth, who was head of the Board of Trustees in England and took a great interest in the institution.

Q. *Who started the Moonlight Schools?* I. H.

A. The Moonlight Schools in the mountains of Kentucky and Tennessee were established by Mrs. Cora Wilson Stewart. They have done much to reduce illiteracy among the adults of that region.

Q. *Please explain the Union Pacific Scholarships.* G. K.

A. The Union Pacific System offers agricultural scholarships in the following States: California, Montana, Nevada, Nebraska, Kansas, Colorado, Wyoming, Utah, Idaho, Oregon, and Washington. Annual scholarship awards are made to students of agriculture in vocational high schools. A $100 scholarship award and a $50 award are made.

Q. *Does Harvard University limit the size of its freshman class?* L. D. C.

A. The Harvard catalogue says: "It is necessary to restrict the size of the freshman class, but no earnest student of firm resolve should hesitate to apply for admission. Each individual applicant will be cheerfully reviewed by the committee, and much weight attached to the character, personality, and promise of the student, as well as the scholarly attainments."

Q. *How many foreign born children are attending school in the United States?* H. N.

A. In the 1930 Census there were 389,749 school children between the ages of 5 and 20 of foreign birth attending school in the United States.

Q. *What is meant by the honor system of schools?* E. C. D.

A. The honor system as applied to schools is a phase of student gov-ernment whereby the students pledge themselves to handle their own affairs and be responsible for good deportment without the constant attendance of a professor. This is particularly true at examination time, when the students promise not to cheat, even though a professor is not in the room.

Q. *Is the practise of cribbing for examinations a modern practise?* W. A. H.

A. On the contrary a recent silk handkerchief presented to the Field Museum of Natural History, covered with thousands of Chinese characters, was identified as having probably been used as a crib to enable a Chinese student of the Kang-hi period—1562–1722—to pass his civil service examination.

Q. *For what purpose is the Paul Block gift to Yale to be put?* T. G. N.

A. One hundred thousand dollars was given by Mr. Block, prominent newspaper publisher, for a program of studies in the field of journalism leading to the coordination of the newspaper function with courses in economics and the social sciences.

Q. *What is the shield which forms part of the seal of the University of Pennsylvania?* S. D. C.

A. It is, with slight modification, the coat-of-arms of William Penn. The original charters of the University were granted by the Penn family as proprietors of colonial Pennsylvania, and two members of the family were also among the early trustees of the institution.

Q. *Does the R. O. T. C. tend to create a militaristic attitude in students?* E. M.

A. A Study of the Educational Value of Military Instruction in Universities and Colleges shows that more than 10,000 college graduates who completed the R. O. T. C. course in military science and tactics give full recognition to the educational values derived from the course.

Ninety-three and six-tenths per cent of the students attested that the training does not create a militaristic attitude, but that it does furnish graduates with a sense of individual responsibility toward national welfare and security.

Q. What are the duties of a governess? M. A. D.

A. A governess is employed to train and instruct children and frequently to assist in light household duties. Formerly a governess was primarily a teacher, but with the increase in the number of good schools the office has changed to a great extent. When children are attending school the duty of the governess is to accompany them to and from classes, assist in the preparation of lessons, and the care of their wardrobe. In a home where there are children of pre-school age, the governess dresses and feeds the children and supervises their exercise in parks or playgrounds.

Q. What were the ragged schools referred to in English novels? S. E.

A. The Ragged Schools were maintained in Great Britain by voluntary contributions for the education of destitute and neglected children. The idea is said to have originated with John Pounds, a poor cobbler, who used to gather the ragged children in his district and teach them as he worked. With the introduction of the compulsory education act in 1870, their usefulness was largely destroyed and many were merged into the free schools.

Q. Where was the first training school for occupational therapists in the United States? E. J.

A. The first school of this kind established in this or in any other country was the Henry Favill Training School of Chicago. Mrs. Eleanor Clark Slagle was its director.

Q. Does Germany still receive Rhodes Scholarships? S. N.

A. Owing to Germany's action in the European war an act was passed in 1916 cancelling the German scholarships and allowing them to Alberta, Saskatchewan, the Transvaal, the Orange Free State, and to the towns of Kimberley and Port Elizabeth alternately.

Q. What name is given to a college where a student works part of the time and goes to school part of the time? A. H. J.

A. Such colleges are called co-operative.

Q. What college has an Institute of Human Relations? H. B.

A. The Institute of Human Relations was established at Yale University in 1929. It is devoted principally to the study of biology, sociology, psychiatry, and psychology.

Q. When was speedwriting first introduced to the public? N. V. A.

A. It was invented by Emma B. Dearborn, and introduced to the public in 1923 under the name of the Steno Short-Type System.

Q. How did the Rhodes Scholarships originate? G. E. B.

A. John Cecil Rhodes was a South African financier and statesman. He bequeathed the bulk of his great fortune for the endowment of a large number of scholarships at Oxford University, with the intention of bringing about the complete union of the English-speaking races for the peace, enlightenment, and uplift of mankind. He died in March, 1902.

Q. Upon which side of the mortar board should students wear the tassel? E. G.

A. The Collegiate Bureau of Academic Costume says that the tassel should be worn on the left side for the doctor's, master's, and bachelor's degrees and also by students without degrees. There are several colleges that have made a local ruling in accordance with which the students wear the tassel on the right side and upon the conferring of the degree, change it to the left. This is a matter of local concern.

Q. How did the ten Upson Scholarships at Rutgers originate? J. N. U.

A. The Irving S. Upson Scholarships at Rutgers University were established in 1922. They originated through the desire on the part of a number of Alumni to provide aid for worthy young men on the basis of Rhodes' Scholarships. For four years funds were provided by interested Alumni. After that the scholarships were given directly by the University. They are awarded by a Committee of the faculty.

Q. Where did the custom originate of providing undernourished school children with meals? A. D.

A. The feeding of needy children of school age was first started in France by the institution of cantines scolaires. Pioneer work of a similar kind was established at Manchester, Bradford, London, and other large towns in the later years of the 19th century. In the United States, school lunches were primarily intended for children suffering from malnutrition, but of recent years, educational authorities have realized that the provision of proper food for all pupils is now a part of the general educational movement.

Q. How did it come about that graduation exercises were called Commencement? D. L.

A. Originally it was really a commencement as it marked the inception of the pupil graduate as a teacher and his recognition as such by his master and other members of the profession.

Q. Into how many terms is the school year at Oxford University divided? M. C.

A. Into four. Michaelmas term, October 10 to December 17; Hilary or Lent, January 14 to the day before Palm Sunday; Easter term, Wednesday after Easter to Friday before Whitsunday; and Trinity or Act term, from the day before Whitsunday to the Saturday after the first Tuesday in July.

Q. What is the National Home Study Council? M. M.

A. The National Home Study Council is the banding together of the outstanding correspondence schools and several resident schools under fair play standards, to protect ambitious people from deception and imposition, and constantly to advance the standards of home study schools.

Q. Do the students with high scholastic marks or the average students turn out to be more successful financially? C. H.

A. In a study of 809 graduates of the Massachusetts Institute of Technology, it was shown that there is a definite correlation between scholastic ability and success. Taking graduates of the years 1917 to 1929, from the start the money-makers stood out as men of the upper fifth of the class. Three years out of college they averaged $3000 annually, and at ten years $8500. In contrast, the lowest fifth made $1700 at three years and $2400 at ten years.

Q. What is the La Verne Noyes Foundation? H. S.

A. The La Verne Noyes Foundation, established July 5, 1918, at the University of Chicago, provides tuition scholarships for veterans of the World War or their descendants.

Q. Does teaching offer much opportunity as a profession? D. S.

A. The profession of teaching offers a wide variety of opportunity. The teacher may specialize in the instruction to the youngest children, in the kindergarten, in the primary grades, or in the nursery school which is growing both in importance and also in numbers. Since a majority of the nation's children never go into high school the greatest social opportunity for promoting the education of the country lies in the grade schools. Secondary school teaching differs from elementary school teaching in the broader scope of the subject matter taught and in the difference in psychological approach to the adolescent group. College graduates are universally preferred for secondary school teaching. Teaching in special schools offers various opportunities for important service; schools and classes for the deaf, the blind, the crippled, the retarded, the mentally defective, all require teachers of exceptional ability and specialized training.

Q. What colleges have residential quarters for students where the language they are studying is spoken exclusively? E. L. K.

A. The New Jersey College for Women, Wheaton College, Wellesley, and the University of Wisconsin have adopted the language house plan.

Q. What Indian school corresponds to the colleges of the white race? T. H.

A. Haskell Institute most nearly approaches college standards.

Q. How long ago was Antioch College reorganized along its new progressive line of part study and part work? G. E.

A. In 1920, Arthur E. Morgan, president of the college, instituted the new system, and in 1921 the plan was in operation.

Q. What school is owned by P. E. O.? B. K.

A. Cottey Junior College at Nevada, Missouri, is owned and administered by the organization.

Q. Are girls eligible for Rhodes Scholarships? H. E. T.

A. The Scholarships are given to men only.

Q. Are Soviet universities open to foreign students? M. M. T.

A. Soviet universities and educational institutions are open to qualified foreign students, provided they can meet all necessary expenses. However, only a limited number of foreign students are being accomodated, owing to crowded living conditions in the educational centers of the Soviet Union. The Union is not encouraging students to come to Russia.

Q. Does the college for the deaf in Washington, D. C., fit its students for self-support? J. L. L.

A. The Gallaudet College for the Deaf in Washington offers full courses which enable graduate students to be self-supporting. The entrance requirement is high school graduation and the passing of an entrance examination. The course of study extends over five years.

Q. When did modern shorthand come into vogue? V. W.

A. In England modern shorthand originated during Queen Elizabeth's reign. A system was invented by Timothy Bright. Other systems were invented by Thomas Shelton about 1630 and John Byrom in 1767. Most of the early systems were orthographic or alphabetic. The first published system using a phonetic base was that of William Tiffin in 1750.

Q. Why do college seniors wear caps and gowns? N. B.

A. The movement was essentially a student movement to provide a senior badge and to improve the commencement week exercises, take the place of the dress suit, and revive the traditions of a continuing and related university life. It was approved particularly by the students on account of its being uniform, which overcame all differences of dress and made for democracy. It was seen that the gowns added grace and overcame awkwardness in speaking and that the general effect was to make university functions more characteristic, interesting, and impressive to all beholders.

Q. Who is the Superintendent of Schools in Alaska? C. C. B.

A. The Governor of Alaska is ex-officio superintendent of public instruction. The general supervision and direction of the schools is vested in a territorial board of education consisting of five members, of whom the Governor is ex-officio chairman, with a commissioner of education chosen by them as chief executive officer.

Q. Please tell something about the school that Owen D. Young gave to Van Hornesville, N. Y. R. M.

A. Mr. Young's object in building the school in his home town was to give the boys and girls advantages not formerly to be had and to teach them to live successfully and happily. The building is of Georgian Colonial style. None but native labor was employed in the construction. On a bronze tablet in the entrance hall are the names of all the men who had a part in the building, names of the members of the school board, and others. Some of the furnishing is copied from antiques in Mr. Young's home. As the school is to be a center of community life, the assembly hall is equipped with a moving picture screen and pictures are shown twice weekly. All conveniences are afforded including two swimming pools. A teachers' house, beautifully equipped and of the same style of architecture, adjoins the school building.

Q. When was the University of Paris founded? B. W.

A. Tradition says that the University of Paris dates from 780, but authentic annals seem to commence about 1107.

Q. Which is the oldest agricultural college in the United States? H. D.

A. Michigan State College, dedicated May 13, 1857, is the oldest.

Q. Which college was the first to establish a course in hotel administration? R. A. J.

A. The world's first four-year course in hotel administration was established at Cornell in 1922.

Q. When were examinations first given in schools and colleges? B. S. H.

A. The earliest type of examinations which prevailed were oral. A disputation or a definition of a thesis were the first forms that the examination took in medieval universities. The written examination was unknown at the universities probably until 1702, at which time it was introduced by Bentley at Trinity College, Cambridge.

Q. What work does a dental hygienist do? M. W.

A. This work is a development in preventive medicine and consists in practical treatment and education in the care of the teeth.

Q. What are known as tool subjects by educators? H. R.

A. The subjects which are necessary tools in securing an education, such as reading, writing, arithmetic, and grammar.

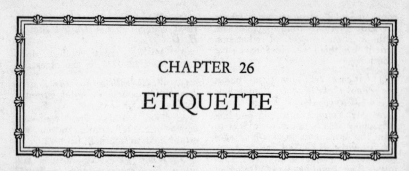

CHAPTER 26

ETIQUETTE

Q. How long does a hostess wait for a tardy dinner guest? C. B.

A. Formal rules of etiquette state that a hostess need wait only 20 minutes for a tardy guest before beginning the dinner without him.

Q. Is it considered ill-bred to complain to an usher when people persist in talking while attending a talking picture? J. C.

A. The people who are talking are the ones who are ill-bred. The managers of many motion picture houses request the disturbers to be quiet or leave.

Q. I am interested in the correct use of the title, Lady. B. L.

A. Armiger's "Titles" says that the title, Lady, is held by all peeresses under the rank of Duchess, by all daughters of the three highest ranks of the peerage, and by the wives of Baronets and Knights.

Q. When attending a tea, should one leave a card? L. B.

A. When a guest at a tea, one leaves a visiting card on the tray held by the servant who opens the door or lays the card on a table in the hall.

Q. Should one accompany a guest to the front door when he is leaving? F. B.

A. If one is living informally it is hospitable to accompany a guest to the door of the house or apartment when he is leaving. A hostess whose home is conducted upon formal lines bids good-bye to her guest at the door of the drawing-room.

Q. To whom is it correct to give the title, Right Honourable? A. D.

A. This title (which precedes all other titles) is given to all Privy Councillors.

Q. Is it correct for a maid to say "Mrs. Dextere is not at home," when the caller knows that Mrs. Dexter is at home? J. M.

A. This conventional phrase means merely that Mrs. Dexter is not at home to visitors.

Q. Should a man, let us say a Senator, rise when a woman visitor enters his office? A. H. D.

A. A good rule to observe is thus phrased by Braddy: "It is unnecessary for a man to rise every time one of the girls in his office enters his private audience room, but he should always rise to receive a visitor, whether it is a man or a woman, and should ask the visitor to be seated before he himself sits down."

Q. Should both hands be put in a finger bowl at once? W. R.

A. The fingers of one hand at a time should be dipped lightly into a finger bowl.

Q. If I were to write to the Pope, how would I begin the letter? L. F. H.

A. The correct ecclesiastical usage is as follows: Address: "His Holiness Pope Benedict V," or "His

166

Holiness the Pope." The Salutation is "Your Holiness," or "Most Holy Father."

Q. *When one has not met the first member of a receiving line, should one introduce one's self?* M. D.

A. In this situation, one should say, "I am Mrs. ——"

Q. *How should one bring a business letter to the attention of a certain person?* A. W. C.

A. Write Attention of Mr. —— on the same line as the salutation or beneath it to the right.

Q. *How should an engraved card announcing an engagement be worded?* N. T. W.

A. This type of card should not be used.

Q. *Should a person knock before opening a door into a business office?* R. L. B.

A. The door is opened without knocking.

Q. *Are patty shells eaten?* G. W. A.

A. If they are made of pastry, they are eaten with the fork.

Q. *Does a woman wear a hat in a restaurant?* M. C. F.

A. This is always correct.

Q. *Does one eat an olive from a fork or in the fingers?* M. V.

A. An olive is held in the fingers.

Q. *Will you please tell me if after a woman's husband dies she is addressed as Mrs. Mabel Smith or Mrs. George Smith?* J. M. S.

A. The fact that the husband of a woman has died, in no way affects the name by which she is known socially. Mrs. George Smith continues to be Mrs. George Smith. Of course, except on a legal document or an hotel register, the woman herself does not use this form. She signs her name Mabel Smith, and if it is necessary that she be identified as her husband's widow, she writes in parentheses at the left of her signature (Mrs. George).

Q. *Is it considered vulgar or ill-bred to call one's parent Dad or Daddy?* R. E. P.

A. Thirty-five or forty years ago the title Dad or Daddy was not in good form. Today, however, both are regarded as extremely proper and are preferred by many parents. To address one's father as Dad or Daddy implies no discourtesy, indicates no lack of rearing, and is by no means vulgar.

Q. *When gloves or mits are worn, should they be removed while eating?* G. H.

A. They should.

Q. *In applying face powder, should one use a considerable quantity on the nose?*

A. A beauty expert advises against this. She explains that only a small amount of powder should be used on the nose; otherwise it is over-emphasized.

Q. *When speaking to the President of the United States, what form of address does one use?* I. M. D.

A. One says "Mr. President" and usually adds "Sir" later in the conversation.

Q. *What is the little hammock for, that one finds in a pullman berth?* M. E. D.

A. In it one places whatever he chooses—articles of attire, books, a folding umbrella, etc.

Q. *If I am dining in a café, and my napkin slips from my lap, should I pick it up?* M. C. S.

A. A waiter will give you a fresh one. He will also pick up the napkin from the floor.

Q. *Is it correct to use just the title, "Doctor"?* M. G.

A. One should never say, "Good morning, Doctor." The surname should always be added to this title.

Q. *How does the Vice President rank, for example, at a dinner?* A. L. L.

A. Emily Post says: "When the Vice President is not representing the President, he ranks as the head of the Senate and is placed necessarily below the Chief Justice who, as head of the Supreme Court, outranks the Senate."

Q. *May one use a handkerchief at table?* M. R. M.

A. If it is necessary, one may use a handkerchief at table, but it should be used as unobtrusively as possible.

Q. *Should one wear a necklace—"a choker" for example—when wearing pendant earrings?* A. A. R.

A. To avoid what one authority calls "the Christmas tree appearance," a woman wearing pendant earrings should wear no chain or string of beads around her neck.

Q. *We must choose an inscription for the façade of our hospital. What is appropriate?* A. C. L.

A. Near Boston is a hospital over the main entrance to which is this brief inscription: "Man tends. God mends."

Q. *When writing a social letter on a typewriter, should one type his name?* W. H. H.

A. One should use ink for the signature.

Q. *What is the correct way to eat a sandwich? Should fork or fingers be used?* F. L. H.

A. It depends upon the time, place, and company. The general rule for eating sandwiches is to use a fork if one is provided and it is possible to do so.

Q. *How are pomegranates eaten?* I. D. B.

A. Margery Quigley and Mary Clark advise: "Do not let the fact that they or other new models are not an article of your daily diet feaze you for a moment. Instead, repeat to yourself, 'Peel the fruit and quarter it, then eat it with your fingers. Remove pits or seeds from your mouth with thumb and first finger. If the fruit is juicy, expect a finger bowl.'"

Q. *Does a woman sit at the right side or left side of a vehicle when driving with a man?* A. V.

A. In Europe, the woman sits at the right. Except in official life, this rule is not closely followed in the United States.

Q. *Should a master of ceremonies rise or remain seated when making announcements at a banquet?* L. H.

A. A master of ceremonies always rises when functioning as such. If he has occasion to make an announcement or to make some comment which should be heard by all the guests, he stands as a matter of courtesy.

Q. *In taking a month's cruise, when does one tip—at the end of the voyage, or as one does in an hotel?* M. E. B.

A. Fees on shipboard on a cruise or extended trips should be given at intervals of, say, two weeks instead of waiting until the end, as is customary on a transatlantic voyage. The amount will vary according to the location of the stateroom. A reasonable standard for such fortnightly tips would be the amount which would normally be given for the same service on a transatlantic voyage.

Q. *In eating soup should the spoon be drawn toward one or away?* O. W. B.

A. A soup spoon is dipped into the surface of the soup and moved toward the farther edge of the plate.

Q. *Is it good manners to type personal letters?* H. S.

A. The custom has not been fully established. Years ago it was regarded as being in questionable taste to send a typewritten social letter. Now, however, the use of the typewriter is so general that the attitude of the public has largely changed, many people typing all letters except formal ones.

Q. Is it all right to thank people verbally for wedding presents? T. H. D.

A. It is not. A personal letter must be written for each present.

Q. Are good manners inherent or acquired? D. W. D.

A. John Erskine in "What Education Means to Me" says: "All good manners have something histrionic in them; they are not natural; they are a performance, and the best inspiration toward acquiring them is a fine desire to be agreeable to others."

Q. Is it correct to say "yes ma'm" or "yes sir"? L. L. B.

A. Whether or not one says "yes ma'm" or "yes sir" depends to a large degree upon the section of the country in which one lives. For example, many cultured southern families use this form of reply. In some sections of the United States it is used only by domestics, or those of an inferior social grade. Some parents teach their children to say "yes, mother" or "yes, father," "no, Mrs. Smith," etc.

Q. Please settle the question as to whether a salad plate goes to the right or left of the dinner plate. B. W.

A. There is no arbitrary rule in regard to the matter. In fact, certain writers on etiquette say that it is quite permissible to shift the salad plate from one side to the other if the side at which it is served does not prove to be convenient.

Q. Please give form of formal invitations for use at a Colonial party. H. L. H.

A. In the museum of the D. A. R. Continental Hall is a copper plate made in 1767 upon which an invitation to a dance is engraved. The form is: Mr. and Mrs. Blank—Present their Compliments—to Miss Doe —And Ask the Favour—of Miss Doe's Company—at a Dance—at the Town House—on Thursday at the Commencement.—N. B. This Admission to be delivered at the Door.

Q. Please list some expressions to avoid in a business letter. A. T.

A. Sarah Taintor and Kate Monro say that fortunately these hackneyed expressions are disappearing from modern letters: "Yours of the 13th inst. received; In reply to yours of the tenth, would say; Under separate cover; Enclosed you will find; Trusting to hear from you soon."

Q. Is it correct for a gentleman to assist a lady by carrying her wraps, or any packages that she happens to have? W. F.

A. It is correct for a man to carry a woman's wraps or packages. It is, however, not necessary for him to do so, and some women prefer to carry their own.

Q. Is it correct to use both "Mr." and "Jr." with a man's name? A. L.

A. The fact that the title "Jr." is used with a man's name in no way affects the use of the title "Mr." It must also be used.

Q. In writing to her divorced husband, whose name is John Smith, how should a woman begin the letter? L. M. P.

A. She would write "My dear John." This is a conventional phrase which has no real significance.

Q. When one wishes to furnish a reference, should he ask for permission to use the name of the one referred to? C. W.

A. One always asks for permission to use the name of the individual which is given as reference.

Q. Suppose I find I have a meat bone or a fishbone in my mouth. What then? A. H. D.

A. Remove it by grasping it between the thumb and first finger. Lay the bone on the edge of the plate.

Q. Which salutation is more formal for a letter—"Dear Mrs. Jones" or "My dear Mrs. Jones"? A. N. M.

A. "My dear Mrs. Jones" is considered the more formal salutation.

Q. May one break bread or crackers into soup?

A. This should not be done.

Q. In addressing letters to members of the Supreme Court what form of salutation should be used? F. W.

A. In the case of the Chief Justice, the form should be "My dear Mr. Chief Justice" and in the case of the other Justices, "My dear Mr. Justice."

Q. Should the inner envelope of a wedding invitation be addressed? D. C.

A. It bears the name but not the address of the person to whom it is sent.

Q. How wide should a mourning band be? H. C.

A. It is from 3½ to 4½ inches wide. It is of dull broadcloth on overcoats or winter clothing, and of serge on summer clothing.

Q. When a man is not sure whether an occasion calls for a Tuxedo or full dress clothes, which should he wear? F. R.

A. He should wear the swallowtail. It is not a question of being overdressed. The swallowtail is appropriate for either formal or informal occasions, while the dinner jacket is not.

Q. How should a wedding invitation be declined? J. B.

A. Emily Post says that an invitation to the church only, requires no answer whatever unless the wedding is so small that the invitation is a personal note. An invitation to the reception or breakfast is answered on the first page of a sheet of note paper; although it is written by hand, the words must be spaced as though they were engraved. The regret reads as follows: "Mr. and Mrs. Richard Brown —regret that they are unable to accept—Mr. and Mrs. John Huntington Smith's—kind invitation for—Tuesday the first of June."

Q. Please make it clear whether a son who bears the title, junior, continues to use it after the death of his father? O. M. T.

A. Following the death of his father, whose name the son bears, the son discontinues the use of the title junior.

Q. How should the visiting card of a woman who has divorced her husband read? W. H. A.

A. She may use the full name of her husband if she chooses. Usually she prefers, if her name was Anna Brown, and her married name is Smith, to have her cards engraved Mrs. Brown Smith or Mrs. Anna Brown Smith.

Q. At what age should a boy cease to call his parents, Papa and Mama, and adopt the more formal Father and Mother? B. B.

A. There is no set time. Whenever a boy is old enough to feel self-conscious about it, he is old enough. Some men continue to use the informal terms. In these days, most children are taught to say Father and Mother when they are infants, but family terms necessarily enjoy considerable latitude of expression, and personal preference controls their use in the home, at least.

Q. Must a woman wear black when attending a funeral? C. B. B.

A. In ordinary circumstances, a woman no longer finds it necessary to wear black unless she is to be seated with the family. Dark clothes should, however, be worn.

Q. What rule governs the use of the title, Esquire? N. D. L.

A. "The Secretary's Handbook" says: "The title, Esquire, is used with the following government officials: Chief clerks and chiefs of

Bureaus of the Executive Department, Commissioners of the District of Columbia, Mayors of cities, American diplomatic officers below the grade of Minister, American consular officers, practicing attorneys of the American Bar."

Q. What is meant by drinking a toast "with all the honours three"? M. E. M.

A. The reference is probably to the cheers with which a toast is greeted. Some toasts are drunk standing, such as a toast to one's country, and are often received with hurrahs three in number, or in case of great enthusiasm, with three times three.

Q. At what age should a baby be christened? M. H. D.

A. "Etiquette" says that in other days of stricter observances a baby was baptized in the Catholic and high Episcopal church on the first or at least second Sunday after its birth. But today the christening is usually delayed at least until the young mother is up and about again; often it is put off for months and in some denominations children need not be christened until they are several years old. The usual age is from two to six months.

Q. Is it good form to spread jelly on bread at the table? E. P. H.

A. It is never correct to spread jelly on bread. Jelly is conveyed to the mouth on the tip of the fork. One, for example, eats a portion of bread and this is followed by a small portion of jelly.

Q. When were calling cards first used? J. H. G.

A. It is believed that something similar to the modern calling or visiting card was used by the Chinese or some other Oriental people in very early times. It was first used in the Western World by the Germans in the 16th century and was soon adopted in France and elsewhere. The French, under Louis XIV, used very elaborate and ornate cards. When England took up the use of the cards in the 18th century simplicity was made the standard.

Q. As a signature on Christmas cards, where should the wife's name appear? B. H. J.

A. Authorities differ on this subject. One says: "Although whenever the titles Mr. and Mrs. are used together, as name or address, Mr. comes first, the wife's name comes first as a signature."

Q. How do the clothes worn by the best man differ from those worn by the groom at a wedding? M. P.

A. The best man wears the same kind that the groom wears with one small exception—the groom's boutonniere is slightly different and more elaborate.

Q. Where should one grasp a goblet? A. D. T.

A. A goblet should be grasped firmly in the middle.

Q. Is it permissible for a bride to exchange her wedding gifts? M. B. D.

A. She should never change the presents chosen for her by her family or by the groom's family, unless especially told that she may do so. However, to keep a number of one kind of gift, when in need of another, is said by one authority to be "putting sentiment above sense."

Q. Is it proper to break a soft-boiled egg into a cup or should it be eaten from the shell? L. P.

A. In Europe, boiled eggs are eaten from the shell and Europeans do not consider our method of serving soft-boiled eggs correct. Nevertheless, in the United States an egg cup or glass is the usual accompaniment of boiled eggs and its use is generally countenanced.

Q. Are artichokes eaten with the fingers? P. A.

A. Artichokes are always eaten with the fingers; a leaf at a time is pulled off and the edible end dipped in the sauce, and then bitten off.

Q. Is it improper to ask a married man to be best man at a wedding? E. G.

A. A man usually asks his best friend to be best man, even though he is married. Should any entertaining be done for the bridal party, the wife of the best man should be included.

Q. How should the cards be engraved that the Governor of a State uses in his official capacity? G. M.

A. They should be engraved "The Governor of Virginia" or whatever the State may be. No name is used.

Q. May a half slice of bread be buttered at the table, or should it be broken again? J. T. C.

A. The correct procedure is to break from the piece of bread a single morsel, which is then buttered.

Q. Is it proper to wear the wedding ring first on the finger or the engagement ring? L. D.

A. The usual custom is to wear the wedding ring first and the engagement ring above it. The engagement ring is removed before or during the marriage ceremony, then replaced after the wedding ring has been put on.

Q. What is the proper way to eat corn on the cob? L. A. T.

A. One should be careful to select a piece which does not require the support of both hands. If an entire cob is offered to one, it should be held in the napkin and broken. One places on the corn enough salt, pepper, and butter for one or two morsels.

Q. I have just become engaged to a young man whose family I do not know. Should I write to his mother or should the first advance be made by his family? L. L.

A. Your fiancé has doubtless communicated with his family to the effect that he has become engaged. It is the duty of the man's family immediately to call upon the prospective bride and her family, if it is possible to do so. If it is not, the family of the prospective groom communicates immediately with the fiancée of the son.

Q. How long should a wedding ring be worn after the husband has died? R. F. M.

A. A widow continues to wear the wedding ring during her lifetime unless she becomes engaged to marry a second time. Following the announcement of her engagement, she ceases to wear her first wedding ring.

Q. When one finishes a meal, where should the napkin be placed? How should one dispose of knife and fork when the dinner plate is removed? R. E. R.

A. When one has finished a meal, the napkin is laid at the right or the left of the plate, preferably the right side. The knife and fork are laid a little to the right of the center of the plate. The tines of the fork point upward. The sharp edge of the knife faces the center of the plate.

Q. At a dining table where men and women are seated alternately, should all the women be served first? D. A. S.

A. Guests at table should be served in regular sequence regardless of sex.

Q. Is it proper to carry meat to the mouth with the fork in the left hand? J. A. R.

A. It is purely an American custom to shift the fork from the left hand to the right hand when eating. It is correct to retain the fork in the left hand. Many children are now being encouraged to do this.

Q. In writing a business letter to a Spanish, German, and an Italian firm, what phrase should I use in the salutation?

A. Muy Senores Nuestros; Geehrte Herren; Spettabile Ditta.

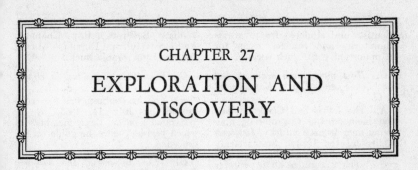

CHAPTER 27

EXPLORATION AND DISCOVERY

Q. How much did the expedition of Columbus cost, and how does it compare with modern expeditions? C. H.

A. Fitzhugh Green calculated that it cost backers of Columbus about $2115 to discover America in 1492. The Scott Antarctic Expedition cost $500,000; the Amundsen-Ellsworth Expedition about $200,000; the Nobile "Italia" Expedition $300,000; while the cost of Byrd's Antarctic Expedition was more than a million dollars.

Q. How much time do Mr. and Mrs. Martin Johnson, the explorers, spend in civilization? S. N. G.

A. The Johnsons estimate that they have spent in civilization about three of the twenty years that they have been married. During their expedition to the pigmy country they remained two years making sound pictures.

Q. How much did Sir Hubert Wilkins pay our Government for the use of the submarine, Nautilus? S. J. M.

A. The Nautilus was one of the submarines to be scrapped under the London Naval Treaty. Sir Hubert Wilkins paid the United States Government a dollar a year for its use.

Q. How long after the North Pole was discovered was it that the South Pole was reached? E. C.

A. About two years. Admiral Robert E. Peary reached the North Pole in April, 1909. The South Pole

was first reached in December, 1911, by Roald Amundsen.

Q. Has any explorer reached both the North and South Poles? A. C. S.

A. Captain Roald Amundsen is the only man who reached both poles.

Q. For how long a time did Stefansson live on a meat diet? J. K.

A. He lived four hundred days at one time without tasting vegetable food.

Q. Is William Beebe, the explorer, married? T. K.

A. His wife is Elswyth Thane, the novelist.

Q. How long after Amundsen discovered the South Pole did Scott reach it? R. R.

A. About a month. Amundsen reached it on December 14, 1911, and Scott on January 18, 1912.

Q. How is the personnel of the Smithsonian and National Geographic exploring expeditions made up? I. N.

A. In the Smithsonian a prominent scientist who is a member of the staff is given charge of an expedition and his personnel is selected generally from scientists already in the employ of the Government under the Civil Service. The National Geographic Society's expeditions are in charge of noted experts who have a large following of scientists and students from various laboratories and colleges, eager for an opportunity for such service.

Q. *How many men accompanied the Lewis and Clark Expedition?* A. G.

A. The Lewis and Clark Expedition included the two officers, nine young men from Kentucky, fourteen soldiers of the United States Army who had volunteered their services, two French watermen, an interpreter and hunter, and a black servant belonging to Captain Clark.

Q. *How many members were there of the Donner Expedition to California which was snowed in on the mountain top in the Sierras and how many survived the experience?* J. K. O.

A. Eighty persons comprised the expedition. Starvation and illness reduced the company to 15. Capt. Donner, the organizer, starved to death and his wife was driven insane.

Q. *Who measured the depth of the Dead Sea?* L. J. D.

A. William F. Lynch, an American explorer, in 1848, conducted an expedition, equipped by the United States Government, to the Jordan and Dead Sea. He claimed to be the first to examine the shores and to sound the depths of the sea.

Q. *Where is Mt. Lindbergh?* R. C. C.

A. Mount Lindbergh is located in the Antarctic region and was explored by Rear Admiral Richard E. Byrd.

Q. *Who discovered the Grand Canyon of Arizona?* J. E. S.

A. The Canyon was discovered by Garcia Lopez de Cardenas in the autumn of 1540.

Q. *Please give the names of some well known explorers who also write books.* H. B.

A. The following are both authors and explorers: William Beebe,

Gregory Mason, Bertram Thomas, William Seabrook, Roy Chapman Andrews, Julian Duguid, Martin Johnson, and Frank Buck.

Q. *Who first succeeded in climbing the Matterhorn?* J. L. C.

A. The Matterhorn was first conquered on July 14, 1865, by E. Whymper's party, three members of which perished with the guide on the descent.

Q. *Who discovered the Sargasso Sea?* A. H.

A. Columbus was the discoverer. His ships were entangled in the Sea for two weeks. Today, though the weeds are thickly matted in some sections, a vessel could not become hopelessly involved in the tract because the patches are not continuous. It is believed by many authorities that the seaweed was originally carried by winds and currents from the Caribbean Sea and the Gulf of Mexico.

Q. *Please give the history of Admiral Byrd's ship, the City of New York.* C. S. M.

A. Admiral Byrd in the National Geographic says: "We searched the world for the best ship, and located the stocky bark, which we renamed the City of New York, in Norway. Since 1885 this 512-ton vessel has been weathering rough seas and the Polar regions. Her hull is wedge-shaped, enabling her to rise when the ice clutches her in its tremendous pressure. It is reinforced with timbers 34 inches thick. I know of no other ship with sides that thick."

Q. *How long ago was the Arctic trip made by Charles Hall?* W. J. E.

A. On July 3, 1871, Charles Travels Hall sailed from New London in the Polaris in command of an expedition to the North Pole. The Polaris passed through Smith Sound into Kane Sea, then through Kennedy and Robeson Channels to the Polar Sea, and August 30, 1871, reached latitude 82°11' N., the highest point then attained by any vessel. The expedition went into winter quarters at Thank God Harbor, Greenland. Hall became ill October 24, 1871, on the return from a sledge journey to Cape Brevoort and died of apoplexy, November 8, 1871.

Q. *At what point was the Mississippi River first seen by a white man?* M. H.

A. It was reached in 1541 by Fernando de Soto near the present site of Memphis, Tennessee.

Q. *Did Peary have any white men with him when he reached the North Pole?* J. F.

A. His party for the final dash included no white men. He took Matthew Henson, his colored servant, and four Eskimos.

Q. *Who discovered Catalina Island?* J. W. C.

A. The Island of Santa Catalina, lying off the coast of Southern California, is 50 miles south of Los Angeles. It was discovered in 1542 by Juan Rodriguez Cabrillo, a Portuguese explorer, in the service of Spain, and named San Salvador. It was visited by Sebastian Vizcaino 60 years later and named Santa Catalina in honor of St. Catherine of Sienna. Its area is about 55,000 acres. The surface is hilly and well-wooded. The island contains many deep gorges.

Q. *Who was the Arctic explorer whose frozen body was found in the summer of 1931?* V. H.

A. It was Salomon August Andree, who left for the North Pole in the balloon Ornen, July 11, 1897, from Virgo, Spitsbergen. The frozen bodies of Andree and his companions were found August 6, 1931, on White Island, and removed to Norway for burial.

Q. *When was Cumberland Gap discovered?* G. S.

A. Daniel Boone discovered this passageway through the mountains in 1769 while on a hunting trip. Six years later he and his companions blazed a trail through the gap, which was afterwards known as the Wilderness Road and played an important part in the Civil War.

Q. *Was the Boy Scout chosen to go on the Byrd Expedition in college?* G. F.

A. Paul Siple, of Erie, Pa., was the Boy Scout selected for the Byrd Expedition. He was 19 years old September 15, 1928, when he left with the expedition. He was a Freshman at Allegheny College, Meadville, Pa. He was also assistant scoutmaster in that city, having been a Boy Scout for seven years. He is credited with having 59 merit badges.

Q. *When did the exploration of interior Africa begin?* F. McG.

A. Until the seventh century A.D., the desert was an impassable barrier between the Mediterranean countries and Central Sudan. The first African expedition on record is mentioned by Herodotus as having been sent out by Pharaoh Necho about the seventh century, B.C., to circumnavigate the continent.

Q. *When was the first expedition fitted out to find the Northwest Passage?* N. G.

A. Probably the earliest attempt to discover the Northwest Passage and incidentally to define the location of the North Pole was made by a Portuguese named Corte Real about 1500. In 1585 a company was formed in London called "The Fellowship for the Discovery of the Northwest Passage."

Q. *Who discovered the Painted Desert?* M. R.

A. It was discovered by Coronado in 1540. This area has been added to the Petrified Forest National Monument in Arizona.

Q. *Who financed Admiral Byrd when he flew to the North Pole?* V. T.

A. Several wealthy Americans, including Edsel Ford, John D. Rockefeller, Jr., and Vincent Astor financed the expedition, which established a base at Kings Bay, Spitsbergen. From there, Byrd, accompanied by Floyd Bennett, flew to the Pole and back on May 9, 1926, a distance of 1360 miles, in 15½ hours.

Q. To what body of judges were Admiral Peary's proofs of reaching the North Pole submitted? A. W. F.

A. Peary submitted records of his observations to a committee consisting of members of the National Geographic Society and the Superintendent of the United States Coast and Geodetic Survey. This committee reported that Peary's material supplied proof that he had attained the North Pole on April 6, 1909.

Q. Who discovered the Isle of Trinidad off the coast of Brazil? B. W.

A. Trinidad was first discovered by the Portuguese but never claimed or made use of until 1700 when the English astronomer Halley, in the course of a scientific cruise, raised the British flag there. In 1895 Great Britain annexed the island for a cable station site. This, however, was opposed by Brazil and by mutual consent the dispute was submitted to the King of Portugal who decided in favor of Brazil. The island is 680 miles east of the Coast of Espirito Santo, Brazil. It is four miles long and two miles wide.

Q. Did Kit Carson go with Fremont on his fourth expedition? E. W.

A. Kit Carson accompanied John Charles Fremont on his first three expeditions. He did not accompany him on the fourth. Bill Williams, who had been engaged at Pueblo for the fourth expedition in 1849 by Kit Carson, went reluctantly because he believed that the passage of the mountains at that season of the year

was very difficult, if not impossible. The expedition encountered severely cold weather and endured a great deal of suffering. Eleven men died as the result, and in February the scattered survivors were finally gathered at the pueblo of Taos, New Mexico. Kit Carson lived here and aided them. Fremont was cared for in Carson's house.

Q. Where is Livingstone buried? I. McD.

A. He is buried in Westminster Abbey.

Q. Who authorized the first excavation in Pompeii? A. L.

A. King Charles III authorized the first excavation at Pompeii, 1748.

Q. Where was Nansen, the explorer, buried? C. R. S.

A. Dr. Nansen died in Oslo, Norway, May 13, 1930. His body was cremated.

Q. How did Captain Sir George Hubert Wilkins gain his knighthood? M. F. S.

A. Captain Wilkins was born in Australia. He has been engaged in Arctic exploration for many years. In April, 1928, he flew from Alaska to Spitsbergen and for this feat was knighted by King George V of England.

Q. How old was Roald Amundsen at the time of his death? B. K.

A. Roald Amundsen was born in Norway, July 16, 1872. It is probable that he met his death in the Arctic wastes on the night of June 18, 1928, while searching for the Nobile Expedition.

Q. Where was Shackleton, the explorer, buried? D. W. R.

A. Sir Ernest Shackleton's grave is at Grytviken, on South Georgia Island.

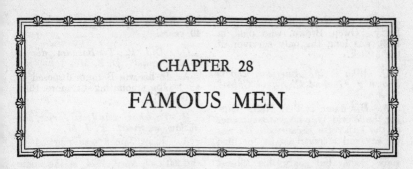

CHAPTER 28

FAMOUS MEN

Q. *What family is called "the royal family of the United States"?* A. C.

A. On account of their great wealth and their generous benefactions, this pleasantry has been used in referring to the Duponts. There are 74 individuals of this name in Wilmington, Delaware, most of whom, either by their present holdings or expectations, are millionaires.

Q. *How many wives and children did Brigham Young have? Did he die a rich man?* L. M.

A. He was reputed to have left $1,000,000 and 19 wives. He was the father of 57 children.

Q. *Was Knute Rockne born in this country? Where was he educated?* A. M.

A. Knute Rockne was of Norwegian descent. He was born in this country. He was a graduate of Notre Dame University.

Q. *When did Blondin, the celebrated French rope performer, come to this country?* I. N. A.

A. Blondin crossed Niagara Falls on a tight rope in 1859. He returned to the United States on two other occasions, the last time being in 1888.

Q. *Does John D. Rockefeller, Jr., look like his father?* T. K. L.

A. He has the long head, the broad brow, and strong nose of his famous parent, but there the likeness ends. He is a man of medium height and square build. The thin tight lips of the elder Rockefeller are not part of the son's countenance.

Q. *Did Admiral Byrd really make a trip around the world alone when only a boy?* S. M. G.

A. When 12 years of age he visited a friend in the Philippines and returned to America by way of Ceylon, Red Sea, Port Said, the Mediterranean Sea to Boston. He thus made a complete trip around the world alone.

Q. *Where is William Penn buried?* A. H. H.

A. William Penn, his two wives and seven of his eleven children, are buried in Jordan's Churchyard, two miles from Beaconsfield, Buckinghamshire, England.

Q. *Who were the men chosen by H. G. Wells as the great lights in history?* W. W.

A. When asked by Bruce Barton to name the half dozen men in history who really deserve to be called great, H. G. Wells chose Jesus of Nazareth, Buddha, Asoka, Aristotle, Roger Bacon, and Abraham Lincoln.

Q. *How many children did John Brown of Civil War fame have?* F. H. B.

A. John Brown was married twice and had twenty children, eight of whom died in early childhood. His sons aided him in all his undertakings and two were killed at Harper's Ferry. Owen Brown, who died in 1889, was long the only survivor of the attack.

Q. *Who is the American who is known as General Chang in China?* C. A.

A. His name is Bert Hall. During the World War he was a member of the Lafayette Escadrille. He was an ace and received credit for nine planes. Hall has been General Chang since 1929, but only his closest friends have known it. He is styled as aviation's first soldier of fortune and has battled under half a dozen flags.

Q. *Was James Smithson, founder of the Smithsonian Institution, an American?* R. M. F.

A. No, he was an Englishman and had never visited the United States. Nevertheless, when he died he left his fortune of $550,000 in trust to this country "to found an establishment for the increase and diffusion of knowledge among men."

Q. *What was Weston's best record for a day's walk?* R. H. B.

A. Edward Payson Weston's longest day's trip was 82 miles. This distance was traveled in 1867 on his walk from Portland, Maine, to Chicago, Ill. Weston at this time was 28½ years old.

Q. *How tall was the Dutch giant, Van Druesen?* M. Z.

A. Van Druesen, the Dutch giant who died at the age of 28, was said to be the tallest man in the world. He measured 8 feet 9 inches.

Q. *Who was court dressmaker to Empress Eugenie?* E. L. B.

A. Worth is credited with having designed the gowns of Empress Eugenie.

Q. *What was the nationality of Father Damien?* N. S.

A. He was a Belgian priest who devoted years of his life to the lepers of Molokai. Finally, he contracted the disease and died at the age of 49 years.

Q. *Did P. T. Barnum die a wealthy man?* D. E. M.

A. In his will Barnum disposed of an estate amounting to more than $4,000,000.

Q. *To whom was Jesse James, the outlaw, married?* P. J. M.

A. Jesse James was married to his first cousin, Zerelda Mimms, on the 24th of April, 1874, at the home of a neighbor near Kearney, Missouri.

Q. *Did Paul Revere practice dentistry along with his other trades?* H. F.

A. In the Journal of the American Dental Association Dr. Arthur Black quotes an advertisement taken from the Boston Gazette for August 29, 1768: "Whereas many Persons are so unfortunate as to lose their Fore Teeth by Accident and otherways, to their great Detriment, not only in Looks but in speaking bothe in Public and Private; This is to inform all such that they may have them replaced with false Ones that look as well as the Natural and answer the end of speaking to all Intents by Paul Revere, Goldsmith, near the Head of Dr. Clark's wharf, Boston."

Q. *Who was Sam Patch?* L. G.

A. Sam Patch was a lad widely known for daring leaps and dives. Born in 1807 in Rhode Island, he became a cotton spinner in Paterson, N. J. A jump from a bridge into the Passaic River brought him such notoriety that he traveled about leaping from bridges and diving from topmasts of ships. He was killed in 1829 when attempting a jump of 125 feet into the Genesee River.

Q. *What was Harry Houdini's name before he changed it to Houdini?* W. S.

A. His name was Eric Weiss. He was the son of the Rev. Dr. Mayer Samuel Weiss, a Jewish rabbi. Houdini went on the stage as a trapeze performer when only eight years old, and soon after began his practice of legerdemain.

Q. *How did Harry Lehr become the arbiter of New York society?* S. S.

A. Lehr became secretary to Mrs. William Astor, and later, director of the lavish entertainments of Mrs. Stuyvesant Fish. He made a fortune through commissions as a wine agent. Witty and audacious, he put gaiety and originality into the social entertainments of the nineties.

Q. *To whom was the nickname "Fighting Quaker," applied?* G. I. F.

A. It was often said of John Bright, British statesman in the Victorian era, that "if he had not been a Quaker he must have been a prizefighter." He was eloquent, humorous, and pugnacious.

Q. *Is Theodore Roosevelt left-handed?* E. S.

A. The secretary to Theodore Roosevelt, Jr., says that he is not left-handed, and that she has never heard it said that the late Theodore Roosevelt was left-handed.

Q. *Was Sir Thomas Lipton born in Scotland or Ireland? How did he make his fortune?* J. G.

A. Sir Thomas Lipton was born in Glasgow, Scotland, of Irish parentage. In 1876 he opened a grocery store in Glasgow and from this his business expanded to include many stores in Great Britain, as well as tea, coffee, and cocoa plantations in India, rubber estates in Ceylon, and a pork-packing establishment in Chicago.

Q. *How did Martin Luther die?* E. A. G.

A. He died as a result of exposure while attending a dispute at which he arbitrated between the Counts Albrecht and Gebbard of Mansfield. He successfully accomplished his mission and preached several times to crowded congregations, but the exposure to inclement weather on the way to Eisleben and protracted negotiations proved too great and on the early morning of February 18, 1546, he passed quietly away.

Q. *How long did MacSwiney's hunger strike last?* B. N. Y.

A. The Lord Mayor of Cork, Terence MacSwiney, died as the result of a hunger strike in Brixton jail 5:40 A.M. October 25, 1920. His strike lasted 74 days.

Q. *When and where did Samuel Pepys live? What did he write besides his diary?* J. F.

A. Samuel Pepys lived from 1633 to 1703, in London. He occupied a position similar to that of Secretary of the Navy in the United States. Except for the Diary, in six volumes of shorthand, published after his death, he wrote only one work—Memoirs of the Royal Navy.

Q. *What great man besides Lincoln was born in 1809?* D. P.

A. Alfred Lord Tennyson and Charles Darwin were born in 1809.

Q. *Was Joseph Addison, author of the Spectator, intemperate?* G. D. N.

A. Addison, like most literary men of his time, was intemperate. Thackeray said of him: "If he had not that little weakness for wine, why we could scarcely have found a fault in him, and could not have liked him as we did."

Q. *What became of the man who first engraved the Lord's Prayer upon the head of a pin?* K. M. B.

A. The Lord's Prayer, 69 words, 397 letters, counting punctuation marks, was engraved in 12 lines on the head of an ordinary pin by Charles Howard Baker, of Spokane, Washington. The engraving cannot be read without the aid of a powerful magnifying glass. Baker was at one time an employee of the United States Government in the Bureau of Printing and Engraving. He spent 3 years and 11 days completing this work. The pin at present is the property of Charles J. Seymour, a friend of Baker's. Seymour carries the pin from place to place for exhibition purposes.

Q. Was the Roman Emperor Nero possessed of any redeeming traits? I. R. A.

A. Contrary to the usual belief, at the time of his presentation to the Roman Senate, Nero was "justly praised for his modesty, filial feeling, clemency, liberality, and affability." His mentors, Seneca and Burrus, had endeavored through his early youth to curb the passions of ambition, cruelty, and lust which were afterwards to consume him.

Q. Was Mendelssohn the correct name of the composer, and of what nationality was he? D. A. C.

A. Felix Mendelssohn-Bartholdy, born 1809, in Hamburg, Germany, was a German. His grandfather Moses Mendelssohn, and his father Abraham Mendelssohn, were Jews. According to his biography, his father caused Felix, his brother, and two sisters to be baptized as Lutheran Christians.

Q. What was the ultimate aim of Alexander the Great? K. F.

A. Alexander sought to subject the entire world to the Greek spirit, to stamp the customs, the language, the culture, and even the thoughts of the Greeks upon surrounding nations. For this purpose poets and philosophers accompanied his armies. "In the deserts of Bactria, and Syria, and Libya, he founded Greek cities."

Q. Was Charles James Fox an inveterate gambler? B. S.

A. Charles James Fox was a typical gambler of his period, about 150 years ago. He won heavily at the race track but lost at cards. At one time his father had to pay $700,000 of his gambling debts. Later his friends raised $350,000. In addition, he lost all his winnings and his estate. He entered Parliament at the age of 19, became a cabinet member at 21, and gambled through a lifetime of great political activity in the course of which he became Foreign Minister and, save for the dislike of the King, would have been Prime Minister of England.

Q. Who were the Hartford Wits? A. J.

A. This name was given by the cultivated circles of the United States to a group of Connecticut professional men and literary aspirants, who lived in Hartford or met there for converse and collaboration, from shortly after the Revolution till toward 1800. The exact composition of the group is not uniformly agreed upon, but the unquestioned members were Richard Alsop, Joel Barlow, Theodore Dwight, Lemuel Hopkins, and David Humphreys. Benjamin Trumbull, the historian, is sometimes added.

Q. What English King is called "the father of his country"? T. I. M.

A. Alfred of England is also affectionately remembered as the father of his people, "Who listened to all complaints, who redressed all wrongs, the philosopher who raised up a barbarous age toward the height of his own mind and founded the civilization of England."

Q. Who was said to be the master of all arts? U. T.

A. Emerson gives this title to Michaelangelo Buonarroti: "The four crowns of architecture, sculpture, painting, and poetry."

Q. Did Premier MacDonald ever work in the coal mines? If not, what kind of manual labor did he perform? A. D.

A. Ramsay MacDonald, Premier of Great Britain, did not work in the coal mines. He was born and spent his early days in Lossiemouth, Scotland, which is a fishing and agricultural village. He did the usual work of a boy of poor circumstances until 12 years of age, obtaining a fairly good education at the district school.

After that he went to London and did any work which he could secure, until obtaining a clerkship which finally resulted in his entering politics.

Q. *What Frenchman of the past is sometimes compared with the Russian statesman Stalin in ruthlessness and cruelty?* V. R.

A. Jean Paul Marat, born 1744, one of the leaders of the Jacobin party in the French Revolution, was insatiable in his desire to destroy utterly all the aristocracy or capitalistic class, demanding "300,000 heads." He was absolutely honest, asking neither honors nor friends. At the height of his power he was assassinated in 1793, while seated in his bath, by Charlotte Corday.

Q. *Is the Roman historian, Caius Cornelius Tacitus, reliable?* M. C. F.

A. Tacitus is undoubtedly the most reliable of the early historians. He has been compared with Carlyle, having the same satiric brilliance and, at times, bitter philosophy.

Q. *Is Eugene V. Debs dead?* F. M.

A. He died October 20, 1926.

Q. *Was Immanuel Kant an atheist?* B. I. A.

A. Strictly speaking Kant was not an atheist. He was a German philosopher, born 1724, died 1804, and among the cardinal tenets of his philosophy were the beliefs that "Human wisdom is not sufficient to discover what is divine," together with his ideal, "every man his own doctor, every man his own lawyer, every man his own priest."

Q. *When was W. G. McAdoo a Cabinet Member and why did he resign?* R. L. H.

A. The Hon. Wm. G. McAdoo was appointed Secretary of the Treasury by President Wilson in 1913, and served until 1918 when he resigned after the Armistice to return to his legal practice and "rebuild his fortune."

Q. *Where is Gypsy Smith, Sr., living?* E. S. M.

A. His correct name is Rodney Smith and he lives in Cambridge, England.

Q. *Is General "Hell'n" Maria Dawes a very profane man?* F. L.

A. Intimate friends who have known him a lifetime say that he uses no profanity except the conventional Hell and damn of normal conversation and that he has never been known to tell an off-color story.

Q. *Who was Louis Pasteur?* T. Y.

A. He was a French chemist noted for his investigations in bacteriology. It was for him that the process of pasteurization was named.

Q. *When, how, and where did Sandow, the strong man, die?* V. V. L.

A. Eugene Sandow died suddenly in London on October 14, 1925. His death is believed to have been due to the effects of a motor accident several years before, in which he was injured.

Q. *When did Bismarck live?* E. W.

A. Bismarck was a famous German statesman who lived from 1815 to 1898. He is regarded as the founder of the modern German Empire, of which he was the first Chancellor in 1871.

Q. *How old is Theodore Roosevelt who ran for Governor of New York?* P. B.

A. He was born September 13, 1887.

Q. *What was the calling of Herbert Hoover's father?* C. E.

A. He was a blacksmith in Iowa and died before his son was 12 years old.

Q. *When did Malthus live?* B. T.

A. Thomas R. Malthus, an English economist, was born in 1766 and died in 1834. He taught that population tends to increase faster than the means of subsistence and that poverty is inevitable unless the birth rate is lowered.

Q. How old is Mussolini? M. N.

A. He was born July 29, 1883.

Q. Who are the world's greatest thinkers according to modern historians? T. W. D.

A. Dr. Will Durant names Confucius, Plato, Aristotle, Thomas Aquinas, Copernicus, Francis Bacon, Isaac Newton, Voltaire, Immanuel Kant, and Darwin as the world's ten greatest thinkers.

Q. Is it true that Robert G. Ingersoll recanted his atheistic views before his death? S. M.

A. This has been vigorously denied by his family. In a recent biography of Ingersoll is a copy of a letter written by him July 13, 1899, only a few days before his death in which he says, "You are right in thinking I have not changed. I still believe that all religions are based on falsehoods and mistakes. I still deny the existence of the supernatural and I still say that real religion is usefulness."

Q. When Mussolini first considered writing his autobiography, what title did he plan to use? N. H.

A. "Dalla Strada al Potere"— "From the Street to Power."

Q. Was Oliver Cromwell really the great man he has been proclaimed? A. T. G.

A. Undoubtedly during the protectorate of Cromwell, England emerged from a cloud which had become increasingly dark and threatening. Voltaire said, however, of Cromwell: "It was very fortunate for Cromwell that he appeared upon the stage at the precise moment when the English people were tired of kings, and as unfortunate for his son Richard, that he had to make good his pretensions, at a moment when they were equally tired of protectors."

Q. Was John Cabot an Englishman? T. H.

A. Cabot's real name was Giovanni Cabato, and he was born in Genoa, later moving to Venice. When he reached the North American continent in 1497, he was sailing under the flag of England, having gone to Bristol to live about 1490.

Q. How old is Herbert Hoover? L. C.

A. He was born at West Branch, Iowa, August 10, 1874.

Q. Is Ambrose Bierce still living? J. C. R.

A. Whether or not Ambrose Bierce is still living is a matter of conjecture. Many of his friends are confident that he died in Mexico. He entered that country in January, 1914, and was never heard from again.

Q. Did Tweed, the famous New York political boss, die in prison? N. D. E.

A. Tweed died in Ludlow Street Jail, April 12, 1878.

Q. Where and when was Clarence S. Darrow, the criminal lawyer, born and where was he educated? B. T. F.

A. Clarence Darrow was born in Kinsman, Ohio, in 1857. He was educated in the Ohio public schools and gained his legal education largely by working and reading law in various lawyers' offices.

Q. Was John Calvin an Englishman? F. D. S.

A. John Calvin was a Frenchman.

Q. Who is the chief descendant or representative of Sir Walter Scott? F. T. J.

A. The British Library of Information says: "Sir Walter Scott is now lineally represented by the family of his great-granddaughter, the Hon. Mrs. Mary Monica Maxwell Scott, whose eldest son is Colonel Walter Joseph Maxwell Scott of

Abbotsford, C. B., D. S. O., Kara Georg with Swords (Serbian), Legion d'Honneur (Croix d'officier), Croix de Guerre."

Q. Was Will Rogers really the mayor of Beverly Hills? J. V. N.

A. Will Rogers was made the "good will" mayor of Beverly Hills, California, by the Chamber of Commerce, December 21, 1926.

Q. What position did William Howard Taft hold after he was President and before he became Chief Justice of the Supreme Court? H. McW.

A. He was a professor in Yale University.

Q. Is it true that most big business men were born poor? P. G.

A. In tracing the origin of the fifty foremost business men in America, B. C. Forbes has stated that of this number twenty-four were born poor, seventeen in moderate circumstances, and nine were born rich.

Q. When did Lenin die? M. W.

A. He died at Gorky near Moscow, January 21, 1924.

Q. Are there any grandsons of Abraham Lincoln living? R. E. M.

A. Robert T. Lincoln, the only son of Lincoln who lived to maturity, married and had two daughters and one son. The son died while in school abroad. Robert T. Lincoln was the last of the family to bear the name.

Q. Is Kipling related to the former British Prime Minister, Stanley Baldwin? C. A. W.

A. Rudyard Kipling and Stanley Baldwin are cousins, their mothers being sisters.

Q. Was President Coolidge's father a Colonel in the United States Army? E. R. F.

A. Colonel Coolidge did not receive his title as a result of active service in the United States Army.

It is an honorary title and was bestowed upon him for his services on the staff of a Governor of Vermont.

Q. Was John Ericsson an officer in the American Navy? W. T. D.

A. The Swedish inventor refused the rank and pay of an Admiral in the American Navy. He wished to be known as "Captain Ericsson," a rank held in the Swedish Navy.

Q. Where did the first Rockefeller to come to America come from? B. F.

A. John Peter Rockefeller emigrated to America from Germany in 1723.

Q. Where was Mahatma Gandhi born and where did he receive his education? H. R. E.

A. Mahatma Gandhi was born in Probanda, India, October 2, 1869, of an official family. He received a liberal Hindu education and at 19 years of age went to London to study; received a university degree; was admitted to the English bar, where he practised a short time. After that he spent several years in South Africa and became imbued with an intense desire for the nationalization of India.

Q. What famous men have been left-handed? W. R. P.

A. Among the famous men who were known to be left-handed may be mentioned Tiberius, Sebastian del Piombo, Michelangelo, Flechier, Nigra, Buhl, Raphael of Montelupo, Bertillon, and James A. Garfield. Leonardo da Vinci sketched rapidly with his left hand.

Q. When was the prophet Mohammed born and of what nationality was he? I. R. W.

A. There is some dispute as to the exact year of the birth of Mohammed. The traditional date is 570 A.D. He was born at Mecca, Arabia, and claimed descent from Abraham. He was the son of Abdallah, of the family Hashin, and Amina, of the family of Zuhra. His father died before his birth and he was adopted, after the death of his mother, by his wealthy grandfather Abd al Mittalib. He married when quite young, Khadija, a wealthy widow 15 years his senior.

Q. What member of the Negro race is famous as an agricultural chemist? S. W. H.

A. George Washington Carver, educator and scientist, was born of slave parents about 1864; was stolen and carried into Arkansas. He worked his way through high school at Minneapolis, Kansas, and later through college, receiving degrees from several higher institutions. He was elected a member of the faculty of the Iowa State College of Agriculture, and later became a teacher in Tuskegee Institute, Alabama, being now director of the department of agricultural research. Dr. Carver is a member of the Royal Society of Arts, London, and was awarded the Spingarn medal in 1923. He is credited with the discovery of 145 foods, or useful articles, manufactured from peanuts, and through scientific research has demonstrated the possibilities of many southern products which were formerly wasted. He is also credited with the discovery of methods for the eradication of agricultural pests, notably the boll weevil.

Q. Who was the man who fought a duel seated in a chair? M. R. C.

A. Benjamin Constant, the famous republican of the late 18th and early 19th century, and the intimate friend of Madame de Staël. He had been crippled for the remainder of his life by a fall in the French Chamber of Deputies and was unable to stand. Nevertheless, he fought and won a duel seated.

Q. When did Ike Walton, the fisherman, live? H. O. W.

A. Izaak Walton was born in Stafford, England, August 9, 1593, and died in Winchester, December, 1683.

Q. When did Nietzsche live? J. C. McN.

A. Friedrich Wilhelm Nietzsche (1844–1900) was of aristocratic Polish extraction. He was born at Rocken near Lutzen. The elder Nietzsche was a clergyman. Friedrich had a brilliant career at Bonn and Leipzig. When 24 years of age, he was appointed professor of Greek at Bale. Ill health caused his resignation in 1879. Ten years later, he became insane.

Q. Why didn't Thomas Jefferson take part in the political debates of his time? N. E.

A. He disliked such contests and had a poor voice. He preferred to spend his energy in writing rather than speaking.

Q. Did any ancient nation promote research and study in a fashion similar to that of today? E. F.

A. The Greeks and Romans both made large grants for the furtherance of knowledge. Aristotle, who was tutor to Alexander the Great, and himself a rich man, was granted by Alexander the Great an income of more than $4,000,000 to devote to research work and intellectual pursuits.

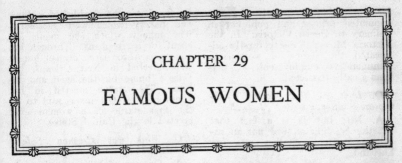

CHAPTER 29

FAMOUS WOMEN

Q. Who are the greatest women of modern times? D. M.

A. Greatness can be claimed for innumerable women, but the four women of our modern age chosen by Emil Ludwig as types in their respective fields are: Florence Nightingale, famous nurse; Harriet Beecher Stowe, author of "Uncle Tom's Cabin"; Marie Curie, discoverer of radium; and Eleonora Duse, dramatic genius.

Q. What is Helen Keller's favorite Bible verse? M. W.

A. She was asked this question and answered, "Come unto Me, all ye that labor and are heavy laden, and I will give you rest." Her favorite chapter of the Bible is the thirteenth of First Corinthians.

Q. Who was the first woman to obtain a medical degree in the United States? C. R. C.

A. Elizabeth Blackwell, who was graduated from Geneva Medical College in 1849, was the first. She and her sister Emily started in New York the Infirmary for Women and Children in 1853, the first institution of its kind conducted solely by women. She was afterward connected with other forward steps in medical education, both here and in England.

Q. Please give some facts about Ella Ewing. M. S.

A. Ella Ewing was known as the Missouri Giantess. She was born in Scotland County, Missouri, of normal parents, and at birth weighed 6½ pounds. She grew abnormally between the ages of 8 and 22 years until she reached the enormous height of 8 feet 4 inches. She wore a number 24 shoe. It took 30 yards of silk to make a dress for her. When she stopped at hotels two ordinary beds had to be placed side by side so she could sleep across them. She made a fortune traveling about on exhibition, and died at the age of 40 years.

Q. Is Queen Mary of England older than King George V? R. C.

A. Queen Mary was born May 26, 1867. King George was born at Marlborough House. London, June 3, 1865.

Q. Was the wife of Thomas Jefferson a rich woman? F. G.

A. Jefferson inherited through his wife from her father 40,000 acres of land and 135 slaves.

Q. How old is Galli Curci? A. M. K.

A. She was born in Milan, Italy, November 18, 1889. She made her début as Gilda in "Rigoletto" in the Constanze Theatre in Rome in 1909.

Q. Who was Emily Faithfull? F. R. T.

A. She was an English philanthropist (1835–1895), who took a great interest in the conditions of working women, and in 1860 set up in London a printing establishment for women. Subsequently she was appointed printer and publisher in ordinary to Queen Victoria. In the Victoria Magazine she earnestly advocated the claims of women to remunerative employment, at that time greatly restricted.

Q. Is it true that Martha Washington could not write? J. L. K.

A. No; but it is a fact that Martha Washington was not an excellent speller. Neither was her husband.

Q. Where does Nell Brinkley live? G. H.

A. Nell Brinkley is Mrs. Bruce McRae, and lives at New Rochelle, N. Y.

Q. Who was the Princess Anne after whom counties and hotels in this country have been named? M. C.

A. It was the Anne who became Queen of England.

Q. Who was the French courtesan who retained her admirers until her extreme old age? T. I.

A. Anne Lenclos, better known as Ninon de Lenclos, lived from 1615 to 1705 and was famed for her beauty and charm. In her old age her house was the rendezvous of the most distinguished personages in Paris. She retained her charm of manners and conversation and her attraction for men into extreme old age.

Q. How old is the present wife of the ex-Emperor William? R. R.

A. Princess Hermine was born on the 17th of December, 1892.

Q. Please publish the story of Margaret Haughey. R. C.

A. Margaret Haughey after being left an orphan and later losing her husband and baby, went to work as a laundress in an hotel in New Orleans. She spent part of every day visiting the orphans' home and taking food to them. She secured this food by asking various merchants

for it. Later she established a dairy and bakery which were successful. The money which she made she spent for her orphans. Through her generosity three large orphan homes were erected in New Orleans, besides a home for the aged and infirm. The statue erected in her honor in New Orleans is said to be the first statue of a woman ever erected in the United States.

Q. Who was Carmen Sylva? P. M.

A. Carmen Sylva was the pen name of Elizabeth, former Queen of Rumania.

Q. How far from Fredericksburg, Virginia, is Mary Washington's grave? W. T.

A. The ground on which the grave of George Washington's mother is situated was originally part of Kenmore Farm, home of her daughter, Betty Washington Lewis. The city limits have been extended beyond the spot and the grave is now in a residential section of the town. The National Mary Washington Memorial Association owns two acres surrounding the grave which is marked by a monument said to be the only monument to a woman erected entirely by women.

Q. Who was Empress Eugenie for whom certain hats were named? H. L.

A. She was the last Empress of the French. She was a very beautiful woman and the acknowledged leader of fashion and society. She made small ostrich-trimmed hats popular.

Q. Where was Madame Curie born? M. D.

A. She was born in Warsaw, Poland, in 1867.

Q. Who were the Biddenden Maids? N. G. T.

A. This name was given to two unmarried sisters named Mary and Elizabeth Chulkhurst, born at Biddenden in 1100, and joined together, as tradition states, by the shoulders and hips. They lived for 34 years. When one died the other, persisting in a refusal to be separated from the corpse of her sister, succumbed after six hours.

Q. What was Carrie Nation's maiden name? M. O'N.

A. Her maiden name was Moore, and her first husband's name was Gloyd, but it was after she married David Nation that she became famous as a saloon-wrecker.

Q. Whom did Ramsay MacDonald marry? Is she living? W. B.

A. Ramsay MacDonald's wife was the daughter of Dr. Gladstone. She was also niece of Lord Kelvin. Mrs. MacDonald has been dead for many years.

Q. Was Lady Astor married before she married William Waldorf Astor? J. C. W.

A. As Nancy Langhorne, she married Robert Gould Shaw in 1897. She obtained a divorce in 1903, and three years later married William Waldorf Astor.

Q. How many times was Mary Baker Eddy married? C. S. B.

A. Mrs. Eddy's first husband was Major George W. Glover. He died in 1843. Ten years later she married Dr. Daniel Patterson, whom she divorced. She did not marry again until 1877. Her last husband was Asa Gilbert Eddy, who predeceased her.

Q. Name the sisters of Lady Astor. C. P.

A. The three beautiful Langhorne sisters of Virginia are Lady Nancy Astor, Mrs. Charles Dana Gibson, and Mrs. Robert H. Brand.

Q. Please give some facts about the life of Lady Drummond-Hay. P. R. Y.

A. Lady Grace Hay Drummond-Hay is the daughter of Sidney Lethridge of Hempstead, England. In 1920 she married Sir Robert Hay Drummond-Hay, a British diplomat and consular officer. After his death in 1926, she took up journalism as a career. Lady Hay was the only woman to cross the Atlantic on the Graf Zeppelin's first trip, and the only woman passenger who circled the globe on the famous graf.

Q. Was there ever a real person called Calamity Jane? F. G.

A. Jane Burke, better known as Calamity Jane, American Army scout and mail carrier, was born in Princeton, Missouri, 1852, and died in Deadwood, South Dakota, August 1, 1903. She was an Indian scout and was an aide to General Custer and General Miles. For several years she was government mail carrier between Deadwood, South Dakota, and Custer, Montana.

Q. Is Nellie Bly still living? W. McA.

A. Elizabeth Cochrane, the famous Nellie Bly, died in 1922.

Q. Please give a short biography of Rosa Ponselle, who has made such a success in London. J. B. M.

A. Rosa Melba Ponselle, dramatic soprano, was born at Meriden, Connecticut, and educated at the public schools in Meriden and under private tutors in New York City. She joined the Metropolitan Opera Company, November, 1918. She was the first American to make a début in a leading rôle with Caruso.

Q. Is it true that Louisa M. Alcott sold her hair? N. D.

A. Miss Alcott and her sisters "always held this treasure as a possible resource in case of need," but the time never came when it was necessary for them to make the sacrifice.

Q. Who was Lady Hamilton? D. W.

A. Lady Hamilton was the wife of the diplomat, Lord Hamilton, and was famed both as the favorite of Lord Nelson, the British naval hero, and as the model of the artist Romney, who painted thirty portraits of her.

Q. *When did Maude Royden preach at the City Temple in London?* E. G.

A. Maude Royden was assistant preacher at the City Temple from 1917 to 1920. She was the first woman preacher in England.

Q. *What has become of Breshkovskaya, the "Little Grandmother of the Revolution"?* T. P. L.

A. She settled in Czechoslovakia after being exiled from Russia by the Bolshevik régime. She is devoting herself to the education of the children of the Carpatho-Russian peasants.

Q. *Will you please give me some information about the Swedish Angel, a nurse in Russia during the Great War?* F. E. W.

A. The Swedish Legation says that the name of the Swedish Angel, a nurse in Russia during the World War, is Miss Elsa Brändström. She is the daughter of the late Swedish Minister to Russia, General Brändström. After the war she bought a castle in Germany, where German war orphans are educated under her supervision.

Q. *Why is Helen Wills Moody referred to as "Little Poker Face"?* K. J.

A. This sobriquet is applied to Mrs. Moody because of the serene austerity of her features.

Q. *Is Gertrude Atherton married?*

A. She was Miss Gertrude Horn, and married George H. Bower Atherton, who is now dead.

Q. *Is the woman known as Madame Sorgue still living?* S. N.

A. Madame Sorgue, the European Syndicalist, died in London in February of 1924. She was variously known as "the stormy petrel," "Madame Trouble," and "The Most Dangerous Woman in Europe." She was the London correspondent of a Belgian newspaper at the time.

Q. *Where did Madame Du Barry, mistress of Louis XV, die?* I. T. R.

A. After the King's death she retired for several years to her mansion at Luciennes with her latest lover, the comte de Crosse-Brissac. She was accused, during the revolution, and was beheaded in Paris December 7, 1793.

Q. *Are Margaret Sanger, of birth control fame, and Margaret Sangster, one and the same person?* D. R. E.

A. They are not. Mrs. Sanger, advocate of birth control, and editor and publisher of the Birth Control Review, was, before her marriage, Margaret Higgins. She married first Wm. Sanger, by whom she had three children; and second J. Noah H. Slee, of New York City, where she at present resides. Margaret Sangster is a religious writer.

Q. *How old is Aimee Semple McPherson?* S. N.

A. According to Who's Who, the evangelist was born in Ingersoll, Ontario, October 9, 1890.

Q. *Was the assassination of Marat, French revolutionist, by Charlotte Corday an act purely of patriotism?* L. F.

A. Charlotte Corday by her early training had become inspired with a deep-rooted hatred against all oppressors. Her feeling against Marat was accentuated on account of the fact that her lover had been accused by Marat as a conspirator against the republic and was assassinated by villains hired for the purpose. She stabbed Marat, while in his bath, July 13, 1793, and was guillotined herself on the 17th.

Q. *Who was Agnes Sorel?* T. T.

A. She was attached to the service of Isabel of Lorraine, queen of Sicily, wife of Rene of Anjou, the brother-in-law of Charles VII. From 1444 until her death in 1450 she was the acknowledged mistress of the king, the first woman to hold that semiofficial position which was to be of such great importance in the subsequent history of the old régime.

Q. *Who was Poppea Sabina?* T. A.

A. She was an infamous Roman beauty who became the wife of Nero and was killed by him in 65 A.D.

Q. *Was Florence Nightingale associated with the Red Cross?* K. G. D.

A. Miss Nightingale was not associated with this organization. She was the daughter of a wealthy family. She became interested in nursing, particularly of the poor. Upon the outbreak of the Crimean War in 1854, she set out for the front with 38 nurses, and at the close of the war established a testimonial fund for the founding of the Nightingale Home at St. Thomas's Hospital, England, for the training of nurses. She died in London, August 13, 1910.

Q. *What relation was Amy Lowell to Abbott Lawrence Lowell, former president of Harvard University?* G. T.

A. Amy Lowell (1874–1925) was the sister of Abbott Lawrence Lowell.

Q. *Is Carrie Chapman Catt, noted suffragist leader, married?* T. N. L.

A. Mrs. Carrie Chapman Catt was the daughter of Lucius and Maria Lane, and was born in Ripon, Wisconsin. She was married first to Leo Chapman, 1884, who died in 1886, and second to George Wm. Catt, 1890, who died in 1905.

Q. *Where is Pavlova, the Russian dancer, buried?* O. V.

A. This "supreme interpreter of the dance" died at The Hague, and her body was brought first to Rotterdam, and then to London on January 28, 1931. Her body lay in state in the Russian Orthodox Church in that city until the following day. A service was held in the chapel of the hospital where she died. A two and a half hour funeral service was

held in compliance with her wish. Her body was cremated and the ashes are held in London, also by her wish, "until the present régime in Russia ends."

Q. *Isn't it true that Marie Louise, of Austria, had a lover with whom she carried on an affair that was generally known?* F. G. A.

A. Marie Louise deserted Napoleon when he was on his way to Elba and returned to Vienna with Count Neipperg. While Napoleon was at St. Helena Marie Louise lived openly with Neipperg at Parma and she bore the count a son shortly after the death of her exiled husband.

Q. *Is it true that Alice and Phoebe Cary died on the same day?* G. J. I.

A. They did not die on the same day, but in the same year, 1871, within three months of each other. Miss Alice Cary was 51 years old at the time of her death, and Miss Phoebe, 47. Both wrote many poems. Miss Alice wrote several novels, and Miss Phoebe numerous hymns.

Q. *What relation was Marion Harland to Virginia Terhune Van de Water?* W. N.

A. Marion Harland was the nom de plume under which Mrs. Edward Payson Terhune wrote. This noted woman died on June 3, 1922, leaving three children, all of them writers of note. Two of them are daughters, Mrs. Virginia Terhune Van de Water, and Mrs. Christine Terhune Herrick, and the other a son, Albert Payson Terhune.

Q. *Was Anna Howard Shaw a physician or a minister of the gospel?* F. B.

A. She was both. She was ordained in the Methodist Protestant Church and received her M. D. from Boston University.

Q. *Please give a sketch of Onoto Watanna.* S. L. R.

A. Onoto Watanna is the pseudonym of Mrs. Winifred E. Babcock.

She was born in Nagasaki, Japan, in 1879, of English parents. She was educated in Montreal and New York City and married B. W. Babcock of New York in 1901. Many of her stories deal with Japanese life.

Q. *Please name some well known men whose wives were older than they were.* V. B. T.

A. The Empress Josephine was older than Napoleon; Queen Catherine of Aragon was older than Henry VIII; Mary Stuart was older than Francis II of France; Jenny Lind, older than Otto Goldschmidt; Disraeli's wife was his elder by fifteen years; Ann Hathaway Shakespeare was eight years older than her husband; Mrs. Warren G. Harding was older than the late President.

Q. *Please give a short sketch of Dorothy L. Sayers who edited the Omnibus of Crime.* J. F.

A. Dorothy L. Sayers, detective fiction writer, was born in 1893 at Cathedral Choir School, Oxford, where her father was headmaster. In 1915 she graduated from Somerville College, Oxford, with first honors in medieval literature. She was one of the first women to take an Oxford degree. In 1926 she married Captain Atherton Fleming, famous war-correspondent. At present this author is engaged in writing a biography of Wilkie Collins.

Q. *Is Helen Taft still a college dean?* T. C. E.

A. Mrs. Frederick J. Manning (Helen Herron Taft) is a Dean of Bryn Mawr College, Bryn Mawr, Pa.

Q. *Please give a short biography of Elizabeth Palmer Peabody.* L. V. B.

A. Elizabeth Palmer Peabody, an American educator, was born at Billerica, Mass., in 1804. She was for the time connected with the school of Amos Bronson Alcott, in Boston, of which she wrote an account entitled, A Record of Mr. Alcott's School; but later she came under the influence of Friedrich Froebel and was one of the most active in introducing the kindergarten system into the United States. The educator died in 1894.

Q. *Where is Emma Goldman living?* M. W.

A. She has a villa at St. Tropez on the French Riviera, and has lived there for some time.

Q. *When did Cleopatra live?* O. W.

A. Cleopatra was born either 68 or 69 B.C. The exact day is not known. She died August 29, 30 B.C.

Q. *Who was the girl who fought during the World War with the Rumanian forces?* M. H.

A. Ecaterina Teodoroiu was known as the Jeanne D'Arc of Rumania. She fought in the front line trenches of the Rumanian Army during the World War. This girl of 16 wore a man's uniform and fought as bravely as her companions, who revered her as a rare and wonderful example of fidelity and courage. She was killed in battle early in the war.

Q. *What relation of the Roosevelts is Mme. Hilda Roosevelt?* T. D. F.

A. This distinguished opera singer is a second cousin of the late President Roosevelt.

Q. *Will you give me the names of three Italian women who are supporters of the Fascisti?* A. L.

A. Donna Maria Christine Rossi, a student of Bologna, Countess Piccolomini, and Donna Soava Gallone are prominent in the movement.

CHAPTER 30

FISH

Q. *How many different kinds of fish are there?* B. F. D.

A. Of the true fishes, or Pisces, there are about 20,000 living species.

Q. *How far do salmon travel?* B. S.

A. A red salmon marked by the U. S. Bureau of Fisheries in Alaskan waters in May, and caught 44 days later in a Siberian stream, was found to have traveled 1300 miles in that time.

Q. *What is the largest fish caught with rod and reel?* L. D. M.

A. A Mako Shark weighing 2176 pounds holds the record. It was caught by W. W. Selkirk in South Africa in 1928.

Q. *How many anglers are there in the United States?* P. A. D.

A. No definite statement can be made. It is believed that at least 10,000,000 people take active enough interest in fishing to be called anglers.

Q. *How high are the falls that salmon jump when swimming upstream?* T. M.

A. Salmon jump falls of from six to eight feet.

Q. *Is it true that fish see but one color, gray?* S. R.

A. The Bureau of Fisheries says that fishes distinguish colors, but whether they see as many colors as we do is not known nor can we say that the colors appear to them in the same way that they do to us. It would be safe to say, however, that fishes can distinguish more than one color.

Q. *What kind of a fish is scrod?* J. J. F.

A. It is a young codfish spilt and prepared for cooking.

Q. *Will sharks follow a ship for many days?* P. G.

A. They have a most extraordinary power of swimming, great endurance, and a rapidity of motion. Many large ones inhabit the open ocean, following ships for weeks.

Q. *How many eggs are there in the average serving of shad roe?* B. R.

A. The average serving of roe in restaurants is half of a large shad roe, or from 10,000 to 15,000 eggs. The total number of eggs in the roe taken from a single fish is from 23,000 to 32,000.

Q. *How fast do fish swim?* R. B.

A. For the medium sized freshwater fishes, the maximum swimming speed appears to be about seven miles an hour, with the possibility of a bound at nearly three times this rate. More detailed observations will be needed to show variations with species, sex, water temperature, physiological conditions, and so on. Among salt-water fishes the swordfish is known to attain a speed of approximately 60 miles per hour. The Bureau of Fisheries says that the dolphin and carp are said to outswim the fastest vessels.

Q. *How does the globefish make itself round?* M. C. W.

A. The globefish or sea-hedgehog has the faculty of inflating its stomach with air or water. The body is covered with tough skin, without scales, but provided with spines. When the stomach is inflated, the fish assumes a globular form and the spines protrude, forming a defensive armor. A fish thus blown out turns over and floats belly upwards, driving before the winds and waves.

Q. *How large do lake trout grow?* C. S. A.

A. Specimens have been known that exceed 100 pounds in weight, but the average is from 15 to 20 pounds.

Q. *What are the young of fish called?* M. H.

A. Young fish are called fry while the yolk sac upon which they first feed lasts, which is usually 30 days. When a fish passes out of this stage, it is called a fingerling. When a fish is a year old, it is called a yearling. When it reaches the age of two years, it is called a two year old, three years a three year old, etc.

Q. *Three deep-sea sunfish were landed in front of the Flamingo Hotel at Miami. One of them weighed 1000 pounds. Is this a record?* J. H.

A. The ocean sunfish is a lazy, clumsy species, with limited swimming abilities. It is easily approached and harpooned. It often attains a weight of 1500 pounds. Since it has no economic value, no particular effort is made to bring sunfish to shore.

Q. *What is considered to be the most dangerous fish?* M. S.

A. It is generally believed that the shark is the most dangerous, but the barracuda, a large savage pike-like fish of the tropical seas, is more apt to attack man than the shark.

It is almost as large as a twelve-year-old boy and its mouth is such that any bite is likely to result in permanent injury.

Q. *How are French sardines canned?* P. F.

A. They are first beheaded and then gutted and assorted for size. They are washed in sea water and dried on wire screens, nets, or willows in the open air. They are then plunged into a caldron of boiling olive oil. When sufficiently cooked, they are drained, packed in tins, tins filled with oil, then hermetically sealed.

Q. *How many goldfish farms are there in the United States?* D. J.

A. Approximately 350.

Q. *What sort of fish is the pompano?* D. C.

A. It belongs to the Jack family and is one of the most prized of the world's food fishes. The name is taken from the Spanish pampano, meaning grape leaf, which the outline of the fish resembles, when viewed from the side. It attains a length of one foot and a half, a weight of two to three pounds, and has white flaky flesh. It is a favorite in Creole cookery.

Q. *How large a shark has been caught?* N. J.

A. The largest shark of record is a whale shark, Rhinodon typus, which weighed approximately 26,600 pounds, having a length of 38 feet and a girth of 18 feet. It was harpooned at Knights Key, Florida, June 1, 1912, by Captain Charles Thompson.

Q. *What are the essential things to be followed in constructing a fish pond?* T. M. E.

A. The following features should be provided for: Water tightness, so that a small inflow will be sufficient making high temperatures during the summer months; a shallow area, from 18 to 30 inches deep, where the fish may nest; a deeper area, of six feet or more, for winter quarters; and a fertile bottom for the growth of aquatic plants, upon which fish food depends.

Q. *Why are fish found dead in forest streams after forest fires?* P. C.

A. After the fire is over and the embers have cooled, rains wash tons of the alkali ashes into the streams and lakes. This fundamental change in the water content kills thousands of fish.

Q. *Is there a name for fish which go from salt water to fresh to spawn?* F. R.

A. Such fish are termed anadromous fish. The Pacific salmon and the shad are examples. Fish which go from fresh water to salt to spawn are called catadromous. The eel is an example.

Q. *How much do salmon weigh?* J. McD.

A. Salmon have been caught as heavy as 40 pounds. Twenty is a good average.

Q. *What is a trot line?* A. D. G.

A. It is a stout line reaching across a stream, or for some distance from one bank, bearing at frequent intervals single hooks hung by short lines.

Q. *Where are the best government bass hatcheries in the United States?* T. C.

A. The state hatcheries at Hackettstown, New Jersey, and Comstock Park, Michigan, and the Federal hatcheries at Tupelo, Mississippi, Orangeburg, South Carolina, and Louisville, Kentucky, are excellent. Louisville's new hatchery is the finest in the country as to buildings and equipment.

Q. *How can one tell when the water in an aquarium needs changing?* E. B.

A. When the bubbles come to the top of an aquarium the water needs more oxygen. The water should be changed and the bottom of the aquarium should be cleaned.

Q. *Why do fish bite?* A. H.

A. American Forests and Forest Life says that contentiousness, water temperature, the angler's skill, tempting bait, and sheer perversity, as well as appetite cause fish to decide whether to bite or not to bite. The pugnacity of some species causes them to strike at objects that get in their way. Feeding is governed to a great extent by temperature changes, and it is well known that fish are more or less inactive when the water temperature is low, requiring little food at such times. During the winter months they take practically no food.

Q. *Has an eel two hearts?* E. H. M. A.

A. The eel has a single heart. It also has in the tail a lymphatic sinus, that is, an enclosed open space filled with lymph. This sinus pulsates and is, therefore, sometimes called the caudal heart. The sinus, however, is a simple structure and does not have the complex mechanism of a true heart.

Q. *Is the trout fishing good in Switzerland?* G. G. S.

A. The lakes and mountain streams of Switzerland abound in trout, especially in the Upper Engandine.

Q. *What kinds of fish are found in the Potomac River?* C. H. H.

A. The following are some of the fish usually found in the Potomac River: shad, black bass, six species of suckers, about six species of catfish, carp, croakers, spots, pike, trout, yellow perch, and sunfish.

Q. *How is the sturgeon caught?* B. R.

A. The Bureau of Fisheries says that the sturgeon is caught by snagging. It will not take any bait. Snagging is done with a hook and line. A very heavy linen thread is used for the line about one-eighth inch in diameter. The hook should be very stout and from three to four inches in length.

Q. What is Bombay duck? A. G. H.

A. It is small dried fish canned in Bombay, India.

Q. Is there a fish called the John Dory? G. F.

A. There is. Its English name is believed to be a corruption of the French jaune doree, in reference to the golden-yellow color of the living fish. The John Dory inhabits the Atlantic coasts of Europe, the Mediterranean, and the Australian seas.

Q. How big does a jewfish grow? K. L. J.

A. Some species of jewfish attain a weight of 500 pounds, notably the black sea bass and the black jewfish.

Q. Is swordfish increasing in popularity as a food? N. L.

A. It has caught the popular fancy and is considered an excellent food.

Q. How can the age of a fish be determined? M. H.

A. There are two ways to tell the age of a fish, but both are technical and the test can be made only in a laboratory. It may be determined by microscopic examination of the scales and second by microscopic examination of the bone in the ear of the fish. The latter test is more technical and can be made only by one experienced in work of this kind.

Q. Does a fish hear and if so, how? H. E.

A. Fishes do hear to a certain extent. The more rapid vibrations of the water they sense with their ears, as sounds. Owing to the great energy of sound waves in water, these pass through the hard tissues of the head and reach the internal ear unimpaired. Thus no other parts of the ear are necessary. The fish ear is primitive in itself, it exhibits in its various conditions several grades of proficiency. The ears of these lower fishes are stimulated only by relatively loud noises such as have been shown to be effective stimuli for the skin. In the higher fishes, the teleosts, the ears are not only stimulated by noises of the kind just mentioned, but they are stimulated by much less intense sounds and sounds in the nature of tones.

Q. What is the nature of a fish's circulatory system? T. L. B.

A. The circulation of fish is practically the same as that of higher animals except that the lungs are replaced by gills. When water passes over the gills the blood takes up the oxygen. In some fish, in addition to gills, there are rudimentary lungs, a supplementary circulation.

Q. Can fish swim backwards? J. B.

A. It is possible for fish to swim backwards. They occasionally back up when swimming, but as a rule do not go far swimming backwards.

Q. If fish will not bite, is it a sign that no fish are present in that particular place at that particular time? K. T.

A. It may often mean that the water is ideal for fish in that it contains a variety of desirable foods and that the bait is lost among so many other objects at which the fish may bite. At such times the angler's skill will be taxed to find some unusually attractive lure.

Q. In what light should a goldfish aquarium be kept? C. M.

A. The aquarium should have a northern or northeastern exposure in summer, while in winter it should be placed where it will get the sunlight for from two to three hours each day. The light should enter the aquarium in about the same way it enters the streams. If too much light is admitted it will stimulate the growth of low vegetation known as algae, which causes the water to turn green.

Q. Are tuna fish found anywhere except on the Pacific Coast? S. M.

A. The tunny is any of several oceanic fishes of the mackerel family, especially the great or common tunny of all warm seas. On the Atlantic Coast of America it is called horse mackerel; on the Pacific Coast it is called tuna.

Q. Please give me some information concerning the water supply for the New York Aquarium in Battery Park. W. M.

A. The aquarium is equipped for heating sea water for tropical fishes in winter, and has a refrigerating plant for cooling fresh water in summer. Flowing fresh water is supplied from the city water system, while the pumps circulate about 200,000 gallons of salt water daily.

Q. A went fishing and sent home fish not cleaned, packed in ice and sawdust. B sent his fish home cleaned. Which is the better way? D. B. S.

A. The Bureau of Fisheries says that if in transporting fish not more than four hours is required, it is not objectionable to send the fish not cleaned. If, however, the time will amount to more than four hours, the fish should be cleaned, giving special attention to the removal of the gills and the blood which is concentrated along the backbone. The viscera should also be removed, and the fish then shipped in ice and sawdust.

Q. What was the name of the particularly fierce fish Theodore Roosevelt discovered on his South American trip? Have any of them ever been brought to this country alive? D. F.

A. The paranha. The New York City Aquarium has specimens.

Q. Why are plants grown in aquariums? L. H.

A. They add beauty and help to purify the water. They give off oxygen which the fish need and take up some of the waste products as carbon dioxide.

Q. What is a hippocampus? H. E.

A. It is a small fish, commonly known as a sea-horse.

Q. Please describe the devil-fish. M. P.

A. The devil-fish is a huge ray of the family Mantidae which have a lozenge-shaped disc broader than long, with the head free from the pectoral fins. It is provided with a pair of anterior processes and the tail is long and whip-like. The two genera and six or seven species are confined to warm seas. The best-known species is Manta birostris, sometimes called the blanket-fish by tropical American pearl-fishers, from their belief that it attacks and devours men after enveloping them in its great wing-like pectoral fins, which reach a breadth of 20 feet. It is common in tropical American waters and occurs on both the Atlantic and Pacific coasts of the United States. The name applies to the Octopus and allied eight-armed Cephalopoda.

Q. Where is the new aquarium in Chicago? N. H.

A. The Shedd Aquarium is in Grant Park, a short distance northeast of the Field Museum. Funds to the amount of $3,000,000 were guaranteed by the late John G. Shedd for the creation of the aquarium. The building contains 132 exhibition tanks.

Q. Does the change of waters account for the fact that the flesh of some salmon is red and of some is pink? P. K.

A. The difference in the color of the flesh of salmon is a difference between various species of the same genus Oncorhynchus, to which all the Pacific Coast salmon belong. The red and pink varieties have the same food value.

Q. Are salt baths good for goldfish? O. K.

A. A salt bath is very beneficial to goldfish as a remedy for parasites and fungus growth which attack them. A solution of 13 ounces of salt per gallon of water is prepared and the fish dipped up and lowered into the bath where they should remain for two or three seconds. They may then be transferred to another vessel containing well aerated water of the same temperature as that from which they were taken. This treatment may be profitably repeated daily for two or three days.

Q. Does a fish have a heart, and if so, where is it located? H. C. M.

A. All fishes have hearts, but in the lowest forms, the heart is reduced to a simple pulsating tube. The heart of a fish is located in the front part of the body, directly behind the neck. It is not necessarily located on the left side, as in mammals, but may be in the middle of the body, or on either side.

Q. Are salmon as plentiful on the Atlantic coast as on the Pacific? R. S. N.

A. Atlantic salmon are not nearly so numerous as Pacific salmon, and the catch in the United States is restricted almost entirely to Maine.

Q. Are the fish in Lake Baikal of Arctic variety? C. K.

A. Fish in Lake Baikal are not typical of Arctic Ocean variety. They are more like the fish fauna of the north temperate region in general; but, in detail, they are peculiar to Lake Baikal because that lake has been isolated for long eons of time and therefore has developed a fauna peculiar to itself.

Q. Are there several kinds of sardines? G. P.

A. Commercially speaking, any small fish of the herring family is a sardine. The herring family includes not only the true sardine or pilchard, but also the sea herring or sild, and the sprat or bristling.

Q. Are fish called skates good to eat? J. P.

A. The Bureau of Fisheries says that skates are good to eat. The part of the skate taken customarily for commercial food purposes is the saddle, which is a portion of the body of the fish immediately behind the head and between the wings.

Q. Are there fish in the Mediterranean Sea? P. W.

A. It abounds in fish, some 400 species having been noted.

Q. How deep in the sea can fish remain alive? F. B. S.

A. Fish are able to live at the greatest known depths of the ocean. Deep-sea monsters are especially adapted to the enormous pressure encountered at the bottom of the ocean.

Q. Can the age of a large-mouth black bass be told by its size? F. R.

A. A black bass 10 to 12 inches in length, weighing a pound or a little over, is about two years old. At three years the bass will be from 12 to 15 inches long and weigh from two to two and one-half pounds.

Q. Are there any fish except guppy-fish which are born alive instead of being hatched from eggs? J. T.

A. Others are the Embiotocidae or surf fishes of the Pacific coast of North America; many of the Cyprinodontidae or top minnows, which are common in most fresh water streams in this country; many sharks and rays found mostly in tropical waters; and many of the small toy aquarium fish such as the guppy-fish.

Q. What is meant by fish and chips? F. E.

A. It is a dinner very popular in England and Canada. The houses or stores which serve this dinner serve, as a rule, no other kind of meals. It is made of filleted white fish, sliced very thin and in pieces about half the size of the hand, dipped in waffle batter made without grease, then fried in deep fat. French-fried potatoes are served with it, hence the name, fish and chips. It is sprinkled with a little vinegar, salt, and pepper.

CHAPTER 31

FLAGS

Q. *In what battle was the American flag first used?* H. H.

A. The U. S. flag was first unfurled on land in the fight at Cooch's Bridge, Del., on September 3, 1777. The spot is marked with a handsome monument.

Q. *When a state is added to the Union, when is the star added to the flag?* R. T.

A. The star is added on July 4th, following the date of admission.

Q. *When a flag is to be placed at half mast, is it run to the top of staff first?* R. A. W.

A. It should be run to top of staff, then lowered to half-staff. When it is taken down, it is first run to the peak and then lowered. A flag should never be allowed to touch the ground.

Q. *How long has the American Flag had forty-eight stars?* D. A. N.

A. The United States Flag has had forty-eight stars only since July 4, 1912, the Independence Day following the admission of the last two states, New Mexico and Arizona.

Q. *Does the flag fly over the National Capitol day and night?* J. G. K.

A. The flag which flies from a staff over the central pediment and in front of the dome of the National Capitol on the east front, and a similar flag on the corresponding side of the dome on the west front, are never lowered, night or day, except

for replacement. Other official flags, by regulation, are lowered at sunset and run up to the peak of the staff at sunrise. That these flags should fly continuously is a matter of custom, which has been followed for many years, until now it has the authority of tradition.

Q. *What became of the U. S. flag carried by United States troops in London, England, during the World War?* L. L.

A. This particular flag is now hanging at President Wilson's tomb in the National Cathedral of St. Peter and St. Paul in Washington, D. C.

Q. *Is the Stars and Stripes the oldest flag now in use?* S. L.

A. It is the second oldest established flag, the Danish flag being the only one which dates further back in an unchanged form. The cross of the Danish Flag was adopted as the national emblem in the year 1219. The changes in our flag are not counted, as the law establishing the flag provided for them. At the time the United States flag was officially adopted on June 14, 1777, there were a good many national flags which had been in use for a considerable period of time, but through changes in government these flags have all since been changed in one way or another. The present British National Flag or "Union Jack" was not adopted until 1801, the date of the union of Great Britain with Ireland.

Q. *In our first flags were the thirteen stars in a circle on the blue field, or were there twelve stars in the circle with the thirteenth in the center?* J. U.

A. Sometimes the stars were arranged in a circle, sometimes scattered, and sometimes in a circle of twelve with one in the center.

Q. *What are the rules for displaying the U. S. Flag when it is not on a staff?* E. P.

A. The Flag Code as adopted by the National Flag Conference provides as follows: When the Flag is displayed in a manner other than by being flown from a staff, it should be displayed flat, whether indoors or out. When displayed either horizontally or vertically against a wall, the union should be uppermost and to the Flag's own right, i.e., to the observer's left. When displayed in a window it should be displayed in the same way, that is, with the union or blue field to the left of the observer in the street. When festoons, rosettes, or drapings are desired, bunting of blue, white, and red should be used, but never the Flag.

Q. *When did the tricolor become the flag of France?* A. R.

A. Marquis de Lafayette brought about the adoption of the tricolor in 1789.

Q. *Where is there an exhibition of our flags?* N. D. B.

A. There has been a partial exhibit of different United States flags since June 4, 1777, in the Arts and Industries Building of the National Museum in Washington, D. C. The Navy Department also has a valuable collection, but the flags in this one antedate rather than follow the year 1777.

Q. *Are all flags spoken of as the colors?* W. R. W.

A. The flag is our National Emblem that is hoisted on a flagstaff. The colors are National or Regimental Emblems carried by foot troops when marching or parading.

These emblems of the mounted organizations are called standards.

Q. *When entering a British port, does an American cargo ship fly a British flag?* F. T.

A. Merchant ships fly two flags. On the foremast is the flag of the port to which the ship is bound, and on the stern mast, the flag of the ship's country is flown.

Q. *Why does the Confederate Battle Flag of 1863 have thirteen stars when only eleven states seceded?* E. A. P.

A. Although the Federal Government considered the States of Kentucky and Missouri as members of the Union, these states actually had representatives in the Confederate Congress and were represented in that body during the life of the organization. These states were considered by the Confederacy as members of that government.

Q. *Where is the enormous flag which was carried in a G. A. R. parade about 15 years ago?* J. T. W.

A. This flag is owned by the City of Canton, Ohio. It is 53½ feet wide and 120 feet long. The stripes measure 4 feet 1½ inches in width and the stars are 5 feet in diameter. The weight of the flag is 150 pounds. This flag was carried in the G. A. R. parade in Washington, D. C., in 1915, and was hung from the dome of the Capitol.

Q. *For what citizens is the United States Flag generally flown at half-staff?* W. C. C.

A. The custom regarding the half-staffing of the United States Flag is that such action is taken only when an important official or national figure has died, for whom national mourning is declared, as in the case of the late William Howard Taft, former President and Chief Justice. In a case such as that of the late Knute Rockne, national mourning was not declared, and consequently the United States Flag was not officially half-staffed. State or organization flags may be flown at half-staff in cases short of national mourning.

Q. *Who furnishes the flag which drapes the casket of a deceased veteran of the World War? C. R. F.*

A. It is furnished by either the Veterans Administration or the War Department. The Veterans Administration customarily supplies the flag if the veteran was not in active service at the time of his death, while the Quartermaster Corps generally furnishes flags for active service men. The flag should not be lowered into the grave with the coffin, but should be removed at the point of the burial service when the casket is started downwards. The flag is customarily turned over to the relatives of the deceased.

Q. *Is it true that each star in our flag stands for an individual state? N. D.*

A. This is not a fact. The stars collectively represent the forty-eight States of the Union.

Q. *Please describe the Hawaiian flag. P. M.*

A. As a territory of the United States, the Stars and Stripes is first. The official emblem of the islands consists of eight horizontal stripes of white, red, and blue, with the Union Jack in the upper left-hand corner.

Q. *When a government official of a foreign country is visiting in this country, how are the two countries' flags flown on his residence? L. T.*

A. The visit of Premier Laval of France is a case in point. The French flag is flown to the left as observed from the street.

Q. *Is it against the law to wash or mend an American flag? J. M.*

A. The United States flag may be laundered and may be sewn if torn. However, if it is in a bad condition so that it will not be a credit to its owner if displayed, it should be decently destroyed, preferably by burning.

Q. *Please name some countries whose flags are blue and white without any red. C. N.*

A. Argentina, Greece, Guatemala, Honduras, and Nicaragua have blue and white flags.

Q. *Please describe the flag of the new Spanish Republic. O. F. M.*

A. It is composed of three equal horizontal stripes—the top red, the center yellow, and the bottom purple.

Q. *How should the flag be flown on Armistice Day? F. J. C.*

A. It should be flown at full staff from sunrise until sunset.

Q. *What were the British and French flags at the time of the American Revolution? M. M.*

A. The British flag was a blue shield with the crosses of St. Andrew and St. George: St. George cross white; St. Andrew, red. The standard of France at this period was white with the golden fleur-de-lis or lily.

Q. *What is the symbolism of the Albanian flag? D. S.*

A. The flag has a red field with a black double-headed eagle. This is an old national emblem of the Albanian people dating back to the time of the Crusades and signifies both spiritual and temporal power. This has an added meaning in Albania, standing for North and South Albania.

Q. *In what house was the flag made which waved over Fort McHenry and inspired The Star-Spangled Banner? C. O. H.*

A. On the northwest corner of Pratt and Albemarle Streets, Baltimore, Maryland, is the so-called Flag House where Mrs. Mary Pickersgill made the flag which floated triumphantly over Fort McHenry throughout its bombardment in 1814.

Q. *Please describe the flag of Afghanistan. E. V. M.*

A. The flag of Afghanistan is a black banner on which appears the

Afghan seal, which consists of a white octagonal-shaped figure upon which is superimposed a black circle within which again is a white mosque.

Q. *When was Flag Day first cele-brated in a public school?* W. McA.

A. Philadelphia was the first to observe the day in the schools, June 14, 1893.

Q. *Please describe the German flag.* L. M. H.

A. The present national flag of the German Republic has three equal horizontal bars of black, red, and gold. The merchant flag is the old monarchal national flag, three equal horizontal bars of black, white, and red, with the new Republic standard in the union portion at the staff end of the black stripe.

Q. *Are the flags of the City of New York and of the Mayor the same in design?* I. O. R.

A. The Mayor's flag is the same in design as the flag of the City of New York, except that upon the middle white bar of the latter there are above the design of the seal in a semi-circle, five blue five-pointed stars typifying the five boroughs of the city.

Q. *Why is a flag called a union jack?* E. C. B.

A. A jack is a small flag used as a signal, hoisted on a jack staff at the bow of a vessel. The union jack was so called because it was a union of the emblems of Great Britain and Ireland.

Q. *What is the Nationalist Flag of India?* H. N.

A. Officially, there is no such flag. Great Britain still regards India as a British-governed empire with not even dominion status. Consequently the only official flag for India as a nation and people is the Union Jack. For certain colonial purposes, as is the case with other member nations of the British Empire, the Union Jack is flown with the colonial badge at the intersection of the crosses, or the red or blue ensign is flown with the badge in the flag. The badge of India is a five-pointed star within a garter and surrounded by golden rays. However, the Indian national-ists have a flag, three horizontal bars of white, green, and red, which has been flown and carried repeatedly in spite of the prohibition of the vice-regal government. This custom is suppressed when possible, and has led to numerous riots and arrests.

Q. *Is it true that the flag which waved at the Surrender of Yorktown was not properly made according to existing specifications?* S. T.

A. The flag waved at the fall of Yorktown, October 19, 1781, had the union proper, but it contained 13 stripes, alternate white and red in-stead of having the red stripes on the edges.

Q. *What is meant by a merchant flag?* W. H. P.

A. It denotes the flag of a coun-try ordinarily used by merchant ves-sels as opposed to the standard flown by vessels of war. In a good many countries the two are the same, though in some cases the man-of-war has the national coat-of-arms displayed in the center or on the union of the flag.

Q. *Why is one flag flown at the Union Station in Washington, D. C., some of the time, and at others, three?* M. McM.

A. The circular plot of land in front of the station containing the flag staffs was originally planned as a part of the station grounds, but was taken over by the Federal Gov-ernment shortly after the station was completed. The Union Station keeps one flag ready for occasions when only one is needed, but on special occasions the Office of Public Build-ings and Public Parks sends two ad-ditional flags and the Union Station then flies all three. A typical occa-sion on which three flags were flown was on the visit of the King and Queen of Siam to Washington.

CHAPTER 32

FOOD

Q. What town has a Sauerkraut Festival each year? J. L.

A. The Sauerkraut Festival at Springfield, Minnesota, has attained fame all over the Northwest. It is stated that as many as fifteen thousand people gather for this celebration. Prominent speakers, stirring music, and a sauerkraut-eating contest are features of the occasion.

Q.. What is pemmican? E. L.

A. Pemmican is a compressed food, made from dried beef, fat, sugar, and dried currants. It is used extensively by Arctic explorers.

Q. Colonial menus mention flummery and sillibub. What were they? F. L.

A. Flummery was a kind of blanc mange, while sillibub was a combination of cream and wine or sweet cider. Frequently the cream was whipped before adding the wine or cider.

Q. What substance gives Worcestershire sauce its characteristic flavor? A. J. M.

A. The characteristic flavor is imparted by the soy bean.

Q. Do yellow and white corn meal have the same food value? B. O.

A. They are similar in composition though they differ in flavor and appearance. White corn meal is milder in flavor. White corn meal is preferred generally in the Southeastern States and in some parts of New England. Yellow corn meal is preferred in the Northern States as a whole, while blue, black, and red varieties have always been used in parts of the Southwest where Mexican influence is marked.

Q. What is jugged hare? C. R.

A. It was originally hare or rabbit stewed in a jug or jar. The term is now applied to a method of canning rabbit or hare. It is cooked with bacon, flour, onion, spices, and water, then sealed in cans.

Q. Is it correct to say cold slaw or cole slaw? J. K.

A. The name is cole slaw. Cole means cabbage, and slaw is from the Danish slaa meaning salad.

Q. Did the Italian invent macaroni? R. B.

A. Macaroni and other pastes are considered typical and peculiarly Italian food, and Italy is probably entitled to the credit for her early appreciation of these foods. However, history credits their first use to the Chinese and their European introduction to the Germans. The Italians are said to have learned the art of making them from the latter. History shows that by the time of the 14th century, Italy was the only European nation enjoying macaroni.

Q. When was the first law promulgated relating to the adulteration of food? C. D.

A. The first protective food law on record was English and bears the date of 1203.

Q. *What are the laxative foods?* H. H.

A. A list of good laxative foods would include oranges, peaches, grapes, plums, apples, pears, prunes, cream, lettuce, tomato, onions, bacon, squash, carrots, peas, spinach, and oatmeal.

Q. *How is bannock made?* R. T. C.

A. Hunter-Trader-Trapper says that no cooks make it alike. Originally it was an old European or Scottish thick bread made of peas, meal, oatmeal, or barley. A modification is made as follows: oatmeal with some wheat flour, a cupful to a spoonful of baking powder, salt to taste, and water. It is cooked in a covered frying pan over a slow fire.

Q. *What is the derivation of the word goulash?* A. G. N.

A. Goulash derives its origin from gulyash, meaning cattle herdsman. The first goulash was cooked at Hortobad, near Debrezcen, Hungary, some five centuries ago by the herdsmen in the open.

Q. *What kind of candy was first made in this country?* P. F.

A. Stick candy was the first confection made in the United States.

Q. *What is the difference between a doughnut and a cruller?* F. H. C.

A. Years ago the difference was marked. A doughnut was made of raised bread dough, to which sugar, spices, and eggs were added; while the cruller was made of a mixture containing baking powder, or cream of tartar and soda. Now the term doughnut is made to include both kinds of fried cakes.

Q. *Do broths so often given to convalescents have any nutritive value?* I. N. O.

A. They have a slight food value but they are mostly stimulating and tonic. When used warm, they favor the secretion of the digestive enzymes and thus may prove of some value.

Q. *What is wild rice used for?* D. T. H.

A. Its principal use is as food for wild ducks and other waterfowl. It is also used to some extent as human food, particularly by some of the Indian tribes of the Upper Mississippi Valley. It is considered excellent to serve as a vegetable with wild duck, fowl, and game.

Q. *What foods are indigenous in America? Is tobacco?* L. M.

A. There has been much controversy concerning the food originally found in the Americas. It is generally agreed that in North America were tobacco, maize, a certain type of pear, and a small variety of tomato. In Central America and the Islands, the early explorers also found tobacco and tomatoes. In South America, particularly Brazil, wild potatoes were found in abundance, so much so that in about 1840 it was necessary to import thousands of these native plants in order to save the potato crop of the world. It was originally thought that bananas were first found in Central and South America and the Islands, but later this theory was the subject of much debate, and it is generally believed today that, while bananas were originally in that section of the world, they were also found in tropical sections of the Eastern Hemisphere at the same time.

Q. *How many lollipops or all-day suckers are consumed yearly in this country?* H. A. P.

A. No statistics are available, but it is known that about two billion sucker sticks are used annually.

Q. *Does salt-water taffy actually contain salt?* G. M.

A. The recipe includes salt. Place in a saucepan 2 cups of white sugar, 1 cupful of white corn syrup, ½ cupful of water. Bring to a boil, then add 1 teaspoonful of glycerine and ¼ teaspoonful of cream of tartar. Boil to about 260 degrees or to a little more than the hard ball stage and not quite to the crack stage.

Pour on a greased platter or a slab and add a tablespoon of butter and one teaspoon of salt. Flavor to suit taste and cool. Pull until of the right consistency.

Q. *Is it wise to use the liquid in which vegetables are canned?* A. C.

A. This liquid should never be discarded. It contains flavor and food value, including mineral salts, and if not served with the vegetables it is suitable for use in soups and sauces.

Q. *Is there any danger in using galvanized pots for cooking purposes?* V. C.

A. Galvanized iron is iron covered with a coating of zinc. The solutions from zinc are poisonous, therefore, the use of galvanized iron for any cooking purpose is dangerous.

Q. *Which foods contain iron and copper?* R. C.

A. The most important sources of iron are vegetables, fruits, eggs, and milk. Among foods containing copper may be mentioned liver, beefsteak, and milk.

Q. *Was barley used in ancient times?* C. N. N.

A. It is said that barley is the oldest food of man. Several varieties, one the sacred barley of the ancients, were known to the lake dwellers of Switzerland. It was cultivated in ancient Egypt, and was also the chief breadstuff of the Hebrews, Greeks, and Romans.

Q. *How may fruit be canned without sugar for persons with diabetes?* M. F.

A. Prepare jars, rubber rings, and tops as usual for any canning process. Select and prepare the fruit as usual, taking care to select firm fruit. Fill the jars with equal weights of fruit and water. Screw on the tops lightly. Sterilize the fruit and jars by placing them in a kettle or boiler of hot water. There should be a rack in the bottom of the kettle to prevent the jars from touching it.

Bring the water in the boiler to the boiling point and boil for thirty minutes. Remove the jars from the boiling water, take off the tops and add boiling water to fill the jars to overflowing. Put on new rubber rings, then put on the tops, seal, and turn upside down until cold.

Q. *Are chowders typically American?* D. F.

A. Chowders, although considered American, did not originate in America. They are supposed to have been made first by the fisher folk of Brittany. Every one in the village brought their contribution for the dish and added it to the common cauldron, and the name chowder comes from the name of their cauldron, which was chaudiere. Our early colonists learned this dish from the French, and so chowders are associated with the history of New England, and are thus linked with America in general.

Q. *Is candy a perishable food?* M. S.

A. Candy is considered perishable in that its sales value is affected by its condition. Candy should not be kept in a hot place and should be given the same care when stored that is given to other perishable foods.

Q. *How is a tomato cocktail made?* S. C.

A. Bring one-quart can of tomatoes to a boil. Rub through a colander and chill. Season with salt and sugar for children. For adults, season with salt, red pepper, and add a little Worcestershire and horseradish if desired. Serve very cold in cocktail glasses at the beginning of the meal.

Q. *Is it necessary to use new rubber rings on glass jars each canning season?* R. B.

A. Rubber deteriorates and it is a mistake to use the rings a second time. The cost of them is small compared with the risk of having fruit and vegetables spoil when old ones are used.

Q. *How many meals are eaten away from home by the average person?* C. O. B.

A. There are no statistics for the entire country. A survey of New York City, however, shows that every sixth meal, on an average, eaten by its more than six million people, is served in a public place. More than 2,000,000 persons eat at least one meal daily away from home.

Q. *How did "Porterhouse" steak get the name?* A. G.

A. The "Porterhouse" steak is said to have originally got its name from a small hotel in Sandusky, Ohio, the Porter House. In 1847 Charles Dickens visited the Porter House and was so pleased with a steak served to him there that he spread its fame through the United States, referring to it as the steak served in the Porter House in Ohio. Afterwards leading hotels and cafés began to call their best steaks "Porterhouse."

Q. *What foods should be included and avoided in planning summer meals?* D. C.

A. It is wise to avoid rich pastries and desserts and to limit meat to one meal a day. Fewer fattening foods should be eaten. Otherwise choose a ration with plenty of vegetables, greens, salads, and fruits in season. It is best to cut out stimulants and depend upon whole milk, buttermilk, water, ginger ale, and fruit juices to quench thirst.

Q. *Will taking canned food to a high altitude cause spoilage?* E. B.

A. It will have no effect upon it.

Q. *How can pumpkins be kept throughout the winter?* A. R.

A. Pumpkins may be kept fresh until spring if gathered just before fully ripe and if the storage place is dry, cool, and protected from frost. The best method is to place them on shelves, seeing that they do not touch each other and occasionally wiping them off with a dry cloth. Peeled, cut-up, sun dried, and properly stored, they can be used all the year.

Q. *Does the freezing of canned food make it unfit to eat?* C. T.

A. It does not. The texture of certain types of food is affected, but the food value is unchanged. Vast quantities of the food taken on the Byrd Antarctic Expedition were in cans, were frozen solid for months, but were in edible condition.

Q. *Could you publish simple directions for making sugar toys?* C. W. C.

A. Sugar toys may be made according to the following directions: 4 lbs. sugar; 2 oz. corn sirup; 1 pt. water. Boil to 240–242°; then stir until cloudy and pour in plaster-of-paris moulds that have been soaked in cold water for 2 to 3 hours and drained.

Q. *How long may lemons be kept?* R. M. I.

A. A lemon may be preserved for years by putting it in a 2 per cent formaline solution or a 5 per cent glycerin solution. The color might not hold permanently. Lemons, if wrapped in tissue paper and kept on trays in a cool, dark place, will keep for a considerable period of time.

Q. *How can one obtain the glossy appearance on chocolate candy?* C. P.

A. Chocolates derive their glossy appearance from careful control of their dipping temperature (about 80° Fahrenheit) and quick cooling at 50° to 65° Fahrenheit, in a relatively dry atmosphere.

Q. *When economy must be effected, what part of the children's diet is most important?* H. T.

A. For children the government home economists say that the food dollar should be divided as follows: 25 cents for milk and cheese, 25 to 20 cents for vegetables and fruit, 15 to 20 cents for bread and cereals, 20 to 15 cents for butter, lard, or other fats and sugar or molasses, 15 to 20 cents for meat, fish, and eggs. A family of adults would need less milk and cheese, and correspondingly more vegetables and fruit.

Q. *What food is used most widely?* L. T. D.

A. Rice is more extensively grown and more widely used than any other foodstuff.

Q. *Describe how meat may be barbecued.* F. L.

A. Barbecued meat is meat roasted over or in front of a bed of glowing coals and basted during the cooking with certain piquant sauces. The fire should be built either in a trench of pit, or in a regular barbecue roaster. A broiler, which may be metal lath or a commercial broiler, is placed over the coals. A hardwood fire is recommended. The meat should be dipped in the sauce, which should be heated, and placed on the broiler. It should be constantly swabbed or basted with the sauce and turned frequently. Allow the meat 20 minutes to the pound for cooking. Thick steaks, and chops of all kinds, venison, chicken, ham, and even small roasts are the favorite meats to barbecue.

Q. *What is the relationship between vitamin D and ultra violet rays?* T. H.

A. Vitamin D, unlike other vitamins, is not plentiful in many of the common foods. Green vegetables do not contain it, nor do fruits or cereals. It can, however, be produced in various foods and in the human body by artificial means. This is because many food materials contain the chemical compound known as ergosterol, which is changed into vitamin D when exposed to sunlight or to the rays of an ultra-violet lamp. The human skin, also, contains ergosterol, and this, it is believed, is the reason why baths in summer sunlight, when the ultra-violet rays are the most abundant, are so effective in promoting bone growth and preventing rickets in children, just as are the foods that are rich in vitamin D.

Q. *Who originated chop suey?* M. M.

A. The truth seems to be that there is no such dish as chop suey known in China, although it is commonly served as Chinese throughout the United States. This has come about in a curious way. It originated at a dinner that Prince Li Hung Chang gave in New York, when he made his trip around the world. Prince Li carried his own chef with him, and the menu was strictly Chinese. One of the dishes especially delighted the wife of the guest of honor, and she asked Li what it was. Prince Li called in his chef, and the chef replied in Chinese, "It is a creation of my own —a chop suey." The words "chop suey" mean a mixture or hash. Prince Li said in English, "It is a chop suey." The American woman spread the news of chop suey, the wonderful dish. The name was taken up by the Chinese restaurants in America and today chop suey is the chief concoction that they serve.

Q. *Why do some farmers' wives use salicylic acid when canning?* I. G.

A. The U. S. Department of Agriculture has made the following statement: "The attention of the Department of Agriculture has recently been called to the widespread use, especially in rural communities, of salicylic acid in preserved foods. The Department is aware that this practice is not confined to salicylic acid under its own name alone, but that large quantities of this acid, and of boric acid as well, are sold under fanciful names as 'preserving powders' or 'canning compounds,' at prices which are much in excess of their real value. In the directions for use the housewife is told to fill the jar with fruit or vegetables, cover with water, and add a teaspoonful of the powder. It is true that these powders may prevent the decay of the fruit or vegetables, but they also encourage uncleanly and careless work, and their excessive use may be attended with very serious effects on the health. It is entirely practicable to put up both fruits and vegetables in such a manner that they will keep indefinitely by sterilizing the products by means of heat, and there is no excuse for running any risk by the use of preserving powders."

Q. Is it safe to leave canned foods in the cans after opening? P. F. A.

A. There is nothing in the can, or in the material going into the structure of the can, that is in any way injurious to health. The United States Department of Agriculture carried on a three-year study which demonstrated that there is nothing about a tin can that can, in itself, cause spoilage or be harmful from the health standpoint. Foods left in an open vessel of any kind should, of course, be kept cold and should be protected from dust, flies, or vermin, which will contaminate food, causing it to spoil. As soon as a can is opened, the food no longer is sterile and is subject to spoilage just as any other cooked food would be if it were improperly cared for.

Q. What sort of food is chipolata? A. C.

A. It is an Italian creation, half sauce and half stew made of carrots, turnips, chestnuts, onion, sausage, mushrooms, artichokes, celery, and strong veal gravy.

Q. How much food does an elderly person need? O. B.

A. A person beyond the age of seventy and weighing 150 pounds will be amply nourished if the day's menu includes the following: 2 moderate servings of vegetables (puréed if necessary); 1 moderate serving of meat; 1 to 2 glasses whole milk; an egg; 4 or 5 slices of bread; two ordinary squares of butter; 1 or 2 servings of fresh or stewed fruit; 2 or 3 teaspoons sugar and cream for coffee or tea.

Q. How did the popular "club sandwich" happen to be called "club"? R. S.

A. The story goes that a hungry man was prowling around in the larder of his home one night when his family was away. He found in the ice-box numerous odds and ends of food. There were cold chicken, slices of bacon, lettuce, tomato, and a jar of mayonnaise. He put these all together on some toasted bread and the result was so satisfactory that the idea was passed along, and soon won popularity with a large public.

Q. Since contests have been conducted to determine the favorite all-American meal, what is the result? I. D.

A. In one contest, the winning menu voted by 25,000 readers consisted of the following: grapefruit and orange cocktail, cream of tomato soup with crackers, roast chicken with dressing, new peas, mashed potatoes, butter, biscuits, lettuce and asparagus tip salad, pumpkin pie, coffee. In another contest, when one single food was to be voted upon, apple pie proved to be the favorite.

Q. Why is a thick soup called a purée? H. T. T.

A. This is a French word meaning porridge.

Q. What are sippets, frequently mentioned in English cook books? H. A.

A. These are small thin fingers of toast, dry and crisp, served with wine, soup, or as a garnish to made dishes such as ragouts and minces.

CHAPTER 33

FOREIGN COUNTRIES

Q. How many new countries were created as a result of the World War? L. K.

A. In Europe proper eleven sovereign states have been created as a result of the World War.

Q. What is the status of the United States in Haiti? A. J. F.

A. The Department of State says that the relation between the United States and Haiti is determined by the treaty made September 17, 1915. By virtue of the treaty the United States will have occupation privileges until May, 1936.

Q. How many counties formed the Irish Free State? N. G.

A. The 26 southern counties were erected into the Irish Free State, and the 6 northern counties constituted the government of Northern Ireland.

Q. How does Turkey compare in size with some of the American States? L. S. D.

A. Turkey in Europe is now slightly larger than Massachusetts, and the entire Turkish Republic is slightly larger than New Mexico and California combined.

Q. What country is known as the Land without Women? T. W.

A. Mt. Athos on the Macedonian coast of the Aegean Sea is so known. This holy mountain has, since the early days of Christianity, been the retreat of monks and no women have lived there.

Q. How long have there been castes in India? W. W. C.

A. It is not known definitely just when castes originated in India. Records are not available until the Vedic Arya period about 1200 B.C. Castes were then in existence.

Q. How many inhabitants has Liberia? L. A. E.

A. This negro republic has a population of about 2,000,000, all negroes, of whom nearly 20,000 are Afro-Americans. The civilized inhabitants number about 50,000, live near the coast, and speak the English language.

Q. Where is Patagonia? E. A. L.

A. Patagonia is a name now generally applied to an indefinite region lying east of the Andes and south of Rio Negro in the Argentine Republic. It was formerly applied to the whole southern portion of the South American continent.

Q. How much of Norway is in the Land of the Midnight Sun? R. S.

A. Norway reaches 300 miles into the Arctic zone, and nearly one-third of the country is in the domain of the midnight sun and winter darkness, but even in the extreme south the summer day is long, and the winter day is short.

Q. When did Mexico become the size that it is at present? B. L. S.

A. The treaty of Guadalupe Hidalgo, February 2, 1848, conveyed to the United States the territory

207

which has since become the States of California, Nevada, and Utah, part of Colorado, and the largest parts of New Mexico and Arizona. Previous to that time, this territory belonged to Mexico. Five years later, the United States purchased from Mexico about 45,000 square miles of southern Arizona for $10,000,000. Since this treaty, Mexico has remained approximately the same size as it is at present.

Q. What is the population of Puerto Rico to the square mile? H. L.

A. Puerto Rico has an area of 3435 square miles and a population of nearly 1,500,000. This makes more than 400 to the square mile. About 78 per cent of the population is rural, only 22 per cent living in cities.

Q. What countries are represented here by ambassadors? J. E. G.

A. The following nations are represented in this country by ambassadors. They are given in the order of length of service at the beginning of 1933: France, Turkey, Germany, Japan, Poland, Great Britain, Peru, Belgium, Brazil, Argentina, Chile, Mexico, Spain, Cuba, and Italy.

Q. What does the name of the country, Venezuela, mean? G. A. T.

A. It means little Venice. It probably was given to the country because of the pile dwellings built by the natives on Lake Maracaibo, which suggested Venice to the early explorers.

Q. Who first gave the name, "the unspeakable Turk," to the Turkish empire? A. S. D.

A. Its first use is credited to Thomas Carlyle in a public letter in 1877.

Q. How many countries belong to the Pan American Union? P. N.

A. This international organization is composed of the twenty-one Republics of the Western Hemisphere. It was organized in 1890.

Q. Which is the correct title—British Empire or British Commonwealth of Nations? S. L. F.

A. The British Empire is the correct designation for the whole aggregate territory linked together by allegiance to the British Crown. The associated self-governing communities of the British Empire are spoken of as the British Commonwealth of Nations.

Q. Is there a complete separation between Church and State in Chile? M. B. T.

A. The final payment due the Church under the separation agreement provided for by the Constitution in 1925 has been paid.

Q. How many people are there in the Irish Free State? S. M.

A. Its population is 2,975,000. Its area is 26,592 square miles. Northern Ireland or Ulster has an area of 5237 square miles and a population of 1,260,000.

Q. What countries form the Little Entente? L. R.

A. Rumania, Yugoslavia, and Czechoslovakia are the three.

Q. How far is it from Juneau, Alaska, to Little America? T. M. N.

A. It is 8281 nautical miles or 9536 statute miles.

Q. To what part of the continent was the name Africa first applied? B. D.

A. It was originally applied to the country in the neighborhood of Carthage, that part of the continent first known to the Romans. Carthage was founded in 800 B.C.

Q. How many people are there to the square mile in China and Japan? G. A. S.

A. The area of the whole territory of the Republic of China is 4,277,-000 square miles, with a population of 400,800,000, giving the population per square mile about 95. However, this is hardly an indication of the great density of population in some parts of China Proper. For instance, the Province of Kiangsu, with 33,-700,000 people in an area of 38,600 square miles, has a density of 874 persons to the square mile, and is the most densely populated political unit in the world. Japan, with an area of 148,756 square miles and a population of approximately 62,940,000, has a density of population of 423 persons per square mile.

Q. Which country has Tacna and which Arica? C. B.

A. By treaty, the province of Tacna was allotted to Peru and Arica to Chile.

Q. They say that republics are ungrateful, but didn't Colombia give Simon Bolivar a big pension? G. H.

A. The Colombian Congress voted Bolivar a pension of $30,000, but he did not accept it.

Q. What is the area and population of Ecuador? G. M.

A. Ecuador has an area of 118,596 square miles and approximately 2,-000,000 inhabitants.

Q. What country increased its area the most in proportion to its former size, due to the World War? R. S.

A. Rumania. It is now the largest Balkan nation. In 1914, its area was 53,489 square miles and its population 7,500,000. In 1919, its area was 122,282 square miles and its population 17,393,000.

Q. What country was called The Sick Man of Europe? C. T.

A. The Turkish Empire was so characterized by Nicholas of Russia in 1844.

Q. Why are inhabitants of the Netherlands called low Germans? L. K.

A. The inhabitants of the Netherlands are chiefly of the low German race which is composed of three branches — Frankish, Saxon, and Friesian. The term, low, is applied to this section of the world because it occupies the low region near the North Sea.

Q. How much of India now belongs to England? M. C.

A. The area of the British provinces of India is 1,094,300 square miles. The area of protected native states or agencies is 711,032 square miles. The total area of India is 1,805,332 square miles.

Q. How does Germany rank in potential military power? G. S.

A. The total military man-power of Germany is estimated at 8,700,000. Four nations rank ahead of her in actual number of soldiers available. The percentage of military manpower of Germany as compared with the population is 13.73 per cent. Sixteen nations rank ahead of Germany in percentage of military man-power.

Q. What countries are called the Bolivarian nations? H. B.

A. Simon Bolivar founded six nations—Venezuela, Colombia, Ecuador, Peru, Bolivia, and Panama.

Q. How large is Palestine? G. F. C.

A. Excluding Transjordan, the area of Palestine is slightly over 9,000 square miles.

Q. What name was first given to Brazil? A. W. D.

A. The country was discovered by Pedro Alvares Cabral in 1500. He named it Terra de Santa Cruz or Land of the Holy Cross, and took possession of it in the name of the King of Portugal.

Q. Is the present day Russia interested in the drama? B. J.

A. It is said that a spontaneous amateur theatre movement has sprung up in the Soviet Union. Performances take place in factory towns. Village club workers write, produce, and act their own plays. There are some 35,000 of these club theatres in cities and towns, and about 30,000 in the villages. Troupes known as Blue Blossers travel about the country performing before local trade unions and peasant clubs. Their repertoire includes songs, acrobatics, dances, and satirical sketches. There are about 10,000 of these. There are about 9,000 motion picture display places in the Soviet Union.

Q. Is the central part of Australia inhabited? R. S. J.

A. There remains a vast territory estimated at a million square miles, in the central and western portions, which is uninhabited and regarded as uninhabitable.

Q. How long has Delhi been the capital of India? T. B. L.

A. This has been a capital of provinces of India almost from the beginning of the history of India. It was made the British capital of India by proclamation of King George V in 1911.

Q. How many colonies did ancient Greece have? K. H.

A. Greece had as many as 250 colonies in the year 600 B.C.

Q. What is the present capital of Turkey? N. M.

A. The capital of Turkey is Angora. Through the adoption of the Latin alphabet, the transliteration of the name of the capital became Ankara.

Q. Can a person go to American Samoa to live and buy property there? W. R.

A. All the land on these islands is privately owned and there is a law forbidding foreigners to purchase such land. The natives are of a high class and can all read and write. The majority are Christians.

Q. Where is the Hejaz? J. W. J.

A. The Hejaz is one of the new Arab states which became independent after the World War. It was one of the first of the Arab nations to be recognized by the great powers and it was represented at the Peace Conference and admitted to the League of Nations. It is located in northwestern Arabia, extending along the Red Sea for several hundred miles. It includes the important cities of Mecca and Medina, both sacred to the Mohammedan faith. The Hejaz is now a part of the dominions of Sultan Abdul Aziz ibn Saud, the leader and king of the war-like Wahabi sect of Arabs who live in the interior of the peninsula. Abdul Aziz ibn Saud captured The Hejaz in 1925 and on January 11, 1926, was proclaimed in Mecca King of The Hejaz and Sultan of Nejd. On September 22, 1932, he changed the name of his dominion to Soudi Arabia.

Q. Where is the Riviera of Great Britain? F. H.

A. The entire southern coastal region of the Counties of Devon and Cornwall is often referred to as the Riviera of Great Britain.

Q. How are the Highlands divided from the Lowlands of Scotland? T. B.

A. The Grampian Hills extending across Scotland from the southwest to the northeast are generally regarded as the dividing line.

Q. What country received the mandate over Syria? J. F.

A. Syria, a former province of Turkey, after the World War was created an independent state and was placed under mandate to France by the Supreme Council of the League of Nations.

Q. Is Czechoslovakia densely populated? S. T. E.

A. The country is slightly larger than Wisconsin and has five and a half times the population of that State. Villages and towns are about two miles apart, and cities of 15,000 to 30,000 population are encountered about every fifteen miles. The average size of farms is about 25 acres.

Q. Does Russia extend as far to the east as China does? M. L. R.

A. The Union of Soviet Republics extends much farther to the east than China does. The Russian port, Vladivostok, is practically as far east as the easternmost part of China. Much of old Siberia lies north and east of Vladivostok.

Q. Where is Liechtenstein? J. T. M.

A. It lies on the Upper Rhine between Austria and Switzerland. On November 7, 1918, the Diet declared its complete independence. By treaty with Switzerland, the latter country administers its posts and telegraphs.

Q. What country is called the Cock-pit of Europe? B. L.

A. Belgium has often been so called because it has been the site of more European battles than any other country.

Q. How does Japan compare in size with Great Britain and Ireland? B. S.

A. Japan proper contains 148,756 square miles, while Great Britain and Ireland contain 121,633 square miles. Japan has 64,450,000 inhabitants, while the United Kingdom has 46,-500,000.

Q. Has Abyssinia's name been changed to Ethiopia? C. D.

A. Ethiopia is in reality the true official name of that country, and Abyssinia is a name applied to it by Europeans. At the time of the recent accession of the present Emperor, His Majesty Heile Selassie I, the name Ethiopia was revived in official usage.

Q. How large is the Principality of Monaco in which Monte Carlo is situated? B. M. S.

A. It has an area of approximately eight square miles, and a population of 25,000.

Q. What country is called the garden of Europe. P. W. H.

A. Worcestershire is called the garden of England on account of its scenery; Touraine the garden of France on account of its fertility; Sicily the garden of Italy on account of its climate; and Italy is called the garden of Europe on account of its scenery, fertility, and climate.

Q. What country is the Land of Cakes? H. J.

A. Scotland, so called from its oatmeal cakes.

Q. How did the separation of Norway and Sweden come about? G. J.

A. Norway separated from Sweden in 1905. On June 7 of that year the King of Sweden refused to sign an act establishing separate Norwegian consulates, and the Norwegian ministry resigned. No one would accept office, whereupon the Norwegian Storthing voted that the union between Norway and Sweden had been dissolved, since the King of Sweden had acknowledged himself unable to form a Norwegian ministry and could not discharge his constitutional functions.

Q. How does the size of Brazil compare with that of the United States? B. D. C.

A. Brazil is larger. The area of Brazil is officially estimated at 3,-285,319 square miles. The total area of continental United States is 3,-026,789 square miles.

Q. What is the area of Egypt? T. D.

A. The area is about 350,000 square miles if the desert regions are included, and 12,226 square miles if only the cultivated and settled areas of the Nile Valley and Delta are considered.

CHAPTER 34

FORESTRY

Q. How many leaves are there on an apple tree? F. L.

A. The New York State College of Agriculture says that it is estimated that a full-grown apple tree has about 50,000 leaves.

Q. Can a tree forty feet tall be transplanted? Can a tree three feet in diameter be moved? D. L.

A. It is possible to transplant a tree forty feet tall if it is properly handled and prepared with enough soil. The Department of Agriculture says that a tree as large as three feet in diameter can be transplanted.

Q. What is the oldest tree in the City of Washington? G. F.

A. The twin sassafras trees in the grounds at the Soldiers' Home, believed to be over a thousand years old, are said to be the oldest trees in the District of Columbia.

Q. What kind of tree grows the fastest? G. S.

A. The balsa. It reaches a diameter of 15 inches in five years and has a very fast height growth.

Q. Is it detrimental to trees to top them? C. H. H.

A. The Forest Service says that, if properly done, the topping of branches is beneficial and improves the appearance of trees.

Q. What kind of tree is the smallest in this country? A. Z. R.

A. The Alpine willow, which does not exceed six inches in height (sometimes only one inch high), is the smallest tree in the United States.

Q. When did the chestnut blight first attack the trees in this country? D. B.

A. It appeared in 1904 and has spread rapidly to all sections to which the tree is native. Experimentation is going forward, hoping to develop a tree which is blight resistant.

Q. How old must pecan trees be before they will bear nuts? S. W. A.

A. Pecan trees may bear a few nuts when three to five years of age, but generally speaking, pecan orchards do not come into commercial bearing until they are about ten years old. With proper care and adequate spacing, the trend in yields is then upward as the orchard grows older.

Q. What kind of trees were the ones which were found petrified in Arizona? B. D.

A. The wood found in the Petrified Forest in Arizona is that of prehistoric coniferous or evergreen trees.

Q. How old are the queer trees in front of Carvel Hall at Annapolis, Md.? S. G.

A. The trees on the front terrace of Carvel Hall are between 250 and 300 years old. They are ailanthus trees, the Chinese Tree of Heaven. No one seems to know how they happened to be planted on the front terrace of Carvel Hall. They were brought from China in a sailing ship considerably over 200 years ago. The house in front of which they stand is the Prince George Street entrance of Carvel Hall Hotel. It was built in 1764 by William Paca, one of the signers of the Declaration of Independence and the Third Governor of Maryland.

Q. *Please publish data concerning the Liberty Tree in Providence, Rhode Island.* C. A. U.

A. The Providence Journal says that on July 25, 1769, the Liberty Tree of Providence was dedicated in front of Capt. James Olney's tree, on Olney Lane, now Olney Street, by the Sons of Liberty. Among the lower branches a platform was built from which speeches against England's rule of the Colonies were made. The tree was cut down about 1825.

Q. *What became of the redwood stump which was in the grounds of the Department of Agriculture in Washington, D. C.?* C. A. C.

A. This is the stump of a giant redwood tree. It has been removed to Arlington Farms, Virginia. The stump was first exhibited at the Columbian Exposition in Chicago.

Q. *Do trees grow on the Canadian prairies?* A. C. W.

A. The prairies were treeless. Now, however, most farm homes have groves and shade trees. The Canadian Government has fostered the planting of trees and now there are well over 100,000,000 trees on prairie farms.

Q. *What species of tree is used as a memorial to a mother?* J. H. E.

A. The white birch has been designated officially by the American Forestry Association as the tree to commemorate mothers, and the tree at Reading, Pa., is called the Initial Mother's Tree. A white birch tree was planted by Solan L. Parkes on the shores of Lake Antietam, near Reading, Pa., on May 13, 1923, and dedicated to motherhood. Originally designed to honor his own mother, it was later designated to honor mothers of the world.

Q. *What kind of wood is deal?* S. R.

A. Deal is fir or pine.

Q. *How much sap can be expected from a sugar maple?* T. H.

A. A Cornell Bulletin says that about fifteen gallons of sap may be expected from each tree on an average, though the yield may vary from five to forty gallons. Normal sap contains about two per cent of sugar. Hence, it takes forty-five to fifty gallons of sap to make a gallon of sirup; a gallon of sirup of standard density contains about eight pounds of sugar.

Q. *How big a trunk did the Charter Oak have?* J. D. K.

A. Charter Oak was nearly seven feet in diameter. It was in Hartford, Conn., and blew down in a storm on August 21, 1856. Its age was computed to be nearly 1000 years. A section of the trunk has been preserved in the rooms of the Connecticut Historical Society; the remainder was kept or sold for small souvenirs. In a hollow of this tree was concealed the Charter of Connecticut, rescued from Andros in 1687, according to tradition.

Q. *How are coffee trees raised?* M. S.

A. Coffee trees are raised from seed grown in nurseries, and when of a size to endure variations of temperature, usually in about six months time, they are transplanted to the coffee orchard, where they begin to bear when three years old and bear fruit for about twenty years.

Q. *Are you sure that the Australian eucalyptus attains a height of 400 feet?* W. N. W.

A. This statement is made. A member of the Forest Products Laboratory staff who spent a year in Australia not long ago used the opportunity to check up on some of the basic facts. The tallest Australian tree he actually measured was 310 feet, and he satisfied himself that the tallest tree ever measured with accuracy in that country was a Eucalyptus regnans, or mountain ash, that grew at Colac, Victoria, and was 346 feet high. A prize offered at the Melbourne Exposition in 1888 for proof of the tallest tree standing at that time was won on evidence for a eucalypt 325 feet high. Measurements by a well-known forester gave 363 feet for the height of a redwood growing in Bull Creek Flat, California. This is the tallest tree in the world on which there is authentic and reliable information.

Q. Is orange-wood the only wood used in the so-called orange-sticks? K. S.

A. These manicure sticks are made of orange-wood, lemon-wood, box-wood, and birch.

Q. What woods are best to use for carving? M. B.

A. The Forest Service says that there are a number of woods which are good for carving, among which are the following: black walnut, yellow poplar, basswood, red gum, and oak.

Q. What is an osier wythe? R. A.

A. This is another name for a willow twig.

Q. Are there several varieties of Japanese cherry trees in Potomac Park in Washington, D. C.? W. F. S.

A. There are twelve varieties.

Q. What does balsa wood look like? J. E. M.

A. It is nearly white or sometimes tinted in red, showing practically no distinction between heartwood and sapwood. It has a silky texture, is rather coarse but straight-grained, and is the lightest of all woods, even lighter than true cork.

Q. Of what wood should chessmen be made? W. C. D.

A. The Forest Products Laboratory says that the best chessmen are probably made from genuine boxwood. This wood is imported in relatively small quantities because of its scarcity and high price. It probably can be readily had, however, in the small sizes required for chessmen. West Indian boxwood should also be suitable for chessmen. This wood is much more common and is considerably lower in price. Among American species, holly is probably best suited for chessmen. This wood is light colored, rather heavy, and quite hard. It carves well and takes a smooth finish.

Q. Please name the various kinds of ornamental hedge. B. M. A.

A. The types of plants most commonly used for hedges in this country are as follows: Deciduous—Privet, Spiraea, Osage Orange, Barberry, Box Elder, Locust, Buckthorn, Cockspur Thorn, and Rose of Sharon; evergreen—Arbor Vitae, Juniper, Boxwood, Hemlock, Spruce, and Holly.

Q. How large do teak trees grow? J. F.

A. The teak tree which is a native of South Asia and the Malayan Islands, is a large forest tree from 100 to 150 feet in height, with a circumference of 20 to 25 feet at 100 years of age. The heart of the tree is the valuable part. It is one of the heaviest woods in existence.

Q. What kind of a tree was the ilex, often mentioned in the Latin classics? B. M.

A. It was a kind of holly.

Q. If a tree is stripped of its leaves, will it still be able to live? M. C. R.

A. The leaves of a tree correspond to the lungs or other breathing apparatus of an animal, since a large part of the tree's respiration is done through the leaves. A tree stripped of all its leaves would die if unable to replace them, although under ordinary circumstances at least part of the leaves would grow back. A plant may be said to die from lack of moisture during a dry spell, which is equivalent to the dying of thirst of an animal.

Q. How large must trees be allowed to grow before they can be cut at a profit? P. L.

A. It is more costly to handle small trees than large ones, and the lumber sells for less per foot when cut. The following smallest sizes should be taken for maximum immediate profit per acre logged: In Arkansas second-growth forest shortleaf and loblolly pine, 12 inches; in Louisiana oldfield loblolly, 15 inches; in Virginia second-growth forest loblolly, 12 inches; in North Carolina oldfield loblolly, 11 inches; in Texas and western Arkansas virgin shortleaf, 10 to 14 inches, according to type and age of stand.

Q. What is a tree called which is not coniferous but does not shed its leaves? S. H.

A. It is referred to as persistent.

Q. What makes the sap run out of the bark on peach and cherry trees? P. T.

A. Gummosis in fruit trees is caused by a number of factors, the most important of which is winter injury. Winter injury is damage to the surface of the tree's bark caused by too quick thawing after a cold spell. This breaks the bark and may cause the sap to exude in places. The remedy is to remove carefully all portions of damaged or unsound bark and to protect the bare parts of the trunk by some preservative such as coal-tar creosote.

Q. What is the Glastonbury Thorn? E. M.

A. It is the hawthorn tree which sprang from the spot on Wearyall Hill at Glastonbury in England where Joseph of Arimathea set his pilgrim's staff while on his mission to convert Britain. As the result of its holy origin, this hawthorn bloomed miraculously at Christmas, the natural blossoming season of the hawthorn being in May and June. During the Cromwellian civil war, the thorn tree was destroyed by a fanatical Puritan but grafts from it were saved, replanted, and persist in their miraculous Christmas blooming in defiance of botanical laws. A stone now marks the spot of the original tree.

Q. What is the real name of the calico bush? C. S.

A. Mountain laurel (Kalmia latifolia).

Q. What kind of a tree is a caragana? C. W. W.

A. It is an ornamental Asiatic tree with delicate pale foliage and yellow vernal flowers. The caragana is easy to grow, drouth resisting, and very difficult to kill, once properly established. In ten years the seedlings properly planted and cultivated, will grow into an ornamental hedge 12 feet high and 10 feet wide, and eventually to a height of 18 or 20 feet.

Q. What is the technical name for a tree which sheds its bark? P. T.

A. A tree which sheds its bark during certain intervals of the year is called a decorticating tree.

Q. Why is yew planted in such abundance around the Folger Shakespeare Library at Washington, D. C.? E. M.

A. Like many other features of the Library, it is in conformity to Elizabethan convention, when the yew was burned in theatres to counteract any offensive odors.

Q. Is the sap of the maple tree flowing up or down when the tree is tapped? J. C.

A. The movement of sap is described generally as follows: It is the watery solution which circulates through the vascular tissue in woody plants. The ascending current consists of the water of imbibition in which are dissolved various salts obtained from the earth. This so-called crude sap passes through the xylem portion of the vascular bundles to the chlorophyll-containing tissues, the leaves in most plants, where the surplus water is transpired into newly formed carbohydrates and proteids through the phloem or sieve tissue to the parts of the plant which may require them, the descending current often being called elaborated sap. From this it will be seen that the sap taken in tapping a tree is the type of sap which has already formed the carbohydrates and proteids and is therefore largely from the descending or elaborated sap.

Q. Why do leaves turn so as to show the under sides before a storm? R. H. R.

A. Prof. Humphreys says that many plants undergo some changes on the approach of rain. The hanging of the leaves so as to show their under sides, when viewed laterally or at a distance, is owing to changes in the leaf stalk on the absorption of moisture. Similarly all noticeable plant changes on which weather predictions are based, result from variations in humidity, temperature, and sunshine. Plant signs, however, are not regarded as reliable guides to coming weather.

Q. The fruit of the ginkgo tree looks like a persimmon. Why is it called a conifer? L. L. C.

A. The fruit of the ginkgo looks like a drupe, superficially, but is very much more like a cone than a drupe in actual structure. The order to which the ginkgo belongs is one of three orders of Gymnosperms or plants with naked seeds, the most important of which is the order of cone-bearing trees or conifers. The ginkgo is closely allied to the conifers and is called a deciduous conifer, or cone-bearing tree which drops its leaves yearly.

Q. Will a dogwood tree which now bears pink blossoms, continue to do so, or will the blossoms be white in a few years? F. M. E.

A. The pink variety of dogwood is now a distinct variety, having been developed from pink specimens of the wild dogwood. The color of the blossoms is probably determined to some extent by soil conditions, but it is reasonable to suppose that a defi-nitely pink variety would continue giving pink blossoms.

Q. What kind of a tree bears the pecan nut? How is pecan pronounced? A. S. N.

A. The pecan tree is a species of hickory. The name is of Indian origin, accented on the last syllable, the a either short or broad.

Q. Does the cypress belong to the pine family? W. H. Z.

A. It does. Any tree of the pine family in Africa is called African cypress.

Q. Is it possible to dye the wood of a tree before the tree is felled? L. A. M.

A. Scientists have dyed living trees with different aniline dyes for more than thirty years in order that they may study the flow of sap, and many different methods of injection have been attempted. Several attempts have been made to put this scheme on a commercial basis. The companies working with the material have been particularly concerned with the coloring of birch, beech, and maple, particularly the sapwood. One of the difficulties of the process is that it is almost impossible to get an even color throughout the tree. As a consequence, the material has been cut up into small articles such as colored wooden buttons, umbrella handles, cigarette cases, candlesticks, etc.

Q. For whom are Douglas firs named? J. D. S.

A. The Pseudotsuga douglasii, closely related to the firs, and often regarded as a fir, is named after the Scotch botanist, David Douglas. He visited the Pacific coast in the first half of the 19th century.

Q. Is it true that trees explode from extreme cold? E. W.

A. They do not explode, but are subject to frost cracks. At times, the cold wood of the tree will contract, in other words it will become frozen. If the sun comes out and shines brightly on one portion of the tree and the rest of the tree is unable to take up the expansion, the result is a crack. Sometimes this cracking makes itself heard. This noise is not comparable to an explosion.

Q. Why do pine trees stay green all winter? D. T.

A. Pine needles are in reality leaves, and contain chlorophyll as other leaves do. The surface of pine needles is tougher than that of other leaves. Thus the chlorophyll is protected during the winter and remains green.

Q. In tapping trees for maple sirup, how many places should be tapped? G. N.

A. Tapping only one place on a tree prolongs the life of the tree. Large first-growth trees may be tapped in two and sometimes three places without injury, but it is disastrous to tap in two places near together, in order to collect the sap from the two in one bucket.

Q. What trees are common in Mexico? R. S.

A. Such a list includes: Yucca, Zapote Chico, Pine, Juniper, Oak, Ahuehuete, Magnolia, Acacia, Myrtle, Mimosa, Bamboo, Spanish Cedar, and Logwood.

Q. Why do forsythia and redbud bushes bloom so early in the spring? O. G.

A. They develop their blossom buds during the previous summer.

Q. Is there a tree called the ague tree? M. N. B.

A. The sassafras tree is sometimes called the ague tree.

Q. How many kinds of elms are there? A. E.

A. There are about twenty species known. They are natives of the North Temperate Zone and of the southern portions of the Arctic Zone. Their southern limits seem to be the Himalayas in Asia and the mountains of southern Mexico. No elms

were found native on the Pacific slope of North America.

Q. What trees grow the largest in the vicinity of Washington, D. C.? T. O. D.

A. Oaks are the largest, generally speaking, although in some areas the tulip trees rival oaks in size.

Q. How does the Department of Agriculture label trees? W. E. U.

A. It uses aluminum tapes tacked on pieces of board which are screwed fast to the tree.

Q. Does the mahogany tree grow in a forest of its own kind or scattered among other species of trees? W. M.

A. Mahogany trees are generally scattered among other trees.

Q. How many trees are there in the Hall of Fame? C. N.

A. The American Forestry Association says that there are now nearly 300 trees which have been brought to its attention and found eligible to enrollment in its Hall of Fame, which is a register of trees of historical interest.

Q. What is the name of the trees that have fan-shaped leaves and line some Washington streets? L. E. D.

A. They are ginkgo trees, and are native to China and Japan. Only the staminate form is used in streets and parks as the pistillate form bears ill-smelling, slippery fruit which is sometimes poisonous to the touch.

Q. How far apart should peach and apple trees be planted? C. N. G.

A. The Bureau of Plant Industry says that peach trees should be planted not less than 20 feet apart; apple trees not less than 35 feet apart.

Q. Where is the famous Endicott pear tree? How old is it? F. L.

A. This tree is at Danversport, near Danvers, Mass. It was planted in 1632 by Governor John Endicott on his land there and is still the property of the Endicott family. William Crowningshield Endicott, owner of the tree, believes that it was planted in Governor Endicott's garden in Salem even before it was planted at Danvers and that it was brought from a nursery in England in 1630.

Q. *How does softwood lumber production compare with hardwood in this country?* W. C. A.

A. More than five times as much softwood lumber is marketed.

Q. *Are the colors of the leaves in the Autumn more brilliant when there is an early frost?* W. P.

A. The colors are more brilliant when there is not an early frost. Temperature and moisture are factors that influence these changes. Color production is not dependent upon frost. In fact more beautiful colors are produced when temperatures do not quite reach the freezing point during this period. An early frost prevents the formation of the special layer of cells, called the abscission layer, at the base of the petiole of the leaf, which cuts off the leaf and at the same time heals the wound. When factors are favorable for the early and quick development of the abscission layer, more sugars are held in the leaves and go to form even more brilliant colors.

Q. *Are there many forests in Egypt?* N. R.

A. There are no forests. The date palm and sycamore are the principal trees. Many other trees, principally fruit trees, have been introduced and flourish when sufficient moisture is furnished.

Q. *In what parts of the country are the most lumber mills?* J. L. B.

A. The National Lumberman's Association says that the main lumber-producing centers are on the Pacific Coast. The leading lumber States are Washington, Oregon, California, Idaho, and Montana. The second center may be called the Southern States—Louisiana leading, then Mississippi, Texas, Alabama,

Georgia, and Florida. These States are noted for yellow pine. The third center is the Lake States—Michigan, Wisconsin, and Minnesota.

Q. *What is monkey bread?* T. P.

A. It is the fruit of the African baobab tree. The pulp has a pleasant acid taste and can be made into a beverage. The trunk of the tree often grows to a diameter of 30 feet. The leaves and bark are used medicinally and the fibre is used by the natives to make cloth and rope.

Q. *How many magnolia trees are there in Mountain Lake Sanctuary?* B. P.

A. There are 2000 magnolia trees and 1500 dogwood trees in this garden. Over a million trees, shrubs, and flowers have transformed this waste of sand into one of the loveliest spots in the world.

Q. *What is metal wood?* G. L.

A. It is a new building material devised by German chemists, the density of which is said to be greater than that of wood. The compound consists of wood which has been blended with low fusing point metals such as lead, tin, or alloys. Its power of swelling and its combustibility are small and it is capable of being wrought like wood.

Q. *Please give a list of rare woods.* W. S. G.

A. A partial list follows: Amaranth, Ebony, Rosewood, Sandal Wood, Snake Wood, Tulip Wood, Palisander, Australian Blackwood, Lignum Vitae, Pear, Indian Laurel, Australian Walnut, Silky Oak, Ceylon Satinwood, Prima Vera, Spanish Cedar, Carreta, Olive, Orangewood, Madrone Burl, and Coco Bolo.

Q. *When and by whom was wood veneer first used?* W. L. D.

A. In the British Museum in London there are examples of Egyptian veneer work that are many thousand years old. Pliny says that veneer came into general use in Rome in his day. It obtained great popularity in the Netherlands, France, and England in the 18th century.

Q. *For what purposes is the wood called lignum vitae used?* P. S. B.

A. It is used for the bearings in machinery and also in bowling alley balls. This most unusual tree is found in South America.

Q. *How much does a mahogany log weigh?* A. H.

A. Those imported from the coast of Africa average from three to five tons.

Q. *What kinds of wood are used by the wood carvers of Germany and Switzerland?* W. G. M.

A. The Forest Service says that they generally use mountain pine, walnut, and basswood.

Q. *What color is ebony before it is finished?* S. D.

A. The sapwood is almost a golden color, while the heart is black. Sometimes the wood is streaked.

Q. *How is teakwood cured?* J. K. M.

A. Since green teakwood would not float as a raft, and if let lie on the ground would season unevenly, it is girdled standing. It is girdled and a broad strip of bark and sap wood taken off annually. Two or three years are required for curing to a point where it will float. It is handled by elephants.

Q. *How often do expert wood choppers sharpen their axes?* J. H. F.

A. The Forest Service says that it depends on many things, such as the axes themselves and the kind of trees which are being felled. Generally, however, the men who fell the trees take their axes in every two or three days. The limbers on the other hand must, as a rule, have their axes sharpened after every day's work. The hard knots in the limbs dull them very quickly.

Q. *How does wood become petrified?* S. McF.

A. When wood or other vegetable matter is buried in soil charged with petrifying material, it becomes saturated with it and the cells are filled with unfiltrated matter. When the wood decays the petrifying material is left, retaining the structure of the wood. The most common petrifying materials are silica, carbonate of lime, and sulphide of iron.

Q. *Does balsa wood absorb much moisture?* S. R.

A. It is very absorbent, and, when placed under water, light pieces may absorb as high as 500 to 600 per cent moisture. Its life is said to be very short under ordinary conditions unless treated with a preservative.

Q. *What is white mahogany?* E. P.

A. The Forest Service says that white mahogany is a trade name for Primavera, which is found on the western coast of Mexico and southward to Guatemala. The wood is moderately heavy and hard, works well, and is said to give little trouble by warping. It is creamy white to yellowish-brown in color. The grain is interlocked, and the pores are of about the same size as in true mahogany, so that the figure produced, especially when finished with a mahogany stain, is similar to that of true mahogany.

Q. *What is persimmon timber used for?* J. E.

A. Persimmon wood is used largely for shuttles in looms, golf club heads, and small children's shoe lasts. Persimmon lumber is often used for parquet flooring, automobile bodies, and furniture.

Q. *What is the name of the heavy wood which cannot be split?* N. T.

A. Owing to the diagonal and oblique arrangement of the successive layers of its fibers, lignum vitae cannot be split. On account of its hardness, durability, and density, it is much valued for the manufacture of ship's pulleys, rulers, skittle-balls, mallets, and similar articles.

Q. What makes wood decay? S. M.

A. Bacteria and certain microscopic plants called fungi grow in the wood and destroy its structure.

Q. What is the process called kyanizing? L. H.

A. It is a process of treating wood with corrosive sublimate to prevent decay. It was named for its inventor, J. H. Kyan, an Irishman, who lived from 1774 to 1850.

Q. Is kiln-drying as good as outdoor drying of wood? W. D.

A. Kiln-drying has all the good features of outdoor drying and is without detriment to the wood. A mild heat is used first with a very high relative humidity often as high as 90°. This regulated weather slows up the surface drying but the heat brings the inside moisture to the surface of the lumber. In this manner the inside and surface shrink together so no strains develop and therefore no checks, cracks, or warping.

Q. What wood is the most valuable in antique furniture? J. C. K.

A. The fact that antique furniture is made of any particular wood is not taken into serious consideration in the valuation of an article. The age and condition are of more importance.

Q. What sort of wood is nagaed? F. J.

A. Nagaed is more commonly known as Honduras-rosewood, genus Dalbergia. It is common in southern and British Honduras and grows on broken ridges along the coast. There are also fairly large quantities inland in strips about two miles wide on either sides of rivers. It is found in several different shades from light brown to very dark brown. It is a fairly large tree, diameters up to 30

and 36 inches being recorded. It is used to manufacture percussion instruments of the marimba type.

Q. Why does a scratch on a mahogany table show yellow or orange? E. K.

A. The natural wood is light in color. When a scratch penetrates the finish, the original color is revealed.

Q. How should hickory saplings be seasoned? J. K.

A. The Forest Service says that the best way to season hickory is to remove the bark and pile the wood up in a shed where it will get a good circulation of air but will not be rained or snowed upon.

Q. In using the Doyle scale are logs measured with the bark? H. W.

A. The Forest Service says that the proper method of measuring logs by the Doyle scale is from the inside of the bark to the inside of the bark.

Q. How should red jasper and petrified wood be polished? C. E. B.

A. They are polished by laps, using carborundum as an abrasive. Tin oxide applied on a felt lap makes a higher polish.

Q. What kind of lumber should be used for forms for concrete work? A. W. R.

A. White pine is best for fine face-work, and quite essential for ornamental construction when cast in wooden forms. Partially dry lumber is usually best. Kiln-dried is unsuitable as it swells when the wet concrete touches it.

Q. Are trees being planted in Hawaiian government forests? S. S.

A. Planting operations on the Hawaiian forest reserves in the past two years required 418,531 trees, an increase of 200,000 over the previous two years. Recent increases in Hawaiian forest reserve areas have brought the total to 980,682 acres.

CHAPTER 35

FRUIT

Q. What is the per capita consumption of oranges in the United States? M. S. D.

A. The average American eats 70 oranges a year.

Q. How long have some of the well-known varieties of apples been raised? A. W. T.

A. The Baldwin apple was raised near Lowell, Mass., about 1750. The Jonathan and Northern Spy were grown in New York, the Grimes Golden in West Virginia, and the Maiden Blush in various places, before 1800. The Red Astrachan was imported from Russia in 1835, the Rome Beauty was grown in Ohio by 1848, the Stayman Winesap appeared in Kansas in 1866, and the Delicious in Iowa in 1895.

Q. What proportion of the lemons used in this country is grown in California? R. F.

A. From 85 to 90 per cent of the lemons consumed in this country is grown in California. Twenty-five years ago, three-fourths of the lemons used in America came from Italy and Sicily.

Q. When were seedless grapes first produced? F. W.

A. The Bureau of Plant Industry says that the sultana variety of seedless grapes was first introduced into this country about 1865. The sultanina was introduced at Yuba City, California, by a grower named Thompson about 1882, and from him this has become known as the Thompson seedless. There is no record of the first production of seedless grapes. This type of grape goes back 800 years in Persia and 2500 years in China.

Q. In the large grapefruit canning factories what becomes of the seeds? V. D.

A. So far they are merely waste, but recent experiments show that they yield an oil that can be used in soap-making.

Q. What kind of a fruit is monastery? A. B. D.

A. Botanically a monastery is known as a philodendron. The taste is similar to both the pineapple and banana. It is brought from Porto Rico and probably is the rarest fruit on the New York market.

Q. Which contains more calories, watermelon or muskmelon? M. G.

A. Watermelons contain 140 calories per pound, while muskmelons contain 185.

Q. What is the largest of the citrus fruits and what is the smallest? S. B.

A. The grapefruit is the largest member of the citrus family and the kumquat is the smallest.

Q. Why are apples called the fruit of Eden? A. V. S.

A. For many centuries it was supposed that the apple was the fruit which Eve under the direction of the serpent ate and gave to Adam to eat in the Garden of Eden. This view is no longer held, many more tropical fruits being suggested as the probable fruit of the garden, among them the pomegranate.

Q. *Where do oranges stand in importance as a crop?* N. H.

A. They stand eleventh in value of all United States crops. Apples lead all fruits in value and oranges are second.

Q. *Please give the origin of the prune.* A. L. D.

A. Louis Pellier, a Frenchman, went to California in search of gold. Missing the delicious plum called the Prune d'Agens, he sent to France for seeds and cuttings. These he grafted with certain varieties of the wild plum in the California hills. His experiments were highly successful and the thriving family now numbers more than 7,000,000 trees in the Santa Clara Valley alone. In the fall of 1929, California paid tribute to the founder of a great industry by erecting a monument to the memory of Pellier in San Jose. The ceremony celebrated the seventy-fifth anniversary of the American prune.

Q. *Of what country is the navel orange a native?* A. K.

A. It is believed to have originated in Bahia, Brazil, as a bud sport of the Selecta variety. It was first propagated by budding about 1820. Its successful introduction into the United States was accomplished in 1870 by William Saunders of the United States Department of Agriculture. Within three years, navel oranges had been sent to California and Florida.

Q. *How can a valuation be fixed upon fruit trees that have been destroyed?* G. L.

A. The Department of Agriculture says that it is almost impossible to fix a valuation on fruit trees destroyed. In the first place, the fruit crop is always an uncertainty depending not only upon weather conditions but also on the peculiarities of the market. One method that has been recommended, which is purely academic but is the valuation used by the Vermont Home Horticulture Society, is that a tree less than one year old is worth $1 and increases in value at the rate of $1 a year thereafter.

Q. *How long have pineapples been grown in Florida?* B. E.

A. The earliest recorded successful planting of pineapples in Florida was made in 1860, when Benjamin Baker, of Key West, obtained a number of slips from Havana and started a small experimental patch on Plantation Key.

Q. *How long does it take a persimmon tree to bear?* J. C.

A. The Japanese persimmon will bear when it becomes four or five years old. The time at which the native persimmon reaches the bearing period is variable. Under the most favorable conditions this tree will bear in from four to six years.

Q. *How are coconuts propagated?* G. W. R.

A. Coconuts are prapagated differently from almost any form of fruit or nuts. The coconut, as it forms in the outer hull, is buried in the ground, and the embryo gams nourishment first from the coconut milk, and as the growth of the plant advances, the white meat becomes soft and spongy and also feeds the young plant. After a certain stage of development has been reached, small roots reach out into the ground and by the time they are sufficiently long and strong enough to feed the nourishment to the plant from the earth, the original coconut has entirely disintegrated.

Q. *How are the different flavors and colors of apples produced?* S. F.

A. The flavors of apples are natural to different varieties but can be influenced by water and excessive tree growth. Much wet weather and heavy growth shading the fruit will cause the flavor to become less pronounced. Colors are natural to fruit and can only be changed by shading or pruning to let in more light.

Q. *How long do orange trees bear?* E. S. B.

A. The average life of an orange grove is from 35 to 50 years. Orange trees under favorable conditions require about 4 years before they bring returns and about 5 or 6 years before they bear fruit to any large extent.

Q. *What are limes used for?* H. D.

A. The lime is chiefly valued as a source of citric acid and for lime juice, which is extensively used on shipboard as an anti-scorbutic. It is also used to make limeade, a pleasant beverage.

Q. *How many olives are grown in Spain?* D. C.

A. Nearly 1,500,000,000 pounds of olives are gathered yearly in the olive orchards of Spain.

Q. *Why are apples from the same tree larger some years than they are in other years?* E. D. T.

A. Extremes in temperature, either hot or cold, tend to check growth, with consequent maturity at smaller sizes. In some years the length of season and amount of rainfall in summer apparently have some influence upon size, but the effect of these factors is not as pronounced as that of temperature.

Q. *How should the zinc covers to fruit jars be cleaned?* F. S.

A. They should be washed, then dipped in a solution of soda, dried, and allowed to sun for several hours.

Q. *Why is it that chopped apples covered with mayonnaise dressing will not turn black?* W. T.

A. The oil in the mayonnaise forms a coating on the pieces of apple that excludes the air. Oxygen in contact with apples produces a chemical effect that turns the apples brown or black.

Q. *Should fruit be ripe for pickle-making?* F. J.

A. Fruit that is slightly under-ripe is better for pickles.

Q. *How long will grape vines produce?* G. H.

A. Some varieties continue fruitful for at least 300 or 400 years.

Q. *Does breadfruit taste like a fruit or a vegetable, and how is it prepared?* J. K. L.

A. The common method of preparing breadfruit in the South Sea Islands is to bake it entire in hot embers and scoop out the inside, which should have a smooth consistence, with a taste comparable to boiled potatoes and sweet milk. With sugar, milk, butter, or treacle it makes a delicious pudding. Breadfruit is also cut in strips and dried. From the strips a flour is made which is used for bread, biscuits, and pudding, or the slices are baked without grinding.

Q. *In what parts of Washington and Oregon are apples grown?* M. C.

A. Apples are grown successfully in every county in both Washington and Oregon.

Q. *Are seedless watermelons a possibility?* F. W.

A. Seedless watermelons have never been produced in sufficient quantities to be of commercial value. Horticulturists and persons with a gardening hobby have been able to grow them for their own pleasure.

Q. *Do watermelons contain vitamins?* P. S.

A. Ripe watermelons supply two vitamins abundantly and contain two others in detectable quantities.

Q. *If oranges are squeezed at night is the juice good to drink at breakfast time?* O. L. T.

A. The Bureau of Home Economics says that orange juice which is squeezed at night and saved for breakfast loses no food value, but due to oxidation some flavor is lost unless the juice is placed in a tightly covered container.

Q. Can Siberian crab apples be kept through the winter? E. W.

A. This particular variety ripens so easily that they do not keep well in cold storage, or any other process known at the present time.

Q. Can you give me a suggestion for something different in the way of a pear salad? R. G.

A. To 2 cups of sliced ripe pears take 1 cup sliced red plums. Mix lightly together and serve with a sweet boiled dressing lightened with a little whipped cream.

Q. How are navel oranges propagated? C. S.

A. The original seedless oranges were produced in Brazil by means of budding and the orange trees of this type in the United States are all descended from two imported Brazilian trees. Buds or budding sticks are taken from seedless orange trees in spring or fall and inserted in two-year-old seedling orange trees of ordinary type. When the buds send out shoots, the seedlings are cut back so that only the budding portions develop.

Q. How old must a banana tree be to bear? H. H.

A. The banana tree begins to bloom 1½ to 2 years after being established. The fruit ripens quickly after blooming.

Q. Are watermelon and muskmelon considered fattening? E.

A. Neither of them is considered fattening.

Q. How are pineapples propagated? W. H.

A. Pineapples are propagated by means of crowns, slips, suckers, and rattoons. The crown is the leafy part of the fruit just below which small plants form and these are left in the field when the fruit is gathered. These are termed slits. In the axles of the leaves are buds and

those developing near the ground make strong plants and are termed suckers. Buds developing from an underground part are rattoons.

Q. Does California or Florida raise more oranges and grapefruit? J. F. M.

A. California raises more oranges and Florida raises more grapefruit.

Q. Please name the fruits whose acids pass through the system unchanged. M. L. G.

A. The foods which contain benzoic acid are namely, plums, prunes, and cranberries. They are acid-forming because benzoic acid is not oxidized or broken down in the process of digestion. Other fruits, even though they taste acid, are not acid forming in the blood because their acid content is oxidized.

Q. Does all fruit ripen a certain length of time after the trees blossom? O. A.

A. There is no coördination between the season of blossoming and ripening of fruits. Some that blossom early may ripen late; others that blossom late may ripen early.

Q. When can the milk of the coconut be drunk? W. N.

A. The Bureau of Plant Industry says that the milk from the coconut is used as a drink immediately after the coconut is opened.

Q. How are citrus fruits colored for market? C. E.

A. It is a delicate process which is carefully done. Kerosene burners are still used to some extent, but ethylene is now often used.

Q. When is the picking season in California for cantaloupes, pears, peaches, plums, grapes, and oranges? J. O. M.

A. The picking season in California for cantaloupes is from April to September, the earliest season being in the Imperial Valley; for pears from June to September; for peaches May to October; prunes and plums from May to October; grapes from June to January; oranges continue during the entire year. The earliest sections for the above mentioned fruit are in the hot interior valleys.

Q. What is a kangaroo apple? K. R. M.

A. It is a plant closely related to the potato, native to Peru, New Zealand, and Australia. The mealy, slightly acid fruit, which is eaten either raw or cooked, is used for food by the native peoples.

Q. What kind of fruit is plantain? C. K.

A. Plantain is a species of banana, the fruit of which is a staple article of food in the tropics. It is larger than the ordinary banana, greenish yellow in color, less sweet, and more starchy. It is cooked in various ways.

Q. How much water should be left in dried apples? T. M. W.

A. According to federal food standards, dried apples should not contain more than 24 per cent water.

Q. How are skins removed from peaches other than peeling? J. W. B.

A. The peaches may be immersed in boiling water for about one minute or until the skins slip easily. Plunge at once into cold water for a few seconds.

Q. Are all muskmelons known as cantaloupes? M. B. O.

A. The use of the term cantaloupe has become synonymous with the term muskmelon, commercially. Technically, however, the cantaloupe is only one variety of muskmelon.

Q. What sort of a fruit is the Calamondin? B. R. S.

A. The Calamondin is a variety of citrus fruit which is unique among citrus fruits in being the hardiest of the acid species now being grown in America. Its dense head with bright green leaves, upright habit, and small fruits resembling tangerines in shape and color, make it one of the most ornamental of the citrus allies. The fruits are bright orange-red, 1 to 1½ inches in diameter, with deep orange flesh. The juice is well flavored and very acid. It is a valuable garden fruit adaptable to those sections where the Satsuma and Kumquat are grown—and is unsurpassed among ade-making fruits.

Q. How long have honeydew melons been on the market? D. R.

A. Honeydew melons were introduced into Colorado from France in 1913 and the culture has spread to every melon-growing state in the Union. These melons prefer an arid or semi-arid region.

Q. Can watermelons be used in making vinegar? B. D.

A. Watermelons have been used successfully for making vinegar, but the juice must be concentrated to about half its original volume to give the proper sugar content.

Q. Is cashew fruit edible? C. V.

A. Cashew fruit is not only edible but very tasty and makes an excellent conserve. It also is used in a beverage very much as lemons are used in this country. When pressed, it emits a valuable sweet oil.

Q. Is the banana an alkali or acid-producing food? E. B. M.

A. The banana is known to be an alkali-producing food. It is a food which has been found to be efficient in reducing the acidity of the body. The banana when fully ripe is a most valuable addition to the diet of young children, particularly those for whom a gain in weight is desirable. It can also be given to infants. This fruit when unripe consists largely of starch, and is therefore difficult of digestion. As the ripening process goes on, a large part of the starch is converted into sugar.

Q. What fruits are most important as foods? D. N.

A. Nutrition and Diet says: "The apple leads among the orchard fruits. It carries small amounts of vitamins

A, B, and C. It has definite laxative properties, probably owing to the large cellulose content. The young apple contains a large amount of starch, but as it ripens this is rapidly converted into sugar until when fully ripe it contains little or no starch. The acid content decreases as the sugar increases. In like manner, its pectin, valuable in the formation of jelly, decreases with the ripening process. The citrus fruits are next in importance to the apple, and their culture is being enormously increased. Oranges come first. They offer an excellent source of readily assimilable glucose, and for this reason orange juice is used when there is necessity for quickly assimilable carbohydrate which will throw the least burden on the digestive organs. The orange contains both vitamins A and B."

Q. *Do pineapples contain vitamin C? C. W. O.*

A. Pineapples are a very good source for vitamin C.

Q. *Why are persimmons astringent? A. M.*

A. They are astringent when green because of tannin contained in the fruit.

Q. *What is the origin of the word, kumquat? L. E. Y.*

A. Kumquat is from the Chinese Kamkwat, meaning gold orange. The word came into English through the Cantonese dialect. This is a specific variety of orange—Citrus japonica—which, as its name indicates, originated in Japan.

Q. *Please name some of the unusual fruits of the tropical zone. G. C.*

A. The sequidilla, the chayote, the akee, breadfruit, jackfruit, mangosteen, sapodilla, and durian are some of the tropical fruits that are not yet common in the markets of the temperate zone. Tomatoes, egg-plants, pomegranates, limes, oranges, lemons, grapefruit, bananas, pineapples, figs, dates, and alligator pears are as familiar as many of the native fruits of the temperate zone.

Q. *What is a plumcot? L. H.*

A. It is a cross between a plum and an apricot.

Q. *Is our persimmon a native fruit? L. T. W.*

A. It is a native fruit and grows wild throughout the eastern United States from Connecticut to the Carolinas and westward to Missouri and Arkansas. The American persimmon is a close relative of the Japanese persimmon, or date-plum, which came originally from China. This tree bears a larger and much less astringent fruit than the American species, and is more tropical, having been grown successfully in southern California.

Q. *How long will a date palm bear fruit? A. E. M.*

A. For one or two centuries. In western Asia and northern Africa dates are an important part of the daily food of the natives.

Q. *What is the origin of the pippin? M. T.*

A. This name was given to a certain class of apples probably because the trees were raised from the pips or seeds. They seem to have been introduced into Great Britain from France, and were little known there until about the end of the 16th century. In the time of Shakespeare pippins were delicacies for the dessert. Sir Hugh Evans in the Merry Wives of Windsor says: "I will make an end of my dinner—there's pippins and cheese to come." The ribston, golden, Newton, and the small Scotch oslin or arbroath pippin are favorite sorts.

Q. *Is the watermelon a native plant? I. L. S.*

A. It is a separate and distinct species of the cucumber family which has been grown in this country for a great many years, but which is supposed to have originated in a wild state in Africa.

Q. *What is the calorie content of the avocado?* W. V. L.

A. The avocado is a native of the West Indies and Central America. It is the only species of this order cultivated for the fruit. The fruit is unusual in that the flesh has a high fat content, 10 per cent on an average. The water content is 81 per cent, and the carbohydrates 7 per cent. The fuel value is high, 512 calories per pound.

Q. *How long will a coconut still in its outer husk keep without rotting?* N. L.

A. Coconuts in the husk will keep indefinitely if kept in a dry place. Such coconuts have been satisfactorily kept for 20 or 30 years.

Q. *Is there a pink grapefruit?* M. S. T.

A. There is a species of grapefruit the pulp or flesh of which is of a pinkish tinge. The food value is the same as the golden grapefruit. The pink variety is being grown to some extent, especially in Texas.

Q. *What fruits are classified as citrus?* M. D. T.

A. The orange, lemon, grapefruit, kumquat, lime, citron, tangerine, and citrange are the best known members of the citrus family.

Q. *How many acres of vineyards are there in Italy and France?* R. A. S.

A. In 1927 Italy had 10,581,400 acres in vineyards and produced 784,-206,000 gallons of wine. In the same year France had 3,351,695 acres in grapes and produced 892,410,000 gallons of wine.

Q. *How can a person tell when a coconut is ripe?* L. F. D.

A. The Bureau of Plant Industry says that coconuts will generally drop from the tree when they are ripe. Tne nuts on the lowest fruiting branches will naturally ripen first. It is very difficult to tell from the exterior of a coconut whether or not it is ripe and the only sure way is to open it. If the coconut is desired for the milk, the nut should be gathered just before ripening; that is, before it is ready to fall.

Q. *Why was the pineapple so often employed in decoration?* S. A.

A. It was supposed to be the symbol of Plenty in the Home.

Q. *How is rhubarb made pink when cooked?* C. B.

A. If the rhubarb is not peeled before cooking, the sauce will have an attractive pinkish color. The skin is edible.

Q. *To how many countries are grapefruit exported from the United States?* B. N.

A. The Citrus Industry says that grapefruit was exported to sixty countries last year. England, Germany, and Canada were the best customers, but among the other buyers were Brazil, Bolivia, Ceylon, Japan, Nigeria, and Liberia.

Q. *Why is pineapple so often mentioned in menus for dieting to reduce?* E. L. H.

A. Pineapple contains fewer calories per pound than most fruits. It contains but 20 calories per pound.

Q. *Are grapefruit grown in Porto Rico?* L. M.

A. Commercial planting of citrus fruits in Porto Rico dates from about 1900. At first, oranges were the principal crop, but in 1928, the citrus production was estimated at 1,235,000 boxes of grapefruit and about 500,-000 boxes of oranges.

Q. *After the fruit is picked, does the banana tree die?* C. L. S.

A. After fruiting, the stem decays or is cut down, and new shoots spring from the root and produce a new crop in a few months.

Q. *What is the usual length of freight haul of the orange crop?* R. N.

A. Long hauls are the rule rather than the exception. Approximately

58 per cent of the oranges shipped are hauled from 2000 to 3500 miles; about 34 per cent travel from 1000 to 2000 miles; and 8 per cent, less than 1000 miles.

Q What part of the United States is best adapted to the growing of olives? C. L.

A. The region in which the olive may be successfully grown for the commercial production of fruit in the United States is not as great as for most frost-hardy fruits and has been confined to portions of California and Arizona, although the trees will live and bear some fruit in portions of all of the southern tier of states of this country.

Q. What are Apples of Paradise? W. M.

A. By tracing the name through the Latin Apples of Hesperides, it has been decided that they were pomegranates. Hesperides has been interpreted to mean "having the structure of an orange" but the ancient orange was not the same as the fruit which we know by that name now.

Q. When is the planting season for pineapples in Hawaii? A. Y.

A. The Department of Agriculture says that, due to the climate of Hawaii, pineapples may be planted any time in the year that the rain is right. In other words, the planting of pineapples is directly dependent on rainfall rather than on weather. It takes a year for the plants to mature and produce fruit.

Q. Should cherry stones be planted as soon as they are removed from the cherries or can they be kept a while without deteriorating? F. T. W.

A. The Department of Agriculture says that cherry seeds should be planted just as quickly as they are removed from the fruit. In this connection, several years ago the Department of Agriculture conducted experiments, planting some seeds immediately after they were removed from the fruit, and others spaced about two weeks apart. It was found that germination was more highly developed in the seeds that were freshly removed, and therefore still moist, than those that had been out for several weeks, and had been allowed to become dry.

Q. In what states of the Union are oranges grown? W. M.

A. Oranges are raised in the southern part of California, Florida, Alabama, Mississippi, Georgia, Louisiana, and Texas. They are too delicate to grow farther north than the 32nd parallel.

Q. Will a fruit tree grow from a seed? M. N.

A. If a fruit tree grows from a seed, eventually it will bear fruit, all conditions being favorable. However, the chances are greatly against the fruit resembling that of the parent tree exactly.

Q. Are there any of the fruits planted by the Mission Fathers still growing in California? J. C. S.

A. Trees of the original planting of Mission olives brought to this country by the Franciscan Fathers a century and a half ago are growing at the San Diego Mission. After Cortez conquered Mexico in 1521, the Jesuit padres soon began their missionary work among the Indians. With them they brought the fruits of France and Spain, among these the pomegranate. All the fruits from the older missions in Mexico were carried northward and planted in the New Mission Gardens in California. In these gardens may still be seen some of the old olive and date trees and pomegranate bushes. In 1792 Vancouver found an orchard at Mission San Buena Ventura in which pomegranates were growing together with apples, pears, plums, figs, oranges, grapes, and peaches.

Q. What is a granadilla? W. S.

A. It is a tropical American fruit, oval shape, of a greenish yellow color.

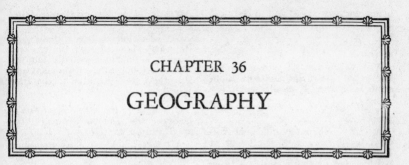

CHAPTER 36

GEOGRAPHY

Q. What is the crookedest river in the United States? G. S.

A. Probably the Nolin River in west-central Kentucky. It crosses the southeastern part of the Big Clifty quadrangle in a course about 20 miles long, though the air-line distance between the points where it enters and leaves the quadrangle is only 6 miles.

Q. Is Reno, Nevada, as far west as Los Angeles, California? C. S.

A. It is farther west.

Q. When Staten Island was bought from the Indians, what did they receive in return? D. D.

A. The Dutch West India Company gave in exchange "some kettles, axes, hoes, wampum, drilling awls, jew's-harps, and divers small wares."

Q. How is the boundary between the United States and Canada marked? A. H.

A. The boundary is 5500 miles in length, of which 3100 miles are land boundary and 2400 miles are water boundary. The land boundary is marked by 5483 monuments and a vista cut through the woods in all forest covered areas; the water boundary is identified by 2530 reference marks.

Q. Which State has the longest coast line? T. B.

A. Maine has the longest, the coast being so indented that its length is about 3000 miles.

Q. Is there a place in the Americas where both the Atlantic and Pacific Oceans can be seen at once? I. M.

A. On a clear day both oceans can be seen from the summit of Irazu, a mountain in Cartago Province, Costa Rica. It is 12,600 feet high.

Q. What place in the Dominion of Canada is farthest south? D. T.

A. Point Pelee, near Leamington, Ontario. It projects ten miles into Lake Erie.

Q. How does the Great American Desert compare with the Sahara in size? B. C. D.

A. The Sahara has an area of about 3,500,000 square miles. The Great American Desert extending from the United States into Mexico, has an area of approximately 1,050,-000 square miles.

Q. Where is the Mississippi River the widest? G. G.

A. The Mississippi River Commission says that, according to the latest survey the widest point on the Mississippi River at bankfull stage was found 77 miles below Cairo, Ill., where the river was 14,420 feet across.

Q. What is the name of the land nearest to the no-latitude, no-longitude point? C. R. D.

A. The Gold Coast of Africa is nearest to 0° latitude, 0° longitude. Accra is probably the nearest place,

229

being located at 5° north latitude and 0° longitude.

Q. *How many volcanoes are there in Iceland?* P. D.

A. Altogether 107 volcanoes are known to exist in Iceland, with thousands of craters, great and small.

Q. *How far from Tokyo is Fujiyama?* N. A.

A. This celebrated quiescent volcano is 70 miles west southwest of Tokyo. It rises to a height of 12,-395 feet and its southern slopes reach the shore of Suruga Bay.

Q. *What is meant by Abyla and Calpe?* R. N.

A. These are the ancient names for the Pillars of Hercules. Calpe, the modern Gibraltar, and Abyla, now Jebel Musa or Ape's Hill.

Q. *How much of the water surface of the Great Lakes belongs to the United States?* G. L.

A. The Great Lakes have a water surface of about 95,000 square miles, of which 33,940 square miles lie on the Canadian side and 60,770 square miles on the United States side of the International Boundary.

Q. *Is the water of Lake Utah fresh or salt?* G. W. B.

A. It is fresh and is one of the principal sources of the Great Salt Lake.

Q. *How long is the Potomac River?* P. B. L.

A. It is about 550 miles in length.

Q. *Is there a river which sometimes flows in one direction and at others flows in the opposite direction?* W. A. E.

A. A stream known as the Cassquiare Canal does so. This is a natural waterway which, varying with the rain, flows now into the Orinoco Basin, now into that of the Amazon. At the flood tide of the Amazon it flows into the Orinoco, while at the flood tide of the Orinoco it flows into the Amazon.

Q. *What is the most celebrated whirlpool in the world?* E. R.

A. Charybdis between Sicily and Italy and Maelstrom off the coast of Norway are perhaps equally famous. The whirlpool at Niagara is probably the most celebrated in the New World.

Q. *What is the meaning of Okeefenokee, the Indian name of the great swamp in Georgia?* H. J. L.

A. Okeefenokee means trembling water.

Q. *Who has supervision over the waters of the Rio Grande and Colorado River which flow in both Mexican and American territory?* L. N.

A. The International Water Commission, United States and Mexico, has been appointed to work out a plan providing for the equitable division of the waters of the Rio Grande, Colorado River, and Tia Juana River, streams which flow on both sides of the international boundary.

Q. *How does Victoria Falls compare with Niagara Falls?* B. C.

A. The chasm of Victoria Falls on the Zambezi River in northern Rhodesia, South Africa, is only about one-half as wide as that of Niagara, but more than twice the depth. The height of Victoria Falls is 256 feet at the right bank and 343 feet in the center. The American fall of Niagara is 1400 feet broad and 185 feet high, while the Canadian or Horseshoe fall is 2600 feet broad and 155 feet high.

Q. *Where are the Kakabeka Falls?* B. L. T.

A. They are on the Kaministikwia River, Ontario, Canada, 14 miles west of Port Arthur. The falls, noted for their beauty, have a height of 130 feet and their width is about 450 feet.

Q. *Where is the Grand Canyon?* B. K. P.

A. The Grand Canyon proper begins shortly after the Colorado River enters the State of Arizona and is entirely within this State. It has a length of over 100 miles. In some places, as at the little town of Grand Canyon where the well known resort is located, the canyon is fully 15 miles broad from rim to rim.

Q. In going from Sydney, Australia, to London, is it nearer by way of the Suez or the Panama Canal? M. O'D.

A. It is a little shorter through the Suez Canal. The distance is approximately 12,000 miles by way of the Suez Canal, and 12,800 miles through the Panama Canal.

Q. Where are the Maritime Provinces? B. L. T.

A. This name is usually applied to the Canadian provinces of New Brunswick, Nova Scotia, and Prince Edward Island.

Q. Is the Gulf of St. Lawrence as large as Lake Superior? C. W. T.

A. The Gulf of St. Lawrence is larger than Lake Superior. Its area is 64,000 square miles approximately and the area of Lake Superior about 31,820 square miles.

Q. Is there an inland waterway from New York to Florida? A. C. L.

A. There is a so-called inland waterway from New York to Florida. This route roughly parallels the Atlantic coast, taking advantage of natural waterways, although canals are built wherever necessary. In some places the route is only four feet deep. It starts from the New York Harbor, follows the Delaware River to Chesapeake Bay, goes through to Albemarle Sound, thence by artificial waterway to Pamlico Sound. It goes outside from Newport, N. C., to Georgetown, S. C., then parallels the coast of Florida.

Q. How many countries are there on the globe? N. B.

A. The number of countries there are on the globe depends on just what one means by the word country. If self-government is meant, there are 77 countries which may be called nations. These include the so-called pocket nations or small independent countries such as Monaco. If by country one means political and geographic divisions, there are of course many more. The full number of these is approximately 170.

Q. How long and wide is the Shenandoah Valley? J. V. N

A. The Valley is more than 100 miles long and varies in width from 20 to 30 miles; included within its area are Berkeley and Jefferson counties, West Virginia, and Frederick, Clarke, Warren, Shenandoah, Page, Rockingham, and Augusta counties, Virginia.

Q. How large is Death Valley? H. N. M.

A. Death Valley proper is about 50 miles long, and averages between 20 and 25 miles in breadth between the crests of the enclosing mountain ranges. It is 276 feet below sea level, and is the lowest point on the continent. The Amargosa River enters the valley through a deep canyon at the south but disappears in the basin.

Q. What is the highest point on the Atlantic Coast of the United States south of Maine? C. F. S.

A. It is Todt Hill, Staten Island, and the altitude is 430 feet above sea-level.

Q. Where was Norumbega? N. F. A.

A. Norumbega was a region along the northeast coast of North America, or its capital city, given on old maps of the 16th and 17th Centuries. The extent of the country varied from a region including the entire coast from near Cape Breton to Florida, to a district in Maine about the Penobscot River. It is disputed whether the name is of Indian, Norse, or Spanish origin.

Q. Is Labrador on the mainland of Canada? C. J. C.

A. Labrador is a territory of the colony of Newfoundland. Newfoundland is an island off the eastern coast of Canada, but Labrador is on the mainland and adjoins the Canadian

Province of Quebec—more exactly, Labrador occupies the entire Atlantic seaboard of Quebec and cuts off that province from the ocean.

Q. What is the name of the peninsula between the Chesapeake and Delaware Bays? E. W. J.

A. It is sometimes called the Delmarva Peninsula, from parts of the names of the three States having jurisdiction over the area.

Q. Has Brazil a state as large as Texas? B. G.

A. Brazil is larger than the United States and is divided into only 20 states whereas we have 48. Three of the Brazilian states are larger than Texas.

Q. How does the area of Great Britain compare with that of Ireland? H. D.

A. Great Britain has an area of 89,000 square miles, while Ireland comprises 33,000 square miles. It is therefore about 2¾ times the size of Ireland.

Q. Where is the highest lake in the United States? P. McG.

A. The highest lake having an area greater than 0.1 square miles, is Tulainyo, 1½ miles northeast of Mt. Whitney, California. The elevation is 12,865 feet, and the area about 0.2 square miles.

Q. How many volcanoes are there on the island of Java? S. M.

A. There are one hundred and twenty-five, thirteen of which are active.

Q. Why was the capital of Turkey changed? M. G. P.

A. The capital of Turkey was moved from Istanbul (Constantinople) to Ankara (Angora) when the Ottoman Empire became a republic after the World War. Istanbul was considered too open for attack and too closely associated with foreign governments to remain the capital of the new Turkish republic. The Turkish Nationalist party under the leadership of President Mustafa Kemal Pasha wished to establish the capital in a location capable of strong defense and in the center of the Turkish nation.

Q. Where is the largest lake wholly within Canada? E. T.

A. Great Bear Lake, in the Mackenzie district of the Northwest Territories, Canada, is the largest lake wholly within Canadian territory. Its area is approximately 12,000 square miles.

Q. What is the depth of San Francisco Bay? P. W. J.

A. The waters of San Francisco Bay are generally shallow far out from the shores, but the Golden Gate and the part of the bay adjoining San Francisco as well as a central channel running through its whole length have a depth of 30 to over 100 feet.

Q. Do the Great Lakes freeze in the winter? J. W. McD.

A. The Great Lakes do not freeze entirely during the winter, but the harbors and often the connecting rivers are closed by ice. The navigable season at the Soo is about seven and one-half months, and at Erie somewhat longer. Lake Superior freezes only in the shallow water along the shores. The northern reaches of Michigan are frozen but the solid ice stops well north of Milwaukee.

Q. What is the north to south span of the Pacific Ocean? T. R. E.

A. The north to south distance of the Pacific from Behring Strait to Antarctica, near Cape Adare, is 15,-500 kilometers, or 8350 nautical miles.

Q. When was the word ocean first used? L. S. G.

A. The word ocean to define the great outer body of water is from the Greek and appears in Homer defining the great stream or river supposed to encompass the disk of the earth and personified as the god of the great primeval water, the son of Uranus and Gaia, and husband of

Tethys; hence the great outer sea as opposed to the Mediterranean. In England before 1400 it was known as the sea ocean. Down to 1640 the great body of water was known as the ocean sea.

Q. What are the Pillars of Hercules? N. T.

A. The Pillars of Hercules are two hills on opposite sides of the Strait of Gibraltar, so called because of the myth that they had been torn asunder by Hercules to admit the flow of the ocean into the Mediterranean.

Q. Is the Kilauea volcano a menace to Hawaii? W. B.

A. It is considered harmlessly active. It affords a marvelous spectacle for tourists. In its latest eruption it is believed that every automobile on the island has made a trip to the volcano.

Q. When were Wilmington and San Pedro annexed to Los Angeles and when was the harbor begun? R. C.

A. Wilmington and San Pedro were annexed to Los Angeles in 1909. San Pedro was recognized as a port as early as 1826. In 1852 the first regular water service between Los Angeles and San Francisco was established. The first government harbor improvements were made in 1877. A deep water harbor was begun in 1892.

Q. Why is the Arctic Ocean so-named? S. T.

A. Arctic is from the Greek arctos, a bear, the reference being to the northern constellation of the Great Bear. Antarctic means "opposed to Arctic."

Q. How large is the Salton Sea? D. McC.

A. The Salton Sea is a lake in the wide Colorado Desert or Imperial Valley in southeastern California. Under ordinary conditions it is a salt marsh covered in places by shallow lakes about 30 miles long, 12 miles wide, and 280 feet below sea level. At times of freshets the lakes expand into a water body covering from 40,000 to 50,000 acres.

Q. Is Mount Popocatepetl a mountain that can be climbed? J. McA.

A. The height of Mt. Popocatepetl is 17,888 feet. The ascent of the volcano is made on the northeastern slope where there are rough roads which are kept open a greater part of the year. At an elevation of about 14,500 feet horses are left behind. Diego de Ordaz was probably the first European to make the ascent. Other exploration trips were made in April and November, 1827, in 1834, and 1848. In 1905 the Mexican Geological Survey spent two days on the slope.

Q. How long have the locks been in use at Sault Sainte Marie, Michigan? L. P.

A. The North West Fur Company built a lock on the Canadian side of the river in 1797–98. The state lock and canal, later widened and deepened by the Federal Government, were opened in 1855. The Weitzel lock was completed in 1881, the Canadian in 1895, the Poe in 1896, the Davis in 1914, and the Sabin in 1919.

Q. How wide is the entrance to New York Harbor? V. R.

A. The entrance from the ocean is seven miles wide, from Sandy Hook to Rockaway Point.

Q. Which is rougher, the Atlantic or the Pacific Ocean? M. B.

A. The zone of greatest storm frequency lies between latitudes 45° and 55°. The most severe storms are the hurricanes that begin in the tropical portion of the Atlantic. The North Atlantic lies in the path of the great procession of cyclones and anti-cyclones of the middle latitudes, and also in the path of the West Indian hurricanes over its lower latitudes, and counterparts of these atmospheric disturbances in the South

Atlantic. The Pacific is subject to sudden and violent storms, especially typhoons, but the frequency of storms is not so great as in the Atlantic.

Q. *Where is Papeete?* E. L. S.

A. It is in Tahiti, one of the most important and populous of the South Sea Islands. The chief town, Papeete, has about 4600 inhabitants. The climate is agreeable and the natural vegetation beautiful and luxuriant. Tahiti is a French colony.

Q. *What is the new canal which is contemplated by France?* W. B. L.

A. Numerous Senators have united in a special committee to advocate creation of a French two-sea canal from Bordeaux, on the Atlantic coast, to Narbonne, on the Mediterranean. Such a canal would make it possible for the French war fleet to go from the ocean to the Mediterranean in less than two days and without passing under the British guns at Gibraltar. It would shorten the route from Great Britain and northern Europe to the Mediterranean, the Suez, and India by 1100 miles. It would provide adequate protection against floods which periodically devastate southwestern France. Cost of the canal would be about $2,000,000,000.

Q. *Was the eruption of Mt. Katmai in 1912 an important one?* K. C.

A. The eruption was one of the largest ever known. The haze caused by this eruption on the Alaskan peninsula was noted in the eastern United States. The Valley of Ten Thousand Smokes which came into being at this time has been set aside as the Katmai National Monument.

Q. *How large is the lock on the North Sea Canal at Ymuiden?* A. H.

A. The North Sea Canal's lock is the largest in the world. It is 1312 feet long and 164 feet wide. The Gatun lock in Panama is 1000 feet long and 110 feet wide. Lock Eight of the Welland Canal is 1380 feet long and 80 feet wide. In lock construction greater engineering prob-lems are related to width than to length as the width determines the size of the gates.

Q. *What are the tolls for the Cape Cod Canal?* A. A.

A. The Cape Cod Canal was purchased by the United States, March 31, 1928, and has since become a free waterway. Since the United States took over this canal the traffic has doubled.

Q. *To what country do the islands of St. Pierre and Miquelon belong?* T. C. U.

A. The small islands of St. Pierre and Miquelon off the southwest coast of Newfoundland are a colony of France. The area of the colony is about 100 square miles, and the population about 4000.

Q. *Where is the seat of government of the French Islands in the Southern Pacific?* C. M. S.

A. It is at Papeete, the chief town of Tahiti, the principal island of the Society Group. Tahiti is the center both administratively and culturally of all the widely scattered possessions in the South Pacific known as French Oceania.

Q. *Where is Corn Island?* D. L.

A. The Corn Islands are a group of two small islands in the Caribbean Sea some distance off the coast of Nicaragua. They consist of Great and Little Corn Island. They were leased from the Nicaraguan Government for 99 years by the Treaty of August 5, 1914, whereby Nicaragua also granted the right to the United States of constructing a canal across her territory. Although by treaty empowered to do so, this Government has never obtained governmental control of the islands which are still governed by a native Nicaraguan.

Q. *How wide is the Seine River at Paris?* M. G. F.

A. The Seine has a width of 540 feet as it enters Paris and 446 feet as it leaves the city. At the island,

La Cite, the river is at its widest, 863 feet.

Q. Where is the Isle of Man? H. R.

A. It is a small island in the Irish Sea, nearly equally distant from England, Scotland, and Ireland. It has an area of 227 square miles, and a population in 1931 of 50,000. The Isle of Man is not considered a part of the United Kingdom of Great Britain and Northern Ireland, but is a separate British island.

Q. How do the rivers of the Western Hemisphere compare with those of the Eastern? T. T.

A. The drainage system of the Americas is the greatest on earth. The Amazon River discharges more water into the ocean than the eight largest rivers of Asia together. The Mississippi River discharges more water than all of the rivers of Europe.

Q. What is the total area of all the islands in the world? J. H. B.

A. It is approximately 4,000,000 square miles. This includes Australia, the largest island. Besides Australia, there are approximately 1,910,000 square miles of islands in the seas.

Q. How many people live on the Aleutian Islands? P. S.

A. The population is about 3000. This group is a chain of about 80 small islands belonging to Alaska Territory, separating the Sea of Kamchatka from the northern part of the Pacific Ocean, and extending nearly 1600 miles from east to west. The total area is 6391 square miles.

Q. What does the name Haiti mean? B. H.

A. Haiti, the name given by the natives to one of the islands of the Greater Antilles, means mountainous or high land. Columbus renamed it Hispaniola and the chief port became Santc Domingo. The island was often called Santo Domingo, until early in the nineteenth century

the original name, Haiti, came into use. Haiti is now the designation of the island and also of the republic which occupies the western four-elevenths of the island. Santo Domingo, officially Republica Dominicana, occupies the eastern seven-elevenths of the island.

Q. How wide is the Potomac River at Washington and where it enters Chesapeake Bay? J. E. H.

A. As it flows past Washington, the Potomac is about 2000 feet wide. When it enters the Bay, its width is about six miles.

Q. How far up is the Missouri River navigable? F. I.

A. It is navigable in summer during flood period as far as Great Falls, Montana, and in low water as far as Buford at the mouth of the Yellowstone River.

Q. Is there really a Devil's Island where there is a prison? B. S.

A. Devil's Island does actually exist. It is located in a group of islands called the Iles Du Salut in French Guiana off the coast of South America. Here is located a French penal station, with administrative headquarters in Ile Royale, nearest the mainland. To the seaward is the Ile du Diable (Devil's Island) noteworthy as the prison of Alfred Dreyfus, confined there in 1894–99.

Q. What was the cost of the locks on the Ohio River? J. J. H.

A. The fifty locks on the Ohio River between Pittsburgh and Cairo were constructed at a cost exceeding $100,000,000.

Q. Please give the name of a popular inland lake resort in Argentina. N. S. S.

A. The most prominent inland lake and resort in Argentina is Nahuel-Huapi, which is the largest of a group of high Andean Valley lakes in the southwest corner of the territory of the Neuquen in western

Argentina. The name Nahuel-Huapi means "Lion Grass" in the native dialect of that region. The lake is nearly 50 miles long from east to west, and about 20 miles from north to south at its widest part. There is a very popular resort called also Nahuel-Huapi at the eastern end of the lake.

Q. *Do people live on Philae Island?* J. M. R.

A. The Island of Philae has no permanent population at the present time. Since the completion of the Assuan Dam in 1902 the Island is submerged except for a few months each year from August to December.

Q. *Is Key West a coral island?* W. S.

A. It is. It is about three and one-half miles from east to west, three-fourths to one and one-fourth mile from north to south, and about 11 feet above sea level.

Q. *What is the highest mountain situated upon an island?* C. O.

A. The highest island mountain in the world is Mauna Kea in the Hawaiian Islands, with an altitude of 13,825 feet above sea level.

Q. *Are there many islands in the Mississippi River?* E. N.

A. There are 747 islands between its source and the mouth of the Red River. Below this point—309 miles from the Gulf—there are only three islands.

Q. *What is the altitude of each of the Great Lakes?* B. C.

A. The approximate altitude of the various Great Lakes is as follows: Lake Superior, 602 feet; Lake Michigan, 578 feet; Lake Huron, 578 feet; Lake Erie, 572 feet; Lake Ontario, 246 feet.

Q. *Where is Tin Can Island?* A. M. S.

A. Tin Can Island is the nickname of Niafou, one of the Tongo or friendly Islands situated in the South Pacific halfway between Samoa and

Fiji. It is a small volcanic island which owes its name to the fact that the islanders' mailbag is a tin can bobbing in the water to be picked up by a passing steamer.

Q. *How does Lake Titicaca compare in size with one of the Great Lakes?* F. A. L.

A. It is about one-third the size of Lake Ontario.

Q. *How much higher than Pike's Peak is Mount Whitney?* B. A.

A. It is 386 feet higher. Pike's Peak has an altitude of 14,110 feet and Mount Whitney, the highest peak in continental United States, is 14,496 feet high.

Q. *Who gave the Lakes of Killarney to the Irish Free State?* L. J.

A. William Bowers Bourn of San Mateo, Calif., presented to the Irish Free State the huge tract of land containing the Lakes of Killarney. The Killarney Estate belonged to Lord Kenmare's family, whose ancestral seat was Killarney Castle. In 1913 the ancient castle was swept by fire and left in ruins. By 1930 the owners of the property were no longer able to pay taxes and Killarney went for sale on the auction block. It was purchased by Mr. Bourn, who now returns it to the Irish government.

Q. *How many islands are there in the Fiji Islands?* E. G.

A. This group in the southern Pacific contains about 250 islands. They form a British crown colony.

Q. *Are the waves on the Great Lakes ever as high as on the ocean?* D. B.

A. Waves have been measured in various parts of the ocean reaching heights of from 30 to 40 feet. In the South Atlantic and South Pacific it is thought that storm waves in their fullest development have reached 50 feet. Lake Superior has the largest waves, and it is thought probable that during severe storms waves may be encountered in deep water of a height of from 20 to 25 feet.

Q. Who first united the Hawaiian Islands under one rule? M. W.

A. King Kamehameha the First conquered all of the islands and brought them together under one rule. He is honored as the greatest of Hawaiian heroes.

Q. Please give the history of Ellis Island. E. M. H.

A. Ellis Island is a small island in the northern part of upper New York Bay, a mile southwest of the Battery. It was sold by New York State to the United States in 1808, and for many years was used as a powder magazine. In 1891 it was an immigrant station. The present buildings were erected in 1897 when the original structures were burned.

Q. In what county are the sources of the most rivers? C. K.

A. Randolph County, West Virginia, claims that more rivers have their origin in that county or nearby than in any known place in the world. From this high land, streams flow in practically all directions.

Q. Where and what is Kahoolawe? N. P.

A. Kahoolawe (pronounced Kaho-o-la-way, with the accent on la) is a lesser island of the Hawaiian group, situated near the southwestern end of the larger island of Maui, to which it is attached politically. There is very little on the island other than a steep volcanic hill in the center, and a lighthouse in a bend of the north shore.

Q. Has the River Nile in Africa many tributaries? W. T. H.

A. The Nile is unique among rivers of the world. Although it is 3500 miles long it has no tributaries for the last 1700 miles of its journey to the sea, largely through desert. Several streams discharge into it above this point. The flow is so light in summer that the mouths of the Nile are entirely closed by dams, but at the height of the flood season or inundation, it is a torrent discharging 13,000 cubic yards per second.

Q. Where is the Island of Majorca? J. W. C.

A. It lies off the coast of Spain 130 miles south of Barcelona. It is a port to which many fruit steamers go. It is 58 miles in length. The population according to the latest census was 253,000.

Q. Where are the highest mountains east of the Rockies? A. C.

A. They are located in North Carolina. Mt. Mitchell is the highest of these, being 6688 feet.

Q. What is the second largest port in the Hawaiian Islands? B. E. H.

A. Hilo is second in size, Honolulu ranking first.

Q. Is Elbrus the same as Elburz? A. R. B.

A. Elbrus is a peak in the Caucasus range in European Russia. It is the highest mountain in Europe, with an elevation of 18,468 feet. The Elburz are a mountain range in north Persia, south of the Caspian Sea.

Q. Distinguish between Orenburg and Oldenburg. N. D. F.

A. Orenburg is a city and district in the Autonomous Soviet Socialist Republic of Kirghiz, one of the eleven autonomous republics of the Russian S. F. S. R. or Soviet Russia proper, the principal constituent republic of the U. S. S. R. Oldenburg is a city and free state, one of the component units of the German Republic.

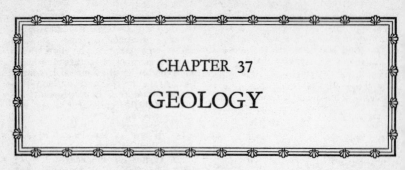

CHAPTER 37

GEOLOGY

Q. *How thick is the ice in the Arctic Ocean? O. B. H.*

A. The entire Arctic Ocean is practically covered by permanent heavy ice or ice pack of an average thickness of six or seven feet, but through pressures and underrunning it may attain or exceed 30 feet in places. The average maximum thickness of sea ice in the Arctic as determined from observations over a period of 18 years at 15 different stations was 76 inches.

Q. *What makes the Red Sea red? A. R.*

A. The dull red tint of the Red Sea arises from millions of microscopic plants called algae.

Q. *What is the name of the geological period in which we live? P. G.*

A. It is the Holocene. It extends from about 20,000 B.C. to the present time.

Q. *How far north and south do the Rocky Mountains extend? E. C.*

A. The Rocky Mountains are an assemblage of mountain ranges which form the backbone of North America. They begin in Mexico and extend northward to the westernmost of the Aleutian Islands. The length of the Rocky Mountain chain from north to south is some 4000 miles and its width between 400 and 500 miles. Within its borders are several mountain systems and a large number of individual ranges, together with several large plateaus, numerous val-leys, parks, and canyons, as well as multitudes of peaks and ridges, mesas, and buttes.

Q. *If all oceans were of the same depth, how deep would the water be? J. A. L.*

A. The average depth of the ocean below sea level is 12,500 feet.

Q. *Are the floors of the oceans covered with mud which corresponds to the soil on land? D. S. L.*

A. They are not except near the coasts. The vast floors of the oceans are covered with deposits of three kinds—a red clay, globigerina ooze, and pteropod ooze.

Q. *I heard Dr. Roy Chapman Andrews speaking of fossil remains found in the Gobi Desert. He spoke of the fact that the animals existed millions of years ago. How is it possible to know when these animals lived? D. B.*

A. Paleontology is a science which treats of the life of the geologic past. The records are read from the rocks themselves. Through observation of processes now going on, geologists are able to approximate how long ago the strata of rocks were formed in which the fossils are found.

Q. *What is meant by saying that a river has ages? F. G.*

A. A river has its stages of development; youth, maturity, and old age. In its earliest stages a river drains its basin imperfectly; as valleys are deepened, the drainage im-

238

proves, so that in maturity the total drainage area is large and the rate of erosion high. Old age is reached when wide flats have developed and the bordering lands have been brought low.

Q. How much of the sea area of the earth is included in the Pacific and Atlantic Ocean? C. T.

A. The basin of the Pacific Ocean comprises about 40 per cent of the whole sea area; the Atlantic Ocean about 25 per cent.

Q. Are the Rocky Mountains growing higher? E. R. L.

A. Probably. The Rocky Mountains are fairly new. Scientists know this because they are so steep. Old mountains are more worn down and have lower forms. The growth of mountains is slow. They are not pushed up suddenly in some grand cataclysm, but rise a few inches in a thousand years.

Q. Is the Mediterranean Sea as salt as the Atlantic Ocean? M. S.

A. The salinity of the Mediterranean Sea is slightly greater than that of the Atlantic, probably the result of greater evaporation. The proportion of the salinity of these bodies of water is 1.029 to 1.028.

Q. What is meant by a moving mountain? O. L.

A. Some mountains have a soft clay base topped with heavy sandstone. The clay becomes water-soaked through seepage and can no longer hold up the weight. Consequently the slope of the peaks steadily rolls down to a less steep inclination as the tremors of the mountain sides shake down gravel from the tops. Meeker's Mountain and Golden Mountain in Colorado are examples.

Q. How is the great size of the Amazon River accounted for? N. L.

A. The great size of the Amazon River is due to some extent to the configuration of the land. The Amazon Valley lies between two parallel ranges of mountains upon whose sides a large number of streams of considerable size flow. These streams have generally a southeastern course and it is probably the eastward flow of the waters which tends to increase the size of the Amazon River. There is no dividing ridge of mountains to divert part of the flow to other directions. The Amazon has at least 200 large tributaries, 17 of which are from 1000 to 2300 miles long. There are innumerable others of smaller size.

Q. Do mountainous states have more area than states which are flat? A. D. S.

A. The Geological Survey says that when land is surveyed for division it is treated as a plane surface. Therefore, a quarter of a section of level land contains the same amount as a quarter of a section of rolling land, but there may actually be more surface or earth in the rolling section than in the level section.

Q. Why are some beaches such as Daytona hard enough to drive a car on while others are so soft that a person walking sinks ankle-deep in the sand? J. J. C.

A. The Geological Survey states that the reason some sand is hard enough for driving and other sand is soft is due to the shape of the grains. Where the grains of sand are rounded, driving is not possible and the sand is soft. At Daytona Beach, the sand grains have sharp corners and the sand forms a hard surface for driving.

Q. How are stalactites and stalagmites formed? E. B.

A. Stalactites are pendent masses formed where water containing mineral solutions drops very slowly. On exposure to the air part of the water evaporates and a deposit of carbonate of lime ensues and as the drop continues to fall from the same spot, a small column of the material forms downward from the cave. Conditions essential to the formation of stalactites are a very slow trickle of water, regular evaporation, and the absence of disturbances, such as currents of air. When the water drops upon the floor of the cave, evaporation still goes on and the drop falling from the roof will always land on the same place so that the pillar of deposit rises vertically. This is known as stalagmite. In course of time the two may meet and in this way a column is deposited.

Q. What caused the Glacial Period? W. J.

A. C. L. Dake, Professor of Geology, University of Missouri, says: "Though several theories of the cause of the Glacial Period have been proposed no one has received general acceptance. The existence of glacial periods in past geologic ages is well established. . . . The time since the close of the Ice Age has been variously estimated, average estimates being around 20,000 years."

Q. How was the Chesapeake Bay formed? A. L.

A. It is what is known as a drowned valley. It was once the valley of the Susquehanna River, which emptied into the sea at the present mouth of the bay. This part of the Atlantic Coast sank, thus changing many physical features.

Q. How much soil is washed down into the ocean each year? V. M. E.

A. Geologists have estimated the amount of soil annually carried into the sea to be more than one billion tons.

Q. Was Natural Bridge in Virginia formed by a river which has since been "lost?" A. N.

A. This is not the explanation. In limestone formations, rainwater percolates through the soil, enters the cracks and crevices in the rock and gradually enlarges them. It often follows some plane of stratification, hollowing out large irregular rooms, then finding a lower level, repeats the process. In places the intervening floor of rock breaks down, and a lofty hall is formed. Then if the roof of this hall falls in, there is a valley bounded with steep cliffs. In some places the floor between the two original levels is left, forming such a natural bridge as the one in Virginia.

Q. How was the Devil's Tower in Wyoming formed? C. W. B.

A. The Geological Survey says that the Devil's Tower of northeastern Wyoming is a small part of a once extensive dome-like sheet of igneous rock which was molten and was formed below the surface. The rock when molten flowed upward through the neck that is probably below the Tower, and as it cooled off and hardened it shrunk and cracked into six-sided vertical columns of rock. During the many millions of years since the cooling of the igneous rock, streams and other processes of erosion have lowered the surface of the land and have not only carried away most of the rock strata inclosing the dome-like sheet but have also carried away most of the sheet itself. The only part that is left is the bold precipitous Tower, the sides of which are strongly fluted by great stone columns.

Q. Were there any people living on earth at the time of the glacial period? G. B.

A. Geologists say that people were known to be living in Europe during the time of the last glacial sheet; however, no traces have been found in North America of human beings at this time. These human beings were uncivilized men of the old Stone Age.

Q. What is an anticline? Can it be detected at the surface of the earth? G. D.

A. The Geological Survey says that an anticline is an upfold in rocks, and such a fold in deposits, that are buried beneath formations of more recent geologic age that were not subjected to the folding, cannot be detected at the surface. Such upfolds—called anticlines—are regarded as favorable to the accumulation of oil and it is for this reason that oil prospectors endeavor to locate such structures.

Q. *How was the Maine Desert formed?* L. M. T.

A. It was formed by a glacial lake or pool. Such a mass as this must have been deposited in a gradually enlarging pool or lake within the ice sheet. The Maine Desert is solid and rather level on top. The smoothness of the surface may be in part due to the waves of the sea sweeping over it, since it occupies a position where it would be much exposed to the waves of the broad bay which then covered the valley of the Royal River to the south of it.

Q. *What causes a line in the ocean, on one side of which the water is rough while on the other it is smooth?* A. J.

A. The Coast and Geodetic Survey says the phenomenon is one that is frequently observed at sea. The cause is usually ascribed to currents, although there may be other reasons involved. The edge of the Gulf Stream is often marked by a very definite line with an abrupt change in temperature and color of water. If the wind is against the current the stream will be rough and choppy while the adjacent water is comparatively smooth. A fine film of oil produces a surface known as a "Slick." Along the edge of this there is often a distinct line.

Q. *What makes volcanoes erupt?* W. S.

A. The ultimate cause of volcanicity is the internal heat of the earth.

Q. *Is it true that lava in a volcano crater is liquid rock?* H. H.

A. Lava is molten rock. Lavas of siliceous nature usually have a pasty or ropy consistency and flow sluggishly after eruption, while basaltic lavas are usually fluid and flow freely. The former build up volcanic cones of steep slopes, as in central France, whereas basaltic lavas form volcanic cones of gentle slopes, like those of Etna or the Hawaiian volcanoes. Some lavas decompose and disintegrate with amazing rapidity and form a fertile soil for the vine. Others, but slightly different in composition, present for centuries a firm unyielding surface to the elements. Lavas may be either compact or vesicular, slaggy, scoriaceous, or pumiceous.

Q. *How many glaciers are there in Glacier National Park?* P. L.

A. There are about eighty, some of an area of five square miles while some cover only a few acres.

Q. *Why are there so many more lakes in some parts of the country than in others?* J. J. D.

A. The most common cause of the formation of lakes is the disturbance of drainage by glacial action. Thus, they are generally abundant in mountain regions or within those areas subjected to ice.

Q. *Are there any other lakes as large as Crater Lake which occupy the basins of volcanoes?* N. P. C.

A. While there are other crater lakes, there is none which compares in size with Crater Lake, which fills the great caldera where once Mount Mazama raised its peak.

Q. *Why is water coming from a deep well cold, when we are told that beyond the earth's crust the temperature increases?* M. A. S.

A. Only a few feet of earth on the very surface is affected by the daily range of temperature. There is then a larger layer upon which neither the surface temperature nor the temperature from the inside of the earth has any effect. Then comes the layer where the temperature of the earth increases one degree for every 50 to 75 feet one goes into the interior of the earth. The cold water comes from the layer which is unaffected by temperatures from within the earth or on the surface of the earth. In some places we have thermo springs where the water comes from a depth below this in the region which is influenced by the heat from within the earth.

Q. *Please give an example of an island which is gradually submerging. F. O.*

A. The Island of Capri offers an unusual example of submergence within historic times. In ancient times a sea cave, now known as Blue Grotto, was used by the Romans as a resort from excessive heat. In order to obtain light an opening was cut in the roof. Since that time the island has sunk so that even the artificial opening is now partially submerged. In some caves of the Bermuda Islands stalactites hang from the roof and extend into the sea water which partially fills the cave. Stalactites obviously could not have been formed in water, proving that at one time the island had a greater elevation. These islands seem to be disappearing, but in this case the process is a very slow one.

Q. *Are there many active volcanoes in the United States? A. G.*

A. There are few active volcanoes in the United States at the present time, but a number have been extinct within times geographically recent. There was an eruption of Tres Virgines, California, in 1857. Mt. Lassen renewed its activity mildly a few years ago. Mt. Hood in Oregon exhales vapor, as does also Mt. Rainier in Washington. Mt. St. Helena, Washington, was in eruption in 1841–42, and Mt. Baker, also in Washington, was reported active in 1843.

Q. *Please explain the presence of oases in a desert. A. E. R.*

A. An oasis in a desert is generally caused by springs or streams rising from a subterranean spring. In the Sahara there are mountains sufficiently high to induce rainfall in the neighboring lowlands, which thus receive sufficient water to support some vegetation. A combination of soil that holds water but prevents evaporation is sometimes found in deserts and greatly favors the formation of oases.

Q. *Why are so many of the natural springs in the West hot? W. L.*

A. It is due to geological conditions, much of the western country being of volcanic origin and affected by volcanic conditions.

Q. *In surveys, is the curvature of the surface of the earth taken into account? H. W. H.*

A. The Geological Survey says that in surveys of small tracts of land no account is taken of the fact that the surface of the earth is spherical. The irregularities of the surface more than make up for the curvature. True north and south lines are not parallel but get closer and closer together as they go north or south from the equator. For large areas the curvature of the earth is apparent. In the General Land Office surveys the curvature shows. The blocks of a square mile are made as nearly square as possible, the error from curvature being all thrown into the northeast corner of each six-mile block.

Q. *Can a ship be held in the Sargasso Sea by the tangle of weeds found there? C. W. P.*

A. The widely credited possibility of ships becoming embedded in the weeds and being unable to escape was disproved by the expedition of the Michael Sars under the direction of Sir John Murray in 1910, which found the surface covered with weeds only in patches, not continuously. The Beebe Expedition later verified this statement.

Q. *What is the difference in sea level of the Pacific and Atlantic Oceans at Panama? J. H. N.*

A. The mean level of the Pacific at the Isthmus has been found to be about eight inches higher than the mean level of the Atlantic. In the month of February the levels are the same, but throughout the rest of the year, on account of current, tidal and wind influences, the mean level of the Pacific ranges above that of the Atlantic. It is as much as one foot higher in October.

Q. What kind of a prehistoric animal was it that was found in an Alaskan glacier a year or so ago? L. H.

A. The remains of a strange animal found on Glacier Island, Alaska, in November, 1930, were identified as those of a prehistoric whale.

Q. How does it happen that there are so many small lakes in the northern portions of the country? B. B.

A. They occur in the portions of the country that were covered by glaciers during the ice age. They consist of accumulations of water from springs, or from drainage of rainfall, or from inflowing streams, sometimes within hollows, gorges, and channels scooped out by the glaciers in their movement, sometimes within valleys or channels, which were more or less completely dammed up by deposits of sand, gravel, boulders, dropped by the glaciers, and sometimes with hollows or depressions, called kettle-holes, in the earth's surface.

Q. Does the portion of ocean near the equator contain more salt than water farther north and south? H. N. S.

A. There are two zones of maximum salinity on the surface waters of the ocean, one north and one south of the tropical belts, separated by a zone of minimum salinity in the equatorial region.

Q. Are the Ozark Mountains the oldest mountains in the world? W. L. L.

A. The Ozark Mountains, or Ozark Plateau, belong with the oldest mountain regions of the world, and denudation is slowly and surely removing the last remains of once lofty mountains. A small area of Pre-Cambrian rocks is exposed in the Saint Francois Mountains. The re-

mainder of the plateau consists of Cambrian and Ordovician Age.

Q. What makes an undertow at an ocean beach? G. S.

A. When a wave rushes up on a beach, the water must recede. Meanwhile, another wave is approaching. This second wave climbs over the water which is running back. This is repeated time and time again. There is therefore a seaward-flowing current set up under the advancing waves.

Q. What does the elevation have to be for high land to be called a mountain? H. R.

A. A mountain is any elevation of land high enough to be very conspicuous in its surroundings. In general, an elevation higher than a hill and often rising with a comparative abruptness, but without great extent of surface at its summit. Popularly, the term is variously used; hills which rise 100 to 200 feet above essentially flat surroundings are sometimes called mountains, as in southern New Jersey and the plains of Texas, while in a mountainous region, as near the Rocky Mountains, elevations of 1000 or 2000 feet are called hills.

Q. When was the Mississippi River formed? A. H.

A. The river, as it now exists, was formed during the latter part of the Ice Age, more than twenty thousand years ago.

Q. Were the Great Lakes at one time a single body of water? S. N. S.

A. The Smithsonian Institution says that at a remote time, the State of Michigan and the adjacent Great Lakes were a vast inland sea.

Q. Were the islands on the west coast of Scotland ever part of the mainland? D. McL.

A. The islands on the western coast of Scotland were originally part of the mainland. The whole western coast of Scotland has sunk.

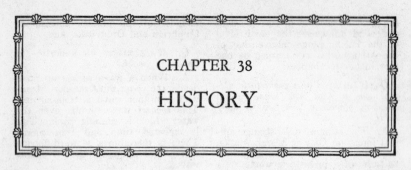

CHAPTER 38

HISTORY

Q. *Did General Grant demand the surrender of General Lee's sword?* O. V. G.

A. Contrary to the popular belief this incident did not occur. In the possession of Robert Underwood Johnson at the time that he prepared Grant's Memoirs were General Grant's signed words in his own handwriting: "There was no demand made for General Lee's sword and no tender of it."

Q. *Is there still extant a tea chest left from the Boston Tea Party?* C. E.

A. There is one on exhibition in the Royall House, Medford, Massachusetts.

Q. *Where did the white man first cross the Mississippi to explore country to the west?* W. S.

A. Cape Rock, at Cape Girardeau, Missouri, marks the spot where the first crossing was made.

Q. *What parts of the United States were originally palatinates?* C. M.

A. Maryland and South Carolina were originally instituted as palatinates.

Q. *Where was a dueling ground known as the Oaks?* H. McK.

A. The Oaks, one of the most famous dueling grounds in the world, was in the suburbs of New Orleans. On one particular Sunday in 1828, ten duels were fought there. Between 1834 and 1844, scarcely a day passed without a duel. The oaks on this ground are still standing. Duels in those days were fought over such unimportant differences, that they would now be regarded as trivial.

Q. *Was Alexander Hamilton ever offered a seat on the bench of the United States Supreme Court?* H. A. G.

A. He declined the position of Chief Justice of the United States Supreme Court.

Q. *Who were considered the greatest scouts of our early days?* H. W. L.

A. Boone, Crockett, Carson, Bridger, Wild Bill Hickok, and Buffalo Bill Cody are the six great names.

Q. *What American city was called The Paris of the Colonies?* I. A. T.

A. This name was applied to Annapolis. From a little settlement on the Severn in 1664, it grew in size and importance until it became the capital of Maryland. By 1750 it was famed for its gayety and luxury and was often referred to as the Paris of the Colonies.

Q. *How many Indians were there in the United States at the time of its discovery by Columbus?* Y. T.

A. There could have been no authentic census of the Indians in 1492. A government expert estimates the number of Indians at that time at 1,115,000.

244

Q. Had Oliver Cromwell a particular interest in the American colonies? E. C.

A. In 1643, he was appointed one of a board of commissioners for the general management of all the English colonies in America. Other duties occupied most of his time at this period.

Q. What was the vocation of Barbara Fritchie's husband? W. D.

A. He was a glove maker. In Barbara Fritchie's home in Frederick, Maryland, several relics of his trade —scraps of leathers and skins, gloves, and the wooden forms used in shaping the fingers of the gloves—are to be seen.

Q. Who chose the name for the State of Tennessee? E. S. G.

A. Andrew Jackson helped draft the constitution of Tennessee, and suggested the name to the constitutional convention. He said that Mrs. Jackson had suggested to him that the State be named for the river of that name which runs through the State. It is an Indian name, meaning crooked spoon.

Q. In how many different places did the Continental Congress meet? P. T. B.

A. Eight. The Continental Congress held sessions in New York City, Princeton, Trenton, Philadelphia, Reading, York, Baltimore, and Annapolis.

Q. What nickname was given to General Cornwallis? D. A.

A. General Greene of the American forces called him "The Modern Hannibal."

Q. How was the news of the capitulation of Cornwallis at Yorktown sent to Philadelphia? Q. A.

A. Tench Tilghman was selected to carry the letter announcing the surrender to the President of Congress, Thomas McKean. Tilghman spread the tidings as he rode. He reached Philadelphia in about four days—October 23, 1781.

Q. Why did Empress Carlotta of Mexico desert her husband at the critical time shortly before he was executed? N. S.

A. In 1863 she went with her husband to Mexico and remained there till 1866, when the dissatisfaction against the empire forced her husband to send her from the land of their adoption to ask help in France. She could obtain no assistance from Napoleon III and went to Rome to appeal to the Pope. Before negotiations there were completed, her health gave way under the strain, and after the end of the empire and the execution of her husband (June 19, 1867) she became totally insane. She died in seclusion January 19, 1927.

Q. Was light ever used as a weapon in a famous battle? A. H. D.

A. The focusing of the sun's rays by curved mirror surfaces was known to the Romans and Greeks, and this was employed at the suggestion of Archimedes in the Battle of Syracuse when the sun's rays were focused on the wooden ships and set them on fire.

Q. How much did England pay for the Hessian soldiers which were sent to America during the Revolution? S. B. T.

A. The Landgrave of Hesse, who sold his troops for so much a head, received more than $2,500,000 for Hessian soldiers lost during the war.

Q. What caused the French Revolution? G. McG.

A. The French Revolution was mainly the result of the oppression of the French people, who rose in revolt against the extravagance and tyranny of the kings and nobles. In addition they had no adequate representation in the legislature. The taxes were heavy, and in 1777 there were as many as 1,250,000 beggars in France. Alarmed by the increasing signs of unrest in the country, the king and some of the nobles began to gather the army near Paris. This so enraged the people of Paris that they stormed the Bastille on July 14, 1789. This is regarded as the beginning of the Revolution.

Q. *What was Peary's first message about the discovery of the North Pole?* W. C. F.

A. The message was "Stars and Stripes nailed to the Pole" and was telegraphed by Commodore Peary on September 5, 1909 from Indian Harbor.

Q. *Please explain briefly the Magna Charta.* A. K. J.

A. In 1215 the English barons rose against the authority of King John of England and compelled him to sign a charter called the Magna Charta, guaranteeing to Englishmen certain rights and liberties which have been held by the English people since that day. The charter was signed at Runnymede, June 15.

Q. *Why did the British wish to capture Washington in the War of 1812?* A. M. G.

A. They wished to create a diversion for the benefit of their northern operations. They were planning an invasion through New York, by way of Lake Champlain.

Q. *How long did it take Magellan to go around the world?* W. W.

A. This journey started in 1519 and took 1093 days.

Q. *Why is Khyber Pass of particular importance?* A. C.

A. It is the most important of the passes which lead from Afghanistan into India. No other pass in the world has possessed such strategic importance, or retains so many historic associations as this gateway to the plains of India.

Q. *Who rang the Liberty Bell when the Declaration of Independence was adopted?* A. B.

A. Andrew McNair, the official ringer of the Liberty Bell from 1759–1776, rang the bell upon the occasion of the signing of the Declaration of Independence.

Q. *Who was in charge of the boats in which Washington and his men crossed the Delaware?* G. M.

A. A patriot, now almost forgotten, John Glover. He rose to the rank of Brigadier General.

Q. *For what purpose did the Scots display the fiery cross?* S. L.

A. Brewer's Directory of Phrase and Fable says that the fiery cross was anciently a signal sent around the Scottish clans in the Highlands summoning them to assemble for battle. It was symbolic of fire and sword. It consisted of a cross, the ends of which had been dipped in the blood of some animal slain for the purpose.

Q. *What dispute between the United States and Great Britain was decided by the Emperor of Germany?* E. D.

A. The dispute between the United States and Great Britain that was arbitrated by a German emperor was in relation to the San Juan water boundary. In 1871 the German emperor rendered a decision sustaining the American claim.

Q. *Where and when did Wild Bill Hickok die?* R. J.

A. He was shot during a card game in Deadwood, S. Dak., August 2, 1876.

Q. *What were the names of the vessels which brought the first colonists to Jamestown, Virginia?* W. B.

A. They were the Sarah Constant, the Goodspeed, and the Discovery. They came to anchor off the island where Jamestown was established on May 13, 1607.

Q. *What is meant by the catacombs of Paris?* G. W. H.

A. The catacombs of Paris are vast excavations extending under the city of Paris, formerly subterranean quarries which furnished the building material for the city. In the latter part of the eighteenth century some portions of the city began to sink, and it was necessary to strengthen the roof of the quarries with masonry. In 1787 the catacombs were arranged to contain the bodies removed from other burying grounds, and it is estimated that upward of 6,000,000 bodies are now preserved in them. The bones are arranged in varied designs along the sides of the galleries.

Q. *Has the United States paid Denmark for the Virgin Islands? E. E. R.*

A. On March 3, 1917, Congress appropriated $25,000,000 to pay for the Virgin Islands. On the 31st of that month a Treasury warrant was made out to the Envoy Extraordinary of Denmark, and this warrant was returned as paid on April 2, 1917.

Q. *What was the longest siege in history? L. O. M.*

A. The siege of Tyre by Nebuchadnezzar, which was carried on for 13 years. The siege was raised in 572 B.C.

Q. *Where is Myles Standish buried? E. R.*

A. In 1931 the bones of Myles Standish were taken from their wooden coffin, placed in a metal one, and then reburied in the cemetery at Duxbury, Mass.

Q. *Where was the State of Deseret? G. N.*

A. This was the name given by the Mormons in 1849 to their settlement in the present State of Utah. Deseret was taken from the Book of Mormon and meant land of the honey bee. In 1850, Congress created the Territory of Utah, and the old name fell into disuse.

Q. *After Columbus discovered the islands off the east coast of America, who was the first to come to the mainland? P. S.*

A. Juan Ponce de Leon landed on the coast of Florida, April 2, 1513. He did not know that it was the mainland. He supposed it was a large island which the Indians called Bimini, but named the region he discovered, Florida.

Q. *What is the oldest American settlement in Alaska? L. N. D.*

A. It is Juneau. It was named for Joseph Juneau, who discovered the quartz and placer riches which have made that district famous.

Q. *After the Battle of Little Big Horn did any man or beast of Custer's Command survive? U. B.*

A. Comanche, the horse of Capt. Myles Keogh, Seventh Cavalry, was the only animate part of Custer's Command that survived. He had three severe wounds but was cared for by the officers and men of the Seventh Cavalry until his death at the age of 28 years.

Q. *Of what nationality was Mata Hari, the German spy? D. D.*

A. While a fiction was created about her birth in India, she in reality was a Dutch girl, Marguerite Gertrude Zelle, born August 7, 1876, at Leeuwarden in Frisia. She married Captain Rudolph MacLeod. After some years of wretched married life, she was deserted and trained herself as a dancer. Her astonishing popularity followed. Eventually she came under suspicion as a German spy during the World War. She was arrested, convicted, and shot.

Q. *Why was it said that if Cleopatra's nose had been shorter the whole face of the world would have been changed? D. E. S.*

A. To convey the idea that if Cleopatra had been less attractive she would not have enslaved Julius Caesar and Mark Antony.

Q. *Where was Charlemagne buried? R. E.*

A. He was buried at Aix-la-Chapelle, his favorite and usual place of residence. He was, according to tradition, buried in a vault of a chapel in a sitting posture on a gold throne, dressed in his full imperial costume.

Q. *Where is George Wythe, signer of the Declaration of Independence, buried?* S. R.

A. George Wythe is buried in the churchyard of St. Johns Church in Richmond, Virginia. The stone which marks the site bears the following inscription: "This tablet is dedicated to mark the site, where lie the mortal remains of George Wythe Born 1726—Died 1806 Jurist and Statesman Teacher of Randolph Jefferson and Marshall First Professor of law in the United States First Virginia signer of the Declaration of Independence Erected by Patriotic citizens of Virginia A.D. 1922."

Q. *Is there a snuff box made from the hoof of Napoleon's favorite horse?* S. A. L.

A. There is still in existence a snuff box made from a hoof of Napoleon's famous charger, Marengo. The hoof is silver-shod and fitted with a silver lid upon which is this inscription: "Hoof of Marengo, barb charger of Napoleon, ridden by him at Marengo, Jena, Wagram, in the Russian campaign, and at Waterloo."

Q. *Did Sir Walter Raleigh visit North America?* E. C.

A. He did not. He sent expeditions to Virginia in 1584, 1585, 1586, 1587, and 1589, but Queen Elizabeth would not permit him to accompany the expeditions. Later, however, he did visit South America.

Q. *What American statesman was the grandson of a king?* D. C.

A. Charles Bonaparte, who was in the Roosevelt cabinet.

Q. *Where was Secretary of State Seward at the time of the surrender at Appomattox in 1865?* W. S. E.

A. The surrender occurred on April 9. On the fifth day of April Seward had been thrown from a carriage. He was picked up unconscious with his jaw broken in two places and his shoulder dislocated. He had many other bruises and strains. His jaw was placed in an iron frame and he could speak with difficulty, if at all, for many days. He was still confined to his bed on the night of April 14th when Lincoln was assassinated, and when the attempt on his life was month was made; in fact, it was nearly a month before he was able to attend a Cabinet meeting even in his own house.

Q. *Of what significance was Blucher's part in the Battle of Waterloo?* W. M.

A. General Blucher was a Prussian field-marshal. When his countrymen rose against the French in 1813, he was appointed to the chief command. In the Battle of Waterloo the victory of the allies was decided by his appearance on the field.

Q. *What proportion of the people in the American colonies were Tories?* M. H.

A. Probably a third of the people of the thirteen colonies remained faithful to the King, and opposed armed resistance from the beginning. These were called Tories and Loyalists.

Q. *What were the casualties in the Battle of Waterloo?* F. B.

A. The exact losses at the Battle of Waterloo are undetermined. The French probably lost over 31,000 persons killed, wounded, and missing. The Allies' losses, according to official returns, amounted to 22,428.

Q. *Had any of the 13 original colonies declared their independence of England before the Declaration of Independence?* N. W. B.

A. Prior to the Declaration seven States had assumed independent governments, and four had drawn up written constitutions, while one, Massachusetts, had adopted a provisional government.

Q. *When was the State of Franklin formed?* G. H. R.

A. It was formed at a conference at Jonesboro, August 23, 1784. John Sevier was the first Governor. Congress ignored requests to be recognized as a State and at the expiration of Sevier's term in 1788, the State of Franklin ended.

Q. *What is the Mecklenburg Declaration of Independence?* N. M. F.

A. It was a declaration of independence from England alleged to have been made at Charlotte, N. C., in May, 1775, by the citizens of Mecklenburg County.

Q. *What was the battle of Chateauquay?* S. R.

A. The battle of Chateauquay took place in October, 1813, during the War of 1812. The United States troops were defeated.

Q. *What were Head's Right Grants?* E. B. W.

A. In early days, every immigrant who came to this country and paid his own way was, in many of the States, given 50 acres of land for his own use and 50 acres more for every other person imported by him. These were called Head's Right Grants. These allotments of land were assignable and this was a common method of acquiring large estates.

Q. *Is Garcia to whom the Message was sent, still living?* W. E.

A. This Cuban patriot died in 1898.

Q. *Was there a battle during the Spanish-American War in which the United States losses were greater than those of the Spanish?* W. S. A.

A. In the battle of El Caney the Spanish losses were 320 while the American losses were about 440.

Q. *When were London and Paris founded?* D. W.

A. The exact dates of the settlements of London and Paris are not recorded. London first rose out of obscurity early after the Roman occupation of Britain in the first century of the Christian Era. Caesar makes no mention of the town, but Tacitus refers to it as having been a place much frequented by merchants in A.D. 61. Paris was formerly known as Lutetia. Caesar describes in his Commentaries how it was burnt during the first Gallic War 52 B.C. During the first century there was reference to Lutetia as a Roman town.

Q. *What was the origin of the Maltese Cross?* A. A. S.

A. This emblem was adopted by the Knights of Malta. They devised a cross made up of four barbed arrowheads meeting at their points.

Q. *In what years did Lafayette come to this country?* M. C.

A. Lafayette came to the American colonies in 1777. He returned to France in 1779, and again returned to the United States in 1780. He visited in this country in 1784 and again in 1824 and 1825.

Q. *Why is it sometimes said that the Declaration of Independence was not signed on the 4th of July?* E. A. M.

A. On July 4, 1776, the Declaration of Independence was reported to the Continental Congress by the chairman, but it was not signed by all the delegates until August 2, some of them having to wait for instructions from their respective colonies.

Q. *Name the six Senators who voted against the United States entering the World War.* R. G.

A. The Senators who voted against the declaration of war with Germany were as follows: Stone, La Follette, Norris, Vardaman, Lane, Gronna.

Q. *At what place in France was the Armistice signed?* W. A. F.

A. The Armistice was signed in Marshal Foch's private car which was on a switch near the Castle of Francport near Choisy-au-Bac, France.

Q. *Has Constantinople ever been out of the hands of the Turks?* B. J.

A. Before its capture by the Turks, Constantinople **was in the** hands of the Romans, Greeks, and Mohammedans consecutively.

Q. *What is the story about the Sepoy Rebellion being caused by the Sepoys being forced to eat meat?* J. W. C.

A. Sepoys are the native British Indian soldiers. In religion they are for the most part Mohammedan and Brahman. One considers the cow sacred, the other is not permitted to eat pork. The Enfield rifles, which were put in the hands of the Sepoys had cartridges greased with tallow and lard. It was necessary for the soldiers to bite these cartridges with their teeth. On May 10, 1857, the Sepoys mutinied in Meerut, when native troops rose and liberated some of their comrades who had been imprisoned for refusing to handle the English cartridges.

Q. *What was the name of the ship from which the tea was thrown overboard in Boston in 1775?* L. M. A.

A. Three ships were involved in the Boston Tea Party, the Eleanor, Beaver, and Dartmouth.

Q. *During the War of 1812 did the New England States threaten secession?* G. T.

A. Andrew McLaughlin says: "It was commonly supposed that it (the Hartford Convention) would plot a disruption of the Union; but it simply drew up remonstrances, and proposed amendments to the Constitution intended to protect a minority of the States against unwelcome Federal legislation."

Q. *What caused the fall of Rome?* M. W.

A. The downfall of the Roman Empire came about gradually. The empire had become so far-flung that the maintenance of legions to guard the outlying territories became an increased burden and expenditure to the people. Taxation was extraordinarily heavy in order to maintain the numerous officials and to keep up the luxurious splendor of the court.

Other symptoms of economic ruin were the decrease of population, thereby diminishing the number of taxpayers and the number of soldiers for legions, the spread of infanticide, the increase of waste lands, and the constantly recurring riots and insurrections caused by these conditions.

Q. *Was Judah P. Benjamin, Secretary of State of the Confederacy, a Senator before or after the Civil War?* N. T.

A. He was a Senator from Louisiana when the war began and withdrew to join the Confederate cause. After the war, he left the country, established himself in England, and was called within the bar as a queen's counsel in 1872. He moved to Paris and died there in 1884.

Q. *What people first became civilized?* W. M.

A. It is not possible to say definitely which is the oldest civilization on earth. The Chinese claim this distinction. As the early history of many of the ancient countries is largely legendary, it may be that there are other civilizations which antedate that of China, such as, for instance, that of Assyria or that of the Aztecs in Mexico.

Q. *Why was a statue erected to Caesar Rodney in Wilmington, Delaware?* J. M. S.

A. Caesar Rodney was one of the delegates from Delaware to the Continental Congress held in Independence Hall, Philadelphia. This Congress was to vote on the adoption of independence. By agreement, unless the majority of the delegates of each individual colony was in favor of adoption of the Declaration, the same would not be done. One of Delaware's delegates was favorable, one was opposed. Caesar Rodney was held at home in Dover due to illness. Word was sent to him by carrier that his vote was needed. He arose from his sick bed and rode without stopping from Dover to Wilmington to Philadelphia and arrived just in time as his name was called on the roll to say "Delaware casts her vote for Independence."

Q. From what countries was the North Russian Expeditionary Force drawn? W. M. S.

A. It consisted of men from the United States, England, Canada, France, Italy, and Serbia.

Q. Please give some information about Haym Salomon. C. M. T.

A. Salomon was an immigrant Jew who was the financial genius of the Revolution. Writing of him, Joseph D. Sawyer says: "From far off Poland came Haym Salomon, the Jew, who had much to do with the finances of the Revolution. Born at Lissa, Poland, in 1740, he arrived in the New World in 1771, four years before the Lexington skirmish. The French appointed him Treasurer of their army in America and he became the financial intermediary between the United States and France." The diary of Robert Morris, born in England, the Treasurer of the Revolution, had disclosed over 70 transactions in Salomon's name.

Q. When was Jefferson Davis in Washington as a public servant? V. D.

A. Jefferson Davis was a representative in Congress 1845–46, when he resigned on account of the Mexican War in which he participated. He was appointed to the Senate in 1847 and elected for the next term. He was Secretary of War in the cabinet of President Pierce from 1853 to 1857, and elected again to the Senate 1857–61, when he resigned on account of the Civil War.

Q. Is it true that Walter Reed Hospital is located on a Civil War battlefield? If so, of what significance was the encounter? F. F.

A. The Army medical center is located on a tract of 109.7 acres of land about five miles northwest of the center of Washington, D. C., on the site of a skirmish of the Civil War known as the Battle of Fort Stevens. This engagement marked the high tide of the advance of the Confederate Forces on the Union capital and is of historical interest owing to the fact that President Lincoln, while viewing the engagement, narrowly missed being shot by a Confederate sharpshooter located in a tree on the present reservation. Unfortunately this historic tree was recently demolished by lightning.

Q. Who was known as the Black Napoleon? T. L. S.

A. Dessalines, whose statue stands in the Champ de Mars, Port au Prince, Haiti. He drove the French out of Haiti and a century after his death his monument was erected bearing the epitaph "Founder of the Republic."

Q. Why did the English decide to colonize in America? L. M. T.

A. Walker's "Essentials in English History" says: "The beginning of English colonization is due to the statesmanship of Walter Raleigh. Although erratic and visionary in many respects, Raleigh saw clearly that attacks on Spanish ports or vessels were a poor method of fighting Spain. He appears to have been the first to conceive the idea of opposing Spain by invading her special domain, the American continent, and erecting there against Spanish dominance a lasting bulwark by planting a series of colonies along its coast. Drake might plunder and burn; but Raleigh preferred to plant and settle. In 1585 he sent Sir Richard Grenville to Roanoke Island with a colony of one hundred persons; in 1587 he sent John White with one hundred and fifty more; and although both these attempts failed, yet they led in the next reign to the more lasting work of the Virginia Company."

Q. Was there a real person named Cyrano de Bergerac? W. C. C.

A. Savinier Cyrano de Bergerac was a French author who was born in 1619 and died in 1655. Edmund Rostand wrote a drama in which de

Bergerac was the hero, and the play was in many ways true to facts. The real de Bergerac was distinguished for his courage in the field, and for the duels he fought. These numbered more than a thousand, most of them fought on account of his monstrously large nose.

Q. Was Washington ever accused of incompetence? R. E. N.

A. During the Revolution, in 1777, an intrigue was organized by Thomas Conway, to displace Washington as Commander-in-Chief of the American Armies by General Horatio Gates. The association included besides Conway and Gates such men as Charles Lee, Thomas Mifflin, and Benjamin Rush, and was known as the Conway Cabal. Washington was accused of gross incompetence and favoritism, but sufficient support was not given these men so that their scheme fell through. Conway was virtually forced to leave the service in 1778.

Q. What was the Webster-Ashburton Treaty? N. E.

A. This treaty between the United States and Great Britain was negotiated in 1842. By it the frontier line between the State of Maine and Canada was definitely fixed, provisions were made for putting an end to the African slave trade, and an agreement was made for the mutual extradition of suspected criminals.

Q. What State first ratified the Constitution? S. N.

A. Delaware was the first State to ratify the Constitution.

Q. How much did the Civil War cost? J. F.

A. In the Civil War, according to Elson, "the expense to the Government reached an average of nearly $3,000,000 a day, and there was a public debt in August, 1865, of $2,845,000,000. These figures take no account of the separate expenditures of the States and cities, amounting to nearly $500,000,000, nor of the expense to the South, nor of the incalculable destruction of property. To all this must be added the interest on the public debt and the pensions paid to the soldiers, to the widows, and the orphans. The total cost of the war no doubt exceeded $10,000,000,000."

Q. How was Ft. Michilimackinac captured by the Indians? S. T.

A. The Indians arranged to play a game of ball within the fort. The squaws stood by with concealed weapons. At a given signal the Indians seized the weapons and attacked the unprepared English, few of whom escaped alive.

Q. What happened to the loyalists at the close of the Revolutionary War? N. O.

A. Many left the country, going principally to England or Canada. Some were reduced to poverty. Some were tarred and feathered. Some were put to death.

Q. What was the Battle of Sailor's Creek and when was it fought? N. S. G.

A. Sailor's Creek was the last great battle of the Civil War. General Sheridan described it as "one of the severest conflicts of the war." It is explained that comparatively little is heard of the battle because it was completely overshadowed by the surrender of the Confederacy only three days later. Such leading generals, as Lee, Meade, Longstreet, Sheridan, Humphreys, R. H. Anderson, Ewell, Gordon, Seymour, Crook, Merritt, Stagg, and Kershaw were engaged. The battle took place on April 5, 1865. The scene was the general neighborhood of Amelia Court House, about 30 miles west of Petersburg, Va.

Q. What State has been under six flags? C. M.

A. Texas served under six flags as follows: Fleur de lis, France; Lions and Castles, Spain; Eagle and Snake, Mexico; Lone Star, Republic of Texas; Stars and Bars, Confederacy; Star Spangled Banner, United States.

Q. Was the encounter between the Monitor and the Merrimac considered an important battle? F. B.

A. Elson says that the battle between the Monitor and the Merrimac was the most famous of all naval duels, and one of the most important in the world's history. This first fight of ironclads had the effect of revolutionizing naval warfare throughout the world.

Q. When was Hawaii discovered? H. W. S.

A. The first white men in Hawaii were the survivors of the crews of two Spanish vessels which were wrecked on the islands as early, possibly, as 1527. Gaetano in 1555 made a landfall here, but Captain James Cook on his third voyage in the Pacific definitely discovered the group in 1778. Cook named the group Sandwich Islands after John Montagu, the fourth Earl of Sandwich.

Q. What was the Addled Parliament? R. A.

A. This was the name given to the second parliament of James I of England because it did not produce a single statute.

Q. Name the foreigners who served in the Revolutionary War on the side of the colonies? H. V.

A. Some of the principal ones were Von Steuben (Prussia), Lafayette (France), Paul Jones (Scotland), Thomson (Ireland), Sullivan (Ireland), Haym Salomon, a Jew born in Poland, DeKalb (Bavaria), Pulaski (Poland), Kosciusko (Poland).

Q. Why was the Colony of Georgia founded? G. W.

A. A charter for the establishment of the Colony of Georgia was obtained from George II of England, June, 1732, by a number of benevolent gentlemen of London, whose design was to found a home for the poor of Great Britain and a place of refuge for the Protestants and other persecuted sects of the continent of Europe. The colony was also intended as a military settlement to protest against the encroachments of Spain upon South Carolina. General Oglethorpe brought over the first 116 immigrants. Georgia was primarily founded as a religious asylum and refuge.

Q. How was the purchase price of Alaska paid? F. D.

A. Payment for Alaska was made by means of a draft on the Assistant Treasurer of New York, dated August 1, 1868, for $7,200,000. The draft was drawn in favor of "Edward de Staecke, Envoy Extraordinary, etc.," who represented the Emperor of Russia.

Q. What American girl enlisted in the Continental Army, for the whole term of the Revolutionary War? R. B.

A. Deborah Samson enlisted thus in October, 1778. The military authorities supposed of course she was a young man. She was received and enrolled in the Army as Robert Shirtliffe.

Q. Who are known as the Financiers of the War of 1812? M. T.

A. Three of the principal financiers of the War of 1812 were David Parish, John Jacob Astor, and Stephen Girard.

Q. Was the issuance of the emancipation proclamation legal? S. K.

A. The legal effect of this proclamation was and is extremely doubtful. However, the adoption of the 13th Amendment to the Constitution providing that slavery and servitude should not exist in the United States settled that point.

Q. Is it true that Henry Clay was not the author of the Missouri Compromise? G. H. U.

A. It is quite true that Henry Clay was not the author of a first Missouri Compromise passed in 1820, although he is given credit for a suggestion which was utilized by the Senate in a bill to admit Maine as a free State and Missouri as a slave

State. As the result of this controversy a joint committee was appointed which agreed to admit Maine and Missouri separately, leaving the Thomas amendment to the Missouri bill which provided slavery in all the remainder of the Louisiana territory north of thirty-six degrees and thirty minutes north latitude (the southern boundary of Missouri).

Q. *Is there a noted Benedict Arnold in American history other than the one known as The Traitor?* W. W. K.

A. Benedict Arnold was the first Governor of Rhode Island under the Royal Charter in 1663, more than 100 years before the treason of the Revolutionary War General of the same name. The earlier Benedict Arnold was three times Governor of Rhode Island and twice President of the colonies of Portsmouth and Newport before the State was integrated. He was celebrated as the best linguist in the Indian tongues of his time.

Q. *Did Sir Francis Drake command the British Navy at the repulse of the Spanish Armada?* G. T.

A. While Sir Francis Drake is celebrated in history as being the most spectacular ship captain engaged against the Armada, he was not in command. Lord Howard was Admiral of the British forces.

Q. *Who were the cliff dwellers?* J. W. D.

A. The term cliff dwellers is used to designate the supposed extinct builders of the numerous cliff ruins scattered throughout the canyons of the Southwest, along the upper rivers of the Colorado and Rio Grande, in Utah, Colorado, Arizona, and New Mexico. For a long time their origin was a subject of much discussion, but recent investigation has proved that these ruins are not the work of any extinct race, but were built by the immediate ancestors of the modern Pueblo Indians, some of whom notably the Hopi, still have their villages on the summits of almost inaccessible mesas. Evidences of cliff dwellers have also been found in various parts of Europe, having existed during an early period in the history of men.

Q. *What history is connected with the good ship Adventure?* J. E. D.

A. Adventure was the name of the ship commanded by Captain Kidd. This famous pirate sailed from Plymouth, England, in April, 1696, in the galley Adventure, carrying 30 guns and a crew of 80. He put in first at New York and later went to Madagascar. He was eventually put to death for his piratical exploits.

Q. *When was the Reign of Terror?* J. W. S.

A. The Reign of Terror was the period in France beginning about March, 1793, when the Revolutionary Tribunal was appointed, and ending in July, 1794, with the overthrow of Robespierre and his associates. During this time a great number of persons, principally of the aristocracy, were executed.

Q. *When and by whom was Aguinaldo captured?* J. A. H.

A. Aguinaldo, the leader of the Philippine insurrection, was captured March 23, 1901, by Brig. General Frederick Funston at Palawan, Province of Isabella, Luzon, and brought to Manila on April 19, 1901. Aguinaldo formally took the oath of allegiance to the United States.

Q. *Were many Americans privateers in Revolutionary times?* M. P.

A. Channing's History says: "More than two thousand American privateers ranged the seas at one time or another. They swarmed in the West Indies; they cruised along the Atlantic coasts; they sought their prey in the British Channel and the North Sea. . . . In 1781, the Cabots of Beverley received six hundred thousand riales of vellon for their half share in five prizes, the Gardoquis getting the rest. The Derbys of Salem got over sixty thousand dollars on account of prizes that were sold at Bilbao."

Q. *Why is it said that the Bunker Hill Monument commemorates a battle which was never fought? F. G. P.*

A. Back of the village of Charlestown rose an elevation called Breed's Hill, while still further back was a higher elevation known as Bunker Hill. On the evening of June 16, 1775, Col. Prescott led his regiment and some other soldiers to Bunker Hill, but possibly because the soil was refractory at that point the detachment proceeded to the eastward extremity of Breed's Hill. When the detachment reached this hill at midnight, it began to throw up embankments and the battle known to us as the Battle of Bunker Hill is really the battle of Breed's Hill.

Q. *Where was Ft. Blunder? N. C.*

A. The fortifications were started in 1816 at Rouses Point, N. Y., under the supervision of Colonel James Totten, a United States engineer. It was believed that the fort would be of great strategic value, but in 1818 it was found that the fort was located within the limits of Canada and work was abandoned. It was known for many years as Fort Blunder. Its correct name is Fort Montgomery. By the Webster Treaty of 1842 the fort was ceded to the United States.

Q. *Was there ever such a thing as King Arthur's Round Table? F. L. L.*

A. King Arthur was a half-legendary king of the Britons, supposed to have reigned in the 6th century. Nothing is absolutely known of his history and his existence has sometimes been denied altogether. The opinion now generally accepted by scholars is that the evidence of Nennius stated the fact correctly. He tells of an Arthur who was "Dux bellorum" and led the armies of the British kings against the Saxon invaders whom he defeated in twelve great battles. The number of knights that the Round Table seated varied.

Upon some occasions there were 12 and at others 50 or even as many as 150.

Q. *Please give some information about the massacre of St. Bartholomew. E. McC.*

A. This massacre of the Huguenots occurred April 24–25, 1572. It grew out of feuds in France between the House of Guise and the Roman Catholics on the one hand, the House of Conde and the Huguenots on the other. From the tower of the royal palace the signal was given for the carnival of blood, which lasted several weeks. Statistics concerning the number of deaths occasioned by the massacre of St. Bartholomew vary from 2,000 to 100,000.

Q. *What was the Battle of Golden Hill? M. W.*

A. The Battle of Golden Hill is ranked by some writers as the first conflict of the War of the American Revolution. This took place on January 18th, nearly seven weeks before the Boston Massacre. The British soldiers killed one citizen and wounded three, after the soldiers had destroyed a liberty pole set up by the Sons of Liberty.

Q. *What were the names of the men who captured Major John Andre? D. J. S.*

A. He was captured by three American militiamen named John Paulding, David Williams, and Isaac Van Wart.

Q. *How many men were killed in the fight between the Monitor and the Merrimac? V. Z.*

A. There were virtually no casualties on either side. After Lieut. Worden, the commanding officer, had been blinded as a result of a shot, the Monitor withdrew and the Merrimac steamed back to Norfolk.

Q. *Where was the Mason and Dixon's Line? E. S. A.*

A. Mason and Dixon's Line is the popular name of the boundary line surveyed between November 15, 1763, and December 27, 1767, by two

English mathematicians and surveyors, Charles Mason and Jeremiah Dixon, to settle the constant dissensions between the Lords Baltimore and the Penn family, the lords proprietors of Maryland and Pennsylvania respectively. It runs along the parallel in latitude 39° 43′ 2.3″, and was originally marked by milestones, every fifth one bearing on one side the coat of arms of Penn and on the other those of Lord Baltimore. The name was afterwards currently applied to designate an imaginary boundary line between the free and the slave States.

Q. Who was Gasparilla? W. B. J.

A. Gasparalios Gasparilla was an officer of high rank in the Spanish Navy until 1782, when having been detected in stealing the crown jewels, he stole a ship and turned pirate. He stopped at Charlotte Harbour and built a fort where he kept many men prisoners. In 1821 the United States broke up his pirate kingdom, and the booty of 30 million dollars was divided. He tried to sail away, and to escape capture he wound a piece of anchor chain about his waist and jumped overboard, and was drowned.

Q. Had Napoleon any children by his second wife? T. W. N.

A. Napoleon II was the son of Napoleon I and his second wife, Archduchess Marie Louise of Austria. After the fall of the Empire, he lived in Austria with his mother and was given the title, Duke of Reichstadt. He died at the age of twenty-one.

Q. Why was the Battle of the Wilderness so called? M. S.

A. The Wilderness is the name of a large forest in Spottsylvania County, Virginia, where the Battle of the Wilderness was fought during the Civil War.

Q. What king went into battle although blind? E. H.

A. Reference doubtless is made to King John of Bohemia. As an ally of Philip of France he was at the Battle of Crecy, August 26, 1346, at which the French army suffered overwhelming defeat at the hands of the English. Although completely blind, King John insisted upon being headed into the thick of battle where he died fighting his unseen foes.

Q. What was a bounty jumper in the Civil War? X. S.

A. He was one who upon payment of bounty enlisted in the Army and afterwards deserted from the service. Usually a man who did this successfully once, repeated the performance, until he had accumulated quite a sum of money, or was caught at the game.

Q. Please give a history of Claude Duval, highwayman. A. R.

A. Claude Duval was born in Normandy in 1643. He was sent to Paris in 1657, where he remained until he came to England in attendance on the Duke of Richmond at the Restoration. He soon took to the road, and became famous for his daring and gallantry. He was captured in 1670 in London, and within a week was executed at Tyburn. His body was laid in state in a tavern and was viewed by huge crowds before the exhibition was stopped by a judge's order.

Q. In what towns were the Lincoln-Douglas debates held? A. J. B.

A. Towns where great debates between Abraham Lincoln and Stephen A. Douglas were held with the dates of the debates were: Ottawa, Ill., August 21, 1858; Freeport, Ill., August 27, 1858; Jonesboro, Ill., September 15, 1858; Charleston, Ill., September 18, 1858; Galesburg, Ill., October 7, 1858; Quincy, Ill., October 13, 1858; and Alton, Ill., October 15, 1858. Unofficial debates were also held at Springfield, and Chicago, Illinois.

Q. When and why did Terence McSwiney starve himself to death? S. C.

A. Terence McSwiney, Lord Mayor of Cork, was convicted of

inciting rebellion against the British Crown, and sentenced to a term of imprisonment. He denied the right of England to interfere in Irish matters and entered upon a hunger strike in prison which resulted in his death.

Q. *What was the Annapolis Convention?* T. C.

A. A convention held at Annapolis, Maryland, September 11, 1786, to consider the question of intercolonial commerce and discuss changes in the Articles of Confederation. Since only five States were represented the Convention adjourned after recommending a convention of all the States. This led to the Constitutional Convention of 1787.

Q. *What was the Battle above the Clouds?* P. S. J.

A. It was a part of the Battle of Chattanooga, which lasted from November 23 to 25, 1863. On the 24th General Hooker carried Lookout Mountain. This is known as the Battle above the Clouds.

Q. *Did Citizen Genet ever return to France after he was sent to the United States as the minister of the French Republic?* B. W.

A. He never returned. He became an American citizen, married a daughter of Governor Clinton, settled on the Hudson, and became a scientific farmer.

Q. *How soon after the Revolutionary War did foreign countries recognize the United States?* P. M. P.

A. On February 6, 1778, signatures were affixed to a Treaty of Commerce and a Treaty of Amity and Alliance between France and the United States. The Definitive Treaty between the United States and England was signed at the end of 1783. Although Frederick the Great wrote Franklin that he probably would soon follow France in recognizing the United States in 1778, no recognition was extended until about 1786. A Treaty of Peace and Commerce was signed with the Netherlands in September, 1785. A Treaty of Peace and Friendship was signed by Morocco in January, 1787. A treaty had been signed with Sweden in April, 1783. Russia did not recognize the new country or send a diplomatic representative until 1809.

Q. *I have heard that William Pitt was criticized for appointing Wolfe to lead the Quebec expedition. Is this true?* D. P.

A. William Pitt was severely criticized. Premier Newcastle said, "Pitt's new general is mad." "Mad, is he," returned Pitt, "then I hope he will bite some other of my generals!"

Q. *Please name some of the officers who served in the Confederate Army and were later elected to Congress.* M. R.

A. Lucius Q. C. Lamar of Mississippi, Col. of 18th Mississippi regiment; Henry Watterson of Kentucky, Chief of Scouts in General Joseph E. Johnston's Army; Charles E. Hooker, Colonel of Cavalry—attached to General Polk's command; John T. Morgan, Brigadier-General; Wade Hampton, Lieutenant-General; Joseph E. Johnston, General.

Q. *Who were the Argonauts of '49?* L. F.

A. This was the name applied to the fortune seekers who emigrated to California in the years immediately following the discovery of gold in 1848.

Q. *What was the Whiskey Rebellion?* R. C.

A. The Whiskey Rebellion was an uprising in western Pennsylvania in 1794 against the Federal Government, occasioned by the attempted enforcement of the excise law on domestic spirits.

Q. *What position did Baron von Steuben hold in the Continental Army?* M. N.

A. Baron von Steuben arrived at Portsmouth, N. H., December 1,

1777. He offered his services to Congress and began drilling the inexperienced soldiers at Valley Forge. In May, 1778, he was appointed Inspector General or drill master. He prepared regulations for the order and discipline of the troops.

Q. *Were any settlements made in Brazil by citizens of the United States after the Civil War?* R. T.

A. According to the New York Herald for July 7, 1867, it was estimated that 1800 had left for South America during the first six months of 1867, but the source of this estimate is not given and can not therefore be verified. Most of them, however, settled in a few colonies in Brazil, chief of which were Para, Espiritu Santo, and Sao Paulo.

Q. *What message did Emily Geiger carry?* H. F.

A. After General Greene was forced to retreat from Ninety Six, South Carolina, he sent a messenger to General Sumter to join him at Orangeburg where united they might be successful against the British. A young girl, Emily Geiger, carried the message on horseback through the woods through General Rawdon's lines to General Sumter on the Wateree River.

Q. *What Indian tribes inhabited Alabama at the time of the coming of the white man?* S. W.

A. The Chickasaws, Choctaws, Creeks, Cherokees, Apalaches, and Alabamas were occupying the territory now included in Alabama when De Soto passed through in 1540.

Q. *What was the Underground Railway?* C. A.

A. The Underground Railway was an arrangement for assisting runaway slaves to escape. It consisted of many different routes across the free States. The stations, twenty miles or more apart, were usually private homes in the garrets or cellars of which, or in nearby caves or haymows, the fugitives were kept and fed during the day, and from which they were sent on their way at nightfall.

Q. *Did other candidates receive votes for the Presidency of the Confederate States when Jefferson Davis was elected?* C. C.

A. Jefferson Davis and Alexander H. Stephens had been appointed provisional President and Vice President, and when elected to office received all the votes of the eleven States that voted.

Q. *Did the reporters in the House of Representatives ever carry little inkwells on their thumbs when recording the speeches of the members?* W. H.

A. Some of the reporters in the House of Representatives still use a pen in taking the speeches. A small inkwell is held in the palm of the left hand and steadied by a thong around one of the fingers.

Q. *I heard an old Civil War soldier speak of the "Zouaves" in that war. What was he referring to?* D. S.

A. In the Civil War, the name was applied to a member of one of certain volunteer regiments assuming the name and in part the characteristic dress of the French Zouaves.

Q. *When was Babylon at the height of its power?* M. D. P.

A. Babylon, originating in antiquity, was perhaps at the greatest of its power 2340 B.C. After many vicissitudes it was invaded and conquered by Cyrus, the King of Persia, 558 B.C.

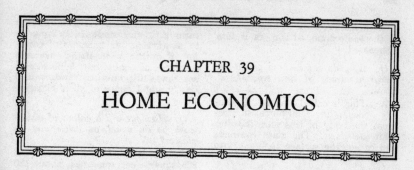

CHAPTER 39

HOME ECONOMICS

Q. *How much light do dirty windows cut out?* S. P.

A. Lewis Carris, of the National Society for the Prevention of Blindness, says that in many shops the light is cut down one-quarter because the windows are not washed regularly.

Q. *Is there any easy way to prolong the life of a cracked dish?* W. W.

A. If boiled for about 45 minutes in enough sweet milk to cover it the cracks will glue together and become invisible and the dish will stand almost as much ordinary usage as before.

Q. *Is dry air in a house destructive to rugs?* L. O.

A. One of the contributory causes of wear in rugs is air without moisture. Wool, in its natural state, holds 35 per cent water. Lack of sufficient humidity causes the rugs to fuzz out, thus losing part of the wool woven into them.

Q. *How should old-fashioned pewter ware be cleaned?* R. J. K.

A. Pewter is a soft metal and only very fine scourers such as fine whiting, rouge, or fine rottenstone mixed with oil should be used for cleaning it.

Q. *How should rattan, grass, and willow furniture be cleaned?* N. E.

A. Use a stiff brush or vacuum cleaner to take out the dust. Then wash with thick lukewarm soapsuds containing a little borax, using a scrubbing brush. Rinse thoroughly and set in the sun to dry.

Q. *Please name some pieces of furniture which are purely American in type.* S. N. R.

A. The butterfly table, the comb-backed Windsor chair, and the rocking chair originated in America.

Q. *In the absence of pistachio flavoring, how can it be imitated?* C. A. L.

A. Vanilla and almond combined give pistachio flavor.

Q. *Can cocoa be substituted for chocolate in a recipe?* H. P. H.

A. The Bureau of Home Economics says that one-half cup of cocoa plus one-half teaspoon of shortening is equal to one ounce or one square of chocolate.

Q. *What kind of a chair should be used with a Governor Winthrop desk?* F. W. T.

A. A John Hancock, an American ladder-back, or a Chippendale claw-foot chair would be appropriate. Possibly a Chippendale would be best.

Q. *What period is known as the golden age of furniture?* E. S.

A. During the latter half of the 18th century, Chippendale, Heppelwhite, Sheraton, and the Brothers Adam produced distinctive furniture in England. Some of the finest furniture made in France, and America as well, was designed and constructed at the same time, so the era is thus designated.

Q. Why do some china dishes develop hundreds of tiny cracks? P. E. N.

A. This is called crazing. It usually occurs in semi-porcelain, because the body of this ware is softer than the glaze. The glaze contracts and causes the surface to break into a network of fine cracks.

Q. What are the various types of canopies on four-poster beds? M. H. M.

A. They are field top, tent top, and square tester.

Q. What will prevent dry rot in floors? R. F. K.

A. The Forest Service says that to prevent dry rot in floors, the wood should be treated with a preservative before it is used, and there should be air vents in the foundation so that the air will not be confined beneath the floor.

Q. Rain water leaked into my automobile and caused mildew to form on the upholstery. What will remove it? T. J.

A. The National Association of Dyers and Cleaners says that usually mildew can be removed from automobile upholstery first by brushing to remove the excess and then sponging with soap solution made slightly alkaline with ammonia.

Q. Why does slamming the oven door make a cake fall? A. L.

A. If an oven door is slammed when a delicate-structured cake is baking, the tiny air cells are broken and the cake falls.

Q. What are sweeping compounds? A. G.

A. There are several patented compounds for sweeping. They are largely composed of sawdust and silicious material, together with some bonding medium, such as rosin, oil, or tar. Bran and sand are also usual ingredients. The following formula is suggested: Melt 2 ounces of paraffin wax in 2 quarts of paraffin oil over a water-bath; then add 6 ounces of coarse salt, 5 pounds of sea sand, 10 pounds of sawdust, and finally add 1 ounce of oil of eucalyptus.

Q. How far will a gallon of whitewash go on wood, on brick, and on plaster? N. A.

A. On wood, it will cover about 225 square feet; on brick, about 180 square feet; and on plaster, about 270 square feet.

Q. Is it possible to remove marks on china which have been caused by cutting food with a knife? H. E. D.

A. It is not possible to remove what is called cutlery marking.

Q. What will soften rubber that has hardened with age? S. G.

A. The Bureau of Standards says that rubber which has become hardened cannot be restored to its original condition. The hardening is due chiefly to oxidation of the rubber by the oxygen of the air. New substances, which are not like rubber, are formed.

Q. When was the willow ware china first made? A. M. P.

A. The willow pattern appeared about 1780 and immediately became popular.

Q. How many pounds of meat does it take to make a pound of beef extract or bouillon cubes? R. P. S.

A. The Institute of American Meat Packers says that meat is not concentrated into bouillon cubes. Only a small part of the meat is soluble by the methods used in manufacturing beef extracts and bouillon cubes. The dilute extracts are evaporated and are finally sold in the paste or cube form. When made into cubes, there may be from 50 to 75 per cent salt in the cube. This is necessary since the extract, itself, is pasty and cannot be made dry. Liebig, who originated the extract, said that it took 34 pounds of meat to give one pound of extract. If all of the material in meat which is soluble in hot water were extracted and made into meat extract, it would take nearly 30 pounds of meat to give one pound of extract.

Q. Is the ground floor of a house and the first floor the same? R. W.

A. In America they are the same, but in England the first floor is the floor above the ground floor.

Q. What can be used to clean windows that will not leave them streaked? J. S.

A. Various cleaning mixtures may be used. Clear water, or clear water with a few drops of ammonia, or with a little dissolved washing soda (about one tablespoon to a pail of water); and on very cold days the cloth may be moistened with wood alcohol. This last makes a most efficient cleaner, but it is expensive. Soap is less satisfactory because it leaves a film over the surface of the glass. Try to clean windows when the sun is not shining on them directly, as it causes uneven evaporation of moisture and gives a streaked surface.

Q. Why are some flat-irons called sad irons? E. S.

A. The word sad used in connection with iron means heavy or weighty.

Q. What is meant by the sheet test for jelly? E. S. T.

A. To make the sheet test take up a small amount of juice in a spoon, allow it to drop from the side; when the drops flow together and form a sheet or film from the spoon the jelly is done.

Q. How may marks made by hot dishes be removed from a table? H. K.

A. Good Housekeeping Institute says: "First rub the spots well with a good furniture polish or wax, or with camphorated oil. Next remove the excess polish or oil with a clean soft cloth. Wring a soft cloth out of clear lukewarm water and put three drops of ammonia on the cloth. Rub the spots carefully with this cloth and follow immediately with another clean cloth, moistened with polish or wax."

Q. Why do floors creak? A. W.

A. Squeaking floors are often not properly secured at the joists, or not properly supported. Sometimes finishing nails may be driven in to make them more secure and to overcome this trouble. If the boards are of uneven thickness, the floor often creaks.

Q. Please tell me how to take care of a washing machine after it is used. I. D.

A. According to directions of the Bureau of Home Economics, the machine should be rinsed thoroughly with hot water, operated for a short time, then drained and dried. The drain faucet should be left open and the lid propped up an inch or two to allow a free circulation of air. The cylinders should be removed and thoroughly dried as well as the metal tubs. If there is a centrifugal drier, it should also be carefully wiped in preparation for the next using.

Q. How thick should a mattress be? P. F.

A. Five inches is satisfactory for service and comfort.

Q. Does the word, sterling, on silver destroy the value of the piece as an antique? D. S.

A. It would depend upon the piece. The word, sterling, appears on Chester silverware as early as 1690. It is also found on silverware made in Cork, Ireland, at the end of the 17th century.

Q. What will remove water glass from stone crocks? W. W.

A. The water glass deposit on the stone crocks may be removed by the use of a mineral acid, which may be purchased at a drug store. Hydrochloric acid is the one used most often in the household. If purchased in the concentrated form, it is quite corrosive, so care should be taken not to get it on the skin or clothing.

Q. How can I refinish a child's blackboard? L. E. G.

A. Paint the board with ordinary black paint such as will dry with a gloss; then apply a coat of black paint, mixed with turps instead of oil, which will dry a dead black.

Q. How can hard sealing wax be removed from glass tubes and corks? C. B.

A. Denatured alcohol is probably the best solvent for sealing wax.

Q. Is there any easy way to make a new hole in a sewing machine belt? M. G.

A. Heat a hat pin very hot and thrust it through the leather. A larger implement can then be used.

Q. What will remove oil stains from concrete floors? S. H.

A. The Bureau of Standards says that it knows of no method that will entirely remove oil stains from concrete. The stains can be partly removed by soaking the concrete with gasoline, then taking up the excess by means of a porous material like blotting paper. By repeating this process several times at intervals a good portion of the oil can be removed.

Q. Why did a certain kind of cook stove get the name of range? L. C. S.

A. Range is a word applied by the Pennsylvania Dutch to the six-plate stove, implying a larger range of space permitted by this particular type of stove than was possible with the four-plate stove which was previously used.

Q. How should paper patterns be shortened for a small person? T. L. B.

A. Fold a tuck in it half-way between the armscye and the waist-line, and another tuck half-way between the waistline and the bottom. In cutting, straighten the seam lines as necessary. If a shorter sleeve is required than that of the pattern, take tucks half-way between the elbow and armscye, and half-way between the elbow and wrist, so that the elbow always remains in the correct position.

Q. How may paint be removed from brushes after it has hardened? I am referring to oil paints and varnishes. N. S. G.

A. Oil paints and varnishes containing much linseed oil cannot be successfully removed after they have dried on a brush. Certain treatments will soften the hardest material to some extent, but the bristles must be scraped to clean them thoroughly. Sometimes the bristles can be separated by soaking the brush in raw linseed oil for a day or two and then washing with hot turpentine. Soaking a brush for 12 to 24 hours in a warm solution containing a pound of sal soda in three pints of water frequently softens it so that it may be washed with soap and water. Some painters believe that a mixture of soda ash or sal soda with borax or trisodium phosphate is less harmful. Lye or caustic soda ruins the bristles.

Q. What is the origin of the well and tree design so often seen in silver platters? E. V. S.

A. This is a device intended to catch the gravy and juices from the meat so that the gravy can be served readily as wanted. The well and tree form is that which is best adapted to the purpose. The design has no other significance. The origin is unknown.

Q. What causes explosions of kerosene stoves? E. T. H.

A. The Department of Commerce says that explosions of kerosene stoves are usually due to overheating the stove to a point above the vaporizing temperature of the kerosene, or using as fuel some mixture which has an evaporating point near room temperatures. By carefully cleaning the stove so that the air passages are open, and by using a good grade of kerosene, explosions can be avoided.

Q. *Will water rot rubber?* J. D. S.

A. The Bureau of Standards says that water will not rot rubber. The Bureau has rubber bands which have been under water for four years and are still usable. Some rubber compounds swell considerably when kept under water, and are thus weakened.

Q. *What are tortillas?* R. J. D.

A. Tortillas are large round cakes of popular consumption in Mexico. They are made by soaking corn grains until soft, then crushing them into a paste, generally by working them with a roller or similar instrument on a large stone, and shaping them into the desired size and cooking on iron or earthen plates.

Q. *What is the best way to treat linoleum to make it last?* M. M.

A. Waxing will help to make linoleum last a long time. Wash with steaming hot water and apply wax while the linoleum is warm. Apply after each washing.

Q. *Is there a good soap substitute on the market?* H. A. B.

A. Soap bark is perhaps the most valuable soap substitute. It is on the market in the form of chips, powder, or long, flat pieces. When extracted with hot water, a solution containing a lather-forming material called a saponin is obtained. This has detergent power, and, since it is very mild in its action, is suitable for delicate fabrics.

Q. *How should screens be cared for? These are not copper screens.* W. B.

A. Screen doors and window screens, when being stored away for the winter should be thoroughly brushed and cleaned and perfectly dry. When the screens are taken out in the spring, they should be brushed and cleaned before hanging and if a light coat of screen paint is applied before they are put up, the screens should last indefinitely. In doing this, any little spot that might have a tendency to rust would be covered and thus prevented from rusting or deteriorating.

Q. *Do the colors in Chinese rugs have any particular significance?* R. E.

A. The Chinese have six symbolic colors: Red signifies fire and the South; black, water and the North; blue or green, wood and the East; white, metal or mist and the West; yellow, Earth and the Center.

Q. *Why do some woolen blankets have an offensive odor?* B. R.

A. Usually any offensive smell in this connection is due to dressing oils which have turned slightly rancid, and can be removed by any proper drycleaning method.

Q. *What causes the green appearance of bathroom fixtures?* S. D.

A. The green corrosion on nickel fixtures in bathrooms is a form of oxidation. It would indicate that the nickel has been worn off, leaving spots exposed to the elements. It should be cleaned with an abrasive from time to time, or the parts should be re-nickeled.

Q. *How should an old black walnut chest of drawers be refinished?* V. S.

A. A modern practice is to remove the coats of paint, smooth the wood, and apply raw linseed oil.

Q. *How many yards of material does it take to curtain a five-room house?* P. N.

A. About 60 yards.

Q. *Why is furniture called period furniture?* A. N.

A. The term is suggestive of the attempt, developed since 1850, to classify various types of antique furniture in groups according to the period of their origin and popularity. These groups are named either after the monarchs, English or French, under whom given styles of furniture flourished, or after the designers of certain styles.

Q. Can pewter be mended? A. C. C.

A. An expert in metals says that pewter can be mended, but as the melting point is extremely low, it requires careful handling by a skilled worker.

Q. What can be done for sticky leather seats? S. C.

A. They may be carefully cleaned with benzine or gasoline and, when perfectly dry, varnished with a good grade of varnish.

Q. What kind of fire extinguishers should be used in the home and how should they be kept? A. S.

A. A fire marshal gives the following instructions for the proper care of fire extinguishers: Fire extinguishers should be kept on a hook off the floor and out of the reach of children. They should be of the acid and soda type and the kind approved by the Underwriters of America. The label on the extinguisher will show whether it has been approved or not by the Underwriters. It is necessary that it be recharged once a year. This may be done by an electrician.

Q. For what purpose is a prayer rug used in this country? W. S. R.

A. A prayer rug is, in the home of an American, used merely as a scatter rug or, if it is especially beautiful or valuable, hung on the wall as if it were a tapestry. It might also be gracefully arranged on a baby grand piano.

Q. When old silk stockings are used to make a rag rug, how are the stockings cut? T. J. M.

A. The stockings are cut in strips about one-half inch wide, starting at the top and circling down in an unbroken strip to the heel. This should be wound up in a ball as it is cut. The rug is either crocheted, knitted, or braided, and the mixture of colors made as desired, sewing the end of one color to another and working it in.

Q. When were marble-topped stands and tables popular? L. C.

A. They were at the height of their popularity in the 1870's.

Q. I notice that the bristles of my hair brush have turned yellow. What caused this? R. S.

A. Authorities say that the reason that the bristles have turned yellow is because they have been washed with too strong a soap.

Q. How were the old samplers made? G. B.

A. The old-fashioned sampler consisted of a square of linen or perforated canvas. Designs were stamped on the material and filled in with different colored worsteds, the stitches forming little x's. On the finest material this would almost give the effect of a painting.

Q. How may paint be removed from glass? W. J. P.

A. To remove paint from glass, use three parts of American potash to one part of unslaked lime. Lay this on with a stick and let it remain for some time. Paint spots may also be removed by rubbing them with very hot, sharp vinegar. The milled edge of a silver coin will also remove small paint spots on glass.

Q. The fence in our back yard is whitewashed and we find that it rubs off on the children's clothes. What can we do to remedy this? K. D. C.

A. Alum added to whitewash will prevent its rubbing off.

Q. How was cooking done in the old brick oven which had no fire under it? M. L. H.

A. The old-fashioned outside oven had a domed chamber built of brick and heated by means of light wood and sticks burned inside. When the bricks were well heated, the ashes and embers were raked out, the floor swept, and the food to be cooked introduced by a flat wooden shovel with a long handle, and the door was then closed.

Q. What temperature should a slow oven be? A hot oven? M. N.

A. A slow oven means one with a temperature of from 250 to 300 degrees Fahrenheit; a moderate oven, one of from 300 to 350 degrees; and a hot oven is from 400 to 450 degrees.

Q. How can hard rubber articles be mended? W. J. B.

A. The Bureau of Standards says that hard rubber may be joined by a bond of new hard rubber. A cement is prepared by adding one part of sulphur and three parts of crude rubber to 50 parts of carbon bisulphide and three parts of alcohol. Several applications of the cement are applied to the surfaces of the broken parts. These are finally joined and held under pressure at a temperature of 160° Centigrade for four hours. A mixture of equal parts of gutta percha and bitumen dissolved in carbon bisulphide may also be used to cement the broken portions.

Q. Can baking-powder biscuits be made up and kept in a refrigerator, then baked a week or ten days later? B. E. G.

A. The Bureau of Chemistry says that baking-powder biscuit dough cannot be mixed and placed in an ice box for a week or ten days, as the gas, liberated when the baking powder comes in contact with the moisture, would escape. It would be possible to keep such a mixture over night but it is not advisable to attempt to keep it longer.

Q. Why do the windows of a room sweat if a gas heater is used? W. H. S.

A. The Bureau of Standards says that water is formed during the combustion of gas and remains in the atmosphere of the room when a gas heater is employed. This water condenses on the surface of windows or other cold objects, the temperature of which is less than the saturation temperature of the water in the atmosphere. The same effect will be produced by supplying water vapor to the atmosphere from any other source. This difficulty can be prevented by venting the products of combustion from the heater to the outer air, or to a certain extent, at least, by using window sash with a double pane so that the inner pane with which the air of the room comes into contact does not reach so low a temperature.

Q. What are the names of the old hand-wrought hinges? S. D.

A. A few of them were: H, HL, butterfly, strap, and ram's horn.

Q. What is pectin, the substance used in preserves? M. H. B.

A. It is a substance which appears in many vegetable tissues as a constituent of the sap or cell wall. Hard, tart, ripe apples or oranges and lemons are usually used in the making of pectin. Apples need not be peeled. The outer yellow rind of oranges or lemons is not used, nor the edible fruit. The white peel is the part used.

Q. Should raw meat be covered when put in the refrigerator? A. D.

A. Meat should be unwrapped at once and put in the coolest place in the refrigerator. A loose sheet of waxed paper may be laid over it.

Q. When a cake recipe calls for brandy, what may be substituted for it? M. H.

A. Cider, rum flavoring, cooking wine, or fruit juices are used in place of brandy in fruit cake.

Q. What can be done for leather which mildews? E. D. B.

A. Keep the leather articles in a well ventilated, dry, light place. When first detected, the mildew should be washed off with soap and warm water, or simply wiped off with a moist cloth and the leather well dried.

Q. How can I get rid of the ice on the brine pipes in a refrigerator? H. K.

A. In order to defrost the pipes, stop the motor and let the ice melt off.

Q. What is the best method for cleaning metallic cloth and trimmings? O. G.

A. There are several practical methods of restoring metallic trimmings, but the following will prove as satisfactory as any: Mix chloroform and jewelers' rouge to make a stiff paste. Apply the paste to the trimmings or cloth with a soft brush or rag, rub lightly. Brush or rinse the powder out with gasoline.

Q. How much does a roast of meat shrink while cooking? C. S.

A. The Bureau of Home Economics says that it depends upon the oven temperature; that is, when meat is roasted from start to finish in a very hot oven the shrinkage is greater than when the meat is first seared at a high temperature and then finished slowly with the temperature rapidly reduced. For example, if, after beef ribs have been seared in a hot oven, the temperature is rapidly reduced so as to finish the cooking very slowly, the shrinkage of the meat when rare is only about one-eight of the fresh weight; whereas if the roasting goes on to the end in a hot oven the shrinkage is about one-fourth of the fresh weight.

Q. What could be used to remove the odor from musty casks and barrels? N. T.

A. Have the casks well scrubbed with boiling water in which a little soda ash has been dissolved. If they are not wanted for immediate use, let them stand exposed to the air, one head out, for a month. There is no greater purifier than the atmosphere. Then head up, slightly steam, blow off, and send to the cellar to be filled. If wanted for immediate use, scrub, then gently fire until well heated through, steam as before. If not wanted for use, when finished put in about one pint of bisulphite of lime and water, one to four of water, and they will keep well in a cellar for 12 months.

Q. When were pieced quilts first made? T. P.

A. The history of quilts is involved in a tradition of long centuries of slow progress. No positive reference to patchwork or quilting is found in western Europe prior to the time of the Crusades, but from the 11th century these arts become more and more conspicuous in the needlecraft of nearly every country in western Europe. Noticeable progress was made in the design of quilts during the Middle Ages in Spain. Some of the finest specimens of quilts of this period have been preserved in Persia.

Q. What color paint will make a room lightest? A. D. O.

A. The Bureau of Standards says that white paint will give the lightest room and light tints will give more light than dark tints or solid colors.

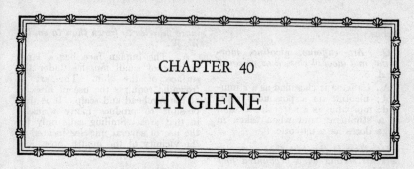

CHAPTER 40

HYGIENE

Q. *How often do people have colds?* D. D.

A. Colds are so prevalent that they average a loss of ten days' activity to each individual yearly.

Q. *How many primary human emotions are there?* F. D. B.

A. There are three—fear, anger, and love. All others are merely linguistic modifications of the original three.

Q. *Would it be safe to use an unsterilized needle when removing a sliver or splinter?* W. D.

A. It is not safe to use an unsterilized needle for this purpose. By sterilizing by heat or by immersion in alcohol, sterilization is simple.

Q. *Is it better to use a hard or soft bed?* B. N. R.

A. Dr. Donald Laird, head of the department of psychology at Colgate University, has come to the conclusion after experiments that at least two hours of rest every night may be saved by sleeping on a good, soft bed. He found that a soft bed will build up as much mental energy in six hours as a hard bed will build in eight.

Q. *At what age do men do their best work?* H. A.

A. There is no golden age, but a study of the achievements of 381 of the greatest men of history showed, according to Professor E. L. Thorndike, that the "masterpiece age" averaged about 47.5 years.

Q. *Are people often made sufficiently ill from sunburn to keep them from work?* S. T.

A. Dr. Charles F. Pabst says that 200,000 working days are lost yearly because of illness due to sunburn.

Q. *Is the man of today taller than the average a thousand years ago?* G. V.

A. To judge by such skeletons as have been recorded so far, even the stature of prehistoric man presents little difference from that of modern inhabitants of the same areas.

Q. *What years are considered middle age?* M. Z.

A. Government physicians say that generally they consider the middle age of a person from 40 to 60 years.

Q. *How many nerves are there in the human body?* D. J. G.

A. The number is countless. In general it may be stated that there are 12 pairs of cranial nerves, which with their branches supply the entire body.

Q. *Which nervous impulse travels faster, sound or feeling?* D. W.

A. Feeling travels faster.

Q. *How tall is a woman who is considered tall, short, or of medium height?* M. A. S.

A. A woman is considered short who is from 4 feet 11 inches to 5 feet 3 inches; medium from 5 feet 3 inches to 5 feet 5½ inches; tall from 5 feet 5½ inches to 5 feet 10 inches.

Q. *Are caffeine, nicotine, morphine, and alcohol classed as poisons?* C. A. S.

A. Caffeine is classified as a stimulant; nicotine as a poisonous alkaloid; morphine as a narcotic; alcohol as a stimulant, and when taken in large doses as a narcotic.

Q. *How is the fact that a runner gets his second wind accounted for?* R. M.

A. The Public Health Service says that by second wind is meant an adjustment of the heart rate to the intake and outgo of air in the lungs.

Q. *What causes double-jointedness?* V. S.

A. It is caused by loose ligaments around the joints. People possessing such ligaments have a wider latitude of movement around the joints than most people and can twist themselves into positions which would not be possible for ordinary persons.

Q. *Why are some people so much more ticklish than others?* G. S.

A. It depends upon the sensitiveness of the nervous system. Susceptibility to tickling is also partially under the control of the will. If no restraint is exercised, hypersensitiveness is apt to result. Considerable resistance can be developed.

Q. *What causes a dimple?* K. M.

A. A dimple is a slight depression or dent in the surface of the human body, caused by the adherence of the skin to the deeper tissues, most frequently on the cheek or chin.

Q. *What are the divisions of the circulatory system of the human body?* H. E. R.

A. The central pumping station, or heart; the distributing system, or arteries; the terminal fine divisions of the system which deliver blood to the tissues, called capillaries; and the collecting system, or veins.

Q. *Why does it take so many more muscles to frown than to smile?* W. W.

A. The human face has a large number of small muscles under the surface of the skin. The art of frowning requires the use of muscles of the forehead and scalp. It is thus possible to produce many wrinkles in that area. Smiling calls only for the use of several muscles located in the vicinity of the mouth, nose, and eyes.

Q. *Why is horseback riding considered beneficial?* F. L.

A. Riding on horseback is a good form of exercise and is especially beneficial in stimulating the function of the gastro-intestinal tract. The rhythmic vibration which the gait of the horse imparts to the rider's body seems to be of benefit to the muscles and to the internal organs.

Q. *Does the voice of a person change when he is at a high altitude?* O. S.

A. It is a common lecture experiment in courses in physics to fill the lungs with hydrogen and speak a word or two. The quality of the voice is much altered and its loudness diminished, because of the low density of the hydrogen. There should be a similar effect in rarefied air.

Q. *Is a cold shower bath to be preferred to a warm shower?* C. C.

A. Not everyone can stand a cold shower. A warm shower—with soap —is recommended because it cleanses the skin and has a beneficial effect on the muscles, circulation, and mental alertness. A cold shower afterwards closes the pores and is stimulating to most people.

Q. *How many calories does an adult need each day?* B. F.

A. As a rule it is appropriate to assume that an American man or woman who leads a quiet life at home with little exercise requires about 2500 calories. If engaged in sedentary occupation 3000 calories are required. A moderate amount of exercise or a laborer doing light work needs about 3500 calories. For hard work, 4000 calories or more are necessary.

Q. *Is the blond type disappearing in America? D. C. S.*

A. Dr. C. F. Pabst says that outdoor life and indulgence in athletics, together with the intermingling of the dark-skinned races of Southern Europe with our own, will produce the brunette as the reigning beauty of the future.

Q. *How do ductless glands discharge their secretions? M. E.*

A. They are discharged directly into the circulating blood. The endocrine or ductless glands are now believed to control the characteristics which make one person differ from another mentally and physically.

Q. *In what part of the body is most of the calcium? A. W.*

A. The bones and teeth contain 99 per cent, while the remainder exists as soluble salts in the fluids and soft tissues.

Q. *What are the things to which human beings have instinctive fear reactions? Z. S.*

A. There are two things which call out a fear response—a loud sound and a loss of support.

Q. *What is meant by dying a natural death? T. C.*

A. The Public Health Service says that all deaths from diseases are spoken of as natural causes of death. Other causes of death are those resulting from accident or violence.

Q. *What is the earliest age that a person may be immunized against typhoid fever? A. R. E.*

A. Medical authorities say that the time to immunize against typhoid fever is any time after the third month of life.

Q. *What association in England corresponds to the American Medical Association in the United States? P. L. M.*

A. The British Medical Association, London.

Q. *Has diet any effect on the singing voice? W. W.*

A. Musical America says "Only in so far as it affects the health generally."

Q. *At what period in life does the brain grow fastest? K. F.*

A. According to Dr. Daniel J. McCarthy, professor of medical jurisprudence in the University of Pennsylvania, the brain grows ten times as fast during the first five years of life as during any later period.

Q. *What is the name of the groove in the face between the nose and the mouth? E. R.*

A. The term is filtrum.

Q. *Is vegetarianism a new health idea? F. M.*

A. Vegetarianism is not a new cult. It was known as early as history in ancient India and was advocated by Plato, Plutarch, and others. It became a cult in England under George Cheyne in 1671.

Q. *Who has jurisdiction over the Leper Island? N. F. L.*

A. The so-called Leper Island at Molokai is under the jurisdiction of the Territorial Board of Health of Hawaii.

Q. *Are blondes and brunettes determined by the color of their hair, eyes, or complexions? H. R. T.*

A. A blonde is described as a person of fair complexion, with light hair and eyes, while a brunette is one having brown or olive skin and brown or black hair and eyes.

Q. *What is the difference between nutrition and nutriment? E. S.*

A. Nutrition is the process by which growth is promoted and waste repaired in living organisms. Nutriment is that which furnishes the substance for the process.

Q. *How much more will a person weigh after a meal?* L. M.

A. His weight will be increased exactly by the weight of the food.

Q. *When was it discovered that sphagnum moss had a healing property?* H. D.

A. The antiseptic value of sphagnum moss is said to have been discovered accidentally as early as 1013. During the battle of Clontarf, near Dublin, the moss was used as an expedient for stopping the bleeding from wounds. It was discovered that such wounds healed more readily than those treated otherwise.

Q. *In what period of growth does a boy eat more than a man?* C. M.

A. A boy between 9 and 13 years of age requires just as much food as a man, and between the ages of 14 and 19 he will require more than a man does.

Q. *In what kind of unconsciousness is artificial respiration resorted to?* T. D. C.

A. The Public Health Service says that the principal causes of unconsciousness in which artificial respiration is used are the following: Asphyxiation due to the inhalation of gas, unconsciousness due to drowning, and unconsciousness due to electric shock.

Q. *What has been America's greatest contribution to medicine?* S. P.

A. That would be a matter of opinion, but one of America's great contributions was the discovery of the use of anaesthetics for operations.

Q. *Should babies be encouraged to walk as soon as possible?* B. S.

A. Walking is a natural function and should not be forced upon an infant. Premature walking strains the legs and feet and causes foot deformities. The average child will learn to walk when the feet and legs have become sufficiently strong.

Q. *How far would the blood vessels in a human body extend if all were placed in one line?* H. G.

A. It has been estimated that there is a length of over 2000 miles of blood vessels in the human body.

Q. *Is the eye or the ear more sensitive to impression?* G. C. F.

A. The eye is 16 times more sensitive than the ear.

Q. *How long does it take a nerve impulse to reach the brain?* A. S.

A. In human beings it takes about eight one-thousandths of a second. In lower animals the speed is much less.

Q. *Do people spend more money for drugs and medicine ordered by physicians or for things of that sort which they think they need themselves.* D. W.

A. According to the Committee on the Cost of Medical Care, the annual bill for medicine in the United States is $715,000,000. More than 70 per cent of the total expenditure for drugs and medicine is for self medication. The average cost for medicines and medical care is $21.32.

Q. *What is the weight of the skeleton of an individual of average height and mature age?* H. C. W.

A. The weight of an adult male skeleton is usually from ten to twelve pounds. A skeleton with light bones would weigh a pound less; a skeleton with heavy bones would weigh a pound more.

Q. *How large a single fee has been paid to a physician?* M. J.

A. One of the largest single fees ever paid a physician was that paid by Catherine of Russia. The fee paid to a physician to inoculate Catherine and her son against smallpox was $50,000, an additional sum of $10,000 was allowed for traveling expenses, and the physician was granted $2500 as an annual pension for life.

Q. What is a normal adult's pulse, temperature, and respiration? B. M. L.

A. The average temperature of a normal adult person is 98.6° F.; the average normal pulse is 72 beats per minute; the average normal respiration varies from 16 to 18 times a minute.

Q. What color are bones? V. G.

A. Fresh bones usually are a reddish color. Old, dry bones are usually gray or white.

Q. How long has castor oil been used as a medicine? W. T.

A. It was known to the ancient Egyptians and used 2000 years B.C. as a remedy.

Q. When was the first hospital founded? D. M.

A. It was founded by St. Basil in 369 A.D. and consisted of a large number of buildings with houses for physicians and nurses, workshops, and industrial schools. It was the first hospital, in the sense we know them today, of which there is any record.

Q. What are proprietary medicines? W. A. L.

A. They belong to a class of medicinal preparations which are put up in uniform packages and offered for sale under a distinctive trademarked name. Many of these remedies are widely used and are frequently prescribed by physicians and are usually combinations of well-known drugs. The number of proprietary patent medicines on the market is more than 50,000.

Q. Who was the first physician to perform an operation for appendicitis? C. W. D.

A. The year 1838 was distinguished by the first operation for disease of the appendix as such. The first decisive step in the direction of modern methods was taken by a London physician, named Han-

cock. The first operation on the appendix performed in the United States was done by R. J. Hall of New York, on May 8, 1886.

Q. Do doctors live longer than other people? L. A. H.

A. According to the Metropolitan Life Insurance Company, physicians have no advantage in longevity, as one might expect because of their profession. On the contrary, they do not live as long as the ordinary policy holders. At the age of thirty, when a physician begins his career, the doctor's expectation of life is two years less than that of the general population.

Q. How many doctors and how many hospitals are there in the United States? J. J.

A. The American Medical Association says that in 1931 there were 156,440 physicians and 6,719 registered hospitals in the United States.

Q. What are birthmarks? L. A. R.

A. They are blemishes with which people are born. They are in reality a number of small blood vessels near the surface of the skin.

Q. How long has the flu been known? J. McC.

A. Medical writings indicate that influenza has been recognized since 400 B.C.

Q. What is the largest hospital for the insane in the United States? T. C.

A. Dr. William Allen White of St. Elizabeth's Hospital says that the largest hospital for the insane in the United States, if not in the world, is the Manhattan State Hospital, Ward's Island, New York. It has between 6000 and 7000 patients.

Q. Why are doctors' prescriptions written in Latin? S. S. L.

A. It is because for many centuries Latin was the language of learning. At the present time, due to this fact, it is the one language which is universally studied by those engaged in the legal, medical, and many other learned professions. Consequently a French doctor would understand the terms of a prescription equally as well as a Czechoslovakian doctor.

Q. What is the capacity of the stomach? R. C.

A. The Public Health Service says that the capacity of the stomach depends upon the size of the person and varies from four to five pints.

Q. Does a person actually think in words? M. N.

A. The Public Health Service says that since a person thinks in his mother tongue, it must be concluded that he thinks in terms of words.

Q. How many pairs of muscles does a person have? P. F.

A. There are between 300 and 400 pairs of muscles and a number of single muscles.

Q. How many people in the United States have defective speech? L. B. D.

A. It is estimated that at least 1,000,000 persons have some form of speech disorder, and of these, approximately 500,000 are school children who stammer or stutter.

Q. Please explain the feeling that you have been some place before when you know you have not. R. M.

A. The condition you describe is known as paramnesia. It is a common experience, and, briefly explained, the reaction depends upon a little trick of the mind manifested by a momentary loss of a sense of time and space. The individual enters into an experience or a situation, obtains a fleeting impression of this situation, then the attention is momentarily attracted to something else. The period of time may be almost infinitesimal. Then upon the return of the attention to the original situation this lapse of time is lost to the individual and the period between the two experiences seems occasionally to expand into a long period, even into the remote past.

Q. Do more men or more women have simple goiter? E. R. T.

A. The Public Health Service says that simple goiter is more prevalent among women.

Q. What is the earliest record of a surgical operation? R. N.

A. Garrison's History of Medicine says that certain pictures engraved on the doorposts of a tomb near Memphis, Egypt, are regarded by their discoverer, W. Max Muller, as the earliest known pictures of surgical operations (2500 B.C.) and antedating these are the well-splinted fractures of the 5th dynasty (2750–2625 B.C.)

Q. What is the skin disease characterized by disappearance of the pigment in splotches, thus leaving white areas? A. C. A.

A. It is called vitiligo, which means piebald skin.

Q. Can a right-handed person by practice make his left hand as dextrous as his right? N. M. X.

A. The Public Health Service says this cannot be done, but practice will increase and improve the use of the left hand.

Q. Which is the longest muscle in the human body? F. L. H.

A. The longest muscle in the body is the sartorius which runs from the upper part of the hip to the inner aspect of the knee.

Q. How many people in the United States have defective hearing? G. S. W.

A. The American Otological Association says that there are 10,000,000 people in the United States whose hearing is impaired.

Q. What is the average weight of the liver of a human being? M. M.

A. From 3 to 3½ pounds, or about 1/40 the weight of the body.

Q. At what age does the brain reach its full size and weight? P. E.

A. The brain reaches its full size and weight at about the same time the rest of the body matures. That is between the ages of 22 and 25 years.

Q. Why do fever blisters appear on the lips rather than on other parts of the body? H. F. L.

A. Fever blisters appear on the mouth instead of elsewhere on the body because the lips are more easily parched due to the thin covering of skin over the blood vessels.

Q. What is the term used to describe a person who sunburns but does not tan? M. M.

A. The term is heliophobe. A person who sunburns repeatedly without acquiring a coat of tan comes in this category. Such a person should exercise care to avoid exposure to hot sunshine.

Q. What is the word that means the putting to an easy and painless death, babies that are hopelessly defective and people who are suffering intensely with incurable diseases? A. G.

A. The term is euthanasia, is of Greek derivation, and means a painless, happy death.

Q. What is the disease that can be contracted from wild rabbits? T. B.

A. Tularaemia is the disease that is contracted through handling or dressing wild rabbits which have the disease.

Q. Is a person suffering from delirium tremens insane? J. A. J.

A. Delirium tremens is a form of acute insanity due to alcoholic poisoning.

Q. What is meant by the bends, and how does this disease affect one? H. L. N.

A. Bends, or caisson disease, is suffered sometimes by deep sea divers. It is due to too rapid a decrease in air pressure, causing bubbles of gas to form in the blood, which if they lodge in the heart or brain, may cause paralysis or death.

Q. How many pharmacists are there in the United States? M. G.

A. The Committee on the Cost of Medical Care says that in 1931 there were 115,000 licensed pharmacists.

Q. What is meant by an accredited hospital? E. I. T.

A. An accredited hospital is one that comes up to certain standards considered necessary for effective results by some organizations such as the American Medical Association, the State Board of Health, or the State Board of Nursing Examiners.

Q. Where is the blood in the human body cleansed and purified? G. H. D.

A. The lungs cleanse and purify the blood.

Q. How many hay fever sufferers are there in the United States? W. E. B.

A. There are approximately five million.

Q. How much air is there in the lungs between breaths? E. J. H.

A. The reserve supply of air in the lungs may amount to 2600 cubic centimeters, while the new air breathed in at each inspiration amounts to 500 cubic centimeters.

Q. Is a person's heart on the left side, as usually thought, or is it in the middle of the body? E. S.

A. Normally, the heart in a human being is slightly more on the left side than on the right, about one-third on the right side of the center of the chest, and two-thirds on the left side.

Q. How does the inner surface of the lungs compare with skin surface of the body? W. C.

A. The inner surface of the lungs amounts to 90 square meters. This is about 100 times the skin surface of the body.

Q. *Please name some famous people who have suffered from tuberculosis. A. S.*

A. Chopin, John Calvin, John Wesley, the Brontë sisters, Elizabeth Barrett Browning, Simon Bolivar, and Andrew Jackson are a few who have had the disease.

Q. *Are there other leper colonies as large as the one on Molokai? D. P.*

A. The colony on the Island of Molokai is the largest in the world.

Q. *How many people become permanently disabled through accident and disease each year? E. D.*

A. The Federal Board for Vocational Education says that in the United States 355,000 become physically handicapped each year.

Q. *Who discovered that tuberculosis was caused by a germ? C. R.*

A. The German physician, Robert Koch, isolated the germ, and announced its identification at a meeting of the Berlin Pathological Society, March 24, 1882.

Q. *When and where did Pasteur announce his conquest of hydrophobia? L. A. B.*

A. In 1884, at the Copenhagen Medical Congress.

Q. *What race has the greatest resistance to tuberculosis? H. G.*

A. The white race. Negroes, Indians, Eskimos, and Siberian Kalmucks were very susceptible when they first came in contact with the white race. This racial tendency is best explained by the lack of contact with the diseases of white men. The white man, by a process of evolution and survival has reached a higher degree of resistance to diseases.

Q. *At what age are children most susceptible to diphtheria? S. C.*

A. Most of the cases occur in the group of children under five years old. The Public Health Service urges parents to have children immunized against diphtheria.

Q. *How long does it take the blood to circulate through the human body? F. W.*

A. The Public Health Service says that the blood in the human body is usually about one-thirteenth of the body weight and requires from one to one and one-half minutes to circulate through the entire body.

Q. *When was trench mouth discovered? B. D.*

A. About 1897, but did not take an epidemic form until the World War, at which time it was more common than were typhoid and malaria during the Spanish-American War.

Q. *Is hay fever an hereditary disease? B. L.*

A. It is due to an inherited sensitivity of the mucous membrane of the eyes, nose, and bronchial tubes. Inheritance determines largely whether or not an individual will develop hay fever and at what time in life symptoms of the malady will occur.

Q. *When was the last case of yellow fever in the United States? F. McN.*

A. The Public Health Service says that there has not been a case of yellow fever since 1905.

Q. *When was it discovered that diseases were the result of natural causes? G. T.*

A. It was not until the time of Hippocrates, some four or five hundred years before Christ, that the Greeks began to attribute disease to natural rather than to supernatural causes.

Q. *Is scurvy usually fatal? V. B.*

A. On the contrary, even in desperate cases of scurvy it is said that recovery is hopefully anticipated when the deficient vitamin C is supplied.

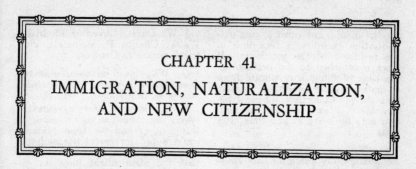

Q. *Are Indians citizens of the United States?* R. L.

A. All North American Indians born within the territorial limits of the United States were given citizenship by the Act of June 2, 1921.

Q. *If a child of an alien is under 21 at the time of his father's naturalization but does not live in this country does he acquire citizenship?* J. Q.

A. A child of an alien does not acquire citizenship unless he is under the age of 21 and is a resident of the United States. If he should come to the United States during his minority after his father had secured his naturalization papers, he would become a citizen at that time.

Q. *Can an Englishman come over here, be naturalized, then return to England and be a British subject again?* S. G.

A. A British subject who has become an American citizen by naturalization may return to his native land and after a residence there of five years may again become a British citizen by naturalization.

Q. *Can an alien who entered the United States illegally ever secure naturalization papers?* J. E.

A. If he entered the United States before June 3, 1921, he may apply to the Immigration Bureau, Washington, D. C., and have his arrival registered. This will cost $20.00. He may then apply for naturalization papers.

Q. *If a foreigner comes to this country as a student, may he remain and become naturalized?* E. A. L.

A. An alien student who enters this country on a student passport is permitted to remain here only until he has completed the studies for which he was given permission to enter.

Q. *Is the process of naturalization the same in all the States?* R. W.

A. Naturalization procedure is the same in all States since it is provided for by Federal law. Each court, however, is the judge of whether the applicant appearing before it has met the requirements of the law.

Q. *Is a passport necessary to a United States citizen who goes to Mexico?* D. I.

A. Although it is not necessary for a citizen of the United States to secure a passport before entering Mexico, he must secure certain travel documents from a Mexican consul in the United States.

Q. *If a woman who was a citizen of the United States, but lost this citizenship through her marriage to an alien before September 22, 1922, is left a widow, of what country is she considered a citizen?* C. L.

A. If this woman has not acquired any other nationality by affirmative act she may reacquire citizenship by naturalization. However, she needs no declaration of intention and no certificate of arrival. There is no

275

residence requirement. The petition may be filed in any court having naturalization jurisdiction regardless of the residence of the petitioner. If there is attached to the petition, at the time of filing, a certificate from a naturalization examiner stating that the petitioner has appeared before him for examination, the petition may be heard at any time after filing.

Q. Will you please tell me how the immigration quota for each country is figured? E. R. E.

A. Congress, in enacting the national origins law fixed an arbitrary limit of 150,000. That number was to be distributed among the European countries according to a complex ratio, based upon the total number of immigrants and their descendants from the beginning of governmental records as related to the total population at the time of the 1920 census. Each country might have a share proportional to its contribution to the total population as it existed in 1920. The share of each country was determined by a careful analysis of the first census of 1790, the records of immigration since 1820, and estimates of the number of descendants both of the population recorded in 1790 and of subsequent arrivals. A provision was included in the law that no country should have a quota less than 100. This raised the final quota figure to 154,714, or slightly in excess of the maximum aimed at.

Q. Please name some naturalized American citizens who became famous. A. P.

A. There are so many of these that we can name only a few. James J. Davis, U. S. Senator and Former Secretary of Labor, Wales; Jacob Gould Schurman, former American Ambassador to Germany, Canada; Mary Antin Grabau, author, Russia; John McCormack, singer, Ireland; James Couzens, U. S. Senator from Michigan, Canada; Samuel Gompers, late labor leader, England; Franklin K. Lane, late Secretary of the Interior, Canada; David W. Davis, Governor of Idaho, Wales; Charles P. Steinmetz, electrical engineer, Germany.

Q. Why must an alien wait two years before applying for citizenship papers in this country? L. S.

A. An interval of two years between the time an alien came to this country and the time when he could apply for first citizenship papers was considered wise in order that the alien might have an opportunity to become familiar with our customs and laws and to determine fully whether he desired to remain and become a citizen.

Q. How much head tax does an immigrant pay? Has the amount always been the same? O. K.

A. Section 1 of the Act of August 3, 1882, imposed a head tax of 50 cents on an immigrant to this country. This was increased to $1.00 by an Act approved August 18, 1894, and has been raised at various times since until it is now $8.00.

Q. At what age may an alien apply for citizenship papers? S. S.

A. If he has been in the United States two years, he may apply at the age of 18. His final papers cannot be secured until he reaches the age of 21.

Q. Can Chinese become naturalized in Hawaii? J. P.

A. Chinese cannot be naturalized in Hawaii since the naturalization laws of the United States apply to that country as well as to the United States.

Q. How much does it cost to secure a copy of one's citizenship papers? F. N.

A. A copy of a naturalization paper which has been lost, mutilated, destroyed, or stolen may be secured by the payment of $10.00. If a person wishes to secure a certificate of derivative citizenship, he must in addition to the $10.00 pay a $5.00 fee for the necessary certificate of arrival showing lawful entrance for permanent residence.

Q. Which State received the greatest variety of early immigrants? W. K.

A. No other colony had so many immigrants of different races and religions as Pennsylvania. There were Dutch, Swedes, English, Germans, Welsh, and Irish; Quakers, Presbyterians, Catholics, Lutherans, Mennonites, and Moravians.

Q. Was citizenship lost by a woman who was a citizen of the United States and married an alien previous to March 2, 1907? A. R.

A. Some authorities claim one thing and some another. The court in Boston has decided that such a marriage involved no loss of citizenship. On the other hand a court in Los Angeles has ruled that the woman in such a case lost her citizenship. The Department of Labor favors the view that there is no loss of citizenship. The Department of State claims that there is a loss of citizenship. As a decision is required in any particular case, the woman should apply for naturalization papers (it will not be necessary for her to apply for first papers, only second papers) and the court before whom her case is heard will decide whether she is a citizen (and for that reason cannot secure such papers), or whether she is entitled to receive them.

Q. What portion of the immigrants who come to this country live in the cities? J. C. R.

A. It is estimated that nearly 60 per cent of the immigrants live at least temporarily in the cities of the United States.

Q. Was there any opposition to an unrestricted immigration policy prior to the Civil War? O. D.

A. In the 1830s a political movement developed against "increasing foreign influence." It resulted in the "Native American" or "Know Nothing" movement of the 1850s. In 1845 a labor paper published at Fitchburg, Mass., protested against unrestricted immigration and the use of immigrants as strike breakers.

Q. Can aliens who served in our Army during the World War be naturalized without taking out first papers? C. P.

A. Those aliens who served in our Army during the World War and who have received honorable discharges may secure second citizenship papers without going through the formality of securing first papers until May 25, 1934. No fee is charged for the issuance of these papers.

Q. Are husbands of American citizens exempt from the quota? L. E. C.

A. Husbands of American citizens are exempt from quota restrictions if the marriage shall have occurred prior to July 1, 1932.

Q. Has the city of Danzig a quota by itself? W. A. F.

A. The Free City of Danzig has its own quota of 100 per annum.

Q. From what countries do we receive immigrants without quota restriction? E. V. C.

A. Persons born in the following countries may enter the United States as non-quota immigrants: Dominion of Canada, Newfoundland, Republic of Mexico, Cuba, Haiti, Dominican Republic, the Canal Zone, and independent countries of Central and South America.

Q. If a man has been in this country for twenty years, does he automatically become a citizen? E. H.

A. No alien ever automatically becomes a citizen of the United States because of length of residence.

Q. What is an alien? D. M.

A. Under the immigration laws the term alien includes any individual not a native born or naturalized citizen of the United States, but does not include Indians of the United States not taxed, nor citizens of islands under the jurisdiction of the United States.

Q. When was the first law passed in this country that affected immigration? E. M. W.

A. Until 1819 no law was passed in Congress which affected the immigrant. An act then adopted, though applying to all passengers, was in reality a law regulating immigration, because then nearly all passengers were immigrants. For several years a large percentage of all persons starting for the United States had been dying en route, owing to lack of provisions and because of overcrowding on shipboard. The purpose of this law was to overcome these evils. It provided that only two passengers could be taken on board vessels coming or going from ports of the United States for every five tons of such vessel, and that a sufficient supply of water and provisions must be carried for the use of the passengers and the crew.

Q. Can an alien who has served in prison ever receive citizenship papers? L. N.

A. This is a question for the court to decide. The alien must prove that he has been a man of good moral character for the five years immediately preceding the issuance of his final papers.

Q. If an alien refuses to take an oath to bear arms in defense of the United States, will his naturalization papers be withheld? O. C.

A. The Supreme Court has ruled in several cases, notably those of Douglas Clyde Macintosh, Marie Averil Bland, and Rosika Schwimmer, that one who will not take this oath does not meet the requirements imposed on applicants for citizenship by the Naturalization Act.

Q. May an alien hold property in the United States? F. B.

A. Each State has its own laws in regard to the ownership of property by aliens. In general the states recognize the right of aliens to hold land particularly where treaties exist between the United States and the countries from which the aliens come. Most of the States, however, place some restrictive provisions on this ownership. For instance, a limit is sometimes placed on the number of acres which can be held.

Q. What is the immigration quota for Scotland? D. J.

A. There is no special immigration quota for the Scotch. They are included in the British quota.

Q. May a Filipino be naturalized in the United States? P. N.

A. There are no provisions for the naturalization as citizens of the United States of persons in the Philippine Islands. In the case of Hidenitsu Toyota vs. United States 268 United States 402,410, the United States Supreme Court held that Filipinos other than those rendering service in the United States Navy, Marine Corps, or Naval Auxiliary Service (this service is specified in Section 7 of the Naturalization Laws) are ineligible to naturalization since they are not white persons or of African nativity or descent.

Q. Where did most of the German immigrants settle? C. S.

A. They did not all settle in the large cities; many pioneered into the open Western areas, settling along the Ohio and Mississippi Valleys, forming large and prosperous communities at Cincinnati, St. Louis, and other places.

Q. What is the origin of the name of Ellis Island? S. T.

A. According to a sketch on the origin of the name of Ellis Island, by Aloys Maerz. This island, which was also known by the name of Gull Island, Oyster Island, Dyre's Island, and Bucking Island, received the name of Ellis Island from Samuel Ellis, a butcher of Manhattan. Mr. Maerz states that no record has been found of the exact date of the naming of the island, but it is known from an advertisement that it was possessed by Samuel Ellis as early as February 21, 1785. His residence at that time, according to the advertisement, was No. 1 Greenwich Street at North River near Bear Market.

Q. Must an alien pay a head tax on returning to this country from a visit abroad? C. T.

A. Any alien who leaves this country to go abroad under the provisions of an alien permit to reënter must upon his return again pay the head tax. However, aliens lawfully admitted and having bona fide residence in the United States who have visited Canada, Newfoundland, Cuba, or Mexico for a temporary period, not exceeding six months, may not be required to pay this head tax.

Q. When was the first naturalization act passed? S. B.

A. The first Congress of the United States on March 26th, 1790, enacted a law establishing a rule for the acquisition of United States citizenship by those of foreign birth.

Q. How may a citizen of the United States who served in a foreign army during the World War be repatriated? W. T.

A. He may be repatriated by simply going before any court and taking an oath of allegiance to the United States.

Q. May an alien from a race inadmissible to citizenship be naturalized if he has an honorable discharge from the army or navy? C. F.

A. During the World War some judges held that military and naval service entitled persons to receive naturalization papers irrespective of racial or other requirements of the naturalization law. However, it has since been held by the Supreme Court of the United States that persons having had this service and not otherwise eligible are not entitled to be naturalized.

Q. Who was the first Pole to come to the United States? I. O.

A. It is said that the first Pole who came to the United States was a young man whom the Dutch colonies of Manhattan in 1659 engaged as a schoolmaster for their children.

Q. May a relative act as witness for one securing citizenship papers? B. C.

A. This depends on the court. Witnesses must be acceptable to the court where application for citizenship papers is made.

Q. Does the adoption by United States citizens of a foreign born child confer citizenship on the child? A. P.

A. A minor child of foreign birth and parentage does not acquire United States citizenship through legal adoption by a citizen of this country.

Q. Why did President Wilson veto the laws requiring immigrants to pass a literacy test in 1915 and 1917? S. B.

A. In his veto message in 1915 he said: "Those who come here seeking opportunity are not to be admitted unless they have had one of the chief of the opportunities they seek, the opportunity of education. The object of such a provision is restriction, not selection." Congress passed a second bill over his veto in 1917.

Q. Under what authority has the number of immigrants permitted to come to the United States been so stringently limited since 1930? C. E.

A. The American consuls abroad have enforced that provision of the Immigration Act of 1917 which calls for exclusion of aliens who are likely to become public charges. The application of this policy to the quota countries of Europe was announced by the President on September 8, 1930. The President made public a State Department memorandum in which it was said that: "In abnormal times, such as the present, when there is not any reasonable prospect of prompt employment for an alien laborer or artisan who comes hoping to get a job and live by it, the particular consular officer in the field to whom application for a visa is made will, before issuing a visa, have to pass judgment with particular care on whether the applicant may become a public charge, and if the applicant cannot convince the officer that it is not probable, the visa will be refused."

Q. What were the principal causes of the beginning of migration from Europe? P. N.

A. In modern history the spirit of adventure and the search for gold first led men to leave European countries. Next trading centers were established and colonization naturally followed.

Q. What proportion of the white foreigners who are living in the United States have become naturalized? F. S.

A. Nearly three-fifths—58.8 per cent—of the 13,366,407 foreign-born white persons living in this country have obtained naturalization papers.

Q. After a person has been naturalized can he be deported if he commits a crime? T. J.

A. A naturalized citizen of the United States is not subject to deportation.

Q. If a woman was naturalized fifteen years ago through her marriage to an American citizen and now divorces her husband, will she lose her citizenship? E. L. M.

A. She will not.

Q. If a child is foreign-born, her father dead, and her mother takes out naturalization papers, does the child become an American citizen? F. L.

A. The Naturalization Bureau says that if after the death of the father of an alien child, the mother is naturalized before the child becomes of age, the child automatically becomes a citizen of the United States.

Q. What occupations have Greek immigrants generally entered? A. N.

A. Most Greek immigrants when coming to the United States have started selling candy, fruits, and flowers from baskets on the streets. Later they acquire pushcarts and still later candy or confectionery stores. Eventually many become merchants. Thousands of Greek immigrants have worked as mill and foundry hands, on railroad construction, and as laborers. They also engage in shoe shining establishments. The tendency is to branch out into the following lines: Wholesale grocers, cigarette manufacturers and tobacco merchants; restaurants, steamship companies, banking, and moving picture theatres.

Q. Does the Chinese Exclusion Act apply to the Hawaiian and Philippine Islands? F. O.

A. These exclusion measures were applied to the Hawaiian and Philippine Islands in 1900 and 1902 respectively.

Q. Will the Government return aliens to their native lands if they cannot support themselves here? D.

A. The law provides that any alien not subject to deportation who has fallen into distress or has needed public aid from causes arising subsequent to entry and who is desirous of being removed to his native country may on the order of the Commissioner General with the approval of the Secretary of Labor at any time within three years after entry be so removed at Government expense. There is no provision for aliens who have been here for a longer period of time.

Q. When and why was Emma Goldman deported? S. K.

A. She was tried for conspiracy against the draft law in 1917. She was sentenced to serve two years in a Federal prison and was fined $10,-000. Upon her release from prison, she was deported in January, 1920.

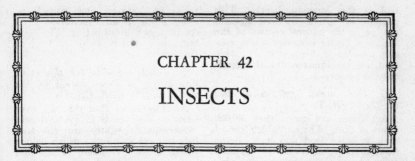

CHAPTER 42

INSECTS

Q. If a flea were the size of a man, how far could it jump? M. G.

A. Professor William Heckler, who has trained fleas, says that a healthy flea would jump what would to us be the equivalent of half a mile.

Q. How far does a fly travel from its breeding place? R. A. B.

A. The Bureau of Entomology says that a house fly will travel a mile or so from its breeding place. If carried by a strong breeze, it may travel several miles.

Q. Is there a certain color that annoys bees? B. W.

A. Persons who have to handle bees are warned that it is best to avoid black clothing, since that color seems to excite bees; a black felt hat is especially to be avoided.

Q. Do swallows carry bedbugs? J. W.

A. Swallows do not carry bedbugs. However, they have their own parasites which resemble bedbugs.

Q. Who owns the rarest collection of butterflies in the United States? S. T.

A. The late Dr. William Barnes, a surgeon of Decatur, Illinois, devoted practically half a century to collecting what is the finest assemblage of North American butterflies in the world. Dr. Barnes' widow has been offered $50,000 for the specimens by the United States Government. Upon her acceptance, they will be brought to Washington and placed in the National Museum.

Q. Can insects communicate with each other? W. L.

A. It is believed that many of them can, especially bees and ants.

Q. How many species of insects are there? D. W.

A. Estimates of the total number of insects, described and undescribed, range from two to ten millions. Over half a million have been described.

Q. Should a hornet's nest in the eaves of a house be removed? J. V.

A. The Bureau of Entomology says that hornets should not be disturbed nor destroyed unless they are actually annoying members of the family. If their nest is under the eaves on the outside of the house and no one is being stung by them, they should be left alone since they are very valuable in destroying injurious garden insect pests.

Q. Has a parasite been found which will exterminate the Japanese beetle? P. B.

A. The Department of Agriculture says that this problem has been given attention since 1920, and at last one seems effective. Tiphia popilliavora was one of the first parasites introduced and one which gave little promise at first. After a slow start, however, it is now increasing rapidly and gives much promise as an important factor in the biological control of the Japanese beetle. This parasite is particularly well adapted for use in the natural control of the Japanese beetle because it is a specific parasite of this pest in its native land, and in this country this tendency is preserved.

Q. *How many varieties of flies are there?* H. T.

A. There are more than 30,000 kinds of flies. Their conduct toward man is both good and bad. Some flies destroy injurious plants and some destroy harmful insects. Indians, at one time, lived off the young of a certain fly.

Q. *Please tell me how to get moths out of a fur collar.* L. G.

A. There are several methods that can be followed. A simple one is to place the fur over a warm radiator or on the top of a lighted gas oven with a very low flame. The moths will come to the surface and may be brushed off. Place the garment in the sun for several days.

Q. *Is the sting of a bee in its head or in its tail?* H. P. B.

A. It is located at the tail-end of the abdomen.

Q. *For what purpose do bees make honey?* W. P.

A. Honey is a sweet substance prepared by bees for food for themselves and their young, and it is made from the sweet juices of blossoms which is mixed with secretions from the mouths of the bees.

Q. *Are insects in the woods better off in a winter which has snow or one in which the ground is bare?* S. L.

A. They benefit by a winter of heavy snow. The snow protects the insects during their dormant period from changes of temperature and penetrating winds.

Q. *Do moth millers eat clothing?* C. T.

A. Moths eat only when in the larval or worm stage. The winged moth never eats, for its mouth is not made for eating. One winged or adult moth in an experiment lived for 77 days without eating. The male moth lives nearly twice as long as the female.

Q. *What accounts for the small flies found in Pennsylvania in the winter time?* E. E. C.

A. The small flies that fly over snow in the woods in Pennsylvania mountains in winter are not true flies but are stone flies which belong to the order Plecoptera. These flies have four membranous wings where true flies have two. During the warmer days in winter they fly about. The young remain under stones until, upon reaching maturity, they shed their skins and appear in adult form. These flies estivate in the warmer weather.

Q. *What should be done to exterminate lice which appear on rose bushes?* R. N.

A. The most effective control of green aphids or plant lice is spraying with a nicotine or pyrethrum extract, several reliable kinds being on the market. If a nicotine sulphate extract is used, use a small amount of soap (one cubic inch to a gallon of water). Whether nicotine or pyrethrum is used, the spray must be applied as a fine, forceful spray to hit the insects.

Q. *Do bees destroy grapes?* S. D. R.

A. The Bureau of Entomology says that bees do not destroy grapes. Their mandibles are too soft to break the skin of grapes and the punctures frequently seen are generally caused by birds. The bees will flock to the grapes after they are punctured since the juice is attractive to them.

Q. *Are there flesh-eating ants in Africa?* N. H.

A. The safari ant belongs to the sub-family Dorylinae of which the genus Dorylus with several subgenera frequents nearly all parts of Africa. These ants usually make only temporary nests but spend most of their time wandering in long files. The size varies from quite minute forms to over one-half inch in length. The mandibles are very strong and the ant also has a powerful sting, and a swarm is able to kill animals or birds that it may come upon. These ants sometimes enter houses in search of vermin and on these occasions the people leave till the ants are through. The same general type of ant occurs in almost all the tropical countries except on islands. The female is without wings, which makes its distribution to islands impossible.

Q. *How long does it take for bees to develop from eggs?* C. E. W.

A. In their metamorphosis, bees pass through four stages, namely, egg, larva, pupa, and adult. The queen develops in 16 days, the worker in 21, and the drone in 25 days.

Q. *What is the Mormon cricket?* W. S. V.

A. The Mormon cricket was so named because of its attack in 1848 on an early Mormon settlement near the present site of Salt Lake City. It threatened the extinction of the colony until a flight of gulls appeared from Salt Lake and exterminated the pest. Because of that, a monument was erected to the gulls. This insect marches in large, orderly armies, but at times will leave good feeding ground for a comparatively barren area.

Q. *How soon after hatching does a house fly reach its full size?* L. L. B.

A. The common house fly is full size when it hatches from the pupa and does not grow any larger. When it hatches it is distorted and it takes from 15 to 30 minutes to straighten out. The fly is not sexually mature until from 3 to 5 days after it hatches.

Q. *How long do grasshoppers live in the tropics where there is no cold season to destroy them?* M. M.

A. In the tropics, the natural span of life of grasshoppers and other in-

sects may be somewhat lengthened by the fact that death is not hastened by the coming of cold and freezing weather as it is in temperate or frigid regions, and also because the period of metamorphosis extends over an average longer period of time. But as a rule the life of single-brooded insects is not over a year in any climate.

Q. *Are fireflies of any value?* S. A. H.

A. They destroy larvae and insects, which are their natural food. In addition to this, they have a value, dead or alive, in China and Japan, where they are used in the manufacture of drugs, poultices, and pills, peculiar to the practice of Chinese medicine. Firefly grease (Hotaru-no-abura) is used by woodworkers for the purpose of imparting rigidity to objects made of bent bamboo. In China and Japan, the catching and selling of fireflies during the summer months is of such extent as to be considered an industry. The chief center of the industry is in the region about Ishiyama, near the Lake of Omi, where a number of merchants ship the fireflies to Osaka and Kyoto. Each house employs from sixty to seventy fly catchers, and experts are known to catch as many as three thousand in a single night.

Q. *What makes a bee hum?* W. M.

A. The sound is due to the very rapid vibration of the bee's wings.

Q. *How high a temperature is needed to kill insect life?* F. G.

A. Practically any form of insect life is killed by a temperature of 125°F., continued for three or four hours.

Q. *What is the difference between biting and sucking insects?* A. L. M.

A. The biting or gnawing insects are those which actually masticate and swallow some portion of the solid substance of the plant, as the wood, bark, leaves, flowers, or fruit. They include most of the injurious larvae, many beetles, and the grasshoppers. The sucking insects are those which injure plants by the gradual extraction of juices from the bark, leaves, or fruit, and include the plant-bugs, aphids, scale insects, thrips, and plant-feeding mites. These insects possess, instead of biting jaws, sucking beaks or bristles.

Q. Has the drone bee a mother and father? E. R. B.

A. The queen bee lays both fertilized and unfertilized eggs. The unfertilized eggs hatch into drones. Hence, drones may be said to have no father or it may be said that the queen bee is both the father and the mother.

Q. Are red lady-bird beetles injurious to plants? M. E. T.

A. There is a widespread belief that these beetles are the parents of injurious plant life, on account of their abundant association with these pests during the growing season. This is not true, as the lady beetles are one of the best natural controls against aphids. Well-grown adult lady-birds require from 50 to 80 plant lice for their daily meal. They also eat the eggs of many injurious insects. They should be encouraged.

Q. Is the white butterfly considered a pest? G. C.

A. The common cabbage worm is quite widely known to gardeners. Many do not know that the white butterfly, common in the vicinity of cabbage plants, is the parent of this pest. The caterpillar becomes the white butterfly which in time lays the eggs from which come a later brood of caterpillars.

Q. Describe the tapestry moth. N. G.

A. The tapestry moth is not so common in the United States as the case-making or the webbing clothes moth, and is larger than either of them, having a wing expanse of about three-fourths of an inch. It is more strikingly colored. The head and basal third of its forewings are black,

while the outer two-thirds of the wings are creamy white, though more or less obscured on the middle with gray. The hind wings are uniformly pale gray.

Q. How long have cockroaches been known? W. S. D.

A. Orthoptera are among the oldest of fossil insects. Cockroaches were numerous and varied in Paleozoic time.

Q. How long do adult mosquitoes live? E. G.

A. Mosquitoes live but a few weeks in adult form.

Q. Will hot water destroy moth eggs? M. G.

A. Water boils at 212°F. At 115° a person finds water almost too hot to hold his hand in it. Fabrics that will not be injured by water can be freed of living clothes-moth eggs and larvae by being dipped for 10 seconds in water heated to 140°F. Care, however, must be exercised to have and keep the water at this, or a greater, temperature. Larvae and eggs in flannel dipped for 10 seconds in water heated only to 122°F. remain unaffected.

Q. When do caterpillars spin their cocoons? R. H.

A. There are many kinds of butterflies and moths, all of which develop from caterpillars, and these have varying habits and times of spinning their cocoons.

Q. Are butterflies found in cold countries? N. E.

A. Both butterflies and mosquitoes, common in warm regions, have been known in extreme Arctic regions. A small kind of butterfly has been found in Ecuador at an elevation of 16,500 feet.

Q. Do flies ever serve any useful purpose? M. O'S.

A. A new kind of fly was recently sent to the Smithsonian Institution for identification. This fly has been discovered to be very effective in attacking a species of caterpillar which destroys cocoanut palms in the Federated Malay States. It appeared to be an entirely new variety and has been christened Ptyschomyia remota.

Q. When did the boll weevil enter South Carolina? C. E. D.

A. In 1917. By 1921 it had spread over the entire State.

Q. What is ant rice? F. T. B.

A. Ant eggs are known as ant rice in some parts of Africa and constitute one of the principal foods of the natives.

Q. Do cotton planters receive official advance notice of the emergence of the cotton boll weevil each year? G. N.

A. While for some years the Department of Agriculture issued a bulletin from its Tallulah, La., experiment station, calculated to inform cotton planters of the strength of boll weevil emergence each spring, the service has been abandoned.

Q. Does a caterpillar turn to a butterfly, or a butterfly to a caterpillar? M. W.

A. The adult female butterfly lays eggs which after a period of about a week or less develop into rapid-growing caterpillars, each of which molts several times before it becomes full size. The animal at this stage is known as a larva. After a life of a few weeks, the caterpillar stops eating and begins to spin a so-called cocoon in which it hangs until the last molt. This stage is known as the chrysalis or pupa. After a week or more of inactivity, the exoskeleton is split and the adult butterfly emerges.

Q. Is there any method of destroying cockroaches without the use of poisons and repellents and fumigants? W. A. J.

A. Various forms of traps have been employed very successfully. These devices are all so constructed that the roaches may easily get into them and cannot afterwards escape.

The destruction of the roaches is effected either by the liquid into which they fall or by being doused with hot water.

Q. How many species of ants are there? A. P. M.

A. There are more than 3500 species of ants.

Q. How can sand flies be eradicated or controlled? W. J. R.

A. No method has been devised. In July, 1930, an appropriation of about $16,000 was made available by Congress for an investigation of this matter by the Bureau of Entomology. It will be several years before this study is complete and any publication appears.

Q. Does the boll weevil fly at night? Is it attracted by light? J. W.

A. The boll weevil is entirely helpless and without power of locomotion in its larval stage, when it infests the scales and bolls of cotton plants. In its adult stage, it moves from place to place by flight and does fly at night as well as in the daytime. However, the boll weevil, unlike other weevils of the same group of insects, is not attracted by light and consequently cannot be snared in this manner.

Q. How many colonies of bees can one man take care of? A. O. F.

A. One man can do practically all of the work required for 350 or 400 colonies, even during rush seasons.

Q. At what season of the year is there danger of moths in upholstered furniture? H. J. F.

A. At all seasons, because once infested the damage may continue indefinitely. Moth eggs hatch in from four to eight days in warm summer weather, in about the same time in warmly heated buildings, and in about three weeks in cold weather, but the larvae develop over a period of from 40 to 175 days, and they do the damage. The Bureau of Entomology has issued a new elaborately illustrated booklet that covers the subject thoroughly, giving preventive measures and methods of eradication.

Q. Please describe a praying mantis. N. S.

A. In appearance, it is quite unlike any other insect. The head pivots in all directions on a threadlike neck. The body is very long and slender and is supported by six long legs, the front pair of which are used for grasping its prey. When in repose, these front legs are held in the position a person assumes when kneeling to pray. When full grown, the insect is about three inches long and a pale green color.

Q. What is the real name for the June bug? G. M.

A. The June bug or June beetle is any of several species of large brown melolonthine beetles of the genus Lachnosterna and related genera. The larvae of these beetles live underground and feed upon roots of grasses and other plants.

Q. In what year were the locusts the worst in the United States? A. P.

A. The most disastrous locust year was 1874.

Q. What are the natural enemies of mosquitoes? F. B.

A. The common goldfish and silverfish destroy mosquito larvae and should be put in artificial ponds. Top-minnows of several species have been introduced successfully in several localities and feed on larvae. There are many predatory aquatic insects that feed upon larvae while others catch the adults. Certain birds prey on the adults, and bats eat them.

Q. How many lenses has a bee in its eyes? L. T.

A. The worker has 3000 to 4000 lenses in its eyes; the drone, 7000 to 8000; a queen about 5000.

Q. Please give directions for making a fly spray. J. L. McC.

A. The following is a recipe for an insecticide which is a contact spray

fly killer: 1 pound of half open pyrethrum flowers and 2 gallons of kerosene. Soak the flowers in the kerosene 48 hours and drain off the liquid. To this or similar fly sprays may be added either oil of rhodium, oil of wintergreen, or oil of contronella for a pleasing odor.

Q. How much calcium arsenate is used as an insecticide in the United States? Z. P.

A. The Bureau of Chemistry says that calcium arsenate is one of the most largely used insecticides in this country at the present time. More than 30,000,000 pounds are used annually, chiefly in dusting cotton for boll weevil control. Some calcium arsenate has even been sprayed by airplane.

Q. What is the insect which attacks antique furniture? H. W.

A. The insect which attacks antique furniture as well as other types of seasoned hardwood is the lyctus powder-post beetle.

Q. Do butterflies have a fragrance? B. S.

A. Fragrance in butterflies, though rivaling that of flowers, is not nearly as certain a quality. Many specimens are without odor, while others resemble the smell of sweet grass, jasmine, syringa, mignonette, orange blossoms, or balsam.

Q. Do ants sting or bite? A. E. W.

A. In ants, a sting is sometimes present as in the Poneridae, which sting like wasps and bees, but in the workers of the ordinary ants, it is either vestigial or entirely wanting. Some ants secrete an active poison, formic acid. This they inject into the wound made by their jaws in biting.

Q. Is it possible for any insect to live inside of a lime? W. E. C.

A. It is quite possible. The Mediterranean fruit fly, which is causing so much damage in the citrus orchards, is just this type of insect.

Q. *When was it that grasshoppers were so numerous in Kansas?* L. B. S.

A. When agriculture began to be established generally in the Great Plains region of the United States, lying west of the Mississippi River and east of the Rocky Mountains, during the decade 1870–1880, a migratory species of grasshopper, commonly known as the Rocky Mountain locust, frequently swooped down from its breeding grounds on the benches of the mountain range. in such great swarms as to destroy practically all cultivated crops over vast areas of country, reducing thousands of families almost to starvation.

Q. *How many legs has the common house fly?* E. M. E.

A. It has six.

Q. *What country was the original home of the honey-bee which we have in this country?* N. N.

A. It was a native of southern Asia, probably including the eastern shores of the Mediterranean Sea.

Q. *Where do flies go in winter?* G. R.

A. It has been proved that most flies die in winter. It is likewise certain that some few of them find places of warmth and protection, live through the cold season, and start new generations in the spring. If these few could be killed, the millions that follow them would not be born. This idea is the basis for the campaign for killing flies in the spring. One fly killed in the spring may mean millions fewer in August.

Q. *What can be done to exterminate slugs which leave slimy trails in cellar and garden?* M. F. S.

A. All decayed boards, débris, bricks, and old flowerpots which serve as hiding places should be removed and air-slaked lime dusted liberally throughout the infested area. Moreover, a poisoned bait, such as boiled potato sprinkled with white arsenic or Paris green, should be distributed in this area. Collect the masses of translucent, yellowish eggs found in dark and damp locations and destroy them.

Q. *How much do honey-bees weigh?* D. H.

A. Honey-bees weigh about 5000 individuals to the pound. So the average weight of a honey-bee would be a little less than one three-hundredths of an ounce.

Q. *How large is the seventeen-year locust?* S. J. S.

A. It is about one inch long when full grown and is marked with black and yellow.

Q. *Will a small water-lily pool in a garden near a house breed mosquitoes?* E. S.

A. It is advisable through the summer season to keep several goldfish in such a pool who will feed on any larvae of mosquitoes, if present, as well as add to the attractiveness of the pool.

Q. *Is it bad luck to kill crickets?* B. M.

A. Crickets are often considered an emblem of good luck and cheer, and for this reason it may be considered bad luck to kill them. There is, of course, no more truth in this than in any other superstition. Actually, however, crickets are not harmful insects since they will not harm clothing or other articles of value unless driven to it by the absence of any other food.

Q. *How long do butterflies live?* S. H. F.

A. Although some species are said to live as long as ten months, authorities say that the average life of a butterfly is about four or five weeks.

Q. *What is the best mixture to keep mosquitoes away?* S. H.

A. The following is used with excellent results: oil of citronella, 1 ounce; spirits of camphor, 1 ounce; oil of cedar, ½ ounce. A few drops on a Turkish towel or wash cloth hung near the head of the bed usually suffices. Its efficacy wears off after several hours, so it is well to renew towards daylight. The yellow fever mosquito begins to bite at daylight, so the extra dosage is particularly necessary in the South.

Q. *What are hellgramites?* F. P.

A. They are the larval form of the Dobson fly. They are found under stones in swift streams and are an excellent bait for bass. Hellgramites can be kept alive for a considerable time in floating bait boxes or in wet grass.

Q. *How much honey by weight should a colony of bees produce?* F. P. B.

A. The average production is about 50 pounds, but under favorable conditions 100 pounds might be produced.

Q. *Why do mosquitoes bite some people and not others?* H. M.

A. The apparent immunity or susceptibility of individuals to mosquitoes is due to body odors which attract or repel.

Q. *How high in the air does life exist?* C. S.

A. Recent government experiments conducted with airplanes have found insect life 20,000 feet, or nearly 4 miles, in the air. This space fly is practically colorless. What it lives on has not been determined.

Q. *Has a fly two kinds of eyes?* T. F. W.

A. The greater part of the head of a fly is occupied by the eyes, some several thousand in number, described as compound. Between the compound eyes, and near the top of the head is a triangular arrangement of three simple eyes.

Q. *What is a boll-weevil?* C. S.

A. It is an insect which lays its eggs in the bud of the cotton plant. Out of these eggs come worm-like larvae which eat the growing bud and prevent the production of cotton fiber. In American slang, boll-weevil

is a term sometimes applied to a person who is a pest.

Q. *How does the drug store beetle get its name?* S. L.

A. Because it eats nearly all kinds of drugs. It is a very general feeder and has been said to "eat anything except cast iron."

Q. *What is the largest insect known?* V. C.

A. In wing expanse alone, the moth Erebus agrippina with a spread of 11 inches is the largest insect known today. If size is to be gauged by bulk combined with body-length, the beetle Macrodontia cervicornis which ranges up to 6 inches in length is perhaps the largest known.

Q. *Is there any way of preventing insects in window boxes?* R. N.

A. Whitewashing the inside of boxes before filling them in the spring will help to keep out insects and prevent rotting of the boxes.

Q. *How can we get rid of big black roaches in our cellar?* R. L.

A. The Bureau of Entomology says that one of the most effective simple means of ridding premises of roaches is dusting with commercial sodium fluoride, either pure or diluted one-half with some inert substance such as powdered gypsum or flour.

Q. *Does the print on newspapers keep moths away?* B. P.

A. There is no foundation for this belief. Any firm wrapping paper or several thicknesses of newspaper will serve. The important things are to have the garments clean, freed from moths, and carefully wrapped so that there is no possibility of moths crawling in. Clothes moths will not eat into paper to attack clothing.

Q. *How was it discovered that the Mediterranean fruit fly had entered the United States?* H. D. I.

A. It is stated that the first warning of this pest's entry into the United States came from Orlando, Florida. A group, which included a distinguished entomologist, had secured some grapefruit from an experimental station. It was found that the fruit was dried and riddled with canals. Specimens of the fruit were dispatched to Washington for examination. An official of the State Plant Board of Florida obtained specimens of the adult fly, sending them by air mail to the U. S. Department of Agriculture. Here they were identified as the destructive Mediterranean fly and the Federal Government took precautions at once to restrict and eradicate this insect plague.

Q. Does Canada find it necessary to wage war on insects which attack crops? G. H. M.

A. It does. Some of the chief insect enemies are grasshoppers, the wheat stem sawfly, wireworms, the pale western cutworm and his ally the red-backed cutworm, the bertha armyworm, the early cutworm, the Colorado potato beetle, the imported cabbage butterfly, and the root maggot.

Q. How does a bee find its way home? S. L. L.

A. The bee finds its way home by its sense of direction. When it leaves the hive it circles around and then flies off. Each hive has its own odor which helps the bee to identify its hive.

Q. What States were the first to try tick eradication? C. D. C.

A. The Division of Tick Eradication says that the first states were Virginia and North Carolina, in 1906. The origin of the arsenic dip to kill ticks is claimed to have been Australia. It was used in the United States until 1911 at which time it was permitted to be used in inter-

state movement. This was its first official federal recognition.

Q. Please publish a description of the Japanese beetle, which is causing such havoc. A. W. E.

A. The adult Japanese beetle is about three-eighths of an inch in length and about the same in width. It is bright metallic green in color, with coppery brown wings.

Q. Is a spider an insect? D. D.

A. A spider is not an insect, but an arachnid. The phylum Arthropoda, or jointed invertebrate animals, has three principal classes, Insecta, Arachnida, and Crustacea. The class Arachnida includes such familiar creatures as spiders, order Araneida, scorpions, order Scorpionida, and harvestmen, or daddy longlegs, order Phalanjida. True spiders are distinguished from insects by possessing four (instead of three) pairs of walking legs, and by having the body divided into only two main divisions separated by a narrow waist: a cephalothorax, bearing the legs, mouth parts and eyes, and an unsegmented abdomen, which is short and rounded, and bears two or more spinnerets at the posterior end, for spinning silk threads. Spiders are predacious, and have poison glands near their jaws, some being able to inflict bites painful or even dangerous to man. The young develop without a metamorphosis, such as is typical of insects.

Q. Is it true that the Colorado potato beetle has not appeared west of the Rockies? K. N.

A. The Bureau of Entomology says that this important enemy of the potato and other vegetable crops has reached Washington and Oregon, but it does not yet occur in California.

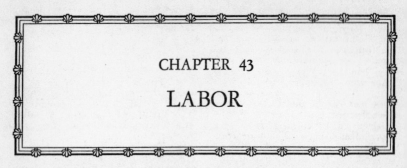

CHAPTER 43

LABOR

Q. *Is there any factory operated entirely by machinery?* L. T.

A. A factory for the production of rayon yarn is nearly completed in New Jersey. In this factory production may be carried on for 24 hours a day without a single worker.

Q. *How many hours a day would each adult person in the United States have to work if the employment were equally divided?* I. O.

A. According to Technocracy, the adult population of this country would have to work only four hours a day for four days a week to supply us with all our material needs.

Q. *In the United States are more persons employed in manufacture or agriculture?* O. D.

A. According to the 1930 Census, 10,482,323 persons were employed in agriculture, and 14,317,535 in manufacturing and mechanical industries.

Q. *How much does the payment of old age pensions cost the citizens?* F. T.

A. The annual per capita cost of old age pensions ranges from 4 cents to $1.35 per inhabitant.

Q. *What foreign countries have systems of unemployment insurance?* I. C.

A. The following countries have some system of unemployment insurance: Austria, Bulgaria, Germany, Great Britain and Northern Ireland, Irish Free State, Italy, Luxemburg, Poland, Queensland, Belgium, Czechoslovakia, Denmark, Finland, France, Netherlands, Norway, Spain, Switzerland.

Q. *What are real wages?* S. O.

A. The amount of purchasing power represented by nominal wages is the real wages.

Q. *In the construction of new buildings what is the relative cost of labor and material?* A. O. P.

A. For fifteen cities studied by the Bureau of Labor Statistics in 1931–32, it was found that 63.6% of the money spent in the erection of buildings went for material and 36.4% for labor. The percentage received by labor was slightly higher on residential than on non-residential buildings.

Q. *How many coöperative societies are there in the world?* S. C.

A. Data covering the various phases of the coöperative movement throughout the world show more than 400,000 societies of all types in 37 countries.

Q. *Which States in the United States of America do not have laws regulating the number of hours women shall work?* H. T. L.

A. Alabama, Florida, Iowa, and West Virginia do not have such laws.

Q. *Do women receive as much pay as men for the same work?* C. F.

A. According to Miss Mary Anderson, women receive one-third to one-half less pay than men for the same work.

Q. *How many are employed directly and indirectly in the manufacture of automobiles?* N. K.

A. There are 4,030,000 persons so employed.

Q. *By whom was Cooper Union founded?* J. W.

A. It was founded by Peter Cooper for the instruction of the working classes of New York shortly after the middle of the last century.

Q. *Has any one ever proposed that labor be paid by the year instead of by the hour, day, or week?* W. G.

A. Senator Couzens, of Michigan, recently referred to such an idea when he said: "If every industry were to pay its men by the year instead of by the hour or day, industry would find a way to stabilize its production so that it got its money's worth."

Q. *Where or how did the strike originate?* F. P.

A. The first appearance of the strike in history was the strike of secession of the plebeians against the patricians in Ancient Rome 494 B.C.

Q. *What occupations are not open to women?* F. A.

A. A publication of the Census Bureau lists many occupations in which it is unusual for women to be employed. Some of these are: Blacksmith, baggageman, boilermaker, brakeman, butcher, conductor on railroad, coppersmith, electrician, locomotive engineer or fireman, fireman in fire department, forester, garbage man, hostler, pilot, plumber, railway mail clerk, stone mason, street cleaner, tinsmith.

Q. *When did the American Federation of Labor have its largest membership?* W. J. C.

A. In 1920 when the members numbered over 4,000,000. The reported membership of the American Federation of Labor at the Boston Convention, October 6, 1930, was 2,-961,096. In 1932 there were about 2,520,000 members.

Q. *Please name the Secretaries of Labor.* W. F. V.

A. William B. Wilson, 1913; James J. Davis, 1921; William N. Doak, 1930.

Q. *What is a Yellow Dog contract?* C. H.

A. There are different kinds of contracts known by this name, but in general this is an agreement between the employer and the employee that the employee will not join a union while he is an employee of the employer, that he will not associate or confer with union labor leaders or union labor members so long as he is in the employ of the employer. There is often also a portion that the employee may not leave without certain notice to the employer, but that the employee may be dismissed without notice.

Q. *What was the doctrine of Laissez-faire?* U. T.

A. Laissez-faire may be defined as the doctrine which demands the minimum interference by the government in economic and political affairs. The doctrine arose at the end of the 17th and the beginning of the 18th centuries as a protest against the excessive regulation of industry by government action.

Q. *How long have there been trade unions in England?* I. R. H.

A. Trade unions were legalized in England in 1824, but such organizations or combinations of wage earners for the purpose of maintaining or improving the condition of their employment have existed continuously from the latter part of the 17th Century. The earliest actual record of such a combination is that of the woolen workers of the southwest of England, which is mentioned as existing in 1700 and frequently referred to in Devonshire, Somerset, Wilshire, and Gloucestershire throughout the 18th Century. The London tailors can be shown to have been in continuous combination from at least 1720, when an Act of Parliament was passed to restrain them.

Q. *What were the causes of the strike of cotton weavers in Lancashire, England, during the late summer and fall of 1932?* O. G.

A. The basic trouble was generally conceded to be twofold: The overcapitalization of the industry in the boom period following the war and the growing competition in the world market, where the cheaper products of the oriental countries were displacing English cottons. It was essential, the employers said, that costs should be reduced. The employees agreed, but insisted that this should be done through a reorganization of the industry and that the savings which could be effected through a cut in wages were so small relatively that it was not worth while to submit to it unless it were coupled with some more far-reaching movement.

Q. *What important things did Woodrow Wilson do for labor?* M. C.

A. The Adamson Eight Hour Law, enacted during his administration, was one; the creation of the National War Labor Board to handle industrial controversies during the World War was another.

Q. *How do industrial accidents in the United States and Great Britain compare?* P. L.

A. With twice as many persons employed in factories and workshops as in Great Britain, industrial accidents in the United States annually are 13 times greater, according to information made available at the Women's Bureau, Department of Labor, November 21, 1932.

Q. *What effect has the operation of old age pensions on other means of relief?* W. D. S.

A. It has a decided effect. Undoubtedly these laws prevent thousands of persons from having to enter almshouses. It also affects the number of persons entering private homes for the aged. It is said that in some States a new type of agency is developing, namely, the licensed boarding house.

Q. *When was the Department of Labor organized?* B. S.

A. Originally the Bureau of Labor organized in 1885, was a part of the Department of the Interior. In February, 1903, the Bureau was transferred to the Department of Commerce and Labor. The Department of Labor was established separately by act of Congress approved March 4, 1913.

Q. *What is labor turnover?* G. O.

A. According to a definition of the Bureau of Labor Statistics, "labor turnover for any period consists of the number of separations from service during that period. Separations include all quits, discharges, and layoffs for any reason whatsoever. To compute the percentage of labor turnover for any period, find the total separation for the period considered and divide by the average of the number actually working each day throughout that period, then multiply by the proper factor to reduce to a yearly basis."

Q. *What are labor colonies?* G. T.

A. These are agricultural communities, common in Europe but almost unknown in the United States. They are maintained for the purpose of giving employment and training to individuals who because of misfortune or inefficiency have difficulty in earning a living. The oldest of these colonies are the four in Holland which have a membership of over 2000, and were established about 75 years ago.

Q. *Who were the Six Men of Dorset?* B. F. S.

A. They were farm laborers who about 150 years ago banded together to demand of their employers meat to eat at least once a week. They were prosecuted for conspiracy and sentenced to long terms of penal servitude.

Q. What is Technocracy? B. T.

A. It is a functional organization of engineers who have made over a ten-year period an extensive analysis of our industrial and agricultural growth, applying a quantitative measure to the social mechanism.

Q. How many foreign countries have systems of pensions or insurance for old age? U. D. S.

A. At least 39 countries have established some form of old age pension according to data available here.

Q. What were the principal questions discussed at the International Labor Conference held in Geneva in April, 1932? P. H.

A. The agenda of the conference contained four items: Fee charging employment agencies; invalidity, old age, and widows' and orphans' insurance; juvenile employment in non-industrial occupations; and the revision of the convention for the safety of dockers.

Q. What are the different stages of economic history? A. G. B.

A. Many attempts have been made to divide economic history into different stages through which mankind passed in arriving at modern industrial civilization. The basis of this classification is the increasing power of man over nature and from this standpoint the stages are: Direct appropriation; the pastoral stage; the agricultural stage; the handicraft stage; the industrial stage.

Q. When was the Women's Bureau organized and what is its function? H. D.

A. It was organized in July, 1918, as a war service and made a permanent bureau in June, 1920. This Bureau is charged with the responsibility of developing policies and standards and conducting investigations in the industries of the country which shall safeguard the interests of women workers and thus make their service effective for the national good. It represents and advises the Secretary of Labor in all matters concerning women in industry, and is charged with maintaining close contact with other agencies which deal with special phases of the problem, including other divisions of the Department of Labor. It works with and through the state departments of labor.

Q. Is our minimum-wage system patterned after that of any country? D. D.

A. The Women's Bureau says that the minimum-wage system in this country is a direct outgrowth of the wage regulations for all workers in specified industries that developed in New Zealand and Australia at the end of the nineteenth century. Whereas there are many differences between the laws to be found in the United States and those of the other countries, American legislation has profited largely by the more mature foreign experience.

Q. Is a labor exchange the same thing as an employment bureau? S. P.

A. The term is sometimes erroneously applied to employment bureaus. Properly the term was given to a class of institutions founded in 1832–1835 designed to bring about an exchange of products of labor without the use of money. The basis of the value of each product was the amount of time spent in producing it.

Q. In what year did the Pullman strike occur? A. L.

A. The famous Pullman strike took place in 1894.

Q. How many States have adopted some form of old age pensions? M. C.

A. California, Colorado, Delaware, Idaho, Kentucky, Maryland, Massachusetts, Minnesota, Montana, Nevada, New Hampshire, New Jersey,

New York, Utah, West Virginia, Wisconsin, and Wyoming have provided for the payment of old age pensions.

Q. *Does the Adamson Act apply only to train service employees?* N. C.

A. Although the Adamson Act provides for an eight hour day only to train service employees, the basic eight hour working day has been extended to all railroad employees.

Q. *Has any State adopted an unemployment insurance law?* I. T.

A. On January 28, 1932, the first unemployment insurance law adopted by any State in the Union was approved by the Governor of Wisconsin. Unless employers of at least 175,000 employees establish voluntarily some unemployment insurance plan which meets the standards prescribed by the act, it will automatically become compulsory on July 1, 1933.

Q. *In what industry has the 5-day week been adopted to the greatest extent in the United States?* N. S.

A. From a study of 44,025 establishments representing 102 industries or industrial groups it appears that the automobile industry has the largest proportion of employees on the 5-day week, namely 67.2 per cent.

Q. *What was the Godin idea of profit-sharing between capital and labor?* C. L. B.

A. Godin, a French socialist, established a coöperative association in 1859 and by 1886 had fully established profit sharing. By his plan, profits in excess of 5 per cent on capital were to be divided between labor and capital in the ratio of aggregate wages to aggregate minimum profits.

Q. *When did the biggest strike of anthracite coal miners take place?* N. B. B.

A. The longest and costliest strike in the anthracite industry began September 1, 1925, and was settled February 12, 1926. It lasted 164 days, involved 158,000 workers, and caused a loss of $200,000,000 to the operators and $188,600,000 in wages. The total loss is estimated at $1,000,000,-000.

Q. *When was the term industrialism first used?* R. L.

A. It was first applied by Saint-Simon and his followers to the modern régime.

Q. *Have the laws placing legal restrictions upon hours of labor of men in the United States been held constitutional by the Supreme Court?* T. S.

A. The laws have been upheld quite generally when there was a reasonable basis for the restriction and the purpose was to protect the lives and health of the workers or society in general.

Q. *Have the unemployment insurance systems in foreign countries broken down during the depression?* M. D. R.

A. Unemployment-insurance systems in foreign countries have carried on through the depression, although changes have been necessary in some of the systems to meet the demands caused by the increasing number of unemployed. In some instances benefits have been curtailed and contributions increased, while in several of the systems, including those of Great Britain and Germany, the "means" or "need" test, by which unemployed persons are required to prove their need for financial aid, has been introduced.

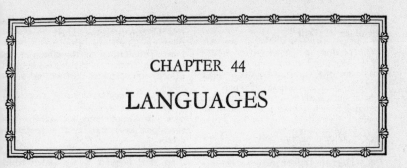

CHAPTER 44

LANGUAGES

Q. How many different languages are spoken in the world? V. S.

A. Authorities differ widely as to the number of languages and dialects that are spoken in the world at the present time. Some give the number as 1000; others as high as 5000 and 7000.

Q. Most European countries have a number of languages. Is there any one in which a single language is spoken? C. E.

A. Portugal is the only European country having a single language.

Q. What are the official languages of the League of Nations? M. A. R.

A. English and French.

Q. Were Latin and Greek the only languages spoken in the time of Christ? R. E. G.

A. There were many others, such as Babylonian, Phoenician, Egyptian, Hindustan, Chinese, Hebrew, Aramaic, etc.

Q. How many dialects are spoken in India? J. P.

A. India has 220 vernacular languages.

Q. When did French become the language of diplomacy? C. A. S.

A. As the language for treaties and foreign intercourse between nations, it became general in the time of Louis XIV (1643–1715). At conferences of representatives of various nations there are interpreters present to make the proceedings clear to each member. Treaties are generally translated into all the languages of the countries represented.

Q. How long has there been a written language in Hawaii? C. C. H.

A. The Hawaiian is one of the Polynesian languages. The written language dates from the time of the arrival of missionaries in 1820. The alphabet consists of 12 letters which are pronounced as in Latin.

Q. What is the Greek word for God? M. B.

A. In Greek this word is Theos, English words of like meaning tracing their derivation to it.

Q. Into how many languages has the Koran been translated? H. H. H.

A. The Koran has been translated into English, French, German, Eastern languages of India, and dialects of Arabic, Egyptian, Turkish, Syrian, and Persian.

Q. What system of pronunciation was used by the Egyptians? F. S. P.

A. All pronunciation is conjectural. It is customary to give the vowels the same value as in German. The consonants are given the same value as in English.

Q. What does the word Calcutta mean? J. K.

A. The Hindu of Calcutta is Kalighatta. Kali is the name of an Indian goddess to whom a temple has been erected in Calcutta. Ghatta is the Hindu for ghat or landing place.

Kalighatta means, therefore, "landing place of Kali."

Q. Is there a Canadian language? H. J. M.

A. English is the language generally spoken in Canada. French was spoken in some sections, and has changed into a patois that is distinctive.

Q. How many languages are spoken in the Philippines? A. F. T.

A. English and Spanish are widely spoken, English being the commercial and official language. There are something like 85 native dialects; a few of these are distinct languages, each spoken to-day by approximately 500,000 people.

Q. What is the. official language of the Irish Free State? J. D.

A. Gaelic is the official language.

Q. How is hello said in other languages? M. L.

A. When the word is used by foreigners it is given as nearly the English pronunciation as possible. The French do not sound the "h."

Q. When did Latin cease to be. a spoken language? C. R. K.

A. It ceased to be a spoken language in 580 A.D., but remained the organ of general literature until the early part of the 17th Century. The last great philosopher who wrote entirely in Latin was Leibnitz (1646-1716).

Q. From what languages is English as spoken in America derived? A. D.

A. English as spoken in this country is derived from many sources. Our speech has a Saxon base. Approximately 20 per cent of the words in conversational use are derived from Latin. We have many literary and ecclesiastical Latin terms and technical words derived from the Greek. A greater part of our household and poetical words are Saxon. There is a strong French influence originally introduced by the conquest of the Island of Britain by William the Conqueror, the Duke of Normandy. There are also in our language numerous words brought by colonists from the Netherlands, and also Spanish and Indian words.

Q. Do the Czechs use Cz in their written language? W. W. R.

A. Jessie Mothersole, in "Czechoslovakia," says that the Czechs themselves do not use Cz at all in their written language, but C with a breve over it. The Cz is an older form still used in Poland and it is easier for English printers.

Q. What language is spoken in Guam? N. C. P.

A. The natives speak a native language called Chamorro. English is the official language, but Spanish is spoken.

Q. What is the official language of Palestine? B. W.

A. There are three official languages in Palestine: English, Hebrew, and Arabic, and all public documents are translated into these three languages.

Q. Which Spanish dialect is considered the best? T. A. C.

A. There are five principal dialects, the Asturian, Leonese, Aragonese, Andalusian, Castilian. Castilian is the standard literary speech.

Q. Are Yiddish and Hebrew the same? R. E. B.

A. Yiddish is spoken by a large number of Jews of German or Polish ancestry, and is quite commonly spoken, but it is not the natural language of the Jewish people, who speak modern Hebrew. The Jews who left Germany in the Middle Ages for the Slavic lands of Bohemia, Poland, Galicia, and Lithuania, spoke besides Hebrew, the Middle High German. In course of time, Hebrew and Aramaic and Slavic words became customary, and a certain modification of the sound of the German words also took place, and by the 16th century a world-defined dialect or language known as Yiddish had become common. It was not adopted as a literary language until the 19th century.

Q. *In the time of Shakespeare, how many people used the English language?* A. T.

A. In the time of Shakespeare, English was spoken by fewer than 6,000,000 people. At the time of the Revolutionary War, more people in the world spoke French, German, Spanish, or Russian than the English language.

Q. *What language has the largest vocabulary?* L. F.

A. The English language has the greatest number of words.

Q. *Is there a Scotch language?* R. G. B.

A. The name "Scotch language" is often applied to the Celtic speech of the Scotch Highlanders, also known as Gaelic. It also refers to the dialect or dialects of the English spoken in the Lowlands of Scotland.

Q. *In what part of the country do the most high school students elect to study French?* L. R.

A. Nearly 36 per cent of all students enrolled in the public high schools reporting from New England study French, as against slightly less than 8 per cent in the North Central States, less than 3 per cent in the Southwest, and 13.2 per cent in the nation as a whole.

Q. *Is the French spoken in Canada the same as that spoken in Paris?* A. S. B.

A. The French language as spoken in Canada differs in several respects, principally in the matter of certain colloquialisms, from the French of Paris.

Q. *What German dialect is considered the standard pronunciation?* G. E.

A. In Germany there is no standard of pronunciation that is acknowledged and absolutely followed by the mass of intelligent people. The so-called standard of some people is the pronunciation of the stage, which again, is divided into the pronunciation of tragedy and comedy. In the latter, of course, is heard the more natural pronunciation of everyday life. The sectional differences are very marked, but in general there is a North German and a South German pronunciation.

Q. *What are the Romance languages?* C. O'N.

A. The languages derived from the Latin are the Romance languages, which include Italian, Spanish, Portuguese, French, Provençal, Rumanian, Romansch, and Ladin.

Q. *What is the Swiss language?* G. F.

A. The principal languages of Switzerland are German, spoken by 71 per cent of the people; French, by 21 per cent, and Italian by 6 per cent. Other languages are Romansch and Ladin. By the Federal Constitution of 1848 and 1874, German, French, and Italian are recognized as national languages.

Q. *What is meant by lingua franca?* L. E. M.

A. It is a term used for a language used in any country secondary to the principal language of the country.

Q. *How many Irishmen speak the Gaelic language?* W. J. R.

A. At present about 1 per cent of the population speaks Gaelic only; 86 per cent English only; and about 13 per cent both languages. Since the establishment of the Irish Free State, Irish is being taught in schools, with the idea of the eventual restoration of Irish as the vernacular of the country.

Q. *Do we speak English or is our language called American?* W. E. N.

A. English is the official language of the United States. It has been suggested by some philologists that the speech of the Americans be termed the American language, but no definite action has ever been taken in this respect. Words and phrases that are peculiar to the United States are termed Americanisms.

Q. Which languages are considered most melodious? M. L.

A. Opinions differ to some extent. One linguistic expert says that he considers Italian, Turkish, and Telugu (a language of southern India) the most melodious.

Q. Which of the Latin dialects became the Italian of today? A. B.

A. This dialect is the Tuscan, the native language of Dante. The language of Tuscany, more particularly of Florence, is thus the classical language of Italy; it was established as such by grammarians who chose it chiefly because the "Three Crowns"—Dante, Petrarch, and Boccaccio—used it.

Q. Is English spoken exclusively in the British Isles? I. G.

A. The language of the people of the British Isles is English with few exceptions. There is a large proportion of Welsh-speaking people in Wales, many of whom are bilingual. Gaelic is still spoken on the west coast of Ireland, and in the highlands and islands of Scotland, according to the 1921 census, there were 10,314 people speaking Gaelic only.

Q. How many dialects are spoken in France? S. W.

A. There are seven in the north of France, and six in the south. These dialects have distinct divisions, amounting in all to seventy or eighty.

Q. Is there a language known as Afrikaans? B. M.

A. Afrikaans is the name given to the language spoken and written by the descendants of Dutch, French, and German colonists who settled in South Africa prior to the British occupation of 1806. It is also known as Cape Dutch. Afrikaans was developed from the seventeenth century dialects of the province of Holland.

Q. Where is the Flemish language spoken? L. O. R.

A. The Flemish language is spoken in the northern half of Belgium and by more than 200,000 people in the Nord Department of France.

Q. What foreign languages are the most necessary for a singer to know? M. K. M.

A. The Musician says that Italian, German, and French are the most important.

Q. What language is spoken by the most people in the vicinity of Jerusalem? L. M. S.

A. Arabic is spoken by the greatest number of people in Palestine near Jerusalem.

Q. What is the predominating language in Mexico? M. E.

A. The Spanish language is the predominant one in Mexico. However, American business houses there handle much correspondence in English.

Q. What is a language called in which entire thoughts are combined in one word? P. K.

A. It is called holophrastic. American Indian tongues are examples of this. They often compress a whole sentence into a word, the length of which is often remarkable.

Q. Which language is older, Latin or Greek? J. F.

A. Greek is considerably older than Latin, which is shown by the fact that Latin was profoundly influenced by Greek during its development.

Q. How does the Catalan language differ from Spanish? P. C.

A. It is generally assumed that Catalan was imported from Roussillon into Spain during Carolingian times, but there is a contrary view that it was originally developed in Spain and introduced into Roussillon by Catalan immigrants. It is a Romance language, an off-shoot of Provençal. Philologically Catalan differs from Spanish in that it lacks the characteristic diphthongs. One of its distinctive features is its tendency to suppress many of the consonant and unaccented vowel endings so common in Spanish.

Q. What are the "Prakrit" languages? G. F.

A. The term is applied to the vernacular languages of India as opposed to the literary Sanskrit.

Q. What language is spoken in Yugoslavia? J. V.

A. The principal language is what is known as Serbo-Croatian. It is spoken by nearly nine million out of a total of twelve million people.

Q. Is Sanskrit a Hebrew word? M. B. S.

A. It is an ancient Hindu word and signifies perfection or perfect. The Hindu word is Sanskrita. Sanskrit was from the earliest times a classical language and between 2000 and 1500 B.C. was the language used in writing of the Vedas or sacred books of Hindustan.

Q. Which of the many dialects of early England is the one upon which the language is based? R. E.

A. When Chaucer used the Midland dialect for his Canterbury Tales, he made it the standard for modern English.

Q. What language did the ancient Ethiopians speak? J. L. T.

A. They spoke a language known as Ethiopic, also called lesana Ge'ez, the tongue of Ge'ez. It is closely allied with the languages of Southern Arabia and represents the southwestern branch of the southern division of the Sem languages.

Q. In what South American country is Portuguese spoken? B. K.

A. It is spoken in Brazil. All other South American countries use Spanish.

Q. I received a locket from Australia bearing the inscription, Kiaora. What does it mean? R. H. G.

A. The word Kiaora is a Maori term used in toasts. It may be interpreted as be well, or, be happy.

Q. How many languages are spoken in Africa? J. P.

A. About 275 are known.

Q. What is the native tongue of the Rumanians? C. S. B.

A. The native language of the Rumanians is Rumanian, a Romance language related to Italian and the extinct Dalmatian. The language is divided into four main dialects—the North or Daco-Rumanian, which is Rumanian Proper; South Rumanian or Vlach; the Meglen dialect; and Istrian or Dalmatian Rumanian.

Q. What is the meaning of Mavourneen? A. P.

A. Mavourneen is derived from two Irish words, mo and mhurnen, meaning my darling.

Q. What kind of language is Anglic? E. R.

A. Anglic is a new international language proposed by Prof. R. E. Zachrisson in 1930. It is based on an analysis of all English words in general use, without adding new letters to the alphabet, at the same time keeping the continuity with the conventional English orthography. It embraces the most common of the existing spelling variants, introducing at the same time a few new diagraphs—uu, dh, zh—which have to do the duty of new letters. Anglic has 50 letters or letter combinations to represent the 40-odd sounds that occur in English words in current use.

Q. When was Latin first written? E. B.

A. It was reduced to writing about the 6th century B.C. by the use of an alphabet derived from the Greek alphabet of the town of Cumae in southern Italy. Latin became a literary language during the 3rd and 2nd centuries B.C.

Q. Is a person at 50 too old to learn a foreign language? A. E.

A. Professor Thorndyke says that extensive experiments with adults learning algebra, science, foreign languages, and the like in evening classes, and with adults learning typewriting and shorthand in secretarial schools, support the general conclusion that ability to learn rises till about twenty years, and then, perhaps after a stationary period of some years, slowly declines. The decline is so slow (it may roughly be thought of as one per cent per year) that persons under fifty should seldom be deterred from trying to learn anything which they really need to learn by the fear that they are too old. And to a lesser degree this is true after fifty years also.

Q. Which language is easiest to learn, French, German, or English? J. C.

A. French is possibly the simplest. The German grammar is extremely complicated and English pronunciation is difficult for certain foreigners. The English language also contains a great number of colloquialisms used in every-day speech, which take some time to acquire. All languages do not contain the same number of words. The English language contains approximately 700,000 words; German dictionaries contain about 300,000 words; French 210,000 words.

Q. Is Slovak a distinct language? R. T.

A. Slovak is so closely allied to Czech that most scholars describe it as a dialect. This alphabet is founded on the Czech. Slovak books were rare before the War, but since the formation of the Czecho-Slovak State many have appeared.

Q. Is it essential for a student to master a foreign language? R. D.

A. In a recent address Dr. Henry Grattan Doyle of George Washington University made the following statement: Not only are foreign languages the indispensable tools for international dealings of all kinds, but a knowledge of foreign languages and literature is the gateway to the understanding of foreign culture, foreign civilization, and foreign psychologies. . . . Students should begin their study early and should continue at least four, and preferably six, years.

Q. Did the broad a of the English originate with the Irish? A. W.

A. Prof. Grandgent of Harvard University says that the earlier English "ah" became short a by the 16th century. Until 1780 or thereabouts the standard language had no broad a. Benjamin Franklin, who recorded in 1768 the pronunciation of his day, knew no "ah." Evidence indicates that it appeared again in London speech between 1780 and 1790. There is no basis for the statement that it originated with the Irish.

Q. When was modern Italian first spoken? P. M.

A. The modern Italian language is developed from the Latin. The earliest definite traces of Italian speech may be found in a document of Monte Cassino, dated 960. Tuscan and especially Florentine has been the classical literary language almost from the beginning of the national literature. During the first half of the 13th century the mass of lyrical poetry was produced by the Sicilian school at Palermo at the Court of the Emperor Frederick II. In the second half of the century the seat of lyrical poetry was transferred to Tuscany. The modern Italian literary language, however, is founded on the Florentine dialect which was the language of Dante.

Q. Is modern Greek the same as the Greek of the ancients? P. N.

A. It differs greatly from the Greek spoken in classical times.

Q. Who spoke Latin as a language and how long was it used? E. S.

A. Originally Latin was spoken by the inhabitants of the ancient city of Rome and by the tribe called the Latini who lived on the plain of

Latium, south of the Tiber. Various other languages were at the same time used in Italy. Gradually as the Romans conquered the neighboring Italian towns, and their power increased, the Latin language spread through Europe. Latin was spoken in Central Italy probably as early as 10 or 15 centuries before our era. It ceased to be a living tongue about the 8th century of our era.

Q. When was the Gaelic language at its height in Ireland? N. S.

A. Deasmumhan O'Cleirigh says that as a living language it reached its acme of perfection in the 17th and 18th centuries. Thereafter, it declined as there was a law against its use. Now, Gaelic is the official language of the Irish Free State.

Q. Was German ever considered seriously as the language for the United States? F. J. G.

A. Although there was a discussion in the Continental Congress in regard to the use of the German or English language in the colonies, and a motion was made in favor of using the German language, the matter never came to a vote. Only in Pennsylvania was the German element more than a small minority before the Revolution. Perhaps a third of the settlers in Pennsylvania were Germans. Although the German language persisted in the speech and in the press in Pennsylvania, the English stock outnumbered all the others from 1760 to 1790.

Q. Is there a basic language in Africa? R. F.

A. Ethnologists have failed so far to find a common root language of the African or negro people. There are many dialects and in many cases a dialect used by natives of one tribe not far removed physically from another is unintelligible to the other tribe.

Q. What are the Papuan languages? H. G.

A. The Papuan languages are those spoken in New Guinea and the adjacent islands, and in the Solomon group.

Q. Please. tell something about the Portuguese language. J. M. S.

A. The Portuguese language is a Romance language resembling the Spanish and paralleling it rather closely in grammar. The Portuguese vocabulary shows considerable borrowing from the French. According to the latest estimates there seem to be 11 vowel sounds and some 26 consonantal sounds. One of the marked features of Portuguese as compared with other Romance languages is the loss of the intervocal l and n, thus quaes represents the Latin quales and pessoa the Latin persona. An interesting phenomenon of Portuguese is the appearance of a personal or inflected infinitive, which makes possible a very succinct construction comparable to the Latin accusative and infinitive.

Q. How many people speak the Celtic languages? T. C. M.

A. They are spoken by about 3,-500,000 people.

Q. What is the official language of the Belgian Congo? E. R.

A. The official language is French.

Q. What is Volapuk? D C. D.

A. Volapuk was a proposed universal language and was invented about 1879 by Johann Martin Schleyer of Constance, Germany. The name means "world speech." Volapuk was received with great favor immediately after the scheme was published, but later declined.

Q. How many words should be acquired in a scholastic year of study of a foreign language? K. M. J.

A. One college informs us that it considers one thousand words a fair vocabulary for each year of the foreign language instruction. Most of the first year books contain a vocabulary of about one thousand to twelve hundred words.

Q. *In what positions is command of a foreign language a prime vocational asset?* G. S.

A. The American Foreign Service, service with a foreign government, interpreterships, journalistic work with foreign-language papers, employment as nursery governess, and translator. This last is extremely monotonous and underpaid. The highest salaries in the vocation go to technical translators of scientific material.

Q. *On which syllable are words in Esperanto accented?* W. B.

A. In the plan followed in building words in Esperanto, the accent was placed always on the syllable next to the last.

Q. *Is there a difference between ecclesiastical Latin and classical Latin?* V. B.

A. Ecclesiastical Latin differs from classical Latin in various ways, these changes being due principally to the origin and derivation of ecclesiastical Latin. Originally the Romans spoke the old tongue of Latium known as the prisca latinitas. In the 3rd century B.C., Ennius and a few other writers trained in the schools of the Greeks, made certain changes and encouraged by the cultured classes thus developed the classical Latin. The mass of the Roman people, however, continued to speak the old tongue and after the 3rd century there were two separate idioms. The necessary contact between the two classes produced still a third. When the church developed a Latin it was necessary to employ a language which would appeal to the masses as well as to the literary class, hence some of the factors of each idiom were used.

Q. *Why do some languages die out?* P. T. B.

A. The death of a language is caused by the decadence of the people using it. Conquest and settlement by other peoples often change languages considerably or obliterate them.

Q. *What is meant by the Gaeltacht in the Irish Free State?* G. C. F.

A. The word Gaeltacht refers to a district in Ireland where the Gaelic language is spoken. This is a seaboard district on the south coast of Ireland and includes the counties of Donegal, Mayo, Galway, Kerry.

Q. *Who was considered the best Latin grammarian?* C. T.

A. Priscian was the most noted of Latin grammarians. He belongs to the early part of the sixth century, teaching Latin at Constantinople, probably at the Imperial Court, since he received a government salary.

Q. *Why is the Latin language preferred in medicine?* L. P. J.

A. Latin is used in medicine because of its unchangeableness; because it is an old language; and the most universal.

Q. *How many words are there in the Italian language?* A. F.

A. Italian dictionaries contain about 140,000 words. English dictionaries contain about 700,000.

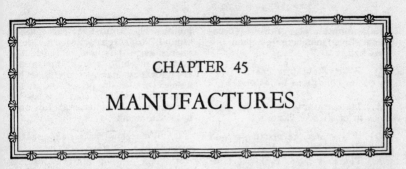

CHAPTER 45

MANUFACTURES

Q. *How long has iron been used?*
E. H.

A. An iron blade probably 5,000 years old has been found in one of the Egyptian pyramids. Since iron or steel implements rust away in time little evidence of early use remains, but the antiquity of iron smelting is very great.

Q. *Is Los Angeles a manufacturing center?* C. P.

A. The city of Los Angeles and environs have some 6000 factories.

Q. *Who introduced the broom into America?* S. P.

A. Records found in a diary in North Hadley, Massachusetts, show that Benjamin Franklin introduced the broom into America. The diary related that a woman acquaintance of Franklin sent him from India a whisk broom with broom corn seeds on the stalks. He planted the seed and passed the stalks among his friends, making round brooms by winding thread around several stalks.

Q. *What State ranks first in manufacturing?* N. H.

A. New York State ranks first of all the States in manufacturing, both as to number of wage earners and as to value of the product.

Q. *Where was the first shirt factory in the United States and who ran it?* M. C.

A. The first shirt factory of which there is a record was owned by David and Isaac N. Jordan, merchants in New York City. They frequently received from the South orders for shirts which they employed seamstresses to make. In 1832 they started a factory for making stock shirts. In 1840 another firm in New York City began manufacturing shirts, and in 1845 the first shirt factory was opened in Troy.

Q. *What is the leading industry in Ohio?* I. C.

A. The leading industry in Ohio is petroleum refining.

Q. *In what countries besides the U. S. are chocolate and confectionery manufactured on a large scale?* C. E.

A. These are manufactured on a large scale in nearly all of the British Dominions, Switzerland, Holland, Germany, France, and Belgium.

Q. *In what country did the meat packing industry originate?* L. C.

A. The packing industry originated in the United States many years ago when pork was packed in barrels for the West Indies.

Q. *Is there any manufacturing in the Philippine Islands?* O. D.

A. There are many sugar and rice mills. Manufactures also include candles, embroideries, pearl buttons, fibre textiles, cotton textiles, tailoring, luri mats.

Q. *For what is wood flour used?* W. R.

A. Among the products in which wood flour is used are imitation precious stones, lamp shades, eyeglass frames, fountain pens, furniture ornaments, toys, manicure sets, and billiard balls.

Q. *What State first enacted laws governing conditions in factories?* F. T.

A. Massachusetts was the first State to enact such laws.

Q. *Where was the first paper mill in the United States?* C. A.

A. The first paper mill was built in 1690 at Germantown, Pa.

Q. *From what year does the so-called factory system date in this country?* E. V.

A. It seems probable that until about the year 1850 the bulk of general manufacturing in the United States was carried on in the shop and in the household by the labor of the family or individual proprietors, with apprentice assistants, as contrasted with the present system of factory labor, compensated by wages and assisted by power. However the factory system was introduced into this country in the latter part of the 18th century. In 1789 Samuel Slater, who has been called "the father of American manufactures," set up in Pawtucket, Rhode Island, the first complete cotton machinery to operate in this country.

Q. *Where did the silk industry originate?* F. G.

A. The silk industry originated in China and has existed there from a very remote period.

Q. *Is much photographic apparatus manufactured in the United States?* D. F.

A. Estimates indicate that approximately $95,000,000 worth of photographic apparatus and supplies is manufactured in the United States annually.

Q. *What is kapok?* H. C. P.

A. Kapok is the down from the seed pods of the Randoe tree, grown chiefly in Java, but to some extent in Ceylon and the Philippine Islands. The United States imports around 700,000 tons per year. Due to its resilience it is used in the manufacture of pillows and mattresses. Its buoyancy makes it useful in the manufacture of life preservers. It has been found recently that it is an excellent insulating material for both heat and sound.

Q. *What country uses the greatest amount of silk?* H. S.

A. The United States consumes much more silk than any other country.

Q. *Name some of the by-products of the packing industry.* M. G.

A. A list of the principal by-products of the packing industry includes all kinds of leathers, artificial teeth, beef extract, buttons, candles, canned edible products formerly wasted, combs, crochet needles, dice, drum snares, fertilizer, gelatine, glue, glycerine, hair for brushes, handles for knives, handles for razors, hair for upholstering, hairpins, imitation stag horn, inedible grease, laundry soaps, musical strings, napkin rings, neatsfoot oil, nursing rings, oleomargarine, pancreatin, pepsin, perfume, pipestems, rennet, stock feeds, suprarenal—worth more than $4000 a pound—tennis strings, thyroid tablets, toilet soaps, umbrella handles, wool.

Q. *What is the meaning of cooperage?* E. B.

A. This is the trade of making casks of staves and hoops. Pliny ascribes the invention of cooperage to the inhabitants of the Alpine Valley.

Q. *From what is commercial salt manufactured?* H. F.

A. Commercial salt is mainly manufactured from natural brine and rock salt.

Q. *What sort of material was serge originally?* H. R.

A. The material originally designated by the name serge must have been silk. Before the 16th century it is mentioned chiefly as material for hangings, bed-covers and the like. Afterwards it often was used in reference to the clothing worn by the poorer classes.

Q. What is maizolith? M. N.

A. Maizolith is a name for artificial wood. It is derived from "stone made from corn."

Q. What are the longitudinal and transverse threads of fabric called? M. B.

A. The longitudinal threads are called warp, caine, twist and organzine. The transverse threads are called weft, shoot, woof, filling, and tram.

Q. Please name over ten most important industries. M. F. V.

A. According to the 1929 Census of Manufactures the industries ranked according to the value of products are as follows: Motor vehicles, meat packing (wholesale), steel works and rolling mills, foundry and machine shop products, printing and publishing, petroleum refining, electrical machinery, clothing (women's, not elsewhere classified), motor vehicle bodies and parts, bread and other bakery products.

Q. When was glass first manufactured? S. R.

A. It cannot be said with any certainty where glass was invented. It probably originated in Egypt.

Q. When did the manufacture of artificial silk begin? S. H.

A. The development of artificial silk on an extensive industrial scale began with the discovery of viscose by C. F. Cross and E. J. Bevan in 1892 and certain inventions developed in 1900. By 1910 viscose had made a strong start with 20% of the world's output.

Q. When were artificial pearls first made? O. E.

A. Fine artificial pearls were first made in western Europe in 1680 by Jacquin, a rosary-maker in Paris.

Q. What city ranks first in the manufacture of iron and steel products in the United States? H. Y.

A. Pittsburgh.

Q. Why is tweed so called? R. M.

A. Published statements concerning the origin of the word are not in accord. It seems probable that tweed is a trade name originating in an accidental misreading of tweel (a form of twill) helped by association with the river Tweed.

Q. When did the manufacture of silverware begin in the United States? C. H.

A. Silverware manufacture in the United States dates from 1842.

Q. Is there an artificial corundum? A. O.

A. Artificial corundum is known by various trade names such as alundum, aloxite, lionite, borolon and oxaluma.

Q. What does chiffon mean? B. N.

A. The term chiffon has a different meaning in different countries. In France it means a rag; in Roumania, a bleached cotton shirting; in Germany and Austria, a stout fine plain woven linen fabric with a smooth tissue; in the United States, a delicate, gauzelike silk tissue.

Q. What is the principle involved in the manufacture of Axminster rugs? C. S.

A. The Axminster principle involves the use of a wide loom which produces mechanically a fabric in which the tufts are tied with a Ghiordes knot, exactly as in Oriental hand-looms.

Q. How much fuel and power is used in manufacturing? L. C.

A. American manufacturing industries spent $1,498,228,952 for fuels of all kinds in 1929, a special report of the Census of Manufactures shows. In addition, manufacturing industries spent, in 1929, $475,634,377 for kilowatt hours of electric energy generated outside their own plants, principally in public-service power plants. A large part of this energy was generated by the consumption of fuel in public-service power plants, but neither the quantity nor the cost of this fuel is covered by these figures.

Q. What is the origin of satin? A. T.

A. Hirth suggests that the Arabs may have confused the name of Zaitun, a city in China with the Cantonese sze-tun.

Q. Who was the first manufacturer of jewelry in the United States? D. F.

A. Epaphras Hinsdale of Newark, N. J., is believed to be the first regular manufacturer of American jewelry. This was about 1790.

Q. Please name some of the products manufactured of wood. S. C.

A. Smokeless powder, oils, insulating materials, rayon, cellophane, dye-stuffs, soap.

Q. Why is Birmingham, Alabama, such an important industrial city? R. G.

A. The industrial development of Birmingham is based on immense mineral deposits. All the materials needed for making steel are found in close proximity. Pig iron and steel are the leading products although 2000 different commodities are produced in the Birmingham district.

Q. Is there any manufacturing in Arkansas? S. D.

A. The United States Census of Manufactures, 1929, reported 1,731 establishments and products valued at $208,897,033. The leading industry is the manufacture of lumber and timber products, including furniture.

Q. Where are the principal furniture manufacturing centers in the United States? A. F.

A. Chicago, Ill., New York City, N. Y., Grand Rapids, Mich., Rockford, Ill., Jamestown, N. Y., High Point, N. C.

Q. Where did the art of Batik originate? S. C.

A. Some believe that it originated in China and others believe that it is an outgrowth of methods employed many centuries in India.

Q. Is there any petroleum refining in Louisiana? M. Y.

A. The leading industries of Louisiana are petroleum refining, sugar refining, and lumber and planing mills.

Q. When did hosiery become a factory product in the United States? R. B.

A. Although a stocking loom had been imported into Pennsylvania by John Camm about 1723 and several others were introduced during the Revolutionary War, the business did not expand rapidly until 1831 when the power loom came into use.

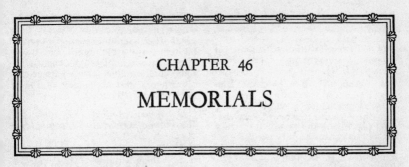

CHAPTER 46

MEMORIALS

Q. What memorial has the most wreaths placed upon it? G. L. L.

A. It is believed that the Tomb of the Unknown Soldier in Arlington Cemetery has been decorated more often than any monument or memorial, taking into consideration the length of time it has been built. Scarcely a day passes that a wreath is not placed upon the tomb, and often two or three are laid there upon the same day.

Q. How long is it believed that the statues of our nation's heroes which are being carved in the Black Hills will last? N. W.

A. It is estimated that the memorial will endure 500,000 years.

Q. Please give the dimensions of the Lincoln statue in the Lincoln Memorial. J. C.

A. The dimensions of the Daniel Chester French statue of Abraham Lincoln in the Lincoln Memorial are as follows: It is a seated figure upon an oblong pedestal about 10 feet high, 17 feet from front to back, by 16 feet wide. The plinth between the pedestal and the bottom of the seat is 1 foot 7 inches thick. The statue is 19 feet high from the top of the plinth to the top of the head. The extreme width of the statue, including the drapery over the chair, is 19 feet.

Q. Where is the Portal of Peace? A. L. H.

A. The Portal of Peace is a massive concrete structure in the form of a gateway. It is located at Blaine, Washington, and was dedicated September 5, 1921, in honor of the peace between the United States and Canada, which had lasted for more than 100 years without a break. The memorial, which cost $40,000 stands 100 yards from the international boundary where the 49th parallel meets Boundary Bay.

Q. Where is the tombstone statue of Nancy Hanks, the great trotter? E. L.

A. It is in John E. Madden's graveyard near Lexington, Ky.

Q. Please tell something about the Buckingham Fountain in Chicago. A. L. D.

A. This fountain in Grant Park was given to the city by Kate Buckingham in memory of her brother. Built at a cost of about $750,000, it is said to be the most beautiful and spectacular fountain in this country.

Q. Has any country other than France a perpetual flame to honor its World War dead? B. M. M.

A. Roumania has a perpetual flame in Bucharest and Belgium has one in Brussels.

Q. What was done with Carrie Nation's famous hatchet? N. A.

A. After her death Mrs. Nation's portrait and a hatchet which the police had taken from her, were placed in the archives of the Kansas State Historical Society at Topeka, and a memorial fountain was erected on the spot where she was first arrested in Topeka.

Q. *Upon what kind of rock is the Mount Rushmore Memorial being carved?* B. H.

A. Mount Rushmore in the Harney Range, is the loftiest elevation of solid granite between the Rockies and the Atlantic Seaboard. It rises 7000 feet above sea level.

Q. *Where is the building which is a memorial to women of the World War?* C. M. G.

A. The memorial building in Washington, D. C., which commemorates the services and sacrifices of women in the World War adjoins the Red Cross memorial to the women of the Civil War. The new structure is a handsome marble building.

Q. *What is the memorial to John Burroughs in the garden of Henry Ford?* S. L.

A. The memorial to the late naturalist at Fair Lane, the Ford country home near Dearborn, is in the form of a rockery. Rocks from Mr. Burroughs' boyhood home were brought for this purpose and there is a statue of him in the garden.

Q. *Please describe the tablet which has been erected to Walt Whitman in Brooklyn?* E. C.

A. It was erected by the Authors Club at the corner of Fulton and Cranberry Streets, Brooklyn, where the first edition of "Leaves of Grass" was published in 1855. Its central figure is an idealized head of the poet, with flowing hair and beard. Surrounding it are symbolic representations of four of Whitman's poems, "Old Ireland," "O Captain, My Captain," "Passage to India," and "Democracy."

Q. *Please describe the Harding Memorial.* J. T. S.

A. It is said that the $800,000 Harding Memorial at Marion, Ohio, is among the finest of its kind in the world. It is a circular building 102 feet in diameter and 57 feet high,

set in a ten-acre landscaped park. There is no roof, but twenty-four great doric columns, each containing 53 tons of marble, mark the outer circumference. Twenty-two fluted ionic columns constitute an inner circle, wherein rest the bodies of President and Mrs. Harding.

Q. *Who provided the funds for the Titanic Memorial in Washington?* T. D.

A. Twenty-five thousand American women furnished the funds as a memorial to the men who gave their lives that women and children might be saved.

Q. *Of what material is the Washington Masonic Memorial at Alexandria, Virginia, made?* H. N.

A. The exterior is of Conway pink granite from New Hampshire, the hardest granite known to the building trade.

Q. *Please describe the Columbia War Memorial dedicated on Armistice Day, 1931, in Potomac Park, Washington, D. C.* P. T.

A. Its height is approximately 45 feet; diameter 45 feet. Height of columns, 22 feet; diameter of columns, 4 feet. Vermont marble was used in the construction. The floor is composed of white Vermont marble and pink Tennessee marble. The approximate cost was $137,000 exclusive of the landscaping.

Q. *Is the Arc de Triomphe in Paris the largest triumphal arch in the world?* L. L.

A. It is. This arch is 147 feet high and 149 feet wide.

Q. *Does a sculptor actually cut a marble statue himself?* C. R. H.

A. A sculptor executes a model; an artisan called a stone-cutter is usually the one to reproduce this model in marble. Except for a few finishing touches, the sculptor does not touch the marble reproduction of his model. For example, the stone-cutters who are famous as the Piccirilli Brothers actually carved the figure of Lincoln by Daniel Chester French which is in the Lincoln Memorial. It is true that certain of these brothers are so fine that they are above the artisan class and are among the well known sculptors of the modern American school.

Q. How many acres are there in the Nancy Hanks Lincoln Memorial where her grave is located? S. C.

A. There are 85 acres in the tract set apart at Lincoln City, Spencer County, Indiana, in memory of the mother of Abraham Lincoln.

Q. If the figures being carved on Mount Rushmore were full length, how tall would they be? P. M. H.

A. Senator Norbeck, in speaking of the memorial, said that each figure of the group scales to the proportion of men 465 feet high, fading into the ledge at the waistline, the tops of the heads being upon the skyline.

Q. Has a light been erected in Detroit in honor of Thomas Edison? P. B.

A. An illuminated fountain to the honor of Thomas A. Edison has been erected in Grand Circus Park, Detroit.

Q. Who made the statue which Americans gave to France as a memorial to the Battle of the Marne? E. J.

A. The colossal statue was sculptured by Frederick William Mac-Monnies. It is called France Defiant and is near Meaux.

Q. Where is the largest war memorial in the world? S. M. C.

A. It is said to be the one unveiled in 1932 at Thiepval, France. The monument bears the names of 73,413 British soldiers whose last resting place is not known. The dead, in whose memory the monument was built, fell in the battles of Thiepval, Beaumont-Hamel, Courcelette, Authuille, Aveluy, Grandcourt, and Pozieres, in 1916. Just behind the memorial is a new cemetery in which are buried 300 British and 300 French soldiers, symbolizing the comradeship in arms of the two nations.

Q. Has Hawaii a memorial to the song Aloha Oe? H. R.

A. On September 16, 1929 a bronze memorial plaque with the words and music of Aloha Oe was dedicated in Hawaii. The plaque bears a likeness of the late Queen Liliuokalani, last ruler of the Hawaiians, who wrote the song fifty years ago. The ceremony took place on the 67th anniversary of the marriage of Liliuokalani to Governor John Owen Dominis. Henri Berger, then 85 years old, the organizer of the Royal Hawaiian Band and the music master who wrote the score for Aloha Oe and many Hawaiian melodies, participated in the dedication.

Q. Have the Mexicans created a memorial to the late Dwight Whitney Morrow? H. F.

A. A group of his Mexican friends presented to the United States Embassy in Mexico City a bronze tablet in memory of this former American Ambassador to Mexico who brought about an increased understanding and good will between the two countries. The tablet has been affixed to the chancery wall facing the Embassy.

Q. How tall is Bunker Hill Monument? B. E. A.

A. Its height is 221 feet.

Q. To whose memory has a tablet been placed at Culebra Cut? M. S.

A. Gaillard Cut which was formerly known as Culebra Cut was named after Lt. Col. David Dubose Gaillard, Corps of Engineers, U. S. A., who was the Engineer in charge of the work at that section of the Panama Canal. A bronze tablet dedicated to his memory was unveiled on February 4th, 1928, at a prominent place on the rock face of Contractors' Hill (formerly called Culebra Hill), 103 feet above the normal surface of the Canal at that point. The tablet was provided by Mrs. David Dubose Gaillard and family and the Third U. S. Volunteer Engineers Memorial Association composed of members of the regiment commanded by Lt. Col. Gaillard during the Spanish War.

Q. Who designed the "Flambeau de la paix," erected at Neuville-Saint-Vaast? D. H. A.

A. The sculptor, Yrondy. From a pile of rocks emerges a forearm and hand. The wrist bears the familiar identification disc and chain. In the hand is a conventionalized torch.

Q. Please give some information in regard to the memorial arch to the war correspondents in the Civil War. C. A. F.

A. The War Correspondents' Arch was erected by Mr. George Alfred Townsend on his mountain estate, Gapland, Maryland, in 1896. The inscription reads: "To the Army Correspondents and Artists, 1861–65, whose toils cheered the camps, thrilled the fireside, educated the provinces of rustics into a bright nation of readers, and gave incentive to narrate distant wars and explore dark lands. Erected by subscription 1896."

Q. Who designed the tombstone erected at the grave of President Wilson's first wife? W. J. G.

A. The beautiful memorial to Ellen Axson Wilson was designed by the American sculptor, Herbert Adams.

Q. Please give some information regarding the Morgan Memorial. M. W.

A. The Morgan Memorial is located in Boston, Massachusetts. Unique as an institution, Morgan Memorial is unique also in its inception. It was born in the mind and heart of one who was noted at once for his eccentricity of character and his devotion to humanity. It was in the early sixties that Henry Morgan launched the enterprise which today bears his name. He was known as an independent Methodist Episcopalian, which means that he was not taking regular appointments at the hands of the Episcopal authorities, but worked where he pleased and under such conditions as he desired. A free lance he preached wherever he deemed wise, and here in the south end of Boston he found his chief field of operation. Many years have elapsed since then and Morgan Chapel has become Morgan Memorial and the work has expanded from a religious service until it covers practically the whole wide range of modern social activities.

Q. To whom was the Lion of Lucerne erected as a monument? H. G. R.

A. The model for the Lion of Lucerne was executed by Thorwaldsen. The lion is carved out of the side of a grotto. The memorial commemorates the defense of the Tuileries in Paris, August 10, 1792, by the Swiss guards. All were massacred by the mob.

Q. What is the design of the memorial window to President Roosevelt at Oyster Bay? H. T. S.

A. The window in the Masonic Temple, of which President Roosevelt was master, depicts a knight in full armor with sword sheathed, standing before a tall castle. The symbolism is, Roosevelt prepared to defend his principles. The lower central panel has the Presidential eagles.

Q. Does Henry Bacon's face appear in a mural in the Lincoln Memorial? G. F. B.

A. The head of the architect, Mr. Bacon, appears in the decoration on the north wall in the fourth figure in the group at the left of the angel.

Q. In what form is the Walter Camp Memorial at Yale? C. D. N.

A. A massive gateway leading to the Yale Bowl and athletic fields is the memorial given by American colleges and schools, uniting with graduates of Yale, to honor Walter

Camp and the traditions of college sport which he exemplified.

Q. Who erected Perry's Victory Memorial? B. S.

A. This memorial at Put In Bay, Ohio, was erected by the United States Government and the States of Ohio, Pennsylvania, Michigan, Illinois, Wisconsin, New York, Rhode Island, Kentucky, and Massachusetts commemorating the Battle of Lake Erie, September 13, 1813. It is 352 feet high, and cost over a million dollars.

Q. Has Cornell University a memorial to her War dead? A. N.

A. Cornell University has erected a War memorial to the 264 Cornell men who lost their lives in the World War. It commemorates also the active military service of 9000 former students. The memorial is in the form of two towers, one for men who served in the Army and one for those who served in the Navy. There is a connecting cloister in which are carved the names of the dead. The towers are flanked by two buildings which are residential halls for men.

Q. Of what material is the Lincoln Memorial near Hodgenville, Ky., built? M. K.

A. It is built of Stoney Creek, Connecticut, granite.

Q. What is the cost, date of erection, and dimensions of the Arch at Valley Forge, Pa.? L. M. L.

A. The so-called National Arch at Valley Forge was authorized by an Act of Congress June 25, 1910. One hundred thousand dollars was appropriated and it was stipulated that the Arch must be completed by November, 1913. It is 60 feet 9 inches high, 50 feet wide, and 19 feet thick. The archway itself is 21 feet wide and 32 feet 9 inches high.

Q. Where is the Westinghouse Memorial? Please describe it. A. C.

A. The memorial to George Westinghouse, inventor, is in Schenley Park, Pittsburgh. The main unit of the memorial, a bronze statue, was created by Daniel Chester French. It rises twenty feet from a Norwegian granite base and depicts a figure of the subject. At his side are two figures, representing a skilled workman and an engineer. Facing this group, is the figure of an American youth studying the achievements. The setting for the memorial was designed by Henry Hornbostel of Pittsburgh. The Piccirilli brothers of New York constructed the models of the units for casting. The six panels, portraying the achievements of Mr. Westinghouse, were designed by Paul Fjeldi. Subscriptions of employees of the Westinghouse industries in the United States and Canada made the memorial possible.

Q. What prompted the people of Charleston, S. C., to erect a statue to William Pitt, Earl of Chatham, during the Revolutionary War? E. A. S.

A. Chatham, although a member of the British House of Lords, was friendly to the American cause. Charlestonians were especially fired by a sentence in one of his speeches saying: "If I were an American as I am an Englishman, while a foreign troop was landed in my country I never would lay down my arms—never, never, never!"

Q. Please describe the monument to the Wright Brothers at Kitty Hawk, N. C. M. M.

A. It is a magnificent triangular granite shaft sixty feet high surmounted by an airways beacon. It will serve as an aid both to aerial and marine navigation. It was dedicated November 19, 1932, twenty-nine years after the Wright Brothers made the first flight in the history of the world in which a machine carrying a man raised itself by its own power into the air in free flight. The monument is but a short distance from the site of the first white settlement in the United States.

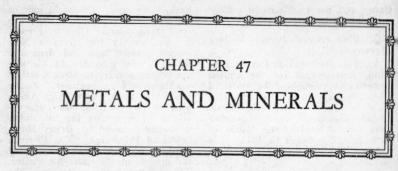

CHAPTER 47

METALS AND MINERALS

Q. What is the most abundant metal yielded by the earth's crust? T. A.

A. Aluminum. Although not discovered as a separate metal until 1824, science has since determined that there is more aluminum than any other metal.

Q. What are the most precious stones? A. Y.

A. The Bureau of Mines states that the ruby, emerald, diamond, and sapphire are the most precious stones.

Q. What was the first American city to have gas? F. A. M.

A. Baltimore, Md., in 1816.

Q. Are there at present any burning coal mines? L. M. B.

A. There are many burning coal mines. The most famous is the Anthracite Mine at Summit Hill, Pennsylvania, which has been burning since 1860. A coal deposit near Brownsville, Pennsylvania, is said to have been burning since before the Civil War.

Q. Why won't asbestos burn? S. G.

A. It is a mineral, and like most minerals, is noncombustible.

Q. How were the South African diamond fields discovered? E. C.

A. The South African diamond fields were discovered near Kimberly in 1866, when a child picked up a stone weighing 21¼ carats, which was sold in the rough for $2500. In 1868, a Hottentot negro found a diamond

of 83½ carats. He sold it for $2000 to a dealer who got $56,000 for it. The stone has been valued since at $125,000 and is the famous Star of South Africa.

Q. What is the difference between a synthetic and an imitation stone? D. K. M.

A. A synthetic stone has the same chemical composition as the natural jewel, but is made by man instead of by nature. An imitation stone has much the same appearance as the true gem, but is of an entirely different composition.

Q. Please give the comparative explosive power of a pound of gun powder and a pound of nitroglycerine. L. P.

A. The Bureau of Mines says that nitroglycerine has eight times the explosive power of gun powder in the comparison mentioned.

Q. How many kinds of rays does radium give off? N. H.

A. Radium gives off three kinds of rays: Alpha rays, or rapidly moving atoms of helium; beta rays, the atoms of electricity; and gamma rays, similar to X-rays.

Q. How many bushels of corn does it take to give as much heat as a ton of coal? J. B.

A. The Bureau of Mines says that shelled corn has a heating value of approximately 6000 B. T. U.'s per pound as compared with 13,000 B. T. U.'s in a pound of coal. At this rate it would take between 60 and 65 bushels of corn to equal one ton of coal.

Q. *Who was the first man to discharge an explosive located at a distance, by an electric current sent over a wire?* P. S.

A. Benjamin Franklin.

Q. *What is a rose-cut diamond?* D. H. S.

A. It is one which is quite flat underneath, with its upper part cut into 12 or more facets, usually triangles, the uppermost of which terminates in a point.

Q. *If diamonds and coal are both carbon, what is the difference between them?* T. S.

A. Coal is impure carbon. A diamond is pure carbon, crystallized. That is, the diamond has its carbon atoms arranged in a definite form and rigidly fixed in that position.

Q. *Can gas stoves be used in rural districts where gas is not piped?* A. W. S.

A. Artificial gas is being sold to persons outside the reach of city gas mains and has proved very successful. It is delivered in large containers.

Q. *How many gold mines are there in the United States?* S. T.

A. There are nearly 3500 non-ferrous mines at the present, and of these 2134 are principally gold producers.

Q. *When was helium discovered?* H. P. T.

A. It was first discovered in the sun's atmosphere in 1868 by Jansen and Lockyer. It was discovered on the earth in 1895.

Q. *What people first made tools of iron?* F. A. H.

A. It is thought by archaeologists that the Assyrians were the first people to use iron freely in the manufacture of tools and weapons. They had knives and saws of hardened steel. The art of hardening and tempering steel was a familiar one in Homer's time.

Q. *Why is kerosene so called?* H. B.

A. The name is from the Greek word, Keros, meaning wax. It was formerly obtained from the distillation of mineral wax.

Q. *Where is tin found in the United States?* L. P.

A. Alaska is the only portion of the United States in which tin is found.

Q. *What material is used in polishing diamonds?* E. T.

A. Diamond powder is used. This is obtained from the diamond cutting process and by crushing inferior diamonds. The diamond powder is applied with oil.

Q. *What is the symbolism of the various precious and semi-precious stones?* K. S. K.

A. One list gives the following: Garnet, credited with endowing the wearer with constancy and fidelity; amethyst, betokens sincerity; bloodstone or aquamarine, courage and truthfulness; diamond, innocence; emerald, happiness; pearl or moonstone, health and long life; ruby, a contented mind; sardonyx or peridot, felicity; sapphire, wisdom; opal or tourmaline, hope; topaz, fidelity; turquoise or lapis lazuli, prosperity and success.

Q. *What minerals are more valuable than gold?* W. S. H.

A. Beryllium, platinum, radium, palladium, osmium, iridium, and vanadium are more valuable than gold.

Q. *What are quicksands?* W. S.

A. Quicksands usually occur on flat shores underlain by stiff clay or other impervious materials. They appear to be formed by the continued collection of water within the sand bank which is prevented from running off by the underlying impervious layer. The grains of quick-sand have rounded surfaces. Quick-sand is of very light weight. The infiltrated water separates and lubricates the particles, rendering them unable to support heavy weight.

Q. *Is all steel made from iron ore?* J. S.

A. The Bureau of Standards says that it is. Steel is made from pig iron by first burning out the impurities and then adding known amounts of other elements, such as carbon. There are many varieties of steel, each having different characteristics, as for instance, high tensile strength, elasticity, extreme hardness, etc.

Q. *When was radium discovered?* J. E. S.

A. Radium was first obtained from pitchblends by Monsieur and Madame Curie and Monsieur Bemont in 1898.

Q. *What gases have the greatest lifting power?* P. C.

A. Helium and hydrogen. Hydrogen is more powerful, although helium is the more satisfactory as it is inflammable and inert. Helium will lift 0.066 pounds per cubic foot under ordinary conditions, while hydrogen will lift 0.071 pounds per cubic foot.

Q. *Has aluminum been used for clothing?* B. O. N.

A. Aluminum brocades have been put upon the market in some places. They are woven of fine aluminum threads. The metal has been neutralized and has been made capable of stretching through layers of cellulose superimpressed upon it. Thin aluminum is also much used for the outside covering of shoes, pocketbooks, and vanity bags.

Q. *How large a nugget of gold has been found?* W. D. P.

A. The largest recorded piece of gold ever found was a nugget called the Welcome Nugget taken from the Bakery Hill, Ballarat, Victoria, Australia, on June 11, 1858, at a depth of 180 feet from the surface. It weighed 2195 troy ounces and was also one of the purest ever recorded, being 99 per cent pure.

Q. *When was iron first discovered in what now is United States territory? When and where was the first foundry established?* P. B.

A. Sir Walter Raleigh, searching for gold, discovered iron ore in what now is North Carolina in 1585. The first iron works was established at Falling Creek, near Richmond, Va., in 1619, by the Virginia Company. Indian troubles resulted in early suspension of operations. The first successful and permanent iron works was established near Lynn, Mass., in 1643. John Winthrop, son of the famous Massachusetts Governor, was the builder of the works.

Q. *How much does a cubic foot of solid gold weigh?* T. R.

A. Pure gold weighs 1204 pounds per cubic foot.

Q. *What causes oil to flow from wells after the wells are drilled?* W. D. P.

A. Gas pressure forces the oil upward. When the gas in a well is exhausted, the oil ceases to flow. It is estimated that only one-fifth of the oil in a pool is thus forced to the surface. Lately, oil companies have learned to capture the gas and pump it back into the oil pool, where the pressure is restored.

Q. *When were diamonds discovered in Arkansas?* J. W. M.

A. Diamonds were discovered in Murfreesboro, Pike County, Arkansas, in 1906, and over 10,000 have been found.

Q. *Are fairy stones actually found, or are they manufactured in the cross form?* J. W. R.

A. They are found in cross form in their natural state. The stones are a mineral hydrated iron-aluminum silicate in the orthorhombic system. They have a subvitreous to resinous lustre and are brown or black in color. The crystalline varieties are frequently cruciform, owing to twinning. The proper name for such stone is saurolite, which is a combination of two Greek words meaning cross and stone.

Q. Has anything ever been discovered to do away with carbon monoxide gas? M. P.

A. It has been stated that Dr. J. C. W. Frazer of Johns Hopkins University has announced the discovery of a catalyst that will convert carbon monoxide gas passing over it to harmless carbon dioxide. The efficacy of this catalyst is said to have been demonstrated under a variety of driving conditions and in confined spaces, the equivalent of closed garages.

Q. What are the chemical properties of duralumin? B. C.

A. The chemical properties of duralumin are copper, 3.5 to 4.5 per cent; manganese, 0.4 to 1 per cent; magnesium, 0.2 to 0.75 per cent; aluminum, 92 per cent, minimum.

Q. What is the composition of pewter? J. H.

A Pewter is composed of tin and lead, with an alloy of brass or copper which gives, particularly to old pewter, a mellow glow. The usual mixture is 6 to 4 parts tin to 1 of lead and an old formula was 30 parts of brass to 1000 parts of tin. A hardening process has been discovered which is a trade secret which is apparently able to overcome the softness of pewter which was one of the great causes of its decline in the making of utensils.

Q. Please give a short history of the oil burner. A. J. G.

A. Oil has been used for fuel and for heating from a very early period, but the mechanical development of the oil burner dates from the middle of the 19th century, its widespread use in the United States from about the year 1922. Public interest was attracted to the possibility of oil burning with a very considerable increase in the oil production of California and Texas about 1900. Small burners were soon produced and larger ones for power and heat. The first attempts at commercial oil burning were crude. They were followed by natural-draught vaporizing burners and a later development was the mechanical-draught automatic burner, the foundation of the modern domestic oil heating industry.

Q. What is the weight of the largest nugget of gold found in California? C. K.

A. The National Museum has a record showing that the largest gold nugget found in California was found in the Monumental Mine in Sierra County and weighed 1596 troy ounces.

Q. What minerals are included in the scale of hardness? W. K.

A. The hardness of a solid substance may be measured by its capacity for scratching, or being scratched by other substances. The well-known minerals included in the standard comparative scale of hardness are talc, gypsum, calcite, fluorite, apatite, feldspar, quartz, topaz, sapphire, diamond. For scientific work, more exact methods are used.

Q. What was the first house illuminated by gas? B. R. F.

A. The home of William Murdock in Redruth, England.

Q. Is the radium used in the treatment of cancer and that used in the making of watch dials the same? H. G.

A. Radium used in the treatment of cancer is the same element that is employed in making luminous materials.

Q. What products are yielded by a barrel of crude oil? L. S.

A. The Bureau of Mines says that the average yield would be gasoline 26 per cent; kerosene 9 per cent; fuel and gas oil 48 per cent; miscellaneous oils 6 per cent; lubricating oils 4 per cent; losses 4 per cent; wax, coke, and asphalt 3 per cent.

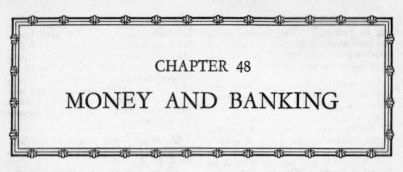

CHAPTER 48

MONEY AND BANKING

Q. When have tokens been issued because there was a shortage of small coins in the country? W. L.

A. At two periods since the nation began to coin money, there has arisen a stringency of small coins, which made it necessary for business firms to supply their wants by the issue of copper tokens redeemable in legal money by the firms which issued them. The first period to witness such an issue came in 1837, when many business houses had prepared for their use copper tokens of the size of the large copper cent. The types of these tokens then, as usually, were of two principal classes, the one strongly political with devices and inscriptions giving vivid expression to the partisan slogans of the day; while the other bore simply the advertisement of the merchant who issued them. Again, in 1863, the dearth of small coins gave rise to an enormous issue of such tokens, at that time again in the module of the current bronze one-cent piece.

Q. When is the term country bank used? V. G.

A. In classifying the national banks the Comptroller of the Currency designates as a country bank one which is not situated in a reserve city or a central reserve city.

Q. What is a compensated dollar? H. O'N.

A. The term compensated or stabilized dollar was coined by Prof. Irving Fisher of Yale in his book, Stabilizing the Dollar. It is a theoretical dollar having a constant purchasing power. The theory of the compensated dollar is to convert the present gold standard into a true commodity standard, that is, to standardize the dollar as a unit of purchasing power. Thus, there would be a gold dollar of constant purchasing power with varying weight instead of a gold dollar of standard weight and varying purchasing power.

Q. What is the total amount of money in circulation in the United States?

A. At the end of October, 1932, the total amount of money in circulation in this country was $5,627,-581,274. This amounted to a per capita circulation of $44.99.

Q. When was paper money first issued in this country? V. H.

A. Adopted as a matter of necessity, and not from choice, by Massachusetts Bay Colony in 1690, it was gradually issued by other colonies until in general use by all.

Q. Why is it said that the wealth of the country is controlled by women? W. L.

A. It was estimated that in 1931 more than 41 per cent of the individual wealth of the country was controlled by women. Out of ninety-five billion dollars of life insurance policies in force, in eighty out of every hundred cases the beneficiaries were women. Among some of the largest corporations women comprise more than one-half of the stockholders.

316

Q. *What is a cashier's check?* M. E. S.

A. It is a common form of exchange. It is a check upon a bank signed by its cashier. The cashier's check is a guarantee of the bank that the amount stated is in the bank and can be drawn out upon presentation of the check.

Q. *When did it become legal to charge interest for money lent in England?* A. A. T.

A. In the time of Henry VIII. Before this interest had been charged for generations, by legal fictions of partnership, breach of contract, etc. The first English permissive statutes fixed 10 per cent as the legal limit which could be charged.

Q. *How long has the weight and fineness of the gold coins of our country remained the same?* S. W. O.

A. The weight and fineness of the gold dollar unit has been continuous since established by law of January 18, 1837.

Q. *Is it illegal to date a check ahead?* J. W. T.

A. There is no law against it. If a check is given on March 15th and dated April 1st, the bank does not pay the check until April 1st. If on April 1st, there are no funds in the bank, the check is returned marked "No Funds."

Q. *Where is the gold reserve of France kept?* V. W. A.

A. Specially constructed vaults have been provided to house the gold reserve of France. These vaults are in a big chamber covering 2½ acres, 200 feet below the earth's surface. Above the ceiling is first 40 feet of water and then 50 feet of solid rock. This safety deposit has been built since the World War. A place was planned which would not only be safe from bombs but where the bank force guarding it would be safe from gas attack. A supply of fresh air is drawn into the vault chamber through a secret source. The fact

of the vaults being under water is explained as resulting from the flow of a river beneath the city of Paris. This was discovered when the Opera House was built just before the War of 1870.

Q. *What is commercial paper?* G. H. C.

A. Commercial paper is a general name for checks, drafts, notes, bills of lading, bills of exchange, warehouse receipts, treasury warrants, orders for delivery of goods, certificates of stocks and bonds, etc., and is sometimes applied to contracts and agreements.

Q. *When were the first United States coins made?* D. J. W.

A. The first United States coin was made in 1793.

Q. *Who originated the Christmas Savings plan used in banks?* M. J. McD.

A. The first Christmas Club that operated in any banking institution in the United States was installed in the Carlisle Trust Company of Carlisle, Pennsylvania, by Mr. Merkle Landis, Treasurer of that company. Shortly thereafter an organization was formed with headquarters in Harrisburg, Pennsylvania, known as the Landis Christmas Savings Club Company, which was recently consolidated with the Christmas Club, National Bankservice Corporation.

Q. *Do banks accept gold coins as deposits on any different basis than they accept silver coins or paper currency?* M. T.

A. In the case of a small deposit a bank probably would accept, for instance, a $10 to $20 deposit in gold coin on the basis of the sum stamped on its face. In any considerable sum, however, the bank would weigh the gold coins. Gold wears off easily. If a $100 deposit in gold coin weighed a little light, credit on the bank book would be given for only $98 or $97 or whatever the subtraction through wear might show. This is not necessary in accepting deposits of silver or paper because the Government guarantees the value of these. Gold must stand on its own weight and fineness and, therefore, is the standard.

Q. When were the initials V.D.B. put on the Lincoln pennies? L. L. W.

A. The initials on the back of the 1909 one-cent piece are V.D.B. They are the initials of the designer, Victor D. Brenner. The first issue of these one-cent pieces carried the initials, but it was decided that the initials were too conspicuous and an order was issued not to place them on the new coins.

Q. Can a demand note be paid before the lender calls it? P. C.

A. A promissory note payable on presentation may be paid off at any time.

Q. What currency reform did Woodrow Wilson sponsor? E. W.

A. President Wilson sponsored the basic currency reform embodied in the Federal Reserve System. It became a law in December, 1913, and the 12 Federal Reserve Banks opened the following November.

Q. Since England is off the gold standard, have her gold coins the same value as they had? S. M.

A. They have unless they have lost weight through abrasion.

Q. When was the largest amount of per capita circulation of money in the United States? C. E. G.

A. The largest per capita circulation of money was in 1920, when the average per capita circulation for the year was $51.38. For the month of October, 1920, it was $53.21.

Q. Are standard silver dollars minted anywhere besides in the United States? S. T. M.

A. The Chinese Government Mint at Nanking has undertaken the minting of standard silver dollars bearing the Chinese superscription. All minting by provincial mints has been or-

dered suspended, the work being concentrated at Nanking. A modern mint has been established with American machinery under direction of experts from the United States.

Q. If paper money is kept in an air-tight container, will it disintegrate when exposed to the air? G. A.

A. It would not unless some deteriorative agent has been included within the container.

Q. Why is the $2.50 gold piece no longer made? S. W. L.

A. By Act of Congress passed April 11, 1930, the $2.50 gold piece was discontinued. The coin was discontinued because it was not desired for circulation or commercial purposes. It was used mainly as a gift during the Christmas season and in January these coins were again returned to the vaults of the bank.

Q. Why is a person who collects or studies coins called a numismatist? C. N.

A. The word has a Greek derivation, being composed of two words which mean current coin.

Q. Is it against the law to make metal money into jewelry? B. D.

A. There is no penalty attached to the destroying of coins of the United States. There is a penalty for mutilating coins and restoring them to circulation. The penalty depends upon the individual case.

Q. How can old coins be cleaned before being offered for sale? M. D. W.

A. A coin catalogue says that one should "never attempt to clean, polish, or improve a coin. Cleaning always detracts from the value and has been known to make a good coin practically worthless."

Q. Did Canada go off the gold standard when England did? W. E. S.

A. The change in the status of the British monetary system makes no difference to Canada's system because Canada still maintains the gold standard. The British unit is the pound; the Canadian unit the dollar. The Bank of England no longer is able to redeem pound notes at full face in gold; the Canadian Treasury so far has been able to redeem its dollar currency at par. Canada has a separate Government and a separate Treasury, a separate coinage and a separate currency, and a separate gold reserve.

Q. In counting our stock of gold, are sums being held here for other countries included? F. H.

A. Earmarked gold is gold held in one country or bank and marked as belonging to someone else. Foreign earmarked gold in this country is not counted in monetary stock.

Q. What rate of interest does a government bond pay? Where are such bonds bought? E. L. R.

A. Government bonds do not all pay the same amount of interest. At advertised times they are sold by the Treasury. During the period that subscription books are closed the purchase of United States Government bonds must be made in the open market, through any reliable bank, trust company, or reputable bond dealer, at the prevailing market price, which is quoted in the financial columns of papers which are published in the United States.

Q. What is meant by legal tender? K. M. B.

A. Legal tender is money which may be legally used in the payment of a debt and which the creditor must accept.

Q. At what date were gold quarters and half dollars coined? M. W. D.

A. No 25 cent or 50 cent gold pieces have ever been issued by the United States Government. Between 1830 and 1875 gold half dollars and quarter dollars were issued by private parties. These pieces never were legal tender, although they passed as currency at a time when there oc-

curred a shortage of coins with which to transact business. The issue of private gold coins never was sanctioned by the United States Government.

Q. Who first had a coinage system? E. C. C.

A. The cubes of gold employed by the Chinese may have been the earliest coins. Modern authorities, however, accept the view of Herodotus that gold and silver coins were first used by the Lydians about the 6th century B.C.

Q. Why should not money secured by land be used instead of money secured by gold? G. E.

A. The experience of history is that land values are not stable and could not constitute a standard. Land worth $1000 an acre in 1920 now is down to less than $100 in many cases. Gold is a standard which remains precisely the same.

Q. How much is saved by the use of the smaller size of paper money? G. M.

A. The estimates show that there is a saving of one-third in the cost of production. One-third less of the highly expensive and distinctive paper is required and one-third less ink, and the shipping weight is reduced by a third. A 50 per cent saving is effected in the actual printing process. Notes are printed in large sheets and afterwards cut into single notes. The old size bills were printed 8 to the sheet. The new size are made 12 to the sheet. What the lengthened life of the smaller notes will be, as the result of less folding, creasing, and cracking, must be determined by experience, but it is expected a substantial saving will result.

Q. For whom was The Chase National Bank named? R. J. T.

A. The Chase National Bank of the City of New York was organized on September 12, 1877, by John and Samuel Thompson, well known bankers of that period who also founded the First National Bank in 1863. The new bank, capitalized at $300,000, was named for Salmon P. Chase, Secretary of the Treasury under Lincoln, and opened on September 20, 1877, at 117 Broadway. Mr. Chase, himself, however, had no official connection with the Bank.

Q. *To settle a bet, please state whether in the stamping of coins, the metal is hot or cold. J. D. G.*

A. The office of the Director of the Mint says that the metal is cold at the time the coins are stamped.

Q. *May a bond be purchased direct from the Treasury? R. B.*

A. It can be only when the subscription books are open. The newspapers always publish a notice at such time. After the books at the Treasury close, bonds can be bought through local bankers and brokers, at the market price.

Q. *How large a box would it take to hold one million silver dollars? E. D.*

A. The Department of the Treasury says that 250 cubic feet are required to store one million silver dollars.

Q. *Why did the government discontinue the practice of laundering the paper money? E. McC.*

A. It was found that the process shortened the life of the money and dulled the engraving.

Q. *When was the silver dollar first coined? N. S.*

A. The coinage of the United States silver dollar was commenced in 1794.

Q. *Is a check drawn on the Treasury of the United States ever outlawed on account of date issued? K. B. M.*

A. The Department of the Treasury says that if a check drawn on the Treasury of the United States is not presented within three years after the date of issue, it is counted as an outstanding liability, and it is then necessary for the individual to send the claim to the Comptroller General of the United States, Treasury Department, Washington, D. C., who issues the check. The above information does not apply to interest checks.

Q. *How long has paper money been used? I. B.*

A. Paper money is believed to have originated in China. Marco Polo, the famous traveler, was the first to report in Europe the existence of paper money in China. It was subsequently introduced into Persia. It is recorded that as early as 119 B.C. there was introduced in China Phi-pi or "value in skins." These were small pieces of skin of deer, a Chinese square foot in size, whose price was fixed at a sum approximately equal to $5.

Q. *How much are $4000 in German marks worth? W. S. B.*

A. If they were issued by the old German Reichsbank, they have no value. The new Reichsmark is worth a little over 23 cents.

Q. *Are British consols similar to United States bonds? J. F.*

A. British consols are obligations of Great Britain just as United States bonds are obligations of the American Government.

Q. *Is a holder of a United States bond which is registered reimbursed if it is stolen? H. B. R.*

A. Registration protects the owner of a United States bond from loss or theft, and holders generally are urged, wherever practicable, to take advantage of the privilege of registration. In case of the loss or theft of a registered bond, unless assigned in blank or for exchange for coupon bonds without instructions restricting delivery, the Treasury Department will give relief to the owner in accordance with the provisions of paragraphs 83 to 85 of Department Circular No. 300. Holders of registered bonds receive interest checks drawn on the Treasurer of the United States in payment of interest as it falls due, and their names are all recorded on the books of the Treasury Department.

Q. *What has become of the banking house of Rothschild?* R. N.

A. It still flourishes. However, so many great joint stock company enterprises have arisen, doing vaster business, that the old personal firms are overshadowed. The Rothschilds have no counting house in the United States although they have correspondents. They operate largely in England and on the continent.

Q. *When was the first Morris Plan Bank established?* E. B. R.

A. The first Morris Plan Bank was established in Norfolk about 1910, and different Morris Plan Banks or companies have been organized at various times since until there are over one hundred Morris Plan Banks.

Q. *When was the Bank of England founded?* H. E. M.

A. It was established in 1694 to finance William and Mary.

Q. *Who founded the Mitsui Bank?* J. V. R.

A. The story of the family goes back more than 250 years. Takatoshi Mitsui conceived the plan which resulted in the great House of Mitsui. He inherited a pawn shop from his father. His ambition was to have an exchange house, but it was very difficult for an outsider to break into a business of this kind. He began, therefore, by opening a drapery shop in Honcho in 1670 and established a money exchange department. In less than ten years he had won a place among exchangers. In May, 1683, he opened an exchange house in Surugacho. In 1686 another one opened in Kyoto, and in 1691 one in Osaka. He provided that each exchange house should have a member of the Mitsui family at its head and each of these in turn should be succeeded by a member of the Mitsui family. In February, 1872, five young members of the Mitsui family were sent to the United States to learn the banking business. The following year the First National Bank in Japan was opened by Mitsui-Gumi and Ono-Gumi. In 1876 the Mitsuis established the first private bank in Japan.

Q. *In stock market parlance, what are "cats and dogs?"* N. E. S.

A. The term is applied to miscellaneous securities of a low speculative value.

Q. *What is meant by disagio?* B. D.

A. It is the discount charged for cashing foreign or depreciated currency. Also a discount upon a depreciated currency, and for abrasion in metallic currency.

Q. *Where is the World Bank?* F. H.

A. The Bank for International Settlements, also known as the World Bank, was organized as a result of the Paris Conferences for the purpose of supervising reparations payments, and also to serve as a joint agency for the central banks of the world and for the clearance of accounts among them as well as the establishment of a centralized management of their gold The headquarters of the bank is at Basle in Switzerland.

Q. *What is a coöperative bank?* T. W.

A. A coöperative bank is a bank in which the depositors are not paid interest on their deposits, but are given, in lieu of interest, a share in the profits of the bank.

Q. *How many bank failures have there been in this country since the Civil War?* R. D.

A. According to the Annual Report of the Comptroller of the Currency, the total number of bank suspensions in the United States since 1864 was 10,949. These failures include failures up to the end of the fiscal year 1931. During the calendar year 1931 and from January to

October, 1932, there was a total of 3,497 bank suspensions.

Q. *Is there a Federal law which prohibits the issuance of a check for less than one dollar? G. P.*

A. There is a Federal law stating that "no person shall make, issue, circulate, or pay out any note, check, memorandum, token, or other obligation for a less sum than one dollar, intended to circulate as money or to be received or used in lieu of lawful money of the United States and every person so offending shall be fined not more than $500 or imprisoned not more than six months, or both, at the discretion of the court." Many individuals and even the Government make checks for an amount less than one dollar, but they are not intended to circulate but are only intended to pay the amount of the check to the person the check is made payable to. A check is not lawful money and consequently cannot be passed as lawful money. A check is a personal credit instrument used in place of money.

Q. *Does a five dollar gold piece contain five dollars worth of gold? E. I. T.*

A. When it leaves the mint it contains exactly five dollars worth of gold. The value of the alloy is insignificant.

Q. *How many cubic feet are there in a stack composed of a million one dollar bills? F. McE.*

A. One million bills of the small size currency can be contained in 35 cubic feet when packed and wrapped by the Bureau of Engraving and Printing.

Q. *What is a bank call?*

A. It is the demand which the State Superintendent of Banks sends to all banks and trust companies at any time during each quarter of a year for sworn balance sheets showing their conditions on a given date. The Comptroller of the Currency issues the bank call for national banks.

Q. *What was the money called which was paid to a captor of a person captured on a vessel of war or a pirate? B. S.*

A. It was called head-and-gun money.

Q. *What is the world's newest monetary unit? W. W.*

A. The Union of South Africa which, heretofore, used the English currency system of pounds, shillings, and pence, has set up a new unit called the rand. In addition a silver double florin, a silver florin which divides into 100 bronze cents, 50 cent pieces of silver and silver 20 and 10-cent pieces as well as bronze coins worth 1, 2, and 4 South African cents are provided. The rand is a gold coin having a value equivalent to 10 florins or 2 British shillings or 50 cents in American money. A South African cent is worth half what an American cent is worth.

Q. *Is it possible to get coins made in specified years from the Department of the Treasury? G. R.*

A. It does not keep coins segregated according to years.

Q. *Why does the weight of paper money vary? A. H.*

A. The weight varies as much as five per cent due to several factors. The blank paper varies slightly in thickness and weight. Notes printed from new plates contain more ink than notes printed from worn plates. The moisture content, also, varies according to atmosphere.

Q. *What should a boy study who wants to be a banker? A. K.*

A. The American Institute of Banking states that a student who wishes to become a banker should follow a curriculum which includes economics, elementary and advanced banking, commercial law, negotiable instruments, and accounting.

Q. *What is knife money? C. B.*

A. It is a form of bronze currency long in use in China. Money knives were highly ornamented and bore characters on the blades indicating their value in the money market. The handles were usually in the form of a disk with a hole in the center so that the knives could be strung on a cord with other such money.

Q. *Please give complete list of United States mints. J. C. F.*

A. The mints of the United States are under control of a Bureau of the Mint at Washington, D. C., which was established in 1873, and is in charge of a Director of the Mint. The minting establishments of the United States, the marks by which their respective coins are distinguished, and also the dates of organization, and in some cases the dates of their suspension, are as follows: the Mint at Philadelphia, no mark, 1793; New Orleans, La., mint-mark O, 1838, suspended, 1861, reopened, 1879, closed, 1910; Charlotte, N. C., mint-mark C, for the coinage of gold only, 1838-1861; Dahlonega, Ga., mint-mark D, for the coinage of gold only, 1838-1861; San Francisco, mint-mark S, 1854; Carson City, Nev., mint-mark CC, 1870-June 30, 1893; Denver, Colo., mint-mark D, 1906.

Q. *How many Columbian half-dollars were made for the Chicago World's Fair? V. S.*

A. There were 4,052,105 made.

Q. *Why is money sometimes called lucre? H. I. J.*

A. It comes from the Latin lucrum, meaning gain.

Q. *Was Continental currency redeemed by the United States? N. L. G.*

A. The various issues of Continental currency were never redeemable by the United States as re-organized under the Constitution. By the Act of August 4, 1790, it was receivable at the Treasury in subscriptions to a loan at the rate of $100 in Continental money for $1.00 in specie. By the Act of March 3, 1797, it was declared that said money should be receivable as above until December 31, 1797, and no longer.

Q. *What was the goloid dollar? A. A. B.*

A. It was an experimental pattern—in fact there were two, one struck in 1878 and one in 1880. The proportional amalgam of the first goloid dollar was 16 1/10 grains of silver, 1 9/10 grains of copper, to one grain of gold. The second goloid dollar had proportionate 24 grains of silver to one of gold. The plan never had the sanction of Congress nor was it ever reported to that body.

Q. *What was Henry Ford's scheme for issuing paper money? L. B.*

A. When Henry Ford was seeking to buy the Muscle Shoals plant in Alabama from the Government, he suggested that the forty million dollars necessary to complete the dam could be issued in greenbacks based on the potential earnings of the plant. He stated at the time that the currency could and should be based on natural resources. The idea is not a new one. Fiat money has been tried out repeatedly.

Q. *What is the gold point? L. F.*

A. It is the point of difference in international trade balance affecting a foreign exchange. For example, when the bills one nation owes to the other get more than 11/64th of 1 per cent out of exact balance, gold must be shipped or one currency will go down and the other up. That point is the gold point.

Q. *Why was the trade dollar coined? When was it discontinued? G. B. B.*

A. Silver trade dollars were coined in response to a petition addressed to Congress by western trade bodies through the medium of the California Legislature, by which it was expected that this coin, because struck on the same standard as the Mexican dollar (420 grains 0.900 fine) which circulated freely in China and Japan, would assist their trade with the Orient. For four years following the enactment of this law, 1874–1877, no standard silver dollars were coined, but about 35,000,000 trade dollars were struck. The expected results from the trade dollar were not realized, and many of them went into circulation at home. In 1886 they were withdrawn from circulation and recoined into standard dollars.

Q. *Were the coinages of ancient Babylon, Greece and Rome gold or silver?* W. W. L.

A. The coins of the Babylonian Empire were both gold and silver. In Rome from 268 B.C. onward the sestertius was the unit of money. It was at first a small silver coin, but under the Empire a brass sestertius was issued. Silver was the standard coinage of ancient Greece. Gold was rarely coined in Greece proper, but it was largely minted by Alexander the Great and his immediate successors.

Q. *Why is English pound called sterling?* F. A. G.

A. The term, pound sterling, derives from an early English coin known as the esterling, which was introduced into British trades by the Esterlings or Saxons who came out of the East. It was a coin which was maintained at a steady, fixed content. It contained approximately a pound of silver, originally. The term might more properly be expressed as an Esterling pound.

Q. *What was used for payment in this country before we had a coinage?* E. A. H.

A. The product most extensively employed in the place of coined money was the tobacco of the southern colonies, especially of Virginia. For several years nearly all of the business of that colony, both domestic and foreign, was carried on by means of tobacco, until the enormous production of the plant made restriction on its use as money necessary. Powder and bullets were also used as money throughout the colonies, in some of which the legal tender of bullets in payment was limited to a small number. In Massachusetts, and among the New England colonies generally, grain, fish, and furs were in common use as means of exchange; and not only in the settlement of private debts but they were receivable for taxes as well. Wampum, which served the Indians in nearly all their business transactions, was early recognized in New England and valuations placed upon it from time to time by the General Court.

Q. *Which pays better dividends, preferred or common stock?* N. H. A.

A. Preferred stock pays a certain specified dividend which is assessed before common stock receives any dividend. For this reason it is a safer investment than common stock, but common stock often pays much higher dividends, since its value fluctuates with the earnings of the concern.

Q. *What is bimetallism?* A. M.

A. It is the concurrent use of two metals, usually gold and silver, as the legal monetary standard of a country at a fixed relative value, both metals being legal tender and being subject to free and unlimited coinage.

Q. *How may counterfeit bills be detected by the average person?* F. L.

A. The present issue of currency has distinctive fibers distributed across and near the ends of the note. This is one of the best tests of a genuine bill. No counterfeiter can put in silk threads to imitate the genuine bill. The paper of the counterfeit is always of inferior quality as the Government has the best and most perfect system of manufacturing the highest grade paper. The medallion, rulings, and circular ornaments on a genuine bill are mathematically correct and are made from a machine upon which $150,000 was spent in the production, and is, therefore, beyond the reach of counterfeiters. Engraving by hand can never imitate this work. It is said that the portraits on counterfeit bills are not as perfect as those on legal ones. The first thing to do in examining a suspected bill is to feel the paper. It should have a strong texture. Look to see whether the printing on the suspected bill is clean-cut. The seal on the bill should be clear and bright.

Q. *What does the term, cover, mean in connection with stock transactions?* N. J.

A. It is a word which is used when one is in the act of buying in a stock which had previously been sold short—in other words, a stock which had been sold with the hope that the market in that stock would subsequently decline and would thus afford an opportunity for its purchase at a lower price, with the difference between its sale and purchase price representing a profit on the transaction.

Q. *What does the brokers' term cleared mean?* E. M.

A. As used by brokers it means a stock which is paid for; that is, free from any debt such as brokers' fees, handling charges, etc.

Q. *Were Lincoln pennies made in 1922?* L. G. R.

A. Lincoln pennies were made in 1922 but only $71,600 worth.

Q. *What is the difference between the British pound and the guinea?* W. T. K.

A. The pound sterling is a unit of 20 shillings and the guinea of 21 shillings. There are no paper guineas. Both are in use and it is customary for a British tradesman to quote a price in guineas to a man known to be wealthy or of high position while quoting the same number of pounds as the price to a poorer and humbler purchaser. Thus the man who is charged 10 guineas for a purchase pays 210 shillings while he who is charged 10 pounds pays 200 shillings.

Q. *How long have the dimes been coined which have the fasces on the back?* N. W. C.

A. The design was adopted in 1916.

Q. *How long do depositors have to wait to recover their money or part of it after a bank fails?* C. M.

A. The Comptroller of the Currency says that statistics kept over a period of years show that an average period of five years and six months is required to liquidate failed banks. The shortest time is ten months.

Q. *How did the cost of the Civil War compare with that of the World War?* A. M. E.

A. The peak of the national debt, borrowed to wage the Civil War, was $2,238,954,794. The peak of the World War debt was $25,234,496,274. In neither case do the figures represent total cost as all the millions spent in Civil War pensions since 1865 and the millions in veteran relief since 1918 are part of the real cost. The respective debt peaks indicate the immediate cost.

Q. *What are Lombard loans?* A. T.

A. Loans which have a large element of speculation in them and which, for that reason, bear a higher than average rate of interest. The name comes from Lombard Street, the old Wall Street of London, where money lenders made such loans.

Q. *What was the amount of the Confederacy's first war loan?* D. R.

A. Even before Ft. Sumter was fired on, President Jefferson Davis of the Confederacy asked the Southern public to subscribe to a loan of $15,000,000. While war had not begun at the time it was regarded as inevitable.

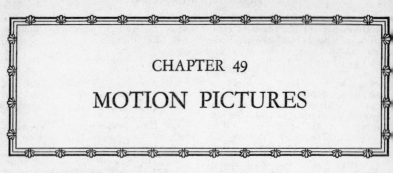

CHAPTER 49

MOTION PICTURES

Q. *Who was the first moving picture actor to be known widely by name?* H. P.

A. John Bunny was the first.

Q. *When was the first long motion picture shown in America?* H. S. B.

A. Queen Elizabeth, with Sarah Bernhardt in the title rôle, was the first four-reeler exhibited in this country. It had its initial showing in New York City, July 12, 1912.

Q. *How long have there been colored movies?* M. P.

A. The effort to produce colored films is as old as the industry. From time to time different processes have been introduced, and while none is considered perfect, several have met with approval. The commercial career of color dates back to 1909.

Q. *Who was the first person to pose for a motion picture under contract?* H. A. S.

A. It is believed that James J. Corbett, heavyweight champion of the world, was the first motion picture actor under contract. In the early days of the industry, it was recognized that action was the most important element needed to catch the popular interest.

Q. *Why are church weddings in movies always in Catholic or Episcopal churches?* T. F. B.

A. It is because the services of these two denominations make more effective pictures than would the services of some of the other denominations.

Q. *What was the first movie taken in Los Angeles?* G. P.

A. Monte Cristo, a Selig production starring Hobart Bosworth.

Q. *What was the first historical film made in the United States?* L. S. T.

A. Will Hays says the first historic films made were those of President McKinley's inauguration.

Q. *Please give some of the other names that motion pictures were called when they were first introduced.* B. S.

A. Some of the names were kineoptican, animatograph, cinematograph, nickelodeon, and biograph.

Q. *What is Marie Dressler's real name? Where was she born?* M. E. G.

A. Her name is Lelia Koerber. She was born in Cobourg, Ontario, Canada.

Q. *What was the first picture in which Mary Pickford appeared?* M. L.

A. Her first screen appearance was in "The Violin Maker of Cremona," filmed by the Biograph Company, and directed by D. W. Griffith.

Q. *Are there any talking pictures done in Yiddish?* R. C.

A. A complete Yiddish all-talking and singing picture program has been given in New York City. One and two reel pictures opened the program, which closed with the seven reel feature with a title the Yiddish equivalent of Eternal Fools.

Q. *Is Charlie Chaplin a Jew?* H. A.

A. The American Hebrew says that he is a Jew. It says: "A Jewish gamin in Whitechapel, both his parents having been 'stagers,' this sprig of humanity was in vaudeville at seven."

Q. *How is fog made in the movies?* R. B.

A. Vaporized mineral oil, blown through the air by large propellers, is used.

Q. *How many feature films are produced in the United States each year?* G. M.

A. About 600. From 2500 to 3000 short plays are also made annually.

Q. *What is the weekly world attendence of motion picture theatres?* S. L. L.

A. The Motion Picture Almanac for 1932 says that the approximate world attendance weekly is 185,000,-000 persons, and the approximate weekly attendance in the United States is from 65,000,000 to 90,000,-000 persons.

Q. *What salary does Marie Dressler get?* E. S. W.

A. Miss Dressler's salary is reported to be $5,000 per week and she is almost continuously engaged.

Q. *How many extras are on the rolls at Hollywood?* M. M.

A. Photoplay says that there are about 17,500 extras listed at Hollywood's Central Casting Bureau. Only 833 of them average one day's work per week during a year.

Q. *How much does it cost the motion picture producers to give the newcomers screen tests?* M. O. B.

A. Photoplay says that it costs Hollywood almost $1,000,000 a year.

One test averages about $300 and only one person in a thousand has made the grade on the screen.

Q. *What proportion of movie audiences is made up of children?* H. McL.

A. The average weekly attendance in motion picture theatres in 1931 was approximately 75,000,000. The juvenile attendance, that is, of children from 5 to 12 years, makes up less than 5 per cent of the total movie audiences.

Q. *What are the duties of a script clerk in the motion picture industry?* O. P.

A. Above all, a script clerk, who is almost always a girl, must be an expert stenographer. She has charge of the script during the making of the picture and is constantly at the director's side. She takes notes on costumes, action, dialogue, the length of the running of a scene, directions that go with each scene as made for the cutter. It is quite an important job in the studio.

Q. *What is the longest time that a motion picture has run in New York City?* A. J. R.

A. The Film Daily Year Book, 1932, says that the longest run for a picture was "Zwei Herzen im ¾ Takt," (Two Hearts in Three-Quarter Time), with an engagement of fifty weeks at the Europa Theatre.

Q. *What are meant by rushes in motion picture parlance?* L. H.

A. The Film Daily Yearbook says that rushes are advanced prints. They are scenes processed immediately after taking, for the assistance of the director.

Q. *Were African or Indian elephants used in filming Tarzan?* L. W. C.

A. One of the outstanding differences between the African elephants and Indian elephants is the great size of the ears of the African species. However, the African elephant has never proved tamable and has never become the friend of mankind that the Indian elephant is. In filming a picture such as Tarzan it was necessary to use Indian elephants, but to make them appear like African elephants artificial ears were fastened on.

Q. *When were news reels first popularized?* E. H. B.

A. The news weekly came on the screens of the United States in 1910 when Pathe Freres of Paris circulated a weekly issue of their Pathe Journal. Brief pictures of troops taken by camera men during the Spanish American War were the prototypes of the news weekly.

Q. *What is the liquid used to imitate beer, champagne, and whiskey in the movies or on the stage?* J. C.

A. Usually near beer is used for beer; ginger ale for champagne; and cold tea for whiskey.

Q. *Who is the richest actor in Hollywood?* F. H.

A. Harold Lloyd is reputed to be. He is said to be worth $12,000,000. Mary Pickford's fortune is estimated at $5,000,000.

Q. *What are quickies? Where is Poverty Row?* R. B.

A. Quickies are pictures made by the cheaper independent studios. Poverty Row is the legendary street on which all independent studios are commonly supposed to be located and where many quickies are made.

Q. *What is the value of the investments of motion picture stars in real property?* L. L.

A. Los Angeles statisticians figure that film stars' investments in real property total about $20,000,000.

Q. *Are silent pictures still being made?* H. M.

A. Some few—but very few—are still being made for amusement purposes. A considerable number of silent films are made for educational and industrial purposes.

Q. *What is Greta Garbo's real name?* T. B.

A. It is Gustafesson.

Q. *What was D. W. Griffith's business or profession before he entered the motion picture field?* C. C.

A. He had been a newspaper reporter and had abandoned that profession in an effort to get a start as a dramatist. He played small parts to support himself and began to write scenarios. In 1908 he joined Biograph as actor and director.

Q. *How many States have their own motion picture censorship boards?* E. D. R.

A. Six—Kansas, Maryland, New York, Ohio, Pennsylvania, and Virginia. A number of municipalities also have such boards.

Q. *Why are motion pictures given different endings in America and in Europe?* B. V.

A. English-speaking peoples prefer happy endings; Germans like unhappy endings; while Latins want logical endings, however unpleasant they may be. Films are often changed for export trade with these facts in mind.

Q. *What was Douglas Fairbanks' real name?* R. L. F.

A. His name was Ullman, but he has now had the name, Fairbanks, legalized.

Q. *Is Harpo Marx deaf and dumb?* R. E. P.

A. He is not. He is a pantomimist.

Q. *What kind of a signal is used in motion picture studios to warn people that a sound picture is being taken?* P. R.

A. In most of the studios there is on the walls near to the stage whereon the sound pictures are made, a flashing signal of a red light the purpose being to notify all within sight that the sound camera is in operation. On the jamb of many of the doors leading into the sound stages are signs somewhat resembling the exit signs in theatres, on which the word "Silence" is made to stand out. When the sound camera is in operation, these signs on the doors flash red.

Q. Is El Brendel, the movie actor, a Swede? M. H.

A. He is an American. He was born in Philadelphia, Pa., March 25, 1891. He has made a specialty of Swedish characters since 1917. He made his vaudeville debut in 1911. He fought during the late war and returned to his Swedish rôles. Strangely enough, Brendel is neither German nor Swedish, but is of Pennsylvania Dutch ancestry.

Q. Does Jerusalem have movies and what kind? R. B. L.

A. There are 16 sound movie theatres in Palestine and three silent. Nearly all are in Jerusalem, but Haifa and Tel-Aviv also have theatres. The foreign colony likes the general run of pictures such as are shown in the United States, but the native population insists upon outdoor thrillers. Jazz music is popular.

Q. What was the name of the black animal in "Bring 'Em Back Alive"? M. R.

A. It is a black leopard, which is a freak, and occurs infrequently but is said to be one of the most vicious animals known to man.

Q. In settlement of a little dispute, can you explain to me just how reverse action in movies is produced? What I have reference to is the bringing of a diver out of the water and back on the diving board. H. E.

A. The usual way of making reverse action in motion pictures is to turn the camera bottom side up and run the film through in the regular way. When the printed positive from this film is projected in the normal way, it will of course be reversed and all the action will be moving in the opposite direction. This same effect may be obtained by running the film through the camera (not inverted) from the take up magazine backward to the heat magazine. All cameras, however, are not equipped with a take up on the upper magazine and the first method has to be resorted to.

Q. How did Zasu Pitts get her first name? T. R.

A. The father of Zasu Pitts had two sisters, one named Eliza and the other Susan. Her mother decided to take the last syllable of the one name and the first of the other and give it to the child.

Q. What are the cobwebs made of which are used in old houses in the movies? W. D.

A. They are made of finely shredded asbestos.

Q. Where was Bela Lugosi born? How old is he? H. L.

A. He was born in Lugos, Hungary, in 1884.

Q. How did the Four Marx Brothers get their names? F. L. M.

A. There were five brothers, Chico, Harpo, Groucho, Gummo, and Zeppo. The first four named were billed as the Four Marx Brothers in 1913. In 1915 Art Fischer, the monologist, gave them their nicknames. Chico was so called because of his fondness for chicken; Harpo because he played the harp; Groucho because of his serious countenance; and Gummo because he always wore rubbers. Gummo retired, and when another brother took his place they called him Zeppo after a circus freak seen in childhood. The real names of the brothers are Julius (Groucho), Arthur (Harpo), Leonard (Chico), Herbert (Zeppo). Milton (Gummo) is now in business.

Q. What are the motion picture screens made of? J. W. F.

A. The average theatrical screen used in the large motion picture theatres is made of prepared fireproof white material which is porous to permit the sound to filter through. The material is called alabastine.

Q. *What is the amount of film manufactured and used annually in the United States?* **D. E. L.**

A. The approximate amount is, according to the Motion Picture Almanac, 1932, 6,000,000,000 linear feet.

Q. *Who directed Greta Garbo in her first picture?* **F. C.**

A. G. W. Pabst directed her first picture, Street of Sorrow, in 1925.

Q. *How many motion picture theatres are there in the United States, both silent and those equipped with sound apparatus?* **M. D. M.**

A. In 1932 there were 13,223 sound-equipped motion picture theatres in the United States and 5,295 silent theatres. Of the 5,295 silent theatres, 3,757 are not operating; of the total number of sound-equipped theatres, 1,582 are not operating.

Q. *Does Lowell Sherman come of a family of actors?* **R. A.**

A. His father, John Sherman, was a theatrical producer, associated for many years with the Baldwin Theatre in San Francisco. His mother, Julia Louise Gray, was an actress, while his grandmother, Kate Gray, was leading lady for Junius Brutus Booth, father of Edwin Booth.

Q. *How long has Harold Lloyd been making motion pictures?* **E. M.**

A. For fifteen years. In this time he has had but six leading ladies— Bebe Daniels, Mildred Davis (whom he married), Jobyna Ralston, Ann Christy, Barbara Kent, and Constance Cummings.

Q. *When was the motion picture, The Birth of a Nation, first presented?* **W. Z.**

A. It was released March 3, 1915.

Q. *Please give a short biography of Leslie Howard.* **F. W.**

A. He was born in London and attended Dulwich College. He enlisted in the service when war broke

and was invalided out in 1917. After acting in the provinces a while, he made his London début in Pinero's The Freaks. He appeared for the first time in New York in 1921 in The Wren. His real name is Leslie Stainer. He is also a playwright and author of numerous magazine articles.

Q. *How tall are most of the motion picture actresses?* **E. B.**

A. Most of them are of heights between 5 feet and 5 feet 5 inches. A few are shorter and a few are taller.

Q. *Are many of the movie stars foreign born?* **J. J.**

A. A great many of them are. To name a few, there are: Charlie Chaplin, Maurice Chevalier, Greta Garbo, Marlene Dietrich, Norma Shearer, Ramon Novarro, George Arliss, Marie Dressler, Mary Pickford, Clive Brook, Dorothy Mackaill, Paul Lukas, Victor McLaglen, Fifi Dorsay, Dolores Del Rio, Lupe Velez, Elissa Landi, Maureen O'Sullivan, Pola Negri, Boris Karloff, Leslie Howard, Bela Lugosi, Jill Esmond, Lawrence Olivier, Ivan Lebedeff, Reginald Denny, Rockcliffe Fellows, Alec Francis, Jean Hersholt, Montague Love, Antonio Moreno, Greta Nissen, Warner Oland, Ernest Torrence, H. B. Warner, and Ronald Colman.

Q. *Are Jackie Cooper's parents actors?* **G. T.**

A. The American Magazine says that his mother, the former Mabel Leonard, was a child actress. At twelve she was in vaudeville, and at fifteen an accomplished pianist and accompanist. She married Johnny Cooper, a vaudeville actor, and formed a team with him. Johnny Cooper died six years ago.

Q. *Are the big feature pictures shortened in the smaller theatres and communities?* **T. D. C.**

A. The Motion Picture Producers and Distributors of America say that practically all regular feature pictures are shown identically wherever they are run. Very rarely, only in case of a picture of extraordinary length which is shown in the legitimate theatres as a road show attraction, is it necessary to shorten it for general distribution. This, however, does not occur once in a hundred pictures.

Q. *Did Ronald Colman serve in the World War?* **W. M.**

A. He was a member of the London Scottish Reserves prior to the World War and was invalided home after two years' service at the front.

Q. *How can broken motion picture film be mended?* **C. R. H.**

A. Broken parts may be cemented together with a translucent cement.

Q. *Is Boris Karloff a Russian?* **E. M.**

A. This actor, who took the part of the monster in Frankenstein, was born in London, England, November 23, 1887. He has dark brown hair, brown eyes, and his real name is Pratt.

Q. *Who made the first speech recorded for talking pictures?* **B. R.**

A. Will H. Hays, President, Motion Picture Producers and Distributors of America, made a short speech as an introduction to John Barrymore's Don Juan, the first Vitaphone talking picture, and is therefore the first to have made a speech for the talkies.

Q. *Please give the names of the fifty greatest motion pictures that were selected by David Wark Griffith?* **M. F.**

A. At the request of the New York Evening Post, the noted film director listed the following motion pictures that he considers the finest yet produced: Stella Maris, The Birth of a Nation, War Brides, Intolerance, Quo Vadis, Avenging Conscience, The Four Horsemen of the Apocalypse, The Miracle Man, Broken Blossoms, Passion, The Mark of Zorro, The Dark Angel, Driven.

The White Sister, Greed, Way Down East, Smilin' Through, Tol'able David, Robin Hood, Orphans of the Storm, The Covered Wagon, Merry Go Round, The Hunchback of Notre Dame, Down to the Sea in Ships, Little Old New York, The Sea Hawk, Monsieur Beaucaire, The Marriage Circle, The Ten Commandments, The Kid, The Merry Widow, The Last Laugh, The Big Parade, The Valiant, Wings, Variety, Beau Geste, Stella Dallas, What Price Glory, The Way of All Flesh, Ben-Hur, Seventh Heaven, The Patriot, Sunrise, The Crowd, The King of Kings, Disraeli, Hallelujah, Grass, All Quiet on the Western Front.

Q. *Of what descent is Richard Barthelmess? What are his chief successes in the movies?* **C. S.**

A. He is of Bavarian descent. His father was an importer, his mother an actress. His first successful part in pictures was in War Brides. Among his silent pictures are Broken Blossoms, Tol'able David, The Enchanted Cottage, The Bright Shawl, The Patent Leather Kid, Fury, and Scarlet Seas. His talking pictures have been Weary River, Drag, Young Nowheres, Son of the Gods, The Dawn Patrol, Cabin in the Cotton.

Q. *How are the old silent movies made over with sound? I understand The Birth of a Nation now has sound.* **D. E.**

A. Usually when sound is added to silent pictures they are re-made. Dialogue is written for them and they are re-enacted. The Birth of a Nation is an exception. Sound effects, not dialogue, were prepared and added to the film or put on disks which are synchronized with the film.

Q. *Please give a complete list of Lon Chaney's pictures.* **B. M.**

A. Lon Chaney's first work of any importance was in Western pictures such as Riddle Gawn, Hell Morgan's Girl, and False Faces. He first came to prominence in The Miracle Man. Subsequently he appeared in Treasure Island, The Penalty, The Hunchback of Notre Dame, The Phantom of the Opera, Ace of Clubs, Oliver Twist, The Shock, He Who Gets Slapped, The Unholy Three (silent version), The Blackbird, Tell It to the Marines, Laugh, Clown, Laugh, The Monster, Mr. Wu, London After Midnight, The Tower of Lies, While the City Sleeps, The Unknown, The Road to Mandalay, West of Zanzibar, and The Unholy Three (talking version).

Q. Which motion picture company is the largest in the world? R. S.

A. The Motion Picture Producers and Distributors of America says that it is impossible to answer the question as they do not know whether the company producing the largest number of pictures, having the widest distribution of product, or the largest studio is meant. Among the largest American companies are Paramount-Publix Corporation, Fox Film Corporation, Warner Bros., Metro-Goldwyn-Mayer Distributing Corporation, First National Pictures, Inc., United Artists Corporation, and Universal Pictures.

Q. What is Paul Muni's real name? C. L.

A. Muni Wisenfrend is known in motion pictures as Paul Muni.

Q. Does the film for a sound picture last as long as for a silent picture? A. R.

A. At the present time it does not. The life of sound prints is from 50 to 75 days, while the silent print lasts from 90 to 120 days.

Q. What is the rental price for a first-run motion picture? C. T. E.

A. The rental price of a first-run feature motion picture depends on the size of the theatre, the neighborhood, the clientele of the theatre, the length of run, etc. There is no set rental price for any picture anywhere except by agreement between distributor and exhibitor. If the film is rented on a percentage basis, that percentage is agreed upon by the distributor and exhibitor.

Q. Please give a short biography of Will Rogers. H. C. D.

A. He was born at Oolagah, Indian Territory, November 4, 1879; son of Clem Vann and Mary (Schrimpsher) Rogers; educated at the Willie Hassell School, Neosho, Mo., and the Kemper Military Academy, Boonville, Mo.; married Betty Blake November 25, 1908. Began his stage career in vaudeville at Hammerstein's Roof Garden, N. Y., 1905.

Q. Did Gary Cooper go to college? M. C. F.

A. He was a student at Grinnell College, Grinnell, Iowa, for two years.

Q. Did Houdini appear in motion pictures? J. M.

A. Mrs. Houdini says he made a number of pictures, all containing stunts and escapes. The Master Mystery was a serial featuring Houdini in practically every kind of an escape, trick, stunt, or illusion that he did.

Q. Who is the strongest man in Hollywood? B. T. S.

A. Tom Tyler is considered the strongest man in Hollywood, as one would be who can "muscle up" 240 pounds in one hand. He is an expert horseman, having spent much of his time at his father's ranch in Wyoming. He has also played a lot of football and is a field star of note.

Q. What was Greta Garbo's occupation before she went into the movies? C. V. M.

A. Greta Garbo left school when 15, and worked in a department store selling hats. She played minor parts in the movies and was recommended for a scholarship in the Dramatic School in Stockholm. She studied for six months and later came to Hollywood in 1925.

Q. In movie parlance what is meant by the terms "dubbing up" and "dumping up" pictures? A. T.

A. The sound pictures are developing a vocabulary of their own. It seems that scenario writers and photographers sometimes turn out scenes that go over the heads of average movie fans. So the picture is "dumped up" by making the scenes and phraseology simple enough for any moron to understand. "Dubbing up" a picture is the addition of sound features to old pictures.

Q. Name the first photoplay in which John Barrymore appeared. G. T. V.

A. His first screen production was Raffles, The Amateur Cracksman.

Q. Do the Canadian people have the same moving picture favorites that we have in the United States? J. T. S.

A. An authority on the subject says: "The favorite stars of Canada are such players as Alice Joyce, Mary Pickford, Douglas Fairbanks, Norma Shearer, Janet Gaynor, Clive Brook, Percy Marmont, and that type of player."

Q. Is Ramon Novarro related to Dolores Del Rio? B. A. B.

A. Both come from Durango Mexico, and they are second cousins.

Q. How tall is Victor McLaglen? L. A. C.

A. He is six feet three and weighs 215 pounds. It is said that he was the shortest of five brothers.

Q. Was The Birth of a Nation based on some novel? P. H.

A. The motion picture, The Birth of a Nation, was based on a novel called The Clansman, by Thomas Dixon.

Q. Is the sound film ever used to record legal contracts? A. N. L.

A. A permanent sound film contract was recorded when Mary Lewis, opera star, was engaged to appear in talking pictures. Both the offer and acceptance were stamped on a film in picture and synchronization.

Q. Is Edwin Carewe, the movie director, an Indian? H. A.

A. We are informed that he is half Indian.

Q. Of the Laurel and Hardy team of comedians which is the Englishman and which the Southerner? S. P. K.

A. Stan Laurel was born at Ulverston, England, June 16, 1895. Oliver Hardy was born in Atlanta, Ga., January 18, 1892. Hardy is 6 feet 1 inch tall and weighs 284 pounds, while Laurel is 5 feet 9 inches and weighs 150 pounds.

Q. What is a "horse opera"? Y. G. F.

A. Motion pictures known as "Westerns" are sometimes referred to as "horse operas."

Q. In what picture did William Powell play his first rôle? J. S.

A. With John Barrymore in Sherlock Holmes in 1921.

Q. How many cameramen are there in Hollywood? L. C.

A. The American Cinematographer says there are close to 1,000 cameramen of varying classification in Hollywood.

Q. What was the first successful Vitaphone play? A. M.

A. The first successful photoplay produced on the Vitaphone was Don Juan, starring John Barrymore. It was first shown at the Warner Theater, New York City, August, 1927.

Q. In making moving pictures why are white clothes never worn? B. S.

A. White clothing is not allowed for the screen. The first rule of every studio is an avoidance of dead-white material. White, catching the artificial lights, produces halation and in the finished picture shows a ghostly shadow which seems to follow the players. Women choose any sort of light shade rather than white. This is the reason why white screen clothing is a light yellow. Light yellow photographs a clear white. Light pink and blue photograph a dainty white.

Q. Why does Hoot Gibson always wear gloves in his pictures? W. J. S.

A. Cowboys always wear gloves to protect their hands from wind and rope burns. Gloves are as much a part of their wardrobe as hats and boots.

Q. Please give a biography of Maurice Chevalier, the French screen star. M. P.

A. He was born near Paris, France, 1893. He is 5 feet 11 inches tall and weighs 165 pounds. He has brown hair and blue eyes. He is married. His stage career began at the age of 12. He became the idol of the French theatregoers. He fought in the World War and received a decoration for bravery. Since coming to America, his talking pictures have been received with enthusiasm.

Q. Please give a list of the different phases and types of work connected with the Motion Picture Industry. J. N.

A. There are at least a hundred classifications of work in the industry. Among them are actors, authors, directors, producers, cameramen, electricians, continuity writers, painters, assistant production managers, plasterers, sculptors, cartoonists, assistant directors, make-up artists, costumers, stars, featured players, character actors, "extras," riders, aviators, divers, auto drivers, motorcyclists, iron workers, assistant cameramen, art directors, architects, scenario editors, supervisors of production, title writers, casting directors, publicity men, interior decorators, cleaners, watchmen, motor truck drivers, gardeners, hair dressers, wig makers, wood workers, firemen, engineers, superintendents of plants, foremen, musicians, draftsmen, film cutters, tinters, developers, printers, physicians, metal workers, dressmakers, mechanics, readers, errand boys, lawyers, washers, laboratory managers, inspectors, machinists, telephone operators, shipping and receiving clerks, general sales managers, assistant sales managers, district sales managers, branch sales managers, salesmen, inspectors, stenographers, postal clerks, clerks, wrappers, bookers, bookkeepers, exploitation managers and assistants, projectionists, foreign managers and assistants, translators and news reel editors, and others.

Q. How old is George Arliss? Has he always played old man parts? E. M.

A. Mr. Arliss was born in London, England, April 10, 1868. He went on the stage in 1887 at the age of 19, and toured America for the first time in 1910. He has not always played the part of an old man.

Q. Which of Mary Pickford's early films made her famous abroad? L. D.

A. While A Good Little Devil and Tess of the Storm Country established her as a great star, it was The Poor Little Rich Girl which made her fame world wide.

CHAPTER 50

MUSIC

Q. How many Christian hymns are there? R. M. D.

A. A Dictionary of Hymnology says that the total number of Christian hymns in the 200 or more languages and dialects in which they have been written or translated is not less than 400,000.

Q. Which one of the many marches written by John Philip Sousa is his favorite? J. C.

A. Commander Sousa said that if he had any preference at all he would name Stars and Stripes Forever. This march earned him $300,000 in royalties. The Washington Post March has had the largest sale of any of his compositions, but he sold it outright for $35.

Q. Which operas are sung oftenest at the Metropolitan? T. F.

A. A review of Gatti-Casazza's twenty-four seasons, shows that Aida leads with 170 presentations; La Boheme is second with 151; Pagliacci third with 149; and Madam Butterfly fourth with 143.

Q. What piece of music is most often requested as a concert number? H. H.

A. Hans Hanke, concert pianist, says that it has been his experience that the most requests are made for Liszt's Liebestraum.

Q. Who imported the first pianos known in America? S. T.

A. In 1784 John Jacob Astor of New York imported the first pianos.

They were small four and one-half to five octave square pianos with eight legs.

Q. How many singers are there in the Mormon Tabernacle Choir? R. K. S.

A. The choir consists of 400 unpaid singers. It has been in existence many years, but its first broadcast was made in 1928.

Q. In the song, Comin' Through the Rye, is rye a river or a field of grain? S. W. S.

A. It refers to the fording of the little River Rye. Custom established a toll of kisses to be exacted from lassies who were met in crossing the stream on the stepping stones.

Q. What is the highest price ever paid for a Stradivarius violin? G. A. H.

A. The Etude says that it is impossible to state the exact amount. There are rumors of sums all the way from $25,000 to over $100,000.

Q. What was Caruso singing when he had a hemorrhage of the throat, from which he never entirely recovered? C. R. M.

A. Enrico Caruso, famous opera singer, was singing in the opera, Pagliacci, playing the rôle of Canio (Punchinello) when just as the opera began he noticed the welling of blood in his throat. He tried to go on, mopping the blood from time to time, but finally had to leave the stage. He had burst a blood vessel in the back of the throat and he never recovered, although, he did not die for some time afterwards.

Q. *Is American jazz music played over the radio in Russia?* G. L.

A. It is absolutely taboo on the Russian radio which features symphonic music by the finest orchestras.

Q. *What is the origin of the bugle call, Retreat?* C. S.

A. It is of very ancient origin and is one of the few calls known to have been used by the Crusaders.

Q. *What instrument is considered the most important in an orchestra?* N. T.

A. The violin is so considered, and the first violinist ranks next to the conductor.

Q. *When was the Star-Spangled Banner made the national anthem?* J. H.

A. It was made the national anthem of the United States by Act of Congress, signed by the President, March 3, 1931.

Q. *How long has Gloria in Excelsis been sung?* L. S.

A. It is one of the oldest Christian doxologies, eastern in origin and in use for more than 1500 years.

Q. *Is jazz a particular type of music?* G. M.

A. The Etude says that Paul Whiteman has defined it most definitely not as a particular type of music but as a method of playing music.

Q. *Does the word music occur in the Bible? What was the first musical instrument?* L. D. N.

A. The word music occurs 15 times in the King James and Revised Version of the Scriptures. It can not be definitely stated exactly what the first musical instrument was, but undoubtedly crude instruments were used by paleolithic man, a primitive flute of reindeer horns being found in a cave which was inhabited during the stone age, also many prehistoric horns of metal have been unearthed among the relics of the Bronze Age.

Q. *When were hymns first written?* C. S.

A. The writing of hymns can be traced to man's first worship of a Supreme Being. Hymns were written in ancient Egypt to the Sun God, Ra.

Q. *How long did it take the author to compose the words to America?* L. R.

A. Dr. Samuel Francis Smith composed the poem when he was 24 years old. He wrote the words to fit the music found in a book of German songs. He is quoted as saying that he composed the eight verses in about half an hour. The first four are the ones usually sung, or the first two and the fourth.

Q. *What was the first opera written in America?* E. L. D.

A. Leonora composed by W. H. Fry (1813–1864) was the first American grand opera. It was produced in Philadelphia in 1845.

Q. *What is the meaning of the word, transpose, as applied to music?* L. A. C.

A. It means to change the key in which the music is written.

Q. *Who wrote the Communist song, The Internationale?* L. Z.

A. The Communist hymn was written by Eugene Pottier, a Frenchman.

Q. *Please name some popular songs that are reminiscent of classical themes.* S. W.

A. Paul Whiteman writes that Handel's Messiah and I Dreamt That I Dwelt In Marble Halls furnished the themes for Yes, We Have No Bananas; Chopin supplied Alice Blue Gown; Avalon is Tosca; Marcheta is reminiscent of The

Merry Wives of Windsor; and The Love Nest is Tschaikowsky.

Q. Who wrote the hymn, Abide With Me? N. N.

A. Rev. Henry F. Lyte (1793–1847), an English curate, in broken health, had been ordered to take a trip to a more southern climate. After his final Communion service, he dragged himself to his room, and before leaving gave to a relative copy of the words, Abide with me, Fast falls the eventide, which he had written, recording his own feelings during the twilight of that Sabbath day. Soon afterward while on this journey, he died at Nice, France.

Q. What bands in England and France are the most famous military bands? M. N.

A. Probably the Coldstream Guards Band and Grenadier Guards Band fill the position in England and the Garde Republicaine Band in France.

Q. Is it correct to include the Star-Spangled Banner in a medley of songs? G. J. S.

A. The leader of the Marine Band says the Star-Spangled Banner should never be played as a medley with other songs. At least two bars must elapse before playing the Star-Spangled Banner. There are no official regulations regarding the playing of such hymns except in the Army, Navy, and Marine Corps.

Q. Is Hail to the Chief played when a Governer enters a hall or auditorium? J. H.

A. Hail to the Chief is reserved to mark the entrance of the President of the United States.

Q. Who wrote Kathleen Mavourneen? J. S.

A. This famous Irish song was written by Mrs. Julia Crawford and the music was composed by Frederick Nicholls Crouch, who first sang it at a concert in Plymouth, England, about 1832. He received five guineas ($26.25) for the song. In 1866 the plates were sold at auction for $2660.

Q. What is the story back of By the Waters of Minnetonka? G. G. P.

A. What We Hear In Music says: "This is based on an actual Indian theme. The song tells of the interesting old Indian legend of the young lovers of the Sun and the Moon Tribes who loved each other against the tribal law and how, to escape, they fled together, and sank into the lonely waters of a tranquil northern lake. There they were united forever, and the blue skies looked down and smiled upon their love.

Q. Did Paganini make violins? S. K.

A. Nicolo Paganini, Italian virtuoso, was a musician, not a maker of violins. His violin was a very fine Guarnerius violin which he bequeathed to the municipality of Genoa, Italy, the town where he was born, and it is preserved there as one of its most valuable possessions.

Q. What especial music is played at the inauguration of a President? R. P. G.

A. The Star-Spangled Banner, the President's March, and Hail to the Chief are included.

Q. What is the penalty for using a copyrighted musical composition in a theater without permission? M. R.

A. The copyright laws provide that any person who infringes a copyright musical composition shall be liable in damages to the copyright owner in an amount not to exceed $5000 nor less than $250.

Q. Does the Marine Corps train men for its band? G. T.

A. It does not train men for the Marine Band. The men in this band are accomplished musicians and are often graduates of well-known music schools. Instruments are furnished although a good many of the musicians prefer to use their own.

Q. *How many members are there in the U. S. Army Band, the Navy Band, and the Marine Band?* D. C.

A. Each organization has 76 members.

Q. *When were the first open air concerts given in this country?* S. W.

A. The Etude says that they took place in New York City in 1765.

Q. *When did bands originate?* I. M. M.

A. John Philip Sousa said that according to historical records the beginning of the modern wind band may be traced from Central Europe in the Middle Ages. Traveling minstrels gathering at great fairs, church festivals, and state occasions often organized impromptu bands. These, Commander Sousa continued, were possibly the first of the modern bands.

Q. *Please give a brief history of the harp.* M. L.

A. It is the oldest of stringed instruments. The Bible mentions Jubal as the inventor. The harp has been used by all nations in one form or another. The improvements which have rendered the modern harp an efficient musical instrument are due to Sebastian Erard, who in 1794 took out a patent for a harp with seven pedals, and again in 1808 for a double-action harp with the same number of pedals, each of which effects two changes in the pitch of the strings. Various improvements over Erard's harp were made during the 19th century.

Q. *Please name some of the collections of famous violins.* V. L. M.

A. One of the greatest collections of valuable violins in the world is owned by the Rudolph Wurlitzer Company. The following also have valuable collections of instruments, including violins: Carl Fischer Collection of Stringed Instruments; The Crosby Brown Collection of Musical Instruments, Metropolitan Museum of Art; Frederick Stearns Collection of Musical Instruments; and the Rodman Wanamaker collection of violins was recently acquired by Dr. Thaddeus Rich, of the Rudolph Wurlitzer Company.

Q. *How much does a complete set of devices for a trap drummer such as one sees in jazz orchestras cost?* O. J.

A. The late John Philip Sousa said that while some trap drummers spend as much as $2000 on their instruments, the 44 pieces which go to make up a set can be purchased for $1,689.15.

Q. *What is the highest toned wind instrument?* M. K.

A. The piccolo is the highest toned wind instrument. After the piccolo, the highest toned are the soprano oboe and the sopranino saxophone in F.

Q. *How many parts or pieces are there in a violin and what are they?* E. K.

A. Bachmann's Encyclopedia says that there are 70. They are: Belly, 2 pieces (sometimes 1); back, 2 (sometimes 1); ribs, 6; inside blocks, 6; inside linings, 12; inside bass bar, 1; purfling, 24; finger board, 1; neck and scroll, 1; nut, 1; lower nut, 1; tailpiece, 1; loop, 1; tailpiece button, 1; pegs, 4; strings, 4; bridge, 1; and sound, 1.

Q. *What was the first stringed instrument to be played with a bow?* T. T.

A. An ancient violin-like instrument with three to six strings, used in Ireland and Wales, was the first. It was called a crowd.

Q. *What instruments are included in the term wood-winds?* T. S.

A. They include the piccolo, flute, oboe, English horn, clarinet, bass clarinet, bassoon, and contra-bassoon.

Q. *How is the falsetto voice produced?* R. C.

A. The falsetto voice is a head voice as distinguished from the normal or chest voice. It is produced by tightening the ligaments of the glottis.

Q. *Are negro spirituals always of a religious character?* W. D. N.

A. They are not. While southern negroes are intensely religious, many of the songs of negro origin do not deal with religious subjects.

Q. *Are the vocal cords of a man longer or shorter than those of a woman?* J. H. R.

A. The length of the vocal cords of men is estimated at $\frac{7}{12}$ of an inch and of women at $\frac{5}{12}$ of an inch. This is a factor in the pitch of voices. It is highly probable that a slight difference also exists between bass and tenor, and between contralto and soprano, but it is difficult to measure with sufficient accuracy.

Q. *How long has Handel's Messiah been sung in London?* N. W.

A. The first performance was given in 1749. Since that time it has been a custom in London to perform that work with greatly augmented chorus and orchestra each year at Christmas.

Q. *Please name some of the hardest tenor solos.* A. L.

A. Among the most difficult are Celeste Aida by Giuseppe Verdi from the opera Aida; Vesti la Giubba from the opera Pagliacci by Leoncavallo; Cielo e Mar from La Gioconda by Ponchielli.

Q. *What was the first opera?* A. E.

A. The first opera, Daphne was composed in 1594 by a coterie of cultivated amateurs of Florence. In their second opera Euridice solo singing was first introduced.

Q. *How do grand, light, and comic opera differ?* H. K.

A. Groves's Dictionary of Music gives the following information concerning the difference between certain types of opera: Comic opera—a term used indiscriminately to de-note a musico-dramatic work of an amusing nature. It is not the English equivalent to the French opera-comique, for that term includes works into which seriousness and even tragedy may enter; the type is rather the opera-bouffe. Light opera is a term often employed for works in which sentiment counts for more than high spirits, although the latter is not necessarily absent. Grand opera is an opera with continuous music and of a serious nature.

Q. *When were Isaac Watts' hymns first published?* N. V.

A. Isaac Watts first published his volume, Hymns, in 1707.

Q. *How old is the Guido Scale?* W. M.

A. This scale of musical notation was invented by Guido d'Arezzo, an Italian Benedictine monk, who lived from 990–1050.

Q. *Why did the great composer, Handel, turn from opera to oratorio?* R. R. K.

A. Minute Sketches of Great Composers says: "Up to his fiftieth year Handel wrote opera endlessly and so shrewdly calculated commercial gain and popular favor that wealth and fame were his for the asking, although only the 'Largo' and one or two arias survive on today's programs. It was his failure as opera director in London which drove him to write oratorios. In 13 years he produced 19—Israel in Egypt, Herakles, the Messiah, and Saul (including the famous Dead March), being the best known." Music authorities say that England has always been oratorio minded rather than opera minded.

Q. *What inspired Schubert to write Who Is Silvia?* A. B.

A. This is one of his best known compositions of its kind. At the writing of the piece, Schubert was unquestionably in love with the name, Silvia, or his conception of her. The song was inspired by Shakespeare's Two Gentlemen of

Verona. It is said that the song inspired Arthur Sullivan to write Orpheus and His Lute. Who Is Silvia was published shortly after Schubert's death together with three songs of 1827 (later called Opus 106) which were dedicated to Marie Pachler, Schubert's kind hostess in Graz.

Q. How old is Irving Berlin? J. J. S.

A. He was born in Russia in 1888.

Q. How many hymns did Fanny Crosby write? O. V. N.

A. Fanny Crosby, the blind hymn writer, wrote some 2000 songs and hymns. Her most popular hymn is Safe In The Arms of Jesus.

Q. How long have batons been used in conducting an orchestra or band? M. P.

A. Grove's Dictionary of Music and Musicians says: "We can trace the history of conducting as far back at least as the 15th century by which time it had become customary to beat time to the Sistine Choir at Rome with a roll of paper called a sol-fa. Ornithoparcus writing in 1516 describes Tact as a certain motion of the hand of the chief singer according to the nature of the marks, which motion directs a song according to measure."

Q. How many of the different instruments are used in a symphony orchestra? R. R.

A. The average number of players for each type of instrument is as follows: Violins, 35; cellists, 10; violists, 12; double basses, 8; flutes, 2; oboes, 2; clarinets, 2; bassoons, 2; horns, 4; trumpets, 4; trombones, 3; tuba, 1; timpani, 1.

Q. What are the usual instruments in a dance orchestra? M. J. O.

A. The average dance orchestra consists of from five to nine pieces and the instruments vary, usually consisting of piano, violin, drums, banjo, saxophones, and cornet or trumpet.

Q. What is a jug band? K. S.

A. It is a band which uses jugs for musical instruments. Musical tones are produced by expert blowing into the jugs.

Q. What is meant by the coronach? I. M. F.

A. This is the Gaelic name for the lament or dirge formerly sung or played on the bagpipes on the occasion of a funeral of an Irish or Scottish person. Sir Walter Scott in the Lady of the Lake has one of the finest coronachs extant.

Q. Why is the tune, Garryowen, associated with General Custer? A. S. R.

A. Sound Off, compiled by Edward Arthur Dolph says: "Garryowen is the most famous regimental march in our Army. For more than half a century this rollicking old Irish tune has been inseparably joined with the name of George A. Custer in the Annals of the 7th Cavalry. In 1868 the 7th under General Custer was engaged in a campaign against the Cheyennes near Washita, Wyoming. On the morning of November 26th after a long hard march through the knee deep snow, the regiment discovered the camp of Chief Black Kettle. At dawn just as the bugles were sounding the charge, the band struck up Garryowen. To its stirring notes the 7th charged the camp from three sides, and completely defeated the Indians. Eight years later Custer heard his favorite tune for perhaps the last time when, with General Terry, he and the 7th marched out of Fort Lincoln on the ill-fated expedition which was to end in the massacre of Little Bighorn."

Q. What are the degrees given in music? R. N.

A. The musical degrees most frequently conferred in English speaking countries for work in music are Mus. B.—Bachelor of Music, and Mus. D.—Doctor of Music. Less frequently the degree Mus. M.—Master of Music is granted. In Germany the Ph. D. degree is granted instead of Mus. D., thus placing specialized work in music on a par with other studies.

Q. What manager brought Paderewski to this country for his first American tour? P. E. L.

A. Daniel Mayer, internationally known concert manager, brought Paderewski to this country for his first American tour in the winter of 1891–92. Daniel Mayer, who died in London at the age of 72, had managed more than 1500 musical artists. Among the artists who have been under his management are Pavlowa, Mischa Elman, Levitski, Josef Hofmann, Kreisler, de Pachmann, Nikisch, Caruso, Carreno, Saraste, d'Albert, Busoni, and the Denishawn dancers.

Q. What duty must be paid upon sheet music printed abroad? R. C. F.

A. The United States Customs Office says that if the composers are foreigners 15 per cent duty is charged. If composed by Americans but printed abroad 25 per cent duty is asked.

Q. Where is the birthplace of Efrem Zimbalist? P. P. M.

A. Zimbalist was born at Rostoff on the Don, Russia, April 9, 1889.

Q. Do the various keys in music express different feelings or emotions? G. W.

A. There is a general belief that certain keys do express particular emotions best, and many composers consciously or unconsciously employ them. The minor keys as a class are sad, somber, and melancholy, each having particular attributes. In the major keys, C. is simple, naive, and commonplace; G. is rural, merry; B. flat, noble, elegant, graceful; E flat, sonorous, vigorous, chivalrous; and so on.

Q. Who was the first musician to be knighted? F. R. B.

A. Henry Bishop, an original member of the Philharmonic Society of London, and for many years the leader at Covent Garden, was the first to be knighted on account of his musical contributions. He wrote no less than 130 operas, farces, ballets, and adaptions. My Pretty Jane and Lo! Hear the Gentle Lark are still popular, the latter being included in the repertoires of modern coloratura prima donnas, such as Melba, Alma Gluck, and Galli-Curci.

Q. Is the music to the Marines' Hymn taken from some opera? R. N. I.

A. The melody of the song, From the Halls of Montezuma is that of the Couplets des Hommes d'Armee from Offenbach's opera bouffe Genevieve de Brabant.

Q. How old is Fritz Kreisler? Where was he born? L. G.

A. The violinist was born in Vienna, in 1875.

Q. What is a chantey? C. D.

A. It is a sailors' song, sung to lighten or enliven the sailors' tasks. The leader or chantey-man sings a line or two and the sailors sing the chorus as an accompaniment to the work in hand.

Q. What is the difference between a professional and an amateur musician? P. K.

A. The same rule applies to musicians that applies to other lines of endeavor. A professional is one who uses his art as a gainful occupation, while an amateur pursues his art for love of the art and love of work.

Q. Who established the Peabody Conservatory of music in Baltimore? W. C.

A. The conservatory is George Peabody's gift to the city of his adoption. The founder was born in Massachusetts in 1795, a poor boy. At the age of 20 he went South to seek his fortune and settle in Baltimore. Here he laid the foundations of the great wealth he was some day to possess. His death was in 1869 and during his life he gave away from eight to nine millions of dollars. Students now come to this conservatory from 34 states, China, Hawaii, and Philippine Islands.

Q. What is pibroch playing? C. N.

A. It is the playing of a wild, irregular form of martial music played by Scottish Highlanders on the bagpipe. Usually the air is profusely ornamented with variations.

Q. Is it better for a child to take a half-hour music lesson or an hour lesson? E. T.

A. The Etude says that the half-hour lesson, or one only slightly longer, is satisfactory for most pupils.

Q. What is the difference between melodies and harmonies? I. H.

A. Melodies are produced by notes in succession, harmonies by notes in combination.

Q. How old was Jascha Heifetz when he first played the violin? R. McN.

A. He commenced playing the violin at three, completed the course at the Royal Music School in Vilna, Poland, at the age of seven, and after study with Professor Leopold Auer in Petrograd, was a mature artist at the age of ten.

Q. Is music printed from type or is it done from engraved plates? D. E.

A. Inexpensive music is usually printed from type. The better class of music is reproduced from plates.

Q. Please tell something of the Curtis Institute of Music in Philadelphia. S. A. C.

A. The Curtis Institute of Music, of which Josef Hofmann is director, was created in 1924 under an endowment of $500,000 by Mrs. Mary Louise Curtis Bok. The endowment was later increased to $12,500,000. Its avowed purpose is "to hand down through contemporary masters the

great traditions of the past—to teach students to build on this heritage for the future." The faculty list contains the names of many world-famous virtuosos. Free tuition is granted to all students. Admission is limited to those whose natural musical talent gives promise of developing to a point of artistic achievement.

Q. What is a ballad? R. C. C.

A. A reference book on music says: "Ballad—originally used to signify a song with simple melody and accompaniment—now applied to songs of story-telling content as well as to instrumental compositions in which the narrative idea is present."

Q. What is an intermezzo? R. C. N.

A. It is a song or chorus or a short burlesque, ballet, operetta, or the like given between the acts of a play or opera.

Q. In what year was Gatti-Casazza made director of the Metropolitan? S. B. P.

A. Giulio Gatti-Casazza was made general director of the Metropolitan Opera House in 1908.

Q. What is the name of the 13-year-old-boy who has been appointed professor of the violin by Mussolini? C. E.

A. He is Willi Cornides Von Kreinrach. He was appointed as professor of the violin at the new Juvenile Academy of Music in Rome, Italy.

Q. On sheet music, when it says lyrics by so-and-so, does this refer to the music or the words? M. M.

A. Lyrics are the words of the song.

Q. How old is the hymn heard every Sunday night over the radio called Now the Day is Over? M. W. F.

A. This hymn first appeared in 1861 in Hymns Ancient and Modern. It was written by the Rev. Sabine

Baring-Gould for the children of the Sunday School at St. John's, Horbury Bridge, Yorkshire, England, and was then known as The Evening Hymn For Missions. Rev. Sabine Baring-Gould was born in 1834 and died in 1924.

Q. What is meant by counterpoint in music? S. D.

A. It is the art of combining two or more melodies with the main theme according to the rules of harmony. Broadly, it is the art of writing part music.

Q. How long has music been taught in the public schools? R. L. H.

A. Music was first taught in public schools about 1855-60.

Q. Are Russians particularly fond of music? R. B.

A. In Russia music has always been closely connected with the lives of the people. From the time of birth through all the events of life until death claims them, they move to a musical accompaniment. The return of spring is celebrated by a sort of choral dance, termed the khorovod; marriage, being a most important time, brings forth many songs, such as The Birchwood Splinter (Lootchina), Glorification, The Matchmaker (Svatoushka). There are boating songs, laboring songs, lullabies, and dance songs. Most of the dance tunes are in the major mode, the slow tunes, and these are best liked in the minor.

Q. Why are various selections of music called Humoreske? P. T.

A. Grove's Dictionary of Music and Musicians says of the word Humoreske (Humoresque): "A title adopted by Schuman for his Op. 20 and Op. 88, No. 2, the former for piano solo, the latter for piano, violin, and violin-cello. Heller and Grieg have also used the term for pianoforte pieces—op. 64 and opp. 9 and 16 respectively. There is nothing particularly 'humorous' in any of these, and the term 'caprice' might equally well be applied to them. Rubenstein also entitled his Don Quixote 'Humoreske,' but the 'humor' is there of a more obvious and boisterous kind."

Q. What does the musical term, fret, mean? H. K.

A. A fret is one of the narrow ridges of wood, metal, or ivory crossing the fingerboard of the mandolin, guitar, zither, etc., against which the strings are pressed by the fingers to shorten their vibrating length and thus raise the tone.

Q. When did Paderewski make his American début? C. H. K.

A. This master musician made his American début, November 7, 1891.

Q. How often did Ole Bull come to America to play? D. J. W.

A. This Norwegian violinist came to America five times between 1843 and 1879. He died in 1880.

Q. Where was Walter Damrosch born? H. P. W.

A. He was born in Breslau, Germany, January 30, 1862.

Q. When was the first piano made? T. S.

A. The first pianoforte was made by Cristofori of Italy and exhibited in 1709. At almost the same time, a piano was exhibited in Paris, and a similar instrument was claimed to have been constructed by the German, Schroeter.

Q. How many times was Adelina Patti married? C. R. M.

A. According to her biography, she was married three times. Her first husband was Henri, Marquis de Caux, whom she married in 1868; she was divorced from him in 1885, then married Nicolini, the tenor, who died in 1898; in 1899 she married Baron Cederstrom, a Swede, whose title she bore when she died, September 27, 1919. Madame Patti was born in 1843.

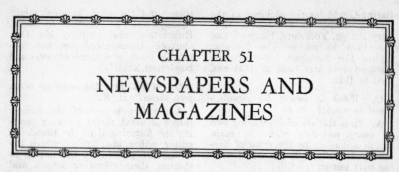

CHAPTER 51
NEWSPAPERS AND MAGAZINES

Q. How many newspapers use the dispatches of the Associated Press? F. B.

A. Frank B. Noyes, President of the Associated Press, says that it serves about 1200 daily newspapers in the United States, and a few outside this country.

Q. What is the membership of the National Press Club? H. D.

A. This world-famed organization of newspaper men has about 2,000 members who reside in Washington, in every State of the Union, and in many foreign countries.

Q. What newspaper has the largest daily circulation in America? T. D.

A. The New York News, tabloid, has the largest circulation—1,343,871 daily. Of the standard-size newspapers the Chicago Tribune heads the list with 813,708 daily.

Q. What was the first American newspaper printed in a foreign language? R. T.

A. The Philadelphia Zeitung. Benjamin Franklin established it in 1732.

Q. How much did it cost to supply the newspapers with the account of the Republican Convention in Chicago, 1932? B. A. S.

A. In a special story to Editor and Publisher, Marlen Pew said that the press spent about $200,000 a day in covering the G. O. P. convention. He said there were 726 reporters present, constituting 38 per cent of the floor assembly, also that the Mayor of Chicago put two ambulances at the disposal of the newspaper photographers to rush the photographic plates from the convention hall to the airport where planes were waiting to carry them to various cities.

Q. How old is the Gridiron Club? A. R.

A. This popular dining society, whose membership is limited to forty newspaper men, gave its first banquet on April 23, 1885, during the first administration of Grover Cleveland.

Q. What city publishes the most daily newspapers? F. S.

A. Paris. It is said that Paris has as many daily newspapers as London, New York, and Berlin combined.

Q. How do the creators of newspaper comic strips market their drawings? M. G.

A. When comic strips first were introduced in American journalism, such artists as F. W. Opper and James Swinnerton, who created Happy Hooligan and Little Jimmy, drew for a single newspaper. As the popularity of the strips increased, syndicates took over their distribution, the artists receiving large increases in salary with often a percentage of profits. The King Features Syndicate, Chicago Tribune Syndicate, McNaught Syndicate, NEA Service, and similar large or-

344

ganizations distribute strips such as Bud Fisher's Mutt and Jeff, George McManus' Bringing Up Father, Sidney Smith's Gumps, Frank King's Gasoline Alley, Harry Tuthill's Bungle Family, Gene Ahern's Our Boarding House, Rube Goldberg's Boob McNutt, and other famous features.

Q. What publication has the largest circulation? M. D.

A. The American Weekly, distributed through the Hearst Sunday papers, claims the greatest circulation in the world. It is said to reach over five million families every week.

Q. Who was the first baseball editor? W. J. G.

A. The late ex-Senator William Cauldwell, editor and proprietor of the old New York Sunday Mercury, was the first man to write and print anything on baseball. His articles were first published in 1853. Everything relating to baseball prior to that time is merely hearsay.

Q. What group of chain-owned dailies has the largest list of papers? S. N.

A. The Scripps-Howard and the Scripps-Canfield interests have the most papers, but the Hearst chain has the largest circulation.

Q. What paper was the first to be sold on the streets in this country? H. S.

A. The New York Sun.

Q. What persons are eligible to the press galleries at the Capitol? C. W. F.

A. The occupation of the galleries is confined to bona fide correspondents of reputable standing in their profession, who represent daily newspapers or newspaper associations requiring telegraphic service. The press galleries are under control of a standing committee of correspondents, subject to the approval and supervision of the Speaker of the House of Representatives and the Senate Committee on Rules. The Congressional Directory lists

389 correspondents as members of the Press Gallery.

Q. What newspaper was the first to bulletin election returns? B. E. T.

A. The New Orleans Picayune, now the Times-Picayune, had the first newspaper bulletin board displaying election returns in 1848.

Q. Please name some of the leading weeklies of the country. O. C.

A. Among the leading weeklies are The Saturday Evening Post, Collier's, New Yorker, Literary Digest, Liberty, and Time.

Q. How many negro newspapers are there in the United States? P. C.

A. A recent compilation lists some 250.

Q. What was the first monthly magazine to sell for ten cents? W. M.

A. Munsey's Magazine was the first monthly of its class to sell for ten cents.

Q. Why is a certain edition of a newspaper called the bulldog? D. R. W.

A. Editor and Publisher says that it probably got its name in the late 90's when the New York World, Herald, and Journal fought to get out editions that would catch the mails going out of town. It was said that they fought like bulldogs —hence, the bulldog edition.

Q. To whom is the saying accredited—"When a dog bites a man, that's not news, but when a man bites a dog, that's news"? D. McD.

A. It is attributed to Charles Dana, former editor of the New York Sun.

Q. What is the meaning of such words or letters as "etaoin shrdlu" so often seen in newspaper columns? D. B. D.

A. This is known as a pi-line. Newspapers are set on linotypes, the type being cast in metal, one complete line forming a solid slug. There is no such process as erasure possible. When a typographer makes an error he knows the entire line must be reset. He drags his finger along the keyboard to complete a line and release the machine for a new line. The letters on the keyboard run etaoinshrdlu and mean nothing. In making up, this line should be removed but sometimes remains by mistake, and appears in the paper.

Q. *What is meant by the term by-line?* J. F.

A. A by-line is the signature of the writer. Most newspaper dispatches are plain statements of news not attributed to any individual. Some state that they are written, for instance, —By Frank R. Kent, Walter Lippman, Gould Lincoln, George R. Holmes, Frederic William Wile, William Philip Simms, Clinton W. Gilbert, David Lawrence, Ray T. Tucker, Paul Y. Anderson, Carlisle Bargeron, Leroy T. Vernon, or Robert E. Armstrong.

Q. *What is the oldest newspaper west of the Mississippi?* A. C. C.

A. The oldest one which is still being published is the Arkansas Gazette, founded in 1819 by William E. Woodruff. There were six papers west of the Mississippi by that time, but none of them is still being published.

Q. *When was the first medical journal published in this country?* E. B.

A. The Medical Repository was the first. It was a quarterly and was first issued in 1797. It continued publication until 1824.

Q. *Do many American newspaper men attain distinction as authors of books?* W. B. S.

A. Probably 80 per cent of all successful authors have had early newspaper experience and training. Among them are Sinclair Lewis, recipient of the Nobel Prize for Literature in 1931; Will Irwin, Irvin Cobb, Edna Ferber, Elmer Davis, George Ade, Forrest Wilson, James Hay,

Christopher Morley, and Don Marquis. Many who have become recognized authors continue journalistic work, such as Mark Sullivan, Henry L. Mencken, Frank H. Simonds, Claude G. Bowers, William Allen White, Gene Fowler, Jr., J. Fred Essary, and Ludwell Denny.

Q. *When were editorials first printed in newspapers?* M. T.

A. John Dillingham, an English journalist, invented the leading article or editorial, one of which landed him in prison in 1645.

Q. *What is the name given to the upper left-hand corner of the editorial page of a newspaper or other similar publication, where the subscription rates appear?* A. S.

A. It is known as the masthead.

Q. *What magazine runs a column called the Port of Missing Men?* G. V. S.

A. The Red Cross Courier runs this column devoted to advertising for missing people.

Q. *Is the Police Gazette still published?* G. A. R.

A. The National Police Gazette ceased publication with Vol. 140, No. 2843, February 6, 1932.

Q. *What was the first press association or news agency?* W. E. D.

A. The first news agency is believed to have been that organized by Charles Havas in Paris in 1835, when he began translating articles for the French press. In 1840 Havas established news service by carrier pigeons between Paris, London, and Brussels.

Q. *Please name some of the best known cartoonists in this country.* W. W.

A. Some of the better known cartoonists are: John T. McCutcheon, Winson McCay, J. H. Donahey, J. N. (Ding) Darling, Herbert Johnson, Clifford K. Berryman, F. W. Opper, H. T. Webster, John Held, Oscar Caesar, Rollin Kirby, H. M. Talburt, D. R. Fitzpatrick, Percy Crosby, Nelson Harding, and Charles R. Macauley.

Q. How many publications are there in the United States devoted to some trade or business? I. O'D.

A. There are about 1800 such publications devoted to some industry, trade, profession, or specialized service.

Q. How long has the Searchlight, the magazine for blind children, been published? M. B. L.

A. This juvenile quarterly is published in Braille by the New York Association For the Blind. It was started more than twenty years ago, and is now a full-fledged publication, containing essays, poems, scientific articles, and reprinted stories from popular children's magazines.

Q. What magazine is the most popular with seamen? D. B.

A. The National Geographic comes first. Sailormen seem to enjoy seeing the pictures of places where they have been and reading about them.

Q. What is the average yearly earning of a newspaper whose daily circulation averages around 10,000, and which sells for two cents? J. W. G.

A. Editor and Publisher says that the average yearly earning is $60,-000.

Q. When was the first two-cent daily newspaper published? P. L.

A. In 1833, Horace Greeley, Francis V. Story, and H. D. Shepard started the Morning Post in New York City. It failed in three weeks, but is said to have been the first two-cent daily ever published.

Q. What is a columnist? H. F.

A. A columnist is a writer who conducts a special department of humor, sports, or gossip under a permanent title. Some of the best known columnists are: Arthur Brisbane, O. O. McIntyre, Heywood

Broun, Arthur (Bugs) Baer, Grantland Rice, Karl Kitchen, Franklin P. Adams, H. I. Phillips, Robert H. Davis, Ted Cook, Jay House, and Walter Winchell.

Q. Are there many schools of journalism in the United States? M. T.

A. More than 120 schools and universities now have departments or courses in journalism.

Q. How many members has the American Newspaper Publishers' Association? F. S.

A. This Association has approximately five hundred members.

Q. How many foreign-language newspapers are there in the United States? H. S.

A. There are about 1300.

Q. When was the first college paper or magazine published in the United States? H. E. S.

A. The precursor of college periodicals was the Dartmouth Gazette, published in 1800, which numbered among its editors, Daniel Webster. The first regular American college magazine is said to have been the Literary Cabinet begun at Yale, November 15, 1806, and published until October, 1807. The first Harvard periodical was the Harvard Lyceum, published from July 14, 1810, to March 9, 1811.

Q. What is the Associated Press? D. D.

A. The Associated Press is a cooperative organization formed to gather news for the daily papers. Even before the Civil War the New York newspapers realized that each was paying large sums of money for news that was accessible to all. Accordingly, provision was made for a joint agency which acted as a sort of clearing house through which each paper gave to all other papers that were members of the agency any news that it might receive. This formed the nucleus for the later organization known as the New York

Associated Press. In 1865 the western papers incorporated their agency known as the Western Associated Press, and there were several minor associations which formed a general alliance centered in the New York association. In 1892 a stock association was formed, and in 1900 this was changed to a mutual association.

Q. What are the publications owned by the Curtis Publishing Company? P. F.

A. The Ladies' Home Journal, The Saturday Evening Post, The Country Gentleman, the Public Ledger newspapers, the Philadelphia Inquirer, the New York Evening Post. It also owns the Public Ledger Feature Syndicate.

Q. What newspaper in the United States first printed financial news? F. E. L.

A. On June 13, 1835, the New York Herald, edited by James Gordon Bennett, printed an article on the state of the money market, which gained wide attention. Despite considerable opposition, this became a permanent feature. This paper was the first to publish the stock lists and a daily financial review.

Q. What proportion of the manuscripts submitted to them do magazines actually buy? S. H. J.

A. That would depend upon conditions. The editor of one national weekly states that his magazine purchases approximately .004 per cent of the manuscripts submitted to it from year's end to year's end. He adds that from 80 to .90 per cent of fiction submissions comes from people of no professional experience or training whatever.

Q. When were newsboys first employed? C. E. K.

A. Apparently they have been employed from an early period and were known in Great Britain in the 18th century. In Scotland, paper criers or caddies sold newspapers and also provided news gossip. At the close of the 17th century they were incorporated in Edinburgh into a society, but it eventually became a nuisance and was dissolved in 1710. The word newsboy appears in English literature as early as 1812.

Q. About how much reading material is there in the average newspaper? F. H.

A. Journalism says that a 24-page paper consists of from 80,000 to 100,000 words, exclusive of advertisements, or as many as the average novel.

Q. How many feature and picture syndicates are there? W. H.

A. There are more than one hundred picture and feature syndicates in the United States as listed in the Editor and Publisher.

Q. Are there many books published on journalism and advertising? A. K.

A. There are more than 300 standard and recent books on journalism and advertising. The subjects range from the history of American journalism to news writing and advertising copy.

Q. Please name the chief news services in the United States. C. W.

A. The chief news services in the United States are the Associated Press, United Press, and International News Service.

Q. What states have the largest number of daily newspapers? S. G.

A. New York leads with 192 daily newspapers, followed by California with 178, Pennsylvania 159, Ohio 144, Illinois 131, Texas 125.

Q. How many daily newspapers are there in the United States? G. M.

A. There were 1,923 daily newspapers in this country at the beginning of 1932. There were also 513 Sunday papers. Due to consolidations, this number has declined somewhat since the last figures were compiled.

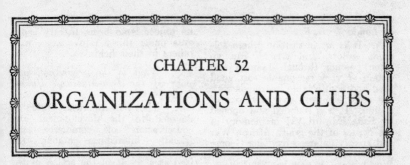

CHAPTER 52

ORGANIZATIONS AND CLUBS

Q. Why was the Caterpillar Club given this name? M. W.

A. The Caterpillar Club is composed of aviators who have resorted to parachutes to save their lives in airplane disasters. The name was chosen because it is the caterpillar that spins the silk of which parachutes are made.

Q. What is the Associated Press? Z. R. T.

A. The Associated Press is a co-operative, non-partisan, and non-political association of newspapers. All member papers contribute the news of their locality for the general good and pay a weekly assessment for the service. The service consists of telegraphic information as soon as possible of all important happenings to such newspapers as are members of the association. The membership is considered a great privilege. The Associated Press controls private wires exceeding 22,000 miles for day service and 28,000 miles for night service. Over 50,000 words are received and transmitted daily. The president and board of directors serve without salary.

Q. Does the work of the Volunteers of America and the Salvation Army overlap? F. R. W.

A. The work of the Volunteers of America is especially among prisoners and those who are released from prison and who find it hard to obtain work or homes. It is not a branch of the Salvation Army but is at present under the management of General Ballington Booth (a son of the founder of the Salvation Army, General Wm. Booth) and his wife, Maud Ballington Booth. The headquarters of the association is at 34 West 28th Street, New York City.

Q. Are Roosevelt and Hoover Masons? R. W.

A. Herbert Hoover is not a Mason. Franklin D. Roosevelt is a Mason.

Q. Do they have Girl Reserves and Girl Scouts in England? R. L.

A. There are Girl Reserves in England, and also Girl Guides who correspond to our Girl Scouts. The Girl Scouts, the American sisters of the Girl Guides of Europe, were organized in 1912 by Mrs. Juliette Low, a friend and associate of Sir Robert Baden-Powell, the father of all Scouting, who urged and inspired the undertaking.

Q. Please tell something of the work of the Valley Forge Historical Society. P. A.

A. It was organized June 19, 1918, for the preservation and publication of documents relating to Valley Forge, and for the development of the spirit of Valley Forge through education in American history and in American ideals and institutions. It maintains as part of its work the Valley Forge Museum of American History and the Washington Memorial Library. The President is Rev. W. Herbert Burk, D.D., Valley Forge, Pa.

Q. *What is the Union Jack Club of London?* B. F.

A. It is an institution where soldiers, sailors, and airmen can go when passing through London and obtain at very reasonable cost good food and comfortable bedrooms with the usual comforts and privileges of a club. It was founded and opened by King Edward VII in memory of the heroes of the South African War and greatly enlarged by King George V in memory of the men lost in the World War. It now has 826 beds.

Q. *Are Rotary Clubs organized in foreign countries?* S. B. C.

A. Rotary Clubs have been established in 42 countries of the world. In 1927 the clubs numbered 2658.

Q. *Does General Pershing belong to any fraternal orders?* W. C.

A. He is a 33rd degree Mason.

Q. *Please give me information regarding the national headquarters and activities of the Quota Club.* L. B. N.

A. Quota is an international organization similar to the men's Rotary Club. It is composed of business and professional women who have distinguished themselves in their particular line of business or profession. Only one of each classification is eligible to membership in a local Quota Club and the person holding the classification must be an owner, manager, or an executive.

Q. *What is the Commission on Interracial Coöperation?* S. M.

A. It is an organization of white and colored people in the South, attempting to adjust racial differences through conference and coöperation between influential white and colored leaders. It has been in existence for 10 years. Its headquarters are at 409 Palmer Building, Atlanta, Georgia.

Q. *What is the P. E. N. Club?* S. M. A.

A. It is a society in London, of which John Galsworthy was president. The initials stand for Poets, Playwrights, Editors, and Novelists and its object is to bring literary aspirants under thirty into contact with others in their fields.

Q. *What is the origin and purpose of the Pan-American Union?* L. L.

A. The Pan-American Union is devoted to the development and conservation of commerce and friendly intercourse among the American Republics. It was organized as a result of the action of the first Pan-American Conference held in Washington, D. C., during the autumn and winter of 1889–90. The Union is an international organization maintained by the United States and twenty other republics of Central and South America with headquarters in Washington, D. C.

Q. *What is the object of the Sentinels of the Republic?* I. R.

A. The principal object of this organization, which was established in 1922, is the "conservation of the constitutional rights of the citizens of the United States and opposition to any infringement, public or private, upon such vested rights." There are said to be over 9,000 members, and the headquarters is the National Press Building, Washington, D. C.

Q. *When the president or chairman of an organization leaves the chair to take part in the debate of a question under consideration, should he resume the chair when he has finished his remarks?* T. H. G.

A. To safeguard his reputation for impartiality he should not return to the chair until the question under debate has been disposed of and the result announced by the chairman pro tem.

Q. *How old is the American Federation of Labor?* K. M.

A. The American Federation of Labor dates from November 1881 when the Federation of Organized Trades and Labor Unions of the United States and Canada was formed. The American Federation of Labor as such did not come into existence until 1886, but in 1889 it acknowledged the continuity of its existence by dating the proceedings to 1881.

Q. *Is there an organization of atheists in this country?* J. H. G.

A. There is an organization with the title, the American Association for the Advancement of Atheism.

Q. *Please name the German organization whose purpose is to restore monarchies.* W. W.

A. The Steel Helmets, Escherich Organization, and the Swastika have such aims. In Hungary, the Awakening Magyars have the same purpose.

Q. *What was the origin of the British Coöperative Trading System?* L. R. E.

A. This organization was founded in Manchester, England, 1843, after an unsuccessful strike had been carried on by the mill-workers of Lancashire. About forty strikers were organized who contributed about 25 cents a week until $140 had been acquired, when a coöperative store was opened. Four unemployed employees conducted the business without salary. By 1921, the capital stock of the coöperative organization in England was $400,000,000, and the four unpaid employees had grown to 190,000 paid employees.

Q. *What was the first fraternity in the United States?* A. B. T.

A. The first American college fraternity of which there is a record was the Flat Hat Club that appeared at the College of William and Mary in 1750 and continued in existence until after 1772. It was secret, literary, and social. The oldest Greek letter fraternity in this country now in existence is the Phi Beta Kappa, organized in 1776.

Q. *Who can belong to the F. F. V's?* K. C.

A. These are the descendants of those who came to Virginia in a superior capacity previous to 1620.

Q. *What is a correct order of business for an ordinary society or club?* A. D.

A. Roll call, reading of minutes of previous session, reports of officers, receipt of communications, bills, etc., reports of standing committees, reports of special committees, unfinished business, new business, program, and adjournment.

Q. *When was the first peace society formed?* A. P. S.

A. The first peace society of the world was founded by David Low Dodge, of the United States, 1815. The Massachusetts Peace Society was founded the same year, and the American Peace Society by William Ladd, in 1828.

Q. *What is the significance of the organization known as the Society of the Daughters of the Barons of Runnymede?* W. C. C.

A. The society was organized in 1915 by Mrs. Robert G. Hogan of Catonsville, Maryland, who conceived the idea of an organization for women similar to a men's organization, the Baronial Order of Runnymede, which was organized but undeveloped on account of our entry into the World War. The membership is limited to those who can trace their ancestry in a direct line to a Baron who in the year 1215 A.D. compelled the signing of the Magna Charta by King John at Runnymede. The organization is American.

Q. *Is there a difference in eligibility requirements of the Veterans of Foreign Wars and the American Legion?* C. T. C.

A. The eligibility requirements are not the same. To belong to the Veterans of Foreign Wars it is necessary that the soldier has seen foreign service such as in the World War, Spanish-American War, Mexican engagements, Philippine Island occupation, China Expedition, Nicaraguan campaign, etc. Recently a special ruling has been passed making Civil War veterans eligible out of courtesy. To belong to the American Legion it is necessary that one be a veteran of the World War and have an honorable discharge.

Q. When and where were the Knights of Pythias founded? N. T. N.

A. The Knights of Pythias were organized to spread the doctrines of friendship, charity, and benevolence. It was founded, Washington, D. C., February, 1864, by Justin Henry Rathbone, and four associates, and was founded on the story of Damon and Pythias, taking as its motto: "Friendship even unto death." Its present membership is estimated at 600,000.

Q. What should the constitution of a woman's civic organization include? A. G. N.

A. The constitution should, in its several articles, state the name of the organization, its object, the classes and qualifications of its members, its officers and the method of their election and term of office, its standing committees and the method of their selection and their duties, its regular meetings and how special meetings may be called, and how the constitution may be amended.

Q. Did the Society of Friends do relief work during and after the War? S. M.

A. During the War it was active in relief work in France, Germany, Holland, Poland, and Russia. After the War it did a great deal of reconstruction work, hospital work, and relief work among the destitute.

Q. What is the Society of the Cincinnati and what was George Washington's connection with it? D. O.

A. The Society is an hereditary patriotic Society organized in 1783 by the American and foreign officers of the Continental Army assembled in their cantonment on the Hudson River near Fishkill, New York. The objects of the Society were: "To perpetuate as well the remembrance of the Revolution as the mutual friendships which have been formed under the pressure of common danger. . . ." Since most of the officers were returning to their farms which they had left to fight for the Republic, they named their organization the Society of the Cincinnati after their Roman prototype, Lucius Quinctius Cincinnatus. George Washington was the first President-General.

Q. When was the Daughters of Rebekah founded? L. B. P.

A. The Daughters of Rebekah was founded at South Bend, Indiana, in 1857 by Schuyler Colfax "to reconcile women to the pledge of secrecy made by their husbands by inducing them to take similar obligations."

Q. When was the first building and loan association formed in this country? C. S.

A. It was formed on January 3, 1831, at Frankford, Pennsylvania, by three citizens and called the Oxford Provident Building and Loan Association. There are now over 12,000 such associations in the United States, and 8,000,000 homes have been financed within the 100 years since the first one was formed.

Q. Who founded the Order of Moose? When did Senator Davis become a high officer of the organization? T. C.

A. The Loyal Order of Moose was founded in 1888 at Louisville, Kentucky, by Dr. J. H. Wilson. James J. Davis became its director general in 1906.

Q. Is the Camp Fire Girls an organization of wide ramifications? F. L.

A. It has members in every State of the Union and in seventeen foreign countries.

Q. What does Kiwanis mean? W. W.

A. It finds its origin in a word in one of the Indian languages—Keewanis. This may be translated in English, to make oneself known. In the Kiwanis Clubs, it is interpreted as the accomplishing of worth-while things. Their slogan is, "We Build."

Q. How does a family organization function? M. O.

A. Many family organizations are regularly incorporated bodies. Reunions are held regularly and on special dates to celebrate events connected with the family history. Regular officers are appointed and business meetings held. A genealogy of the family may be compiled and papers or pamphlets prepared on prominent members of the family or events of special interest with which they were connected. The family gatherings are also largely social.

Q. What, if any, is the connection between the A. F. L. and the I. W. W., and where is the headquarters of each? E. L. S.

A. There is no connection whatever between the American Federation of Labor and the Industrial Workers of the World. The A. F. of L. headquarters is A. F. of L. Building, Washington, D. C., and the headquarters of the I. W. W. is 90 E. 10th Street, New York City.

Q. What is the Order of the Purple Heart? F. D. R.

A. The Order of the Purple Heart was first established by George Washington, at Newburgh, New York, August 7, 1782, during the War of the Revolution, for military merit. This order was reëstablished on February 22, 1932, by President Hoover. The emblem consists of the figure of a heart on purple cloth, or silk, edged with narrow lace or binding, which is to be worn on the coat facings of recipients, over the left breast.

Q. What should the minutes of an organization include? A. W.

A. The essentials of the minutes are: Name of organization; time and place of meeting; kind of meeting, whether regular, special, adjourned, etc.; the fact of the presence or absence of the regular chairman and secretary, and the names of their substitutes, if they are absent; whether the minutes of the preceding meeting were read and approved; all main motions made at the meeting, except those that were withdrawn, and points of order and appeals, whether sustained or lost, and all other motions not lost or withdrawn; usually the names of members introducing main motions are recorded, but not the names of seconders.

Q. What is the Federal Council of Churches? H. F.

A. The Federal Council of Churches of Christ in America was organized at Philadelphia, 1908. Thirty denominations united for the purpose of enabling churches coöperatively to obtain results which they could not hope to do alone; to express the fellowship and unity of the Christian church; to unite the Christian bodies of America into service for Christ in the world at large; to encourage devotional fellowship and mutual counsel; and to secure a larger combined interest for the churches of Christ in all matters affecting the moral and social condition of all people. The headquarters is 105 East 22nd Street, New York City.

Q. What is the significance of the spinning wheel emblem of the D. A. R.? C. V.

A. The 13 spokes represents the 13 original States and the projecting ends of the spokes the 13 stars in the first flag, the spinning wheel being emblematical of woman's work during the Revolutionary period.

Q. What kind of an organization is P. E. O.? D. L. H.

A. P. E. O. was founded January 21, 1869, at Mt. Pleasant, Iowa, by seven girls. At first it was simply a secret society of a local school, but spread until at the present time it is reported to have 30,000 members scattered through the different States. Its present object is the acquisition and disposition of an educational loan fund whereby young girls past high school, who have not the means to secure higher education, may make a loan for one or two years to carry them through the preparatory college classes.

Q. What is the National Economy League? E. C. N.

A. The National Economy League is a self-organizing body, the object of which is to aid in bringing about economy in government expenditures. Delegates from 30 States attended the first meeting to form a country-wide organization of the League. Rear Admiral Richard E. Byrd termed the League a "National coalition of citizens to supply an effective method of correcting the gross governmental mistakes that are making this depression chronic." Its purpose is also to bring about Government economy by eliminating allowances to veterans not actually disabled in war service and preventing immediate payment of the bonus.

Q. What are Alpine Clubs? A. N.

A. Alpine Clubs are societies established primarily to promote a spirit of fellowship among lovers of the sport of mountaineering, and also foster mountain exploration and scientific research. They are to be found in most of the leading countries. The largest Alpine Club in the United States is the Appalachian Mountain Club. On the Pacific Coast are the Sierra Club, the Mazamas, and the Mountaineers.

Q. Is there a League for the prevention of suicide? D. W. G.

A. There is a Save-A-Life League with headquarters at 299 Madison Avenue, New York City.

Q. Please supply me with addresses of communistic societies in the United States, on the order of the Brook Farm experiment. J. O.

A. The principal communistic societies of the United States are the Amana Society, organized 1714 in Germany, headquarters, Amana,

Iowa; the Shakers or true believers, founded in England in 1770, headquarters, Mt. Lebanon, New York; and the Oneida Community, headquarters, Oneida, New York.

Q. What are some of the achievements of the Grange? T. R.

A. Strictly speaking this is not the correct title of the agricultural organization, the official title being Society of Patrons of Husbandry. The Grange is equivalent to the term lodge used in other fraternal orders. It originated in a secret association of farmers founded at Washington, D. C., December 4, 1867, through the influence of Oliver Hudson Kelly, a Minnesota farmer who was deputed by the Government, 1866, to make a tour of inspection through the southern States and to report upon their agricultural conditions and the best means of improving them. From this small beginning the organization has grown to its present enormous proportions, and claims as a part of its achievements, the creation of the Department of Agriculture as a Cabinet office, the founding of State Agricultural Experiment Stations, and of the Interstate Commerce Commission.

Q. How old is the nude cult of Germany? A. J.

A. It started about 1900. Most of the cities have groups, Berlin having 20. The movement has approximately 25,000 members.

Q. Is the present Ku Klux Klan a continuation of the organization of the Civil War Period? J. F. V.

A. The Ku Klux Klan originated in Pulaski, Tennessee, first as a social organization, and afterwards as a means of preserving the white supremacy and combatting the misrule which arose during the reconstruction period. It became corrupt and fell largely into the hands of a lawless element of society. It was suppressed by the Force Bill, passed by Congress, April 20. 1871. The later organization known as the Ku Klux Klan claims as its principle "the enforcement of the laws of the Constitution, and the bringing together into an organization all those possessing one hundred per cent Americanism."

Q. *Are all boys eligible to the organization known as De Molay?* B. R.

A. The Order of De Molay is an organization to which sons of Masons and their chums, over 16 years of age, are eligible. The object is to commemorate the fidelity and patriotism of Jacques de Molay, a Knight Templar of the middle ages, who allowed himself to be put to death, rather than reveal the secrets of his Order.

Q. *Why is the hour of eleven observed by the Elks?* E. G. M.

A. Originally the Elks were known as The Jolly Corks, a club of men composed exclusively of actors who usually met in New York on Sunday nights in friendly fellowship, and they formed a club and the custom was established of drinking to the absent ones at 11 o'clock every Sunday night, and as a result thereof remembrance of absent members became one of the principles of the present great Order of Elks, and the custom is regularly observed in Elks homes and clubs and Lodges.

Q. *Just what is the objective of the Rockefeller Foundation?* G. T.

A. The Rockefeller Foundation was incorporated May 14, 1913, and originated in a trust fund established by John D. Rockefeller of $100,-000,000, which has been greatly added to since. Its object is to provide and manage funds for the purpose of promoting the well-being of mankind throughout the world. Some of the great achievements have been the establishment of medical research which greatly helped to ameliorate the sufferings of the soldiers in the World War, and the campaign for the extermination of hook worm, which is one of the most destructive parasites.

Q. *What is the Everywhere League?* H. H.

A. It is a correspondence club for the hard of hearing. It has about four hundred members. It is conducted under the auspices of the American Federation of Organizations for the Hard of Hearing, Inc.

Q. *Is there an association of towns named for towns in England?* L. S.

A. There is a Namesake Towns Association in connection with the English-Speaking Union of the United States. It was organized to promote friendly relations between the cities and towns of America and England bearing the same names.

Q. *What is the salary of the head of the American Red Cross?* J. A.

A. When Judge John Barton Payne became Chairman of this great organization in 1921, it was with the stipulation that he would receive no salary, and would pay all of his own expenses.

CHAPTER 53

PATENTS, TRADE-MARKS, AND COPYRIGHTS

Q. Can an individual secure a patent without employing an attorney? L. P.

A. The Patent Office advises inventors to employ a competent attorney to aid in procuring patents, because generally an application cannot be prepared properly except by some one trained in this work. It is also advised that great care be exercised in this selection. The value of a patent depends largely upon skillful preparation of specifications and claims.

Q. Did Abraham Lincoln ever take out a patent? N. H.

A. Abraham Lincoln received a patent, No. 6469, on Camel and Floating Dock on May 22, 1849.

Q. How long did Thorvald Solberg serve as Register of Copyrights? R. L. C.

A. He was appointed to the position when it was created in 1897 and held it until he retired upon his 78th birthday, April 22, 1932.

Q. How many countries are signatories of the International Copyright Union? W. J. A.

A. There are 30, counting Great Britain as one. Her self-governing dominions, however, are individual members.

Q. Is an improvement on a machine patentable? S. D.

A. In the case of Smith vs. Nichols, 21 Wall. 118, the court said "A new idea may be ingrafted upon an old invention, be distinct from the conception which preceded it, and be an improvement. In such case it is patentable. The prior patentee cannot use it (the patented improvement) without the consent of the improver, and the latter cannot use the original invention without the consent of the former."

Q. What does the term "interference" mean in connection with a controversy over a patent application? M. N.

A. An interference is a proceeding instituted to determine the question of priority when two inventors are making practically the same claims for a patent.

Q. Who invented the suction type of rubber heel? B. D.

A. John George Tufford conceived the idea of making the inner surface of a rubber heel concave so that suction would keep the edges tight against the shoe without cement.

Q. When was the first publication copyrighted in this country? D. J. I.

A. Noah Webster was the first to take advantage of the Copyright Law. His Grammatical Institute of the English Language, published in 1783, was so protected.

Q. Does a copyright notice have to appear in a certain place in a book? M. D.

A. The Copyright Law is specific as to the place where the copyright notice shall appear and as to the

356

form that the copyright notice shall take. Many court decisions have been handed down ruling that if these specific requirements are not followed, the copyright is invalid. Other decisions have established that publication without proper notice is a dedication of the material to the public.

Q. Has the Patent Office any publication? P. L. R.

A. Each week the Patent Office publishes the Patent Office Gazette which lists the patents issued each week. This publication sells for $10 a year without index and $11.50 with index. Single numbers may be purchased for 25¢.

Q. How long may the ownership of a patented invention be contested? B. L.

A. The true ownership of a patented invention may be contested within two years after the patent has been issued.

Q. How long ago were cross-word puzzles invented? C. M. F.

A. Something similar to the cross-word puzzle is said to have taken up much of the time of the Hindus and Chinese as long ago as 1000 B.C. The American Indians also played some kind of criss-cross game with grains of corn when the first white men arrived on this continent. Magic squares played an important part in the occultism and mysticism of the Middle Ages. These seem to have been the predecessors of the cross-word puzzles of today.

Q. How do writers of columns, comic strip artists, political commentators, and similar newspaper contributors protect their material? A. McD.

A. While the former practice was to copyright such material, there is a growing practice of registering titles as trade-marks. The theory is that the contributor's regular readers look for the distinctive column heading or title and that if this is protected against use by another, there is no

necessity for protecting the actual material printed or displayed from day to day. The Patent Office now lists some 6000 such trade-marked captions.

Q. Can a copy of a patent be secured? F. R.

A. After a patent has been issued, uncertified copies of the specifications and accompanying drawings, if in print, may be secured for 10¢ from the Patent Office, Washington, D. C.

Q. In case one makes a synopsis, or abstract, or summary of a printed book, and publishes the same and offers it for sale—is there then any infringement of copyright law or other rights of the author whose work is thus reviewed? N. M. L.

A. Section 6 of the Copyright Law states definitely that abridgements have been held to be an infringement of copyright.

Q Who was the official who offered to resign from the Patent Office many years ago because he thought everything had been invented? W. H. W.

A. This is one of the legends of the Patent Office, but cannot be absolutely authenticated or ascribed to any certain official. However, Commissioner of Patents Ellsworth in his report to Congress dated January 31, 1844, said: "The advancement of the arts from year to year taxes our credulity and seems to presage the arrival of that period when human improvement must end."

Q. What is infringement? L. O.

A. In the case of Johnson vs. Brick & Tile Co., 237 Fed. at 671, quoting Rogers on Patents, 137, the court said "Infringement is the unauthorized making, using, or selling for practical use, or for profit, of an invention covered by a valid claim of a patent during the life of the patent. It may involve any one or all of the acts of making, using, and selling. It is therefore an infringement for an unauthorized person to make a patented machine for use or for sale, though in fact it is neither used or sold."

Q. When was the loom invented? S. F.

A. The ancient Egyptians wove with a primitive loom. The first successful power loom was invented in 1785 by Edmond Cartwright.

Q. Is the Billiken protected by patent? M. F. B.

A. A patent for the Billiken No. 39603 was issued October 6th, 1908, to Florence Pretz.

Q. In what year did Rudyard Kipling get a trade-mark for the elephant's head? J. J.

A. His trade-mark was registered on January 18, 1901. The number is 35770.

Q. By what rule should a person be guided, in adopting a trade-mark, in endeavoring to avoid infringement of a trade-mark already in use by some one else? H. P.

A. The courts have said that a person entering a field of endeavor already occupied by another should, in the selection of a trade-name or trade-mark, keep far enough away to avoid all possible confusion. Whether there is an infringement of a trade-mark does not depend upon the use of the identical words, nor on the question as to whether they are so similar that a person looking at one would be deceived into the belief that it was the other. The courts incline to hold that infringement occurs if one adopts a trade-name or a trade-mark so like another in form, spelling, or sound, that a person, with a not very definite or clear recollection as to the real trade-mark, is likely to become confused or misled.

Q. For what purpose was the gyroscope invented? P. D.

A. When first invented, the gyroscope, then called rotascope, was used as a scientific toy to illustrate the dynamics of rotating bodies, the composition of rotations, etc. A delicately mounted form of the above apparatus invented by M. Foncault, is used to render visible the rotation of the earth on account of the tendency of the rotating wheel to preserve a constant plane of rotation, independent of the earth's motion. This same principle is made use of in an instrument invented by Dr. H. Auschutz-Kampfe, designed to replace the mariner's compass or to serve as a check upon its accuracy.

Q. Which were invented first— daguerreotypes or ambrotypes? E. F. S.

A. Daguerreotypes were in use prior to ambrotypes. The former were invented by Daguerre in 1839; the latter by Scott Archer of London in 1851.

Q. What have American women done in the field of invention? S. R.

A. While the first American invention was patented by a man, the records further state that the process was "found out by Sybille his wife." This patent was granted by the British Government to Thomas Masters for an invention for cleaning and curing Indian corn. For 19 years after the enactment of the patent law in 1790 not a single one of the 10,000 patents issued was granted to a woman. The first successful application for a woman was recorded in 1809 and was for a method of weaving straw with silk or thread. Even for a quarter of a century afterwards there were less than a score of patents granted to women. Women have patented inventions relating to power machinery, a belt drive, a flexible shaft coupling, a solar heating plant, a reversible turbine, automobile contrivances, machinery for harvesting and planting, kitchen and household appliances.

Q. What is a monomark? A. D.

A. It is a comon trade-mark used by British manufacturers or contemplated for use by them. The letters B C M are understood to represent the name British Commercial Monomark.

Q. By whom was the safety pin invented? Was the inventor a Christian? H. H. B.

A. Many forms of fibulas or brooches found by archaeologists in tombs, ruins, and elsewhere, are closely similar to modern safety pins. Fibulas are among the earliest metallic objects of antiquity. It probably is correct to say that no one knows or ever will know in what year fibulas or so-called safety-pins were invented, or by whom, and at best it can only be inferred that the first inventor was a heathen, or at any rate non-Christian. In recent times one form of safety pin was patented to T. Woodward under date of May 7, 1842; another form to I. W. Stewart, under date of August 16, 1870; and another form to W. H. Hockensmith under date of August 29, 1871.

Q. Who invented the yoyo? H. S.

A. The yoyo is a simple adaptation of the device popular through the centuries under various names. The popularity of the toy in recent years seems to have originated with a Mexican youth, Pedro Flores, who working in a Santa Barbara hotel, whittled a primitive yoyo out of wood, and placing a cord around the groove, amused the guests of the hotel.

Q. Who invented the zipper? A. R.

A. The term zipper is properly applied only to the overshoe made by the B. F. Goodrich Company. The hookless fastener to which this name is often applied was invented by Whitcomb L. Judson in 1893. It was later improved and patented by Gideon L. Sundback.

Q. When and where were scissors first used? H. C. A.

A. It was formerly believed that scissors were invented in Venice in the 16th century, but records show that implements similar to our modern scissors were in use very much earlier than this period. In the remains of Pompeii, shears were found made of iron and steel, as well as bronze. Scissors were also in use in various oriental countries from a very early period. It is stated that those manufactured in Europe were copied from the Persian. The oriental scissors were very much ornamented and frequently in the form of a bird, the blade forming the beak.

Q. Who made the kewpie and why was it so named? G. D.

A. Rose O'Neill put the first kewpie on the market in 1912. The name is a diminutive for cupid.

Q. When was the first carpet sweeper made? L. B.

A. Carpet sweepers of a crude pattern were made in England hundreds of years ago, but not until 1876 was this device seriously considered as a time saving, labor saving, household article. To Mr. M. R. Bissell is due the credit of producing the first carpet sweeper that did the work properly.

Q. Who invented the robot? J. M.

A. Eric Robot was created in 1928 in England by Captain William H. Richards.

Q. Are trade-mark laws in other countries similar to ours? O. G. C.

A. In discussing the principles of trade-mark laws existing in the world, two separate systems of law have to be considered, one system being that in force in the United States, Great Britain, France, and a few other countries where the first user of a trade-mark is protected, and the other system where ownership is based on registration of the mark. This latter system is used more generally throughout the Latin countries of the world. The law of the United States is practically unique in one respect, in that it requires as a basis of the right to register that the mark shall have been applied to goods sold in interstate or foreign commerce, this requirement following the clause of the Constitution in which trade-mark rights are recognized.

Q. *Is a man's own name a valid trade-mark?* K. J.

A. Yes, if written, printed, or impressed in a particular or distinctive manner, or in association with a portrait of the individual, and as thus used it will be registered by the United States Patent Office upon application for registration.

Q. *When were trade-marks first registered under laws of the United States?* H. S. G.

A. In 1870, under the Act of July 8, 1870. During 1870 there were 121 registrations under that law, the first thereof (No. 1) under date of October 25, 1870, by Averill Chemical Paint Co. of New York, N. Y. Prior to the enactment of such law, protection was sought to be secured in a few instances through taking out patents for designs for trade-marks. The Act of July 8, 1870 within a few years was declared void by the U. S. Supreme Court (Trade-Mark Cases) as unconstitutional. The subsequent Act of March 3, 1881, was superseded by the Act of February 20, 1905, which was supplemented by the Acts of May 4, 1906, and March 19, 1920, all of these three being now in force.

Q. *Who invented the paper bag?* G. A.

A. The paper bag is said to have been invented by Miss M. E. Knight.

Q. *What are the principal inventions of Thomas A. Edison?* W. M. L.

A. The incandescent lamp, phonograph, carbon telephone transmitter, microphone, motion pictures, an alkaline storage battery, many appliances and improvements for the transmission of electric light, heat, and power.

Q. *Who invented the ice-cream freezer?* D. L.

A. It is generally believed that the first ice-cream freezer was patented by Nancy M. Johnson in 1843. However, there is a memorandum in Washington's Cash Book to the

effect that he purchased an ice cream machine May 17th, 1784.

Q. *How many inventions had Thomas A. Edison?* L. B.

A. There is no way of telling how many inventions of Thomas A. Edison are in use. He is said to have been the most prolific inventor in the United States and was granted more than 1000 United States patents, some of which are famous throughout the entire world.

Q. *When was the first sewing machine made?* A. G.

A. It is probable that the first sewing machine was made by a man named Thomas Saint, who was born July 17, 1790. It was made of wood but resembled the later successful machines in that it had an overhanging arm, vertical ray, reciprocal needle containing thread, and automatic feed. It had a notch instead of an eye in the needle. A hole was punched with an awl for the needle to pass through. It produced a single thread chain stitch. In 1830 a sewing machine was patented in France and later in the United States which was successful enough to be employed in the manufacture of clothing for the French Army. In 1841 a machine using an eye pointed needle was invented. In 1846 Elias Howe patented a sewing machine containing most of the essential features of the modern machine.

Q. *What is a shop right?* B. F.

A. If an employee uses the time and equipment of a shop for producing an invention a shop right is automatically created on behalf of the owner of the shop.

Q. *What important inventions were made in England at the time of the Industrial Revolution?* F. G. M.

A. In 1770 Hargreaves patented the spinning jenny; the water frame was invented by Arkwright in 1769; Crompton's mule was introduced in 1779. Watt obtained his first patent for an improvement in the steam engine in 1769, and six years later it was successfully applied to cotton manufacture.

Q. Who invented vestibule trains? C. L. M.

A. George Mortimer Pullman, who built the first sleeping car, also put into execution the idea of vestibule trains.

Q. Is it wise to manufacture and sell a newly invented article before applying for a patent? O. F.

A. According to Section 4899, U. S. Statutes "Every person who purchases of the inventor, or with his knowledge and consent constructs any newly invented or discovered machine or other patentable article prior to the application by the inventor for a patent, or who uses or sells one so constructed, shall have the right to use and vend to others to be used, the specific thing so made or purchased without liability therefor."

Q. Can a patent be secured for a new use of an old mechanism? J. D.

A. Such a discovery is not patentable unless a better result is obtained.

Q. Will the first person to file an application for a patent for a certain invention always be the one to receive the patent? L. H. J.

A. He will not. He will, however, be the senior party in an interference controversy.

Q. Is a patent assignable? P. O.

A. If a part or whole interest in a patent is transferred for a valuable consideration, the instrument by which this is done is called an assignment.

Q. If an inventor has insufficient funds for a patent and secures financial backing from another person, should the two file an application as joint inventors? R. F.

A. If a patent is secured by two persons who claim to be joint inventors, whereas only one is the inventor and one is the financier, the resulting patent is rendered invalid. The sole inventor should apply for a patent and make a proper assignment of the agreed interest to the other party.

Q. Can a patent be secured for a medicinal compound? P. M. A.

A. A patent for a medicinal compound is obtainable only in rare instances. Such medicine must be beyond the skill of an ordinary physician.

Q. What is a design patent? K. O.

A. A design patent is given one who has invented a new, original, and ornamental design for an article of manufacture, such as an ornamental design on wall paper, rugs, or furniture.

Q. Is there danger in manufacturing an invention while the application for patent is pending? L. K.

A. The principal danger in manufacturing an invention while the patent application is pending is that one may become involved in an interference procedure.

Q. What are the penalties for infringing a copyright? H. O.

A. Any person who wilfully and for profit shall infringe any copyright or who shall knowingly aid such infringement shall, upon conviction, be punished by imprisonment not to exceed one year or by a fine of not less than $100 nor more than $1000, or both, in the discretion of the Court. Imprinting or affixing a false notice of copyright subjects that person to a fine of $1000. Innocent infringement subjects that infringer to the surrender and destruction of the unauthorized copies and to the payment of damages in sums ranging from $10 up to $5000. Wilful infringement subjects the infringer to damages in excess of $5000 in the discretion of the Court and in accordance with the extent of the wilful infringement.

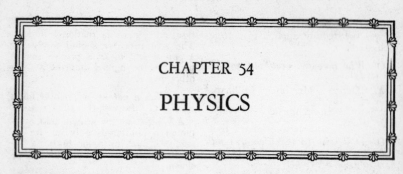

CHAPTER 54
PHYSICS

Q. How long does it take sound to travel over telephone wires from San Francisco to New York? C. J.

A. It takes .02 to .07 seconds for unloaded and loaded open wire line respectively.

Q. When a photograph has begun to fade, can anything be done about it? W. W.

A. The fading is usually caused by improper fixing and washing. To prevent further change fix in a hypo bath of usual strength for 10 to 20 minutes and wash in running water for one hour.

Q. Why do the colors in cloth appear brighter and deeper when wet? D. W.

A. Cloth appears brighter and deeper in color when wet because the minute droplets of water fill up the spaces between the threads and refract the light.

Q. Do the frosted electric light bulbs give as much light as the clear ones? M. Z. M.

A. The inside-frosted lamps give very nearly the same light output as do clear lamps of the same size and efficiency rating. There is a loss of light a little less than two per cent.

Q. Why is blue called a cool color? G. A. P.

A. All colors are produced by vibrations of rays of light. Those vibrating less than 470 billion times per second produce a red sensation and are described as warm. As the number of vibrations increases shades of orange, yellow, green, blue, and violet appear. The slower the rays move the greater amount of energy is contained by the light. The more rapid vibrations contain less energy and therefore are a smaller tax upon the eye and produce colors which are described as cold.

Q. Is it possible to take a picture through a microscope with an ordinary camera? R. H. S.

A. It is possible to take a picture through a microscope. Remove the camera lens and fit the camera to the eyepiece end of the microscope; focus the microscope on the camera ground glass and photograph as usual.

Q. What is the frequency of a sound which can be heard most distinctly at the greatest distance? R. D. W.

A. The Bureau of Standards says the distance at which a sound can be heard depends principally upon the sensitiveness of the ear to sounds of different pitches. Ordinarily the human ear is most sensitive to sounds of a frequency of from 1000 to 2000 cycles a second. The soprano high C is approximately at the lower of these two frequencies.

Q. Is it possible to create a perfect vacuum? T. L. S.

A. It is not possible to create an absolutely perfect vacuum. This is at present a mere intellectual concept. No physical or chemical method has been devised for effecting the absolute removal of every trace of matter from any portion of space having finite measurements. By the use of a good modern air-pump a degree of exhaustion can be obtained which is so perfect that no residual matter can be detected except by the most delicate testing. The Sprengel pump invented about 1865 is able to produce a vacuum so nearly perfect that the residual pressure probably does not exceed the 400,000,000th part of an atmosphere.

Q. What is specific gravity? E. E.

A. It is the weight of a body compared with the weight of the same volume of water. Thus the average specific gravity of rock is 2.77, meaning that a cubic foot of rock weighs 2.77 times as much as a cubic foot of water.

Q. How cold is cold? P. P.

A. Cold is a term used to designate a temperature below the normal, the normal being based on the sensations of the human body.

Q. Could you tell me what light is? C. L. W.

A. Light is physically defined as radiant energy, which is capable of producing the effect of vision. Light waves consisting of vibrations in the ether sent out by the sun and other luminous bodies strike the retina of the eye, cause the optic nerve to vibrate, and produce the sensation of sight.

Q. Are gyroscopes the fastest turning wheels in existence? T. H. S.

A. The speed at which gyroscopes turn is from 10,000 to 20,000 revolutions per minute. Small internal grinding wheels are sometimes driven at 50,000 revolutions per minute.

Q. When two small objects are floating near each other in a basin of water, why are they suddenly drawn together as if by a magnet?

A. The weight of the floating particles stretches the surface of the water, forming a dimple. When the two particles come close enough, the two dimples coalesce into one throwing the particles together. The action is due to surface tension, in virtue of which the surface is constantly striving to reduce its exposed area to a minimum.

Q. Can heat rays be reflected with a mirror the same as light rays can? E. F.

A. The Bureau of Standards says that they can. The loss depends upon the reflecting surface. All polished metals reflect from 90 to 95 per cent of the infra-red (heat) rays. The reflection of visible light varies over a wide range, but may be from 90 to 98 per cent for highly polished silver.

Q. I recently read something about the flattest thing in the world. What is it? J. H.

A. The flattest surfaces in the world are three disks in the Bureau of Standards made from clear fused quartz or silica glass.

Q. Is it possible to light a cigarette with steam? D. S.

A. It is possible. This was demonstrated by Dr. Andrade of the Royal Institution of London, who produced high pressure steam hot enough to set fire to a match or a cigarette. The steam which escapes from a tea kettle is not really steam. It has ceased to be steam since it has condensed to tiny drops of liquid water. Water steam is invisible gas.

Q. Can sounds such as a clap of thunder or the purr of a cat be measured? C. E. G.

A. The frequency of vibration of any sound having a definite pitch can be accurately measured by means of a microphone and an oscillograph. Many sounds, such as a clap of thunder or the purring of a cat will be complex sounds consisting of mixtures of sound of different pitches. Such sounds can be recorded on the oscillograph and analyzed into their simple components whose frequencies can be determined.

Q. What makes snow stick together in a snowball? F. O.

A. A snowball is formed by the regelation of the particles forming it. Pressure lowers the freezing point and melts the particles which bear upon each other. Then the freezing point rises and the hard ball is held together.

Q. Can a man pushing against an ordinary brick wall move it even in the slightest degree? W. P.

A. There would be some deflection. An instrument constructed at the Bureau of Standards, Washington, can measure the amount of deflection of a brick wall 40 inches thick under the pressure of one finger. This instrument is so delicately adjusted that if one person looks into the eyepiece while another walks across the floor the deflection is apparently so great that the whole building seems to be swaying back and forth as though made of cardboard.

Q. Why is a soap bubble round? How many surfaces has it? What causes the play of colors? J. D. F. S.

A. A liquid surface by virtue of the surface tension tends to become as small as conditions will permit, and a sphere has a smaller surface than any other solid of equal volume. This explains why a soap bubble is round. A soap bubble has two surfaces, one inside and one out. A soap bubble has many mirror surfaces and light falling on it is reflected back and forth from them so that there is interference among the various trains of light waves. This produces the variety of colors.

Q. Do carpets and rugs in a choir loft reduce the reverberation of sound? T. N.

A. The Bureau of Standards says that carpets and rugs absorb sound and have the effect of reducing the reverberation time of a room. The area of the floor covering in a choir loft of average size would hardly be large enough to have any deadening effect upon the reverberation in the church as a whole. Musicians generally prefer to have their immediate surroundings bare and reverberant.

Q. What is superheated steam? D. J.

A. It is steam at a temperature higher than the condensing point corresponding to its actual volume and density, so that it will expand and do work without being condensed.

Q. What was the Florentine Experiment? R. G. A.

A. The Florentine Experiment, in physics, was an experiment made in 1661 to test whether or not water was compressible. Water was enclosed in a globe of thin gold, afterward hermetically sealed. In compressing the globe the water, instead of yielding, forced its way through the pores of the gold and stood in drops on the outer surface.

Q. How much does a cubic foot of air weigh? D. L.

A. One cubic foot of air at 32° F. and atmospheric pressure weighs 0.080728 pound.

Q. What is the expansive force exerted at the moment of freezing of water? H. G.

A. The sudden expansive force exerted at the moment of freezing is sufficiently great to split iron water pipes, being probably not less than 30,000 pounds per square inch. There have been instances of its splitting cast tubular posts of iron bridges and of ordinary buildings.

Q. When using double glass to prevent frost in cold weather, what is the proper distance to have between the two glasses? W. A. T.

A. The Bureau of Standards says that the most efficient spacing between double glass is ¾ inch.

Q. How far does a man have to fall to gain maximum speed? A. B.

A. An experiment was conducted at Wright Field to determine how fast a man falls when dropped from a great height. The velocity was found to be considerably lower than that deduced from the theory of falling bodies. Were there no atmosphere a man would fall 16 feet the first second; 64 feet in two seconds; 256 feet in four seconds; 1024 feet in eight seconds, etc., the distance increasing as the square of the time. Due to the resistance of the air, however, there comes a time when the velocity is no longer increased. This is known as the terminal velocity, and was found to be less than 200 miles an hour. It was reached after the man (dummy) had fallen 1600 feet.

Q. *Is air ever visible?* V. N.

A. Sometimes it is. When thrown into agitation by heat, it may be seen rising from a stove or from the heated ground.

Q. *Can water be compressed?* N. H. M.

A. Water is very slightly compressible. Its compressibility is from 0.000040 to 0.000051 for one atmosphere, decreasing with increase of temperature. For each foot of pressure distilled water will be diminished in volume 0.0000015 to 0.0000013. Water is so incompressible that even at a depth of a mile a cubic foot of water will weigh only about half a pound more than at the surface.

Q. *Who first had the idea of colors graduated on a music scale?* D. N.

A. Graduation of colors on a musical scale was first suggested by Sir Isaac Newton and has been followed by a multitude of others.

Q. *If a metal ring which is perfectly round is magnetized, where will the north and south poles be?* W. H. K.

A. If a ring of ferromagnetic material is magnetized by means of a toroidal coil wound upon it, and if the material is uniform in magnetic properties throughout, there will be no magnetic poles. If magnetized in a solenoid or between the poles of an electromagnet, the poles will be at opposite ends of a diameter.

Q. *What is the difference between potential energy and kinetic energy?* R. C. G.

A. Energy is the capacity for performing work. It may be either potential, as in the case of a body of water stored in a reservoir capable of doing work by means of a waterwheel, or actual, sometimes, called kinetic, which is the energy of a moving body. Potential energy may also exist as stored heat, as stored mechanical energy, as in fuel, or as electrical energy, the measure of these energies being the amount of work that they are capable of performing. Actual energy of a moving body is the work which it is capable of performing against a retarding resistance before being brought to rest and is equal to the work which must be done upon it to bring it from a state of rest to its actual velocity.

Q. *How many degrees hot is a red hot coal?* F. L.

A. The phrase red hot is used popularly to designate any temperature between 700° C. and 1000° C. Above 1000° C. the phrase employed to describe an object would usually be white hot although the color would still be primarily red or reddish yellow. A lump of coal would first become visibly red at about 600° C. in a very dark room, although one would have to look closely in order to see the light given off at this temperature.

Q. *What is the meaning of the word Mazda in connection with an electric light bulb?* A. M.

A. The followers of Zoroaster believed that Ahura Mazda (Wise Lord) was, to quote from their Avesta or Bible, "The Supreme Deity, the All-Father, existent before the world arose, and from whom the world emanated, its course governed by His all-seeing eye." The good spirit, Mazda or Armazd, represented light and life, and created all that was good and pure. All other gods were subordinate to Mazda. According to the Westinghouse Lamp Company, "just as the original Ahura Mazda typified supremacy and beneficence, so the word Mazda today is understood to mean a standard of quality and of helpfulness, and has been frequently mentioned as not the name of a thing, but the mark of a service."

Q. *How long does a sound remain perceptible in the air?* M. L.

A. The length of time that a sound will remain perceptible after the source of sound has ceased operating depends upon several factors—the volume of the room, the nature of its interior finish, and the intensity of the initial sound.

Q. *How are very high temperatures and low ones measured?* J. T.

A. The Bureau of Standards says that high temperatures are measured by means of thermocouples, optical pyrometers, pyrometric cones, etc., and that temperatures below the freezing point of liquids are measured by the gas thermometer.

Q. *Is the water in a bucket perfectly level on top?* E. B.

A. The surface of the water in a common bucket is not perfectly level, but slightly concave. Due to capillarity and surface tension the water rises a little at the sides of the bucket.

Q. *Does an electric bulb become less efficient when old—that is, is more current used for the amount of light produced?* S. W. F.

A. An electric light bulb deteriorates with age and becomes less efficient, that is, it gives less light in proportion to the current consumed. Minute particles of the filament are deposited on the interior of the bulb.

Q. *What is the Magnus Theory?* F. L. D.

A. The Magnus principle denotes the action observed when a wind current is directed against a rotating body and is familiar in such phenomena as the pitching of a curved ball. By rotating a surface on which the wind is incident, the air currents on one side are deflected so that a suction is produced which serves to increase the force acting. In other words, by varying the speeds of rotation to the direction of rotation of the surface, the magnitude of the force is altered.

Q. *Why will two walls four feet apart, built to any great height, and plumbed straight up be farther apart at the top than at the bottom?* E. A. S.

A. The Bureau of Standards says that the reason that two walls starting at four feet apart at the base and plumbed straight up for any great height will be farther apart at the top than at the base is because the plumb bob points to the center of the earth.

Q. *What causes the report when an electric light bulb is broken?* J. M. L.

A. The vacuum type bulb produces a report when it is broken, this being caused by the outside air rushing into the vacuum.

Q. *What are the Magdeburg Hemispheres?* T. G. V.

A. In 1654, Otto von Guericke of Magdeburg performed an experiment before the Imperial Diet at Ratisbon in which he took two hollow hemispheres of copper or brass, rubbed the edges with grease, fitted them closely together, exhausted the air in the globe thus formed through a stopcock in one of the hemispheres, and showed that the hemispheres were held together with tremendous force. With hemispheres a foot in diameter this force is approximately one ton.

Q. *What would be the result if all the colors were blended together?* L. B. L.

A. The Bureau of Standards says that all the colors of the spectrum blended together give white. If all the colors of a paint box are mixed together the result is generally a drab dark brownish color.

Q. Who was the first physicist? R. B.

A. With Thales of Miletus the science of physics is said to have begun. An ancient fragment says, "Thales, who went to Egypt, first brought science into Greece. Much he discovered himself; of much, however, he transmitted the beginnings to his successors. Some things he made more general, some more comprehensible."

Q. Is anything dropped from a height considered a freely falling body? G. J. D.

A. A freely falling body is one moving only under the influence of gravity. This condition can be obtained only in a vacuum since air always offers some resistance.

Q. Please define gravitation. B. S.

A. Gravitation is the name given to the mutual attraction between different bodies of matter. The attraction is universal, and the Law of Universal Gravitation may be stated as follows: Every particle of matter in the universe attracts every other particle with a force that varies directly as the product of the masses of particles and inversely as the square of the distance between them.

Q. Why does water when passing from a basin into a drain pipe assume a rotary motion? H. C. V.

A. The rotary motion of water passing down a pipe is caused by the shape of the opening and the friction on the sides. The direction in which it runs depends upon how it started and it is not always the same direction.

Q. Does the water in waves move across the surface of the ocean or is it only the motion which travels? E. S. M.

A. Wave motion in a liquid represents a continuous handing on from particle to particle of a disturbance in the medium, without actual transfer of the medium itself. This may be demonstrated by throwing a stone into the water. It will be seen that waves run out in circles from the point at which the stone submerged. These waves seem to be actually moving, but if a chip be thrown on the surface of the water, it will be found that its motion is up and down and not in an outward direction.

Q. Are any of the ordinary light rays lost when an electric light bulb is placed behind a piece of clear plate glass? F. J. F.

A. The transmission factor of smooth clear glass is about 92 per cent in perpendicularly incident light, the loss being that reflected at the two surfaces. The amount of light transmitted varies with the angle of incidence and the refractive index of the glass. The reflector will absorb from 10 to 40 per cent of the light incident upon it, depending upon its surface.

Q. Is indirect lighting the best for close work? What color should the walls be for ease on eyes? J. T. S.

A. The American Standard Code of Industrial Lighting recommends an illumination of from 10 to 15 foot-candles on the work plane for close work in offices. To avoid eye strain the illumination should not be less than 6 foot-candles, but higher illumination increases the rapidity and accuracy of office work. Indirect lighting is not necessarily the best form of lighting for an office. Two things are essential for good lighting, viz., sufficient intensity and absence of glare. Under proper conditions semi-indirect lighting, or even direct lighting, may be satisfactory. Indirect lighting is more costly to install and maintain than semi-indirect or direct lighting. Walls should not be white or dark in color. A light buff is a good color for walls. Ceilings should be white. Walls and ceilings should have matt surfaces.

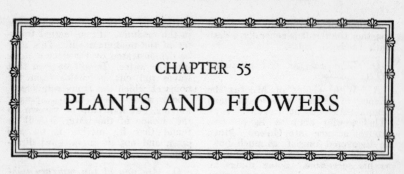

CHAPTER 55

PLANTS AND FLOWERS

Q. *Has a national flower been selected for the United States?* S. R. D.

A. Not officially. The American Nature Association conducted a vote for a national flower and out of one million expressions, there was a preponderance in favor of the wild rose. The second choice was the columbine.

Q. *How large has a rose bush been known to grow?* W. C.

A. The American Rose Annual says that at Whittier, California, is the largest known rose bush in the world. It is a Lamarque and is five feet around the trunk at one and one-half feet above the ground. Its branches cover a large house and it is estimated that there have been 180,000 blossoms on it at one time.

Q. *What is the largest flower in the United States?* F. L.

A. There would be a divergence of opinion regarding this. About the largest is a species of magnolia known as the umbrella tree, which has flowers varying from 8 to 15 inches in diameter.

Q. *When was the thistle adopted as the emblem of Scotland?* W. B.

A. It is said to have been adopted by the Scotch as early as the Eighth Century in commemoration of an unsuccessful night attack by the Danes on Stirling Castle. Their presence was unsuspected and was revealed through the barefooted scouts treading on the thistles and suddenly crying out. The alarm was given, and the Scots fell upon the party with terrible slaughter.

Q. *Who obtained the first patent on a plant under the new law?* T. C.

A. It was granted in August, 1931, to Henry F. Bosenberg of New Brunswick, N. J., for a new variety of ever-blooming rose.

Q. *Can four-leaved clover be propagated?* A. J. D.

A. This is possible. Four-leaved clovers will not come true from seed, as they are mutants or sports, but can be propagated by cuttings.

Q. *How many kinds of orchids are grown in the United States?* C. S.

A. There are estimated to be 3000 species of orchids under cultivation, and over 75 different varieties of wild orchids in the United States and Alaska.

Q. *How many seed catalogues are mailed to prospective purchasers each year?* M. A. H.

A. Annually, about 75,000,000 seed catalogues are distributed. To a great extent, this is a mail order business.

Q. *What is the record size for a dahlia?* B. T. B.

A. It is said that the largest dahlia recorded is a Fort Monmouth fifteen and one-half inches across. At a Englewood, N. J., show three Fort Monmouth blooms came in first, second, and third for size. The first, mentioned above; the second, fifteen inches; and the third, fourteen and one-half inches.

Q. *Please give the names of some flowers which are amusing, such as kiss-me-over-the-garden-gate.* F. K.

A. Here are some more: Dutchman's breeches, bachelor's button, Johnny-jump-up, painted lady, bleeding heart, old man, Venus's chariot, Queen Anne's lace, love-lies-bleeding, milk maid, Jack-in-the-pulpit, London pride, Venus's fly trap, Turk's-cap lily, the Devil's bit, queen-of-the-meadows, Quaker ladies, friar's cap, and obedient plant.

Q. *What can be planted on a raw steep bank to hold it? Something which grows rapidly.* T. O'B.

A. Honeysuckle is often used. Pockets should be dug into the banks and the vines planted. They grow rapidly, make a pleasing bank, and flower once or twice a year.

Q. *Of what country is the sweet pea a native?* J. N.

A. The sweet pea is a native of the island of Sicily, and was first mentioned in 1695, by an Italian monk, who sent seeds to England and Holland. The seeds of sweet peas became an article of commerce as early as 1724.

Q. *Who produced the Shasta Daisy?* H. R. F.

A. Luther Burbank was the originator.

Q. *Is it possible to grow a plant from an avocado seed in water?* S. M.

A. A handsome house plant can be grown from an avocado seed. The seed must be suspended in the water so that only part of it is immersed. The plant has large bright green leaves.

Q. *How many kinds of asters are there?* M. S.

A. There are over 250 species of asters. They are native of temperate regions, being especially abundant throughout the United States. Asters belong to the family Compositae, and are so named from the radiate or star-like appearance of the flowers. The China aster is also a member of the family Compositae, and is a native of China.

Q. *Why will ivy live in water?* M. B.

A. The Bureau of Plant Industry says that ivy planted in water gets its sustenance from the air, the water, and from the stored up material in the plant itself. Ivy planted in water will not continue to grow indefinitely. It will, however, under favorable conditions thrive for quite a while, the length of time depending upon how much plant food there is in the plant and in the water.

Q. *Of what is a lei made?* A. G. D.

A. Lei is an Hawaiian word meaning a wreath or garland of flowers. The true Hawaiian lei is made of fresh flowers and is used both in welcoming guests and bidding them farewell.

Q. *Is it true that putting aspirin tablets in the water will revive cut flowers which have begun to fade?* D. H.

A. The Bureau of Plant Industry says that in so far as they retard fermentation they will have this effect. Salt or sugar acts in the same way. But the treatment recommended is the daily changing of water and cutting of the stems, as this is the best method known for keeping flowers fresh. A low temperature is also helpful.

Q. *Are yellow jasmine and oleander poisonous?* M. B.

A. The Department of Agriculture advises us that yellow jasmine contains certain alkaloids which would cause toxicity if taken internally and caution should consequently be used concerning it. The oleander, however, is deadly poisonous and should never be kept on lawns or around houses where children may have access to it.

Q. *What kind of flowers will grow where the soil is poor?* **T. L.**

A. Such flowers as the following are suggested: Love-lies-bleeding, prince's feather, Joseph's coat, Cape marigold, godetia, dwarf nasturtium, portulaca, Scotch pink, sweet alyssum, garden balsam, and calliopsis.

Q. *Does the arrangement of flowers have special significance in Japan?* **T. A. G.**

A. It does. Flower-masters teach flower arranging and a course is included in the curriculum of nearly all girls' schools in Japan.

Q. *How are carnations dyed green?* **C. T.**

A. Placing the stems of white carnations in a weak solution of iron sulphate or copper sulphate will turn the blossoms green. An aniline dye which is soluble in cold water may be used instead. For different shades, try different proportions.

Q. *What is the floral emblem of Alaska?* **G. C.**

A. By an act of the legislature, approved in 1917, the wild native forget-me-not is the territorial and floral emblem of Alaska.

Q. *What flowers and trees are in danger of extinction in the United States?* **W. K.**

A. Some of them are: Columbine in Colorado, trailing arbutus in middle west, trillium and fringed gentian throughout the United States, holly through the south, and dogwood, particularly in the eastern and middle Atlantic States.

Q. *Does any other naturalist compare with the late Luther Burbank in accomplishments?* **B. L. E.**

A. For more than half a century Ivan Vladimirovich Michurin of Koslov, Russia, has been doing similar work. He has evolved 300 new fruits, berries, garden plants, and flowers, and although an old man is continuing experimental breeding. He has produced 25 new kinds of grapes and 52 new varieties of cherries. Before the revolution in Russia, he was visited by botanists of the United States Department of Agriculture.

Q. *What chemical will destroy grass on a tennis court?* **K. M.**

A. An effective chemical has been found to be calcium chloride. If this is applied at the beginning of the tennis season, it may be mixed with the top soil at the rate of at least two pounds to a square yard of surface.

Q. *What is the last sentence in Ingall's Blue Grass?* **W. J. A.**

A. "It yields no fruit in earth or air, and yet, should its harvest fail for a single year, famine would depopulate the world."

Q. *How can cannas be kept so that they will bloom again next year?* **V. E. B.**

A. Cannas should be lifted from their summer quarters just as soon as the foliage is blackened by the first frosts. Cut off the flowering stems about six inches from the ground. They should be closely packed together in boxes, using dry sand, and stored away where frost will not affect the rhizomes.

Q. *What is the name of the violet which is cultivated and sold by florists?* **H. W. J.**

A. The violet which is commonly used by florists is the European variety, Viola odorata. This is the common sweet violet which has been cultivated in Europe for hundreds of years.

Q. *Is there such a thing as a green rose which has not been artificially dyed?* **B. A. G.**

A. A type of green rose known as Viridiflora originated in Baltimore about 1850, and was mentioned by the National Rose Society in 1914. The petals are small, pointed, set thickly, and of the same color as the foliage of the rose, a dark pea green. The flower is of medium size and double, and is of vigorous growth. It may be considered more as a botanical freak than as a separate variety.

Q. *What flowers are used in southern Spain at Christmas time?* C. K.

A. Scarlet geranium and heliotrope answer in southern Spain the purpose of Christmas holly and mistletoe.

Q. *Does a campaign of publicity help to any extent in an effort to keep people from picking wild flowers and tree blossoms?* E. M.

A. The Wild Flower Preservation Society points to the campaign launched to preserve dogwood in Washington, D. C., and the surrounding country. It has been so successful that few branches are broken from the trees and the woods are increasingly beautiful each year when the trees are in bloom.

Q. *How many kinds of goldenrod grow in the United States?* A. L.

A. There are about 125 varieties of goldenrod, most of which are found in this country. They are cross-fertilized by butterflies and bees, and are typical insect-pollinated plants. The pollen gives a positive hay fever reaction, but, not being wind-borne, can cause hay fever only upon direct inhalation.

Q. *How was pink dogwood developed?* W. H.

A. The Forest Service says that pink dogwood originated from the white by grafting and may be considered a sport. This means that dogwood of a pink tinge was grafted on to other dogwood of a pink tinge, the color thereby being deepened.

Q. *How long has the chrysanthemum been cultivated?* G. C.

A. The chrysanthemum is the national flower of Japan where it has been known in cultivation for at least 2000 years. The conventional-

ized symbol of the chrysanthemum is used as the national coat of arms, the 16-petalled form of which is used only by members of the Japanese Imperial family.

Q. *How do florists arrange when they telegraph flowers for their patrons?* C. E. T.

A. Members of the Florist's Telegraph Delivery Association each have membership lists and also reports on the current prices and seasonal flowers in the different sections of the country. When a customer orders flowers to be wired, the order is telegraphed to the fellow member in the city named. He allows the florist first consulted 20 per cent commission on the order. There is in Detroit a clearing house where all accounts are settled. If the monthly balance is in favor of the florist, he receives a check and if there is a balance against him, he receives a statement.

Q. *What is a xerophyte?* T. A. L.

A. This term is compounded from two Greek words meaning "dry," and "plant," and refers to any drouth-loving or desert-inhabiting plant such as a cactus. Xerophyte is used on contradistinction to hydrophyte, a water-loving plant, halophyte, a plant inhabiting salty soil, and mesophyte, a plant requiring moderate moisture. It is to this last class (the word meaning "middle plant") that the great majority of plants belong.

Q. *What is the state flower of Florida?* H. O'N.

A. The orange blossom.

Q. *What is the soapberry plant?* C. T.

A. It is a shrub or tree of the genus Sapindus—native of tropical America. The pulp of the fruit contains saponin and is used in washing textile fabrics.

Q. *Why can Spanish moss grow on a telephone pole?* D. F. W.

A. Spanish moss can thrive on telephone poles because it is a true epiphyte. An epiphyte is a plant which derives the moisture required for its development from the air.

Q. How did the dandelion get its name? R. G. L.

A. Bailey's Standard Cyclopedia of Horticulture says that the word dandelion comes from the French "dent de lion" meaning lion's tooth which refers to the teeth on the leaves of the dandelion plant.

Q. Is there a plant which bears blue flowers which will grow and bloom in water? D. M. T.

A. The water hyacinth is a type of water plant that floats on the surface and sends out roots which contain air sacs, thus enabling the plant to float and not depend on an anchor. The flowers are blue or lavender and resemble the flowers of the hyacinth, hence the name.

Q. What color is the Thomas Edison dahlia? N. M.

A. This spectacular new dahlia named after the inventor is a rich royal purple.

Q. Please give a history of the pansy. R. R.

A. The commercial pansy of to-day is a development of a small flower native to Europe, variously named. It is a direct descendant of the heartsease of the English gardens and the Johnny-jump-up, and was probably brought to the United States by the earlier settlers.

Q. What is the flower that outlines the hedges around the Pan American Building in Washington, D. C.? A. D. H.

A. It is Phlox sublata.

Q. What is meant by the macchi of Corsica? C. S.

A. The macchi is the dense tangle of arbutus, myrtle, thorn, laurel, broom, and other flowering shrubs, with which the mountain sides of Corsica are covered. The aromatic fragrance of it can be detected far out at sea. It was to this fragrance that Napoleon referred upon his deathbed, when longing for the island of his birth, he said that he would know it by the smell of its soil, even though he were blindfolded.

Q. Please describe the Cherokee Rose. G. W. S.

A. It is a climbing rose naturalized in the southern United States. It has shining, usually trifoliolate leaves, and fragrant white flowers.

Q. What can be done for leaf blight in irises? M. E. M.

A. All dead leaves should be removed and the tops cut back in late fall or early spring. The fungus lives no place else. If the old leaves are destroyed, the source of the blight is removed.

Q. Where did the iris grow originally? V. A. J.

A. From the study of geographical distribution of the iris, it appears that the two centers of original location are central and southern Europe, and the Orient, especially China. For the most part, however, the exotic species are thoroughly at home on the American continent and in certain sections have established themselves as freely as any native plant.

Q. What is the flower of the District of Columbia? N. M.

A. The American Beauty rose.

Q. How long have dahlias been cultivated in European gardens? P. K.

A. Dahlia history commences in 1791, when Cavanilles, the director of the Botanic Garden of Madrid, Spain, described the flowering of a set of dahlia roots received in 1789 from Vicente Cervantes, of Mexico. Dahlias first reached England in 1798 through the agency of the Marchioness of Bute. This had little effect on the history of the plant, however, as all these plants perished from a lack of proper understanding of their needs. They were reintroduced successfully in 1804, through the interest of Lady Holland.

Q. Why was the leek selected as the national flower of Wales? W. B.

A. One story is that St. David, patron Saint of the Welsh, on one occasion caused his countrymen under King Cadwallader to distinguish themselves from their Saxon foes by wearing leeks in their caps.

Q. Is there such a thing as a rose resembling a carnation? T. M.

A. The Carnation Rose was found at the Château of the Abbey of St. Nicolas-aux-bois in 1912. The National Horticulture Society of France awarded it the Certificate of Merit in 1922.

Q. Where does the pasqueflower grow? S. N.

A. The pasqueflower is strictly a western spring blossom. Its chief range is over the plains of the Platte and the upper Missouri. It is found in the western mountains as high as the plateau of Yellowstone Park. Eastwardly it crosses Minnesota and Iowa and its easternmost habitat, so far as is known, is on the prairie hills overlooking the Apple River in northern Illinois.

Q. What is the national flower of Lithuania? C. S.

A. The national flower emblem of Lithuania is the rue, in Lithuanian ruta.

Q. What is the local name of the hibiscus, Hawaii's national flower? A. H.

A. The flower emblem of Hawaii is the pua alcalo.

Q. Which roses are superior, own-root roses, or budded or grafted roses? S. G.

A. Many florists think own-root roses are best. They are not so susceptible to disease as the others are likely to be.

Q. How are water lilies transplanted? E. B.

A. Water lilies should be lifted during the early spring and planted in a location similar to that in which they were grown. When planted in an artificial pool they are usually placed in boxes containing about one cubic foot of soil consisting of a mixture of garden loam and well decomposed cow manure. They should if possible be planted not less than two feet deep in water so that they will not freeze.

Q. Are roses peculiar to any one region or country? L. P.

A. Wild roses of many varieties are found in abundance in practically all the temperate regions of the earth.

Q. Can narcissus be kept and made to bloom a second time? G. R. W.

A. The Bureau of Plant Industry says that narcissus bulbs may be forced to bloom the second time, provided they are well taken care of. They should be allowed to mature in the pots and allowed to rest the usual time. They should be planted in the fall of the year.

Q. What is hydrotropism? P. S.

A. Positive hydrotropism is the property in growing organisms of turning toward a moist surface—negative hydrotropism, away from a moist surface.

Q. What size are crimson clover seed? D. K.

A. About the size of a pin head.

Q. What does microphyllous mean? T. T.

A. It is a Greek word meaning small leaf.

Q. At the Pan American Building in Washington the grass looks so well. What kind of grass seed is used? W. H. D.

A. The lawn is formed of equal parts of Italian rye and red top. The lawn is well kept and watered.

Q. What flowers grow wild in California? V. M.

A. Some of the wild flowers of this state are: clarkia, California poppy, blazing star, baby-blue-eyes, white daisy, wild Canterbury bells, blue lupine, scarlet honeysuckle, white evening primrose, and California fuchsia.

Q. *Why not grow all fruits and shrubs from seeds?* O. M.

A. Where improvements have been made these qualities are not transmitted through the seed but are perpetuated through the buds. Hence the necessity of using parts of the plant itself by budding, grafting, and layering.

Q. *What kind of grass is used between the blocks in a stone walk?* H. A.

A. The best kinds are creeping bent or colonial bent used with red or Chewings fescue.

Q. *Is a rose bush without thorns a rarity?* F. B.

A. The Bureau of Plant Industry says that it is not rare. Some species have few or no thorns.

Q. *Are there white and yellow Darwin tulips?* F. V.

A. Originally, the Darwin tulips contained no whites and no yellows, but at the present time both colors are in the group.

Q. *How long has the poppy been known?* C. B.

A. Fred Richards says: "Since the days of the Sumerians, some five or six thousand years before the birth of Christ, the poppy was known, and in 700 or 800 B.C. it was not altogether ignored as a medicine. By 100 B.C. knowledge of the narcotic qualities of the drug was no longer a secret and Virgil writes of "the sleep-giving poppy."

Q. *What is the national flower of Germany?* J. H.

A. The Kaiserblume, which was the favorite flower of the Emperor Wilhelm I, is considered the German national flower. This is the blue flower which grows wild in cornfields and is called cornflower, bluebottle, bluebonnet, and bachelor's-button in this country. It is sometimes cultivated. Its scientific name is Centaurea cyranus.

Q. *How many varieties of gladiolus are there?* F. G. L.

A. In 1931 the American Gladiolus listed over 7000 varieties, of which probably 3000 are for sale by various growers. Of this 3000, perhaps 100 are outstanding.

Q. *What mixture of grass is recommended as a tough durable turf for an airport?* A. S. H.

A. The United States Department of Commerce recommends an evenly proportioned mixture of the following grasses: Canada Blue Grass, Fancy Kentucky Blue Grass, Fancy Red Top, Meadow Fescue, Hard Fescue, Sheep Fescue, Red Fescue, and Pacy's Perennial Rye Grass. For the best results the exact mixture should be determined by an experienced landscape gardener after a careful examination of the soil. For the cheapest runway surfaces of reasonably good quality, earth oiled with an asphaltic base oil is probably the solution.

Q. *What kinds of flowers keep best after they have been cut?* A. N.

A. Roses, orchids, lilies, carnations, chrysanthemums, spring flowers, and calendulas are the longest keeping of the flowers, according to the findings of A. M. S. Pridham and J. C. Ratsek of the New York State College of Agriculture. With the exception of the chrysanthemum, all of these flowers should receive a slanting cut at the base of the stem and be placed in deep, cool water which should be changed daily. The chrysanthemum stem should be mashed and then placed in cold water.

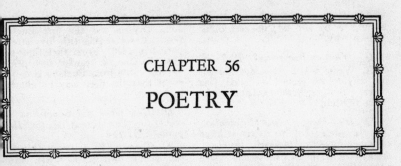

Q. *Whose poetry is most widely read?* L. D.

A. Probably Omar Khayyam's comes first. His quatrains are read, recited, and sung in all parts of the world.

Q. *Who bought a manuscript of Eugene Field's for a large sum during the World War?* L. D. M.

A. The manuscript of Little Boy Blue, perhaps Eugene Field's most popular poem, was bought at a war bazaar, by John McCormack for $2400.

Q. *In what circumstances was the poem, Mighty Lak' a Rose, written?* R. G. V.

A. It was written by Frank Stanton, Sr., at a time when his infant son was very ill. He is quoted as telling of it as follows: "One night when I came home from the office I stole upstairs to his crib and looked down into his feverish little face and I tell you my heart nearly broke, for fear he was going to die. His mother and grandmother were standing by me, and he was asleep. 'Isn't he the sweetest little fellow? He's just like a rose,' said his grandmother. I went to my room, picked up a piece of copy paper, and the poem wrote itself."

Q. *Please state where the smithy was that is mentioned in Longfellow's poem.* C. D. N.

A. Ernest Longfellow in his book "Random Memories" says: "A short time ago I saw in an English newspaper that the village smithy was in a certain English village that was named; as a matter of fact, as everybody knows, it was on Brattle Street, Cambridge, Massachusetts."

Q. *Where is the author of Home Sweet Home buried?* R. H. T.

A. The body of John Howard Payne is buried under the trees of Georgetown, D. C., in Oak Hill Cemetery where Payne used to walk with his friends.

Q. *Who wrote Carry Me Back to Old Virginny?* H. F. N.

A. This was the work of the negro poet James Bland.

Q. *How deep was Shakespeare's grave dug?* C. H. T.

A. The poet's grave in the little church at Stratford was dug 17 feet below the pavement of the chancel.

Q. *In his early life, in what work was Walt Whitman employed?* C. N. E.

A. In early life he was engaged as a printer, carpenter, and journalist. During the Civil War he volunteered as Army nurse.

Q. *What was the poem on the reasons for drinking that is attributed to Dean Henry Aldrich?* B. S.

A. This great churchman, who in 1692 was Vice-Chancellor of Oxford University, wrote a Latin epigram translated as follows: "If on my theme I rightly think, there are five reasons why men drink. Good wine;

a friend; because I'm dry or lest I should be by and by; or—any other reason why."

Q. *What is free verse?* P. T. N.

A. Verse which does not depend on rhyme or meter is called free verse. It does, however, have a certain rhythm.

Q. *Isn't there a poetical quotation to the effect that no house is large enough for two families?* H. G.

A. In Will M. Carleton's Over the Hill to the Poorhouse are the lines, "And a very little cottage one family will do, but I never have seen a house that was big enough for two."

Q. *What does William Butler Yeats preach as "the language of poetry"?* M. S.

A. The doctrine of simple words, the diction of the best human speech.

Q. *Where is the manuscript of the poem If I Should Die?* B. S. H.

A. The manuscript of this sonnet by Rupert Brooke is regarded as being so precious that it is preserved in the British Museum. It lies between a Dickens' manuscript and the Diary of Captain Scott.

Q. *Who was the first poetic writer in this country?* M. H. B.

A. F. V. N. Painter in his Poets of the South gives the honor to George Sandys. He came to Virginia in 1621. Sandys was practically the only poet in the south until the Revolution.

Q. *Please explain the Poet Laureateship of England.* R. M. R.

A. The origin of the laureateship is involved in obscurity. In early days the word laureate came to mean in English eminent. It was thus generally, although not always, applied in a literary sense. Medieval kings had poets or minstrels attached to their households who received pensions although their appointment was not official. In this way Ben Jonson was looked upon as the first laureate, but the title seems never to have been really conferred on him John Dryden was the first English poet to receive the title by letters patent in 1670. From that time the post became a regular institution A press cable from England is to the effect that the post may be allowed to lapse.

Q. *How much did Longfellow receive for The Wreck of the Hesperus?* H. T.

A. Twenty-five dollars. This was the poet's own price. The editor wrote in accepting the poem: "Your ballad is grand. Enclosed are $25 the sum you mention, for it, paid by the proprietors of the New World in which glorious paper, it will resplendently coruscate in Saturday next. Of all American journals, the New World is alone worthy to contain it."

Q. *What poem did Coleridge regard as the finest in the language?* D. W.

A. Blanco White's sonnet, To Night, was so regarded by the poet.

Q. *What did Kipling write which offended the King so that Kipling was never offered the poet laureateship?* W. T. J.

A. According to rumor it was Kipling's poem The Widow at Windsor which kept Kipling from being appointed poet laureate.

Q. *Was Coleridge's The Ancient Mariner an entirely original work, or was it based on a legend or something of that sort?* H. H.

A. Coleridge embodied the dream of a friend in The Ancient Mariner and the suggestion of the shooting of the albatross came from his fellow poet, Wordsworth.

Q. *Is the man to whom Casey at the Bat was written still living?* N. D.

A. Casey at the Bat was written as a tribute to Henry Chadwick of Brooklyn who is called the father of baseball. Mr. Chadwick died in 1908.

Q. *What is the foundation for the poem, Evangeline? S. A. S.*

A. The poem, Evangeline, is based on a true story, which traveled from Canada to New England by word of mouth, finally reaching Hawthorne, who did not care to use it for a romance and turned it over to Longfellow. The story has founded a national legend which has kept alive the memory of an episode which would otherwise have been forgotten.

Q. *Which did Milton prefer—Paradise Lost or Paradise Regained? H. E. W.*

A. The poet preferred the latter.

Q. *How early did Tennyson start writing poetry? A. N.*

A. When he was only 12 years old he wrote a poem which was a translation from Claudian's Prosperine. A number of his early poems are in Latin, presumably based on school tasks.

Q. *Was Keats buried at night? E. N.*

A. The regulation requiring a night burial for non-Catholics was suspended in the case of Keats. He was buried at nine o'clock on a Sunday morning—or fifteen o'clock by the former Roman method of reckoning time.

Q. *Who wrote the poem containing the lines, "I measure every grief I meet with analytic eyes; I wonder if it weighs like mine, or has an easier size"? H. S. C.*

A. Emily Dickinson is the author of the poem, the title of which is I Measure Every Grief I Meet.

Q. *Who was the first American woman to publish a book of poems? T. B. G.*

A. Anne Bradstreet was the author of the first book of poems by a woman. She was the first literary woman to win a reputation among her English and American contemporaries. Her book appeared in London in 1650.

Q. *Who wrote "In the spring a young man's fancy lightly turns to thoughts of love"? H. P.*

A. Tennyson. It is from Locksley Hall.

Q. *In Caliban upon Setebos Browning uses an apostrophe at the beginning of nearly every sentence. Why does he do this? D. K.*

A. The pronoun referring to Caliban is omitted where the apostrophe is thus used. Writing of it, George B. Ives says that so far as his experience is concerned, this is a unique case of the use of this device. Ives disapproves of it.

Q. *I find a poem named Vasant Panchami. What does this mean? S. W.*

A. Sarojini Naidu, in a footnote in her volume of poetry, The Sceptred Flute, says that the Vasant Panchami is the Spring festival when Hindu girls and married women carry gifts of lighted lamps and new-grown corn as offerings to the goddess of Spring, and set them afloat on the face of the waters.

Q. *What was the verse which Coleridge wrote to illustrate the varieties of metrical feet? T. Y. F.*

A. "Trochee trips from long to short; From long to long in solemn sort Slow spondee stalks; Strong foot, yet ill able Ever to come up with dactyl trisyllable Iambics march from short to long; With a leap and a bound the swift anapests throng."

Q. *How did Scott happen to write Lochinvar? D. S. D.*

A. It was a part of the metrical romance, Marmion. For this romance in verse, Scott was offered 1000 pounds before it was begun.

Q. *What is polyphonic prose? Was Amy Lowell the first to write it? F. C.*

A. The term polyphonic prose is sometimes used as the equivalent of vers libre or free verse. Free verse was by no means originated by the late Amy Lowell. There are examples of it in ancient literature, such as the Old Testament.

Q. *Where was Longfellow living when he wrote The Old Clock on the Stairs?* A. D.

A. It was written in his Pittsfield, Mass., home.

Q. *What is the significance of the name Prospice, the title of one of Browning's poems?* L. M.

A. It is interpreted as meaning "Look Forward."

Q. *Why is lyric poetry so called?* T. G.

A. The name was given by the Greeks to a kind of nonnarrative poetry chanted or sung to the accompaniment of the lyre. The term has come to be used with less restriction, passing to poetry unaccompanied by music but constructed on the system of musical measure, then to any short poem of limited scope of emotion, without regard to musical adaptation.

Q. *Where did Edwin A. Robinson write Tristram?* R. E.

A. Tristram was written in the Poets' Studio at the McDowell Colony, Peterborough, N. H.

Q. *Was Pindar considered a great poet?* E. M.

A. As Homer was the great epic poet of the Greeks, and Sophocles their tragic poet, so Pindar was their lyric poet. His fragments represent nearly every kind of lyric poem.

Q. *Who wrote "Give me men to match my mountains"?* W. R.

A. Samuel Foss wrote the poem about which you have inquired.

Q. *How much time elapses in The Lady of the Lake?* W. K.

A. Each canto represents one day.

Q. *Why should Lamb have called Spenser, the poets' poet?* W. T.

A. Charles Lamb was an enthusiastic admirer of Edmund Spenser and regarded his flights of fancy and imagery as so far above other poets' efforts that it required the high artistic sense developed by studying the art of writing poetry to appreciate Spenser.

Q. *What was the rhyme repeated so often in connection with the eight-hour day movement?* W. H. W.

A. Possibly you refer to the English jingle, "Eight hours for work, eight hours for play, eight hours for sleep, eight bob a day."

Q. *What are the three classes of poetry?* W. O. C.

A. The three principal classes of poetry are epic, dramatic, and lyric. An epic poem is a long narrative poem dealing with events in the life of the hero or heroine. For example, Evangeline and the Ænid are epics. A lyric is a brief poem which expresses the sentiment of the poet. As Doctor William A. Wilbur expressed it, "An epic is always the story of someone other than the poet." This is contrary to the lyric. The word drama means the deed. A dramatic poem is one the emphasis in which is upon action.

Q. *When did Joyce Kilmer die?* D. D.

A. He died in the fighting along the Ourcq on July 30, 1918.

Q. *Has America many poets?* E. H.

A. William Ellsworth says: "It may be said that, in round numbers, the verse of about five hundred people appears yearly in American magazines—thousands send in manuscripts, only to have them returned; the number may be anywhere from twenty thousand to fifty thousand. About two hundred volumes of verse appear in the course of a year, but publishers say that not one-quarter of them are profitable; perhaps one-eighth, twenty-five, are bought by quite a number of people, that is, there are twenty-five poets in our population whom people really want to read. Let us consider that one person in five thousand is sending verse to magazines, one in 250,000 gets it printed, one in 600,000 issues a book of poems, and one in five million is a real poet."

Q. *What poet is called "The Elizabethan of To-day"? D. F.*

A. Perhaps you refer to Sara Teasdale of whom Jessie Rittenhouse writes in The Bookman: "She is the Elizabethan of To-day—one of the purest and clearest voices in our poetic literature."

Q. *Who wrote the verse, "Drink to me only with thine eyes," etc.? O. I. L.*

A. Ben Jonson wrote the lines to which you refer, but Philostratus in one of his Letters uses very similar phrases—"Drink to me with your eyes alone. And if you will, take the cup to your lips and fill it with kisses, and give it so to me."

Q. *Is William Blake's place of burial known? T. N.*

A. The bodies of the poet and his wife lie in a pauper's grave in Bunhill Fields, Finsbury. A tombstone marking the spot was unveiled on the 100th anniversary of the poet's death.

Q. *What is the oldest and most popular of French forms of poetry? E. O.*

A. Louis Untermeyer says that it is the ballade (not to be confused with the ballad).

Q. *How old was Elizabeth Barret when she married Robert Browning? V. T.*

A. She was forty in February, and married the following September. Robert Browning was six years her junior.

Q. *Please explain the use of "L'Envoi" in a poem. T. G. N.*

A. The phrase, L'Envoi, is applied to a separate stanza which concludes a poem. The lines contain a moral or an address to some individual. In the days when the troubadours sang in France, they were apt to conclude their song lyrics with a direct address to the person to whom they were singing; hence, it grew to be a custom to begin the envoi with the phrase, "Oh Prince."

Q. *Has any poet other than Shakespeare drawn a picture of the Ages of Man? J. T.*

A. Shakespeare's description of the transition from infancy to old age was later than many others, including Horace in Ars Poetica, Plato in the Dialogues, Socrates in Axiochus. In the Mishna the "ages" are given as fourteen by Jehuda, son of Thema. A more modern version than any of these is found in Le Chemin de Valliance by Jean de Courcy. A copy of this is in the British Museum.

Q. *Who was the poet who, before his death, burned all of his verses? B. F.*

A. Francisco de Figueroa did so, but they were afterwards collected and published from copies in the hands of his friends.

Q. *When and where was the poet Shelley buried? C. P. C.*

A. "Shelley's body," says The Dictionary of National Biography, "was cast ashore near Viareggio on July 18, 1822, and, after having been buried for some time in the sand, was on August 16, in the presence of Byron, Hunt, and Trelawney, cremated to allow the interment of the ashes at Rome. This took place on December 7, immediately under the pyramid of Caius Cestius. . . . The heart, which would not burn and had been snatched from the flames by Trelawney, was given to Mary Shelley and is in the keeping of her family."

Q. *What is the poem about "The lad I used to be"? D. A. R.*

A. It is Sometimes, by T. S. Jones, Jr. "Across the fields of yesterday He sometimes comes to me A little lad just back from play—The Lad I used to be And yet he smiles so wistfully Once he has crept within I wonder if he hopes to see The man I might have been."

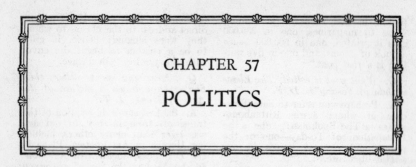

CHAPTER 57
POLITICS

Q. What was the adjuration of the Washington police to Coxey's army in 1894? F. O. G.

A. The army of the unemployed was asked by the police, "Please keep off the grass."

Q. Please explain the so-called Lame Duck Constitutional Amendment. R. S.

A. The so-called Lame Duck Amendment was designed to do away with the three months' session of Congress which convened in December after the election in November. Since this amendment became a part of the Constitution the new Congress will convene on the 3rd of January following the election in November. The President will be inaugurated on January 20th.

Q. What speaker of the House was elected Vice President while he was presiding as Speaker, besides John Garner? G. S.

A. Schuyler Colfax. He was Speaker during the 38th, 39th, and 40th Congresses. He was elected Vice President with Grant November, 1868. He retired as Speaker March 3, 1869.

Q. Is Franklin D. Roosevelt a member of Tammany Hall? A. G. N.

A. President Roosevelt says that he is not now and never has been a member of Tammany Hall. He adds that there is, strictly speaking, no such organization as Tammany Hall. There is a Society of Tammany which is a patriotic organization dating from the Revolutionary War. This society owns the "hall" which it rents to the New York County Democratic Organization. It is this latter organization that is commonly known as Tammany Hall.

Q. Who was the Great Commoner in politics? F. S. A.

A. Contrary to general opinion William J. Bryan's title was "Commoner" without the prefix "great." "Great Commoner" was applied to Gladstone, Henry Clay, and others.

Q. How many tax free cities, towns, and villages are there in the United States, due to the amounts of revenue received from municipally owned utilities? J. A. H.

A. The Public Ownership League of America lists 68 towns, cities, and villages which are exempt from local taxation by reason of the surplus earnings of their municipally owned projects, including light, power, water works, and gas. This does not, however, mean that such municipalities are also free from state or county taxes.

Q. What per cent of the eligible voters vote in England, Australia, Germany, Belgium, Switzerland, Denmark, France, and Italy? E. N.

A. In England, Scotland, and Wales three-fourths of the total possible vote was cast in the last elections. In Australia from 82 to 92 per cent voted; in Germany, 82 per cent; Belgium, 90 per cent; Switzerland and Denmark, 76 per cent;

France, 70 per cent; Italy, 64 per cent.

Q. *Why are the District of Columbia and the detached territories given votes in the national party conventions, when people living in them cannot vote for President?* J. W. H.

A. Many residents of these places have a great deal of influence in the political parties of their choice, and it is considered fair to permit them voice in the naming of the candidates and the formation of the policy of the party.

Q. *How many people in Washington, D. C., maintain voting residences elsewhere?* E. R. C.

A. It is estimated that approximately 60,000 people living in the District have voting residences elsewhere. The population of the District of Columbia was about 500,000 in 1932.

Q. *Please publish the popular vote for Hoover and Smith in 1928.* J. E. M.

A. Hoover, 21,429,109; Smith, 15,005,497.

Q. *Please give a definition of a lobbyist.* F. S.

A. The following are among the prize-winning definitions submitted to the Forum in a recent contest: A lobbyist is one who uses his personal influence with members of a legislative body in order to secure the passage of measures which will be of benefit to him or to the interests which he represents; a lobbyist is one who by persuasion, argument, or artifice seeks to influence the thoughts and actions of a governing body for the benefit of private or public interests.

Q. *What is the difference between filibustering and log-rolling?* K. B.

A. Filibustering is the name given to retarding legislation by taking up the time in lengthy speeches, which delays the vote until too late. Log-rolling is a term given to the practice of combining to assist in getting through one measure in return for help in getting another measure passed in which the other party is interested.

Q. *Are there more women voters than there are men in England?* F. W.

A. Under the new law there are about 2,000,000 more women than men voters in England. Heretofore only women 30 years of age or over have been permitted to vote. The new law enfranchises women at 21.

Q. *Who were the Mugwumps?* M. A. S.

A. The Mugwumps were a faction of the Republican party who refused to support James G. Blaine, and supported Grover Cleveland Mugwump is an Algonquin word meaning chief.

Q. *What was the real name of Henry Wilson, Vice Presidential candidate with President Grant, in his second term?* C. B.

A. Henry Wilson's name was Jeremiah Jones Colbath. He did not like the name and had it changed to Henry Wilson by act of the state legislature.

Q. *What was the mistake in the printing of a tariff bill, that cost the Government a large sum of money?* C. O. B.

A. The blunder to which you refer occurred in a tariff bill about 1874. There was a section enumerating what articles should be admitted free of duty. Among those specified were "all foreign fruit-plants, etc.," that is, plants for transplanting, propagating, or experiment. The enrolling clerk in copying the bill accidentally changed the hyphen to a comma, making it read "all foreign fruit, plants, etc." In consequence, for a year until Congress could remedy the mistake, all oranges, lemons, bananas, grapes, and other foreign fruits were admitted free of duty. The misplacement of the comma in this place cost the Government about $2,000,000.

Q. *Which campaign was known as the Hoop-la?* J. M.

A. In 1840 a great effort was made to interest the general public by songs, torchlight parades, and general "hoop-la." The whigs wore coonskin caps and marched, with floats carrying log cabins with a barrel of hard cider near the door, and a live raccoon chained to the roof.

Q. *Have the last two Vice Presidents cast votes in the Senate?* J. J.

A. The librarian of the United States Senate says that practically all Vice Presidents have, on various occasions, cast the deciding or tie vote, both Vice President Dawes and Vice President Curtis having cast such votes several times. The last tie vote cast by Mr. Curtis was in connection with an amendment to the tariff.

Q. *Did President Wilson veto the 18th Amendment?* E. D. B.

A. An amendment is not submitted to the President. The 18th Amendment became a law through passage of both houses of Congress by a two-thirds vote, and ratification by three-fourths of the legislatures of the States. The Volstead Act which was an enforcement act was vetoed by President Wilson and passed over his veto.

Q. *Does United States citizenship automatically confer the right of suffrage?* R. J.

A. It does not. States grant the right to vote.

Q. *Is voting compulsory in any country?* W. C. C.

A. In 1893 Belgium passed a law making voting compulsory with penalties for failure. In Spain voting has been compulsory since 1908 with a tax increase for failure. Certain Australian provinces and Swiss cantons and, since the war, Czechoslovakia, Denmark, Holland, Hungary, Luxembourg, Argentina, Honduras, Mexico, New Zealand, and Tasmania have had compulsory voting laws. Senator Capper has proposed a law adding 1 per cent to the income tax of persons failing to vote.

Q. *At the time our Government was founded were there two parties?*

A. From the beginnings of the Government there have been at least two political parties or points of view. The earliest were known as the Federalist which advocated a strong central government with a great amount of control of the States, and the Republican Party which was an equally strong advocate of the right of the States to be self-governing in all domestic affairs and to permit federal supervision or government only as far as national defense and security, as well as the integrity of the Union, required.

Q. *Is it necessary for a Senator to resign his office in order to become a candidate for President or other official?* D. B. M.

A. There is no law which obliges a candidate for office to resign his seat in the United States Senate.

Q. *What papers written by a famous magazine author set forth the opposition of the Whigs to our war with Mexico in 1846?* T. A. R.

A. The Bigelow Papers by Joseph Russell Lowell, humorously set forth the opposition of the Whigs.

Q. *Who were the Straightouts?* K. F. E.

A. They were a small faction of the Democratic party who refused to support Horace Greeley, when he was nominated for the Presidency. The party held a convention in Louisville, Kentucky, and nominated Charles O'Conor and John Q. Adams.

Q. *What are the advantages of a six year or longer term for the President, and the prohibition of reëlection?* A. B.

A. Some of the advantages which are claimed are: First, the lack of incentive to work up a party machine for reëlection; second, the longer period during which the policy of the administration as known can be counted upon; third, the elimination of all attempts to influence the mind of the President by a hope of further political advantage or patronage; fourth, the elimination of the cost of elections by one-third or one-half, according to the term, and the greater stability of business.

Q. What was the object of the Greenback Party? I. L. K.

A. After the Civil War the condition in the United States caused unprecedented rise in the value of notes of the United States redeemable in gold. It was proposed in 1868 to make bonds, not specifying the term in which they were payable. The Greenback party was formed definitely in 1874, and in 1876 nominated Peter Cooper, of New York, for President. He polled 81,737 popular votes.

Q. How is the pork barrel supposed to benefit Congressmen? C. E. A.

A. The expression refers to the practice of making appropriations for work in various parts of the country from which members of Congress are enabled to give employment to persons in that section.

Q. Has an American-born woman married to a foreigner the right to vote? Q. S. L.

A. It depends upon the date of marriage. If she was married before September 22, 1922, she lost her United States citizenship, but if she was married after that date she retained her citizenship and is entitled to vote if she meets the requirements of the State of which she is a resident.

Q. What crimes result in disfranchisement of voters? J. R. K.

A. Voting is governed by state law with variations as to reasons for loss of vote in several States. All of the following crimes are listed as causes of disfranchisement: Arson, bigamy, burglary, counterfeiting, larceny, incest, manslaughter, mayhem, murder, perjury, rape, robbery, sodomy, subornation of perjury. Georgia and South Carolina disfranchise any person marrying another of colored blood.

Q. What is the Ohio Idea? E. G.

A. From 1868 to 1876 the Democratic Party's demand for paper money and the taxation of government bonds was so insistent that the inflation movement was commonly known as the Ohio Idea.

Q. Explain the difference between a plurality of vote and a majority of vote? F. P. H.

A. A plurality vote is more votes than the number cast for the next highest candidate. A majority vote is more than half of all votes cast.

Q. How long had Susan B. Anthony been prominent in woman suffrage before she attempted to cast a vote? R. E. F.

A. Susan B. Anthony became a leader in 1848, but it was not until 1872 that she made the test by voting at the polls. She was arrested and fined, but was not jailed for refusing to pay her fine.

Q. In the balloting for candidates for the Presidency, the press reported half and quarter votes. How was this done? A. C.

A. It frequently happens that a political party desires to honor more of its members by appointment as delegates to the national conventions than the quota allotted to a State covers. In such cases it is frequently arranged that two and sometimes more individuals are sent as delegates, each having a half or other part vote as the case may be. When uninstructed delegates are sent these fractions of votes are added in the final tabulation of the votes.

Q. What was La Follette's platform when he ran for President? M. C.

A. He ran for President as the nominee of the Progressive Party. His platform in brief was as follows: Public ownership of water power and railways; strict public control of national resources; the recognition of agriculture as a basic industry of the country; the abrogation of the power of the Supreme Court to nullify legislation.

Q. *Why is the rooster used as the Democratic emblem?* E. B. T.

A. The bird is regarding as heralding victory, also the dawn of a new day.

Q. *Are National Committeemen and Committeewomen paid for their services?* R. H.

A. They are not paid for their services.

Q. *Did former Governor Smith of New York have a precedent for his tactics in dividing the New York Democratic support for President Roosevelt by announcing his own willingness to run?* S. A. H.

A. In 1879 when the Democrats nominated for Governor of the State a man personally objectionable to Honest John Kelly, then leader of Tammany Hall, Kelly had himself nominated in addition, thus dividing the party vote, electing the Republican nominee, and disciplining the party.

Q. *What is the difference between the Republican and Democratic parties?* W. A. T.

A. A magazine contest by an impartial committee of both Republicans and Democrats awarded the prizes to the following definitions: Democratic viewpoint: "A Democrat believes in the doctrine of state's rights, a tariff on luxuries for revenue only and equality in all laws enacted; while a Republican believes in a strong, centralized government, a high protective tariff on manufactured articles, and legislation favoring special or vested interests." Republican viewpoint: "A Republican believes in a strong Federal Government, protection of industry, free speech, press and religion; continued separation of church and state, law enforcement, a high standard of living, and economy in government."

Neutral viewpoint: "A Democrat seeks to find in the interpretation of principles as established by Jefferson, Cleveland, and Wilson, the ideal government, while a Republican seeks the same result in the interpretation of principles as set out by Lincoln, Roosevelt, and Coolidge."

Q. *Has any man ever been nominated for the Presidency by a national convention and refused to run?* T. A. R.

A. In 1872 a Democratic convention at Louisville, which had refused to accept the nomination of Greeley at Baltimore, nominated Charles O'Conor of New York, a Catholic. O'Conor refused the nomination by telegraph, but the convention proceeded to nominate him anyway. In the subsequent election he received thousands of votes in 23 states.

Q. *Did the late Speaker Nicholas Longworth support his father-in-law, Theodore Roosevelt, when the latter bolted the Republican Party and was the Progressive candidate for President in 1912?* T. S.

A. He did not.

Q. *Did the term carpetbagger originate in the reconstruction after the Civil War?* O. T. R.

A. This term of derision was used long before the Civil War, and was applied in the west to denote promoters of wild cat banks or stocks, whose earthly possessions were contained in the carpetbags with which many times they arrived at the place they desired to exploit.

Q. *What is the name applied to the system of lawmaking, which consists of a legislature of two houses?* A. T.

A. The two-chambered system is known as the bicameral system.

Q. *What was the political doctrine of Machiavelli which bears his name?* J. C. C.

A. Niccolo Machiavelli, a Florentine statesman who lived from 1469 to 1527, believed that any means, however treacherous and despotic, were justifiable when employed to maintain a strong central government.

Q. *If all the Roman Catholics were to vote for the same presidential candidate, how many votes would it amount to?* J. E. H.

A. There are about 18,000,000 Roman Catholics in the United States. About half of them are of voting age. If all were eligible to vote, and exercise the privilege, it would amount to about 9,000,000 votes.

Q. *Is it necessary that a person be able to read and write in English in order to vote in this country?* E. C. A.

A. Each State may make its own laws with respect to suffrage qualifications, so long as no provision of the Constitution is violated. There are several States, of which New York was the first, which make it a positive requirement that a voter shall be able to read and write the American language. Other States include: Alabama, Arizona, California, Connecticut, Delaware, Florida, Georgia, Louisiana, Maine, Maryland, Massachusetts, Mississippi, New Hampshire, North Carolina, Oklahoma, Oregon, South Carolina, Virginia, West Virginia, and Wyoming.

Q. *What members of the Constitutional Convention never attended it?* M. E. T.

A. There were ten who did not attend: John Pickering, Benjamin West, Francis Dana, John Neilson, Abraham Clark, Patrick Henry (declined), Richard Caswell (resigned), Willie Jones (declined), George Walton, and Nathaniel Pendleton. Sixteen members of the Convention attended but did not sign the Constitution.

Q. *What appointments does the President make?* D. G. G.

A. The President appoints, without consent of the Congress, his private secretary and the Librarian of Congress. The President, with the concurrence of the Senate, appoints about 16,000 persons a year. These include ambassadors, consuls, judges, collectors of customs, Cabinet officials, district attorneys, marshals, territorial governors, postmasters of certain classes, Treasurer of the United States, Comptroller of the Currency, Superintendent of Mints, Commissioner of Internal Revenue, Interstate Commerce Commissioners, Commissioners of Mines, Pensions, Patents, Federal Trade, Indian Affairs, all bureau chiefs, all military and naval officers, and many others.

Q. *What is meant by the terms rights and lefts as applied to Socialists?* M. L.

A. In any organized movement the moderates or conservatives are known as the rights or members of the right wing, while the liberals or the radicals are designated by the term lefts or left wing.

Q. *Did a negro ever serve as chairman of a national political convention?* M. T.

A. John R. Lynch of Mississippi, on motion of Henry Cabot Lodge, seconded by. Theodore Roosevelt, was chosen Temporary Chairman of the National Republican Convention at Chicago in 1884, the convention which nominated James G. Blaine. Lynch was three times a member of Congress and held other offices. He was an army paymaster with the rank of captain.

Q. *Has there ever been a movement toward abolishing the Electoral College?* M. T.

A. There have been several motions in the House and Senate looking for a change in the system of electing a President, one as early as 1803. In 1868 a motion was made for the direct election of President, again in 1874, and 1877. President Jackson included a recommendation to abolish the Electoral College, and for the direct election of the President, in each of his annual messages to Congress from 1829 to 1836.

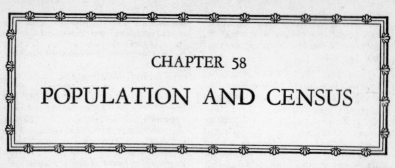

CHAPTER 58

POPULATION AND CENSUS

Q. *In the 1930 census were people counted where they were found at that time, or where they had homes?* J. K. N.

A. The district where a person actually had a home was credited with the count. If the person did not have a permanent residence he was counted in the district where he was found.

Q. *How many families move in a year?* A. M.

A. Martin H. Kennelly says that about 2,150,000 American families change their home sites in a year.

Q. *Where is a sailor who has no permanent home listed as a resident under the official census?* J. K. L.

A. The crews of vessels in the American merchant marine were enumerated as such and counted as a part of the population of the port from which the vessel operated.

Q. *When was the first United States Census taken?* M. G. W.

A. In 1790.

Q. *How many enumerators were needed for the 1930 census?* C. R. S.

A. Approximately 100,000 enumerators were required for local purposes.

Q. *When was the first census taken in Great Britain?* L. P.

A. The first complete census in Great Britain was not taken until 1801. Before that time, authorities

had estimated the English population in 1570 at 4,160,221, and 1670 at 5,773,646. The census of 1801 showed the population of the United Kingdom to be 10,500,956. Since then the census has been taken every ten years. The last one was made in 1931.

Q. *Where are the people in penitentiaries counted in the census?* S. W.

A. They are counted in the penitentiaries, jails, and prisons in which they are when the census enumeration is made and added to the population of the cities in which the institutions are located.

Q. *What proportion of the population of the United States is under thirty years of age?* A. D.

A. According to the Census of 1930, 55.7 per cent of the population of the United States is under 30 years of age.

Q. *How many cities are there in the United States having a population of 100,000 or more?* F. J. D.

A. There are 93. Of these 5 are 1,000,000 or more; 8 are 500,000 to 1,000,000; 24 are 250,000 to 500,000; and 56 are 100,000 to 250,000.

Q. *In a city of 10,000, how many boys and girls would there be between 15 and 24 years of age?* F. W. S.

A. About 20 per cent or about 2000 persons would normally fall in this age group.

Q. Is the population of the East Side of New York City increasing or decreasing? C. M.

A. In 1910 the population was 531,615; in 1930 it had dropped to 249,755.

Q. Is Great Britain losing or gaining population? T. S.

A. She is gaining. Not only is the native population gaining, but for the first time in the recorded history of British immigration and emigration, the tide has turned back to the British Isles, 53,000 more persons entering the United Kingdom in 1931 than leaving. Most have returned from other parts of the Empire. For as long as records stand, each year has seen a strong movement outward until now.

Q. Which has a larger population —Moscow or Leningrad? C. M.

A. According to the latest census, Moscow, Russia, has a population of 2,025,947 and Leningrad has a population of 1,614,008.

Q. What was the population of Europe before the World War? What is it now? H. L.

A. The population of Europe before the World War (1912) was 380,-000,000. The population in 1932 was approximately 550,000,000.

Q. How many of the inhabitants of the Philippines are Americans? M. A. T.

A. The latest population figures show 5776 Americans out of a total population of 10,314,310.

Q. Upon what basis is the center of population figured? G. K. P.

A. The term, center of population, as used by the Census Bureau, is that point which may be considered as the center of gravity of the United States; in other words, the point upon which the United States would balance, if it were a rigid plane without weight and the population distributed thereon, with each individual being assumed to have equal weight and to exert an influence on a central point proportional to his distance from the point.

Q. How many people live in Australia? H. T.

A. About 6,500,000.

Q. Is it true that in Great Britain the census is taken within twenty-four hours? A. C.

A. In Great Britain a certain day is designated for the taking of the census. For the census of 1921, the enumeration was made on June 19. The preliminary report was made public in August.

Q. What is the exact meaning of revered senior as used by the enumerator of a census of the inhabitants of Maryland in 1776? L. N. G.

A. The National Genealogical Society says that the abbreviation, R^d senr., standing for revered senior, is generally accepted as meaning grandmother.

Q. Which country is the largest in the world and which has the largest population? G. N.

A. Russia (U.S.S.R.) with an area of 8,144,228 square miles is the largest country in the world. China with over 400,000,000 population has the greatest population.

Q. Are the Philippine Islands increasing in population to any great extent? F. G.

A. According to the 1930 census the population of the Philippines is 12,604,100. In 1920 it was 10,350,640.

Q. What do the experts say is the greatest population that the earth could support? P. B. M.

A. Prof. Robert R. Kuczinski, of Berlin, one of the recognized authorities, has stated that, assuming that there are fifteen billion acres of arable land and that 1.5 acres on the average are sufficient to support an individual, the maximum population would have to be placed at less than ten billions. "Even allowing for all conceivable advances in technique, and assuming that all human effort will be directed to the maintenance of a maximum number of people," he says, "it seems impossible that the earth could sustain more than six times its present population, or about twelve billion people."

Q. *What percentage of the population of the United States continues to live in the State where born? F. L.*

A. On a percentage basis 67.3 per cent of the total population resides in the States where born, 20.7 per cent born in other States, and the remainder foreign-born, or at sea, or in detached territories.

Q. *What is the population of the world? O. D.*

A. The International Statistical Institute of the League of Nations estimates the world's population at about two billion.

Q. *What is the daily increase in the population of the United States? C. M.*

A. It is estimated that the population increases at the rate of one person every 36 seconds. There is a birth about every 14 seconds and one death every 22 seconds. Immigration and emigration figures affect the rate slightly.

Q. *Where is the country which has the densest population in the world? E. G.*

A. Java is one of the Dutch East Indies. It is the densest populated land mass in the world, 648.4 to the square mile.

Q. *What country has the smallest population per square mile? G. R.*

A. Of the principal countries, Australia, with a population of 2.1 per square mile; Libya has 1.3 and Southwest Africa 0.8.

Q. *How many more men than women are there in the United States? How many in England? H. C.*

A. There are 1,499,114 more men than women in the United States. In England and Wales the situation is reversed and there are 1,670,243 more women than men.

Q. *How many cities are there in the world with a population of 1,000,-000 and over? H. M.*

A. Twenty-nine. Rome and Mexico City recently passed the million mark.

Q. *What was the population of the world in the time of Christ? H. B.*

A. There are of course no actual statistics as to the population of the world at the time of Christ. Little of the world was known at that time to the nations which have since recorded and made history. An estimate placed the number at 50,000,000 in the known world.

Q. *How does the population of Soviet Russia compare with that of India? G. A. M.*

A. Russia has about 160,000,000, while India has about 350,000,000.

Q. *What State in the Union is the most populated? W. K. F.*

A. New York leads with a population in 1930 of 12,588,066. Over half the population lives in New York City.

Q. *What countries besides the United States have a population composed of more men than women? A. C. N.*

A. Men predominate slightly in Canada, Egypt, South Africa, Japan, India, and Australia.

Q. *What proportion of the population of the United States is concentrated in cities of 100,000 or over? D. H. J.*

A. Over one-third of the population is dwelling in such large communities.

Q. *Which State has the densest population? W. T.*

A. Rhode Island leads with 566.4 persons to the square mile. Massachusetts is second. No State compares in density of population with the District of Columbia with 7,292.9 persons to the square mile.

Q. How many white people are there in the world? S. M. T.

A. The most recent estimate gives 725,000,000 people of the white race.

Q. What is included in urban population? G. F. J.

A. Heretofore it has been defined by the Census Bureau as including all cities and other incorporated places having 2500 inhabitants or more. For use in connection with the 1930 Census, the definition has been extended to include townships and other similar political subdivisions (not incorporated as municipalities) which have a total population of 10,000 or more and a population density of 1000 or more per square mile.

Q. How many people have lived in the world since its creation? F. M.

A. It has been estimated that in the approximately 1800 generations since 4000 B.C., 2,000,000,000,000 people have lived in the world. It is impossible to state, even as an estimate, the number of human inhabitants of the earth since its creation, or more accurately since the beginnings of human life, since this has not yet been definitely dated.

Q. What state or territory of the United States has less than 100,000 population? J. A.

A. Only one State, Nevada, and one territory, Alaska, are in this class. Nevada had 91,000 and Alaska 60,000 in 1930. The populations of the detached territories or possessions of the United States range from 10,-000 in American Samoa, to 12½ million for the Philippine Islands.

Q. Where are the center of population and the geographical center of the United States? E. T.

A. According to the Census of 1930 the center of population in the United States is 2.9 miles northeast of Linton, Greene County, Indiana. The exact geographical center of the United States is 18 miles north of Smith's Center, Smith Co., Kansas.

Q. Taking the whole world and distributing the population evenly, how thick would the population be? E. W.

A. It would be 38.4 persons to the square mile.

Q. Have early predictions of the growth of American population been justified? W. C. C.

A. Opinions have been expressed in the past on both sides but most probably were over-enthusiastic. In his first annual message to Congress President Lincoln declared: "There are already among us those who, if the Union be preserved, will live to see it contain 250,000,000." In his second annual message Mr. Lincoln predicted that by 1920 the population would have reached 187,000,000. At that time it was only 105,710,000. The geographers now set the probable static maximum at from 160,000,000 to 180,000,000.

Q. What cities in China have more than a million population? C. L. W.

A. Hangchow, Hankow, Peiping, Hongkong, and Shanghai.

Q. How many people are there in the United States who are one hundred years or more of age? M. M.

A. In the 1930 census, there were 3964 reported. Of these 1180 were white, 2467 were negroes, and 317 were of other races. In all races it was shown that more women reach an advanced age than men.

Q. How long ago did Turkey start taking a census? D. K.

A. In 1928 Turkey decided to take its first census. The Turks employed drastic methods. The entire population was imprisoned on the day of the census; no one was permitted on the streets except guards and census takers. Business and industry came to a halt. In Constantinople it was not until the count was complete at 10:15 P.M. that the people were released from their homes by the signal guns.

Q. Are there more widows or widowers in the United States? E. W.

A. The Census of 1930 gave the number of widows in the United States as 4,734,207 and that of widowers as 2,025,036.

Q. What is the average family size in the United States according to the population report of the last census? D. W. H.

A. According to the Census of 1930, the number of families in the United States totaled 29,980,146. The population per family was 4.1.

Q. At the time the United States was formed, which State had the largest population? M. F.

A. Virginia led with a population of about 568,000. Massachusetts was second with about 410,000. Pennsylvania was third with 350,000; then came Maryland, 254,000; New York, 239,000; Connecticut, 209,000. The other States had smaller populations.

Q. How many people live within fifty miles of New York City? L. T.

A. The New York Region, which includes all people in New York City and within a radius of fifty miles, has a population of 11,500,000.

Q. How many inhabitants to the square mile has South America? J. S.

A. On the whole, it possesses only 10 inhabitants to the square mile. Central America has about 45, and the United States about 41.

Q. Are there more Jews than Italians in New York City? H. B.

A. In 1930, the Jewish population of New York City totaled 1,765,000 and Italian 1,070,355.

Q. Which Canadian province has the largest population? L. L. S.

A. In 1931, Ontario led with a population of 3,426,488. Quebec was second with a population of 2,869,-793. These two provinces contain more than half the population of Canada.

Q. Are more people leaving cities and moving to the country, or is the trend city-ward? A. T.

A. In 1931, it is estimated that 1,472,000 persons moved city-ward and that 1,679,000 moved farm-ward. Thus there was a gain of persons on farms.

Q. How much did the population of Hawaii increase between 1920 and 1930? P. T.

A. About 44 per cent. In 1930 the total population was 368,336, of which 81.4 per cent was native born.

Q. What cities in the United States have a population exceeding 500,000? E. H.

A. The following have: New York, Chicago, Philadelphia, Detroit, Los Angeles, Cleveland, St. Louis, Baltimore, Boston, Pittsburgh, San Francisco, Milwaukee, and Buffalo.

Q. What was the population of Chicago at the time of the Chicago Fire? E. G.

A. The big fire in Chicago was in 1871. In 1870 the population of Chicago was 298,977.

Q. What population must a town have before it is called a city? L. G.

A. The Bureau of the Census says that the population has nothing to do with the matter of a town being called a city. This is a matter of state legislation. The Post Office Department says that a town must have 10,000 population before it can be given city mail delivery.

Q. How many of the inhabitants of Hawaii are pure-blood Hawaiians? R. E. L.

A. There are 22,636. There are 28,224 part-Hawaiians. The remainder of the total population of Hawaii of 368,336 is made up largely of Caucasians and Japanese.

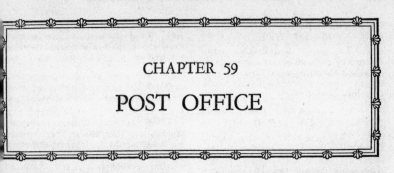

CHAPTER 59

POST OFFICE

Q. When does a letter come under the protection of the Government—when the stamp is placed on it, or when it is put in the letter box? S. G.

A. The Post Office Department says that mail does not come under the protection of the Government until it is dropped in the mail box. Simply placing a postage stamp on a letter or package does not in any way insure protection by the United States Postal Service, nor is the Government in any way responsible for it.

Q. How should a letter be addressed, and how much postage is required to send it around the world via East and via West? H. J. A.

A. It is not permitted to send a letter around the world. The Postal Guide states that postal cards or letters addressed to go around the world are prohibited in the regular mails in all foreign countries.

Q. Is England connected with India by air mail? M. O.

A. Air mail service between England and India was established in 1929. This route is one of the longest air routes in the world. It stretches 5,000 miles across 10 countries.

Q. When money is found in letters sent to the Dead Letter Office, is it often possible to send it to the proper person? D. C.

A. About 55 per cent of the money found in letters is restored to the rightful owners, and nearly 99 per cent of the letters containing checks, drafts, and money orders are either returned to the senders or delivered to the addressees.

Q. Who was the first postmaster of the United States? B. E.

A. July 26, 1775, the Continental Congress established the Post Office with Benjamin Franklin as the first Postmaster General. On September 26, 1789, Samuel Osgood was the first postmaster appointed under the Constitution.

Q. Where are our postage stamps made? K. R.

A. All United States postage stamps are made at the Bureau of Engraving and Printing at Washington, D. C.

Q. What will become of the exceedingly valuable collection of stamps owned by King George at his death? Is it the property of the Crown? W. W.

A. King George's collection is his own personal property, purchased from his own private funds or acquired by personal gift. He can bequeath it as he chooses, either whole or in part. So far as is known none of his immediate family shares his intense interest in philately.

Q. What is the inscription on the New York Post Office? M. G. B.

A. It is "Neither snow nor rain nor heat nor night stays these couriers from the swift completion of their appointed rounds."

Q. *What kind of paper is used to make our stamps?* H. Y.

A. The paper used in the manufacture of postage stamps is made of bleached chemical wood fiber derived, at the present time, from North Carolina pine trees.

Q. *Where was the Edison stamp first put on sale?* J. F. D.

A. The first sale of the Light's Golden Jubilee Two-Cent Stamp was held at Menlo Park, New Jersey. The stamp was struck by the Government to commemorate the fiftieth anniversary of Edison's perfecting of the incandescent lamp.

Q. *What do stamp collectors mean when they talk about "first day covers"?* F. L.

A. A first day cover is an envelope with a stamp of a new issue that has been mailed and the stamp canceled on the first day the new stamps have been placed on sale. Some collectors have blocks of four stamps of each denomination on each envelope.

Q. *What does the postal term "nixie" indicate?* H. B.

A. Nixie is the term used by postal employees to designate mail which cannot be delivered or returned without special treatment.

Q. *Is there a post office by the name of Santa Claus?* L. E. M.

A. Santa Claus post office is located at Santa Claus, Indiana. This post office is used a great deal during the Christmas holidays.

Q. *What is the composition of the gum used on postage stamps?* W. W. N.

A. The gum consists of 58% dextrine, 38% water and 4% glucose.

Q. *How are stamps made on the intaglio web press?* B. M. D.

A. This press is probably the most amazing piece of machinery ever devised for work of this kind. In a continuous operation this press wets the paper, inks in and wipes the plate, prints the impression, dries the printed product, applies the gum, dries the gum, and winds the finished product in a roll at the end of the press.

Q. *What are the names of some of the commemorative stamps?* C. G.

A. Some of the commemorative stamps are Columbian Series, Lexington-Concord, Norse-American Centennial, Valley Forge, Molly Pitcher Surcharged, Civil Aëronautics, Thomas Alva Edison, General Von Steuben, General Pulaski, Red Cross, Washington Bi-centennial.

Q. *How will the new Chicago post office building compare with others in size?* H. T. B.

A. It will be the largest post office in the world. When completed the structure will contain approximately 2,309,000 square feet of floor space covering an area of practically 50 acres. It will be 800 feet long, 350 feet wide, and 200 feet high. It will have nine stories in the rear and twelve stories in front.

Q. *When was the first air mail route established in the United States?* S. M.

A. The first air mail route was established on May 15 and 16, 1918, when Lt. George Boyle and James C. Edgerton made the first air mail trip from New York City to Washington, D. C. However, the first aërial mail delivery in the United States took place September, 1911. The pilot was E. L. Ovington.

Q. *What is the Philatelic Agency?* M. E. R.

A. The Philatelic Agency was established in December, 1921, for the purpose of supplying collectors and dealers with United States postage stamps and other stamped paper of current issues and such discontinued issues as may be on hand. So far as possible, well centered postage stamps will be supplied. Postage stamps are sold at face value, plus return postage and registration fee. The Philatelic Agency is connected with the Post Office Department, Washington, D. C.

Q. *Who employs the air mail pilots?* P. C.

A. Air mail is carried under contract and air mail pilots are employed by the contractors.

Q. *What is the star route in the postal service?* P. R.

A. It is a post route on which the mails are carried under a formal contract awarded to the lowest bidder tendering sufficient guarantees for faithful performance in accordance with the terms of the advertisement, and requiring due celerity, certainty, and security in the performance of the service.

Q. *Does the United States belong to a postal union?* H. T. T.

A. The United States and practically all of the countries of the world are united in the International Postal Union for the reciprocal exchange of mails.

Q. *What is the franking privilege?* G. P.

A. It is the privilege of sending mail free. The person who enjoys the privilege has a facsimile of his signature printed upon the envelopes used for his mail. These and cartons bearing the facsimile are accepted by the Post Office Department without payment of postage.

Q. *Do members of Congress have free unlimited use of the mails?* C. R. N.

A. The free use of the mails by Congressmen must be for official business.

Q. *Does the Post Office Department own the mail cars or rent them?* R. P.

A. The Post Office Department says that the mail cars are owned by the railroad companies. The rent paid the railroads for the carrying of mail is fixed by the Interstate Commerce Commission.

Q. *Was the term philately coined by stamp collectors?* L. T.

A. A French stamp collector named Herpin is credited with making this word in 1865. It was coined from Greek words and means "the love of study of all that concerns prepayment," the love of stamps.

Q. *Is the postmistress at Wakefield, Virginia, related to George Washington?* F. W. K.

A. Miss Julia L. Washington, postmistress at Washington's birthplace, is descended from George Washington's half-brother, Augustine.

Q. *How can return postage be sent to a correspondent in Europe?* H. C. M.

A. United States stamps are not good on mail from foreign countries to the United States. In order to send return postage it is necessary to use an international reply coupon, which may be secured from the Post Office.

Q. *Are competitive examinations given for the position of Post Office Inspector?* N. M. G.

A. This position is filled by promotion within the Post Office Department.

Q. *What postmaster has the distinction of having served the longest term as a postmaster?* C. T. F.

A. J. N. Van Zandt. The date of his appointment was April 23, 1866.

Q. *Is there a law against putting Christmas seals on the address side of letters going to foreign countries?* R. H.

A. There is a Post Office ruling to the effect that Christmas stamps or other adhesive stamps or labels in aid of charitable objects must be affixed to the back of all mail articles and not to the address side of the covers. Unless the foregoing condition is complied with, articles bearing non-postage stamps will not be dispatched from this country, but will be returned to the sender, if known; otherwise they will be sent to the Division of Dead Letters.

Q. *Please explain the process of floating stamps used by collectors.* J. K.

A. In floating stamps to remove the paper particles which adhere to used stamps, use a fairly shallow pan and put in about one-half inch of water. Place the stamps in face up —that is have the paper that is to be soaked off on the water side. In this way after they have soaked for a couple of hours, the particles of paper may be detached by using a pair of tweezers.

Q. *Please give the history of Postal Savings.* W. F. G.

A. The Postal Savings System was inaugurated in the United States by Act of Congress of June 25, 1910, during the administration of William Howard Taft and was started under Postmaster General Frank H. Hitchcock in 1911.

Q. *Are joint accounts permitted for postal savings?* E. D.

A. The Post Office Department says that postal savings can only be placed under one name. Joint accounts are not permitted.

Q. *To what period or event in Washington's life do the different portraits on the new issues of postage stamps refer?* M. J. B.

A. They do not refer to specific events. They are copies of the most famous portraits for which Washington sat during his lifetime.

Q. *Is there any living American whose portrait has graced a United States postage stamp?* L. W.

A. The Post Office Department does not use the portraits of living persons on United States stamps.

Q. *How much does the Post Office Department pay for the wax paper used in books of stamps?* S. B. C.

A. The Bureau of Engraving and Printing says that it pays approximately 11 cents per pound for the wax paper that is used to separate the stamps in the stamp books. The Bureau uses about 14,000 reams per year and the number of pounds in a ream varies from 6 to 8 pounds.

Q. *Is it true that a postage stamp is not a stamp?* D. E. F.

A. The term, postage stamp, as used at the present time, is something of a misnomer. When the adhesive stamp was first introduced it was known as a label. The stamp is really what we call the postmark.

Q. *How many women have had their portraits on United States postage stamps?* D. S.

A. Only three women have been portrayed on postage stamps in the sense that distinct honor has been paid individual women in the designing of postage stamps. The portrait of Martha Washington has been used on a stamp in two of the regular series, and the likeness of Queen Isabella appeared on the $4 stamp of the Columbian commemorative issue. In addition, the central design of the 5 cent denomination stamp of the Jamestown series is a representation of Pocahontas. While other female figures have appeared in the designs on postage stamps, like the Red Cross issue, for example, in no case other than the first three mentioned has the likeness of a woman known by name been used.

Q. *Who suggested the installation of rural free delivery?* D. E. C.

A. It was first officially suggested by Postmaster General Wanamaker in his annual report for the fiscal year 1891. The first rural free delivery of mail was established October 1, 1896, simultaneously at Charleston, Uvilla, and Halltown, West Virginia.

Q. *How is mail sent to Alaska?* E. G. N.

A. All mails for Alaska are dispatched from Seattle, Washington. During the season of navigation all classes of mail are forwarded. During the winter season (from about October 1 to May 1), on account of the difficulty of transportation to remote sections, the dispatch of mail for Alaska, except for offices on the southern coast and those located along the railroads and adjacent thereto, is limited. Valuable parcels can be taken by express to Nome and other points at all times of the year via airplane from Fairbanks, Anchorage, or Seward.

Q. How are fourth class postmasters appointed? A. G. S.

A. On October 15, 1912, they were put under Civil Service.

Q. Which Presidents have had their portraits on stamps? E. J.

A. George Washington, Thomas Jefferson, James Madison, James Monroe, Andrew Jackson, Zachary Taylor, Abraham Lincoln, U. S. Grant, Rutherford B. Hayes, James A. Garfield, Grover Cleveland, Benjamin Harrison, William McKinley, Theodore Roosevelt, Warren G. Harding, Woodrow Wilson, and William Howard Taft.

Q. How many commemorative stamps are struck of one kind? E. G.

A. The number of commemorative stamps to be issued is specified by the Post Office Department. The number is not always the same as there is a greater demand for certain types of commemorative stamps.

Q. Why is a picture of Pulaski on one of our postage stamps? R. E. Y.

A. The Post Office Department says that the stamp was issued in honor of General Pulaski, because of his heroism displayed in the American Revolution. In 1777 he joined Washington's Army as a volunteer. He performed distinctive service in the Battle of Brandywine and received from Congress promotion to the rank of Brigadier General, in command of a division of cavalry. He later formed an independent Corps of Cavalry and Light Infantry, known as Pulaski's Legion.

Q. Has the Post Office Department ever been self-sustaining? A. H. N.

A. According to the Annual Report of the Postmaster General, there was an audited postal surplus during the years 1882, 1883, 1911, 1913, 1914, 1916, 1917, 1918, and 1919.

Q. What does the Battle of Fallen Timbers stamp commemorate? L. M. C.

A. The Battle of Fallen Timbers commemorative stamp issued by the Post Office Department is a memorial to General Anthony Wayne, and to commemorate the 105th anniversary of this battle. "Mad Anthony" Wayne of Revolutionary War fame was called upon to end the Indian trouble at the frontier, when Harmar and St. Clair had failed. He began his campaign in Ohio in the fall of 1793. In 1794 he was active on the Maumee, and on August 20th defeated the Indians decisively at Fallen Timbers, and in August, 1795, he and 127 of the Northwestern tribes signed the Treaty of Greenville by which the United States acquired a large tract of property.

Q. What does the Sullivan postage stamp commemorate? R. S. R.

A. It marks the one hundred fiftieth anniversary of the Sullivan Expedition in New York during the Revolutionary War. This special 2-cent stamp bears a portrait of Major General Sullivan.

Q. What does it mean when a letter is returned with the word fraudulent stamped upon it? K. B.

A. It means that a fraud order has been issued against the addressee.

Q. Is the postage stamp a form of taxation? T. E.

A. The entire revenue derived from the sale of postage stamps is applied to the cost of maintaining the Post Office Department and handling the mail. With an increase in postage rate beyond the expense of postal service, such stamps are a form of taxation.

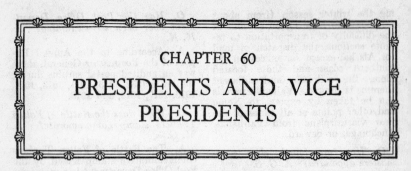

CHAPTER 60

PRESIDENTS AND VICE PRESIDENTS

Q. Who made the shortest inaugural address? H. K. N.

A. George Washington's second inaugural address was the shortest in the history of this republic. It contained 134 words.

Q. Did President Coolidge use shorter sentences than President Lincoln? C. B.

A. State papers of the Presidents show that the average number of words to a sentence used by President Coolidge was 18, while the average number used by President Lincoln was 26.6.

Q. What was the epitaph which Thomas Jefferson wrote for himself? C. A. H.

A. "Here was buried Thomas Jefferson, author of the Declaration of American Independence and of the statute of Virginia for religious freedom, and father of the University of Virginia."

Q. What was Roosevelt's favorite hymn? A. M. A.

A. James Amos writes: "I have heard various hymns named as his favorites. But the one he was always singing to himself, or trying to sing, was 'Nearer My God to Thee.'"

Q. What President vetoed the greatest number of bills during his term of office? E. S. M.

A. President Cleveland vetoed 496 bills during his term as President. During his first term, he vetoed 301 bills, nearly twice as many as had all

his predecessors combined. The majority of these were private pension bills, and only two of them were passed over his veto.

Q. Who was the oldest President of the United States, and who was the youngest? B. E. K.

A. The oldest President when inaugurated was William H. Harrison, 68, and the youngest, Theodore Roosevelt, 42.

Q. Have the Presidents of the United States had more sons or daughters? K. J.

A. The children born to Presidents of the United States have been 66 sons, and 45 daughters. Six Presidents were childless.

Q. How much did George Washington pay for his pew in Christ Church, Alexandria, Virginia? K. N. B.

A. George Washington's pew cost him 36 pounds, 10 shillings, which would amount to about $146, with the English pound at par.

Q. Have two Presidential candidates been nominated from the same State except Harding and Cox from Ohio? J. N. O.

A. It has happened twice before that two Presidential nominees have been chosen from the same State at the same time. These were Abraham Lincoln and Stephen A. Douglas from Illinois in 1860, and Theodore Roosevelt and Alton B. Parker from New York in 1904.

Q. *Is it necessary for a President-elect to dispose of all securities and get out of business before entering upon his term of office?* H. R. L.

A. It is not necessary for a President-elect to dispose of any securities or holdings of property which he might possess. It is necessary for him to resign from all active participation in business affairs during his term as President.

Q. *Can a Chinese, Japanese, or Negro born in the United States become President of the United States if elected to that office?* D. M. N.

A. A native-born person of Chinese, Japanese, or Negro birth is eligible to be President of the United States if so elected.

Q. *How many consecutive generations of President Harrison's family contained Benjamin Harrisons?* C. M. A.

A. There were five consecutive generations of Benjamin Harrisons.

Q. *At what time have the most Presidents been alive?* G. T. S.

A. When Lincoln was inaugurated. Then five Presidents were alive—Van Buren, Tyler, Fillmore, Pierce, and Buchanan.

Q. *Is there a law against a third term in the United States?* P. D.

A. The phrase "third term" usually is interpreted to refer to the Presidency. There is no law against a third term as President, but the example of Washington and subsequent accumulated tradition frown on it. However, the State of Delaware forbids by statute a third term for its governors. The constitutions of 17 States contain provisions limiting consecutive service of governors.

Q. *Can the President of the United States be summoned as a witness in a lawsuit?* W. W.

A. The precedent is against such a practice. Thomas Jefferson, when President, was summoned to Richmond to testify as a witness at the trial for treason of Aaron Burr. He failed to return the summons explaining that for the President to be subject to the beck of courts would leave the state without a head. This has since been regarded as a ruling precedent.

Q. *Which State has furnished the most Presidents?* G. A. A.

A. There have been more native Virginians in the White House. They were: George Washington, Thomas Jefferson, James Madison, James Monroe, William H. Harrison, John Tyler, Zachary Taylor, and Woodrow Wilson. Ohio ranks second with Ulysses S. Grant, Rutherford B. Hayes, James A. Garfield, Benjamin Harrison, William McKinley, William H. Taft, and Warren G. Harding.

Q. *How many Roman Catholics have been nominated for the Presidency of the United States?* O. M. K.

A. There have been two, Charles O'Conor in 1872, and Alfred E. Smith in 1928.

Q. *Which of the Presidents were Grand Sachems of Tammany Hall?* F. M. T.

A. The Kitchi okeinaw, or Great Grand Sachem, was an honorary office conferred by the Tammany Society upon the following Presidents of the United States: Washington, John Adams, Jefferson, Madison, Monroe, John Q. Adams, and Jackson. The office was abolished after President Jackson's term.

Q. *How large was the log cabin in which Abraham Lincoln was born?* A. K. D.

A. Its dimensions, outside, were 12 by 17 feet, and it was composed of 143 logs. It is housed in an impressive marble memorial.

Q. *What was President Roosevelt's comment on living in the White House?* G. S.

A. H. L. Stoddard quotes Theodore Roosevelt as saying: "You don't live there. You're only Exhibit A to the country."

Q. *What Presidents visited foreign countries before becoming Chief Executives?* R. T. E.

A. John Adams, Thomas Jefferson, James Monroe, John Q. Adams, Martin Van Buren, William H. Harrison, Zachary Taylor, Franklin Pierce, James Buchanan, Ulysses S. Grant, Theodore Roosevelt, William H. Taft, Warren G. Harding, Herbert Hoover, and Franklin D. Roosevelt.

Q. *In what cases has the election of President or Vice President been thrown into Congress because of a lack of majority in the Electoral College?* L. B. S.

A. The House elected Thomas Jefferson in the tie with Aaron Burr and elected John Quincy Adams when not one of Adams, Clay, Jackson, or Crawford had a majority. While, in 1836, Van Buren had a majority for the Presidency, the Vice Presidential vote was divided so that the election was thrown into the Senate which chose R. W. Johnson of Kentucky. The Hayes-Tilden controversy was sent to the House of Representatives, no decision was reached and a commission was appointed which decided in favor of Hayes.

Q. *Which Presidents of the United States occupied a cottage in the Soldiers' Home grounds as a summer residence?* H. F.

A. Presidents Lincoln, Hayes, and Arthur. In those days, the Soldiers' Home was in the quiet country, but today it is in a populous section of the city of Washington. It is three miles from the Capitol.

Q. *Was President Grant receiving army pay at the time of his death?* H. T.

A. When he became President, Ulysses S. Grant resigned from the Army. In March, 1885, by special legislation, Congress restored him to the rank of General and retired him on full pay.

Q. *Has Herbert Hoover ever been a citizen of England? Has he ever voted the Democratic ticket?* C. A. R.

A. Hoover has never at any time in his life been a citizen of any other country than the United States. His first vote was cast in 1920 for President Harding. He has not voted the Democratic ticket.

Q. *Who was the youngest Vice President to be inaugurated?* T. R.

A. The youngest Vice President at the date of his inauguration was John C. Breckenridge, of Kentucky, whose age was 36 years.

Q. *What Presidents have made world tours after their terms of office expired?* P. R. W.

A. President Grant, after his term expired, sailed with Mrs. Grant and his son, Jesse, on a trip around the world, lasting over two years. President Roosevelt made an extended foreign tour after his retirement from office in 1909.

Q. *How many of our Presidents lived to be 70 years old?* N. F.

A. Thirteen. John Adams lived to be 90; Thomas Jefferson, 83; James Madison, 85; James Monroe, 73; John Quincy Adams, 80; Andrew Jackson, 78; Martin Van Buren, 79; John Tyler, 71; Millard Fillmore, 74; James Buchanan, 77; Rutherford B. Hayes, 70; Grover Cleveland, 71; and William Howard Taft, 72.

Q. *What is the famous limerick of President Woodrow Wilson?* G. L.

A. The limerick to which you refer was: "For beauty I am not a star, There are others more handsome by far, But my face, I don't mind it, For I am behind it, It's the people in front that I jar."

Q. *Did Thomas Jefferson, as well as George Washington, speak against a third term?* C. McQ.

A. Although the legislatures of five States adopted resolutions favoring the reëlection of President Jefferson for a third term, he in a famous letter dated December 10, 1807, said: "That I should lay down my charge at a proper period is as much a duty as to have borne it faithfully."

Q. *To what religious denomination has the greatest number of Presidents belonged?* L. R. G.

A. The largest number of Presidents have been members, through baptism, of the Protestant Episcopal Church. They were George Washington, James Madison, James Monroe, William H. Harrison, John Tyler, Zachary Taylor, Franklin Pierce, and Chester A. Arthur.

Q. *Has there been a President of the United States of entirely Irish ancestry?* D. M. J.

A. Both the father and mother of Andrew Jackson emigrated from Carrickfergus, County Antrim, North of Ireland, 1765. President Jackson's father died a few days before the birth of Andrew Jackson, in 1767.

Q. *Which Presidents presided over the Senate as Vice President, before succeeding to the Presidency?* K. A.

A. John Adams, Thomas Jefferson, Martin Van Buren, John Tyler, Millard Fillmore, Andrew Johnson, Chester A. Arthur, Theodore Roosevelt, and Calvin Coolidge, all presided over the Senate.

Q. *Did President Wilson make more than one trip to Europe while President?* F. S. M.

A. He went twice. He sailed December 4, 1918, returning February 25, 1919. He sailed again on March 5, 1919, returning July 8, 1919.

Q. *Did former President Roosevelt make a speech in which he said that there was no room in the United States for German-Americans?* M. D.

A. In a speech in St. Louis in 1916, he declared that there was no room in the United States for German-Americans or Irish-Americans or any other hyphenated Americans, but room only for those who were Americans and nothing else. As early as 1890 he had given utterance to much the same sentiment.

Q. *A New York columnist says President Andrew Johnson was not impeached. He's wrong, isn't he?* P. H. W.

A. President Johnson was impeached by the House of Representatives, but was acquitted by the Senate in the impeachment trial. The Constitution gives the House the sole power of impeachment and the Senate the sole power of trying impeachment cases. An impeachment is similar to an indictment in that an official who has been impeached is not necessarily guilty, any more than is a person who has been indicted by a grand jury.

Q. *Did Lincoln kneel during the pastoral prayer at Dr. Gurley's Church?* A. J. W.

A. When Dr. Phineas D. Gurley offered the pastoral prayer, Lincoln always stood as a mark of respect.

Q. *Why did not Washington accept from the French King the large carpet made for the President?* P. D.

A. Gifts from foreign powers could not be accepted by the President. Washington, therefore, declined the carpet. It was then sold to Judge Yates of Lancaster, Pa. It is now in Mt. Vernon.

Q. *Do ex-Presidents of the United States receive pensions?* C. T.

A. They do not.

Q. *What kind of clothes did George Washington wear when he went hunting?* P. G.

A. His costume consisted of a blue coat, scarlet waistcoat, buckskin breeches, top boots, velvet cap, and whip with a long thong.

Q. *Did Lincoln attend the midweek prayer meeting of any Washington church?* N. A. R.

A. He attended the service of the New York Avenue Presbyterian Church. Lincoln sat in a small room adjoining that in which the service was held. Thus his presence was kept private and no political capital could be made of his attendance.

Q. How many countries now have presidents? W. F.

A. There are now 38 countries with governments headed by presidents.

Q. When did President Hoover attend Leland Standford? D. E. C.

A. He entered the newly founded Stanford University, at Palo Alto, Calif., at its opening in 1891, where he was the first student at Encina Hall, the boys' dormitory. He entered the department of geology and mining. He received his B. A. degree in 1895.

Q. Please publish the letter to her new daughter-in-law which Martha Washington wrote. H. M. W.

A. "My dear Nelly:—God took from Me a Daughter when June Roses were blooming—He has now given me another daughter about her age when Winter winds are blowing, to warm my Heart again. I am as Happy as One so afflicted and so Blest can be. Pray receive my Benediction and a wish that you may long live the Loving Wife of my happy Son and a Loving Daughter of Your Affectionate Mother. M. Washington."

Q. Are Sundays counted in the ten days that the President has to sign a bill? P. T. N.

A. The Constitution says "If any bill shall not be returned by the President within ten days (Sundays excepted) after it shall have been presented to him, the same shall be a law, in like manner as if he had signed it, unless the Congress by their adjournment prevent its return, in which case it shall not be a law."

Q. How tall were George Washington and Abraham Lincoln? W. M. S.

A. At the time of his death George Washington was 6 feet 3½

inches. It is probable that he was considerably taller during the prime of life. Abraham Lincoln was 6 feet 4 inches.

Q. How much livestock did George Washington keep on his farm? N. O.

A. The will of Washington, made in the year of his death, listed more than 1000 head of livestock of all kinds, valued at $15,000.

Q. Where did Lincoln make the speech in which he said, "Let us have faith that right makes might?" C. T. W.

A. At Cooper Union in 1860.

Q. Was Scripture read or a prayer offered at the Inauguration of George Washington? N. B. S.

A. Not at the inauguration ceremony. After making the inaugural address, George Washington with the company assembled adjourned to St. Paul's Church where prayers were read by the Bishop.

Q. Who was the first dark horse President? D. S. V.

A. James K. Polk. In the 1844 Democratic convention, a majority was instructed for Martin Van Buren but not the necessary two-thirds. After nine ballots the deadlock was broken and Polk, not before regarded as a contender, was given New York's vote. State after State swung over until Polk, on the final ballot, received every vote in the convention.

Q. Did Andrew Carnegie provide pensions for former Presidents or widows of Presidents? A. R.

A. Andrew Carnegie in his will left an annuity of $5,000 to Mrs. Preston (formerly Mrs. Cleveland) and to Mrs. Roosevelt. He left an annuity of $10,000 to ex-President Taft. He did not provide any pensions for Presidents and Presidents' wives.

Q. How tall was George Washington's father? V. C.

A. Nancy Turner, in The Mother of Washington, quotes an acquaintance of Augustine's as saying, "Six feet in height he was, of noble appearance and manly proportions, with the most extraordinary muscular power. Over at the Principia Iron Works where he acted as agent, he used to lift up and place in a wagon a mass that two ordinary men could hardly have raised from the ground."

Q. Were Washington's hands large? M. M.

A. Helen Nicolay quotes Lafayette as saying that General Washington had the largest hands he ever saw on a human being.

Q. Who has the power to impeach a President of the United States? M. D.

A. The House of Representatives under the Constitution has the sole power to bring an impeachment.

Q. Does the President of the United States pay an income tax on his salary? V. B.

A. The salary of the President of the United States is not taxable. Any other income which he may have is taxable. The Bureau of Internal Revenue says that the law regulating the matter states that the President's salary cannot be reduced during his term of office. This is construed in such a way as to exempt his salary from income tax.

Q. Did President Wilson kneel before the Pope when in Italy? G. C.

A. President Wilson did not make obeisance to the Pope of Rome during his interview with that dignitary in 1919. The Pope received Mr. Wilson most graciously and they conversed together for a short time.

Q. Why is there no Vice President in case his office is vacated? W. A. W.

A. Because the Constitution makes no provision for the filling of the vacancy. One of the functions of a Vice President is to preside over the Senate. In the case of his death or disability, the Senate elects a President Pro Tem from that body.

Q. Did George Washington have god-children? F. R.

A. In 1747 Washington "was godfather to a child in baptism." In 1748 he was godfather to his niece, Frances Lewis; in 1751, to his nephew, Fielding Lewis; in 1760, to another nephew, Charles Lewis.

Q. How is the President's salary paid to him? M. D.

A. The President of the United States receives his salary once a month by check.

Q. Was George Washington a highly educated man? L. L.

A. He was not. Writing of Washington, Corbin says: "His interest in popular education was no less ardent than was Jefferson's and took on a peculiar quality from the fact that he thought of himself always as one of the uneducated. His solicitude for the schools of Virginia and for a national university is expressed in many eloquent and noble passages and in liberal bequests."

Q. Was Jefferson reluctant to relinquish the office of President? W. D.

A. On this subject Jefferson wrote to his friend, Dupont de Nemours: "Never did a prisoner, released from his chains, feel such relief as I shall on shaking off the shackles of power."

Q. What Presidents besides Woodrow Wilson were teachers earlier in life? F. S.

A. John Adams, Garfield, Arthur, Cleveland, and McKinley, as well as Woodrow Wilson, taught school in their early years. Lincoln and Harding also taught for a short time.

Q. Was not John Hanson really the first President? J. M. F.

A. John Hanson, born in Green Hill, Md., 1715, was a Representative in the House of Delegates of Maryland from 1757 to 1781, and a delegate from Maryland to the Continental Congress, 1781 to 1783, serving as President of that body in 1781, the first to hold this office after the adoption of the Articles of Confederation, but not under the Constitution. George Washington was the first President of the United States under the Constitution and was the first President elected according to the provisions of the Constitution.

Q. *How many degrees from colleges or universities has President Hoover?* J. H. G.

A. When Mr. Hoover became President he had received 26 degrees, nine of them from European universities.

Q. *Didn't Taft resign from Roosevelt's Cabinet before he had been in the Cabinet a year?* J. H. G.

A. Taft became Secretary of War February 1, 1904. In November following he tendered his resignation because he thought that a political speech he had made in Connecticut might embarrass President Roosevelt as a candidate for reëlection, but Roosevelt would not accept the resignation.

Q. *Was Lincoln in favor of woman suffrage?* S. B. T.

A. As early as 1836, Lincoln made a speech in which he said: "I go for all sharing the privilege of the government who assist in bearing its burdens. Consequently, I go for admitting all whites to the rights of suffrage who pay taxes or bear arms, by no means excluding females."

Q. *How many Presidents of the United States are buried in Arlington?* J. O.

A. William Howard Taft is the only President buried there.

Q. *What President of the United States lived the longest?* L. K.

A. John Adams, who died at 90, holds the longevity record for Presidents. Monroe came next, his age at death being 85.

Q. *Why was the father of the late President Coolidge known as Col. Coolidge?* A. V. R.

A. John C. Coolidge obtained the title of Colonel from service on the staff of Governor Stickney of Vermont. He occupied several public offices, among them state representative, state Senator, tax collector, deputy sheriff, school director, and assistant postmaster.

Q. *Why was George Washington's birthday changed from February 11 to February 22?* E. B.

A. It was because of the non-acceptance of the revision of the calendar by England and her colonies. The revision of the calendar under Pope Gregory was made in 1582. It was not adopted by England and her colonies until 1752. In the meantime a difference of eleven days between the old and new calendars had occurred.

Q. *Please give the religious affiliations of President and Mrs. Hoover, and explain why they were married by a Catholic priest.* D. C. S.

A. In 1899, Mr. Hoover, a young engineer, had had a job in Australia, and was returning to San Francisco. He was to leave immediately for China to take up another position, so cabled his fiancée, Lou Henry, that he wished to be married without delay. The cable message miscarried, and upon his arrival quick action was necessary. There being no other clergyman in the town of Monterey, California, where the marriage was to take place, a Catholic missionary priest, Rev. Raymon Maria Mestries, who was also a civil official, performed the ceremony, after he had obtained a special dispensation from his bishop, as neither Mr. Hoover nor his bride was a Catholic. Mr. Hoover is a Quaker. Mrs. Hoover is an Episcopalian.

Q. *How many Presidents have been college fraternity men?* C. McC.

A. Nine. Chester A. Arthur, Psi Upsilon; Grover Cleveland, Sigma Chi; Calvin Coolidge, Phi Gamma Delta; James A. Garfield, Delta Upsilon; Benjamin Harrison, Phi Delta Theta; William McKinley, Sigma Alpha Epsilon; Theodore Roosevelt,

Delta Kappa Epsilon and Alpha Delta; William H. Taft, Psi Upsilon; Woodrow Wilson, Phi Kappa Psi. Franklin Delano Roosevelt is a member of Alpha Delta Phi.

Q. *Do Mrs. Calvin Coolidge, Mrs. Herbert Hoover, and Mrs. Franklin Roosevelt wear their hair bobbed?* T. K.

A. None of them has her hair bobbed.

Q. *Was Washington confirmed? Did he receive Holy Communion?* S. K.

A. Canon Dunlap says: "George Washington, although never confirmed, received the Communion as often as circumstances permitted."

Q. *Which Presidents were elected by the House of Representatives?* H. D.

A. Two Presidents have been elected by the House of Representatives, Thomas Jefferson in 1800, and John Quincy Adams in 1824. The Hayes-Tilden controversy was decided by an electoral commission.

Q. *Why did Bryan resign from Wilson's Cabinet?* W. A. H.

A. As one biographer put it: "Increasing irreconcilable differences over the policy of the United States toward Germany before the entry of America into the War, culminating in a disagreement over the second Lusitania note, brought about a breach between Bryan and President Wilson which never again was closed. Bryan resigned his post as Secretary of State June 8, 1915."

Q. *Is it true that France was paid $1,000,000 for repairs made necessary after the occupancy of the Hotel Crillon by President Wilson and his retinue?* A. K. S.

A. The Government of the United States did not pay the French government $1,000,000 for repairs, etc., on the hotel occupied by President Wilson during the Paris Peace Conference. All settlements were made with the Societe de Louvre, the owners of the Hotel Crillon. In Senate Document 330, 66th Congress, Third Session, there is a full report of all expenditures made by the American Commission to negotiate peace. By reference to that document it will be learned that the total amount paid for rent, damages, breakage, losses, etc., for the period from December 1, 1918, to December 31, 1919, was $288,-651.29."

Q. *Has a Democratic President entertained a negro at the White House?*

A. Karl Phillips, a Commissioner of Conciliation in the Department of Labor, says that Grover Cleveland entertained Frederick A. Douglass and C. H. J. Taylor, during his terms of office.

Q. *Why was Andrew Jackson's group of close friends called a kitchen cabinet?* G. C. H.

A. The explanation has been given that "all the members of the Cabinet were men with whom Jackson could smoke and converse at random without the restraint of a council and clashing minds."

Q. *How many of our Presidents have been book collectors?* L. B. J.

A. According to a statement made by Dr. A. S. W. Rosenbach, of Philadelphia, Washington, John Adams, and Jefferson, were noted book collectors. Herbert Hoover also has a large collection of books.

Q. *Was President Garfield a minister of the Gospel?* F. S.

A. Before entering college, he united with the Disciples Church in which he had been brought up and, according to the usage of that denomination, though never formally ordained to the ministry, he often preached.

Q. *Have any of the Presidents of the United States served as diplomatic representatives to Great Britain?* R. N.

A. Four Presidents have been diplomatic representatives of the United

States prior to their Presidency—James Monroe, 1803; John Quincy Adams, 1815; Martin Van Buren, 1831; James Buchanan, 1853.

Q. Please name the wives of the last few Presidents who were college women. E. C.

A. Mrs. Cleveland was a graduate of Wells College; Mrs. Taft's musical education was unusually complete; Mrs. Roosevelt attended female seminaries; Mrs. Coolidge is a graduate of the University of Vermont; Mrs. Hoover is a graduate of Leland Stanford University, California.

Q. Who decided that President Wilson should represent the United States at the Peace Conference? G. C. B.

A. President Wilson notified Congress that he intended to be the representative of the United States and head the Peace Mission to Paris in 1918.

Q. How much did Jefferson spend on wine during his Presidency? D. C.

A. T. E. Watson in his biography of Jefferson says that he and his guests drank $10,855 worth of wine while Jefferson was in office.

Q. Did our early Presidents live longer than the later ones? E. S.

A. Taking the Civil War as a dividing line, the average length of life of the early Presidents was 73.8 years. The average life of Presidents since the Civil War has been 61.67 years.

Q. What President left the United States while in office? W. C. A.

A. Presidents who have left the confines of the United States while in office were: Roosevelt—visited the Panama Canal Zone and went to the City of Panama; Taft—crossed the border into Mexico and dined with President Diaz at Juarez; Cleveland—on a fishing trip exceeded the boundary of the United States; Wilson—Peace Conference in Europe; Harding—British Columbia, Canada; and Coolidge—Cuba.

Q. Is there a law against a President's taking the oath of office on Sunday? A. T.

A. There is not. President Wilson was the last President to do so.

Q. Does the President have to utilize all the money that is appropriated for his traveling expenses each year? If not, does he get the money that is left? M. J. McI.

A. The President does not have to use any more of his traveling and entertaining expenses than he cares to. The balance remains in the Treasury.

Q. Does the selection of a President's secretary have to be approved by the Senate? C. E. B.

A. This is an appointment that a President makes without consent of the Senate.

Q. How many Vice Presidents have become Presidents of the United States? J. H. G.

A. Nine Vice Presidents have become Presidents, three by election and six by death of Presidents. Two of those who succeeded to the Presidency as a result of the death of Presidents, Theodore Roosevelt and Calvin Coolidge, were later elected Presidents.

Q. How long has Secret Service protection been given to the family of the President? M. V. H.

A. Before 1919, protection was extended only to the person of the President. Since that time, the executive family has been included.

Q. How old was President Coolidge at the time of his death? H. T.

A. He was born July 4, 1872, and died January 5, 1933. He was in his sixty-first year.

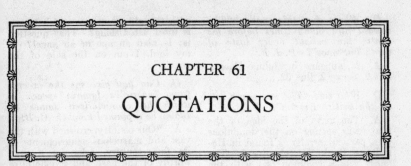

CHAPTER 61

QUOTATIONS

Q. Who said "Nothing is certain but death and taxes"? W. E. D.

A. This is attributed to Benjamin Franklin.

Q. Is "Blessed is the bride that the sun shines on" a very old expression? B. R.

A. It is an old Scotch saying, known as early as the 17th century. It runs as follows: "Blessed is the bride that the sun shines on. Blessed is the corpse that the rain falls on."

Q. Who originated the saying "Nothing succeeds like success"? K. C. I.

A. The words were used in reference to the first operation under ether performed by Dr. John Collins Warren at the Massachusetts General Hospital on October 16, 1846.

Q. Who said "What this country needs is a good 5-cent cigar"? F. W.

A. This well-known saying was originated by Thomas R. Marshall, Vice President of the United States during the Wilson administration.

Q. Who said war's legitimate object is more perfect peace? S. B.

A. The expression is attributed to Gen. William T. Sherman.

Q. Who was it who replied "It always has" when he was asked whether he thought it would stop raining? F. D. S.

A. The story is told of the late Senators Spooner, of Wisconsin, and Allison, of Iowa. They were leaving the Capitol one evening and it was raining heavily. "Do you think it will stop?" asked Spooner. "It always has," answered Allison.

Q. Can you quote the reply of Speaker Tom Reed when he declined the invitation to make a speech before the Blue Grass Club of Kentucky? A. T.

A. "I shall not accept the invitation tendered me by the Blue Grass Club. The reason is very simple. I have been told that during the late disturbances they said that if they had me in Kentucky they would kill me. I do not wish to be killed, especially in Kentucky, where such an event is too common to attract attention. For a good man to die anywhere is of course a gain, but I think I can make more by dying later and elsewhere."

Q. What is the source of the phrase, "the young idea," in referring to children or youths? B. V. R.

A. In Thomson's The Seasons, in the spring canto, appear the lines: "Delightful task to rear the tender thought, to teach the young idea how to shoot."

Q. Who said "What you do speaks so loud, I cannot hear what you say"? M. C. B.

A. It is a paraphrase of "What you are stands over you the while and thunders so that I cannot hear what you say to the contrary" in Social Aims by Ralph Waldo Emerson (1803–1882) first published in 1876.

Q. *Where does this appear—"The coward dies many times before his death, the valiant never taste of death but once"? P. J. F.*

A. It appears in Julius Caesar, Act 2, Scene 2, line 32.

Q. *Who said "The sun never sets on the British Empire"? B. U.*

A. The germ of the idea of the sun never setting on the dominions of a particular ruler is found in Herodotus, Book VII, chapter 8. The boast was a common one with the Spaniards in the 16th and 17th centuries and is frequently alluded to in the literature of other countries. John Wilson, who wrote under the pen name of Christopher North, (1785–1854) in his Noctes Ambrosianae, number 20, April, 1829, says "His Majesty's dominions on which the sun never sets." This appears to be the first use of the expression in English literature.

Q. *Who said "the public be damned"? E. G.*

A. The phrase is accredited to Wm. H. Vanderbilt, famous railroad magnate, and was his amused retort when asked whether the public should be consulted about luxury trains.

Q. *Who said, in part, "My tongue cleave to the roof of my mouth and my right hand lose its cunning"? C. H. W.*

A. It is in the Bible. The 137th Psalm, 5th and 6th verses are: "If I forget thee, O Jerusalem, Let my right hand forget her skill. Let my tongue cleave to the roof of my mouth, If I remember thee not; If I prefer not Jerusalem Above my chief joy." The Psalms are accredited to King David.

Q. *What is the saying about being on the side of the angels? A. A.*

A. The quotation was used by the British Prime Minister Benjamin Disraeli in a speech at the Oxford Diocesan Conference, November 25, 1864, when he said "What is the question now placed before society with the glib assurance which to me is most astonishing? That question is: Is man an ape or an angel? I, my lord, I am on the side of the angels."

Q. *Can you give me the excerpt from Ingersoll's famous speech in which he characterized James G. Blaine as a plumed knight? C. B.*

A. "Our country, crowned with the vast and marvelous achievements of its first century, asks for a man worthy of the past, and prophetic of her future; asks for a man who has the audacity of genius; asks for a man who is the grandest combination of heart, conscience, and brain beneath her flag—such a man is James G. Blaine. . . . Like an armed warrior, like a plumed knight, James G. Blaine marched down the halls of the American Congress and threw his shining lance full and fair against the brazen foreheads of the defamers of his country and the maligners of his honor."

Q. *Who said "Every tub must stand on its own bottom"? E. H. F.*

A. The phrase is accredited to Dean Swift in his Tale of a Tub.

Q. *What American statesman said "Damn your principles! Stick to your party"? F. E. C.*

A. It was not an American statesman. Lord Beaconsfield (Disraeli) said that to Bulwer-Lytton when the latter told the prime minister he could not vote for a certain parliamentary measure because it was against his principles.

Q. *Please set me straight about the author of "If a man write a better book" etc. Was it Elbert Hubbard or Emerson? W. E. W.*

A. Elbert Hubbard said "If a man can write a better book, preach a better sermon, or make a better mousetrap than his neighbor, though he build his house in the woods the world will make a beaten path to his door." The Roycrofters said Mr. Hubbard had in mind the following lines from Emerson, but having no copy of Emerson at hand at the time he quoted as above: "If a man has good corn, or wood, or boards, or pigs to sell, or can make better chairs, or knives, crucibles, or church organs than anybody else, you will find a broad, hard-beaten road to this house, though it be in the woods."

Q. Upon what occasion was "I would rather be right than be President" said? E. A. B.

A. This was the reply of Henry Clay to some of his friends who urged that his advocacy of the compromise of the tariff of 1833 would injure his chances of election to the Presidency.

Q. Where does one first find the phrase "First in war, first in peace and first in the hearts of his countrymen"? A. R.

A. John Marshall's address on the death of Washington concluded with the House resolutions drawn by Lighthorse Harry Lee. Their resolutions included the phrase quoted. Marshall's address marks the first application of the phrase.

Q. Who said "Never put off until tomorrow what you can do today"? M. E. T.

A. It is from Chesterfield's Letters to his Son—December 26, 1749. He wrote, "Know the true value of time; snatch, seize, and enjoy every moment of it. No idleness, no laziness, no procrastination. Never put off till tomorrow what you can do today."

Q. Please give the story of Franklin's toast likening George Washington to Joshua. J. A. T.

A. At the conclusion of the war, Franklin, the English minister, and the French minister were dining together, and a toast from each was requested. The British minister began: "George III, who like the Sun in its meridian, spreads a lustre throughout and enlightens the world." The French minister followed: "The illustrious Louis XVI, who like the moon, sheds mild and benignant rays upon and influences the globe." Franklin then followed: "George Washington, Commander of the American Armies, who like Joshua of old commanded the Sun and Moon to stand still— and they obeyed him."

Q. Who remarked "We must hang together or assuredly we shall all hang separately"? C. J. R.

A. Benjamin Franklin thus expressed himself to John Hancock at the signing of the Declaration of Independence, July 4, 1776.

Q. Who said, "John Marshall has made his decision; now let him enforce it"? H. W. R.

A. It is ascribed to President Andrew Jackson and its occasion was a decision of the Supreme Court in one of the cases involving the Cherokee Indian Nation and the State of Georgia. The Supreme Court had found in favor of the Indians but, as the interests of the United States, as well as those of the State of Georgia, were believed by Jackson to be superior, the Indians were gradually displaced from their lands in spite of the treaty.

Q. What was the statement by some famous divine to the effect that only by sobriety may freedom be attained? J. D.

A. William Magee, Archbishop of York in the last century, said: "It would be better that England should be free than that England should be compulsorily sober. For with freedom we might attain sobriety, but, in the other alternative, we should entirely lose both freedom and sobriety."

Q. What is the quotation about plucking a thistle and planting a rose which is attributed to Lincoln? M. W.

A. In the spring of 1865, a number of men who had resisted the draft in western Pennsylvania were pardoned in a batch by President Lincoln. His friend, I. H. Speed, who had heard the touching pleas of two women petitioners in the case, observed that he wondered how the President stood the anguish of such pleadings when he was, at heart, so sensitive. "I have, in that order," said Lincoln, "made people happy and alleviated the distress of many a poor soul whom I never expect to see. Speed, die when I may, I want it said of me by those who know me best, that I always plucked a thistle and planted a flower when I thought a flower would grow."

Q. When did Capt. Lawrence say "Don't give up the ship"? M. S.

A. The shortest and most desperate sea battle of the War of 1812 was fought off Boston Light June 1, 1813. It was over in fifteen minutes. The Chesapeake struck her flag, but not before nearly all her officers were killed or wounded. Capt. Lawrence had been but recently assigned to this boat. Mortally wounded, he said, "Tell the men to fire faster and not to give up the ship; fight her till she sinks." He was taken to Halifax a prisoner, and died there June 5th.

Q. Who said, "Had I a loaf of bread, I would sell half and buy white hyacinths to feed my soul"? C. C. B.

A. This is attributed to Confucius.

Q. Where can I find the quotation which starts "Yet each man kills the thing he loves"? D. K.

A. It is in "The Ballad of Reading Gaol" by Oscar Wilde.

Q. Who is the author of the quotation, "All the world loves a lover"? W. P.

A. It is in the essay, "Of Love" by Ralph Waldo Emerson.

Q. Who said, "A public office is a public trust"? W. H. R.

A. Dorman Eaton in his Spoils System and Civil Service Reform, chapter 3, entitled "The Merit System," uses the expression "A public office is a public trust." The origin of this expression is assigned to many. According to some it was first used by Charles Sumner in a speech in the United States Senate May 31, 1872. According to Col. John S. Wolfe, of Champaign, it originated in a decision of Justice Samuel D. Lockwood of the Illinois Supreme Court, prior to 1840.

Q. What is the entire quotation, part of which is "Better that ninety-nine. guilty persons go free than one innocent person suffer"? M. K.

A. The quotation appears as a proverb in Wood's Dictionary of Quotations, Phrases, and Proverbs ascribed to the Persian. Christy's Dictionary of Proverbs lists it as Old Danish. Both of these give the text the same: "It is better that ten guilty go free than that one innocent should suffer."

Q. Please quote Joel Chandler Harris' words about what should be said when a man dies. C. W.

A. "Do not say, when a man dies that he is no more, but that he is forever."

Q. Who said, "Every country has the government it deserves"? H. S.

A. This is a translation from the French and was contained in a letter written by Joseph de Maistre in 1811.

Q. When did Grant say "I propose to fight it out on this line if it takes all summer"? S. M. A.

A. He sent this dispatch to Washington on May 11, 1864, during the battles of Spotsylvania Court House.

Q. What is the quotation to the effect that men must be taught without their suspecting it? M. J. M.

A. "Men must be taught as if you taught them not. And things unknown propos'd as things forgot." Alexander Pope's Essay on Criticism part III, lines 14 and 15.

Q. Who said "Corporations have no Souls"? N. P.

A. This is attributed to Richard Coke, famous British lawyer. "They (corporations) cannot commit treason nor be outlawed, nor be excommunicated, for they have no souls." Hence the phrase "Corporations have no souls to save and no bodies to kick."

Q. Who said, "I am fond of children—except boys"? R. T.

A. Lewis Carroll.

Q. Please quote Talleyrand's definition of good coffee. M. B.

A. "It must be pure as an angel, strong as love, black as the devil, and hot as Hell."

Q. Who said "I will find a way or make one"? T. R.

A. This is accredited to Hannibal. When his plan for taking his army across the Alps into Italy was questioned, he said that he would find a way or make one. He accomplished the feat, appearing on the plains of Italy with 26,000 men—half the army with which he had started.

Q. What is the story connected with the saying, "Said the Governor of North Carolina to the Governor of South Carolina, 'It's a long time between drinks'"? D. P.

A. The story with respect to the remark of the Governor of North Carolina is as follows: The Governor of South Carolina required the return of a fugitive slave. The Governor of North Carolina hesitated because of powerful friends of the fugitive. He gave a banquet to his official brother. The Governor of South Carolina in a speech demanded the return of the slave and ended with "What do you say?" The Governor of North Carolina replied "It's a long time between drinks." It is also attributed to Judge Aedanus Burke.

Q. What was the King's retort to the famous burlesque epitaph—"Here lies our Sovereign Lord the King, Whose word no man relies on, Who never said a foolish thing, Nor ever did a wise one"? S. N. S.

A. The Earl of Rochester was one of the wittiest of courtiers and King Charles permitted him great lati-

tude. The King replied to the sally with the facetious retort—"That is very true; but my words are my own, while my actions are my ministers."

Q. Who wrote "The drying up a single tear has more of honest fame than shedding seas of gore"? J. J. K.

A. It is Byron's. It is in Don Juan, canto 8, stanza 3.

Q. Who was it who said "So little done, so much to do!"? F. D. S.

A. Cecil Rhodes, British colonizer and statesman, is said to have uttered those words as he died at Muizenberg, near Cape Town, March 26, 1902.

Q. Who said "O liberty what crimes are committed in thy name"? M. J.

A. The words were used by Madame Roland immediately before her execution, as she stood before the Statue of Liberty that had been erected in the Place de la Revolution in Paris.

Q. Who wrote "One crowded hour of glorious life is worth an age without a name"? F. F.

A. This is the heading from Chapter 34 of the book called "Old Mortality" by Sir Walter Scott.

Q. What sentence preceded Patrick Henry's immortal "Give me liberty or give me death"? M. F. P.

A. The second revolutionary convention of Virginia was held in St. John's Episcopal Church at Richmond in 1775. Proposals for a peaceful settlement had been strongly advocated. On the third day, March 23, 1775, Patrick Henry, realizing that war was inevitable, overwhelmed the opposition to resolutions for arming the Virginia militia in a speech which has since become famous. He ended, "Is life so dear, or peace so sweet, as to be purchased at the price of chains and slavery? Forbid it, Almighty God. I know not what course others may take, but as for me, give me liberty or give me death!"

Q. What was Napoleon's comment upon the death of Washington? R. C. P.

A. It is translated as follows: "Washington is dead. This great man fought against tyranny; he established the liberty of his country. His memory will always be dear to the French people, as it will be to all freemen of the two worlds; and especially to French soldiers who, like him, and the American soldiers, have combated for liberty and equality."

Q. Who was it during the World War who said "Our backs are to the wall"? O. O.

A. The words "Our backs are to the wall" were used by the British Field Marshal Earl Haig at the Battle of Picardy in 1918.

Q. Who said that trifles make perfection and that perfection is no trifle? L. B.

A. It is attributed to Michelangelo.

Q. Where is the couplet found: "And still they gazed and still the wonder grew, That one small head should carry all it knew"? J. K.

A. It is from Goldsmith's Deserted Village.

Q. Who said "Welcome the coming, speed the parting guest"? P. G.

A. Homer uses the expression in The Odyssey.

Q. What British statesman referred to an opponent as "intoxicated by the exuberance of his own verbosity"? W. G.

A. The quotation to which you refer occurs in a speech made at Riding School, London, July 27, 1878, by Benjamin Disraeli, Earl of Beaconsfield, Prime Minister, 1868, and 1874–80. The speech referred to Gladstone and is as follows: "A sophisticated rhetorician, inebriated with the exuberance of his own verbosity, and gifted with an egotistical imagination that can, at all times, command an interminable and inconsistent series of arguments to malign an opponent and to glorify himself."

Q. Is the correct quotation "Far from the maddening crowd" or "Far from the madding crowd"? B. N. O.

A. "Far from the madding crowd" is correct, if you are inquiring as to the quotation from Gray's Elegy.

Q. Who said "There is no such word as impossible in the French language"? T. C.

A. The familiar quotation is "The word impossible is not in my dictionary" and is attributed to Napoleon.

Q. Please place the following quotation "They also serve who only stand and wait." A. A.

A. It is from a sonnet of Milton's written on his blindness.

Q. What was the famous remark made by a World War General which began: "My right has been rolled up"? H. O. H.

A. The following was written by General Foch in a letter to Marshal Joffre during the Battle of the Marne: "My right has been rolled up, my left has been driven back, my center has been smashed. I have ordered an advance from all directions!"

Q. Who originated the quotation "Learn to smoke slow"? F. H.

A. The English magazine Punch is credited with the origin of the phrase, which is in full—"Learn to smoke slow. The other grace is to keep your smoke from people's faces."

Q. Who made popular the expression "place in the sun"? E. H. C.

A. The phrase was used by the former Emperor of Germany William II, on June 18, 1910, in an address at Hamburg while referring to Germany's acquisition of the Chinese harbor at Kiaochow and other valuable commercial concessions in China. The idea was expressed many years before, however. Pascal, who lived from 1623–62, in his Les Pensees said: "That dog is mine said those poor children; that place in the sun is mine; such is the beginning and type of usurpation throughout the earth."

Q. What is the origin of the quotation "Gibble, gobble, gabble, git"? J. D. S.

A. The expression was coined by Oliver Wendell Holmes in describing an afternoon tea.

Q. Who said, "Sir, no man could be as great as Daniel Webster looked"? T. M.

A. The Duke of Wellington thus remarked after he had seen Daniel Webster.

Q. Who said that all military knowledge could be summed up in three words? A. L. B.

A. The Russian general, Alexander V. Surarov. The three words were "Stoupai i bi"—"Forward and strike."

Q. Of whom was it said that "the English are cutting off the best head of their country"? I. V. G.

A. Richelieu made the remark when he heard of the beheading of the Earl of Strafford in 1641.

Q. Who said that the mind can make a heaven of hell, and a hell of heaven? C. T. P.

A. The quotation is from Milton, and in full, is: "The mind is its own place, and in itself can make a heaven of hell, a hell of heaven."

Q. When his mistress, Mme. Pompadour died, Louis XV made a very cynical remark apropos of her funeral. I cannot find the exact words credited to him. Can you supply them? F. D. A.

A. It was a cold rainy day when the body of the Pompadour was taken from Versailles to Paris for burial. Louis did not accompany the cortege. He stood at a palace window as the procession started and without any expression of regret or sorrow said to an attendant, "The marquise will have a very disagreeable day for her journey."

Q. Who used the expression "God has made us neighbors. Let Justice make us friends"? W. S.

A. This sentiment was inscribed on a photograph of William Jennings Bryan which he presented, when Secretary of State, to Director General John Barrett of the Pan American Union.

Q. Who said "England was made by adventurers, not by its government"? J. G.

A. This is attributed to General Charles Gordon, better known as Chinese Gordon, who was killed in the defense of Khartum.

Q. Of whom was it said, "He rose like a star in the heavens; everybody worshipped him and especially the women"? H. E.

A. K. Nebel, the German writer, said this of Johann Wolfgang von Goethe.

Q. Of whom was it said "All the Frenchwomen dote upon him, and all the men are jealous of him"? T. O. L.

A. Orlouski said this of Frederic Chopin.

Q. Who first said "You can't get blood out of a rock or stone"? M. P.

A. This is an old Persian proverb, first published in 599.

Q. Who said "There, but for the grace of God, goes ——"? W. B. C.

A. The saying "There, but for the Grace of God, goes John Bradford," is attributed to John Bradford in his writings on seeing a criminal pass by. It has also been accredited to Baxter, Bunyan, and John Wesley.

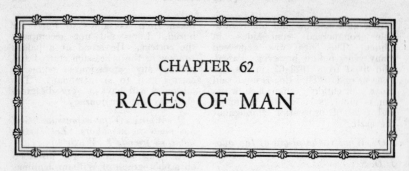

CHAPTER 62

RACES OF MAN

Q. Were the Greeks and Romans astir later or earlier than people of today? T. W. B.

A. Both peoples were busy much earlier in the day than we are.

Q. Are savages strict with the misbehavior of children? A. D. T.

A. In savage life, parents almost never chastise their children. Travelers everywhere have commented upon this.

Q. Do most people in India go barefooted? F. B.

A. Of a total population of 350,-000,000 at least 290,000,000 go barefooted.

Q. Why are German girls always represented as blondes? I. E. H.

A. On the stage and in many instances in fiction the German heroine is flaxen or golden haired. In Berlin, however, a brunette has been selected as the Miss Germany to compete in Paris for the title of Miss Europe.

Q. What races now lead the most primitive lives? C. S.

A. Probably the Bushmen and Hottentots of South Africa.

Q. What are Tex-Mex? B. R.

A. Texas-born Mexicans sometimes are known locally as Tex-Mex.

Q. Are turbans still worn in Persia? W. F.

A. Wearing of the turban in Persia has been abolished by decree.

The Persians are going in for tweed caps.

Q. What kind of food did the Romans in the time of Commodus eat at breakfast time? C. A. C.

A. Among breakfast dishes listed we find a dish of marrow bones, a dozen larks on a dish, a neat's tongue, a dish of fowl, a silver grill with hot sausage, peahens' eggs.

Q. Are Sicilians of Italian origin? M. R. R.

A. Sicilians are a mixture of many nationalities as in early days Sicily was the battleground of all countries. People came from all the northern African and eastern Mediterranean ports as well as all those of Europe to fight.

Q. How many castes are there in India? J. C.

A. At the present time there are estimated to be between three and four thousand social units, and in addition the untouchables who are of no caste whatsoever and considered to be beyond recognition.

Q. Are the Swedish people Teutons? C. F.

A. They are possibly of the purest Teutonic blood in existence.

Q. What are the most valuable contributions by characteristics of the foreign elements in our population? A. G.

A. Opinions would differ. They may be characterized as follows:

412

English, obedience to law; French, thriftiness; Italian, artistic sense; German, industriousness; Russian, imagination; Dutch, placidity.

Q. What savages mutilate their ears? E. M.

A. Very few primitive people leave the ears totally unmutilated. Both the ear lobes are commonly pierced. This is usually done during childhood and a small piece of wood is inserted in the wound which is left to heal. Later this block is removed and a larger one inserted; the operation being continued until the hole is the required size. The greatest distortions are to be found in Borneo and East Africa.

Q. When did the first native of Poland come to this country? K. A. T.

A. It is said that the first Pole who came to the United States was a young man whom the Dutch colonists of Manhattan in 1659 engaged as schoolmaster for their children.

Q. To what tribe do the duckbill women belong? G. Z.

A. The tribal name of these West African negroes is Nazza or Masa. They are also known as the Banana Tribe and because they live near the Ubangi River are referred to as Ubangis. This tribe lives in the jungle in French equatorial Africa between the Ubangi River and Lake Tchad. A group of them was brought to this country and performed for the season of 1930 with a circus.

Q. Into how many races is the human race now divided? C. B.

A. According to Dr. Hrdlicka of the United States National Museum in Washington, three main human races are recognized today—the whites, yellow-browns, and blacks. Each one of these has a number of sub-races or types which are often called races also. The principal of these are: Whites—the Mediterraneans, the Alpines, and the Nordics; yellow-browns—the Mongoloids,

the Malays, and the American Indians; blacks—the Negritoes, Bushmen, African Negroes. Some authorities classify the American Indian as a separate race.

Q. Are many Mexicans now returning to Mexico? C. A. M.

A. The Mexican Government is at present faced with a very serious problem caused by the rapid repatriation of thousands of Mexicans from this country who have returned to Mexico after not finding work here. As many as 10,000 have returned in a single day, and in one month 100,000 returned from the State of California, alone.

Q. Have the Turks given up wearing the red fez? A. B.

A. Kemal Pasha has ordained the complete suppression of this historic headgear.

Q. How did Scotsmen get the reputation of being stingy? A. S.

A. Scotland throughout its history has been a poor country. Its land with small exceptions was infertile, its climate bad, with long hard winters, and short frequently dry summers, and it has also, through its history, been the scene of much strife, both foreign and civil. To surmount such conditions, a people must be of a more frugal, industrious, and persevering habit, and the exercise of these virtues may at times have developed into a hardness and thrift which have been commented on unfavorably and undoubtedly much exaggerated.

Q. What people are Kanakas? M. A.

A. Kanakas is a popular name given to the natives of Hawaii, New Caledonia, New Hebrides, and other islands of the South Seas.

Q. What are the natives of Guam called? N. E.

A. The name applied to the natives is Chamorros. The Chamorro dialect spoken in Guam is a polyglot mixture of Spanish, Malay,

Yaqui Indian lingo, and various Polynesian tongues.

Q. Why are Frenchmen called frogs? B. J. G.

A. During the early years of its history, the streets of Paris were so quaggy that the French court in derision called the inhabitants frogs.

Q. In what sports did the Egyptians indulge? V. S.

A. The people of Egypt were greatly given to hunting and fishing, also throwing of the rounded stones and discus. They were also expert runners.

Q. Of what religion are Ethiopians, and are they polygamous? S. E.

A. In general Ethiopians are Christians of the Coptic or Monophysite type, and are monogamous.

Q. Are any of the dark-skinned people of Africa of white blood? L. O.

A. North Africa is peopled by tribes of dark complexion but of white blood. They are known as a Hamitic group. The more important are the Berbers and the Egyptians, including the Copts.

Q. What is meant by middle peasantry? R. B.

A. This term defines a class of people in Russia. It is composed of wealthier peasants, those who not only work on farms but have progressed to the point that they hire other peasants to work for them. Their status is hard to determine since they are part property owners and part toilers. Occupation and use are titles of ownership; the peasant is not free to develop into an absentee landlord.

Q. Where did the Helvetians live? C. L. D.

A. The Helvetii were a Celtic people who originally dwelt between the Rhine, the Main, and the Hercynian Forest. Later, according to Caesar, they occupied the region between the Jura Mountains on the west, the Rhone on the south, and the Rhine on the east and north. This region corresponds closely with the western part of modern Switzerland.

Q. From what country did gypsies originally come? A. R.

A. Although the gypsies themselves claim Egypt as their native land, it is believed that they originally came from India in the Middle Ages, passing through Egypt to Europe.

Q. Are all Indians of the same shade of brown? A. J. E.

A. They are not. The skin is of various shades of brown, tinged in youth, particularly in the cheeks, with the red of the circulating blood. Newborn infants are of varying shades of dusky red.

Q. Who were known as the Bread and Cheese Folk? M. D. M.

A. This was the name applied to members of the insurgent party in Haarlem, Netherlands, in 1492. This group held temporary possession of the city.

Q. Of what nationality were most of the foreign brides of American World War soldiers? S. A. H.

A. There were the most French brides. Many, however, were English, with a few from practically all the European countries.

Q. Were wigs worn by the Egyptians? D. R.

A. Men and women wore wigs. As a people, Egyptians were expert wig-makers.

Q. Please describe the hair dressing of the Assyrians. M. S. T.

A. Assyrian men covered their hair with gold powder and gold thread. Beards and hair were curled. Their eyebrows were painted. Assyrian women did not wear their hair curled.

Q. To what race do Filipinos belong? A. D.

A. They are Malays.

Q. In early days, did Egyptian women weave materials? N. N.

A. Herodotus says that the Egyptian men remained at home and wove while the women trafficked in the markets.

Q. Who are the Mosquitos of Nicaragua? M. M.

A. They are a people of mixed Indian and African blood.

Q. Have any peoples other than the American Indians practiced painting their bodies as a war preparation? J. K.

A. The ancient Britons stained and dyed their bodies and faces with the juice of the woad plant which was blue in color. The British women also used the dye on their bodies in certain religious ceremonials.

Q. What country was first to set up an institute of race-biology? S. W.

A. Sweden was first. In 1918, the University of Upsala subsidized the research of Professor Lundborg into the lineage of peasant families. The Swedish Parliament later had his work investigated, approved it, and founded an institute making him director.

Q. Are the people who come from Syria called Syrians or Assyrians? H. H. G.

A. They are Syrians. Assyrians were the inhabitants of the ancient empire of Assyria.

Q. Which were more civilized, the Incas of Peru or the Aztecs of Mexico? G. C.

A. Authors differ in their opinions as to whether the Incas of Peru were more civilized than the Aztecs of Mexico. The Peruvians were the best weavers in the world, in fact they were specialists in many lines. The Aztecs had an elaborate calendar system, and were celebrated for their artistic work, as well as for their military prowess. Recent scientific researches conducted in the Sierras have contradicted some of the glowing accounts of the social organizations of the Incas.

Q. Where did the Mayas come from? N. A. L.

A. This is one of the world's ancient mysteries. Research is now going on in the Vatican Library in the hope of tracing manuscripts of priests who visited America at the time of the Spanish conquest. It is hoped that these may prove a key to the Mayan hieroglyphics which have been found. At the time of the conquest the Mayas had a vast literature preserved on scrolls of papyrus. These were gathered and burned by the Spanish invaders. Despite the fact that the Mayas had evolved a complex civilization and had developed astronomy and mathematics to a stage not surpassed by the ancient Egyptians, the source of this civilization is unknown.

Q. From whom did the Hebrews learn the art of wood carving? A. R. R.

A. Robert Casson says: "From the Egyptians, the Jews, no doubt, during their captivity, learned the art of wood carving and the making and worship of idols."

Q. What kind of men were the Tartars in appearance, at the time they conquered Russia? D. M. M.

A. In the 13th century the Tartars were a very much mixed race, but in general the type was swarthy with scant black facial hair.

Q. Are the people who live in Pomorze German or Polish? S. G.

A. Pomorze is that part of Poland which has an outlet upon the Baltic Sea. It separates Eastern Prussia from Germany. Out of 800,000 of the total population, only 12 per cent represents the German element, while Poles compose 88 per cent. Pomorze or Polish Pomerania was part of Poland from the beginning of the 11th century until 1772, except for a period between 1308 and 1454. After the World War the country was given to Poland.

Q. Into what divisions are Russians divided? J. McG.

A. The true Russians are divided into three groups: The Great Russians or Muscovites; the Little Russians or Malo-Russians, otherwise called Ukrainians or Ruthenians; the White Russians.

Q. Are the people of Finland of Mongolian ancestry? C. M.

A. What are popularly called the Finnish people are actually three divisions of a mixed race, the eastern Finns inhabiting parts of Russia and Asia exhibiting strong Mongolian traits. The western Finns appear almost entirely Caucasian with slight traits of Mongolian or Tartar ancestry. The Finns of Finland show a mixture of Caucasian and Mongolian blood. All Finns are classed as white people.

Q. What has become of the Zulus? F. H.

A. Zulus are inhabitants of South Africa where the most extensive occupation by civilization has been made. There are some still there, but they are not organized in such strong tribes as they were formerly.

Q. Is it really believed that the Mayan civilization is a survival of the old Atlantis? K. F. H.

A. The Bureau of American Ethnology says that the Atlantis theory of the development of the Mayan civilization is no longer accepted by Mayan scholars.

Q. Was there ever a race of pygmies in Tennessee? H. S.

A. The existence of a pygmy race in Tennessee is believed to be a fallacy by modern ethnologists. The story owes its origin to the discovery in the early half of the 19th century of numerous small stone coffins containing skeletons, the largest of which measured 24 inches in length

and 9 inches in depth. These were assumed to be the remains of a race of pygmies. However, they have proved to be in many cases the skeletons of children. Those of adults were deprived of flesh according to the common custom in the mound region, then disjointed and the bones packed into a very small space.

Q. From what people are the Basques descended? A. P.

A. The Basques are believed to be a fragment, perhaps the only distinct remnant of the pre-Aryan race or aboriginal people of Europe. Their language is the only non-Aryan language of western Europe. Recent investigations indicate connections with the Berbers of North Africa who are of Hamitic stock.

Q. Is it true that South American aborigines have a process for shrinking and preserving the heads of their slain enemies? C. H. S.

A. This is done by native tribes inhabiting the Amazon jungles. They are known as Jivaro heads and are about the size of an orange.

Q. Where did Nubians come from? E. R.

A. The Nubians were Negroid tribes who formed a powerful empire between Egypt and Abyssinia from the 6th to the 14th century when they were conquered by the Arabs.

Q. What peoples belong to the Caucasian race? A. H.

A. The Caucasian race includes the Teutons, Slavs, Lithuanians and Letts, Romano-Greeks, Spanish, Kelts, Albanians, Armenians, Iranians, Hindus, and Semites.

Q. To what race do Italians belong? F. L. S.

A. They belong to the Caucasian race.

Q. Are modern Greeks of short stature? V. D. G.

A. The true, modern Greek is of tall stature, attractive appearance, and of temperate habits, but the population is to a considerable extent mixed as a result of various incursions and migrations, and in recent times intermixture with other races and commerce has to a great extent removed their distinctive characteristics.

Q. *Do the Chinese worship their ancestors? A. B. S.*

A. They do not consider them as deities to be worshipped; they reverence them.

Q. *What class of people come under the head, the White Russians? F. W. S.*

A. They are considered by Beaulieu to be the purest of the three great Slav divisions, the Great Russians, the Little Russians, and the White Russians. Their dialect is akin to Great Russia. They have light-brown or brown hair with a reddish tinge, and light-brown eyes. Apparently they were so named because of their costume, which consists of white smock, bast shoes with white leggings, and white homespun coat.

Q. *What races are represented in the modern English race? B. H. T.*

A. The modern English race is a mixed one as a result of various invasions, notably those of the Angles and Saxons, the Scandinavian and Teutonic peoples. There are also Norman and Celtic admixtures.

Q. *Please explain the manner in which nomadic tribes of Arabs are organized. G. I.*

A. The organization of the nomadic Arabs is represented by the tribe under the control of a sheikh, an office normally hereditary but sometimes elective. Within the tribe are a number of sections with patrilineal descent, themselves often formed by smaller groups. Each section has its own sheikh subordinate to the tribal sheikh, and much importance is attached to the preservation of tribal and sectional genealogies. The size of a tribe or section may fluctuate from time to time with the popularity and strength of its leader; a strong and just man will attract to his unit families or groups of families from other tribes and these in time may give rise to sections or lose their identity in that of their adopted unit.

Q. *What were the ancient Egyptians' leading contributions to civilization? F. A. G.*

A. Though their literature is extensive and interesting, the most noteworthy work of this most ancient people is the system of architecture and art which developed. The industrial world, too, is under a heavy debt to the early dwellers in the valley of the Nile, for many of the mechanical arts had their beginnings there.

Q. *How long have the people who live in the country we call Germany been known as Germans? C. F.*

A. In English the word German does not occur until the 16th century. Its origin is not definitely known. It may possibly have been the name given by the Gauls to their neighbors.

Q. *Where are the largest Russian colonies in this country? B. S.*

A. They are in New York City, Detroit, Chicago, San Francisco, Pittsburgh, Philadelphia, St. Louis, Jersey City, and Cleveland.

Q. *Who discovered the pygmies in Africa? L. W.*

A. The race of pygmies known as the Akka race was first seen by G. A. Schweinfurth in 1870 in the Mangbettu country northwest of Albert Nyanza.

CHAPTER 63

RADIO

Q. *What country has the best conditions for radio reception?* J. K.

A. It is reported that Sweden has the best atmospheric conditions.

Q. *Was much money expended to rent use of the air for the broadcasting of political arguments and appeals in the 1932 campaign?* C. H. K.

A. It is estimated that between $20,000 and $30,000 an hour was paid for the time used by the major candidates—depending on whether the hook-ups were complete or partial. President Hoover's Detroit speech of one hour and thirty minutes cost about $400.00 a minute.

Q. *Did Enrico Caruso ever broadcast over the radio?* L. M.

A. He sang Siciliana over the radio for Lee De Forest in 1909 from the Metropolitan Opera House.

Q. *How long does it take a radio message to go around the world?* H. R.

A. Only a fraction of a second. The speed of international radio communication has shrunk the world to the dimensions of a room only 75 feet long, as demonstrated in a recent round-the-world broadcast. In this demonstration, the voice circumnavigated the globe from Schenectady to Java and Australia and back again in the same fraction of a second required for the words to echo from a wall of the experimental studio 75 feet from the microphone. This broadcast made the round-the-

world journey in less than one-seventh of a second.

Q. *How short a wave is used for radio broadcasting?* F. K.

A. The shortest wave obtained which has proved successful is between 18 and 20 meters.

Q. *How many radio sets and broadcasting stations are there in the United States?* I. W.

A. The 1930 census figures give 12,078,345 radio receiving sets in use in the United States and a trade estimate puts the number now at more than 15,000,000. There are over 600 broadcasting stations licensed in the United States.

Q. *What are the meanings of the numbers 73 and 88 used over the radio?* T. R. D.

A. Seventy-three means "greetings," and 88 means "love and kisses," and is strictly amateur.

Q. *Who pays for the nation-wide religious programs on the air?* W. E. M.

A. Some religious broadcasts are not paid for on a nation-wide radio program. One broadcasting company gives its facilities without charge for the distribution of Protestant, Catholic, and Jewish programs, none of which is denominational, although the Catholic Hour might be described as sectarian. The Protestant faith, under the guidance of the Federal Council of Churches of Christ in America, was the first to avail itself of a nation-wide network. The first broadcast, with Dr. S. Parkes Cadman officiating, took place about 1926.

Q. *What effect is radio having on the English language?* B. S.

A. Radio has aroused new interest in correct speech and pronunciation. No definite steps have been taken in the United States as yet to standardize English speech as used over the radio, but the British Broadcasting Company of England has established a single standard of radio English by organizing an advisory committee to compose a style sheet for radio announcers. According to David Saranoff, radio has added about 5000 new words to the English language.

Q. *When was the first radio program received in the United States from Italy?* J. R.

A. The National Broadcasting Company says that the first international program ever broadcast from Italy to the United States was staged on January 1, 1931, when Premier Benito Mussolini, speaking from Fascist Headquarters in Rome, sent his New Year's greetings to America through coast-to-coast networks. This was the first program ever heard in this country originating on the Italian mainland. Twice before, however, listeners had heard programs from Italian waters—from the yacht of Senatore Guglielmo Marconi, the father of radio, anchored off the coast of the peninsula.

Q. *Did Admiral Byrd communicate with the United States by radio while his plane was flying over the South Pole?* J. R. H.

A. The Conquest of Antarctica by Air says: "One sunny night, January 25, (1929) Malcolm Hanson, chief radio operator, sent through the first radio message from our plane to New York—the distance record, to that date, for two-way communication with an airplane in flight. WFC (call letters of the Stars and Stripes) signaled WHD, the New York Times station, at 8:15 P.M. Antarctic time, 3:15 A.M. New York time. For 12 minutes the dots and dashes cut through the climate zones, crossed the Equator, and New York flashed back that it had the message verbatim."

Q. *Is a license fee charged for radio reception in Canada?* R. F. T.

A. Until recently there has been a license fee of one dollar, yearly. It is now two dollars. There are over 582,000 licensed radio sets in Canada.

Q. *Please give a list of DX stations.* C. M.

A. There is no such list. DX is a term used simply to designate distant stations. A man is said to be "D Xing" when he is trying to get distant stations late at night when the nearer stations are off.

Q. *Does it cost more to operate a vacuum cleaner or a washing machine than it does to operate an electric radio?* T. C.

A. The cost is about the same during the time of operation. It must be borne in mind that a radio is probably used more frequently and for longer periods than the labor-saving devices.

Q. *What does one pay to use a radio in England?* W. W.

A. The British Broadcasting Company requires each person to pay 10 shillings a year for a license or permit to use a radio.

Q. *What do the French call radio?* S. H.

A. They speak of the T. S. F. This stands for Telegraphie sans fil, which means telegraphy without wire.

Q. *When did radio announcing become a profession?* F. J. H.

A. It is claimed that the pioneer in this field was J. Andrew White, who, on July 2, 1921, announced the Dempsey-Carpentier fight from the ringside in Jersey City. It was estimated that nearly 400,000 persons listened to his word-picture of the fight.

Q. Has the use of radio in police work proved practicable? P. L. W.

A. Radio in police work is constantly proving its practicability and reliability. Major crime convictions have increased due to the fast service resulting from the use of radio. At the end of 1932 police radio stations totaled 100.

Q. Why did the census enumerators ask "Do you own a radio"? G. F.

A. The Department of Commerce wished to obtain an estimate of the number of radios in use. Other commodities such as automobiles are taxed or licensed so that a count is available, but there is no other way to make a fair estimate of radios.

Q. Why is a radio log so called? H. C. C.

A. The name was taken from the log book of a ship at sea. The members of the ship's crew keep a record of the day's happenings and the book in which these happenings are written is known as the ship's log. Radio operators on vessels started such a log for themselves by keeping a record of all stations heard. So instead of calling the book a directory or reference book, it is known as a log.

Q. Has Cairo, Egypt, a broadcasting station? F. K.

A. There have been seven stations operating in Egypt—three in Cairo, three in Alexandria, and one in Port Said. When the new station near Cairo, for which Marconi has a construction permit, is completed, the seven stations will be eliminated.

Q. How many stations broadcast the Pope's address at the time of the opening of the Vatican station? D. A. W.

A. One station (HVJ) broadcast the Pope's address during the opening of the Vatican station, and approximately 300 stations throughout the world rebroadcast the program. The Pope's broadcast was delivered in Latin. He used the Italian pronunciation in his Latin.

Q. How long are the short wave and long wave in radio? R. H.

A. The short wave is any under 200 meters. From 200 to 1000 meters are the intermediate waves, and 1000 meters and up are long waves.

Q. Was the radio as we know it today in use during the World War? R. L.

A. Radios were not used at any time during the World War, except telegraphy and telephony in connection with the Signal Corps of the United States Army. Radio telephony emerged from the World War a thoroughly modernized and refined form of communication.

Q. What is television? J. E. G.

A. As television is today, it is a direct viewing process; in its ultimate form it will be a projecting process. The neon light is one of the major units of the television outfit.

Q. What is meant by a sustaining program on the radio? G. S.

A. Broadcasting companies deliver two types of programs to their associated stations, sponsored and sustaining. Sponsored means that a client of the company has engaged the facilities of the company and associated stations for a program. Sustaining means that it is furnished by the studio.

Q. Are the regular telephone wires used for radio broadcasting? W. M. C.

A. They differ in no way except they are reserved for radio use only.

Q. What are some of the most powerful radio stations in the world? T. S. D.

A. The highest powered stations in England, as in the United States and Canada, have 50,000-watts. The station at Villa Acuna, Mexico, XER, is a 75,000-watt station. A powerful station at Luxemburg, which has completed the erection of a 200,000-watt long wave station, is so constructed that its power can be boosted when desirable to 400,000-watts. Also a 200,000-watt station has been erected at Cesky-Brod, near Prague, Czechoslovakia.

Q. Will television take part in the entertainment world, particularly in the motion picture theatre? M. E. G.

A. Television workers have already demonstrated television in theatres, with fair results. In time, it should be possible to flash news events to theatre audiences scattered throughout the country. Television will provide the instantaneous reproduction of the news event or other feature, while the motion picture will reproduce the recorded event.

Q. Is television patented? F. B.

A. There are a number of companies which hold valuable patents on television. The use of the neon tube and scanning disk is not patented. This part of the art of television was laid down as far back as 1896.

Q. Do many people listen in on radios during daytime broadcasting? R. W.

A. One station has made a test recently and found that the listener-interest was surprisingly high.

Q. What are the duties of staff pianists in broadcasting studios? R. E. T.

A. Requirements may differ in various studios. Those employed by one large broadcasting company play about 150 auditions each week or about five hours every day. They also have certain scheduled times to broadcast and must be prepared to fill in at a moment's notice. For instance, if the daily stock market report should lack five minutes of filling in the allotted time, the staff pianist must be prepared to present a program of piano music lasting exactly five minutes.

Q. If one political candidate buys time to speak over the radio, can his opponent be kept off the air by that station? T. D.

A. The Radio Commission says that the Congress was particularly careful to refrain from imposing anything like a general censorship on radio. Obscene language may be ruled off, and if a station rents its facilities to one political candidate it cannot refuse time to an opponent. Beyond that, and except for deliberate setting of instruments to trespass on other wave lengths, the law permits little interference.

Q. Where are the headquarters of the British Broadcasting Company? P. H. H.

A. Broadcasting House is in Langham Place, London. It is a magnificent new building with all of the latest improvements for broadcasting. The concert hall is the third largest in London.

Q. What is used for grounding a radio in an airplane? S. T.

A. All of the metal parts of an airplane are banned together in such a way as to form a ground for a radio. The larger the plane the better the radio reception.

Q. Does a radio receiver cause fading? G. W. J.

A. Fading in radio is caused by weather conditions. This happens before the signal reaches the receiver. Therefore the receiver is not at fault. Radio signals fade more during the daylight hours than at night, as the sun has some effect on signals.

Q. Which radio station broadcast first? M. M. B.

A. KDKA of Pittsburgh, Pa., is generally known as the pioneer broadcasting station, inasmuch as it broadcast programs long before government licenses were necessary. It is said that the Harding-Cox presidential returns were broadcast from this station November 4, 1920. The first program broadcasting license, however, in this country was issued to Station WBZ of the Westinghouse Company at Springfield, Mass., September 15, 1921.

Q. How does one get a radio license? L. F. D.

A. The Federal Radio Commission says in accordance with an Act of Congress, one applying for a radio license must first apply for a construction permit. After he has been permitted to build and his station is completed, he may apply for a broadcasting license. To be eligible to this license he must fill out an application blank for a certain frequency upon which to operate and give particulars relating to the station. If this is agreeable to the Commission, he may be given a license.

Q. Will fastening a radio antenna in the top of a tree kill the tree? G. H. T.

A. The Forest Service says that it will not harm a tree to fasten a radio antenna in it.

Q. How is the arrangement made for the local announcement, when a nationally broadcast program is going on? M. R. T.

A. In every station receiving a network program there is an announcer standing by to make his station announcement when he receives a cue from the studio where the program originates. In the case of one broadcasting company the cue is usually a few notes on a musical gong. When these are sounded all stations on the network are dropped for fifteen seconds. In this interval each station makes its local announcement.

Q. Where do the Mexicans buy their radio sets? F. K.

A. About 90 per cent of the radio sets in use in Mexico are American made.

Q. Does a monopoly exist in the distribution of radio receiving sets? M. S. M.

A. The electrical goods trade does 88 per cent of the distributing of radio sets but there are a great many companies belonging to this trade so it is not considered that a monopoly with the meaning of the law exists. Firms within the electrical goods trade compete with each other. Automobile companies, hardware stores, furniture stores and amusement goods stores participate in the other 12 per cent of the distribution. Six States have wholesale houses which distribute 70 per cent of all radios.

Q. Is the quartz for radio crystals found in this country? T. I.

A. It has never been found in sufficient quantity to be a commercial commodity. The rock crystal used for this purpose is imported from Brazil and Madagascar.

Q. Who was the first broadcaster? D. A. L.

A. Amateur experimentation by Frank Conrad, now assistant chief engineer of the Westinghouse Company, led to the establishment of Station KDKA which was the first broadcasting station.

Q. Why is Radio City so called? N. G.

A. The official name is Metropolitan Square. It is called Radio City from the fact that the largest single transaction in floor space is in the form of contracts under the terms of which the radio rulers of the nation have leased some 1,000,000 square feet of space in the central office building.

Q. How much educational broadcasting is done? M. A. G.

A. Of more than 600 licensed broadcasting stations, 77 are owned and operated by educational institutions. Nearly 300 commercial stations report a weekly average of approximately 60 hours of broadcasting, including about 13 per cent classed as educational. In addition, several state departments of education employ the radio to some extent, Ohio having a one-hour program for every school day. Lately the first program of the American School of the Air was launched, the audience consisting of 1,500,000 school children. Hereafter instruction will be given twice a week in various subjects, supplementing the regular courses.

Q. Can a radio message pass through a vacuum area? C. L. J.

A. The Bureau of Standards says that an ordinary radio program or message can be received if it has to pass through a vacuum. Electric waves pass through a vacuum even more freely than through space filled with some material.

Q. Do radio listeners hear a speaker as soon as people in his visible audience? F. H. W.

A. The radio listeners of a message being broadcast really get the message a fraction of a second sooner than the speaker can be heard by an audience because electric waves travel faster than sound. The difference is very slight, and sometimes atmospheric conditions may interfere.

Q. How many broadcasting stations has Russia? P. C. B.

A. The system of broadcasting in Russia is under the supervision of the Commissariat for Posts and Telegraphs. Every important city has one or more broadcasting stations, making a total of between 60 and 70.

Q. Please give some directions for one preparing a short talk to give over the radio. S. F.

A. A prominent educator gives the following suggestions for preparation of material for broadcasting: Write out your exact wording. Begin with one or more striking statements. Do not overrate the intelligence of your listeners. Use a few pertinent historical allusions. Give informational details of your subject, even though these seem too simple to you. Anecdotes, short and to the point, are good. Avoid too much generalization. Minimize preachment and advice. Close with three or four short sentences of five or six words each, clinching the main points presented. Revise for clearness and delivery. Reread aloud several times for practice or, better still, memorize the talk. Do not change position while speaking. Sitting position is preferable.

Q. Is a license required to operate a small radio transmitter not capable of transmitting more than two miles in distance? D. H.

A. The law provides that one must obtain both station license and operator's license before he can operate any radio transmitter set.

Q. What is the approximate service of a general service radio tube? R. C.

A. The service of a radio tube is about 1000 hours. Radio tubes wear gradually.

Q. Please explain how corn was popped by radio and why it was placed between jars of ice. R. W.

A. The General Electric Company says that: "The heating of the corn is produced by radio waves of very short wave length. The heat is generated by current induced within the kernels themselves. The purpose of the glass jars, with ice, placed on each side of the corn, was to show that this was so, that is, that the surrounding atmosphere was cold and that the only thing that was heated was the corn itself. The reason that the corn was heated by the short wave radio waves, and the ice water was not, was because of the difference of the electro-conductivity of the corn kernels and the ice water."

Q. What do broadcasting companies do with mail sent to people who broadcast for them? F. L.

A. Each broadcast artist's mail is sent to him direct without being opened. However, the organization maintains a large private post office and mail addressed to the network or stations and mentioning individual artists is forwarded to the artist after being read and contents noted for future reference. Most artists and announcers make it a point, although there is no rule that they should, to return the most interesting of their letters to the private post office for the information of program executives.

Q. When was the first electric radio marketed? W. P. H.

A. There is no established record, but it is believed to have been put out in 1927.

Q. Why do so many radio stations begin with the letter W? M. S.

A. Call letters of radio stations have no significance except that the letters assigned to the United States are all three and four letter combinations beginning with the letter N and with the letter W and all combinations from KDA to KZZ inclusive.

Q. What time is the best to reach folks on the farms with radio programs? M. P.

A. A survey indicates that the noon hour is best.

Q. How does a record for electrical transcription differ from the ordinary phonograph record? W. W. L.

A. Electrical transcriptions are similar to phonograph records and are reproduced electrically in the same manner as a phonograph record would be on an electrically-operated phonograph. They approximate 16 inches in diameter and are rotated at a speed of 33⅓ revolutions per minute in contrast to the 78 revolutions per minute, the speed for the standard phonograph record, resembling the ordinary phonograph record except for size. They differ from phonograph records, however, in the manner of recording in that the phonograph needle is placed near the center of the record and as the record rotates the needle moves outward, whereas the standard phonograph

record operates just the reverse—starting from the outer edge and moving toward the center. Electrical transcriptions are made especially for broadcasting purposes and are not offered for sale to the public.

Q. Can American radios be used in Europe? L. G.

A. Europe has several important stations on wave lengths of between 1340 and 1820 meters in addition to the numbers between 200 and 545 meters, for which most standard American sets are constructed. American sets are also usually designed for use on 110 to 115 volt house-light service, while foreign services are divided among many different voltages, mostly 220. In both these respects means of adapting the standard American set must be provided.

Q. Who have been the recipients of the Diction Award of the Academy of Arts and Letters? B. M.

A. Milton J. Cross won it in 1929; Alwyn Bach, 1930; John Holbrook, 1931; and David Ross, 1932.

Q. Are there regulations making it necessary to announce the fact when records are played over the radio? W. W.

A. General Order #787 of the Federal Radio Commission provides as follows: "All broadcasting stations shall announce clearly and distinctly the character of all mechanical reproductions broadcast by them, the announcement to immediately precede the broadcasting of each record. In such announcements each . . . phonograph . . . record used . . . should be described by the use of the exact words 'This is a talking machine record' or 'This is a phonograph record.' "

Q. Is it possible for anyone to get an audition in radio studios? W. D.

A. One broadcasting company has adopted a new system. Heretofore, thousands of auditions have been granted. A study of the auditions records for several years revealed that all applicants who successfully passed the initial trial were persons with some training or experience. This resulted in the present system which requires an applicant to answer in writing questions as to training, experience, style, and, if a vocalist, quality and strength of voice.

Q. Is there any difference between a radio station and a broadcasting station? G. K. T.

A. All radio stations are not broadcasting stations, but all broadcasting stations are radio stations. All stations using a radio as a means of communication are radio stations. Radio broadcasting stations are those which occupy a certain band within the spectrum, and are used to broadcast programs. The broadcasting division occupies only a portion of the radio spectrum.

Q. What is the average length of program furnished daily over the country by radio? L. G.

A. About 18 hours.

Q. How are chain stations connected? R. O. D.

A. Each station in a radio chain is connected to the central control station by telephone wires, which are different from regular telephone wires in that they are used for no other purpose. The central control stations broadcast to the stations in the chain which rebroadcast to the public.

Q. Does a broadcasting company have a course in correct speech for its announcers? A. B. F.

A. Both the National Broadcasting Company and the Columbia Broadcasting System maintain a course of instruction for their announcers in their New York City studios.

Q. Does much time have to be given to the preparation of a radio program? W. B.

A. It varies with the program. Usually, much more time is given to rehearsal after the program is prepared than the time that will be occupied in broadcasting. It must be fitted with the greatest nicety to the time it is to have.

Q. Is a radio head phone the same as a telephone receiver? S. D.

A. Not in principle. In both, an electric vibration is converted into sound, but the detailed designs are different, and they are not interchangeable.

Q. Why do the radio announcers no longer say "By special permission of the copyright owners"? O. W. O.

A. This announcement was a condition imposed by the American Society of Composers, Authors, and Publishers upon broadcasting stations whenever they performed certain numbers which the song writers had restricted over the air. It serves no useful purpose and was objectionable to the public and broadcasting stations alike. The Society has lifted this condition. It will not be heard by listeners unless the Society decides to impose this restriction.

Q. What is the monetary basis for compensation of radio artists? L. D. M.

A. There is no basic pay. Compensation depends upon the talent, experience, and demand for the artist.

Q. Please explain remote control by radio. R. E. R.

A. Remote control in radio is where the transmitting apparatus is located some distance from the operating key or microphone.

Q. Was Colonel Lindbergh equipped with radio on his flight to the Orient? H. F. B.

A. He carried two radio sets, one for use in the plane with a range from 3000 to 7000 miles, and the other an emergency set for use in case of accident afield or afloat. The latter was crash-proof and watertight.

CHAPTER 64

RELIGION

Q. When was the first Christian church built? J. J.

A. There is some difference of opinion as to what year the first Christian Church was actually built. Many historians are of the opinion that the first church to be actually built was at Antioch, probably about A.D. 50.

Q. What word appears but once in the Bible? T. T.

A. There are a great many words which occur only once. Perhaps the most important word occurring but once is "eternity," Isaiah 57: 15.

Q. Where is the smallest church in the world? R. N.

A. Covington, Kentucky, claims it. Monte Casino Church accommodates only three persons, including the priest.

Q. Who first used the phrase, The Lord's Supper? S. B. F.

A. Saint Paul gave this name to the commemorative ordinance instituted by Christ upon the evening preceding His crucifixion.

Q. Do city or country dwellers attend church more regularly? D. M.

A. According to a survey by Roger Babson, cities of more than 50,000 have an average attendance of only 30 per cent. Cities of 10,000 to 50,000 show a 42 per cent attendance, while in incorporated areas and villages under 2500 population there is an average attendance of 71 per cent.

Q. Are there more men's names or women's names in the Bible? J. F.

A. It is said that the Bible supplies one-half the names of civilized men, and that there are about five feminine names to ninety-five names for men.

Q. Are the Ten Commandments divided in any special way? K. D.

A. The first four Commandments relate to sacred duties, while the other six refer to secular, or our duties to our neighbors.

Q. Is there any special significance attached to the number 40? L. L. T.

A. Forty is a number that has been regarded as peculiarly significant. The idea may have originated with readers of the Bible, who notice that Moses was 40 days on the mount, Elijah was fed 40 days by the ravens, the rain of the flood fell 40 days, another 40 days elapsed before Noah opened the window of the ark, 40 days was the period of embalming, Jonah gave Nineveh 40 days to repent, The Lord fasted 40 days, and he was seen 40 days after His resurrection. Old English law also featured many 40-day periods.

Q. What is the word that appears occasionally in the Bible which has no meaning? G. F. T.

A. We do not find that any word in the Bible has no meaning, but there has been for many centuries controversy as to the precise meaning of the word Selah. This occurs 71 times in the Book of Psalms and three times in Habakkuk. It is variously described as a musical rest, a recommending for the bending of the body in reverence, and as an ejaculation corresponding to hallelujah.

Q. How do scientists explain the great age attained by Methuselah and other patriarchs according to the Scriptures? D. W. R.

A. An interesting solution is proposed by H. G. Wells in his Outline of History. He says that the earliest recorded reckoning was by means of moons and generations of men. If the age of Methuselah was reckoned by lunar months, instead of years, it would bring the ages of the patriarchs down to about the average length of life.

Q. What musical instruments are mentioned in the Bible? T. E. J.

A. Harp, lute, psaltry, sackbut, viol, cornet, dulcimer, flute, organ, pipe, trumpet, shawm, bells, cymbals, tabret, and timbrel.

Q. How are the Washington family Bible and the Martha Washington prayer book protected? B. L. N.

A. There were constructed for them specially made frames in which they are hermetically sealed under glass identical with that found in the Shrine of the Declaration of Independence.

Q. How is the revenue produced which supports the Church of England? J. E. W.

A. The principal revenue of the Church of England is obtained through its large estates and endowments and from tithes. Collections are taken up in the Church of England as elsewhere.

Q. Why is Moses depicted with horns on his head? M. T.

A. Horns on the head of Moses, in some of the early pictures, are accounted for by a blunder in the translation of the Book of Exodus 35: 29-30. In some of the early translations the Hebrew phrase stating that the face of Moses shone or sent forth beams was erroneously translated "sent forth horns." Michelangelo, one of the greatest of painters, used the erroneous translation in his depiction of Moses.

Q. What word appears the oftenest in the Bible? F. C.

A. The word "and" occurs most often. In the King James Version it appears 46,227 times. Of words of importance, Jehovah or Lord occurs most often, appearing 6855 times.

Q. What Presbyterian Church in the United States has the largest congregation? E. L. M.

A. The largest Presbyterian Church in America is the First Presbyterian Church of Seattle, Washington, the membership of which is 8160. The next largest is the Immanuel Presbyterian Church of Los Angeles, California, with a membership of 4334. The third largest is the Central Presbyterian Church of Denver, with a membership of 3225.

Q. Where is the largest museum of Bibles in the world? A. N.

A. The British Foreign Bible Society has the largest museum while the America Bible Society has the second in size.

Q. Has the Little Church Around the Corner any memorial windows to famous actors? H. S.

A. The Little Church Around the Corner has memorial windows erected to Edwin Booth, Richard Mansfield, James Montague, and Joseph Jefferson. The newest memorial window is one to the memory of John Drew.

Q. I have seen the Ten Commandments in rhyme. Can you give them to me? T. R. E.

A. "Thou no Gods shalt have but me, Before no idol bow the knee. Take not the name of God in vain, Nor dare the Sabbath day profane; Give to thy parents honor due, Take heed that thou no murder do. Abstain from words and deeds unclean, Steal not, for thou of God art seen.

Tell not a wilful lie, nor love it;
What is thy neighbor's do not covet."

Q. How large is the largest Bible
in the world? R. H. M.

A. It is said to be the Bible
printed by Louis Waynai and his
daughter, Theresa, of Los Angeles.
It weighs 1094 pounds and is eight
feet high. The makers spent about
two years printing it by hand.

Q. What is the largest Protestant
denomination in the world? M. S. B.

A. The Lutheran. It is estimated
to have over 70,000,000 members.

Q. When was Cruden's Bible Concordance first published? R. B.

A. Alexander Cruden published
his concordance in 1737.

Q. Who wrote "Of making of
many books there is no end"? S. T.

A. This is found in Ecclesiastes,
chapter 12. While the authorship of
this Book of the Bible was long attributed to Solomon, scholars have
not agreed upon this point. In fact,
the modern point of view is that the
Book is a compilation of the writings
of several men.

Q. Where are the manuscripts of
the Bible which were written on
vellum? W. A. B.

A. They are known as the Peshito,
the Alexandrine or Sinaiticus, and
the Vaticanus. One is in the British
Museum, one is the property of the
Russian government, and one is in
the Vatican at Rome.

Q. Please give some of the names
or titles used in describing Jesus
Christ. H. W.

A. There were a great many titles
applied to Christ. Among the best
known are Emanuel, Wonderful,
Counsellor, Mighty God, Everlast-
ing Father, Prince of Peace, Isaiah
9: 6, and by John the Baptist, Lamb
of God. At the time of the crucifixion Pontius Pilate bestowed the
title upon Jesus of King of the Jews,
Luke 23: 38. Jesus described Himself as the Way, the Truth and the
Life, the Good Husbandman, the
Light of the World, the Son of Man,
and the Son of God.

Q. Where was there an exhibition
of Bibles? B. L.

A. At Augsburg, Germany, one of
the chief features of the 400th anniversary celebration of the Confes-
sion Augustana was an exhibition of
Bibles in all languages and dialects,
of all ages, sizes, and prices. Besides
a collection of Bibles in all living
languages, there were copies of the
Vulgate, the Bible in ancient Greek,
in Hebrew, in Low German, in several variations of the Romany
tongue, and 125 different African
dialects. The exhibition was held in
the summer of 1930.

Q. Is the Apostle's Creed in the
Bible? E. M.

A. It is not. It is a compilation
or declaration of faith. In its present form it dates back to the 4th
century.

Q. What was the difference between the major and minor prophets?
A. R. S.

A. The major prophets, according
to Jewish belief, received direct instructions from God, and were given
political authority transcending that
of kings or military rulers. The
minor prophets did not have the
power to command obedience as did
the major prophets. The major
prophets included Moses, Samuel,
Elijah, Elisha, Isaiah, and Jeremiah;
the minor prophets included Hosea,
Joel, Amos, Obadiah, Jonas, Zeph-
aniah, Zacharias, Nahum, Habakkuk,
Sophonas, Haggai, and Malachi.

Q. What is the probable reason
for King David's making reference
to renewing "thy youth like the
eagle's"? P. C.

A. The International Critical
Commentary of the Bible says with
respect to the verse you cite that
the metaphor undoubtedly originated
in the known longevity of the eagle
and the fact that even at the present
time an infirm or ailing eagle is

hardly known. The ancients were superstitious in their veneration of this bird and endowed it with many supernatural powers which do not exist in actual fact.

Q. Is there a place in the Bible where "few" is defined as being "eight"? L. R. K.

A. This is found in the 1st Epistle of Peter, 3: 20: "When a few, that is eight souls, were saved by water."

Q. What is the famous Bible recently taken to Washington, D. C., by Dr. Vollbehr? C. M.

A. It is the Luther Bible which is in three volumes. This Bible was printed for George III of Anhalt, a defender of Luther's reform movement. Lucas Cranach, master artist of the German Reformation, illustrated it lavishly with wood blocks and original miniatures, gorgeously colored. The first four pages of each volume were set aside as an autograph book for the four great Reformation leaders, Luther, Philipp Melanchton, Johann Bugenhagen, and Caspar Cruciger.

Q. Who gave the home of the Bishop of London, Fulham Palace, to the Episcopal Church? A. E.

A. The Manor of Fulham has belonged to the See of London since 631. It is said to have been given to Erkenwald, Bishop of London, by Tyrhtilus, Bishop of Hereford, with the consent of Sigehard, King of the East Saxons and Coenred, King of the Mercians.

Q. How many Catholics served with our forces in the World War? W. A. T.

A. There are no official statistics concerning the religious affiliations of men who served in the military forces of the United States. However, the National Catholic Welfare Council in Washington, D. C., has a record of 800,000 Roman Catholics who served during the War; of 5000 Catholic graves in American cemeteries overseas; of 5124 bodies of Catholics returned to the United States; of a total casualty list of 22,000 Catholics.

Q. Is there a Christian denomination which does not use any hymns in its religious services? W. B. C.

A. One of the distinguishing features of the religious worship of the Associated Reformed Presbyterian Church is that praise is by means exclusively of metrical versions of the Psalms.

Q. I was under the impression that Lent lasted 40 days. Why is it longer than that from Ash Wednesday to Easter Sunday? O. D. G.

A. The period of Lent is 40 days of fasting or sacrifice in addition to the Sundays occurring in the period which are not counted.

Q. What portion of the population of the world is Christian? G. B.

A. The total number of Christians in the world is estimated at about 682,400,000, about one-fourth of the total population.

Q. Why do the churches and monasteries built during the Middle Ages face the west? R. A.

A. The altars of the early Christian Churches faced the east. The principal entrance of the church faced the west. There is a tradition to the effect that the altar was so placed in order that the priest could face the direction from which came Christianity.

Q. Is the number of negro churches decreasing? W. H.

A. In 1916 there were 39,592 churches for negroes with a membership of 4,602,805. In 1926 the number of churches had increased to 42,585, having a membership of 5,-203,487.

Q. In what church was Ralph Waldo Emerson a pastor? J. S.

A. He was assistant and pastor in the Second Unitarian Church in Boston, 1829–32. He arrived at the conviction that the Last Supper was not intended by Christ to be a permanent sacrament and retired. He never had charge of another parish, but he preached as opportunity offered until 1847.

Q. Please explain what is meant by "the visible church." F. D.

A. Visible Church is an ecclesiastical term meaning the Church as seen by man, not as it appears to God. It includes the whole body of professing Christians, while the Invisible Church consists only of those who are worthy in the sight of God to be members of His Church.

Q. Are cathedrals always large structures? H. G. F.

A. A cathedral is the church which contains the official seat or throne of a bishop. As a rule they are large, but a small building can serve, as in the case of the tiny cathedral, of the Byzantine Greek type, at Athens.

Q. When was the first Negro church organized in this country? N. B.

A. The first was a Baptist Church organized at Silver Bluff across the Savannah River from Augusta, Georgia, in 1773.

Q. What is the business of a church court in reference to social reform? M. K.

A. Ecclesiastical courts meet to determine matters of church polity and also the action of the church in conformity with its declaration of principles in regard to social or spiritual matters such as the stand of the church upon marriage, birth control, prohibition, child-welfare, education, confederation, and many other religious principles.

Q. What is the significance of the dove and star used in church windows? P. A. B.

A. The dove and the star have been used in church decoration and architecture from a very early period and their symbolism may be variously interpreted, according to the conception of the artists. The dove represents the new principle of Christianity—its two wings the love of man and the love of God, compassion and contemplation, or active and meditative life. It also stands for the Holy Ghost and the soul. The radiating star is the Star of Bethlehem and therefore represents Jesus Christ. Stars without the rays are often used to represent the Saints.

Q. What churches are united in the Church of Christ in China? N. A. L.

A. It is a union of fourteen different denominational groups, representing the fruit of missionary effort. It was organized in October, 1927, and unites in a single body Presbyterians, Congregationalists, Evangelicals, Reformed, United Brethren, English Baptists, and several other groups. Dr. C. Y. Cheng is Moderator of the Church.

Q. When were the International Study School lessons formulated? W. S.

A. The program was formulated in 1872. At this time, 22 States, one territory, Great Britain, Canada, and missions in India participated. The program, which has been continued, provided for a two-year plan in which lessons should alternate between the Old and New Testaments.

Q. Who determines whether a poet shall be buried in Westminster Abbey? J. S. C.

A. There will probably be no more burials in Westminster Abbey. The dean and the Chapter have been the ones to determine who should or should not be buried there.

Q. How are matters concerning church law handled in England? G. W. L.

A. There is an Ecclesiastical Court in England to which are submitted all matters pertaining to church law, also matters in which the church might be either a plaintiff or defendant. This court also regulates the issuance of marriage licenses and other matters of church discipline. Actually the ecclesiastical law of England is dependent upon the authority of the state, and ecclesiastical courts for the most part are officered by laymen, whose subordination to archbishops and bishops is purely formal. The final court of appeal on ecclesiastical matters is the Judicial Committee of the Privy Council of the Nation.

Q. Why are some churches given names ending in "minster"? R. M.

A. The word originally signified the church of a monastery or convent.

Q. Is it customary to hold a sportsman's service in a Cathedral? R. T.

A. It is most unusual. Such a service, believed to be one of the first, was held recently in Chelmsford Cathedral, England.

Q. Is it possible to divide Palestine according to the faith of the population—Jewish, Moslem, and Christian? B. S.

A. Such a plan has been suggested. Mr. Ben Avi has proposed that 16 cantons be formed—six Jewish, seven Moslem, and three Christian. The object is to place the inhabitants in congenial surroundings, giving each group freedom to govern itself in accordance with its own traditions. All would come under a central government, the Mandatory Power for Palestine.

Q. Is there a Protestant association which has the same object as the Catholic Holy Name Society? M. B. N.

A. There is a new organization among Protestants, Hallowed Name League, with the same purpose—the encouragement of pure and reverent speech.

Q. Why is Friday chosen as a day of assembly by Mohammedans? F. D. N.

A. The observance of Friday as the Moslem day of assembly, corresponding in some respects to the Christian Sabbath, originated in the Mohammedan revelations. According to the instructions of the prophet, Friday was the day Adam was created, the day on which he entered paradise and was expelled therefrom, the day of his repentance, the day of his death, and it is to be the day of his resurrection.

Q. How many names do followers of Islam give to God? T. H.

A. There are 99 Arabic names of God so used.

Q. How many tribes of Israel were in Palestine at the time of Christ? R. N.

A. The dispersion of the tribes of Israel had occurred several centuries before the time of Christ so at that time there were only the United Tribes of Judah and Benjamin living in Palestine.

Q. Is Clarence Darrow an atheist? L. R.

A. Clarence Darrow is an avowed agnostic, which is distinguished from atheism in that the latter makes an entirely negative confirmation with respect to religion, while the agnostic simply states that to his mind nothing has been proved with respect to religion.

Q. Was Mahomet married? H. F. B.

A. Mahomet had numerous wives, the first being a widow, 15 years his senior, whom he married when he was 25. Her name was Khadija. Mahomet did not become a polygamist until after her death.

Q. Was Christ born on Christmas Day? M. E. E.

A. There are no data which would prove conclusively at precisely what time of the year Jesus Christ was born. Many are of the opinion that the birth occurred in March or October. The fact that at the season observed as Christmas now a great Roman feast was held which had been held for centuries, probably influenced the early Christians to celebrate the birth of Christ at this period.

Q. *Where is the largest rosary in the world?* A. S.

A. The Portuguese claim that the largest rosary is that on the monument of the Madonna of Peace in Funchal, Madeira. We know of no other rosary for which the claim is made.

Q. *Is Billy Sunday a Methodist?* A. B.

A. Before entering the evangelistic field, Billy Sunday was a Presbyterian, and is still a member of that church.

Q. *Who founded the Jesuit order?* M. W.

A. Ignatius of Loyola, the founder of the Society of Jesus or Jesuits, was born in 1491 of a noble house at the castle of Loyola, Spain. He was a soldier, and desperately wounded in the war with France, and during his convalescence determined to become a "knight of Christ." He reported divine visions and commissions, and after much hardship succeeded in founding an order which devoted itself to the extension of the faith, particularly undertaking missionary work. This is one of the most powerful of the Roman Catholic religious organizations.

Q. *What were hair shirts made of?* A. B.

A. The Catholic Encyclopedia says that a hair shirt was a garment of rough cloth made from goat's hair and worn in the form of a shirt or a girdle around the loins by way of mortification and punishment.

Q. *What is the Mohammedan call to prayer?* M. M.

A. In the evening it is, "God is most great (four times), I bear witness that there is but one God (twice), I bear witness Mohammed is the apostle of God (twice), Come to prayer (twice), Come to Salvation (twice), God is most great (twice), There is no God but God (twice)." In the morning are added the words: "Come to Salvation, prayer is better than sleep (twice)."

Q. *What does the word Episcopal mean?* E. M.

A. It means governed by bishops, and is taken from the Latin Episcopalis.

Q. *Is a Gentile a Christian?* E. K.

A. The word gentile actually means an alien, an outsider. It was applied by the Jews to anyone not of the Jewish faith. The early Christians applied the term to one either Jewish or non-Christian. The Romans applied it as a civil distinction to all who were not Roman citizens.

Q. *How many religious denominations are there in the United States?* A. Z.

A. In the census, 212 sects were listed. There are some which are so small that they are not counted. These would probably bring the total to about 250.

Q. *Is Ash Wednesday a holiday in South American countries?* H. M.

A. It is. The Monday and Tuesday which precede Ash Wednesday are also holidays known as carnival days. South American countries observe many more holidays than this country does.

Q. *What became of the tablets of stone on which the Ten Commandments were written?* J. F. J.

A. The tablets of stone were a part of the treasures kept in the Ark of the Covenant. The Ark at the time of the capture of Jerusalem by Nebuchadnezzar was either destroyed or carried away and since that time all trace of it and its contents has been lost.

Q. *What is the origin of the Shinto religion?* F. A. H.

A. It is impossible to give the precise origin of the Shinto religion of Japan. This is a mild form of ancestor worship and lists 14,000 gods, and has 13 sects. It appears to have been the native religion of the early Japanese.

Q. *What is the Unpardonable Sin in the Brahmin religion?* L. R. E.

A. The Brahmin code lists four great sins: To oppress a suppliant; to desert a wife; to rob a Brahmin; and to betray a friend.

Q. *How old was Martin Luther when he was excommunicated?* C. McC.

A. He was excommunicated from the Roman Catholic Church in 1522, when he was thirty-nine.

Q. *What is an oblate in the Roman Catholic Church?* R. C.

A. An oblate is one who, not being a professed monk or friar, has either in youth been offered to God and fulfilled that offering, or in adult youth has dedicated himself to the service of God in holy religion. There are oblates of many orders; those of St. Francis are perhaps the best known.

Q. *What is the predominating religion in India?* L. M. J.

A. According to the latest religious census of India the total population was 351,450,689. Of this number 238,330,912 are Hindus; 73,743,-928 Moslems; 4,306,442 Sikhs; and 4,961,794 Christians. There are also sects of Jains, Buddhists, Parsees.

Q. *May a priest refuse to divulge a confidence told him in the confessional? I see a judge recently rebuked a priest for his refusal to reveal what he knew.* J. D.

A. The Sodality Union says: "At no time, under any circumstances can the priest divulge the tiniest sin ever confessed to him. The Seal of the Confessional is one of the church's most stringent laws. No court of law can make a priest break it nor does it try to in any land. The Pope himself would not dare to ask it and asking it, would be refused. . . ."

Q. *Is religious training in Germany required by law or is it optional?* A. M.

A. Since the separation of church and state in Germany as effected by the Weimar constitution, religious instruction is not required by law in the schools, but is given if the parents desire it. Certain periods are set aside for the purpose. The instructors are appointed by the State.

Q. *What caused Maryland to proclaim religious tolerance?* J. D. P.

A. Lord Baltimore, the early proprietor of the Maryland Plantation, witnessed the growth of the Puritan party in the province and in adjacent territories, and fearing the loss of control, proposed to the Assembly the act concerning religion known as the Toleration Act, passed in 1649. This act, however, favored only such bodies as professed trinitarian Christianity.

Q. *Is not the dome of St. Peter's Cathedral in Rome the largest in the world?* W. T. T.

A. A resort hotel has been built at West Baden, Indiana, whose immense dome is 212 feet across, 12 feet greater than that of St. Peter's, which was formerly the largest in the world.

Q. *What are the seven virtues as set forth by the Roman Catholic Church?* B. S.

A. The three theological virtues are faith, hope, and charity. The four cardinal virtues are prudence, justice, fortitude, and temperance.

Q. *How big is the Mormon Tabernacle at Salt Lake City?* F. J. H.

A. The building is elliptical in form, 150 feet in extreme width by 250 feet in extreme length, 80 feet high, and the auditorium has a seating capacity of 8000.

Q. *What is the unpardonable sin?* H. I. A.

A. The unpardonable sin according to Mark 3rd Chapter, 29th verse, is "Whosoever shall blaspheme against the Holy Spirit hath never forgiveness, but is guilty of an eternal sin."

Q. *What precious stones are mentioned in the Bible?* K. A. M.

A. Precious stones in the Bible are: Diamond, beryl, sardius or sardine, topaz, onyx, jasper, sapphire, emerald, carbuncle, adamant, pearl, lacinth or hyacinth, agate, amethyst, chalcedony, chrysolite, chrysoprase, ruby, sardonyx, ligure.

Q. *What kind of work does a colporteur do for a religious society?* D. K. H.

A. A colporteur is a traveling agent of a religious society, who sells cheaply or distributes gratuitously Bibles and other religious reading.

Q. *What is the Catholic prayer for departed souls?* Y. G. H.

A. "Requiem aeternam dona ei, Domine, et Lux perpetua luceat ei," which is translated, "Eternal rest grant him, O Lord, and let light perpetual shine upon him."

Q. *Who are latitudinarians?* W. L.

A. The term is applied to people who attach little importance to dogma and to what are called orthodox doctrines. Latitudinarians were a Church of England party in the time of Charles II, opposed both to the High Church party and to the Puritans.

Q. *How does science explain the manna which fell from Heaven?* S. W.

A. The Realm of the Air says: "It is not uncommon to find the earth or pavement under trees sprinkled with drops apparently due to miniature rain storms, but actually consisting of honey-dew ejected by swarms of aphids, scale insects, or leaf-hoppers. The stuff is sweet and sticky and explains the showers of 'honey' recorded in old chronicles. The manna of the Bible was thus produced by scale insects, which exude from their bodies a clear juice that falls to the ground in drops. These drops harden into sugary grains, which the Arabs of the Sinai Peninsula still gather for use as food and medicine."

Q. *What is an encyclical and what is a decretal?* N. T.

A. An encyclical, in the Roman Catholic Church, is a letter issued by the Pope to the whole church. A decretal is a letter or rescript of the Pope's, determining some point in ecclesiastical law.

Q. *What were palmers?* M. P.

A. Palmers were wandering religious votaries, sometimes members of religious organizations, but sometimes just private individuals, usually under the vow of perpetual poverty, who carried in their journeys a palm branch as a sign of having completed a pilgrimage to the Holy Land. They were held in great esteem and were usually kindly entertained.

Q. *Is the centennial celebration of the Oxford Movement in England sponsored by the authorities of the Church of England?* S. D. F.

A. Unofficially, yes.

Q. *How large a spot is shaved on a man's head to form the tonsure of the Catholic clergy?* B. K.

A. Tonsures vary for different localities and religious communities, from the size of a small coin on the crown of the head to a removal of all the hair except a fringe around the edge. The tonsure is not worn in this country, but is of obligation in Catholic countries.

Q. *Where was the first monastery established?* B. McC.

A. There is no record of the first monastery. Monasticism has existed among various peoples of the world since a very early period and antedates Christianity.

CHAPTER 65

SPORTS

Q. When was the first Kentucky Derby run? V. H.

A. The first Kentucky Derby took place in May, 1875. Aristides won the purse of $3,100 before a gallery of 10,000 people.

Q. How much money did Dempsey and Tunney get in their first and second fights? M. E. B.

A. In the first Dempsey-Tunney fight, Dempsey received $711,868, and Tunney received $204,000. In the second fight Dempsey received $425,000 and Tunney received $990,445.

Q. What is the present motor boat record? C. C.

A. The record is 124.91 miles per hour, established by Gar Wood on the St. Clair River on September 20, 1932.

Q. How many baseballs are used in a World Series game? L. B. P.

A. The number varies with the number of balls that are hit foul, hit for home runs, and are discolored or injured in some way. The average for the World Series games is much the same as during the regular season—almost always between three and four dozen.

Q. When was the first national tournament of the Chicago Fly Casting Club held? S. K.

A. The first national movement for developing skill and accuracy in fly-casting developed in Chicago about 1893 with the formation of the Chicago Fly Casting Club, which held the first national tournament at the World's Fair in that year.

Q. Are there any statistics showing the cost of fox-hunting in England? F. J.

A. The British Field Sports Society says that the annual cost of this sport amounts to between $50,-000,000 and $60,000,000. This includes the permanent maintenance of homes in the country, the keep of grooms and hunt servants, horses, dogs, and the elaborate equipment necessary for this colorful sport.

Q. Who is the greatest football player of all time? A. T. R.

A. It is a matter of opinion. However, a board of twelve of the most competent coaches in the country voted on this and Jim Thorpe of Carlisle was first, with Ernie Nevers, Stanford, and Red Grange, Illinois, tied for second place.

Q. How did golf derive its name? S. R. S.

A. It is probably from the Dutch word kolf, meaning club.

Q. Can a person swim more easily in deep water than in shallow water? M. E. C.

A. Experts have decided that the depth of the water makes no difference.

Q. How many rodeos are held in the United States each year? B. R.

A. There are over four hundred, counting cities, towns, and ranches

435

At least 3,000,000 people attend during the year. Among the best known ones are Frontier Days in Cheyenne, Wyoming; the Roundup in Pendleton, Oregon; and Frontier Days in Prescott, Arizona.

Q. How far can a man walk daily, over a period of weeks? W. O.

A. Edward Payson Weston walked 50 miles a day for 100 days between 1883 and 1884. With modern improved roads, it is probable that this record could now be slightly improved.

Q. How is handicapping done? L. R. S.

A. A handicap is an allowance of time, distance, or weight made to inferior competitors in a sport or race. In horse racing extra weight is imposed on the superior horse in accordance with known previous performances and with regard to age and sex of the animals engaged.

Q. Where did handball originate? M. T. K.

A. Handball originated in Ireland about a thousand years ago and is often considered one of the national games of that country. It is now played by more men in America than anywhere else in the world.

Q. Why do people who go swimming get more sunburned than those who stay out of the water? J. B. K.

A. Persons who go in and out of the water on hot days are liable to be burned more severely than those who stay on the beach or out of the water, as the drops of water on the skin act as small magnifying glasses increasing the power of the rays of the sun, making the burn more severe.

Q. In modern times, how many different kinds of wrestling have there been? M. C. T.

A. In modern times there have been three different styles of wrestling. Graeco-Roman, a combination of ancient Greek and Roman grappling, which now is featured mainly in European countries; Jiu Jitsu, originated in Japan and Catch-as-catch-can, the mode which prevails in the United States and has followers throughout the world.

Q. For pitching horseshoes, what weight horseshoes should be used? D. C.

A. The horseshoes used in pitching shall not exceed 2½ pounds each.

Q. When was Dan Patch born? H. L. C.

A. This famous pacer was foaled at Oxford, Indiana, in 1896. He was a mahogany bay with black points and with a small white star on the forehead. His sire was Joe Patchen and dam, Zelica. He died July 12, 1916.

Q. How old is the game of Lacrosse? G. V.

A. Lacrosse of today was baggataway of yesterday—the oldest game played on the North American Continent. The Canadian Indians originated it centuries ago and called it baggataway. In the later years when the French-Canadians saw it played they referred to it as La Cross because the netted stick that was used resembled a bishop's crozier. The name has lingered.

Q. Please give the seating capacity of the American League Baseball parks. C. W. E.

A. Boston, 28,000; Chicago, 51,-000; Cleveland, 22,000; Detroit, 29,-000; New York City, 65,000; Philadelphia, 33,000; St. Louis, 31,500; Washington, 30,000.

Q. Please describe the bobsleds used in the 1932 Winter Olympic Games. J. A. G.

A. Each four-man bob weighed 485 pounds; each two-man, 352 pounds. The four-man sleds were 11 feet 7 inches long; the two-man, 9 feet. The bobs were 10½ inches above the ground and they steered like automobiles. They were engineered to the fraction of an inch and as carefully and stoutly constructed as any racing car. The bobs cost from $500 to $600 each, depending on the size.

Q. Was Gene Sarazen ever a golf caddy? C. L. S.

A. He was a caddy, a caddy master, assistant professional, and then a professional.

Q. How high should a tennis net be? T. C.

A. It should be 3 feet high at the center, where it should be drawn taut by a strap not more than 2 inches wide.

Q. Are there international rules governing ski contests? E. R.

A. The rules governing ski contests in the United States and Canada are those of the International Federation de Ski. In general it may be said that points are awarded according to the position, style, and grace of the contestants, the distance of their jumps, and their success in avoiding falls.

Q. What is bull-fighting called in Spain? How many bulls are killed in a year? D. J. F.

A. Bull-fighting, the national Spanish sport, is called tauromaquia in Spain. About 1300 bulls are killed annually in Spain. At least 6 bulls are killed at each corrida (bull-fight).

Q. Where did the game of dominoes come from? K. J. H.

A. The game of dominoes is of French origin.

Q. Have jockeys in this country always worn the distinctive clothes that they do now when racing? W. P.

A. In the original charter of the Maryland Jockey Club which dates back to 1745 it is prescribed that jockeys be dressed in the following manner: Jockey cap, silk jacket, pantaloons, and half boots.

Q. How long does it take a batter to get to first base? P. B.

A. Paul Gallico, a sports writer, has studied such problems, and says

that a good man will get down to first in four seconds. A fast man or a left-hander will do it in 3.8 or 3.9 seconds.

Q. Where did the game of throwing the hammer originate? V. D.

A. It is said to have been of Celtic origin.

Q. How old is Jack Dempsey? M. F.

A. He was born June 24, 1895.

Q. What kind of targets are used in archery tournaments? J. J. R.

A. Regulation archer targets are the only ones used in the large tournaments. They are four feet in diameter and weigh from 50 to 60 pounds. They are made of light straw, carefully sewn with bright painted faces.

Q. How long has ping pong been played? L. P.

A. Its invention is credited to James Gibb of England. He brought out the game between 1880 and 1890. It was then called Table Tennis. A sporting goods house manufactured a set in the 90's and gave it the name, ping pong.

Q. Please give directions for lighting a tennis court at night. H. W.

A. A pole 35 to 40 feet in height should be erected at each end of the net. These poles should each hold a reflector containing two 1000 watt bulbs. This would equal four kilowatts per hour. If electric service costs five cents a kilowatt, the cost of operating the lighting would be twenty cents an hour.

Q. Please describe the game of shuffleboard. B. A.

A. Shuffleboard is a popular game among passengers on ocean-going steamers, and is customarily a game played with checker-like pieces and a device shaped something like a garden rake used for pushing them along the deck. A board, marked off with squares, is placed at either end of the portion of the deck on which the game is to be played and the opponents attempt to shuffle their men into the squares marked with the highest numbers. The highest score wins.

Q. *When was chess first played?* L. E. M.

A. Chess is a very ancient game antedating any extant records. Although the first authentic literature on chess came from the Arabs and Hebrews, it was already widespread among the Mohammedan nations. It is probable that it originated in China, passed into India and from there spread to Persia. It was then adopted by the Arab conquerors and introduced into Europe.

Q. *How many forms of canoeing are there?* E. W.

A. There are two forms of canoeing: Paddling and sailing, the greatest number of devotees belong to the paddling class. This is the true type of canoeing because the other calls for sailing skill which seems to belong to the sport that is called yachting.

Q. *How far does the average good swimmer go under water?* M. G.

A. The distance which a person may swim under water varies as to conditions. Probably an average swimmer in a pool can swim 30 feet under water. M. Pauliquen in Paris, France, on November 3, 1912, remained under water 6 minutes, 29⅘ seconds. Jack Trivilla of Avalon, California, swam under water 126.41 yards in 2 minutes 13⅗ seconds at the Salt Water Natatorium in Seattle, Washington, July 25, 1912.

Q. *Who invented the game of billiards?* M. B. D.

A. Frank G. Menke says that those who insist that they are best informed declare that the Egyptians played billiards hundreds of years before the Christian era. There is evidence that the Greeks indulged in billiards about 400 B.C. Billiards, as competitive indoor sport, gained its definite impetus in the United States when there was staged in Detroit a National Championship, on April 12, 1859. This was not a tournament, but a match game for a side bet and a purse, the money totaling $15,000.

Q. *Which can be driven farther, an expensive golf ball or a cheap one?* B. R.

A. The more expensive golf ball can be driven noticeably farther than the cheaper types. The more expensive balls are known as high powered balls—the term being used more or less to express the extreme degree of hardness or resistance to compression to which the centers are wound.

Q. *Please give me Hans Wagner's All Time All American Baseball Team.* P. G.

A. Pitcher, Christy Mathewson; catcher, Johnny Kling; first base, Hal Chase; second base, Larry Lajoie; short stop, Joe Tinker; third base, Jimmy Collins; left field, Fred Clarke, center field, Ty Cobb; right field, Babe Ruth; manager, John McGraw; umpires, Bob Emslie and Bill Klem.

Q. *How is hurling played?* S. H.

A. The hurling field is 140 yards long and 80 yards wide, and scoring is accomplished in two ways. If the ball hurled by the stick, lands in a net strung between the goal posts, it counts for three points; if hurled over the crossbar it is one point. The goal post crossbar is 21 feet wide, the uprights 16 feet high and the crossbar 8 feet from the ground. The game is made up of two 30-minute halves.

Q. *Is horseback riding considered healthful?* R. P. R.

A. An authority on value of exercise says that it exercises the back, abdomen, and thighs. There is only slight demand on nerve control and pulse, blood pressure, and respiration. The mechanical shaking has a distinct therapeutic effect. However, for people advanced in years or in poor health, a physician's advice should be followed as to indulgence in this sport.

Q. *Please tell something of the Amateur Trapshooting Association's headquarters.* S. T.

A. The Amateur Trapshooting Association's headquarters is in Vandalia, Ohio. This is the only sport owning its own home and tournament grounds. This home and equipment is representative of an outlay of approximately $150,000. The ground on which the home is erected was deeded to the association without any restrictions.

Q. *Was Knute Rockne born in America?* A. N.

A. Knute Rockne was born in a small town in Norway on March 4, 1888. He came to the United States with his parents when he was two years old and grew up in and near Chicago.

Q. *How long after meals should a person wait before swimming?* W. H.

A. To avoid stomach cramps, never swim until at least two hours after meals. Swimming immediately after a meal is responsible for cramps which are the cause of many a bather's becoming helpless in the water. From victims of such attacks who have been rescued, it is known that they are unable to use their arms or legs; and, fully conscious of the predicament they are in, are unable to do a thing to help themselves.

Q. *How are points counted in playing a Nassau in golf?* L. R.

A. Nassau system: One point for the first nine holes; one point for the last nine holes; and one point on the match. Three possible points. Generally used in team matches, low ball. In individual handicap matches net low ball.

Q. *At what speed are tennis balls served?* N. C. E.

A. A Y.M.C.A. bulletin published at Saloniki, Greece, says: "In the Davis Cup matches of 1932, an energetic German scientist estimated that the service balls delivered by such net stars as Austin (England) and Prenn (Germany) travelled at the rate of about 68.5 miles per hour, the slower balls resulting from base line rallies travelling at about 31 miles per hour. It was reckoned that the 2000 shots executed during a match between the above players travelled a distance of about 28½ miles."

Q. *How did jiu-jitsu originate?* L. B. F.

A. Its origin is uncertain. It is attributed by some to a Japanese physician who learned the rudiments of the art in China. Others claim that it was in common use in Japan centuries before this time. Most are agreed that jiu-jitsu originated in China but that the Japanese have modified it greatly.

Q. *When was the first important boat race held?* G. K.

A. In 1715 an Englishman named Thomas Doggett instituted boat races among the fishermen on the Thames. The first English regatta took place on the Thames off Ranelagh Gardens in 1775. This was modeled on the Venetian regatta. The first race in the United States occurred in 1811 between two barges —the Knickerbocker of New York and the Invincible of Long Island, the former being the winner.

Q. *What is the Olympic Oath?* R. H.

A. It is as follows: We swear that we will take part in the Olympic Games in loyal competition, respecting the regulations which govern them and desirous of participating in them in the true spirit of sportsmanship for the honor of our country and for the glory of sport.

Q. *Which horse of the progeny of Man o' War has most nearly approached him in physical appearance and track performance?* J. A. E.

A. Miss Elizabeth Daingerfield, who managed the horse after his retirement from racing, says that American Flag most nearly resembles his sire. At Faraway Farm the son was often mistaken for the sire, and vice versa, by horsemen and other visitors. Miss Daingerfield thinks that American Flag also came nearest to reproducing Man o' War's qualities as a race horse although Crusader was more famous and more successful, due to the fact that he was a sounder horse.

Q. *In playing polo, is the ball hit with the side of the mallet or with the head?* H. B.

A. It is always struck with the side of the mallet.

Q. *What is the origin of the ski?* E. L. F.

A. Implements for this purpose were used by many nations of antiquity. Xenophon describes the shoes or pattens of skins with which the horses of the Armenians were shod, to prevent them from sinking into the snow, and Procopius made mention of the ancient Lapps, known in Scandinavia as Skrid-Finnen, or sliders. Snow-shoes have always been used by the Mongols of northwestern Asia. From the evidence of the old Norse sagas they must have been general in Scandinavia long before the Christian era.

Q. *Who originated the card display used by the Naval Academy at football games?* N. H.

A. The card displays were introduced at the Naval Academy during the 1930 football season by Midshipman N. C. Copeland, a member of the 1931 class. However, it was not Copeland's original idea. He received his information regarding these stunts from Stanford University at Palo Alto, California.

Q. *What causes a swimmer to get a cramp?* A. N.

A. The Public Health Service says that cramps are due to spasmodic contractions of the muscles of the abdomen or legs. It is usually felt that specific contractions which produce cramps may be due to chilling or prolonged exposure or prolonged exertion.

Q. *Please give the seating capacity of the National League baseball parks.* C. W. E.

A. Boston, 45,000; Brooklyn, 35,-000; Chicago, 45,000; Cincinnati, 27,-000; New York, 56,000; Philadelphia, 18,000; Pittsburgh, 40,000; St. Louis, 35,000.

Q. *Which heavyweight bout had the most slugging or fighting in the first seven rounds?* T. W. B.

A. John J. Romano, authority on boxing, says while the Dempsey-Firpo contest which took place September 14, 1923, in New York City, lasted but two rounds, it is generally conceded by experts and fans alike that more actual slugging took place in the 4 minutes, odd seconds, than in any boxing contest in the history of the game, as they actually crowded more fighting in one round than in the customary 20 rounds. No fewer than 11 knockdowns were crowded into this battle.

Q. *What strokes are used in paddling a canoe?* C. B. R.

A. Bow Stroke, Jay Stroke, Pushover, Draw, Cross Bow Rudder, Sweep, Backwater, Sculling, and Silent or Underwater Stroke. The recovery is called feathering.

Q. *Is the new thoroughbred Nea Lap, which has been brought here, related to Phar Lap?* W. W.

A. Nea Lap is a full sister of Phar Lap, famed Australian race horse which died following a sensational first victory in America. Nea Lap has been shipped to the stables of John Hay Whitney, and is to be a brood mare.

Q. *When were stilts first used?* S. G.

A. Stilts were originally designed for use in crossing rivers and marshes. As a means of amusement stilts have been used by all peoples in all ages, as well as by the inhabitants of marshy or flooded districts. The city of Namur in Belgium, which formerly suffered from the overflowing of the rivers Sambre and Meuse, has been celebrated for its stilt-walkers for many centuries. Not only the townspeople but also the soldiers use stilts. The home of stilt-walking at the present day is the department of Landes in Gascony; owing to the impermeability of the subsoil, all low-lying districts are converted into marshes.

Q. *How is a surf board made? N. R. C.*

A. A surf board should be 6 feet long, 30 inches wide, and one inch thick. It should be made of a light wood like white pine, white cedar, or spruce. A rope for steering should be placed on the sides about 18 inches from the front.

Q. *Was Burgomaster one of the largest race horses that ever ran on a race track? S. P.*

A. Burgomaster was the largest horse that ever trod a race track. As champion 2 year-old in 1905 he weighed 1300 pounds.

Q. *Did Knute Rockne play football on a regular college team? A. J. P.*

A. He played football all of his four years at Notre Dame. He was the captain of the Varsity Team for the 1913 season.

Q. *What is the width of the adhesive tape used in bandaging the hands of professional boxers? E. A. J.*

A. It varies from one and one-half inches to three inches. The one and one-half inch tape is generally used.

Q. *Is jai alai played to any extent in this country? R. T.*

A. It has been introduced in Florida and along the Mexican border, but has not proved to be as popular as it is in Cuba, or abroad.

Q. *How long has hockey been played? C. D.*

A. A crude form of the game was probably known to the Greeks 500 B.C. About 1875 a game resembling modern hockey began to be played. In 1886, the Hockey Association was formed.

Q. *How old is Earl Sande, the American jockey? B. W.*

A. He was born in Salem, Oregon, in 1889.

Q. *How long have they been having tennis tournaments at Wimbledon, England? C. V. B.*

A. Since 1877.

Q. *When was the National Horse Show of America organized? R. B.*

A. The formation of the National Horse Show of America, controlling body for the sport, came about in 1883, as the result of friendly arguments as to which man, among the wealthy group in that era, owned the best trotter, the best pacer, the best jumper, and so on. The initial show was in old Madison Square Garden, New York, on October 22 to 26, 1883. The democracy of the show was evidenced by the fact that although the main idea was to settle supremacy among blooded horses, all types of horses were invited to participate.

Q. *What are the positions on an ice hockey team? J. G. R.*

A. Goal, defense, defense, center, wing, wing.

Q. *In baseball is the batter allowed to change his way of batting from left-handed to right or from right to left after he is charged with two strikes? M. R.*

A. In a baseball game the batter may change from one batsman's box to another except "while the pitcher is in his position ready to pitch." The fact that two strikes have been called does not alter this.

Q. *Can arrows with metallic shafts be shot from a bow with greater accuracy than arrows with wooden shafts? T. A. C.*

A. A metal shaft may be shot with accuracy, but not so consistently as the wooden shaft. The reason is that the metal shaft does not have the power of recovery inherent in the well seasoned wooden shaft. By recovery is meant the action of the shaft in leaving the bow.

Q. *Who was the first baseball player to steal base by sliding into the bag?* A. M.

A. Robert Addy of Rockford, Illinois, is credited in 1866 with the first, although some historians accord the honor to Eddie Cuthbert of the Philadelphia Keystones, saying he stole a base in 1865.

Q. *When and where was Max Schmeling born?* B. E.

A. He was born in Luckow, Germany, on February 28, 1905.

Q. *Where is the largest sports inclosure in Germany?* R. E. D.

A. It is the Westphalia Hall in Dortmund, in which as many as 12,-000 spectators witness sporting competitions such as boxing matches, riding tournaments, and bicycle races.

Q. *What are seeded players in golf and tennis tournaments?* W. E. McD.

A. In sports, in arranging tournaments, the draw is seeded, that is, it is manipulated so that the superior contestants will not meet in the early rounds.

Q. *What is considered a perfect game in baseball?* J. L.

A. It is a game in which there are no runs, no hits, and none reaching first base.

Q. *Is there a Hole-in-One Club?* K. C.

A. Sporting writers created a hole-in-one club by announcing from time to time that this player or that player had made a hole-in-one. D. Scott Chisholm, editor of Country Life, founded the International Hole-in-One Club.

Q. *How long has the Jockey Club existed?* B. T.

A. It was incorporated under the laws of the State of New York, on February 8, 1894. The first annual

meeting was held December 31, 1894. It now has jurisdiction over all the flat racing in the State of New York. It also ascertains and keeps a record of the pedigrees of horses in the United States. No horse can start in a race at a recognized meeting unless it has been registered and named.

Q. *When and where did fencing originate?* E. S.

A. Fencing has been both a form of sport and a method of deadly combat through the centuries. A manuscript dated 1410, describes fencing as a sport in Germany in 1383. Undoubtedly it was fairly well established by that time and thus its origin must have been at least 50 years earlier.

Q. *In horseshoe pitching, when is a shoe counted as a ringer?* T. A.

A. Rule 17 of the Official Horseshoe Pitching Rules says: "A ringer is declared when a shoe encircles the stake far enough to allow the touching of both heel calks simultaneously with a straight edge and permit a clearance of the stake."

Q. *What material should be used for sails on ship models, and should the hulls be painted or stained?* R. V. S.

A. Sails are generally made of cotton canvas which is snowy white or of linen canvas, the latter probably being more satisfactory. In selecting canvas choose the kind that is opaque and of rough texture. The hulls of ship models are either painted in gay colors or stained.

Q. *Where was Connie Mack born?* O. B. H.

A. Cornelius McGillicuddy (Connie Mack) was born at East Brookfield, Massachusetts, on December 23, 1862, of Irish parents.

Q. *What material is used in the manufacture of baseball bats?* F. J.

A. The standard baseball bat is made of the finest, straight-grained ash, the same material used by the Indians for their bows.

CHAPTER 66

STAGE

Q. Where was the first play given in America? M. B. P.

A. The first dramatic performance given in America was "Beaux's Stratagem," on September 15, 1752, at Williamsburg, Virginia. It was presented by Lewis Hallam and his associates, and was long considered America's best box-office attraction.

Q. Where is the largest closed auditorium in America? F. H.

A. The new Convention Hall in Atlantic City is the largest in the world. The seating capacity in the main auditorium is 40,000. This includes 30,000 on the floor and stage, and 10,000 in the balcony.

Q. What were Sarah Bernhardt's nationality and religion? E. P. R.

A. She was born a Jewess, baptized a Catholic; by birth she was French, and by marriage she was Greek.

Q. How long do the contracts at the Comedie-Francaise in Paris run? S. B. T.

A. An artist who becomes a member of the national theatre of France is obligated to remain a member for twenty years.

Q. What does an owner of a box in the Metropolitan Opera House pay for the privilege? E. W.

A. Each boxholder pays annually a certain sum which goes to pay the taxes on the building and other expenses of a minor character. This annual payment of late years has been $5,220 for each owner. The ownership of a box represents a one-thirty-fifth share in the ownership of the Opera House.

Q. Who was the first actor to play in New York? T. D.

A. Anthony Alston is said to have been the first.

Q. On what stage and what year did Joseph Jefferson, the famous actor, first appear? L. H.

A. The first appearance of Joseph Jefferson on any stage was in black-face, as a partner of Daddy Rice, at the Bowery Theatre, Washington, D. C., in 1832. Jefferson, a tiny boy at the time, was carried on by Rice in a valise, emerging as a miniature Jim Crow and joining Rice in a song and dance.

Q. Are theatres well attended in Russia? L. M.

A. All the theatres of Russia are said to be self-supporting, and authorities say that they know of no theatres having deficits. Every theatre in Leningrad and Moscow is packed to capacity.

Q. Please give the date and circumstances of the death of Eleonora Duse. C. G.

A. During her farewell tour in America her health was so broken that often she had to be revived with oxygen after a performance. She died from the results of a chill at Pittsburgh on April 21, 1924, at the age of 64. She was pitifully anxious not to die far away from Italy, and gave orders, almost with her last breath, to pack quickly so as to catch the boat home. Italian emigrants knelt on the quay as her coffin was lowered on to the battleship Duilio at New York, and national mourning was proclaimed in Italy. Her countrymen desired to see her laid at rest with other illustrious Italians in Santa Croce at Florence, but they respected her wish to be buried quietly at Asolo.

Q. Why do actors and actresses so often use other names professionally? L. M. D.

A. It is extremely important that they use names that are interesting, easily remembered, and not commonplace. Therefore, they often adopt names which they think will find favor with the public.

Q. How much money did Lotta Crabtree leave? E. D. L.

A. She is said to have been the wealthiest player in America. She left $3,000,000, most of it to charity.

Q. Who was the first actor to be knighted? A. P. K.

A. Sir Henry Irving was the first to receive this honor. He was knighted in 1895.

Q. How much was charged for admission to theatres in early Greece? J. K.

A. It is believed that the Greek theatres imposed no admission charge. No mention seems to be made of a charge, and the fact that they were usually community enterprises would indicate free entry.

Q. Was Ford's Theatre in Washington, D. C., ever used for a play after Lincoln's assassination? G. H.

A. No theatrical performance was ever given there after the tragedy.

Q. What is the tradition in the Barrymore family concerning an apple on first night performances? J. A.

A. A catch phrase in the Barrymore-Drew family was "Speak your piece and you will get a big red apple." When Ethel Barrymore was to play her first leading part in New York, John Drew, apropos of the saying, sent her an apple. Throughout Drew's lifetime he never failed any members of the family on first nights. When Ethel Barrymore Colt made her début, her uncle, Lionel, wired the apple from Hollywood; and John Drew Colt, making his first appearance in Scarlet Sister Mary, received one from John Barrymore.

Q. Did John Barrymore outdo the record of Edwin Booth for number of performances in New York City in the rôle of Hamlet? B. H.

A. Mr. Booth's record was 100 performances; Mr. Barrymore's 101.

Q. What was the first character impersonated by a woman on the English stage? B. H.

A. It is said that an actress appeared for the first time as Desdemona in Othello.

Q. Where was the first theatre for grand opera built? C. N.

A. In Venice in 1637. It was named the Teatro di San Cassaino.

Q. How many people did Pompey's Theatre seat? H. S.

A. It is variously stated as seating 10,000, 17,000, and 40,000. It was erected by the great Pompey and completed in 52 B.C. It was the first stone theatre in Rome, and had a marble interior.

Q. What was the first permanent theatre built on Manhattan Island? C. A. C.

A. It was the John Street Playhouse which was built in 1767. It remained until 1799 practically the only theatre in New York City.

Q. With what famous actors did Maud Adams play before becoming a principal star herself? I. B.

A. Maud Adams was the daughter of a famous actress of Salt Lake City, Annie Kiskadden, whose stage name was Adams. Miss Adams was on the stage in child parts, but joined the E. H. Southern Company, of New York, when 16 years of age. She was afterwards with the Charles Frohman Stock Company, and later supported John Drew for five years. Her first great success, as a star, was as Lady Babbie, in "The Little Minister," by J. M. Barrie.

Q. How many performances did the original Floradora production have in New York City? T. R.

A. Five hundred and forty-seven.

Q. When did Florenz Ziegfeld enter the theatrical field? S. H. T.

A. He started in Chicago in 1892, and brought military bands from Europe for the World's Fair in Chicago in 1893.

Q. Did the late Wallace Eddinger ever play in "Little Lord Fauntleroy"? E. B.

A. He was one of three children who originated the title rôle. At the time he was only seven years old.

Q. Please give a short biography of Edwin Booth. J. W.

A. Edwin Booth was one of our most distinguished American actors. He was born at Belair, Maryland, November 13, 1833, and brought up to have a dramatic career by his father. He made his début in Boston in 1849 and in 1851 took his father's place as Richard III at the Chatham Square Theatre, New York City. His productions of Hamlet and other Shakespearean plays were successful, and he is generally regarded as the leading American tragedian. He died June 7, 1893.

Q. What is a Greek chorus? H. J.

A. It was a part of the Greek drama sung by the chorus, typically consisting of a series of odes arranged for antiphonal singing, interspersed between the scenes of the play. Hence, in the modern play, a single character who speaks the prologue and explains or comments upon the course of events.

Q. When was East Lynne first produced on the stage? P. T. N.

A. The theatrical career of East Lynne dates back to March 23, 1863, when it was performed at a New York theatre, Tripler's Hall. Clifton W. Tayleure, a Brooklyn playwright, prepared what was probably the first dramatic adaptation. Lucile Western was the first actress to play the rôle of Lady Isabel.

Q. Where is the largest steel curtain in the country? W. D.

A. Variety says that the one used at Convention Hall, Atlantic City, is. It is 108 feet in width, and is a steel frame covered with asbestos cloth. Next is the one at the Alamac Temple in Los Angeles, covering 104 feet. Solid steel curtains are not generally used or required except in Chicago where there is one 73 feet in width at the Granada Theatre.

Q. What is Earl Carroll's real name? T. E.

A. This is the producer's real name. He has never used a nom de theatre.

Q. Is the revolving stage a new idea in the theatre? M. D.

A. It is said to have originated in Japan about 1600 when the Doll Theatre was a popular form of entertainment. Large dolls were operated by dollmasters in full view of the audience. Intricate scenic effects were devised to which the revolving stage contributed. In 1896 Lautenschlager devised a revolving stage in Munich. Fifteen years ago this form of stage was at the zenith of its popularity, being used by Reinhardt in many of his productions.

Q. In the banquet scene in Macbeth is the ghost of Banquo shown upon the stage? R. S.

A. Both versions of the play, Macbeth, by Shakespeare are given —with the ghost appearing and without it. The Ben Greet players, producers of what is known as pure Elizabethan drama, do not show the ghost of Banquo at the banquet table as this is a deviation from the true Shakespeare. Other companies having in mind the dramatic effect of its appearance, show the ghost of Banquo with weird lighting effects.

Q. *Where was Sir Harry Lauder born?* C. H. C.

A. Sir Harry Lauder (family name MacLennan), the Scottish singer, was born at Portobello, Scotland, on August 4, 1870. After working as a mill-boy and coal-miner he took to the variety stage.

Q. *Please tell something about Lottie Collins who sang Ta-ra-ra-boom-de-ay.* S. H. D.

A. She was extremely popular in the London music halls in the early 90's and came to America at the time of the World's Columbian Exposition in Chicago. The song, Ta-ra-ra-boom-de-ay, which she popularized, was written by Henry J. Sayres, a theatrical press agent for the musical farce, Tuxedo. It is said that Sayres first heard the chorus in a St. Louis cabaret run by a negress. The words were somewhat changed and the song eventually reached Lottie Collins, who made it famous in England in 1891.

Q. *Why is the stage referred to as the legitimate stage?* E. H. R.

A. It is so called in the sense of its being normal, regular, conformable to a recognized standard type. Originally the legitimate drama was that body of plays, Shakespearean or other, that have a recognized theatrical and literary merit.

Q. *Please give a biography of Richard Harrison who appeared in "Green Pastures."* C. D.

A. Richard Harrison was born in London, Ontario, in 1864. His parents were fugitive slaves who had taken refuge in that place. Passing his early school days in London, he later attended the Detroit Training School. While working as a bell-boy in a Detroit hotel, someone gave him a copy of Shakespeare's Richard III, which aroused his dramatic am-

bitions. Later he gave dramatic readings throughout the country. It was while Mr. Harrison was on his way to fill various lecture engagements in schools and colleges that he was offered the chief rôle in "The Green Pastures." This was his first appearance on the stage.

Q. *Where did John Drew make his first and last appearance on the stage?* A. T. H.

A. John Drew made his first appearance on the stage in his mother's theatre in Philadelphia, 1873, when he was twenty, and his last in San Francisco fifty-four years later.

Q. *How did Julian Eltinge happen to become a female impersonator?* H. O. C.

A. Julian Eltinge, whose real name is William Julian Dalton, was born in Boston in 1883. He was employed in a bank in Boston and at that time the different banks' clerks put on a show annually, called the Bank Offices Show. Eltinge (or Dalton) played first in the chorus and later the leading female rôle. He achieved such marked success that he became a professional female impersonator. He began his professional career at Keith's Theater, Boston.

Q. *Are Weber and Fields of German descent?* W. H.

A. They are both Polish Jews.

Q. *What was the name of the actress whom Richard Mansfield married?* C. H. L.

A. Richard Mansfield's wife and leading lady was Beatrice Cameron.

Q. *What actress was it who was famous for reciting "Slide, Kelly, Slide"?* G. T.

A. Maggie Cline.

Q. *How did Sarah Bernhardt lose her leg?* M. I. V.

A. During a performance of Jeanne d' Arc in 1890, Bernhardt injured her right knee in falling while on the stage. At that time it was feared that amputation would be necessary. It did not become imperative until 1915, when the leg was amputated.

Q. *Where did Samual Untermyer build the theatre in memory of his wife?* W. S.

A. The Minnie Untermyer Memorial Theatre is in Jerusalem. It overlooks the Dead Sea and the Transjordanian Mountains, and has a seating capacity of 2200.

Q. *Where and when was the actress, Eva Le Gallienne, born?* A. W.

A. She was born in London, England, January 11, 1899.

Q. *Who started minstrel shows?* C. C. R.

A. Minstrel is a name introduced into England by the Normans, and which comprehended singers and performers of instrumental music, together with jugglers, dancers, and other persons. The Negro minstrel is a species of musical entertainment of a quaint and simple kind, which originated among the Negroes of the South, and was first made popular at public entertainments by E. P. Christy, the originator of the troupes of imitation Negro musicians.

Q. *Did Ellen Terry belong to a theatrical family?* C. D.

A. Both of her parents were actors and she went on the stage at the age of eight.

Q. *Who originated the chambermaid or parlormaid comedy character?* G. E.

A. Kitty Clive, who flourished in the early part of the eighteenth century, was famed for depicting such a character.

Q. *Please give a biography of Ed Wynn.* S. K.

A. He was born November 9, 1886. He attended high school 4 months, business college 6 months, and University of Pennsylvania 5½ months. He ran away from home when 15. Was in vaudeville from 1901 until 1914. Then was in Ziegfeld's Follies and at Winter Garden, and became a star. He has written book, lyrics, and music for his own plays; and was first to broadcast entire production of a musical comedy by radio.

Q. *How tall are Ziegfeld Glorified Girls and how much are they supposed to weigh?* E. R.

A. There are no specified measurements. Their approximate height is 5 feet 6 inches and their approximate weight 120 pounds.

Q. *Please give a brief history of vaudeville.* A. H. F.

A. The American theatrical institution of vaudeville originated in 1883, in Boston, Mass., when a former circus employee, Benjamin Franklin Keith, opened a small museum and show in a vacant candy store next to the old Adams House in Washington Street. He called his first theatre the Gaiety Museum, and its principal attractions were Baby Alice, a midget weighing one and one-half pounds, and an ancient stuffed mermaid. Later among his added attractions were the Circassian Beauties, a chicken with a human face, and a pair of rising young comedians, Weber and Fields, who performed as a team.

Q. *Did Edwin Booth remain on the stage after his brother, John Wilkes Booth, assassinated President Lincoln?* G. S.

A. He retired from the stage, but upon the earnest solicitation of his friends, returned to the boards in 1866. He was a very popular actor. In April, 1891, he retired to the Players' Club, which he founded, and to which he gave more than $250,000.

Q. *Did John Drew ever play any Shakespearean rôles?* R. G.

A. He was greatly admired for his rôle of Petruchio in the "Taming of the Shrew." He also played the rôle of Orlando in "As You Like It" and the King of Navarre in "Love's Labour's Lost."

Q. *What was the earliest English comedy?* C. G. A.

A. Ralph Royster Doyster, written by Nicholas Udall was the earliest. The exact date of its appearance is uncertain, but it was before 1551. It was written to be presented by the boys of Eton College.

Q. *Did Jeanne Eagels ever play on the stage in the same play with George Arliss?* M. T.

A. She played three rôles with him: "The Professor's Love Story"; the rôle of Clarissa in a short revival of "Disraeli": and afterwards Mrs. Reynolds in "Hamilton."

Q. *When was the theatre first known?* A. J. P.

A. The theatre originated with the Greeks and developed in that country together with the drama. At first the theatre was simply a space near the Temple of Dyonysius, where the chorus danced about the altar of the god. Later set places were provided for the performances. During the Middle Ages, theatrical performances began with dialogue additions, acted out in church service for Christmas and Easter. It developed in the 12th century into plays in the vernacular, presenting the chief events in sacred stories. The first admission charges of which there is record was from two to four pence.

Q. *Was there a famous actor many years ago by the name of John Gilbert?* S. B.

A. John Gilbert (real name Gibbs) was a popular actor born in Boston in 1810, died there in 1889. Among his best rôles were Sir Anthony Resolute, Sir Peter Teazle, and Mr. Hardcastle. He gave, wrote Wm. Winter, the best performance of Caliban ever seen in America.

Q. *How long have marionettes and puppets been made?* V. W.

A. The origin of marionettes and puppets has been lost in obscurity. They held a prominent place in the lives of the people of ancient India. They were used in the early Greek

and Roman days and by the Egyptians.

Q. *When was Thurston, the magician, born?* F. S.

A. He was born in 1869. He has been a magician since boyhood.

Q. *When was the first pantomime produced in England?* R. N. B.

A. The first one produced in England was at Drury Lane in 1702. It was called "The Tavern Builders." It was not until 1723, however, that the noted harlequin, John Rich, established the Christmas pantomime. This form of entertainment had long been popular, having been at its height in Rome in the time of Nero.

Q. *When did Alla Nazimova come to this country? How old is she?* F. F.

A. She came to America in 1905 with a Russian company, and was born in Yalta, Crimea, Russia, in 1879.

Q. *Who were the members of the original Floradora sextette?* G. A. C.

A. The girls who sang "Tell Me Pretty Maiden" in Floradora and took the town by storm at the Casino Theatre in 1900 were: Vaugn Tex-Smith, Margaret Walker, Marie L. Wilson, Marjorie Relyea, Agnes Wayburn, and Daisy Greene.

Q. *How long has the Lupino family had members on the stage?* R. J.

A. This family has been connected with the stage for 250 years. In 1679, Georgius Luppino, as he spelled his name, went to London from Italy with a puppet show, and was the first of a long line of stage folks. Two members of the family are in this country—Barry Lupino on the stage, and Lupino Lane in the movies.

Q. *What did Al Jolson do before he appeared at the Winter Garden?* E. McL.

A. Al Jolson traveled with a circus for several years and then with Lew Dockstader's Minstrels. He was in vaudeville before being engaged for the Winter Garden, New York, in 1911.

Q. *How long has Jane Cowl been on the stage? Is she married? G. A. G.*

A. She made her first appearance on the stage in 1903 in "Sweet Kitty Bellairs." She is married to Adolph Klauber.

Q. *Name the actresses that were famous for their interpretation of Ibsen rôles. J. S.*

A. Frau Hennings was the first actress to act the rôle of Nora in "A Doll's House." Mrs. Fiske, Mme. Duse, Mary Shaw, Mrs. Patrick Campbell, Mme. Nazimova, Carlotta Nillson, and Eva Le Gallienne were known in Ibsen rôles.

Q. *Who was the first American to play Hamlet in London? N. A. L.*

A. Steele MacKaye was the first. "Epoch," MacKaye's biography by his son, Percy MacKaye, reveals the father as the inventor of almost all of the modern stage devices; author of Hazel Kirk; a veritable genius who was "one of the most romantic and thrilling figures of the 19th century."

Q. *Does England have an official censor of plays? S. N.*

A. By an Act of 1843, no plays may be acted for hire until they have been submitted to the Lord Chamberlin. He may refuse to license them in whole or in parts. The official who reads them for the purpose of deciding is called the examiner of stage plays. There is a fine of $150 for acting an unlicensed or prohibited play, and the theatre in which it is presented forfeits its license.

Q. *Do' stage people still put belladonna in their eyes? H. W. F.*

A. Present day actors and actresses usually put make-up around their eyes instead of using belladonna and similar things in the eyes.

Q. *Can you tell me whether Ethel Barrymore has ever played in the movies? M. A. C.*

A. Miss Barrymore has played in the following named pictures: The Nightingale, The Awakening of Helena Richie, The White Raven, The Lifted Veil, Whirlpool, The American Widow, The Eternal Mother, Lady Frederick, Our Mrs. McChesney, The Divorcee, The Superwoman, and Rasputin.

Q. *Who was the first actress in America to receive the honorary degree of Doctor of Letters? A. D. E.*

A. George Washington University bestowed this degree upon Julia Marlowe, the first actress to receive it in this country.

Q. *Who was the first manager of the Drury Lane Theatre? Who is the present manager? R. V.*

A. The first manager was Colly Cibber. The old theatre opened in 1663 with The Humorous Lieutenant, with Nell Gwyn in the cast. The present manager is Sir Albert Butt. The theatre was remodeled as late as 1929.

Q. *What were the names of the first Elizabethan theatres? S. A. C.*

A. "The Theatre" was the first built by J. Burbage in Shoreditch in 1576 and was soon followed by "The Curtain" in Finsbury. These were the predecessors of "The Rose and the Swan," and "The Globe and the Fortune," the first and second Blackfriars theatres.

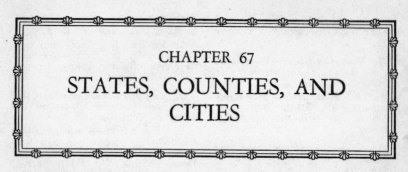

CHAPTER 67

STATES, COUNTIES, AND CITIES

Q. What is the smallest incorporated city in the United States? D. H.

A. Upland, Ark., is believed to be the nation's smallest incorporated city. Official Census Bureau figures for 1930 give a population of 4.

Q. What name appears in the most States as the name of a county? C. B. H.

A. Washington is used the most times. Twenty-nine States have a Washington County.

Q. Please give some illustration that will show the great size of the State of Texas. E. L. C.

A. The distance between the two most remote points in Texas is considerably greater than that from Chicago to either the Atlantic Ocean or the Gulf of Mexico.

Q. Who gave the name Empire to New York State? N. A. L.

A. It is attributed to George Washington, who, in an address in 1784, said ". . . your State (at present the seat of Empire) . . ."

Q. What is meant by a Louisiana parish? F. V. S.

A. Parishes in Louisiana correspond to counties. The word parish is used to designate a district separated and defined by local limitation for civil and political purposes.

Q. What city was known as the city of wooden chimneys? F. J. B.

A. Suffolk, Virginia, had a building boom about the middle of the Eighteenth Century and many chimneys were built of wood because the supply of brick was not equal to the demand. Suffolk thereupon became famous as the city of wooden chimneys.

Q. Which State has only three counties? G. D.

A. Delaware.

Q. Is there a typical American city? M. W.

A. Some time ago the Literary Digest called Zanesville, Ohio, the typical American city, but recently the National Child Health Council, after considering the qualifications of eighty communities, gave Mansfield, Ohio, this honor. It stated that it named Mansfield because of its location, the background of its population, the agricultural communities surrounding it, its history, and its railroad transportation.

Q. Why is Akron, Ohio, so named? S. D.

A. Akron is from a Greek word which means the summit or the peak. The city is appropriately called Akron, because it is on the highest ground in the northern part of the State.

Q. Which county is the smallest in the United States? W. H.

A. New York County, N. Y., is the smallest in the United States and has an area of only 22 square miles. Its population in 1930 totaled 1,867,-312. The county seat is New York

450

City. New York City is incorporated in more than one county.

Q. *Why does Ekaterinburg no longer appear on Russian maps?* P. M.

A. This town where the royal family was assassinated is now called Sverdlovsk.

Q. *What are the five largest cities in California?* F. V.

A. Los Angeles, San Francisco, Oakland, San Diego, and Long Beach.

Q. *How much was paid for the original land upon which Boston was built?* E. E. P.

A. The Rev. Wm. Blackstone, the original settler of the land on which the city of Boston now stands (1623), sold the land to Gov. John Winthrop's colony of settlers in 1634. This land amounted to 800 acres and was sold for 30 pounds (about $150). The Rev. Blackstone then left for Rhode Island where he was also the first white settler and where he died in 1675.

Q. *Was Guthrie ever the capital of the State of Oklahoma?* M. M.

A. Guthrie, the capital of the territory of Oklahoma, was made the capital of the new State of Oklahoma by the Enabling Act of 1906, but in 1910 it was voted to remove the capital to Oklahoma City, where it has since remained.

Q. *When was the City of Philadelphia planned?* R. F.

A. The town of Philadelphia was planned before William Penn left England in 1682. Before 1683 Philadelphia had more than 500 inhabitants.

Q. *When was New Amsterdam renamed New York?* H. T.

A. New Amsterdam was renamed New York and the state government reorganized in 1665, after possession had been taken from the Dutch by the British in 1664. The schout, burgomasters, and schepens were replaced with a sheriff and aldermen and mayor. The actual charter of New York City upon which most of its civic rights were based was granted April 22, 1686.

Q. *When was Reno, Nevada, settled?* H. D.

A. It was settled in 1858 by eastern emigrants who had started for California. It was incorporated in 1869 and chartered as a city in 1901.

Q. *How is Staten Island governed?* W. D.

A. Staten Island was constituted the County of Richmond and had a county government until it became a part of the City of New York under the name of Borough of Richmond.

Q. *In Greater Chicago, how many miles of beaches are there?* R. M.

A. Nearly 30 miles of beaches along Lake Michigan are included in Greater Chicago.

Q. *What city was the first settled in Ohio?* E. U.

A. Marietta was the first settlement within the present limits of Ohio. It was founded in 1788 by Rufus Putnam and a colony from New England under the authority of the Ohio company. It was named in honor of Marie Antoinette.

Q. *How many independent cities are there in Virginia?* H. S.

A. There are now 24.

Q. *For whom were Hampton and Hampton Roads named?* H. E. S.

A. They derived their present names from the Earl of Southampton, one of the leaders of the Virginia Company and a friend or patron of Shakespeare. The name was probably abbreviated to Hampton.

Q. *Please give a list of names of foreign cities whose spelling is changed in English.* C. C.

A. A partial list follows: Havana, La Habana; Marseilles, Marseille; Lyons, Lyon; Rome, Roma; Leghorn, Livorno; Naples, Napoli; Genoa, Genova; Milan, Milano; Turin, Torino; Venice, Venezia; The Hague, 's Gravenhage; Geneva, Geneve; Brussels, Bruxelles; Munich, Munchen; Vienna, Wien; Warsaw, Warszawa; Copenhagen, Kobenhavn; Belgrade, Beograd; Sophia, Sofija; Bucharest, Bucuresti; Moscow, Moskva; Athens, Athenai.

Q. Why is Monterey in California spelled with one r, while the Mexico city has two r's? L. M. W.

A. This seems inexplicable to one unfamiliar with Spanish. The correct spelling in modern Spanish is with the double r, since it is a rule of Spanish phonetics that when any word ending in a vowel is compounded with another word beginning with r, the compound word shall have the r doubled. Monterrey is made up of two Spanish words, monte and rey, meaning mountain and king. Other good examples of this principle are Porto Rican, which in Spanish is one word—Portorrigueno; and Costa Rican, which in Spanish is Costarricense. The explanation of the American spelling of the name Monterey is that it is simpler.

Q. Why is the loop district in Chicago so called? N. N.

A. The business and theatre district was so called because it lay within a loop made by the elevated tracks which come into the center of the city.

Q. Who named the City of Providence, Rhode Island? S. B.

A. It was the first settlement and mother town of Rhode Island. Founded in 1636 by Roger Williams, he named it Providence "in gratitude to his Supreme Deliverer."

Q. What name was first given to Helena, Montana? T. L.

A. In 1864, Helena, Montana, was founded by a band of prospectors headed by John Cowan. At first it was called Last Chance Gulch as they had been looking for gold all through the spring without success and considered this their last chance for that season. On June 15, 1864, an abundance of gold was located.

Q. How long has Olympia been the capital of Washington? M. E. W.

A. The municipality of Olympia became the capital of the newly organized territory of Washington in 1853, and has been the capital of Washington ever since. Washington became a State in November, 1889, and Olympia was incorporated as a city shortly afterwards.

Q. How many cities in the United States are named Madison, Monroe, Jackson, Jefferson, and Sherman? M. C.

A. There are 26 cities by the name of Madison that have post offices; 23 with the name of Monroe; 18 with the name of Jackson; 11 with the name of Jefferson; and 9 with the name of Sherman.

Q. What city is called the City of Five Flags? M. N.

A. Mobile, Alabama. It has been under French, Spanish, British, American, and Confederate flags.

Q. Which are the ten largest cities in Canada? C. B.

A. In order of size they are: Montreal, Toronto, Vancouver, Winnipeg, Hamilton, Quebec, Ottawa, Calgary, Edmonton, and London.

Q. Why is Baltimore called the Monumental City? E. C. D.

A. It had monuments in its square before other cities in the United States had, and also had the imposing monument to Washington.

Q. What is the name of the reconstructed village which Henry Ford is making at Dearborn, Michigan? M. J. L.

A. The official name given Mr. Ford's museum project at Dearborn, Michigan, is The Edison Institute of Technology, which includes the museum, its collection, and the supplementing historic village called Greenfield, which covers approximately 250 acres. The historic village perpetuates the name of Greenfield Township (the birthplace of Mrs. Henry Ford) which was founded in 1826 by Myron Otis, and has since been absorbed by the growth of Detroit. In this village the handicraft arts of the past are presented as they were practised in their original environment of public buildings and residences which in their turn illustrate the development of architectural types. As in all Colonial communities, the public buildings are arranged around a common or green.

Q. Who founded the cities of Quebec and Montreal? G. L.

A. Samuel Champlain founded both cities, Quebec in 1608, and Montreal in 1611.

Q. What are the largest towns in Alaska? C. M.

A. In order of their size, they are Juneau, Ketchikan, Anchorage, Fairbanks, Petersburgtown, Nome, and Sitka.

Q. How many States were there in the Union at the close of the War of 1812? F. J. J.

A. There were 18 States in the Union at the close of the war which ended late in December, 1814.

Q. What State is referred to as the American Riviera? C. B.

A. California is often thus spoken of, because its climate and scenery resemble those of the Riviera. There is also a similarity in the nature of their products.

Q. What is the oldest town in Massachusetts? V. S.

A. Plymouth is the oldest, and Salem comes next.

Q. Why is South Carolina called the Iodine State? R. E. L.

A. An article was published a few years ago in the Journal of Industrial and Engineering Chemistry about the iodine content of the soil in South Carolina, in which it was stated that the soil was rich in iodine and that vegetables grown in the soil were also rich in iodine. Since this time South Carolina has featured this asset.

Q. Could a boundary between two States be changed? L. C.

A. A boundary between two States of the United States may be changed by agreement of the state legislatures, but the agreement must be approved by Congress.

Q. What is the least populous county in Virginia? F. T.

A. Craig County with a population of only 3562 at the last census.

Q. Why is there such an irregular section in the boundary between Massachusetts and Connecticut? A. H. S.

A. This peculiar deviation from a straight line boundary, known as the Southwick Jog, was caused by the straightening out and adjusting of errors in the boundary line between Connecticut and Massachusetts as previously run by compass. A long narrow strip of land was given to Connecticut, and the Southwick Jog ceded to Massachusetts as a parcel of land of equivalent area.

Q. Why does Minnesota extend across a straight line into Canada? H. A.

A. Under the Treaty with Great Britain of 1842, the Commissioners in running out the line when they reached the Lake of the Woods traced the line to the most northern point of the lake in latitude 49°23′55″, longitude 95°14′38″ thence south to the 49th parallel, thence west along the 49th parallel.

Q. What was the origin of the name of the State of Texas? L. M.

A. The name was given to the State on account, according to tradition, of the fact that the Tejas Indians sheltered and protected some Frenchmen, who found refuge with them at the time when the possession of the State was being contested by French and Spaniards.

Q. How did Pennsylvania get the additional frontage on Lake Erie? M. S.

A. Pennsylvania had at first but four miles of territory on Lake Erie. This was at the western end of the county and adjoined the State of Ohio. There was much trouble concerning that portion of Erie County known as the triangle until finally the claims of the Six Nations, Massachusetts and New York became merged in the United States. In March, 1792, Pennsylvania bought the triangle for about $150,000. This gave her nearly 50 miles of frontage on the lake, and more than 200,000 acres of additional land.

Q. Which State ranks first in area and in population? A. M. E.

A. Texas ranks first in area, with 265,896 square miles. California is second with 158,297 square miles. New York State which ranks 29th in area, is first in population. Pennsylvania which is 32nd in size, ranks second in population. Texas ranks 5th in population and California ranks 6th.

Q. Is Kentucky the only State to which the term, Grand Old Commonwealth, has been applied? S. C. J.

A. In United States history, the word Commonwealth is applied to a sovereign self-governing State or nation, and was adopted as the designation of several of the States. States in the United States which officially bear this title are Massachusetts, Pennsylvania, Virginia, and Kentucky. At times all of these States may have been referred to as Grand Old Commonwealth.

Q. How large is Rhode Island? H. T.

A. The extreme length of the State from north to south is 48 miles and the extreme width from east to west is 36 miles. The area is 1248 square miles, of which 1067 square miles are land surface.

Q. When was North Carolina separated from South Carolina? R. F.

A. Carolina was granted to the Lords Proprietors in 1663. In 1710 it was decided to separate the province into North and South Carolina, and to appoint a governor of North Carolina independent of the governor of South Carolina, but the plan was not carried out until 1712. The commission of Edward Hyde as governor of North Carolina independent of the governor of South Carolina was issued January 24, 1712.

Q. Is the State of Florida east or west of the Panama Canal? E. M.

A. The 80th parallel of longitude west from Greenwich just touches the eastern tip of Florida and cuts through the Isthmus of Panama just west of the canal. Therefore Florida is farther west than the canal.

Q. What are the comparative areas of Texas and Alaska? B. B.

A. Texas, with 265,896 square miles is less than half the size of Alaska, with 586,400 square miles. But Texas has almost 6,000,000 people and Alaska only 60,000. An even more amazing discrepancy between area and population of Alaska and a State of the United States is the case of Rhode Island which is one-four hundred seventieths of the size of Alaska, with 1248 square miles, but has over 600,000 people and hence ten times as much population.

Q. Is there a town named Broadway? R. Y.

A. There is an old Norman town in England dating back to the seventh or eighth century by this name.

Q. In what States are there towns named Oshkosh? A. E. R.

A. There is an Oshkosh in Wisconsin and one in Nebraska.

Q. What is the area of the modern city of Jerusalem? W. W. J.

A. The estimated area of modern Jerusalem is 1000 acres, of which one-fifth lies within the walls.

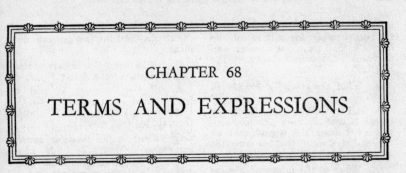

CHAPTER 68

TERMS AND EXPRESSIONS

Q. *What is the story back of the expression "having a white elephant on your hands"?* A. I. W.

A. It is said to have originated in the action of an Eastern potentate who, when he decided to impoverish or destroy a courtier, presented to the individual one of the sacred white elephants. The cost of the custody and upkeep of this animal was so great that its effect was to reduce the courtier to poverty.

Q. *Where do we get the expression "cold shoulder"?* B. P.

A. In medieval days in France it was customary to serve hot roasts when entertaining guests. If the guests outstayed their welcome, a "cold shoulder" was served instead of hot meat.

Q. *Is the expression "flaming youth" a quotation?* C. E. M.

A. It is a quotation from Shakespeare's Hamlet, Act III, Scene 4, occurring in the clause "To flaming youth let virtue be as wax And melt in her own fire."

Q. *What is meant by a "hijacker" as the term is used in connection with liquor smuggling?* C. L. H.

A. A hijacker in the illicit liquor traffic is an individual who robs smugglers and bootleggers of their money or wares. The name is said to be one that was given to a band of hoboes who preyed on men who worked in the harvest fields of the West years ago. The members

hailed their prospective victims with "Hi Jack, what time is it?" and then followed that up by tapping them on the head and relieving them of their money. Railroad detectives called them "hijackers."

Q. *What is the origin of the term "Pig and Whistle" as applied to coffee houses?* W. W.

A. Some authorities believe it to be a corruption of "Peg and Wassail." Peg is from the Low German pegel meaning a measure of liquid capacity, such as was marked by pegs in a peg tankard. Wassail is an old expression of good wishes, also the liquor used for drinking healths.

Q. *To whom do we owe the well-known saying, "Watch your step"?* R. N.

A. The late Theodore Shonts is regarded as the author of this expression.

Q. *Whence the phrase "stand by" used by radio announcers?* P. J.

A. It is a nautical term and has long been used in the Navy. It merely signifies to prepare for orders, or to be at attention.

Q. *What was the origin of the phrase, "A little bird told me"?* T. H.

A. The origin of the phrase which in various forms is found in many countries is said to be the verse of Scripture, Ecclesiastes 10–20: "Revile not the king, no, not in thy

455

thought; and revile not the rich in thy bedchamber for a bird of the heavens shall carry the voice and that which hath wings shall carry the matter."

Q. *What are crocodile tears?* B. S. W.

A. The expression "crocodile tears" is used in reference to insincere grief from the legend told by the old travelers that a crocodile wept over those it devoured.

Q. *What is the origin of the expression, "It would take a Philadelphia lawyer to straighten it out"?* R. M. P.

A. There appear to be many different opinions as to its origin. John Peter Zenger, proprietor of a newspaper of Albany, was indicted for criminal libel, and was successfully defended by Andrew Hamilton, a Philadelphia lawyer, in 1735. The case was epoch-making, as Hamilton established for all time the principles of free press and free speech to which the law of libel should be forever subservient. The New England folks have a saying: "Three Philadelphia lawyers are a match for the very Devil himself." This appears in the Salem Observer, of March 13, 1824.

Q. *Please explain the term cloture.* O. K. E.

A. Cloture is a method of ending debate and securing a vote in the legislature. In the House of Representatives no member may speak on a question for more than one hour in regular session, nor more than five minutes in Committee of the Whole, without unanimous consent. Debate is generally ended by moving the previous question. In the United States Senate there was no cloture rule until the prolongation of debate during the war compelled the adoption of a mild rule which can be used in extreme cases.

Q. *What is zero hour?* H. J.

A. It is the term applied to the time officially appointed for opening an attack in war. This time is kept secret at headquarters and referred to as zero. It is not made known to the troops until the last possible moment.

Q. *Who coined the expression, "the survival of the fittest"?* M. B.

A. Herbert Spencer is said to have coined it in reference to the Darwinian theory of evolution through natural selection.

Q. *What is the meaning of the expression "table d'hôte"?* M. L.

A. It means table of the host. Before inns were numerous enough to accommodate travelers and wayfarers, all householders provided beds and meals for strangers who came to their doors. The traveler was welcomed to the family dining table— to the table of the host.

Q. *What is the origin of the expression "the little red school house"?* M. L. E.

A. In the early days in this country, school houses were small and usually painted red. It is explained that red paint was especially cheap. So many men and women who ultimately attained distinction began their education under these modest conditions and later delighted to pay honor to "the little red school house" that the phrase has become a figure of speech.

Q. *What is meant by Dead Sea Fruit?* A. I.

A. The expression is synonymous with Apples of Sodom. The apple trees around the Dead Sea bore fruit lovely to the eye, but inedible. One explanation is that these apples were a kind of gall. They were rich, glossy, purplish-red in appearance, but filled with an intensely bitter, porous, easily pulverized substance. The term is applied to anything wonderful in contemplation, but disappointing in realization.

Q. *Explain the expression "cute with a worm" or "right cute with a worm."* W. C.

A. The word "cute" is used here to mean clever. The copper coil used in a still is commonly referred to in old English history and among the mountaineers of Kentucky and Tennessee as a worm. Hence when referring to a man who is successfully making "cohn liquor" he is often said to be "right cute with a worm."

Q. When did Woodrow Wilson use the expression that the world must be made safe for democracy? F. L.

A. In his address to Congress, April 2, 1917, President Wilson used the words: "The world must be made safe for democracy."

Q. What is the meaning of the expression "To eat humble pie"? H. M. R.

A. It means to come down from a position you have assumed. "Humble" here is a pun on umble, the umbles being the heart, liver, and entrails of the deer, the huntsman's perquisites. When the lord and his household dined, the venison pastry was served on the dais, but the umbles were made into a pie for the huntsman and his fellows, who took the lower seats.

Q. What is meant by the term "Heaviside layer"? E. W.

A. The Heaviside layer is the layer of ionized air in the upper atmosphere. It was first described by Arthur W. Heaviside, a British scientist, who was experimenting with Sir William Preece in 1892, with parallel telegraph lines.

Q. What does the expression, "Cotton is King," mean? R. A.

A. The expression was used by Senator James Henry Hammond of South Carolina on the floor of the United States Senate in 1858, in reference to the cotton crop bringing in such a large sum of money.

Q. How did the phrase, "They shall not pass," originate? J. J. B.

A. At the end of February, 1916, General de Castelnau was sent by General Joffre to decide whether Verdun should be abandoned or defended. He consulted with General Petain, saying: "They (the Ger-

mans) must not pass." General Petain said: "They shall not pass." In France, the people credit it to General Joffre.

Q. Who is responsible for the maxim, "The customer is always right"? M. C.

A. To Marshall Field, the great Chicago merchant, is attributed this maxim.

Q. What was the origin of the phrase, "The Iron Horse," used in reference to a steam locomotive? S. W.

A. Sitting Bull, the mighty War Chief of the Sioux Indians, coined the phrase, "The Iron Horse." The inspiration came to him after he had his first glimpse of a steam locomotive.

Q. Where is the expression, "A man's house is his castle" first found? W. H.

A. It was first used by Sir Edward Coke, famous British jurist, 1552–1634, in his Institutes, Part III "Against going or riding armed."

Q. What is meant by bushido? G. D. B.

A. Bushido is defined as the unwritten code of moral principles which regulate the actions of Japanese knighthood, the Samurai.

Q. How did the phrase, a "Pyrrhic Victory," originate? L. M.

A. This phrase is used to denote a victory won at tremendous cost and refers to the battle of Asculum in which Pyrrhus, King of Epirus, won a victory over the Romans while sustaining such heavy losses that he is said to have exclaimed "Another such victory and Pyrrhus is destroyed."

Q. What is the origin of the expression, "hue and cry"? M. D.

A. The phrase was employed in English law to signify the old common law process of pursuing a criminal with horn and voice. It was the duty of the aggrieved person to raise the hue and cry, and his neighbors were bound to turn out with him to assist in discovering or in pursuing the offender.

Q. *What is the origin of the expression, "on the level"?* C. T.

A. It is said to have originated in Freemasonry, the level being an emblem of that organization.

Q. *How did the expression, "show the white feather," get its present meaning?* R. W.

A. According to Brewer's Manual the term originated in the 16th and 17th centuries when cock-fighting was a principal sport. Game birds used for cock-fighting are entirely without white feathers and one such chancing to show itself in the plumage of the bird indicated a crossing or inferior bird and therefore probably loss of courage and fighting qualities.

Q. *What is the origin of the expression, "so long"?* G. G. P.

A. It is an English provincialism which was introduced into the United States. J. Redding Ware in his Passing of the English of the Victorian Era speaks of the custom in England of adopting the words of foreigners resident there and Anglicizing them, and mentions as an instance the expression, "so long," which he believes originated in the White Chapel district of London, being a corruption of the Jewish "selah," a phrase which spread all over England.

Q. *Why are campaign orators called spellbinders?* T. S. W.

A. The expression is believed to have originated with an official of the Republican National Committee who applied it to speakers who were always reporting that they had held audiences spell-bound.

Q. *Who were the die-hards?* T. R.

A. In politics, they are the members of a party who stick to their long-held theories regardless of the changes that time and circumstances may make. In particular the name

was applied to the Tories who opposed any reform of the House of Lords, and the Unionists who refused to yield in the direction of Irish Home Rule.

Q. *Who is Jimminy, in the expression, "By Jimminy"?* S. I. K.

A. It refers to the Heavenly Twins of the Zodiac, the Gemini, patrons of ancient Rome.

Q. *What does "to cross the Rubicon" mean?* M. A.

A. It means to take some step from which it is not possible to recede. The Rubicon was a small river separating Italy from Cisalpine Gaul, the province allotted to Julius Caesar. In B.C. 49, when Caesar crossed this stream, he passed beyond the limits of his own province and became an invader of Italy.

Q. *What is meant by the white man's burden?* D. C.

A. This is the name of one of the best known of Kipling's poems. It was written for the inspiration of all who recognize the responsibility of the white to the colored races. It was originally published in 1899.

Q. *Where do we get the expression, "Peace at any price"?* F. N.

A. Lord Palmerston sneered at the Quaker statesman, John Bright, as a "peace-at-any-price man" and the expression has since come to mean any extreme pacifist.

Q. *Who coined the expression "Stop, look, listen"?* H. A. D.

A. Col. J. C. Fuller, vice president and manager in charge of construction of the old Gettysburg and Harrisburg Railroad, now part of the Reading System, says: "In building the Gettysburg and Harrisburg Railroad we were obliged to cross many public roads and were about to prepare a notice to put up at each crossing when my attention was called to a court decision in a suit brought for injury at a crossing. The judge made use of this language—that it is the duty of everyone to 'stop, look, and listen' before crossing a railroad. I at once adopted the words 'stop, look, and listen,' believing it a legal point in determining the responsibility of both the public and the railroad."

Q. *What does the stock market expression, "selling against the box," mean?* G. Y.

A. It means short selling by a person who has the securities he sells, but does not make actual delivery at the time of sale. The box refers to his safety deposit box or strong box.

Q. *What is meant by "sporting one's oak"?* P. L. D.

A. This phrase originated in English universities and means to shut the door as a sign of being engaged. Most rooms at colleges have two doors, the outer one of oak, which is closed when the occupant is away.

Q. *Who coined the expression, "Vanity Fair"?* W. S.

A. Bunyan used it in Pilgrim's Progress, to describe a town fair where all the wares were vanities, and the buyers lovers of vanity.

Q. *Why the expression, "to make a Roman holiday"?* B. J. F.

A. It refers to the custom of the Romans of celebrating victories or other important events by sports in the arena, which often resulted in many deaths and involved much cruelty.

Q. *What is meant by the nautical phrase, "Rope-yarn Sunday"?* J. O'N.

A. It means Thursday. The afternoon of this day is devoted to the making and mending of clothes and is practically a holiday when the ship's company can occupy themselves as they please.

Q. *Why is an inquisitive person called a peeping Tom?* A. W. D.

A. It was originally peeping Tom of Coventry, a person who disobeyed the injunction not to look in the street when the nude Lady Godiva rode by.

Q. *What is the derivation of the expression, namby-pamby?* P. A. L.

A. It was a diminutive reduplication of the name of Ambrose Phillips, an English writer of sentimental verse.

Q. *What is the meaning of the term, cover charge?* E. H.

A. The term is applied to the charge made for the privilege of occupying a place at a café or restaurant table. It is derived from the French word, couvert, which means dinner things such as knives, forks, and spoons, with which a place at a table is set.

Q. *Who coined the phrase the forgotten man?* S. F.

A. It is attributed to William Graham Sumner, who used the expression in a lecture in 1883.

Q. *What is the origin of the phrase, brand new?* C. B.

A. It is a combination of brand, meaning fire and new meaning fresh. Therefore it has the meaning of fresh and bright like a new coin, which has just come from the mint.

Q. *What is the origin of the term, shanghaied?* R. K.

A. The term was applied to a mode of forcibly shipping as sailors men who had been drugged or made drunken, because this practice was largely followed by masters of ships engaged in trade with China, Shanghai being one of the principal ports of call.

Q. *What is meant by the expression, sent up Salt River?* A. C. B.

A. To be sent up Salt River (or Creek) or to row up Salt River (or Creek) is a slang expression meaning to be defeated or to fail in anything; especially applied to political candidates who fail at elections, with a supposed reference to a small stream in Kentucky.

Q. *What is meant by the "fifth estate"? P. J.*

A. This term has recently been applied to that body of persons who are engaged in the preservation and advancement of the organized knowledge known as science.

Q. *What does hidalgo mean? H. T. S.*

A. The term comes from two Spanish words—"hiji" meaning "son" and "d'alguno" meaning "somebody." Hence the term literally means "son of somebody."

Q. *What is the origin of the term, meander? C. M.*

A. In ancient geography it was the name of a river in Asia Minor which was famous for its many windings.

Q. *In modern times, who first applied the word, Hun, to the German? H. T. L.*

A. Kipling. His poem called The Powers (1902) is noteworthy for this first use of the word Hun.

Q. *What is the origin of the expression, The worm will turn? J. L. B.*

A. In the drama Henry VI there is the sentence, "The smallest worm will turn." This quotation from Shakespeare is usually regarded as the origin of the expression about which you have inquired.

Q. *During the World War, what was meant by "four-minute men"? C. L.*

A. The phrase was applied to men who spoke in behalf of the Liberty Loan. They were generally limited to four minute speeches.

Q. *When did the expression, Tell it to the Marines, originate? C. C.*

A. It is traced to Samuel Pepys, secretary of the British Admiralty. He said it originated with Charles II. A returned traveler told his Majesty he had seen flying fish. The King was skeptical and turning to the Colonel of a maritime regiment asked him what he would say. "I should say, sire," returned the sea soldier simply, "that the man hath sailed in southern seas. For when your Majesty's business carried me thither of late I did frequently observe more flying fish in one hour than the hairs of my head in number." Old Roaley glanced narrowly at the colonel's frank, weather-beaten face. Then with a laugh he turned to the secretary and said: "Mr. Pepys, from the very nature of their calling, no class of our subjects can have so wide a knowledge of seas and lands as the officers and men of our royal maritime regiment. Henceforth, whenever we cast doubt upon a tale that lacketh likelihood we will tell it to the marines—if they believe it, it is safe to say it is true."

Q. *When were street cleaners first called white wings? A. D.*

A. This term was applied to the white uniformed street cleaners organized in 1895 by Col. George Edwin Waring for cleaning the streets of New York City.

Q. *Why is the word, mush, used as a cry to dog teams? P. M.*

A. It is a corruption of the French word marchons, the cry of the early French to their teams.

Q. *Why were antimacassars so called? J. F.*

A. Antimacassars took the name from the fact that Macassar oil was a popular hair oil, and it was to protect chairs and sofas from this and other hair oils that doilies were put on the furniture.

Q. *What is a parlor Bolshevist? A. G. S.*

A. He is one who professes radical socialism and encourages it, but does not join in the active struggle to bring it about.

Q. *Why is a bonfire so named? S. P.*

A. Bonfire was originally bonefire, literally fire of bones, and was applied to a funeral pyre.

Q. *What are screevers?* D. C. C.

A. This is the name applied to men who make pastel drawings on paving stones in London.

Q. *What is meant by "the lady or the tiger"?* E. T. K.

A. This is a popular phrase used to express a dilemma. It is derived from a story by Francis Richard Stockton published in 1880, in which the sequel or decision is left to the readers.

Q. *What is argot?* D. E. L.

A. Argot is the French term for what in English is known as slang, especially applied to the dialect of thieves and vagabonds.

Q. *When was the expression, once in a blue moon, first used?* E. T. S.

A. Once in a blue moon was first used by Roy and Barlow in Rede Me and Be Not Rothe in England in 1528. It was formerly used to designate something that will never happen. E. C. Brewer in his book, Phrase and Fable, says: "On December 10, 1883, we had a blue moon. The winter was unusually mild." The expression is now used to mean very seldom.

Q. *How did the slang phrase, to bant, originate?* D. D.

A. This humorous name for dieting with the purpose of losing weight originated in the making of a verb from the name Banting. Banting was the advocate of such a system, which bears his name.

Q. *What was the origin of the expression, on the fence?* C. W.

A. The Richmond Whig is credited with the first use of this expression when it said in 1828: "There are certain administration editors, editors for a long time on the fence."

Q. *How did the expression, dough-face, originate?* N. H.

A. Edmund Randolph, of Virginia, applied the term doughfaces to those slavery supporters who voted for the Missouri compromise. It

was later applied to northerners with southern principles.

Q. *What is the correct term to designate the study of the derivation of family names?* A. M. O'C.

A. Patronomatology is the term.

Q. *What does Ultima Thule mean?* F. V. R.

A. "Thule" which means Norway was the most distant land known to the Romans. The adjective "ultima" means "utmost." United, the two words ultimately came to mean "the extreme end."

Q. *Where do we get the expression, kick the bucket, as applied to dying?* J. H.

A. The expression is said to have originated from the suicide of a man who stood while he adjusted a noose to his neck and then kicked the bucket from under himself and accomplished his purpose.

Q. *How did the expression, free lance, originate?* K. D. W.

A. In the later Middle Ages, bands of knights bearing lances, and men at arms went from state to state selling their services to any lord who was willing to pay for their aid. They were free from allegiance to any one country.

Q. *What is meant by Cheka, a term I frequently see in articles relating to Russia?* M. A. R.

A. It refers to the Secret Service of Soviet Russia. The name is formed from letters of the Russian words Chrezvychainaya Komissia.

Q. *What does mortician mean?* H. A.

A. Mortician is defined as funeral director. It is derived from the Latin mors meaning death.

Q. *I have often seen the expression, Forlorn Hope, associated with battles. What does it mean?* A. C.

A. Forlorn Hope is primarily a military detachment, commissioned or voluntary, for some especially dangerous service. The term thus has come to be employed to any enterprise having little prospect of success.

Q. How did the term, tabloid, originate? E. R. B.

A. It originated as a copyright trade-mark of an English business firm.

Q. What is a "rap" when we say that a thing is not worth a rap? D. T. P.

A. A rap was a counterfeit Irish coin of the time of George I which passed for a half-penny, though not really worth a fourth of that value.

Q. What exactly is meant by the term an Americanism? F. R. D.

A. It was first used by John Witherspoon, President of Princeton University in 1781, to designate any word or combination of words taken into the English language in the United States; or any word or combination of words which becoming archaic in England, continue in good usage in the United States.

Q. What is the origin of the saying, queer as Dick's hatband? B. A. T.

A. We have traced it as far back as 1785 when the expression was "as queer as Dick's hatband that went nine times round and wouldn't meet." The origin of the phrase was not known.

Q. What is the meaning of the term, mob psychology? E. T.

A. The term mob psychology refers to the study of the mental processes of a mob. A mob usually refers to a disorderly or riotous gathering.

Q. What is the significance of the expression, Parthian shot? C. G.

A. The Parthians were a warlike people who specialized in shooting arrows on horseback. Descending at top speed upon the enemy they delivered their darts and dashed on, turning to send arrows as they departed. A Parthian shot has come to mean a parting verbal dart aimed to be received but not returned.

Q. Why is a diploma often called a sheepskin? X. G. C.

A. The word sheepskin is used to describe a diploma because of its being engraved on parchment. Originally parchment was made of the skins of sheep.

Q. What is the origin of the term, dunce? H. A. S.

A. Dunce is a word introduced by the disciples of Thomas Aquinas in ridicule of the disciples of John Duns Scotus, who, although a man of subtle intellect, was held by the more ignorant or prejudiced at the time of the Reformation to be a man of invincible stupidity.

Q. What does oowah mean? D. J.

A. The onomatopoetic expression, oowah, has been coined in imitation of an automobile horn. It is used simply as an ejaculation.

Q. Why did the term, fin de siècle, drop out of popular use? A. M. P.

A. This French phrase became popular in 1889 and signified that the thing to which it was applied was thoroughly up to date. From the very nature of its meaning—end of the century—it lost its appropriateness when the twentieth century came in.

Q. What is meant by the term, Manassa Mauler, as applied to Jack Dempsey? F. C. F.

A. Jack Dempsey was born in Manassa, Colo.

Q. How did the expression, learn by heart, originate? M. M.

A. There are various explanations of the origin of the phrase to learn by heart. Centuries ago the heart was regarded as the seat of the emotions. That which one learned by heart was usually something which made an especial appeal. In other words one greatly wished to retain the memory of it.

CHAPTER 69

TIME

Q. *How many kinds of time are in use?* T. F.

A. Sixty-three kinds of standard time are being used in the world. The majority of the world's population uses one of the 24 scientific systems. India, New Zealand, and several South American countries use a half-hour separation, while some small countries use strictly local time.

Q. *Who first suggested daylight saving?* J. C.

A. It was suggested in France in April, 1784, by Benjamin Franklin in a contribution to the Journal de Paris.

Q. *I have a boy that was born at 12:30 A.M., while we were using daylight saving time. Should his birthday be considered June 2 or June 3?* H. H.

A. In reckoning a birthday, standard time is employed. His birthday would be June 2.

Q. *How is it possible to tell time with a rope?* A. H. H.

A. One of the earliest methods of telling time was that of burning a piece of rope in which knots had been made at intervals. When the rope burned to one knot it was one o'clock. When it reached the second knot it was two o'clock, etc.

Q. *What hours are known as the mischief hours?* S. U. C.

A. Some police departments designate certain hours of the 24 as the time when young boys and men are most apt to get into trouble. From seven to eleven in the evening are looked upon as mischief hours.

Q. *Are cities obliged to use the time of the standard time zones in which they are placed geographically?* A. G.

A. They are under no such obligation. In fact, so many cities deviate from such allocation, that the lines on a map marking the boundaries of the time zones are of little value.

Q. *Why is standard time measured from England?* P. N.

A. The custom of reckoning the prime meridian as that of Greenwich arose because Greenwich is the National Observatory of England. British ships naturally referred their longitude to this meridian and the system spread all over the world. The advantage of having a single system overcame local prejudices.

Q. *When does the fiscal year end?* H. T.

A. A fiscal year is the time between one annual time of settlement or balancing of accounts, and another. Unless otherwise specified the fiscal year regularly ends on December 31st. The United States Government's fiscal year ends June 30th.

Q. *What is meant by summer time?* W. C.

A. This is a popular name for daylight saving time.

463

Q. How long is a moment? F. W. S.

A. In modern times, no exact interpretation has been made of the length of time employed in a moment. In medieval reckoning, it was a 40th or 50th part of an hour. In the 17th and 18th centuries it was often regarded as equivalent to a second.

Q. How is official railway time reckoned in Europe? M. B. G.

A. On the continent, official railway time is based on a 24-hour day, which commences at midnight.

Q. Please give the equivalent of the Swiss watchmaker's ligne. D. L. S.

A. Ligne is the unit of measurement of the diameter of a lens. It is equivalent to ⅟₁₁th part of an inch.

Q. Can a person set a watch to the exact second by receiving the time over the radio? W. W. M.

A. The Bureau of Standards says that the lag in the signals would probably be less than 0.1 second.

Q. Who devised the system of dividing the hour into sixty minutes? A. T. R.

A. The sexagesimal system, counted by sixties, was the method employed by the Babylonians.

Q. What is the time zone called which is directly east of Eastern Standard Time? R. P. B.

A. It is Atlantic Intercolonial Time.

Q. What are the wee sma' hours? A. L. H.

A. The small hours are the early morning hours between midnight and dawn, such as 1, 2, 3, 4 A.M.

Q. Why was the year 47 B.C. called the year of confusion? E. B. R.

A. The year 47 B.C. was known as the year of confusion on account of the necessity of changing the dates of the months and the positions of the months in the year, to revise the ancient calendar and make it conform with the Julian calendar.

Q. Why is the twelfth month called December when decem means ten? A. L.

A. In the Roman calendar, December was the tenth month, and has retained its Latin name as have several others.

Q. When do morning and evening begin? S. I. P.

A. Morning commences at midnight and ends at noon. As used by the U. S. Weather Bureau, the word afternoon refers to the period, noon to 8 P.M., Eastern Standard Time. No definite time is assigned to evening. In common usage it is the earlier part of the night, before bedtime. In the Southern States it is the time between noon and dark.

Q. Are the stars or the sun used for telling time? E. S. W.

A. In astronomy there are three kinds of time—sidereal, apparent solar time, and mean solar time. The first is used for astronomical purposes exclusively; the last is the ordinary time of civil life. Sidereal time is the time defined by the rotation of the earth with respect to the stars and a sidereal day is the interval between the passage of the meridian across a star and its next succeeding passage across the same star. Solar time is defined by the rotation of the earth with respect to the sun. Since the motion of the earth is not uniform, solar time is not satisfactory for daily use and for this purpose mean solar time has been devised. The mean solar day has the average length of all the solar days in the year.

Q. Who has the authority to change the boundaries between the time zones in the United States? P. McM.

A. The Interstate Commerce Commission fixes the boundaries between the time zones. Often the boundaries are made to depart from the half-way position between the standard meridians in order to suit the convenience of the railroads or to meet the demands of the communities affected.

Q. Does the astronomical day begin at noon or midnight? F. E. Q.

A. Astronomers formerly began the day at noon, but recently it was decided advisable for the sake of uniformity to use the same day in astronomical work as is used in civil life, and commencing with 1925 all the national almanacs began the day at midnight.

Q. In discussing calendar reform, what date is being considered as a permanent one for Easter? P. A.

A. The tentative date suggested is the first Sunday after the second Saturday in April.

Q. What make of watch is used by railroad men? H. A. C.

A. There are 37 makes of watches authorized for the use of men employed on one large railroad alone. The specifications for railroad watches do not refer to the make but to the size of the watch, number of jewels, and degree of accuracy.

Q. How can Mohammedan dates be figured from Christian ones? C. F.

A. The Mohammedan era begins July 16, 622 A.D. In making computations, therefore, this sum should be subtracted from the commencement of the Christian year to find a Mohammedan date.

Q. Why does a watch gain time at night? F. F. P.

A. The lower temperature at night causes a watch to gain.

Q. How did the ancient Egyptians divide up the year? W. H. E.

A. The ancient Egyptians had a year determined by the changes of the season without reference to the changes of the moon, containing 365 days, divided into 12 months of 30 days each with 5 supplementary days at the end of the year.

Q. Who invented the banjo clock? F. C.

A. The banjo clock was invented in 1801 by Simon Willard and so-called because of its shape. It was an eight-day non-striking pendulum clock. Willard obtained a patent for it in 1802.

Q. When did we last have eight years between leap years and when will it happen again? O. C. K.

A. The last eight-year interval was between 1896 and 1904. This will occur the next time between 2096 and 2104. Years marking the close of centuries are not leap years unless divisible by 400. The year 2000 will be a leap year.

Q. Who invented the pendulum? T. W.

A. Huygens, a Dutchman born in 1629, was the first practical exponent of the pendulum, employing it in the mechanism of the clock. However, he was not the original discoverer of its properties. Leonardo da Vinci (1452–1520) left notes as to his study of the pendulum, and Galileo (1564–1642) continued these studies.

Q. As the Japanese reckon time, what year is this? R. E.

A. The year 1932 is the year 2592 of the Japanese era.

Q. Is there any watch or clock which keeps perfect time? J. P.

A. No clock or watch keeps absolutely perfect time. Astronomical clocks are very carefully regulated and errors determined regularly by observations of the stars. In distributing time by telegraph and radio, the distributing clock is adjusted to within a few hundredths of a second of the correct Eastern Standard Time.

Q. On what principle does the household electric clock work? L. H.

A. The master clock, which makes practicable the use of electricity for accurate time keeping, regulates the frequency of the alternating current so that there is a definite number of alternations of current per second. The electric household clock has neither springs nor escapements, but in their stead is a tiny synchronous motor, the speed of which is determined by the rapidity of the alternations of current. The motor is connected by a train of gears to the hands of the clock. In effect, the electric clock counts the alternations of current and translates them into seconds, minutes, and hours.

Q. *What is the diameter of the clock in the hall of the House of Representatives?* S. B.

A. It is about 18 inches.

Q. *When was daylight saving time used throughout the United States?* J. S. W.

A. Daylight saving time was operative throughout the entire United States in 1918 and 1919 by Congressional enactment. Subsequently it has been adopted as a state-wide measure by state legislation in a few states, but mostly by local ordinance in the various cities.

Q. *Is it true that the weather can make the spring in a watch break?* H. B.

A. Temperature changes sometimes cause mainsprings in watches to break, through expansion and contraction. There is generally a flaw or weak spot indicated by such a break.

Q. *Please explain why, at the time of the year when the days are lengthening, they take on more of their length in the afternoon than in the morning.* S. J.

A. Forenoon and afternoon are always equal, or very nearly so, by the sun; they are, at times, far from being so, by the clock. The reason for this is that clocks give, not the actual solar time, but the mean or average solar time. Noon by the sun is when the sun is due south; that is to say, noon by the sun is midway or very nearly midway between sunrise and sunset. Noon by

the clock may occur as much as one-quarter hour earlier or later than noon by the sun, the difference being known as the Equation of Time. It so happens that, when the days begin to lengthen in December, noon by the clock is growing relatively earlier at a rapid rate; in other words, is moving toward the time of sunrise and away from the time of sunset; the tendency being to shorten the forenoon and to lengthen the afternoon.

Q. *Are watches adjusted for different positions?* H. A. S.

A. The Bureau of Standards says that the better grade of watches are usually adjusted for three or five positions, while a few are adjusted to two, four, or six positions. The five positions for which adjustments are made are with the watch vertical and the stem or pendant up, with the pendant 90° to the right and 90° to the left of the first position, and with the watch horizontal with dial up and with dial down.

Q. *What is the air played by the chimes of the Westminster clock?* I. M.

A. The chimes of the Westminster clock are the same as the Cambridge chimes, which are founded on a phrase in the opening symphony of Handel's air, "I know that my redeemer liveth" and arranged by Dr. Crotch for the clock of Great Saint Mary's, Cambridge.

Q. *When were alarm clocks invented?* C. R.

A. It is not definitely known when the first alarm clock was made. Alarm attachments are as old as the mechanical clock itself. They were probably adopted for use of the priesthood. According to one authority, the invention is attributed to the Monk Gerbert, as early as 996.

Q. *What is the Canton water clock?* C. K.

A. The water float or clepsydra in Canton dates back some 500 years and has been destroyed and rebuilt many times. It is composed of three copper vessels placed one above the other on step-like platforms. In the bottom vessel is a float with an indicator scale passing through it, which, as the water fills the lower vessel, rises and shows the time.

Q. How accurate must a railroad man's watch be? H. D. T.

A. The requirements of railroads which maintain time inspection are that watches must run within 30 seconds variation a week.

Q. In setting a watch, should the hands be turned forward? M. C.

A. It makes no difference which way they are turned. Turn them in the direction in which the correct time is the nearer.

Q. Why are jewels used in watch movements? C. W.

A. They are there to make the bearings wear-proof. Watches of seventeen or more jewels are considered high grade.

Q. Why is the number four on clocks made IIII instead of IV. G. M. B.

A. It is not definitely known when the practise of using IIII instead of IV on the dials of clocks and watches arose, nor the reason for it. There is a story that a famous clockmaker used the numeral IV. When the clock was shown to the King, however, he insisted upon the change to IIII. This same story has been told in connection with various monarchs. Prof. Milham says that one reason for the change may be symmetry. On the other side of the dial the number VIII is the heaviest number, consisting of four heavy strokes and one light one. It would destroy the symmetrical appearance of the dial to have IV with only two heavy strokes on the other side.

Q. How long have wrist watches been worn? A. F.

A. The origin of wrist watches is uncertain. They are found in antique collections dating as far back as the middle of the 17th century. Originally they were worn by the nobility of Europe.

Q. How did the 24-hour day originate? H. A. C.

A. It is not definitely known just how the day happened to be divided into 24 hours. At the time of the Homeric poems, the day was divided into three parts, the first beginning with sunrise and comprising that part during which the light increased; the second, midday, during which the sun was thought to stand still; and the third period, during which the atmospheric warmth increased. These divisions were later subdivided either by Anaximander or Anaximines, who is said to have made the Greeks acquainted with the use of the Babylonian chronometer or sundial by means of which the natural day was divided into 12 equal spaces. The earliest sundial of which we have knowledge was that of the Chaldean astronomer Berossus, who lived about 300 B.C. Its arc was divided into 12 equal intervals of time. At Babylon the period from sunrise to sunset and also the period of darkness were each divided into 12 hours. According to this arrangement the day hour was in the summer longer than the night hour and in the winter shorter. The Greeks improved upon this system by dividing the whole period into 12 equal hours.

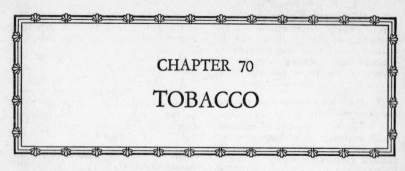

CHAPTER 70

TOBACCO

Q. *How many brands of cigars are there in this country?* C. I. R.

A. The Tobacco Leaf Magazine says that there are about 10,000 brands of cigars in this country.

Q. *How does cigar consumption compare with cigarette use?* K. J.

A. There are about twenty cigarettes smoked to every cigar.

Q. *Has cigarette smoking among children increased or decreased in the past few years?* L. H.

A. It has been estimated that the age for forming the cigarette habit has fallen in the last ten years from 16 to 11 years, and that every year 985,000 child-smokers are added to the cigarette addicts.

Q. *How large a cigar has been made?* C. T.

A. "The Retail Tobaccoist" says that one of the features of the recent exposition held at Seville, Spain, was a cigar made in Cuba by Senor Fonseca which took four and a half months to complete. The cigar is valued at $2,500. It is eight and a half feet long, 50 inches in circumference, and weighs 121 pounds. Ninety-six pounds of tobacco were required for the filler and 25 pounds for wrapper.

Q. *What States have a tax on cigarettes?* R. L. K.

A. These 13 States taxed cigarettes in 1932: Alabama, Arkansas, Georgia, Iowa, Kansas, Mississippi, North Dakota, Ohio, South Carolina, South Dakota, Tennessee, Texas, and Utah.

Q. *When cigarette smoke is inhaled, does it go no further than the larynx or does it enter the lungs?* R. C. O.

A. The Public Health Service says that it depends upon the depth of inhalation. Some persons when they smoke inhale so deeply that the smoke does enter the lungs; others inhale just sufficiently to draw the smoke into the lower part of the larynx.

Q. *Is the smoking of cigars on the decline in the United States?* M. M.

A. Cigar smoking in the United States is declining, but slowly. The consumption in 1914 was 7,174,191,-944; in 1931 it was 6,047,506,432. Meanwhile there has been a considerable increase in population.

Q. *Did the Indians raise tobacco for smoking purposes?* M. C.

A. Upon the arrival of the first Europeans in North America, the natives were observed to make offerings of some plant, generally believed to be tobacco. It was used in the treatment of disease and also offered in propitiation of angry waters, to allay destructive winds, and to protect the traveler. Tobacco was cultivated and smoked in the tribes only by men. To the Indian, the tobacco plant had a sacred character. It was almost invariably used on solemn occasions.

Q. *Who established the first cigar factory in the United States?* E. D. R.

A. The first one was established at Key West, Florida, in 1831, by William H. Wall.

Q. *Where are the largest tobacco centers in the United States?* C. T. C.

A. The three largest tobacco centers in the United States are: Lexington, Ky., which handles approximately 99,000,000 pounds a year; Wilson, N. C., with 77,790,000 pounds; and Greenville, S. C., with 62,365,000 pounds. Of these Lexington is primarily a Burley tobacco market, while the other two are predominantly flue-cured tobacco markets.

Q. *What part of the world's tobacco crop is raised in the United States?* R. H.

A. In 1931, the world crop of tobacco was 1,893,531,000 pounds. Of this, 1,610,098,000 pounds were raised in the United States.

Q. *Did pipes come into use after tobacco was discovered?* E. B.

A. Pipes were used for smoking herbs of various sorts long before tobacco came into use. Specimens of pipes have been discovered in very ancient sites in Europe.

Q. *Why are some cigars called stogies?* H. S.

A. The story runs that the drivers of the Conestoga wagons, which crossed the country, were addicted to the smoking of strong cigars. Often they rolled tobacco leaves into crude cigars. These became known as Conestoga cigars and finally the name, stogy, was evolved.

Q. *Are people smoking fewer cigars and cigarettes?* P. R.

A. In April, 1932, the number of cigars sold was less by 110,028,839 than in April, 1931. Cigarette consumption fell off 1,908,330,926 in the same twelve months. Every kind of tobacco, including snuff, showed a heavy decline for the first time in many years.

Q. *How many cigars does Cuba export?* O. A. B.

A. Less than 50,000,000 were exported in 1931. This is only one-sixth of the number exported about 20 years ago.

Q. *What kind of tobacco is grown in western Florida?* K. C.

A. The tobacco-growing section of western Florida produces profitably a shade leaf grown from Cuban and Sumatran seed which is in great demand in cigar manufacturing.

Q. *Where does Perique tobacco come from?* J. L. B.

A. It is grown in Saint James Parish, Louisiana.

Q. *Is tobacco raised in Australia of as good quality as American tobacco?* H. K. M.

A. The Office of Tobacco Investigations says that the types of tobacco being raised in Australia for cigarette production are not of a quality equal to that of the cigarette tobacco raised in this country. Attempts are at present being made by the Commonwealth government to improve the Australian tobacco situation.

Q. *How many factories in the United States make tobacco pipes?* H. W. H.

A. There are 22 establishments manufacturing an output valued at more than $5,000,000.

Q. *Where are most of the fine meerschaum pipes made?* M. L. P.

A. Meerschaum is obtained in various places, but the best quality comes from Asia Minor. All the pits are exhausted but 250, which are worked by some 900 miners who live there. The mineral is mined in blocks. It is then cleaned, the operation consisting of scraping and cutting the blocks with a sharp instrument or knife. The blocks are then classed as to size and quality. It is then sent to the pipe manufacturers. Most of it is sent to Vienna.

Q. *How should a meerschaum pipe be smoked?* T. R.

A. Ordinarily, the pipe is boiled for coloring in a preparation of wax, which is absorbed, and a thin coating of wax is held on the surface of the pipe, and made to take a high polish. Under the wax is retained the oil of tobacco, which is absorbed by the pipe, and its hue grows darker in proportion to the tobacco used. A meerschaum pipe at first should be smoked very slowly, and before a second bowlful is lighted the pipe should cool off. A new pipe should never be smoked outdoors in extremely cold weather.

Q. *Who was called the pipe man of the United States?* N. T.

A. Edward Hen, who before 1860, was almost the only importer of note of the more expensive pipes, was thus known. William Demuth began the making of pipes in this country in 1861.

Q. *Where is the largest collection of smoking pipes?* M. E. G.

A. Probably the American Museum of Natural History, New York City, N. Y., has the largest pipe collection.

Q. *Why will lighted cigarettes continue to burn on some ash trays and die out on others?* F. McC.

A. The Bureau of Standards says whether cigarettes are extinguished or not when left on ash receivers depends primarily on the condition of thermal contact between the cigarette and the receiver. Also the thermal conductivity and mass of the receiver affect the amount of heat dissipated. The amount of heat conducted away from the cigarette determines whether or not it is extinguished. For example, a cigarette laid on a metal receiver and touching the receiver all along the length would be more likely to be extinguished than one which only touched the receiver for a short distance. Also a cigarette in the same position of contact on a metal receiver would be more likely to be extinguished than one on either a glass or china receiver.

Q. *I notice records of drinking tobacco. How was tobacco prepared as a drink?* D. R.

A. What is now called smoking was at an early period termed drinking tobacco; in fact the term was constantly in use until the middle of the 17th century. It probably originated in the custom of inhaling smoke and allowing it to escape through the nose.

Q. *What is cigarette paper made of?* A. B. S.

A. It is made of linen with a calcium compound.

Q. *Do cigarette manufacturers make their own cigarette cartons?* W. K.

A. They purchase from lithographers the flat cardboards already printed. The flats are shaped into cartons by machinery in the factories.

Q. *What is the name of the part of the cigar cut or bitten off before smoking?* W. L. S.

A. It is called the tip. This part is put on as a protection to the filler tobacco, but has to be removed in order for the cigar to draw.

Q. *Where is tobacco grown in Canada?* C. C. T.

A. It is grown in Quebec and Ontario.

Q. *Who first smoked tobacco in England?* T. G.

A. Ralph Lane, the first governor of Virginia, and Sir Francis Drake brought to the notice of Sir Walter Raleigh the habit of smoking tobacco. Lane is credited with having been the first English smoker, and through the influence and example of the illustrious Raleigh "who tooke a pipe of tobacco a little before he went to the scaffolde" the habit became rooted among Elizabethan courtiers. During the 17th century the indulgence in tobacco spread with marvelous rapidity through all nations.

Q. What was the government revenue from tobacco last year? J. J. J.

A. The internal revenue from tobacco for the fiscal year 1931 was $444,276,000.

Q. What per cent of the tax paid on tobacco goes to the states? M. B.

A. The tax is a federal one and no part goes to the states.

Q. Why is tobacco sold in France in so few places? G. R.

A. Tobacco is a government monopoly and is sold in certain licensed cafés. Such licenses are allotted to ex-service men only. They, however, may sell them.

Q. Does Canada grow her own tobacco? G. M.

A. In 1930, Canada produced 36,716,917 pounds of tobacco. Of this, she exported 5,355,869 pounds. During 1930, she imported 17,435,153 pounds, 90 per cent of which came from the United States.

Q. How many pounds of tobacco does it take to make 1000 cigarettes? A. H.

A. About 2.85 pounds.

Q. What is a cheroot? W. K.

A. A kind of cigar, truncated at both ends, originally made in south India and Manila.

Q. What kinds of tobacco are used in the cigarettes manufactured in this country? T. C. C.

A. There are four types of cigarette tobacco used in American cigarettes. They are Flue-cured, grown in Georgia, North Carolina, South Carolina, and southern Virginia; Burley, grown in Kentucky; Maryland, grown in Maryland; Turkish, grown in Greece, Bulgaria, and Tur-

key, which is imported. Of these types, about 700,000,000 pounds of the first are grown annually, 300,-000,000 pounds of the second (the first two together comprising 1,000,-000,000 pounds), 25,000,000 pounds of Maryland, and 30,000,000 pounds of Turkish imported.

Q. Which will keep better, light cigars or dark cigars? M. H.

A. Light cigars keep their flavor for about six years. Dark cigars keep their natural characteristics for about ten years.

Q. How many cigarettes were consumed in the United States last year? M. T.

A. In 1931, the consumption was 119,672,274,539 cigarettes.

Q. Why can't tobacco be burned and used as fertilizer? B. T. F.

A. The Department of Agriculture says that tobacco ash contains some potash, but the tobacco leaves are so valuable that they would never be burned to produce ash in sufficient quantities to be used commercially as a fertilizer. Stems and undesirable tobacco are often used for the manufacture of fertilizer and are excellent as such.

Q. How many cigars and cigarettes may a person take into Canada, duty free? M. M.

A. Forty cigars or less and 100 cigarettes or less in open package may be taken in for personal use.

Q. How much does a hogshead of tobacco weigh? J. E. B.

A. It usually weighs 1200 pounds for dark-colored tobacco and 1000 pounds for light tobacco.

Q. How can the freshness of pipe smoking tobacco be retained? A. A.

A. Humidors have been designed for this special purpose.

Q. What is the loco weed that Mexicans smoke? S. M.

A. The Mariguana Plant is a species of plant which grows in

Mexico and is prepared as the tobacco in the United States, wrapped, and smoked. It is extremely intoxicating. Its manufacture, sale, or transportation is forbidden and punishable by law.

Q. Are some of our commercial cigarettes rolled by hand? J. O. D.

A. Havana cigarettes are made from the small broken pieces of leaf from the cigar-makers' benches. These cigarettes are rolled by hand. However, foreign cigarettes have almost entirely been supplanted by domestic brands. All the cigarettes made in this country are wrapped by machinery. Some recently devised machines can turn out over 50,000 cigarettes per hour.

Q. How much has the consumption of cigarettes increased in the United States during the present century? W. F. S.

A. In 1901, the consumption was 3,000,000,000. In 1915, it had increased to almost 16,000,000,000. In 1931 the consumption had reached the enormous total of 119,672,274,539.

Q. Are cigarettes doped? H. M.

A. Carl Werner says, "Owing to the prevalence of false notions about so-called doping of cigarettes, it might be well for me to reiterate that in the better grades, there is absolutely no foreign substance of any kind applied to or contained in the tobacco; and that even in the cheaper grades, the tobacco is treated with nothing except glycerine, which is absolutely harmless. And as to the paper used for wrapping the tobacco, it contains no deleterious substance of any kind and is so thin and fragile that the ash, after the paper has been consumed is almost a negligible quantity."

Q. Who took the tobacco plant to Europe? J. A. H.

A. The tobacco plant was taken to Europe in 1558 by Francisco Fernandes who had been sent by Philip the 2nd, of Spain, to investigate the products of Mexico. Jean Nicot, the French Ambassador to Portugal, sent seeds of the plant to the Queen. The services rendered by Nicot in spreading a knowledge of the herb have been commemorated in the scientific name of the genus Nicotiana. While the plant came to Europe through Spain, its use for smoking purposes spread to the Continent from England. Ralph Lane, first Governor of Virginia, and Sir Francis Drake brought it to the notice of Sir Walter Raleigh, who first used it as smoking tobacco, introducing it into England.

Q. What portion of a cigarette is discarded and wasted? S. H.

A. Most cigarette smokers throw away cigarettes when they are about 1¼ inch long.

Q. Why does the under-side of a cigar or cigarette burn faster than the upper when put on the edge of a table? F. M. P.

A. When a cigar or cigarette is placed on a table with the lighted end projecting over, the glow in the under-side progresses a little more rapidly than that above apparently because of the air convection current created around the burning part, which would be more active on the lower portion than on the upper portion. The burning of cigars and cigarettes can be accelerated by applying a gentle breeze to the burning end.

Q. What is meant by wrapper tobacco and filler tobacco? J. S. C.

A. The term wrapper tobacco means that quality of leaf tobacco which has the requisite color, texture, and burn, and is of sufficient size for cigar wrappers, and the term filler tobacco means all other leaf tobacco.

Q. Who was the old Dutchman who had tobacco and pipes buried with him? W. O. H.

A. Mynheer Van Klaes had smoking materials buried with him. It is stated that "At his feet were placed a bladder of the finest Dutch goldenleaf and a packet of caporel; by his sides were laid his china-bowl pipe and a box of matches, and steel, flint, and tinder."

Q. *What constituents are shown by a chemical analysis of tobacco?* H. B. McK.

A. Tobacco leaves, when submitted to chemical analysis, yield nicotine which is its most characteristic constituent, albumin, a gluten-like substance, gum, resin, malic, and citric acids, and a large amount of inorganic constituents, 100 parts of the dry leaf yielding from about 19 to 27 per cent of ash, in which potash, lime, and silica preponderate.

Q. *Can you tell me whether cigarettes were used by Cubans, Mexicans, or other Latin-American people, either men or women, as far back as 1855?* H. H.

A. The Mexican News Bureau says that the use of cigarettes by all Latin-American people, either men or women, dates much farther back than 1855. In fact, it dates back to time immemorial. The oja, a corn-husk cigarette, tobacco ground coarsely and wrapped in the soft inner husk of corn, is used by both men and women and always has been. It is not uncommon to see them smoked by women of the upper class, but not in public.

Q. *For whom or what were Piedmont cigarettes named?* T. A. C.

A. They were named for the Piedmont section of Virginia and North Carolina in the fertile eastern foothills of the Appalachian Mountains, and comprising the old belt where "bright" Virginia tobacco was first known.

Q. *In what States are the manufacture and sale of cigarettes prohibited?* H. H.

A. The Anti-Cigarette Alliance says that at present there are no States which prohibit the manufacture and sale of cigarettes. All States and the District of Columbia prohibit the sale and giving of cigarettes to boys and girls, the ages varying. Eighteen years is the average, however.

Q. *Is tobacco a government monopoly in Japan?* D. M. V.

A. It is, and tobacco imported carries a duty of 355 per cent.

Q. *Is it possible for cigars to be sorted into colors by machinery?* D. N. E.

A. There is a machine which sorts cigars into as many as 30 shades. It consists of a finger which picks up each cigar, a photo-electric eye which measures the color, an amplifying panel, a switching ammeter, and a set of 30 compartments into which the cigars are passed.

Q. *When the new world was discovered, did the Indian group throughout the two continents grow and use tobacco?* C. G.

A. Tobacco was found by European conquerors of the Americas, being used in the West Indies, Central America, and northern parts of South America. It could not be said that all the American Indian tribes knew of its use.

Q. *Is the use of chewing tobacco increasing?* F. D. E.

A. It is not. It has ceased to be an important factor in the tobacco industry. Pipe smoking, too, is declining in popularity.

Q. *What cigarette is the mildest?* M. F. B.

A. Denicotinized cigarettes are the mildest, that is, they contain the least nicotine. Ordinarily manufacturers do not test their cigarettes for nicotine content, so they are not classified as to mildness. Cigarette tobacco is naturally a mild kind of leaf tobacco.

Q. *What is the value of the Cuban tobacco crop?* B. A.

A. It is worth from forty to fifty million dollars yearly.

CHAPTER 71

TRANSPORTATION AND COMMUNICATION

Q. *How many railroad companies are there in the United States?* L. L. T.

A. There were 377 in 1932.

Q. *Do police patrols and fire engines take precedence over mail wagons?* M. E.

A. The police headquarters of the District of Columbia says that at all times fire engines, police patrols, and ambulances have the right of way in traffic; mail wagons, etc., must comply with local traffic regulations. These rules may vary in different municipalities, although in general they hold true.

Q. *In what country do the people use the telephone the most?* R. S.

A. In proportion to the number of telephones, Canadians rank first. They average 250.5 calls per capita annually. The United States has the most telephones, Germany is second, Great Britain and northern Ireland third, and Canada fourth.

Q. *How many telephones are there in the world?* R. B.

A. The total number of telephones in the world is approximately 35,700,000, of which more than 20,-000,000 are in the United States.

Q. *What is the record for speed in laying a railroad track?* C. W.

A. It is said that the track-laying record, made April 29, 1869, in the construction of the Central Pacific—10 miles and 200 feet of track, laid between 7 A.M. and 7 P.M., with a noon rest of one hour—has never been equalled.

Q. *Where was the first union railway station in this country?* L. K.

A. In Indianapolis.

Q. *Kindly advise me what a "P. B. X. operator" is.* A. B.

A. A P. B. X. operator is an operator on a private board exchange such as used in the majority of up-to-date apartment houses, hotels, and offices.

Q. *How much coal does a railroad engine carry?* G. F. C.

A. Modern locomotives have a capacity of from 16 to 30 tons of coal.

Q. *What country was first connected with the United States by transatlantic telephone?* S. F.

A. Great Britain was the first country across the Atlantic to establish telephone communication. Installation in Cuba, a short distance away, preceded the overseas connection.

Q. *How does the modern locomotive compare in size with the first ones made?* R. B.

A. The giant Mallet type is about three times as long and 20 times as powerful as the early type.

Q. *Is there any record of the largest piece of freight ever carried?* B. D. M.

A. It is said that the largest piece of freight ever shipped over a railroad was a tower used in the manufacture of gasoline. This was delivered at Los Angeles from Boston. It is 85 feet high, weighs nearly 80 tons, and was carried on three flat cars.

Q. *Does the United States own the Panama Canal Zone?* M. R.

A. The Panama Canal Zone is not owned by the United States, but it has a perpetual right of occupation, use, and control, for which privilege it pays Panama the sum of $250,000 annually as long as occupancy continues.

Q. *Which State has the most railroad track?* J. P. T.

A. In 1931 Texas operated approximately 17,178 miles of railroad. Texas has greater railroad mileage than any other state. Statistics for the next three States are as follows: Illinois—13,625 miles; Pennsylvania —11,684 miles; and Iowa—10,016 miles.

Q. *Does the Government keep a private railroad car for the use of the President?* D. T. C.

A. When the President of the United States travels he uses the railroad's private car if he is going a short enough distance only to use one railroad. However, if he plans a trip which necessitates the use of more than one railroad, a private car is supplied by the Pullman Company. No special car is reserved for the President of the United States.

Q. *Is there a decrease in number of telephone calls during an electrical storm?* R. E. H.

A. Telephone exchange business may drop off from two to three per cent during an electrical storm. Telephone equipment is so perfected now that very few people hesitate to use the phone during a storm.

Q. *What was the name of the first locomotive made in America?* F. M.

A. The first locomotive built was The Best Friend of Charleston. The second was West Point. The first to "turn a wheel" on American soil was the Stourbridge Lion.

Q. *Is it true that a person in an airplane can see a submarine when it is submerged?* H. P.

A. If the sea is calm and the air is perfectly clear, it is possible for an airplane to see a submarine which is submerged 50 or 60 feet. Only under these favorable circumstances is this possible. Traveling depths of submarines vary. The newer type submarine submerges about 230 feet.

Q. *How much did the first Pullman car cost?* I. M.

A. The first Pullman car was built by George M. Pullman in 1865 at a cost of $20,000. This was hurriedly completed so that it might form a part of the train that bore the body of Abraham Lincoln from Washington, D. C., to Chicago, Illinois, and thence to Springfield, Illinois.

Q. *Are Canadian railways government owned?* J. M.

A. Almost 90 per cent of the Canadian railway mileage is under the control of two systems, the Canadian National (20,747 miles) and the Canadian Pacific (13,667 miles). The Canadian National Railway is government owned. The Canadian Pacific owns and controls hotels, a telegraph system, 84 steamships, and the Canadian Pacific Express Company.

Q. *What proportion of the people in the United States lives on surfaced highways?* D. B.

A. American Highways says that 75 per cent of the population lives on surfaced highways.

Q. *What was the first highway in the United States?* L. O. C.

A. The first important road in the United States, says the Highway Education Board, was the old York Road between New York and Philadelphia, established by the colonies in 1711. The first company incorporated to build and operate a toll road was the Philadelphia and Lancaster Turnpike Company. It was incorporated in Pennsylvania in 1792 and had a road from Philadelphia to Lancaster, a distance of 62 miles. This road was later taken over by the State.

Q. *How many puffs does a locomotive give out in a minute?* J. B.

A. For every revolution of its driving wheel a locomotive gives forth four separate puffs. These are made by the rapid sending out of waste steam from the smokestack. A locomotive with a wheel of average size going 50 miles an hour gives out about 800 puffs a minute. When there are more than 18 per second, the human ear can no longer distinguish them.

Q. *Can anyone who has the resources build a railroad in the United States?* M. W.

A. Not if it is to operate in interstate commerce. The promoters of a railroad must obtain from the Interstate Commerce Commission a certificate of convenience and public necessity before they may sell stock or begin construction. The Commission holds hearings to determine whether a demand for a railroad exists through the territory in which it is planned to build and whether the prospects are favorable for profitable freight loadings.

Q. *When did the horse car disappear from the streets of New York City?* S. P. E.

A. The last horse car was taken off the streets of New York City August 1, 1917. This line was the Madison Street and Avenue Car.

Q. *Who invented the railroad ticket?* A. L. H.

A. In 1836, Thomas Edmondson of Lancaster, England, was stationmaster and booking clerk at the little station of Milton, on the then Newcastle and Carlisle Railway. Feeling the need for a systematic check on the issuance of tickets, he first wrote with pen and ink upon pieces of cardboard the names of the issuing and collecting stations, the number of the ticket, and fare for the journey. He next evolved a case in which the various descriptions of tickets could be safely kept and at the same time conveniently issued. This resulted in the Edmondson ticket case, which remained in use, without improvement, until the invention of an American ticket case in 1874.

Q. *How much of New York's subway system is actually underground?* H. B.

A. New York City has 619 miles of subways of which 313 miles are actual subways.

Q. *What ship first carried the American flag around the world?* N. O.

A. The Columbia, under the command of Capt. Robert Gray, started on this trip in 1787.

Q. *What was the first railroad to do away with the system of indiscriminate issuance of free passes?* S. D.

A. The Pennsylvania is believed to have been the first. Its directors took action to discontinue the issue of passes and free tickets of all kinds on December 13, 1905, the order taking effect on January 1 following.

Q. *What were the lowest steamship passenger rates we have ever had in transatlantic travel?* J. H.

A. A price war in 1904 was carried to a point where a third class passage cost only $10. This is believed to have been the low record.

Q. *What is the longest telephone hook-up now in use?* H. D.

A. It is from San Francisco by way of New York to Australia, more than half-way around the world.

Q. *How many people are employed on the public roads in the United States?* R. A. H.

A. About 300,000.

Q. *What vessel holds the record for crossing the Pacific from Vancouver to Yokohama?* S. A.

A. The Canadian Pacific liner, Empress of Japan, holds the record of 6 days, 19 hours, 43 minutes elapsed time, which lowers the previous record by about 20 hours.

Q. *Why are locomotives now built with so many wheels?* C. H. W.

A. Many wheels are used to reduce the weight at any one point on the rails.

Q. *How many people are employed in the railroad industry?* G. L.

A. The average number of employees in the railroad industry during 1931 was 1,260,758. There are 148 divisions of labor within the railroad industry.

Q. *When was the first elevated street railway built in New York?* G. V. E.

A. The first elevated in New York was a single track line from Battery Place to 30th Street, opened to travel July 2, 1867.

Q. *How many miles of surfaced roads has the United States?* R. A. H.

A. The total highway mileage in the United States in 1932 was 3,009,066. Of this total, 730,000 miles of highway were surfaced.

Q. *What country leads in the electrification of its railroads?* C. A. M.

A. The United States has a slight lead. It has electrified 1870 miles prior to 1933. Switzerland has electrified 1542 miles; France 1048 miles; Italy 1013 miles; and Germany 968 miles.

Q. *Who invented the airbrake?* G. H. D.

A. The airbrake was invented by George Westinghouse, Jr., in 1869. This was known as the straight airbrake. Objections to this led him to invent in 1873 the automatic airbrake. In 1887 he invented the quick action triple valve brake, and in 1897 he placed on the market the high speed brake.

Q. *What ships are included in our merchant marine?* R. T.

A. The term merchant marine is a comprehensive one including all merchant ships sailing under the American flag.

Q. *How many ships can the Panama Canal accommodate?* L. H.

A. At the present time the capacity of the Panama Canal the year round is approximately 48 ships of usual size per day or about 17,000 a year.

Q. *How much did it cost to build the Holland Tunnel between New York and New Jersey?* F. P.

A. It cost $50,000,000.

Q. *What proportion of the railroad mileage has been built in the past forty years?* D. T.

A. Almost one-third of the total has been built since 1892.

Q. *Is there a vehicular tunnel between Canada and the United States?* C. L.

A. The first international vehicular tunnel is the Detroit-Windsor Tunnel.

Q. *How much money is paid in taxes by the railroads of this country?* A. W. H.

A. The taxes paid by the railways of the United States in 1931 totaled $303,560,471.

Q. *How many electric railway cars are there in the United States?* A. N. L.

A. About 94,000, according to figures for 1931.

Q. *Do railroads own or lease Pullman cars?* L. E. D.

A. The Pullman Car Company rents or leases to individual railroads by an agreement or contract with that particular railroad. The respective rights and obligations of the

Pullman Company and the railroads over whose lines its cars operate are definitely fixed by contract. The Pullman Company has 192 contracts with as many different railways.

Q. *How many dry docks in the United States will accommodate the Leviathan? N. H. T.*

A. There are only two dry docks in the United States large enough to accommodate the Leviathan, the dock at the Boston Navy Yard and the dock at the Norfolk Navy Yard. However, the Norfolk Navy Yard is not yet accessible to the Leviathan, because the channel which approaches it needs further dredging in order to allow passage of the Leviathan.

Q. *Please give a list of the world's longest railway tunnels. R. K.*

A. The longest is the Simplon, Switzerland-Italy, 12.26 miles; next comes the St. Gothard, Switzerland-Italy, 9.32 miles; then the Loetschberg, Switzerland, 9 miles; Mont Cenis, Italy-France, 7.98; Arlberg, Austria, 6.23; Moffet, United States, 6.09; Ricken, Switzerland, 5.35; Tauern, Austria, 5.31; Ronco, Italy, 5.16; Tende, Italy, 5.03; Transandine, Chile-Argentina, 5; Connaught, Canada, 5.

Q. *What are the names of the Paris subways? E. O'B.*

A. The Paris subways are the Metro and the Nord-Sud.

Q. *When was railroad iron first rolled in America? T. L.*

A. In 1841, G. W. Scranton of Oxford, N. J., attracted by the rich deposits of iron and coal in the Luzerne Valley, Pennsylvania, bought a tract of land there and established iron works. He was later joined there by S. T. Scranton. W. E. Dodge, a director in the Erie Railroad Company who knew the Scrantons, conceived the idea of having the Scrantons make rails for the Erie Railroad. The company was having difficulties in getting rails from England and the cost was excessive. A contract was made with the Scrantons to furnish 12,000 tons of rails at $46 a ton, which was about half the cost of the English rails. Dodge and others advanced the money to purchase the necessary machinery and the rails were ready for delivery in the spring of 1847.

Q. *Which Indian trail was the longest? H. L. B.*

A. The War Trail of the Six Nations from Chautauqua, New York, to Georgia, is the longest trail known.

Q. *Please give some information regarding stretches of railway without a curve. W. C. P.*

A. Two of the longest stretches of railroad without a curve are: the 72-mile stretch on the Rock Island line from Guymon, Oklahoma, to Dalhart, Texas; at Dalhart there is a quarter degree curve and then it goes on for 25 miles further without a curve. The Seaboard Airline in Florida has 8 curves in 200 miles. It is said that on the Argentine-Pacific Railway to the foot of the Andes, there is a stretch of 200 miles without a curve or a cutting or an embankment deeper than 3 feet. On the Australian Trans-Continental Railway crossing the Nullarbor Plain, there is a straight-away of 300 miles.

Q. *What was done with the dirt taken out when the Panama Canal was dug? K. M.*

A. It was used to fill in swamps and for the Gatun Dam, also for building a causeway at the Pacific end. The dirt was carried to the places desired by 300 dump trains.

Q. *Did any of the early railway trains make speed records? E. E. F.*

A. As early as 1845, a record was made in England of 45 miles in 52 minutes. At one time the train was proceeding at the rate of one mile in 48 seconds or "at the astonishing velocity of 75 miles an hour." In the same year the American Railroad Journal said, "The other day on the London and Birmingham, and on the Great Northwestern Railway, a rate of travel at the speed of 65 miles an hour was accomplished. The express trains on these lines run at the rate of nearly 50 miles an hour, stoppage included." During 1848 the Antelope Engines on the Baltimore and Ohio Railroad made a speed of 60 miles an hour.

Q. *Why is a trackless trolley car system considered better than the old style? T. R.*

A. Three advantages are claimed for the trackless trolley. First, construction costs are only about a tenth of that of a track system; second, the cost of operation is less than that of the standard car or gasoline bus; and, third, the trackless trolley can pull up to the curb for passengers and can go around other traffic.

Q. *When was the first life-boat built and used? R. F. B.*

A. The first life boat is believed to have been one built by Lionel Lukin in England in 1786.

Q. *Which does the most damage to modern highways, heat and cold, or traffic? R. E. W.*

A. Engineers say that traffic does most of the damage to roads.

Q. *When was the first railroad tunnel built? L. T. C.*

A. The first railroad tunnel is the Woodhead Tunnel, which was begun in the spring of 1839. The first train passed through December 2, 1845. This was over what was known as the Manchester, Sheffield, and Lincolnshire Railway, now the Great Central Division of the London and Northeastern Railway.

Q. *What became of the Mayflower, the former presidential yacht? E. H.*

A. After being reduced to a hull by fire it was sold and is now at Wilmington, N. C. It will be reconditioned and preserved as a national relic. The vessel is being planned to exemplify the characteristics of early twentieth century design. When completed, it will visit eastern seaports.

Q. *When did the waters of the two oceans flow together for the first time through the Panama Canal? M. L. W.*

A. Passage was blasted through the last slide at Cucaracha and a line of water was established across the Isthmus of Panama, October 12, 1913.

Q. *What kind of engines do submarines use? C. B.*

A. Submarines use Diesel engines while on the surface, and electric engines, when submerged.

Q. *Has a man been shot out of a submarine tube and reached the surface of the sea alive? W. H.*

A. The Navy Department says that in the Philippines two Navy men freed themselves from a submarine by the means of torpedo tubes and reached the surface alive. However, the greatest depth at which this experiment was tried was forty feet and the water was warm.

Q. *Do ships make the transit of the Panama Canal during the night? M. C.*

A. Ships starting the trip through the Canal during the daylight hours are permitted to finish after dark if they cannot do so before night falls, but ships arriving at night are required to await daylight to start through.

Q. *How low a temperature is maintained in air-conditioned railway cars? C. C. R.*

A. While it is possible to obtain a temperature of 70 degrees, 75 degrees is believed to be as low a temperature as passengers will find comfortable.

Q. *Please give some information about the convict ship, Success. W. L. G.*

A. It was built by the British Government in 1790 at Moulmain, East Indies. When the convict system was abolished the vessel was scuttled and sunk in Sydney harbor, Australia, and lay there for five years.

It was subsequently raised to serve as an object lesson in prison reform. Since that time the vessel has been traveling from port to port as an exhibit. It first came to New York, May 17, 1913.

Q. *How many great roads led into Ancient Rome?* P. D.

A. Rome had five great avenues of approach—the Flaminia, Praenestina, Aurelia, Ostiensis, and Appian Ways.

Q. *What do the whistle signals on a train mean?* T. S.

A. The code of signals, uniform on all railroads is: two blasts (train standing), proceed; two blasts (train running), stop; three blasts (train standing), back up; three blasts (train running), stop next station; four blasts (train standing), test brakes; four blasts (train running), decrease speed; five blasts (train running), increase speed; six blasts (train running), turn off steam; seven blasts (train running), send more steam; eight blasts (train running), brakes sticking.

Q. *If a salvage company raises a vessel, does the cargo and ship belong to it?* R. H. P.

A. If a ship is salvaged whose owner is known that ship belongs to the original owner, and the salvage company must make its arrangements with that company concerning the amount it may collect on the value of the salvaged property. If the owner of the salvaged ship cannot be located, the salvage company has title to the property.

Q. *What year was electricity first used to light the headlights on locomotives?* A. S.

A. Electric headlights on locomotives were first used early in 1886.

Q. *What was the origin of the standard railroad gage of 4 feet 8½ inches and is it universally employed?* N. B.

A. Stephenson, inventor of the steam locomotive, is said to have adopted the gage of his engine from that of his farm wagon wheels. Horse-drawn wheeled vehicles had been of approximately that gage since the days of Roman chariots. Various gages, ranging from 3 feet in the East to 5 feet in California, were employed in the United States for 50 years, but now all save industrial short lines are 4 feet 8½ inches. This is standard over most of the world, but India has a gage of 5½ feet, Russia 5 feet, and Japan 3 feet.

Q. *What was the original cost of the ship, Constitution?* R. M.

A. The total cost of the old Constitution including $93,000 for guns and equipment amounted to $302,719.

Q. *Where is the Oregon Trail?* M. A.

A. The Oregon Trail which is 2000 miles in length, extends from Independence, Missouri, to the Columbia River. For 41 miles it follows the Santa Fe Trail. It originated in the trails of Indians and trappers, a well defined trail existing for some miles made by Verendrye in 1742. Lewis and Clark passed over this in 1804. In 1810 J. J. Astor established trading posts at intervals along the trail. In 1830 Sublette guided the first wagon train over the trail. In 1842 Fremont made his official expedition and under government authority surveyed a practical route to the Pacific coast. The trail was used both by Methodist missionaries and by Mormon pioneers.

Q. *When was the first schooner built in this country?* O. McK.

A. It was built by Andrew Robinson of Gloucester, Massachusetts, in 1713.

Q. *What are the three largest ships run by electricity?* E. B.

A. The three largest electric ships flying any flag are the S. S. President Coolidge, the S. S. President Hoover, and the S. S. Augustus. The S. S. President Coolidge and the S. S. President Hoover are both 653 feet over all; 81 feet in beam; displacement tonnage 31,000; a gross of 23,-000 tons; and a sea speed of 21 knots.

Q. How many steam locomotives operate in the United States and how much does their coal cost? J. C. F.

A. In 1931 there were 55,400 steam locomotives operating in the United States. The cost of locomotive fuel in 1930 totaled $227,527,039.

Q. When was the first transcontinental telephone line established across the United States? H. M. E.

A. The American Telephone and Telegraph Company completed the first on January 25, 1915. It connected New York, Pittsburgh, Chicago, Omaha, Denver, Salt Lake City, and San Francisco.

Q. Who invented the telephone? G. H.

A. The Supreme Court has definitely settled the question of the invention of the telephone. This is credited to Alexander Graham Bell. Italians, however, are equally confident that the honor should be given to Meucci.

Q. When was the first ironclad warship invented? B. T.

A. Yi Soon Sin is believed to have invented the first of the ironclad type. In the 16th century he built a ship of war sheathed completely in metal, for the Korean navy, enabling the Koreans to defeat the Japanese in a great sea fight. Yi's ironclad was built to resemble a dragon, the figurehead on the prow being the dragon's head, breathing fire.

Q. What boat made the famous race with the Robert E. Lee? J. W. S.

A. The Natchez. The race was won by the Robert E. Lee.

Q. Does the Federal Government decide how wide all roads shall be? N. S.

A. The Bureau of Public Roads says that the width of state and county roads is not a federal matter. The Federal Government may have something to say about the width of those roads using federal aid but the width would vary with each road and circumstances.

Q. How much oil does a big passenger ship burn on a trip across the ocean? A. C.

A. The S. S. Majestic, which is one of the largest ships in operation, consumes 7,000 tons of fuel oil in making her six-day voyage between New York and Southampton via Cherbourg.

Q. What is a seatrain? C. L.

A. This name is given to vessels which carry trains of loaded freight cars from one port to another across an ocean. Seatrains in operation range from 450 to 478 feet in length with four decks, on each of which standard-gage railway tracks are laid. Each vessel is capable of carrying 100 freight cars. The ships are loaded and discharged by means of elevators located at each terminal.

Q. On which side of a state highway should a person walk? V. H. S.

A. Pedestrians should walk on the left hand side of the road facing the on-coming traffic.

Q. How did the custom start of telling time on shipboard by ringing a bell? J. A. K.

A. Ship's bells are said to date from the period when the hour glass was used to indicate the passage of time. The glass was empty every half hour and had to be turned over, the ship's bell being struck to mark the time. At present bells are the signals for a change in the watch.

Q. How much coal and water does the average locomotive use in an hour? J. O. F.

A. Trautwine says that a typical powerful locomotive, pulling an average passenger train, evaporates from 25,000 to 30,000 pounds of water per hour, burning from 3500 to 5000 pounds of coal. Passenger engines usually carry fuel and water sufficient for 40 to 50 miles; some, 60 to 70.

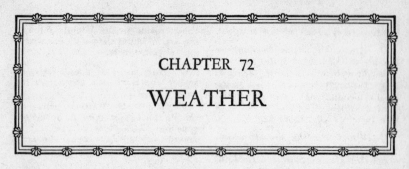

CHAPTER 72

WEATHER

Q. *Where is the coldest place that people actually live?* L. R.

A. Verkhoyansk in the province of Yakutsk, Siberia, is believed to be the coldest inhabited spot in the world. It is known as the Pole of Cold, and temperatures as low as –90°F. have been recorded.

Q. *How far can the sound of thunder be heard?* H. M. H.

A. The Weather Bureau says that thunder is seldom heard more than 20 miles, and usually not over 10 or 15 miles.

Q. *Are there any places on the earth where it never rains?* D. R.

A. Such a place is not known. Even the Sahara Desert is not entirely rainless.

Q. *Are our winters getting less severe?* L. T.

A. The Weather Bureau says that one year differs from another in the weather it brings, and also in respect to almost everything else. However, the average of the weather for any consecutive 20 years is practically the same as for any other consecutive 20 years.

Q. *How much water is there in a dense fog?* C. S.

A. By studying fog off the Grand Banks, it was determined that a block of very dense fog 100 feet long by 6 feet high by 3 feet wide contains about one-seventh of a glass of water. This is divided into about sixty billion droplets.

Q. *Are people ever killed by hailstones?* E. N.

A. Such events are not uncommon. In one hailstorm in India, 250 persons lost their lives.

Q. *What change in temperature is required to make a cold wave?* E. K.

A. Cold wave is a term commonly used in the United States to denote a fall of at least 20 degrees in temperature in 24 hours, bringing the temperature below the freezing point.

Q. *Why are some clouds white, while others are dark?* I. W.

A. The color of clouds depends on the amount of progress made by the droplets composing them toward the formation of actual rain. When the particles of water are so small that they reflect the light, as do crystals, the cloud is white. When the water particles have become larger, and have the size of raindrops, these drops begin to absorb the light instead of reflecting it—the cloud is then dark. A dark cloud may be said to be actually raining; a white cloud indicates that rain may come later, but that the cloud has not yet reached that state.

Q. *When did New York have a record snow storm in March?* J. H. S.

A. The big storm of 1888, commonly known as the New York Blizzard, occurred on the 11th, 12th, and 13th of March of that year. It is regarded as one of the most severe storms ever experienced on the Atlantic coast of the United States.

Q. *How large are the average snowflakes?* G. E.

A. Professor Wilson A. Bentley, pioneer photographer of snow crystals, says that the average snowflake is one-tenth of an inch in diameter.

Q. *How high above the earth does the highest cloud float?* T. S. S.

A. Prof. Humphreys says that rising masses of air cannot ascend beyond the level of the highest cirrus cloud, that is, in middle latitudes above an elevation of about 6 or 7 miles.

Q. *Is there any place on earth where thunder storms never occur?* P. C. R.

A. There is no place without any lightning or electrical storms. Such a storm occurs about once in ten years at the poles.

Q. *Is it possible to have rain when there are no clouds in the sky?* H. A.

A. The Weather Bureau says that it has no record of true rain falling from a clear sky. Sometimes the dripping of dew from trees, and also the drops of liquid falling from insects living on the sap of limbs, have each been mistaken for rain, and give rise to the idea that rain can fall from a clear sky.

Q. *Are any two snowflakes of exactly the same pattern?* L. B.

A. Wilson A. Bentley, who has devoted years to the study of snow crystals, says that duplicates are never found.

Q. *What were the rainmaking schemes? Were any of them successful?* L. B.

A. All rainmaking schemes have proved unsuccessful. As late as 1891, Congress was induced to vote $9000 for experiments in rainmaking. Most of the work was done in Texas by setting off large quantities of dynamite and exploding hydrogen-filled balloons. A little rain fell but weather experts declared it would have fallen anyway. In 1911, the late C. W. Post tried to obtain moisture from the sky by a heavy bombing at Battle Creek, Michigan. In 1903, it was proposed by Australian scientists to install large open pots of chemicals which would generate hydrogen gas that would rise and in doing so create an upward whorl.

Q. *How many terms are used in describing phases of weather?* A. R.

A. C. F. Talman, librarian of the United States Weather Bureau, is collecting words relating to weather. His encyclopedia weather dictionary, when completed, will contain about 15,000 weather terms, including slang, dialect, and scientific names for weather phenomena.

Q. *When was the year without a summer?* E. S. L.

A. It was 1816. While the Weather Bureau was not organized until 1871, much has been written establishing the fact that the summer of 1816 was unusually cold. In the northern States, snow and frosts occurred in every month of the summer.

Q. *How dense are clouds?* F. L. L.

A. The densest clouds are probably not more than one part water to 30,000 parts air.

Q. *Are the winds higher at the North Pole or the South Pole?* C. L.

A. Winds are more constant and have greater force in the vicinity of the South Pole than in the North.

Q. *Why is March such a windy month?* P. G.

A. In March the difference in temperature between the southern and northern portions of the United States is greater than at any other time of the year, hence the difference in atmospheric pressure between these regions is then greatest and the resulting winds strongest.

Q. What phases of weather are covered in the reports furnished to aviators by the Weather Bureau? T. D.

A. The following features are covered: Conditions of sky and weather, ceiling height, horizontal visibility, wind direction and velocity, condition and movement of upper air currents, temperature, barometric pressure, dew point, thunderstorms, squalls, condition of landing fields, fog, cloud formation, smoke, and haze.

Q. What is the lowest authentic barometric reading during a storm? E. L. P.

A. The Weather Bureau says that one of the lowest authentic barometer pressures recorded in recent years was in connection with the hurricane of September, 1929. As the storm passed over Puerto Rico a reading of 27.35 (reduced to sea level) was recorded. During the hurricane at Miami of 1926, the barometer reading was 27.75.

Q. When was weather first predicted? D. B.

A. The idea of charting weather observations was suggested by the German physicist, Brandes, in 1820. The first synchronous weather chart was produced by Prof. Elias Loomis of Yale College in 1843 and represented the weather of eastern United States on February 16, 1842. The term "forecast" was first used in reference to the prediction of weather by Admiral Robert FitzRoy of England at the time when the Meteorological Department began the general issue of weather predictions in August, 1861.

Q. What was the year of the Big Frost, which damaged crops so much? C. F. W.

A. It occurred June 5, 1859.

Q. Please describe the New Orleans storm of 1915 or 1916. A. M. D.

A. On September 29, 1915, a hurricane came from the Gulf of Mexico and struck New Orleans about 8:00 A.M. The wind increased in velocity all day until, between 4:30 and 7:30 P.M., it was blowing from 80 to 120 miles per hour. The barometer fell to 28:11. In 21 hours, 8.36 inches of rain fell. The storm subsided at about 9:00 in the evening. There was heavy rainfall from succeeding storms. In 15 days 22.24 inches of rain fell.

Q. Where should a thermometer be placed in a room? W. P. L.

A. It depends on the existing conditions and the kind of thermometer. For ordinary use the thermometer should be placed to get free circulation around it, that is, in a position to get the most representative temperature. Generally it is placed about five feet high.

Q. Why does the wind blow so furiously around some of New York's tall buildings in the winter time? C. G.

A. The Weather Bureau says that this is because the general wind over the city and round about is strong during the winter, and because the buildings obstruct the free flow and shunt it around their sides and between themselves and other buildings, where it moves faster for much the same reason that a stream of water filling a pipe is fastest where the pipe is constricted or smallest.

Q. Why is the climate of California so different from the rest of the United States? A. K.

A. There are four main factors influencing the climate peculiar to California. According to Dr. McAdie they are as follows: the movements of the great continental and oceanic pressure areas, the so-called permanent highs and lows; the prevailing drift of the atmosphere in the temperate latitudes from west to east; the proximity of the Pacific Ocean; and the exceedingly diversified topography of the country for about 200 miles inland from the coast.

Q. *What makes the wind blow?*
F. L. H.

A. Wind is air in motion. If all parts of the earth were equally heated by the sun's rays, the atmosphere would be equally dense and in a state of perpetual calm. It happens, however, that the sun heats certain areas of the atmosphere more than it does others. The heated portions of the air expand and blow out over the cooler areas. The heavy air of the cool areas is no longer held back by the lighter air of the warm areas and rushes in to restore the equilibrium. Thus winds are formed. The direction of winds is considerably deflected by the rotation of the earth on its axis.

Q. *At what altitude does the air become insufficient for breathing?*
P. D.

A. It is believed that a man can live at an altitude of 25,000 feet for a brief period, if he does no particular work. Army fliers are required by army regulations to begin using oxygen as soon as they reach an altitude of 15,000 feet.

Q. *What is the average time of day when the temperature is the lowest?* *F. W. A.*

A. As a rule the temperature is the lowest just about sunrise. This is due to the fact that, on account of radiation, heat is being given off during the night more rapidly than received from external sources. As this continues until the heat from the sun overcomes this disparity, it is the natural consequence that the lowest temperature should occur just preceding the moment when added heat from the sun overcomes the loss occasioned by radiation during the night.

Q. *How is the velocity of the wind measured?* *M. K.*

A. It is measured by an instrument called an anemometer. It consists of three or four hollow hemispheres on the ends of equal rods at right angles to each other and designed to rotate in a horizontal plane about the point of intersection of the rods. The instrument may be seen turning in the wind at any Weather Bureau Station.

Q. *Does radio have any effect upon the weather?* *B. W. S.*

A. Radio waves have no effect on the weather. How clouds are formed, and how lightning and thunder are produced, are pretty well known in every particular. It is also known that radio does not affect any one of the things that lead to the formation of clouds, or to the production of lightning and thunder.

Q. *How fast do raindrops fall?*
E. J. B.

A. Raindrops never fall faster than 25 feet per second; many of them fall only about 15 feet per second. Suppose then the height of the cloud is 2500 feet, a fairly common height, and that the speed of fall is the greatest possible—very large drops; then the time of fall will be 100 seconds. If the speed is 15 feet per second, the time will be 166.7 seconds. A fair average velocity is 20 feet per second, and the time of fall two minutes.

Q. *Why does thunder seem to roll?* *M. W.*

A. The long duration of thunder is owing mainly to the fact that the several parts of a streak of lightning are at different distances from the observer and that sound travels at the rate of about a mile in five seconds. Reflection of the sound from clouds and other objects also helps to produce the long, drawn-out roll sometimes heard.

Q. *How are the dolls made whose frocks change color as the weather changes?* *H. W.*

A. Some hygroscopes are not mechanical; they owe their hygroscopic properties to their color, which changes with the state of humidity of the air by reason of the application of sympathetic inks. These instruments are often composed of a flower or a figure, of light muslin or paper, immersed in the following solution: Cobalt chloride, 1 part; gelatine, 10 parts; water, 100 parts. The normal coloring is pink; this color changes into violet in medium humid weather, and into blue in very dry weather.

Q. *What causes the Will o' the Wisp?* L. M.

A. The Ignis Fatuus, also known as the Will o' the Wisp, is a luminous appearance generally seen in marshy places or churchyards. It appears after sunset as a pale bluish-colored flame, and floats generally about two feet from the ground, sometimes remaining fixed and sometimes traveling. Many attempts have been made to discover the cause of this phenomenon. Some authorities think it due to the presence of phosphureted hydrogen gas; others, to the combustion of methane. It is probably caused by a number of phenomena arising from different causes. It is seen most frequently in northern Germany, in the swamps and moorland districts of northwestern England, and in the lowlands of Scotland.

Q. *Why are snowflakes sometimes large and sometimes small?* R. W. R.

A. If the temperature is low, the snowflakes are small, flat, and regular. If the temperature is near the freezing point, particularly in the lower layers of the atmosphere, the flakes often mat together and form large clots. If the temperature is still higher, the flakes are often incomplete, as parts are melted off.

Q. *What is a squaw winter?* C. B. H.

A. The term is used to designate the spell of cold weather which often precedes Indian summer.

Q. *How is hail caused?* R. F. C.

A. Summer hail, or true hail, is caused by the rapid uprush of air in a violent thunderstorm, which carries raindrops so high that they freeze. On freezing, they fall back to a lower level where they pick up more water and again are caught in an upward current and carried up to the freezing levels. This is repeated several times until the hailstones get so heavy that they fall through the rising air down to the earth. Winter hail, properly called sleet, consists of frozen raindrops, the rain having fallen through a surface layer of cold air.

Q. *In reporting weather conditions, what is meant by pressure?* W. H. B.

A. It has reference to the atmosphere. Air has weight and exerts pressure equally in all directions. The weight of the atmosphere diminishes with the height and increases toward sea level. Rise in temperature causes the air to expand and become lighter, whereas a drop in temperature results in reverse conditions. Owing to these differences in temperature, the air is constantly in motion and the pressure varies at different points on the earth's surface and is also continually changing at any one point.

Q. *Why do air bubbles appear on a pond of water during certain showers and remain until struck by raindrops?* J. J.

A. When the raindrops are quite large, as they are near the beginning of certain showers, they fall into a body of water with sufficient force to drag after them, as small pebbles do, bubbles of air which are entrapped by the closing water above. These bubbles are small and often do not break immediately. They break when struck by a raindrop, or, sooner or later, even when not struck.

Q. *Must there be dust in the atmosphere in order to have rain?* K. N.

A. Condensation centers, or nuclei, are essential to the formation of cloud, and therefore to rainfall. These nuclei may be dust particles, especially of certain kinds, such as sea salt, or even, it is believed, molecules of certain sorts that have great affinity for water. The air always contains an abundance of such nuclei.

Q. Is snow counted in measuring a year's rainfall? F. S. A.

A. The Weather Bureau says that snowfall that occurs at the government observing stations is reduced to its equivalent in rainfall and included with the latter in determining the amount of precipitation during the year. As a rule the ratio of unmelted snow is 1 to 10, that is, 10 inches of snow will ordinarily make about 1 inch of water.

Q. Why are storms to be expected at the equinoxes? R. V.

A. There is no reason why storms should be more frequent or severe on September 21 or 22 (autumnal equinox) than on September 10 or 11, say, or 29 or 30; nor, in fact, are they. The same is true of the spring or vernal equinox. This whole notion about "equinoctial storms" is erroneous, and it even is uncertain how, where, when, or by whom the idea was started.

Q. What is the difference between clear and fair in a weather report? S. D. T.

A. Clear signifies not only no rain, snow, or sleet ahead, but a sky practically free from clouds, while fair, also promising no precipitation, does not exclude some clouds from the sky.

Q. Is it ever too cold to snow? R. C. C.

A. The greater number of more or less heavy snows come from southerly to easterly winds, i. e., in what is known as the "rainy" portion of the cyclonic or storm area. These winds generally are relatively mild. As the storm passes, the winds come from the northwest, roughly, and are relatively cold. In short, precipitation comes with relatively warm easterly to southerly winds, and clear weather follows with relatively cold northwest winds. If, then, the win-

ter wind is from the northwest, it is cold, and from the wrong direction to give much snow. This, presumably, is the origin of the saying, "It is too cold to snow." This statement, however, is not literally true, for light snows can occur at any temperature, and, indeed, it occasionally happens that heavy snows occur when the surface air is quite cold.

Q. Why is Indian Summer sometimes called St. Martin's Summer? S. McC.

A. The legend of St. Martin relates how on a cold November day, Martin saw a beggar crouching in a church door shivering. Martin tore his cloak in two and gave half to the beggar. This half-warmth provided gave its name to St. Martin's Summer, a semi-summer, which occurs in November.

Q. In what way is snow beneficial? C. A. L.

A. It is a bad conductor of heat, so it protects the ground from cooling while the temperature of the air at the surface of the snow is below freezing. As its presence lessens fluctuations of the temperature of the air, it is naturally beneficial to plants. It provides necessary moisture. When the snows melt in the spring, the volume of water in rivers is increased. The presence of snow on mountains has an important effect on climate.

Q. Is the barometer high or low at the approach of a storm? W. E.

A. In general, it is the rule that falling barometer indicates rising temperature and the probability of precipitation, whereas rising barometer usually indicates clear weather with lowering temperature.

Q. Why is there more wind by day than by night? F. P.

A. Owing to the friction at the surface of the earth, the air near the ground always has less velocity than the air a few hundred feet above it. In the daytime this faster air is mixed up with the surface air by convection induced by surface heating. In this way the surface air is given a greater velocity than it would have if not mixed with the upper and faster wind. At night, when there is no surface heating and no convection, the upper wind, except when quite strong, glides over the lower air which is held relatively quiet by surface friction. When the upper winds are very strong, they mix with the lower air by mechanical turbulence and the surface wind remains as strong by night as by day.

Q. What is the difference in meaning of climate and weather? R. C.

A. Climate is a more general term than weather. The former is the sum and average of the weather which includes daily change in temperature, pressure, wind, and rain. Climate shows a general condition, while weather deals with the special instances of changes in the atmosphere.

Q. Is there any special kind of glass required for thermometers? G. A. L.

A. Authorities say that in thermometers that are to be used for accurate scientific work the bulbs should always be made of one of three kinds of glass. The first type of glass is a French glass which has been demonstrated to be peculiarly adapted for use in thermometer bulbs by the elaborate experiments made by the International Bureau of Weights and Measures at Paris. This glass is known as "verre dur." These other two are made at Jena, Germany, and are known as Jena 16''' and Jena 59'''. These types of glass have similarly proved to be adapted for use in accurate thermometers by the experiments made at the Reichsanstalt in Berlin.

Q. How does the oxygen content of the air in heavily wooded mountain districts compare with that of the air in Pittsburgh? R. M.

A. The difference is very small, too small indeed to be of any special importance. This is owing to the more or less continuous and vigorous stirring and mixing of the atmosphere by winds, convection, turbulence, and diffusion.

Q. Where should a thermometer be hung to record the most accurate outdoor temperature? B. R.

A. It should be hung on the north side of the house, in a sheltered place, such as a porch. The hook should be long enough to keep the thermometer an inch or two from the wall.

Q. Is there any truth in the idea that as the direction of the wind is on March 20-22, so it will be prevailing during the next six months? C. O. B.

A. There is nothing whatever to support this idea, except perhaps in trade-wind regions where the direction of the wind is pretty much the same all the time. And in such places, one day is as good as another as a guide, since all are much alike.

Q. Why is it sometimes as warm when the sun is not shining as when it is? H. A. B.

A. The temperature of the air at a given place depends not only on the sunshine it is then getting but also on its own recent history. Wind from the south on a cloudy day may be as warm as wind from the north on a sunshiny day. This is particularly true, when, as often happens, these winds have come a long way. Furthermore, when it is warm, humid air feels warmer than dry air at the same temperature.

Q. Is any part of the United States free from electrical storms? E. L.

A. So far as known, no part of this country is entirely free from these phenomena. However, they are much more frequently observed in the eastern and central portions of the country than in the far west. In fact, along the immediate Pacific coast, the occurrence of these storms is comparatively rare and it is stated that they are without many of the severe characteristics observed in the more eastern districts.

Q. Where is there the most oxygen in the air? L. S.

A. Oxygen occurs, not in larger percentage, but in greatest weight per cubic foot of air, at the lowest levels, and decreases with increase of height.

Q. Of two flat, vertical walls, one facing east and one facing west, which will get the greater amount of sunshine? D. R. W.

A. They get the same amount, except when the forenoons and afternoons are unequally cloudy, as often is the case, especially in certain regions. For instance, near the ocean in Southern California the forenoons, on the average, are much more cloudy than the afternoons. Here the wall facing west would get more sunshine than the one facing east.

Q. Is it possible to see the end of the rainbow resting upon an object? E. P.

A. The light of the rainbow comes to us from all the water drops the sun is shining upon in the direction of the bow. If the shower is some distance away, the lowest drops may be in line with the surface, land or water, within the shower, in which case the bow, as well known, has all the appearance of standing or terminating upon the surface at that point. But, as implied, this is only an optical illusion, owing to that spot and many drops giving the rainbow colors being in the same direction from the observer.

Q. What is the difference between sleet and hail? J. A. D.

A. Sleet is a drizzling or driving partly-frozen rain, or rain that freezes on the trees and ground. Hail falls usually in connection with thunder storms. It is frozen rain, falling in pellets or hailstones of varying sizes and shapes.

Q. What is meant by the "January thaw"? R. B.

A. In the minds of the general public, the term "January Thaw" is applied to a relatively warm spell in January, but the justification for this is the apparent meteorological fact that in decidedly more than 50 per cent of the years, at least over the northern central and eastern sections of the country, the records show a relatively warm spell of weather occurs in the last week of the month, that is, between the 20th and 28th. The warm spell does not occur at exactly the same date each year, but generally it falls in the latter part of January and is emphasized by being followed by materially colder weather, which occurs on the last days of the month and the first days of February. Of course, in some of the years no such feature exhibits itself, but long records show the tendency to the presence of temperature changes of this character at many stations in the country.

Q. Which is heavier—dry air or moist air? E. M. R.

A. Dry air is slightly heavier than ordinary humid—not foggy—air. The number of molecules in a given volume of air and the same volume of water in the form of invisible gas under the same conditions, is the same. When such water molecules are introduced into the dry air a corresponding number of air molecules are displaced. The atomic weights of oxygen and nitrogen, the principal ingredients of air, are greater than the atomic weight of water vapor. Therefore, since a light substance replaces a heavier one, the total weight is less. Foggy or smoky air is quite likely to be heavier than dry air.

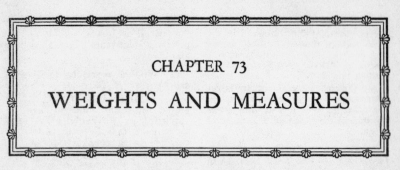

CHAPTER 73

WEIGHTS AND MEASURES

Q. What is weight? R. M.

A. It is the measure of the force with which a body is attracted to the earth. The weight of any body depends on two factors—the quantity of matter which it contains, and its position with respect to the earth.

Q. How many inches in a hand when used to measure a horse? E. F.

A. A hand is four inches.

Q. Where is the International Bureau of Weights and Measures? P. A.

A. By treaty, the United States with 27 other nations maintains the International Bureau of Weights and Measures at Paris on neutral territory in the historic Parc du St. Cloud at Sevres. The bureau is official custodian of the international standards of length and mass, the meter and kilogram.

Q. Do objects weigh more on the ground, under the ground, or at an elevation? J. B.

A. The maximum weight of any object is at the surface of the earth. Weight above or below surface is less than at the surface.

Q. From what point in a city are the measurements of distance taken? H. E. T.

A. Many cities have zero mile stones from which the distance to and from that city is measured. In the county seat, the distance is usually measured to the court house. In other towns and villages the distance is usually measured to the point where the two main streets cross.

Q. Will a gallon can with a dent in it hold exactly a gallon? J. C. C.

A. The Bureau of Standards says that the capacity of a can depends on whether it is dented in or dented out. If a gallon can is dented in, it will hold less.

Q. What is a kiloparsec? C. C. B.

A. A kiloparsec is approximately 6200 light years, figuring the travel of light at 186,000 miles a second.

Q. How large an area is represented by the term, Hide, found in the Domesday Book? W. T.

A. It is generally supposed to equal 120 acres.

Q. Does a wooden ruler change in length with change of temperature? C. C. B.

A. A wooden ruler will expand and contract with change of temperature. The expansion of pine wood is 0.00000276 for each degree Fahrenheit.

Q. What is meant by the calibration of an instrument? W. D.

A. It is the checking or correcting of the scale readings of the instrument.

Q. What is a ligne? B. E. L.

A. Ligne is a French measure of length equal to 2.26 millimeters, or 0.0885 inch.

490

Q. What was the standard for the English pound weight? G. N.

A. The original English pound was derived from the weight of 7680 grains of wheat, all taken from the middle of the ear and well dried. Thus, the grain is the lowest fractional division of the pound. In the time of Henry VII, 7000 grains became the standard.

Q. Who invented the slide rule? W. L. W.

A. It was developed after the invention of logarithms in 1614 by John Napier. In 1620 Edmund Gunter plotted logarithms on a two-foot straight line. The first known slide rule in which the slide worked between parts of a fixed stock was made by Robert Bissaker in 1654.

Q. What were the Thomson Tables which Livingstone took with him to Africa? C. P. C.

A. The Thomson Tables that Livingstone carried on his trip to Africa were tables of logarithms to be used in mathematical computations. Besides the Thomson logarithms, he had with him his Bible and a nautical almanac.

Q. Is a gallon larger in Canada than in the United States? F. J. S.

A. It is slightly larger, as Canada uses the imperial gallon which equals 1.2 United States gallons.

Q. In our household we have three measuring cups, each of which is different in content from the others. How can we ascertain which complies with the Government standard? W. K. W.

A. The proper equivalent for a measuring cup is one-half pint liquid or four fluid ounces. A ready means of determining the accuracy of a measuring cup is by comparison with a standard liquid measure or glass graduate.

Q. What is a milline? W. P.

A. The word is a contraction of million-line, and is a unit of space and circulation, equivalent to one agate line, a column wide, about 2¼ inches, appearing in one million copies of a publication. It is obtained by multiplying the number of agate lines by the number of copies circulated and dividing by one million. The term was defined in a letter of Benjamin H. Jefferson, September, 1921, to Dr. Vizetelly.

Q. How much ground is contained in an arpen of land? M. J.

A. An arpen was an old French measure of land roughly equivalent to an acre.

Q. In surveyors' measure how long is a link? M. D.

A. It is 7.92 inches.

Q. Who divided the circle into 360 degrees? J. S.

A. If not the discoverer, at least the elucidation of the dimensions of the circle and its bisecting into a given number of points, is credited to Euclid, a great mathematician, 300 B.C. Euclid, however, made no specific claim to being the originator of the mathematical proportions described in his elements, text-books of which are standards up to the present time.

Q. Please inform me as to what would be the liquid measure of a so-called jigger, used before prohibition in regard to mixing drinks? A. W.

A. A jigger is a slang term for one dram of liquor.

Q. Has a line any dimension except length? L. M.

A. In mathematics a line is defined as having length, but neither breadth nor thickness.

Q. How long is the Russian verst? S. P.

A. It is a measure of length equal to 0.66288 miles.

Q. What is the origin of our Troy weight? T. T. W.

A. The weights used in the Middle Ages at the fair in Troyes, France.

Q. *What is indirect measurement?*
H. W. M.

A. The Bureau of Standards says that indirect measurement is the measurement of one quantity by measurement of another quantity which bears a definite relationship to the first. Example: Determination of sun's parallax by measuring parallax of Mars.

Q. *How many drops are there in a standard gallon?* C. B. L.

A. The size of a drop is not standard. It varies with the different liquids, therefore it is not possible to say definitely how many drops it takes to fill a standard gallon.

Q. *Why does not the variation in centrifugal force between the poles and the equator affect weights?* J. M. T.

A. The centrifugal effect of the earth's rotation does or does not affect weights according to what is meant by "affecting weights." Weights are not as heavy at the equator as at the poles. This is because of both the rotation and the shape of the earth. As a rule weights are not really used for determining weight, but for the purpose of getting a certain amount of material. When we buy a pound of sugar at the equator we get just as much sugar as if we bought it at the poles, because at the poles both the sugar and the weights would be heavier by the same amount. Therefore, in scientific language, and also in the real purpose for which weights are used in commercial buying and selling, weights are standards of "mass," not standards of weight, and as such the rotation and shape of the earth have no effect— a one-pound weight is a one-pound weight wherever it is taken.

Q. *What is the difference between candlepower and Watt?* E. H.

A. Candlepower is the illuminating power, as of a lamp, or gas flame, reckoned in terms of the light of a standard candle. Watt is the practical unit of electric power, activity, or rate of work; equivalent to 10^7 ergs or one joule per second, or approximately $\frac{1}{746}$ of a horsepower.

Q. *What is a Westphal balance?* S. T.

A. It is an instrument for measuring the specific gravity of minerals, liquids, etc.

Q. *Why has America its present system of weights and measures?* H. H.

A. In the early colonial days of America, the weights and measures used by the colonists were naturally those of the mother country, and in most cases copies of the home standards were brought over and entrusted to the care of special officers of the Commonwealth. In the English colonies, it was usually the yard of 1588 that was employed. At the time of the Revolution, the new country naturally continued with its existing British standards, and although the Constitution gave Congress the power to fix the standard of weights and measures, nothing was immediately done. Thomas Jefferson in 1790 suggested in Congress the establishment of a decimal system. The question was again taken up in Congress in 1817 and 1830. On July 28, 1866, the metric system of weights and measures was legalized by Act of Congress. In 1875 the United States joined with a number of others in the establishment of the International Bureau of Weights and Measures in Paris.

Q. *What is a kilocycle?* H. E. B.

A. Kilo means one thousand. Cycle means a period of time in which a certain phenomenon occurs repeatedly in the same order. In electricity, it is the period of time which is taken for an alternating current to raise from zero to its maximum potential and return to zero again, in one direction, and then go from zero to maximum and return to zero in the opposite direction. Combining the two meanings kilocycle means the above proceedings performed a thousand times a second.

Q. *Is a section of land always 640 acres in the United States?* H. P.

A. The rectangular system of surveys of the public domain of the United States is applicable to all public land states. A section is ordinarily one mile square and contains 640 acres. Lands in the original 13 states never formed a part of the public domain. These may vary.

Q. *What is the average life of electric meters as used in residences?* W. F.

A. A large power company estimates the average life of a house type meter at 22 years. In many cases, however, the development of new types makes it advisable to replace meters before they are worn out.

Q. *How should a huckster's scale be hung?* A. C. T.

A. The Bureau of Standards says that a hanging scale used by a huckster should be so mounted that all parts of the scale will hang free when a load is placed upon the load-receiving element. It should be unnecessary for the operator to hold the scale in any way during the weighing operation.

Q. *What are the different kinds of meters for measuring water?* H. N.

A. Water meters are of three general types, the positive, the inferential, and the proportional. Positive meters measure the actual volume of the water; inferential meters measure the velocity of the flowing water and the quantity is deduced by computation from that record; proportional meters measure a fractional part of the full flow, and are necessarily only approximately accurate.

Q. *Is accurate weight down weight or balance weight?* G. E.

A. When a weight observation is made on a beam or even-arm scale, the position of the beam or of the pans should correspond to their position at zero balance. Such scales should be so balanced at zero load that when they are in equilibrium the beam will be horizontal or the pans will be at the same level. When so balanced down weight will be over-weight.

Q. *How long is the vara?* M. L. C.

A. The vara, which is a Spanish measure of length, equals 33.38 inches or 84.79 centimeters.

Q. *Why do some grains have more pounds to the bushel than others?* L. A.

A. For many years, grains were measured in bushel containers, or peck containers. However, in different states the exact size of these containers varied, and they frequently varied within the same State. Consequently, the Department of Agriculture found it necessary to set some standard amount to the grain. In compiling a standard measurement, it was found that some grains took up more space than others. This necessitated another form of measurement in order to insure accuracy. The answer to this was a table of weights. Now all states use tables giving the pounds to the bushel of the various grains.

Q. *Why isn't a decimal system of units used for circular measure?* J. H.

A. The sexagesimal system of circular measurement has been in existence from a very early period. It was used by the early Greek mathematicians. Their influence was so great that all the medieval astronomers and mathematicians, Christian, Jewish, and Mohammedan, used the same system. When a particular form of measurement has become established through the ages, there is always reluctance in making a change because of the confusion that would be involved, calculations would have to be changed and existing textbooks, tables, and reference books would be out-of-date.

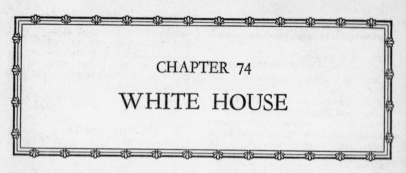

CHAPTER 74

WHITE HOUSE

Q. *Which Presidents died in the White House?* M. T.

A. While other Presidents have died in office, William Henry Harrison and Zachary Taylor are the only ones whose deaths occurred within the White House.

Q. *Does the President of the United States furnish the china used in the White House?* N. W. J.

A. The china and silver used in the White House are supplied by the Government. In some administrations sets have been supplemented, in others entire new sets are ordered. The choice rests with the wife of the President.

Q. *Has any President, before Mr. Hoover, had a desk telephone?* A. N.

A. President Hoover originated the practice of having a private phone on his own desk, putting himself in the position of being better served by telephone and telegraph than anyone else on earth. He has practically instantaneous communication with any part of the United States. Cable connections can be joined up in a minute or two, and the lines are kept wide open 24 hours of the day.

Q. *Was the Russian oak in the White House grounds planted by the Grand Duke Alexis?* R. C.

A. It was not. The oak grew from an acorn of an oak in the grounds of the palace of the former Czar of Russia in St. Petersburg, which in turn had grown from an acorn of an oak which stood over Washington's original tomb at Mt. Vernon. The acorn from Mt. Vernon was sent to the Czar by Senator Charles Sumner of Massachusetts.

Q. *Who selected the site of the White House?* A. T. C.

A. It was selected by President Washington and Major Pierre Charles L'Enfant when they laid out Washington in 1791.

Q. *When was the first plumbing installed in the White House?* I. H.

A. The date is not known definitely. It was installed about 1825.

Q. *Where was the stone obtained that was used in building the White House?* F. R.

A. The sandstone or Virginia freestone used in building the White House, the Capitol, the Patent Office, and the Lee Mansion at Arlington, came from the Aquia Creek quarries, about 40 miles below Washington. These quarries were opened in 1685, and still furnish sandstone for many important buildings.

Q. *Who planted the old trees in the White House grounds?* P. E.

A. The oldest tree is an elm which was planted by President John Quincy Adams. Other elms were planted by Presidents Rutherford B. Hayes and Woodrow Wilson. A sweet gum was planted by Benj. Harrison; oaks by Presidents William McKinley and Theodore Roosevelt, also a beech by President Roosevelt. A Japanese cherry tree

494

was planted by Mrs. Taft, a magnolia by Mrs. Harding, and a birch by Mrs. Coolidge.

Q. What flowers are most generally used in the White House decorations for parties and other entertainments? M. E. M.

A. The recently retired chief of the White House greenhouses, Charles Henlock, says that roses, carnations, freesias, and snapdragons seem to appeal to the majority of the ladies of the White House for decorations. At the wedding at the White House of President Cleveland, pink azaleas were massed.

Q. Please describe the gold piano in the White House. R. C. H.

A. The piano is a concert grand. The makers presented it to the Government. The piano is gilded. It is mounted on three eagles half regardant, with outstretched wings and standing upon square pedestals, draped with laurel wreaths. The case is without moldings, but is adorned with a painted scroll of acanthus in varying tones of red, which serves to bind together the arms of the original States, which, beginning from the right appear displayed upon shields of dull maroon in the order in which they adopted the Constitution.

Q. When the White House was burned in 1814, was it totally destroyed? F. F.

A. Only the walls were left standing.

Q. What do the dates, 1792-1902, in a circle of stars mean? They are in the floor at the White House. L. P. T.

A. They designate that the White House was built in 1792 and was remodeled in 1902. These dates are circumscribed by the seal of the President of the United States.

Q. Does a tourist visiting the White House see the state apartments? H. O. B.

A. It is necessary to obtain a card of permission in order to see the state apartments. The sightseeing parties which visit the Mansion see the lower corridor and the East Room; persons who have cards are shown the state dining room, Blue, Green, and Red Rooms, the East Room, and the long corridor that parallels the state apartments.

Q. How many rooms are there in the White House? B. K.

A. An arbitrary number cannot be given. It depends upon whether storage rooms, cloak rooms, and reception rooms are included. On the first floor of the White House, there is an entrance lobby and main corridor, the East Room, the Green Room, the Blue Room, the Red Room, and the State Dining Room, and the Private Dining Room. On the second floor, there are seven bedrooms and baths in addition to the Library and the President's Study, and a wide hall extending the length of the building. On the third floor are fourteen rooms and seven baths, as well as a number of storage rooms. On the floor below the first floor are cloak rooms, reception rooms, kitchen, pantries, etc.

Q. How does the expense of maintaining the White House now compare with what it was ten years ago? C. C.

A. Senator Harrison made a speech in January in which he said: When Mr. Harding was President, in 1922, $206,000 was appropriated. In 1923 the appropriation amounted to $349,000; in 1924, under Mr. Coolidge, to $450,000; in 1925, under Mr. Coolidge, to $411,000; in 1926, under Mr. Coolidge, to $483,000; in 1932, under Mr. Hoover, to $532,000.

Q. How many windows are there in the White House? M. T.

A. There are 91 windows in the main building of the White House, 70 windows in the west wing, including the Executive Office, 25 in the east wing, excluding the conservatory, 4 large windows in the conservatory, making a total of 190 in all.

Q. *When was the portico on the north front added to the White House? J. M. A.*

A. The White House was burned in 1814. When it was restored the portico on the north front was added; tradition says at the suggestion of Thomas Jefferson.

Q. *What kind of front door has the White House? P. H. B.*

A. The steps leading to the main entrance are stone. The main door is 5 ft. wide, 9 ft. 10 in. high and 2¼ in. thick, and is solid mahogany.

Q. *Did Mrs. Theodore Roosevelt shake hands at the President's New Year's reception? H. V. D.*

A. Mrs. Roosevelt did not shake hands. At her first New Year's reception, she carried a large bouquet of flowers which engaged her hands.

Q. *How are White House aides appointed and what is their salary? G. C. S.*

A. White House aides are chosen from the Army, Navy, and Marine Corps. It is their duty to assist at receptions, and also when foreign delegations make formal calls. The aides may be of any rank and their salaries vary according to their rank and position, but no special compensation is given for their services as aides.

Q. *Who was the most popular baby of the White House? M. B. G.*

A. Baby McKee, the little grandson of President and Mrs. Benj. Harrison, received during his grandfather's term of office, almost as much publicity and attention as Princess Elizabeth of England or Paulina Longworth, the granddaughter of the late President Theodore Roosevelt.

Q. *Was a First Lady ever known as Her Majesty? J. G. R.*

A. This title was never official, but in a description left by Mrs. Joseph Gale, of the Presidential levee, held January 1, 1814, Mrs. Dolly Madison is alluded to and described as her majesty, the phrase being: "Her Majesty's appearance was truly regal, dressed in a robe of pink satin, trimmed elaborately with ermine, and a white velvet and satin turban with nodding ostrich plumes, and a crescent in front. Gold chains and clasps were around her waist and wrists."

Q. *Does a man or woman preside over the housekeeping department of the White House? K. K.*

A. Previous to the administration of President Taft, a steward was in charge, but since that time there has been a housekeeper.

Q. *Is the service of the White House paid for by the President or by the Government? L. F. R.*

A. Cooks, chambermaids, laundry women, butlers, and pantrymen, about 20 in all, are provided by the Government. Such personal servants as the President or his wife may choose to accompany them to the White House are paid by the Executive.

Q. *Which President's family has had the greatest variety of pets at the White House? J. M. T.*

A. The family of President Theodore Roosevelt had the greatest variety actually kept at the White House, including guinea pigs, a kangaroo, rat, alligator, horse and ponies, and many dogs. Also Mr. Roosevelt sent to the zoo black bears, macaws, a lioness, baboon, zebra, ostrich, vulture, leopard, and hawk. President Coolidge had many dogs, also a brindle cat, and Rebecca, the coon. He sent to the zoo a black haired bear, lion cubs, hippopotamus, peacock, baby wallaby, and Ruben, a coon.

Q. *How many guests will the gold table service supply? J. T. S.*

A. The service is said to be sufficient to serve 100 guests, and since the state dining room holds no more guests, the service is ample. The gold service originated with President Monroe.

Q. *Who entertained the King and Queen of Belgium at the White House while President Wilson was ill? P. S.*

A. The King and Queen were not entertained, officially, at the White House during the illness of President Wilson, but by Vice President and Mrs. Marshall.

Q. *What disastrous effect was feared by Abraham Lincoln from the handshaking ordeal of the New Year's reception? C. L.*

A. President Lincoln in 1863 signed on January 1, the proclamation of emancipation. Mr. Lincoln is said to have told Secretary Seward: "If my name ever goes into history it will be for this act, and my soul is in it. If my hand trembles when I sign, all who examine the document hereafter will say 'He hesitated.'"

Q. *Why was the Capitol built so far from the White House? U. R. T.*

A. A fear was expressed by President Washington that if the legislative and executive branches were too close, they might possibly encroach upon each other's time. He advised that the Congressional buildings should be at least a mile from the Executive Mansion. This was before the days of either telegraph, telephone, or automobiles.

Q. *Who held the first New Year's reception in the White House? M. A. C.*

A. The first reception was held in the White House by John Adams, although New Year levees had been held by both Presidents Washington and Adams previously. The first reception was held on the second floor of the unfinished White House, in the oval room. The mansion was entered at the south door.

Q. *Which prominent Negro was entertained at the White House by three Presidents? C. Y.*

A. Frederick Douglas was entertained at the White House in 1864 by President Lincoln, in 1878 by President Hayes, and in 1885 by President Cleveland.

Q. *What is the favorite china of the White House? M. E. L.*

A. The china most often used is the American Belleek, of 1700 pieces. It is a warm creamy ivory, with a double gold border and a conventional motif of the stars and stripes, and the seal of the President in raised gold.

Q. *Which President's wife refused to have wine served at the White House, and was nicknamed in consequence? V. C.*

A. Mrs. Rutherford B. Hayes, from 1877 to 1881, refused to permit wine or spirits to be served at White House dinners or receptions, substituting lemonade. Mrs. Hayes was nicknamed "Lemonade Lucy."

Q. *What are the principal dinners and receptions given at the White House? L. M.*

A. Usually, in their order, are given a dinner for the Cabinet members and their wives, Diplomatic reception, Judicial reception, New Year's Day reception, Vice President's dinner, Diplomatic dinner, reception to the members of the Senate, reception to the House of Representatives, dinner to the Chief Justice and the Supreme Court, dinner to the Speaker of the House, reception to the officials of the Treasury, Post Office, Interior, Agriculture, Commerce and Labor departments, Army and Navy reception.

Q. *What was done with the timber from the White House which was replaced in the recent renovation? H. I. H.*

A. Much of the wood from the White House roof, which was of Virginia white pine, over one hundred years old, has been purchased by people from every section of the country. Much has been made into gavels for the use of organizations. The average price is $1.00 for a piece of pine thirteen inches long, seven inches broad, and four inches in depth, sufficient to make a gavel.

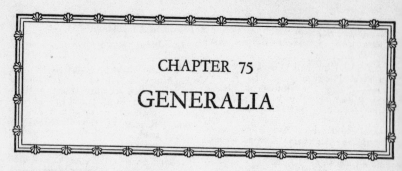

CHAPTER 75

GENERALIA

Q. What people are most law-abiding? *C. C. C.*

A. Generally speaking, the natives of Finland are the most law-abiding. A police system is not found necessary.

Q. Is a person taller when lying down, or when standing up? *S. N.*

A. A person is taller when lying down. Usually the difference is slight, but as much as an inch difference has been noted.

Q. Is it true that spider webs are used commercially? *C. R. N.*

A. Strands of the web of spiders are used for cross lines in microscopes, range finders, and other exacting instruments. The web is wound on a card like thread.

Q. How many telegrams did Col. Lindbergh receive after the kidnapping of his son? *P. E.*

A. Editor and Publisher says that he received 55,000 telegrams from sympathizers over one company's wires. He also received about 3000 letters a day for several weeks.

Q. In what town in Nebraska is everything sold strictly for cash? *T. L.*

A. Bloomfield, Nebraska, is said to be on a strictly cash basis.

Q. Was there an early law against profanity in Pennsylvania? *G. N. A.*

A. In 1794 the legislature passed an act providing that any person over 16 years blaspheming, cursing, or profaning the name of Almighty God should be fined the sum of 67 cents or be confined in the House of Correction 24 hours.

Q. How many acres of land were taken away from owners in the Russian revolution? *S. M. W.*

A. During the revolution, over 1,080,000,000 acres of land belonging to the landowners were acquired by the peasantry. In addition, 48,-000,000 acres belonging to the richer class of peasants were also taken for use in agriculture by the Soviet Government.

Q. How many geese must be plucked to get enough feathers for a pillow of average size? *J. L.*

A. A pillow 22 x 30 inches weighs about 3 pounds. It takes about 18 geese of average size to furnish three pounds of feathers.

Q. What country has neither army nor navy? *R. O. C.*

A. Iceland. The permanent neutrality of this country was established by the Act of Union of 1918 with Denmark.

Q. What was the largest cake ever made? *G. E. L.*

A. Probably the largest cake was that ordered by Frederick William I, King of Prussia, in June, 1730. It is said that this contained 36 bushels of flour, 200 gallons of milk, one ton of butter, one ton of yeast, and 5000 eggs. The finished cake was 18 yards long, 8 yards broad, and more than

498

half a yard thick. It was so large that 30,000 soldiers could not eat it all.

Q. *Does the President of the United States have unlimited use of the radio?* M. P. N.

A. The President may use the radio for broadcasting purposes at any time. This is a courtesy given to the President. If the President is making a speech and his speech runs over the allotted time, he is not cut off.

Q. *How many beads were there usually on a wampum belt?* B. L.

A. Lafitau (1724) says that in his time the usual size of a wampum belt was 11 strands of 180 beads each, or about 1980 wampum beads. There are references to belts composed of 6000 and 7000 beads. The English colonists were compelled to use wampum in trading with the Indians. Three dark or six white beads were about the equivalent of an English penny.

Q. *Is it true that Thomas Jefferson at one time owned the Natural Bridge of Virginia?* M. E. B.

A. A tract of parcel of land containing 157 acres, including the Natural Bridge, was granted to Thomas Jefferson, July 5, 1774, by George III of England, for the sum of "20 shillings of good and lawful money."

Q. *Is the check of nines infallible in mathematics?* J. H.

A. Although casting out nines is a very commonly used method of checking multiplication, addition, subtraction, and division, it is not infallible, and is regarded by mathematicians as only a test and not an absolute proof.

Q. *What was the significance of a yellow ticket in old Russia?* L. L. T.

A. It was a pass given to a prostitute. In Russia, Jews and Jewesses were confined to the "Pale of Settlement." If any Jewish woman was willing to be registered as a prostitute, she was given a yellow ticket

and permitted free and unrestricted residence throughout the empire.

Q. *Why aren't the gondolas in Venice painted in gay colors?* H. M.

A. In 1562 a sumptuary edict was passed by the Great Council of Venice making black the compulsory color of the gondolas.

Q. *Why did Admiral Byrd take an ice-box to the South Pole?* H. M.

A. On his expedition to the Antarctic, Admiral Byrd actually carried with him two ice-boxes, since the food would have been frozen stiff if exposed to the weather. By means of the ice-boxes, it was possible to regulate the temperature.

Q. *How many wives do Mohammedans have?* C. P.

A. Mohammedan laws permit a man to have four wives.

Q. *What was the Roman spectacle called in which ships fought for the amusement of the people?* S. E. L.

A. This was a naumachy. The vessels were manned by gladiators, prisoners, and criminals.

Q. *Who was the last survivor of the Mayflower?* E. C. C.

A. John Alden was the youngest signer of the Mayflower Compact and the last survivor of those who came to this country in that famous boat.

Q. *How many pounds has a man carried?* E. J.

A. P. J. McCarthy, at St. Louis, Missouri, August 4th, 1898, carried on his back, for 8 steps, side stepping, 2250 pounds. He holds the world's record for professional weight lifting.

Q. *How much land did Washington own at the time of the Revolutionary War?* M. G.

A. He owned approximately 40,000 acres in detached areas, mostly in the Ohio Valley, besides the Mount Vernon estate, which embraced 8000 acres, more or less.

Q. *Who was the first American woman presented at the Court of St. James?* W. E. H.

A. Evelyn Byrd, the daughter of William Byrd, was the first American girl presented to the Court of St. James. Presentation at this Court has always marked the peak of attainment in the social world.

Q. *How many beef cattle are killed in a day in a big slaughter house?* J. S.

A. The Chicago plant of one of the largest packing firms is equipped to dress about 250 cattle per hour. On the basis of an eight-hour day, this would be 2000 cattle a day.

Q. *In what lake were the ships found which were lately recovered, after being under water for centuries?* F. A. L.

A. The two ships of Caligula were sunk for 1800 years in the little volcanic lake of Nemi near Rome.

Q. *Why are cups sometimes called mugs?* N. T.

A. In early days the drinking cup was often made in the form of a face, and was therefore called a mug.

Q. *How much damage is done yearly by rats?* J. R.

A. Damage by rats to property and produce in the United States amounts to about $200,000,000 annually. Rats affect a larger percentage of the population than any other pest in existence.

Q. *Where was the first parquet floor laid in America?* W. T.

A. The first parquet floor in America was laid in Monticello, the home of Thomas Jefferson at Charlottesville, Va.

Q. *Are people still being buried in the graveyard of Trinity Church, New York City?* A. W. F.

A. For a great many years burials have not been permitted in the churchyard except in the case of members of old families possessing a Trinity family tomb. A number of famous persons, including Alexander Hamilton, Captain John Lawrence, and Robert Fulton, are buried there.

Q. *How much heat is lost by using gold or aluminum paint on radiators?* E. K.

A. The Bureau of Standards says that it is demonstrated that about 20 per cent of the heat of radiators is lost if they are painted with gold or silver aluminum paint. It recommends a light-colored ordinary house paint.

Q. *What is the record size for a pair of elk antlers?* N. W.

A. The largest pair of elk antlers recorded by the Government was purchased in Colorado Springs in 1897 for the Emperor of Germany. Their length of beam was 67½ inches and there were 12 points. Seven or eight points on antlers are not unusual.

Q. *About how many cats are there in New York City?* A. T. B.

A. The total cat population of New York City was recently estimated by the S. P. C. A. at 1,500,000.

Q. *When was the first ice boat built in the United States?* S. G.

A. The first of which there is authentic record was built by Oliver Booth at Poughkeepsie, New York, in 1790. It was a square box mounted on three runners, shod with rough iron, with a rudder post and tiller of wood.

Q. *What play was George Washington's favorite?* E. T.

A. It is said to have been John Gay's "Beggar's Opera," which was recently played in New York and on tour in celebration of its bicentennial.

Q. *How did "chicken a la king" come to be so called?* R. N.

A. It is claimed that this dish was first prepared for Edward VII, King of England, according to his own recipe, and subsequently became very popular. About 25 years ago, the College Inn Restaurant in Chicago introduced it to this country as a novelty.

Q. Which State had the first State Highway Department? H. E.

A. New Jersey was first, establishing such a department in 1891.

Q. What cities have the least dust? L. S.

A. About five years ago, a survey was made and it was found that Boston, San Francisco, New Orleans, Denver, and Washington, D. C., showed the fewest dust particles per cubic foot of air.

Q. Is it true that a person comes up three times before drowning? R. C. S.

A. The popular notion that a person comes up three times before drowning is a fallacy. He may come up many times, or not at all, depending on various conditions.

Q. What country in Europe has always been at peace? A. C. H.

A. The Republic of Andorra is one of the smallest principalities in the world and is located in the valley of the Pyrenees between France and Spain. It is under the protection of France and governed by the Bishop of Urgal. It was declared independent by Charlemagne about 800 A.D. and has been unmolested since that time.

Q. Please advise the value of Manhattan Island. E. G. C.

A. It has been estimated as having a value of $50,000,000,000.

Q. What are the frog races which are held in California? E. B. G.

A. The frog races are an annual affair called "The Calaveras County Frog Jumping Contests," held on or about the 20th of May at Angel's Camp, California. This little town is the scene of Mark Twain's classic jumping frog tale, and it is probably this story that has suggested the present contests. The last contest was attended by at least 20,000 people and the scene was highly reminiscent of frontier days. A frog named Budweiser again won the world's record and broke his former record by the tremendous leap of 13 feet 5 inches.

Q. What are the five great steps in civilization? H. W. B.

A. As outlined by Dr. Will Durant the progress of mankind is indicated in the following stages: Speech, fire and light, the conquest of the animal, the passage of man from hunting to agriculture, social organization, the moral sense, the sense of beauty, science, writing and print, and education.

Q. Can you give the meaning of a cross and circle which is chalked on a wall by a tramp or vagabond? J. P. B.

A. The symbols employed by tramps are a form of sign language. For example, the cross means that the place so indicated is "good for a handout." This is generally a gate sign. The circle designates coins, and places so marked indicate that money is sometimes obtained there.

Q. What is the oldest continuously inhabited community in the United States? C. A.

A. Dr. Neil M. Judd has made investigations which lead him to believe that Oraibi, Arizona, is. This is an Indian village north of Winslow, and has been in existence since 1370.

Q. Did Shakespeare invent Romeo and Juliet, or was theirs a true story? J. P. M.

A. The story of Romeo and Juliet was not originated by Shakespeare. The story was very popular in Italy before Shakespeare wrote his famous tragedy. It is possible that the original plot was taken from life.

Q. Who designed the seal of the United States? C. S. M.

A. The seal of the United States was designed by a young student of Philadelphia named Will Barton, the brother of Dr. Benj. Barton. He made various designs before the seal in its present form was finally accepted. The designs were presented to a committee consisting of Charles Thompson, Secretary of the Confederation Congress, Dr. Arthur Lee and Elias Boudinot, who in turn reported to Congress.

Q. Is a galvanized iron roof safe in a thunder storm? L. O. S.

A. The Bureau of Standards says that a galvanized iron roof properly grounded will give good protection against lightning. It will be necessary to place air terminals on chimneys and see that all separate parts of the roof, as porch roofs and main roof, are bonded together so that they are in electrical contact.

Q. As an average, how many descendants has an American settler at the tenth generation? N. B.

A.   Greatly differing estimates have been made. Donald L. Jacobus, the New England genealogist, is of the opinion that the total number of descendants of any one colonist of the period from 1620–1640 amounts to over 200,000. J. Gardner Bartlett, from examination of 10,000 families of New England, estimates 78,125 descendants in eight generations.

Q. What is the oldest example of printing still in existence? S. B.

A.   It is believed to be the Kompon-Darani, a Buddhist prayer, printed from wooden type, in 756 A.D., in an edition of 1,000,000 copies, by order of the Japanese Empress Kokes. It is owned by the Art Institute of Chicago.

Q. How high a wave has been recorded at sea during a storm? F. B.

A.   Waves rarely have a greater height than 50 feet, but they appear to be much higher when seen from a ship in the open ocean. These waves frequently have a greater height, however, in breaking upon a rocky coast. The highest wave reported by the Hydrographic Office of the United States Navy Department was encountered in the North Atlantic Ocean, December 22, 1922, by the British Steamship Majestic. Its height was estimated at 80 feet.

Q. What is the origin of the expression double-cross? G. R.

A.   Dr. Vizetelly says that a New York boss in the early 80's testified before an investigating committee that when a constituent asked a favor he made a record of the name and fact, and if he intended to grant the petition he marked a cross after the name. Sometimes he would change his mind, in which case he added a second cross. In his testimony he would say, "I crossed Smith; I double-crossed Jones." Possibly this is the origin of the expression double-cross as used today.

Q. Which was the most important State economically at the time of the Revolution? N. J.

A.   In 1790 when the first census was taken, Virginia, the leading Southern State, ranked ahead of New York both in population and commerce. At that time Virginia had twice the population of New York and was far more prosperous.

Q. Please give some information about Prof. Heckler and his flea circus. E. P. C.

A.   Heckler was born in Switzerland but first saw performing fleas in Germany. He came to the United States when he was 18 years of age and gave his first exhibition about 22 years ago. Ordinary fleas are used. The female is preferred because it is easier to train. About two weeks is required for the training period. Prof. Heckler feeds the fleas with blood from his own right arm. One of these insects, weighing one-half grain, can jump 3 to 4 feet.

THE AMERICAN GOVERNMENT

By Frederic J. Haskin

"THE AMERICAN GOVERNMENT" is one of the world's best sellers among non-fiction books.

It is not a book on civil government. It is not a history.

It is a straightforward story of Uncle Sam at work —what he does and how he does it.

It is generally conceded to be the most authoritative account of the working side of the Federal Government that has ever been written.

It has run through 81 editions.

It has been translated into 11 languages.

It has been made into raised point for the blind, and a moving picture called "Uncle Sam at Work."

It is a standard text-book in schools; an authoritative reference in libraries.

It has been purchased by practically every foreign Government for State use.

It is one of the most popular gift books of this generation, thousands of patriotic readers purchasing copies to present to friends or to use in promoting Americanization.

It has been selected by the General Federation of Women's Clubs as a club study book for 2,800,000 women in America.

All foreign-born persons residing in the United States should read "The American Government."

Every American should not only own a copy of this book but should see that others have it. It should be read and studied by all voters, men and women; by school children and their teachers; by public officials and tax-payers; by farmers and scholars, business men and wage-earners.

GROSSET & DUNLAP • *Publishers* • **NEW YORK**